# CONTENTS

CONTENTS

# ANCIENT EGYPT

## A SOCIAL HISTORY

B. G. TRIGGER, B. J. KEMP,
D. O'CONNOR AND A. B. LLOYD

**CAMBRIDGE**
UNIVERSITY PRESS

# CAMBRIDGE
## UNIVERSITY PRESS

University Printing House, Cambridge CB2 8BS, United Kingdom

Published in the United States of America by Cambridge University Press, New York

Cambridge University Press is part of the University of Cambridge.

It furthers the University's mission by disseminating knowledge in the pursuit of education, learning and research at the highest international levels of excellence.

www.cambridge.org
Information on this title: www.cambridge.org/9780521284271

© Cambridge University Press 1983

First published 1983
Reprinted 1984, 1985, 1986, 1987, 1989, 1990, 1992, 1994, 1996, 1998, 1999, 2001

*A catalogue record for this publication is available from the British Library*

*Library of Congress Catalogue Card Number: 82-22196*

ISBN 978-0-521-24080-2 Hardback
ISBN 978-0-521-28427-1 Paperback

# FIGURES

ACKNOWLEDGEMENTS

Fig. 4.4 is reproduced by courtesy of the Department of Egyptology,
University College London; Figs. 4.5 and 4.7 by permission of the
Egypt Exploration Society; Fig. 4.6 by permission of the author and
the editor of *Mitteilungen des deutschen archäologischen Instituts Abteilung
Kairo*; and Fig. 4.10 by permission of the American University in Cairo
Press.

# PREFACE

Ancient Egypt has proved remarkably resistant to the writing of history which is not traditional in character; which is not, in other words, concerned primarily with the ordering of kings and the chronicling of their deeds. Traditional, narrative history is the inescapable key to man's historic past, but alongside this the twentieth century has seen the emergence of a rich and varied range of alternative approaches, opening up for exploration such fields as social and economic change and the structure of political formations. These alternative approaches mirror the many ways in which we analyse our own contemporary societies; and thus they begin to provide continuity between past and present. If the thread of continuity in the institutions of society is followed far enough into the past, it leads us to the early civilizations of which Egypt was one. Although much of the superficial image of ancient Egypt is of a remote and alien world – and herein lies much of its popular appeal – Egypt was one of a small number of centres which first developed on a significant scale the apparatus of exploitation and of bureaucratic government together with an ideology of social coherence, and so created the basis for all modern states. Egypt has a particular interest because, with relatively little disruption, one can trace the course of development from primitive society to a time when the country became just one part of a wider world of Mediterranean culture where the innovations of formative phases had long been taken for granted.

The difficulties of writing 'alternative' histories of Egypt are, however, enormous. For one thing, the very completeness of the chronological listing of kings which several generations of modern scholars have given us creates an image of knowledge in detail which other kinds of evidence cannot match. The abundance of royal art and architecture compounds the problem with an illusion of familiarity. But the truth is that the names and faces of great and lesser kings are masks that conceal a void. Remove them and any kind of significant continuity in written records which might interest the adventurous historian is gone. What survives illuminates only tiny patches spread across a three-thousand-year tapestry of human striving, inevitably raising the question in each instance: is it typical, can we generalize from it?

Continuity of a different order is, however, provided by the material remains that are open to the archaeologist to explore. But in Egypt archaeology has remained stubbornly the servant of history, having been consistently regarded from the beginning as a means of providing scholars with further texts and royal monuments, and museums with specimens of material culture which illustrate the typical. The idea that archaeology, and especially settlement archaeology, if pursued with sufficient attention to stratigraphy and spatial context, can offer a record of social and economic change that has a validity of its own and is parallel to the images created by written sources has been little pursued until recently, and even now gathers momentum only fitfully. Technical reasons peculiar to the Nile Valley provide some excuse. But at the heart of this failure is the hypnotic power of the images which the monuments and texts of ancient Egypt create. The urge to write something new is rapidly thwarted.

The first three chapters of this book were written for a history in the Cambridge series, namely, volume 1 of the *Cambridge History of Africa*. From a combination of individual preference on the part of the authors and enlightened patience on the part of the volume editor, J. Desmond Clark, the authors followed their own ways in trying to write chapters which addressed themselves more to the broader issues in the study of the past which exist outside Egyptology; and, as well, in view of the series of which the volume was but a single part, which explored Egypt's relationship with African neighbours. If, at the outset, they had written for a book with the present title their contributions might have turned out a little differently in content, though not in tone, and it is this latter aspect that has seemed to us to be the most important.

The first chapter spans the formative age of the Predynastic and Early Dynastic Periods. From the introduction of a south-west Asian-style subsistence economy into the Nile Valley, it follows the development of agricultural communities leading to a few urban centres, the appearance of court art and, through a phase of internal conflict, the emergence of a political state. The second chapter analyses the characteristics of Pharaonic Egypt in the ensuing phase of a mature state still relatively isolated from the outside world. It comprises the periods conventionally termed the Old and Middle Kingdoms and the First and Second Intermediate Periods. One theme of great importance throughout was the resolution of internal tensions between court and provinces, and, at a personal level, between loyal service and private wealth accumulation. It ended in a short period of foreign domination of northern Egypt and of the Egyptian enclave in Nubia. The reaction to foreign rule led to the rapid creation of an empire in Nubia and Western Asia. The third chapter covers the imperial age (the New Kingdom) and its complicated aftermath (the Third Intermediate Period). From a richer body of source material it becomes possible to write more knowledgeably on the structure of government, which embraced a large court and an increasingly powerful priesthood. The post-imperial period witnessed the reappearance of internal political tensions as a major factor, and a new external group, the Libyans, exerting pressure on the north of the country. The final chapter, specially written for this volume, provides an account of society in the Late Period, the last centuries of native rule and recognizably pharaonic culture when Egypt, no longer a dominant military power, experienced periods of defeat and subjugation by rulers from the Sudan, Assyria and Persia. But parallel to military failures, distinctive developments in ideology and society occurred which represent a significant readjustment of traditional forms to greatly changed circumstances. For the first time, too, we have descriptions of Egypt by outsiders, the Greeks, whose accounts are fully utilized in the chapter. The period ends with the conquest of Egypt by Alexander the Great, and the formal entry of Egypt into the Hellenized world.

# CHAPTER 1

# THE RISE OF EGYPTIAN CIVILIZATION

ORIENTATION

Through Pharaonic Egypt, Africa lays claim to being the cradle of one
of the earliest and most spectacular civilizations of antiquity. The aim
of this chapter is to trace the development of this civilization from the
introduction of a south-west Asian-style subsistence economy into the
Nile Valley to its florescence at the beginning of the Old Kingdom,
conventionally dated about 2700 BC. Egyptologists conventionally
divide this span into a Predynastic Period, prior to the traditional First
Dynasty of the Egyptian chronicler Manetho, and a subsequent Early
Dynastic Period, which corresponds with Manetho's first two dynasties.
This division has been justified by assuming that the beginning of the
First Dynasty corresponded with the political unification of Egypt and
marked a critical break in Egyptian history. While it is evident that
political unification played a major long-term role in shaping the
cultural patterns of ancient Egypt, this achievement was part of a
continuum of social and cultural change that was well advanced in late
Predynastic times and reached its culmination in the Old Kingdom.
Because of this, it is profitable to view the entire formative period of
Egyptian civilization as a single unit.

Although the Egyptian script was developed during the Early
Dynastic Period, written sources for this period are extremely limited
and present numerous epigraphic difficulties. Even the succession of
kings and the identifications of the royal Horus-names appearing on the
monuments of this period with the *nebty-* or *insibya*-names given in the
later king-lists are far from certain in many cases (see appendix, p. 69).[1]
For both the Predynastic and Early Dynastic periods the archaeological
evidence tends to be largely restricted to cemeteries in Upper (southern)
Egypt, while in the north the Predynastic Period is mainly represented
by habitation sites that have been found in marginal locations and are
often poorly reported. Few stratified sites have been carefully excavated
and there is a dearth of reliable palaeobotanical or palaeozoological data.
These shortcomings of the archaeological data have recently been

---

[1] For an outline of what is known about the dynastic history of the first two dynasties, see
Edwards (1971, pp. 1–35).

I

discussed in detail by a number of scholars, so that there is no need to repeat their strictures here (see Arkell and Ucko 1965). Because of this, I have chosen to focus on the positive, rather than the negative, aspects of the work that has been accomplished to date.

This synthesis differs from many earlier ones in two important respects. Firstly, all inferences about Egyptian prehistory that are based principally on myths, religious texts and the distribution of religious cults at a later period have been rejected. By treating this material as an accurate reflection of political events in prehistoric times, Sethe (1930) was able to postulate the existence of a Deltaic kingdom the power of which spread over the whole of Egypt long prior to the First Dynasty; however, many alternative and mutually exclusive historical interpretations of the myths he used have been offered (Griffiths 1960, pp. 119–48), while other scholars, notably Frankfort, have rejected the proposition that there is any historical basis to these myths (Frankfort 1948, pp. 15–23). Whatever historical events may have influenced Egyptian religious traditions, they can only be interpreted in the light of what we know about the development of Egyptian culture from other sources. The present study therefore limits itself to archaeological and contemporary epigraphic data.

Secondly, those once-fashionable interpretations that automatically assumed that in antiquity all cultural changes resulted from the intrusion of new groups of settlers into an area have been eschewed. Petrie argued that the Fayum A culture represented a 'Solutrean migration from the Caucasus', which he stated was also the homeland of the Badarian people. The Amratian white-lined pottery was introduced into Egypt by 'Libyan invasions', while the Gerzean culture was brought there by the 'Eastern Desert Folk', who overran and dominated Egypt. Finally, Egypt was unified by the 'Falcon Tribe' or 'Dynastic Race', that 'certainly had originated in Elam' and came to Egypt by way of Ethiopia and the Red Sea (Petrie 1939, pp. 3, 7, 77). In each case, Petrie's arguments were based on alleged connections between a limited number of traits found in Egypt and elsewhere, while the continuities in the Egyptian cultural pattern as a whole were ignored.

Ideas of this sort have continued to exert a strong influence on interpretations of early Egyptian development. On the basis of limited similarities between the Badarian culture and the Khartoum Neolithic, Arkell (Arkell and Ucko 1965) and Baumgartel (1970, p. 471) have proposed a southern origin for the former. Vandier has suggested that an invasion is necessary to account for the development of the Gerzean culture (Vandier 1952, pp. 330-2) and Emery (1961, pp. 38-42) has recently maintained that the Early Dynastic culture was introduced by a 'master race' coming from the east. Each of these suggestions has been specifically denied by other Egyptologists (see Arkell and Ucko 1965). Today, however, a growing number of Egyptologists follow the lead of Frankfort and Kantor in emphasizing the continuities rather than the discontinuities in Egyptian prehistory (see again Arkell and Ucko 1965). While foreign cultural traits can be shown to have diffused into Egypt and become part of the Egyptian cultural pattern during the period we are considering, there is no convincing archaeological or physical-anthropological evidence of large-scale migrations into Egypt at this time. It also now is recognized that cultural diffusion did not necessarily involve large-scale migrations and that in order to understand why traits were accepted at any particular period a thorough knowledge of the recipient culture is essential. The latter point justifies concentrating on the developmental continuities in Egyptian culture in the absence of any clear-cut breaks in the archaeological record.

Prior to the last decade of the nineteenth century, no archaeological finds were known that dated prior to the Third Dynasty. It was in 1894, after a season at Koptos, that Petrie and Quibell began clearing the large cemeteries at Naqada and El-Ballas (Petrie and Quibell 1895). These produced the first clear evidence of the Amratian (or Naqada I) and Gerzean (or Naqada II) cultures. Further excavations revealed these cultures to be widely distributed in Upper Egypt. It was not, however, until Brunton and Caton Thompson had worked in the vicinity of El-Qāw, between 1922 and 1925, that the still earlier Badarian culture was identified (Brunton and Caton Thompson 1928). The village sites of the Northern Egyptian Predynastic Sequence were discovered still later. The Fayum A sites, the only ones for which final reports are available, were excavated by Caton-Thompson and Gardner between 1924 and 1926 (Caton-Thompson and Gardner 1934); Merimda, in the western Delta, by Junker between 1928 and 1939; Ma'adi by Menghin and Amer after 1930; and El-Omari by Debono between 1943 and 1952 (for references to this literature see Hayes (1965, pp. 139-46)). The conviction that Egypt was not an important centre of plant and animal domestication and a consequent shift of interest to south-western Asia are, in part, responsible for the dearth of fieldwork on Predynastic sites in recent years. Since 1952, the most important work on this period has been restudies of earlier data by Baumgartel (1955, 1960), Kaiser (1956, 1957) and Kantor (1965).

3

Studies of Early Dynastic Egypt began with Amélineau's rough-shod excavations of the royal cemetery of the First and Second Dynasties at Abydos, which began in 1895 (Amélineau 1889–1905). This was followed by the systematic re-excavation and publishing of this site by Petrie between 1899 and 1901 (Petrie 1900, 1901a). In 1896–7, de Morgan excavated a large First Dynasty tomb at Naqada and, in 1897–8, Quibell and Green carried out excavations at Hierakonpolis which yielded, among other treasures, the famous slate palette of King Narmer (B. Adams 1974, Quibell 1900, Quibell and Green 1902). Further discoveries were made by Petrie at Tarkhan and other sites and, in 1912, Quibell found traces of large Early Dynastic tombs near the Step Pyramid at Saqqara. Firth began to excavate these tombs in 1932 and, after his death, this work was carried on by Emery between 1936 and 1956 (Emery 1949–58). From 1942 to 1954, Saad cleared a vast Early Dynastic cemetery, containing many graves of less important officials, at Helwan, on the east bank of the Nile opposite Saqqara (Saad 1969).

## Chronology

Unlike in south-western Asia, few stratified sites have been discovered in the Nile Valley that could serve as a basis for working out a cultural chronology for Predynastic Egypt. Merimda appears to have been such a site, but, for the most part, its stratigraphy has gone unrecorded. This leaves the tiny site at El-Hammamiya, which was inhabited intermittently from Badarian into Gerzean times, as the only stratified Predynastic site with any chronological significance.

In an effort to work out a chronology for the graves of the Amratian and Gerzean cultures, Petrie developed his system of 'Sequence Dating', which constituted the first substantial application of the principles of seriation in archaeology (Petrie 1901b, pp. 4–8: for recent appreciations of Petrie's seriation see Kendall 1969, 1971). This system was based on fluctuations in the popularity of different types of pottery from some 900 graves, each containing not less than five different types. On the basis of these fluctuations, Petrie assigned each grave to one of fifty successive temporal divisions, numbered 30 to 80. The time-scale is uncertain, so that it can only be said, for example, that S.D. (Sequence Date) 40 is theoretically earlier than S.D. 41; further, there is no reason to believe that the interval between S.D. 49 and 50 is necessarily the same as between S.D. 60 and 61. It appears that the nearer Petrie's divisions are to the historic period, the shorter periods of time they

4

represent. Petrie placed the transition between the Amratian and Gerzean cultures at about S.D. 40 and saw the transition between the Gerzean and Early Dynastic Period (his Semainean Period) starting about S.D. 65. The beginning of the Early Dynastic Period is now placed at about this stage. In terms of cultural development, the most important feature of Petrie's system is its assumption of enough stylistic continuity and uninterrupted change to permit the construction of a single developmental sequence from Amratian through into Early Dynastic times. This continuity harmonizes very poorly with the importance that Petrie attached to migrations as a principal source of cultural change.

Continuities in varied categories of artifacts suggest that the Badarian culture is earlier than the Amratian one and ancestral to it. The site at El-Hammamiya provides stratigraphic evidence that the Badarian culture came to an end before the end of the Amratian. Kaiser suggests, however, that, since certain types of Amratian pottery are found in some Badarian sites, the two are likely to have been contemporary with each other and represent parallel cultures, or ethnic groups, inhabiting different parts of Upper Egypt (Kaiser 1956, pp. 96–7; see also Hays 1976). Arkell and Ucko (1965) have pointed out that the mixture of pottery could have come about as a result of the contamination of an early site with later sherds and Kantor has argued that the similarities between the two cultures can better be interpreted as evidence that Badarian developed into Amratian (Kantor 1965, pp. 3–4). Brunton also defined a Tasian culture which he claimed represented an earlier phase of the Badarian. It is now generally agreed that the graves which are assigned to this culture, and which have never been found in isolation from Badarian and Old Kingdom ones, do not constitute a valid assemblage (Arkell and Ucko 1965, Kantor 1965, p. 4). This leaves the Badarian as the earliest known Predynastic culture in Upper Egypt.

Petrie's pottery classification has been described as 'the paraphernalia of the Dark Ages' and the cultural chronology derived from his system of Sequence Dating is now highly suspect in some of its details (Lucas and Harris 1962, p. 385, n. 3; Ucko 1967). On the basis of a re-analysis of the Predynastic cemetery at Armant, Kaiser (1957) has worked out an alternative system which differs in many small respects from that of Petrie and in which the Amratian–Gerzean sequence is divided into three stages and eleven sub-stages. On the whole, however, the general cultural sequence that Petrie worked out has stood the test of time remarkably well (Vandier 1952, p. 233).

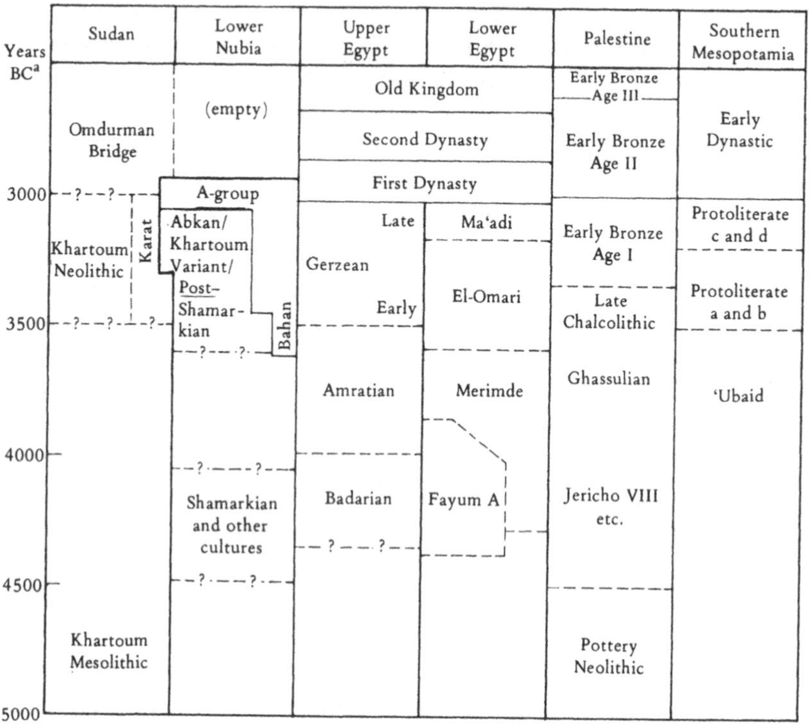

ᵃDates before 3000 BC based on $^{14}$C dates using 5568-year half-life

Fig. 1.1   Relative chronology of Egypt and neighbouring regions.

Not enough material has been published so far to permit a seriation of artifacts from the habitation sites which belong to the distinctive Northern Egyptian Predynastic Sequence. On the basis of similarities in specific types of artifacts, the Fayum A culture has been roughly correlated with the Badarian, the apparently long-inhabited site of Merimda with the Amratian, and El-Omari and Ma'adi with successive stages of the Gerzean (Kantor 1965, pp. 4–6). The main reason for suggesting that Fayum A was earlier than Badarian was the total absence of metal in Fayum A. Metal is also lacking at Merimda and El-Omari, however, which clearly are coeval with the Upper Egyptian Sequence. Although Baumgartel has argued that the Northern Sequence is culturally retarded and that hence all of these sites date much later, radiocarbon datings support the generally-accepted sequence and proposed correlations with the south (Baumgartel 1955, pp. 14–17, 120–2). These dates also provide possible support for the priority of Fayum within the Northern Sequence, since the dates for Fayum A overlap only

6

with the earlier ones from Merimda. The later Merimda dates correlate with the two available for Amratian, while the one date for El-Omari correlates with those for the Gerzean culture (fig. 1.1).

Since the first radiocarbon dates became available, it has been observed that dates for earlier Egyptian historic material are consistently younger than the calendar dates established on the basis of dynastic chronologies. This led some Egyptologists to doubt the applicability of this dating technique to their region or to use it only as a means of establishing relative dates, while others became concerned that the historical chronology might be too long (Hayes 1970, pp. 192–3; H. S. Smith 1964; Trigger 1968, p. 64). Recent calibrations of dated tree-rings of bristlecone pine with the radiocarbon dates that these tree-rings have yielded have indicated major fluctuations in the formation of $^{14}$C, which have now been studied as far back as 5200 BC. These studies indicate that radiocarbon dates are approximately 200 years too recent by the end of the mid second millennium BC and some 800 or 900 years too recent by the beginning of the sixth millennium. While these calibrations remain at the experimental stage, they would place the majority of radiocarbon dates for the Early Dynastic Period between the calendar dates 3400 and 2650 BC. Traditionally, Egyptologists have dated the beginning of this period between 3100 and 2900 BC and the end of the Second Dynasty about 2686 BC (Derricourt 1971, Suess 1970).

If the calibrations that have been suggested for dates prior to 3000 BC are accepted, they would extend the duration of the known Predynastic sequences over a much longer period. Known radiocarbon dates for Fayum A would fall roughly between the calendar years 4700 and 5200 BC; Merimda between 3500 and 5200 BC (and, rejecting one date, between 4600 and 5200 BC); and the single date for El-Omari between 4000 and 4200 BC. Only two dates are available for the Amratian culture, but these fall about 4500 to 4700 BC, while the three Gerzean dates range between 3500 and 4600 BC. Two potsherds from the lowest Badarian level (below the breccia) at El-Hammamiya recently have yielded thermoluminescent dates of $5580 \pm 420$ and $5495 \pm 405$ BC. Five other presumably Badarian sherds from higher levels in the site date, according to depth in the deposit, to between $4360 \pm 355$ and $4690 \pm 365$ BC; while a Gerzean sherd from the still higher 2.5-foot level is dated $3775 \pm 330$ BC.[1] More thermoluminescent dates must be obtained before their implications can be considered.

[1] For details of these determinations see Derricourt (1971). For correct attributions of dates to the Amratian and Gerzean cultures see Arkell and Ucko (1965) and Kantor (1965, p. 5). For

The radiocarbon dates suggest a longer duration for the Gerzean culture than the archaeological evidence indicates is at all likely. The radiocarbon calibrations prior to 3000 BC may be too early. Alternatively, the Gerzean sample is small and the dates were obtained early in the development of the radiocarbon method, using specimens whose radiocarbon content may have been altered by contamination with fossil fuels during long periods of unprotected storage in museums. It may be significant in this respect that the date for a sample collected recently from the Fayum Kom K site is several hundred years more recent than for two samples collected by Caton-Thompson. More determinations will be needed from Egypt, and the proposed calibrations carefully tested, before an acceptable radiocarbon chronology is worked out prior to 3000 BC.

## Environment

The Nile floodplain was formerly believed to have been a vast swampland, unfit for permanent settlements. It was believed that, at first, human beings lived only along the edges of the valley, locating their camp-sites at the foot of cliffs or on rocky promontories. Only as the highlands turned into desert was man forced to settle in the jungle-like valley bottom and to begin the arduous process of clearing it. Passarge and Butzer have come to the conclusion that the topography of the valley is such that swamps were always a minor feature of the landscape, except in the northern Delta. Most of the plain consisted of seasonally flooded natural basins which supported various grasses and brush vegetation during the dry season. The higher levees along the river were covered with trees, such as acacia, tamarisk and sycamore, and the ones that remained permanently out of the water were ideal sites for year-round habitation. Butzer has also obtained evidence which indicates that the Delta has not extended seaward in recent millennia and that physical conditions there in Predynastic times were little different from what they are today. Raised sand deposits would have provided ideal loci for settlement within the inner Delta, immediately adjacent to the rich soils of this area (Butzer 1959, Passarge 1940). These observations run completely counter to Baumgartel's argument that the Delta was

the thermoluminescent datings see Caton-Thompson and Whittle (1975) and Whittle (1975). It should also be noted that the currently accepted, but admittedly somewhat speculative, chronology of early Egyptian history has recently been called into question by Mellaart (1979). On the basis of radiocarbon determinations, Mellaart proposes to date the beginning of the First Dynasty at about 3400 BC and the end of the Second Dynasty at about 2950 BC. Mesopotamian periods are moved correspondingly back in time.

unfit for human settlement much before the Early Dynastic Period (Baumgartel 1955, p. 3).

Instead of there being unremitting desiccation in north-eastern Africa at the end of the last Ice Age, there is evidence of increased rainfall and runoff on the steppes adjacent to Egypt at several intervals thereafter. The first appears to have lasted from about 9200 to 6000 BC, while another began about 5000 BC and, after a dry interval, continued after 4000 BC. Fairly abundant vegetation persisted in the wadis of northern and eastern Egypt until as late as 2350 BC, by which time a level of aridity comparable to the present was established (Butzer 1971, p. 584). At the maxima of precipitation, the northern Red Sea Hills supported tree cover and grazing land, while trees and wild grasses also grew in the wadis on both sides of the Nile and fish lived in the pondings along these wadis (Murray 1951; W. A. Fairservis, personal communication). During such periods, these upland areas and wadi systems, as well as the Nile Valley itself, supported considerable numbers of elephant, giraffe, rhinoceros, ostrich, wild ass and cattle, as well as antelope, gazelle, ibex and deer. That the adjacent deserts had become far more habitable than they are today during the period that saw the rise of Egyptian civilization vitiates the suggestion that an increase in population, resulting from climatic deterioration on the neighbouring steppes, played a major role in encouraging the development of civilization in the Nile Valley (Butzer 1971, p. 594). The moister climate appears to have facilitated the movement of human populations into and through the desert and this, in turn, may have encouraged more communication and more rapid cultural change in the Sahara.

There is considerable evidence that both the river bed and floodplain of the Nile in Egypt have slowly aggraded throughout historic times, as the result of the annual deposit of a thin layer of silt. Although an average rise of 10 cm per century is frequently quoted, Butzer has shown that the rate of deposition has varied considerably from one period to another. Between about 4000 and 3000 BC, the Nile floodplain in Lower Nubia appears to have been six to seven metres higher than at present (Butzer 1959, Butzer and Hansen 1968, pp. 276–8). A review of annual flood heights recorded on the Palermo Stone later in the Old Kingdom indicates a decrease in the average height and volume of the Nile flood during the First Dynasty. Bell (1970) has estimated that the difference between the average flood height of the First Dynasty and that of the Second to Fifth Dynasties is not less than a decline of 0.7 m.

It appears that throughout Egyptian history most settlements have been built on the floodplain, while, in Upper Egypt at least, cemeteries are frequently located in the desert, just beyond the edge of the cultivation. As a result, most living-sites, except those located on high ground or built, like the town of Kom Ombo, on tells formed by the debris of earlier villages, have either been buried under more recent deposits of silt or washed away by changes in the course of the river. This explains the low ratio of Predynastic, and later, living-sites to cemeteries that has been recovered in Upper Egypt (Butzer 1966). It also appears that between 8000 and 5000 BC the Egyptian floodplain was lower than it is today and the valley narrower; hence in most places even the cemeteries that were located along the margins of the flooded land at that time are now buried under more recent deposits of alluvium (Butzer 1971, p. 587; Wendorf, Said and Schild 1970). Butzer has shown that in Middle Egypt, which was hitherto often believed to be uninhabited in Predynastic times, cemeteries of this period are likely to have been either destroyed by shifts in the channel of the river or buried under substantial later deposits of sand and alluvium. Dunes have been particularly active on the west bank of the Nile in this part of Egypt, while, on the east bank, few landforms which would have been close to the edge of the valley in Predynastic times yet which remain unburied by later silts can be found north of Deir el-Gabrawi (Butzer 1961). The Predynastic habitation sites that have survived are all on scarps or embankments several metres above the present alluvium. According to Butzer, their preservation is fortuitous, since it was only sites at this height that have escaped the inundations and lateral expansion of irrigation in recent years.

This suggests that known distributions of Predynastic cultures may be determined more by geological than by cultural factors. For example, it is possible that both the Badarian and Amratian cultures extended almost as far north as did the Gerzean. Moreover, while all the people of Upper Egypt are assumed to have buried their dead on the margins of the Valley, it seems likely that most of the richest and culturally most advanced settlements were built on now-buried levees along the banks of the river and hence have never been discovered by archaeologists. This raises the possibility that the small Badarian settlements studied by Brunton, or the El-Hammamiya site, may be the encampments of simple pastoral groups, living both geographically and culturally on the fringes of a more advanced society. There is good evidence that an important part of the Predynastic settlement at Hierakonpolis extended onto the floodplain, where the settlement was located in historic times (Butzer 1966, Vandier 1952, p. 519).

## Language

Numerous similarities have long been apparent in the grammar, lexicon and phonology of ancient Egyptian and the Semitic languages. Because of this, it is often stated that Egyptian is either a Semitic language obscured by change or a creole language resulting from the mixing, in Predynastic times, of an 'African' and a Semitic language. This African language is sometimes identified as a Hamitic language (which some-times is, and sometimes is not, believed to be distantly related to Semitic) and sometimes as a 'Negro' language (Lambdin 1961, Vergote 1970). Such speculation has been closely related to theories that there were various migrations into Egypt from south-western Asia in prehistoric times and that these have resulted in ethnic and cultural changes.

Borrowings from some Semitic language or languages are well attested in historic times and Kees and others are probably correct in concluding that these languages exerted a strong influence over Egyptian in late Predynastic times, when there is also evidence of south-west Asian influence in the realms of art and material culture generally (Kees 1961, p. 42). There is, however, no evidence of an 'African substratum' in ancient Egyptian, in the sense that it can be proved that all of the similarities with the Semitic languages found in Egyptian are borrowings superimposed on an identifiable, specifically African language. On the contrary, Greenberg (1955, pp. 43–61) has shown that many of these similarities are not borrowings at all, but indicate that both Egyptian and the Semitic languages are derived from a common ancestor. He has also demonstrated that Semitic, ancient Egyptian and Cushitic, found to the east of the Nile (principally in Ethiopia), and Berber and Chadic, found in the western Sudan, constitute five co-ordinate branches of the Afroasiatic (or Hamito-Semitic) language family. It now seems likely that the Cushitic languages constitute not one, but two, major branches of Afroasiatic (Cushitic proper and Omotic) alongside Berber, Egyptian, Chadic and Semitic (Fleming 1969). Greenberg has the impression that Old Kingdom Egyptian and Akkadian are slightly more differentiated than Romanian and Portuguese, which would suggest 5500 to 6000 BC as the time when the branches of Afroasiatic became separate from one another (Trigger

1968, p. 74, based on J. H. Greenberg, personal communication). While no studies of the lexical aspects of proto-Afroasiatic have been undertaken in order to shed light on the geographical point of origin of these languages, the 'principle of least moves' would suggest the eastern Sudan, or perhaps Egypt, as likely areas (Fleming 1969). Alternatively, while western Africa seems an unlikely point of origin, it is possible that, if special economic conditions, or population pressures, existed in south-western Asia, the language family might have been carried westward into Africa from that region. Although it is as yet impossible to trace the spread of Afroasiatic in the archaeological record, it does not seem impossible that Chadic and Berber were carried into the western Sahara during the 'wet phase' that began about 5000 BC.

In any case, it appears quite likely that the Predynastic cultures of Egypt were associated with a people who already spoke Egyptian and that later, specifically Semitic, borrowings were made from a closely related group of languages. These borrowings are, however, much less spectacular than was formerly believed and cannot be construed as evidence of creolization or massive population mergers. Of the hypothesized non-Afroasiatic 'African substratum' no trace exists.

### Physical Anthropology

Just as some linguists have tried to discern an 'African substratum' in the Egyptian language, so some Egyptologists have assumed that the earliest Predynastic population was negroid, and see in any caucasoid element evidence of the later migration of 'Hamito-Semitic' types into the country. Too often there has been a tendency to attribute the cultural development of Egypt to the repeated incursions of people of the latter type. Batrawi, on the other hand, has shown from the careful study of osteological evidence that there was very little change in physical type in Upper Egypt from Predynastic times into the historic period (Batrawi 1945, 1946). Although there was some variation within the population, the Upper Egyptian people were mostly small in stature and had long narrow skulls, dark wavy hair and brown skin. This continuity in physical type does not provide evidence of migration or gene flow, although it cannot rule out the possibility that new groups of similar physical type entered Upper Egypt from time to time.

Skeletons found at Merimda, El-Omari and Ma'adi suggest that the Predynastic inhabitants of the Delta were taller and more sturdily built than the Upper Egyptians and that their skulls were broader. Morant

(1925) saw in such skeletons evidence for the early existence of a 'Lower Egyptian type', which persisted in the north into the Hellenistic period and gradually modified the physical type present in Upper Egypt. The most recent use of physical anthropological findings to advance culture–historical arguments has been Emery's acceptance of Derry's theory of a 'Dynastic Race' as proof that the Early Dynastic civilization was brought into Egypt by a 'civilized aristocracy or master race'. Emery claims that this group may have originated along the Indian Ocean and also may have laid the foundations of the Sumerian civilization (Emery 1961, pp. 39–40). Edwards has suggested more cautiously that 'the fresh knowledge they may have brought with them' accounts for the 'acceleration in cultural progress observable at this time' (Edwards 1971, pp. 40–1). According to Derry (1956), a massively built, mesocephalic people entered Egypt about the start of the First Dynasty, probably from Asia, since they can be identified with the armenoid physical type found in that region. By the end of the First Dynasty, they had penetrated as far south as Abydos and gradually were merging with the indigenous population. It would appear that, in fact, the Predynastic population of Lower Egypt was ancestral to Derry's 'Dynastic Race' and that he was interpreting a basically geographical difference as an irruption of new settlers into the Nile Valley (Berry, Berry and Ucko 1967, Hayes 1965, p. 135). The population of the Delta was probably in contact with south-western Asia in prehistoric times, and settlers may have entered the region and mingled with the local population throughout this period, as they did in later times. This process may explain some of the similarities that Derry noted between these people and the armenoid type, common in Syria and Lebanon. It is prudent, however, to assume that whatever gene flow went on in northern Egypt, at least in later Predynastic times, was incidental to cultural development. To go further and attribute the Early Dynastic culture, or any earlier one, to the appearance of an intrusive ethnic group is to transgress permissible limits of inference.

PREDYNASTIC EGYPT

*Predynastic Subsistence Patterns*

The lower reaches of the Nile and the Tigris–Euphrates valleys are both extensive, but circumscribed, areas of rich, easily cultivated alluvium. As such, they shared the potential of becoming centres of high population density and of early civilizations. In spite of this, the differences between the two areas were very great. The natural floodplain of the Nile Valley was wider and richer than the Mesopotamian one and the annual floodwaters more predictable and less difficult to control. Moreover, salination did not pose a serious problem to the Egyptian farmer as it did in Mesopotamia. Merely by modifying natural basins to retain the floodwaters for longer periods, it was possible to convert the edges of the Nile floodplain into highly productive agricultural land. This was particularly easy to do from Abydos southwards, where these basins were smaller and more easily managed than in Middle Egypt or the Delta. Grain was one of ancient Egypt's principal exports and Herodotus, who travelled widely, stated that the Delta was the easiest land to work in the known world (Butzer 1976, pp. 18–22; Frankfort *et al.* 1949, pp. 39–51, 138–9). Throughout Predynastic times periodic rainfall over the catchments of wadis draining towards the Nile seems to have facilitated a limited amount of agriculture along the margins of the Nile Valley. Farming of this type may have been of no small importance in the early phases of the development of an agricultural economy in this area.

The general settings of Egypt and Mesopotamia were even more different than their river valleys. Mesopotamia was flanked by a series of highly diversified local environments embracing a variety of different altitudes, rainfall patterns and distributions of vegetation. Particularly in the north and west, these included areas that had witnessed the earliest development of sedentary agricultural life. Such diversity was conducive to trade, communication and, under pressure from expanding populations, innovations in subsistence patterns. The relative ecological uniformity of the Sahara and its limited potential for sustaining more than a meagre population even under the most favourable conditions provide a striking contrast with the Mesopotamian hinterland and explain the rudimentary cultural development of this region into later times. While the political, economic and cultural relationship between the Nile Valley and its Saharan hinterland is a subject that deserves careful study, it seems clear that the peoples of the Sahara played a far less important role in the rise of Egyptian civilization than the peoples bordering on Mesopotamia did in that area.

With the development of intensive agriculture in the Nile Valley, its inhabitants became increasingly isolated from their Saharan neighbours by a distinctive and internally highly differentiated way of life; the Egyptians had little motivation, of an economic or any other sort, for much reciprocal interaction with them. To no small degree, the power of the Egyptian state must have rested on the scorn and distrust that the Egyptian peasant felt towards the desert-dwellers and on his inability to adapt to life outside the Nile Valley. Ancient Egyptian civilization reflected in many ways this economic and cultural independence from the cultures of its desert hinterland, which contributed in no small degree to the self-sufficiency and ethnocentrism that, more than for most other early civilizations, were its special hallmarks (Frankfort *et al.* 1949, p. 45).

The lack of geological deposits in the Nile Valley north of Aswan which can be dated to between 8000 and 5000 BC hinders an understanding of the beginnings of a food-producing economy in this area. Moreover, the study of the Predynastic cultures to date has been such that even more recent food-producing sites which lacked or contained only very simple pottery are likely to have been overlooked. It has been pointed out, quite correctly, that there is no reason to believe that the Fayum A and Badarian cultures are necessarily the oldest food-producing cultures in this part of the Nile Valley (Arkell and Ucko 1965). In a recent paper, Clark has reviewed the evidence for the independent origin of food production in the Nile Valley. He stresses the rich faunal resources of the region in early Holocene times and draws attention to the wide range of edible and potentially domesticable trees and plants there (possibly including wild barley). He queries whether this rich environment provided the basis for a population increase that encouraged the subsequent manipulation of these resources or whether, as in parts of sub-Saharan Africa, this very richness of natural resources inhibited rather than stimulated innovation. He also suggests that the rapid adoption of an agricultural complex that was largely of external derivation might have taken place more easily if earlier local experimentation had made the Egyptians aware of the advantages to be gained by doing this (Clark 1971).

In spite of this, direct evidence for what was happening prior to 5000 BC is available only from south and west of the Egyptian Nile Valley. As P. E. L. Smith has explained (Smith 1982), Wendorf has postulated a reliance on wild grains among some late Pleistocene groups in Nubia and Upper Egypt, beginning well before 10000 BC. While putative evidence, in the form of grinding stones, persists into Terminal Palaeolithic times (about 6000–5000 BC), there is no clear evidence of increasing sedentariness or group size. Wendorf has therefore suggested that a trend towards incipient cultivation was reversed when increasing desiccation made wild grains less abundant before the populations of Egypt and Nubia had become fully dependent on them (Wendorf 1968, vol. II, p. 1059; Wendorf *et al.* 1970). Hobler and Hester (1969) have suggested the specialized collecting or incipient cultivation by floodwater farming of unknown grains (perhaps millet, *Panicum turgidum*) at the Dunqul Oasis, west of the Nile, at about 6000 BC. They also suggest that it may have been from this area that ideas of food production were introduced up and down the Nile Valley. Possible cultivation in the Ahaggar has been suggested by pollen grains of *Pennisetum* from Amekni, dated to between 6100 and 4800 BC and by a 'type of cultivated grass' at Meniet from the first half of the fourth millennium BC (Camps 1969, p. 188, also Camps 1982, pp. 566–9; Hugot 1968). Whatever the status of this evidence, collecting wild grass or incipient food production did not lead to the development of sedentary communities in the Sahara; instead the pattern appears to have given way to nomadic pastoralism as domestic animals became available and as the climate of the Sahara deteriorated (P. E. L. Smith 1976).

The best evidence of increasing sedentariness in Holocene times in the Nile Valley is the presumably pre-agricultural 'Khartoum Meso-lithic' culture, whose type-site appears to have been inhabited, at least seasonally, for a considerable period of time. At this site, a wide variety of animal bones were found, bone harpoons indicate that fishing was important and grinding stones are reported, although Arkell believes that these were used only for grinding ochre. The apparently negroid population that inhabited this site also gathered the fruit of wild trees, such as *Celtis integrifolia*. Shelters were constructed of reeds covered with clay, and brown pottery bowls were decorated with wavy lines and later also with dots (Arkell 1949). Related pottery has been found as far north as Dongola and from Kassala, in the east, west to the Ennedi, Ténéré and Ahaggar; some of the latter has been radiocarbon dated to between 6000 and 5000 BC (Arkell and Ucko 1965, Clark 1971, Marks 1968). This pottery is, however, associated with different lithic industries and therefore seems to have diffused among established local groupings. Its wide distribution may bear witness to the growing sedentariness made possible by a highly successful collecting economy which flourished along the southern fringes of the Sahara during a period of increased rainfall, in the fourth millennium or earlier. It must be remembered, however, that the rich resources of the Nile Valley seem to have given rise to at least some permanently occupied settlements in Egypt already in Upper Palaeolithic times (Clark 1971).

The domesticated plants and animals that were of major economic importance in Predynastic Egypt generally seem to have been utilized in south-western Asia at a still earlier period (Wright 1971). The important plant domesticates were wheat, barley and flax (all efficient winter-rainfall crops) and the domesticated animals were sheep, goats, dogs, cattle and pigs. The only obviously locally domesticated animal was the donkey (*Equus asinus*), which is convincingly represented as tame in the art of the late Predynastic period (Zeuner 1963, pp. 375–6). The herding of gazelles has also been suggested for the Gerzean period on the basis of kill patterns, although the true significance of this evidence is far from certain (Reed 1966). There is no evidence of either *Panicum* or *Pennisetum* species in Egypt in early times, despite the alleged use of millet farther west; however, grains of *Echinochloa colonum*, a *Panicum*-type grass, have been found in the intestines of corpses from the Predynastic cemetery at Naga ed-Deir and it has been suggested that this plant was being cultivated as a cereal at that time (Clark 1971, Dixon 1969). It has also been conjectured that the Ethiopian domesticate enset (*Ensete edule*) might have been an important food crop in Egypt before it was displaced by wheat; however, the alleged representations of enset on Gerzean pottery are generally believed to be aloes (Simoons 1965). Whatever steps towards plant and animal domestication may have been taken locally, these domesticates appear to have given way before the superior types of domesticates that had been developed in south-western Asia.

On the basis of evidence from the Fayum, Wendorf is of the opinion that the technological and typological differences between the local Terminal Palaeolithic industry and Fayum A, which is only about 1000 radiocarbon years later, are so great that Fayum A is unlikely to have developed from a local Palaeolithic culture. He therefore suggests that the early Predynastic cultures record the arrival of a new population in Egypt, who brought with them the cultural base from which Egyptian civilization was to develop (Wendorf *et al.* 1970). If, in fact, the Afroasiatic language family originated elsewhere than in Egypt, the appearance of this 'new population' might correspond with the arrival of the first ancient Egyptian-speakers in their historic homeland. Unfortunately, the Fayum is somewhat peripheral to the Nile Valley, so that the transition between the Terminal Palaeolithic and Predynastic cultures may have been somewhat later than it was along the River Nile. In view of the variety of Palaeolithic industries in the Nile Valley at any one time and the long gap that remains in the archaeological record, it seems best to leave open the possibility that, in some fashion, the lithic traditions of Predynastic times evolved from a Palaeolithic culture native to the Nile Valley. It has been suggested that the bifacial technique of stone-working may have spread north from a nuclear area in the Congo and western Sudan during a period of climatic amelioration in the Sahara (Clark 1962). It is also possible that the movement of domesticates across the Sinai peninsula was aided by the wet phase that began about 5000 BC, although an unconfirmed relationship between the microlithic industry found near Helwan and that of the Natufian culture (about 9500–7500 BC) may suggest possible ties between Egypt and Palestine while the latter area was passing through a stage of incipient agriculture and animal domestication. While the Natufian corresponded with a period of climatic amelioration, no evidence of domesticates has been forthcoming, although pig bones occur in refuse heaps (Reed 1966).

Wheat, barley and flax are already present in the Fayum A culture. The only species of wheat prevalent in early times was emmer (*Triticum dicoccum*). A small amount of club wheat (*T. compactum*) has been found at Merimda and El-Omari, but Helbaek is of the opinion that it was a stray, accompanying other crops, which did not establish itself in Egypt (Dixon 1969). Wild emmer (*T. dicoccoides*) occurs in the upper part of the Jordan Valley, while einkorn (*T. monococcum*) seems to have been domesticated in west central Turkey about 6000 BC. Although both emmer and einkorn have been identified as grown at Jericho as early as 6500 BC, only the former made its way into Egypt (J. M. Renfrew 1969). Barley was an important crop in Egypt from early times and occurs in the abdominal contents of a large number of human bodies of Pre-dynastic date from Naga ed-Deir in Upper Egypt (Dixon 1969). The wild ancestor of barley (*Hordeum spontaneum*) is widely dispersed around the fringes of the fertile crescent. Reports of naked barley in ancient Egypt have not been substantiated and four- and six-rowed hulled types appear to be most common. Six-rowed hulled barley requires large amounts of water and thus was suited for cultivation in the Nile Valley. It is reported from Ali Kosh, in Iran, about 6000 BC, but became an established food crop in south-western Asia only after the appearance of irrigation about 5500 BC (Wright 1971). The wild ancestor of flax (*Linum bienne*) occurs in the Kurdish foothills and may have been domesticated there (J. M. Renfrew 1969). Although current evidence favours an Asian origin for all the principal Egyptian cultigens, Vavilov and Sauer have maintained that wheat and barley were first domesticated in Ethiopia (Simoons 1965, Wright 1971). While this now seems highly unlikely, the possibility must be left open that rainfall regimes resulted in distributions of wild plants in early Holocene times different from those postulated on the basis of modern distributions. Some surprises may therefore be in order.

The full complement of domestic animals, except for the donkey, is generally assumed to have been present in Egypt throughout the Predynastic period; however, osteological studies are lacking for most sites. According to Reed, bones of domestic goats are attested with certainty no earlier than the Amratian period, while domesticated sheep and dogs are attested in the Gerzean, and probably domesticated cattle and pigs also. Goat skins have been reported, however, from Badarian sites; dogs, resembling the greyhound or saluki type, are represented on leads on an Amratian pottery vessel; and what seem to be models of domesticated cattle have been found in graves of the same period (Reed 1966, Zeuner 1963, pp. 138, 222).

There is no evidence that the wild ancestor of the goat (*Capra hircus aegagras*) lived in Africa or that wild sheep (*Ovis orientalis*) were ever found south of Syria. Likewise, there is no support for Arkell's suggestion (in Wright 1971) that the dwarf goat, found at the Gerzean site of Tukh and at Esh-Shaheinab, is descended from the so-called 'native dwarf goat' found in Algeria and Zaïre (Reed 1966, Wright 1971). Sheep and goats were both domesticated in south-western Asia considerably earlier than the first known Predynastic cultures and the earliest dated occurrence of one or both these animals in north-eastern Africa is in the Neolithic levels at Haua Fteah (radiocarbon-dated about 4800 BC), while the earliest occurrence to the south of Egypt is at the 'Khartoum Neolithic' site of Esh-Shaheinab (radiocarbon-dated about 3100 to 3500 BC) (Arkell 1953, pp. 15–18; Higgs 1967). While it is possible that these domesticates reached Haua Fteah by way of the Mediterranean and north-west Africa, it is equally possible, and perhaps more likely, that they spread south and west after reaching northern Egypt across the Sinai peninsula. The absence of other domesticates at both Haua Fteah and Esh-Shaheinab further suggests that sheep and goats may have reached north-eastern Africa ahead of other domesticates. Prior to the Middle Kingdom, Egyptian sheep were a screw-horn, hair variety, also known in Mesopotamia. Goats display a range of horn types similar to those found in Neolithic and Bronze Age sites in Palestine (Zeuner 1963, pp. 138, 178).

Zeuner is of the opinion that both long- and short-horned breeds of domestic cattle in Egypt were descended from the native long-horned wild cattle of North Africa (*Bos primigenius*), although Gaillard has argued that a separate subspecies of wild short-horned cattle lived in Upper Egypt during the late Pleistocene (Zeuner 1963, p. 222).[1] Wild pigs also seem to have been abundant in the Delta and Reed believes it likely that these were domesticated by the Egyptians rather than domesticated pigs being driven across the Sinai Desert. It would appear, however, that, even if Egyptian domesticated pigs and cattle were bred from North African wild ancestors, the idea of their domestication must have come from south-western Asia, where there is a definite priority for domesticated pigs and a highly likely priority for domesticated cattle. Although cattle are not milked in parts of West Africa at the present time, there is definite evidence that they were milked in Egypt at least as early as the Old Kingdom.

While the late Neolithic economy of Egypt appears to be an extension of that found in the Near East, an older indigenous pattern of hunting, fishing and utilizing wild plants appears to have played an important role in the subsistence economy of Egypt until the late Predynastic Period. As the population increased and the onset of desiccation began to affect the adjacent deserts, natural plant resources diminished and many species of animals began to die out or were drastically curtailed in numbers. Elephants, giraffes and ostriches seem to have disappeared from both the desert and the floodplain in late Predynastic times, while the remaining savanna-type species, including antelope, ibex and gazelle, were decimated before the start of the Middle Kingdom (Butzer 1958, p. 114). On the other hand, large swamp- and river-dwelling animals, hippopotami and crocodiles, managed to survive throughout the Pharaonic period, although their habitats continued to diminish as a result of land clearance. The disappearance of animals from the floodplain probably resulted, in large part, from the pre-empting of their natural habitats by human beings for fields and for grazing land for their animals. This trend would have been intensified after the First Dynasty by lower flood levels, which resulted in a narrower floodplain. It is uncertain from the archaeological record when an increasing population made it necessary to supplement simple floodplain and runoff cultivation by increasingly modifying natural basins. While the drainage works that Herodotus later claimed were carried out at the beginning of the First Dynasty suggest a long-standing familiarity with the problems connected with large-scale irrigation projects (Baumgartel 1970, p. 482),

---

[1] These are almost certainly female *Bos primigenius* (Reed 1966).

additional proof of this is lacking. Basin agriculture and flash flood cultivation can be practised on a small scale and it seems likely that, as in Mesopotamia, large-scale undertakings were a result of centralized control rather than an important factor in the development of this control (Frankfort 1956, p. 33; Nims 1965, p. 34).

## The Northern Predynastic Sequence

Knowledge of Predynastic sites in northern Egypt is extremely limited. No sites of this period have been discovered as yet in the inner Delta, which was almost certainly the key area of settlement in northern Egypt in Predynastic as it was in later times (Wilson 1955). Most of these sites now either lie below the watertable or are covered by more recent settlements. A small number of sites found at the apex of the Delta and around its margins indicate that in Predynastic times the cultural pattern of this region was different from that of Upper Egypt. The principal sites are, however, few in number and located some distance apart, hence it is not always possible to distinguish clearly between temporal and geographical variations in culture. All of these sites appear to be characterized by undecorated, or simply incised, monochrome red or black pottery. Throughout all of Egypt, early Predynastic pottery tends to lack handles, spouts or fancy lips and to take the form of open bowls, cups and dishes. Later, closed and fancy forms of vessels become more common. There is, however, a total absence in the Northern Predynastic Sequence of the fancy decorated pottery found in Upper Egypt (Baumgartel 1955, pp. 17–18).

The oldest known components of the Northern Predynastic Sequence seem to be the habitation sites of the Fayum A culture.[1] These were located along the northern and north-eastern shores of an old lake level in the Fayum Depression. The encampments seem to have consisted of mat or reed huts erected in the lee of buttes or mounds near the fertile soil along the edge of the lake. Possibly to avoid ground moisture, the communal underground granaries associated with these settlements were located on higher ground some distance from the settlements. Bones of sheep, goats and possibly of domesticated cattle were reported, although none were examined by specialists. The granaries yielded the remains of emmer wheat and six-rowed barley.

[1] For a summary of the archaeological data related to Predynastic northern Egypt see Hayes (1965, pp. 91–146); for Upper Egypt see Baumgartel (1955, 1960) and Vandier (1952, pp. 167–466, 497–609).

While the Fayum A people were clearly agriculturalists and may have kept domesticated animals, they appear to have remained dependent on hunting and fishing to a considerable degree. Large mammals, including elephants, crocodiles and hippopotami, were hunted, and fish and mussels were taken from the lake. Small harpoons and bevelled points made of bone were preserved, but no fish-hooks. The harpoons are said to resemble those from Palestine rather than the kinds found in the Republic of the Sudan and East Africa. Shells, which were used for ornaments, were obtained from both the Mediterranean and the Red Sea. A few amazonite beads do not necessarily indicate contact with the Tibesti region to the west, since this mineral also occurs in the Nile basin (Lucas and Harris 1962, pp. 393–4).

Many of the stone tools are large, thick flakes with notches and denticulates. Sickle flints were set in wooden handles; stemmed and winged arrow-heads and leaf-shaped pieces were bifacially chipped, and celts were chipped and provided with polished cutting edges. Baskets were common and used to line granaries, and rough linen cloth was being manufactured. Pottery was made from coarse, straw-tempered clay and consisted mainly of bag-shaped vessels and flat-bottomed dishes. Some vessels had a burnished red slip, others a plain rough surface. McBurney suggests that the pottery, as well as other aspects of the culture, show connections with the coastal areas of the Levant (McBurney 1960, pp. 233–8). Although the most substantial site (Kom W) was 600 m long, the lack of house structures does not suggest a strongly sedentary settlement pattern. It has been speculated that these sites were probably seasonal ones. To what degree the Fayum settlements were representative of life in the Nile Valley at that time remains problematical. Communal granaries occur in many (but not all) Pre-dynastic sites in Egypt and suggest that village or local groups played an important corporate role in the allocation of resources. Even if few villages were larger than extended kin groups, these corporate activities must have enhanced the status of local headmen (Baumgartel 1970, pp. 482–3).

The earliest evidence of fully sedentary village life in the Nile Valley is the site of Merimda, on the western margin of the Delta. It has been estimated to cover about 180 000 sq. m with cultural debris up to 2 m deep (Butzer 1966, Kemp 1968a). Although the site was dug in arbitrary levels and its stratigraphy not properly recorded, radiocarbon dates suggest that it may have been inhabited for 600 years. In general, the pottery and stone artifacts resemble those of Fayum A, although the shapes and decoration of the pottery are more varied and elaborate. Polished black pottery is found only in the upper layers of the site. The pear-shaped stone mace-heads found at Merimda may be derived from Asian models and are likely prototypes for the later Gerzean ones. A special type of vessel supported by four modelled human feet is also found in the Amratian culture (Kantor 1965, p. 5).

In the early stages, the inhabitants of Merimda appear to have lived in sparsely scattered wind-breaks or pole-framed huts. These dispersed 'farmsteads' frequently became engulfed in sand and, at one point, there is evidence of extensive sheet-flooding resulting from rainfall (Butzer 1966). In the higher levels of the site, the occupation is denser and there is evidence of semi-subterranean adobe huts, whose walls rose several feet above the ground and probably were covered by a pitched roof. Not one of these houses was over three metres in diameter and most were so small they could only have been lived in by one adult or a woman and her children. Clusters of single-adult dwellings, usually occupied by groups of patrilineal, polygamous kinsmen are found in various parts of modern sub-Saharan Africa and analogous settlements appear in the archaeological record of the Natufian and pre-pottery Neolithic cultures in Palestine (about 9000 to 6500 BC). Flannery has queried whether the African compounds may not be surviving examples of a settlement type that once stretched from Palestine into north-eastern Africa (Flannery 1972, Trigger 1965, p. 60). At Merimda a number of these huts were found laid out in ragged rows on either side of what was believed to be a street; but the plan suggests that alternatively they might have been part of a double ring of huts (Vandier 1952, pp. 117–19). Granaries, consisting either of baskets or clay jars buried up to their necks in the ground, were scattered throughout the village and seem to have been associated with individual dwellings. What appear to have been circular clay-lined threshing floors are also reported. Butzer has tentatively estimated that Merimda had a population of 16000, although it is far from certain that the entire site was occupied at any one time or that the occupation was sufficiently dense to support this estimate. Kemp considers it likely that Merimda was a relatively small community. He also demonstrates that the evidence is insufficient to prove that, at Merimda, the custom was to bury the dead within the village in such a position that they faced the hearth of their former home. Kemp (1968a) suggests that a small number of adults may have been buried in the empty spaces that existed between the houses at any one period. Similar practices are attested in Upper Egypt in spite of the importance apparently placed on cemeteries and grave-goods there in Predynastic times. The graves found within the limits of Merimda contained almost no grave-goods.

Approximately contemporary with the final occupation at Merimda is a group of settlements and cemeteries collectively known as El-Omari. These are clustered in and around the mouth of the Wadi Hof, between Cairo and Helwan. In Predynastic times this wadi was probably suitable for growing crops. The pottery is predominantly red or black and almost devoid of decoration, although vasiform and lipped vessels are more common than at Merimda. Most of the stone tool types found at Merimda also occur at El-Omari, although there is a greater emphasis on flake and blade tools, that appears to foreshadow the predominance of blade tools in the still later settlement of Ma'adi. Unfortunately, El-Omari has been less completely explored than either the Fayum sites or Merimda, and only cursory accounts of the excavations have been published. The main settlement, which like Merimda appears to have been lived in for a lengthy period, occupies a gravel terrace sloping down to the estuary of the Wadi Hof. Traces of many oval shelters made of poles and basketwork were found on the surface of the site, as well as various sized pits lined with matting or baskets. These were all probably granaries, although the excavators believed the larger ones to be semi-subterranean huts (Vandier 1952, p. 156). Still larger areas enclosed with reed fences were probably pens for domestic animals. Evidence of an area given over to flint-knapping was found on the outskirts of the settlement. A smaller site, apparently contemporary with this one, was found near two natural rain catchments on one of the highest terraces of the Jebel Hof. Many cores and hammerstones suggest considerable amounts of flint-working, but numerous burials in and around the site, as well as millstones, indicate that it too was a settlement. The relationship between the upper and lower settlements is unclear, although it does not seem impossible that the former was established as a naturally-defended outpost of the latter. Another small, and possibly later, village was discovered in a branch of the estuary of the Wadi Hof.

Bodies were interred within both of the older settlements. In the larger settlement, these burials were made over a long time; some were disturbed by later building on the site, while later ones were placed in granaries of an earlier period. Bodies were generally laid on their left side, head south, as they were in Upper Egypt, but not at Merimda. One skeleton was found holding a staff about 35 cm long and similar to the *ames* sceptre associated with kings and deities in historic times. It has been suggested that he may have been a local headman. Grave-goods were generally sparse, as they were at Merimda. Two cemeteries containing dispersed graves covered with stone tumuli appear to have been associated with the later village.

Ma'adi is located 10 km north-west of El-Omari. Here a sprawling site up to 2 m thick and covering some 18 hectares flourished from late Predynastic into Early Dynastic times. The dwellings at Ma'adi are concentrated in the central part of the site. For the most part, they consist of oval huts or horseshoe-shaped wind-breaks constructed of posts driven deep into the ground to support walls of wattle or reeds covered with mud. Grindstones and storage jars or storage pits were sometimes found inside, or closely associated with, these houses, which continued to be built throughout the history of the site. Two rectangular structures were also noted; one with walls of reeds and straw, the other built of logs laid horizontally. A number of spacious subterranean chambers were dug to a depth of over 2 m into the sandy soil. These were circular to rectangular in plan, were entered by stairways and evidently were dwellings, since they contained hearths, as well as traces of roof-poles. Special storage areas existed on the periphery of the settlement, which recall the segregated granary areas associated with the Fayum A settlements. Pottery storage jars, about 1 m high and buried up to their necks in the sandy soil, occupied the northern outskirts of the settlement. On the south side were numerous storage pits, with vertical or sloping sides and sometimes lined with mud or basketwork. Many of these storage pits contained carbonized grain, but basalt vases, carnelian beads and other valuable items were also found inside them. It has been suggested that the settlement was protected by palisades and ditches. Burials within the settlement were limited, with few exceptions, to the bodies of unborn children and three cemeteries have been found in the vicinity of the town. The grave-goods in the Wadi Digla cemetery are richer than in the other two. A number of dogs and gazelles were buried in graves of their own in these cemeteries.

Hunting and gathering seem to have been less important at Ma'adi than they had been in the earlier sites of northern Egypt. The remains of wild animals are sparse and limited to ibex and to riverine species, such as hippopotami, turtles, fish and molluscs. On the other hand, at Ma'adi there is evidence not only of agriculture and herding but also of advanced craft specialization. A copper axe-head spoiled in casting and masses of copper ore indicate that copper was being processed at

Ma'adi. Ma'adi is the oldest site in northern Egypt in which copper artifacts have been found. Although copper tools and weapons have not survived in large numbers, traces of disintegrated copper artifacts occurred with some frequency in the site. Ma'adi is located at the mouth of the principal wadi leading eastward to the copper deposits of Jebel 'Ataqa and the Sinai and Baumgartel has suggested that a copper industry connected with the first exploitation of the Sinai mines might have been the reason for Ma'adi's existence; however, no evidence has been adduced that indicates that the Egyptians were mining copper in the Sinai peninsula at this period, or to any significant degree in Pharaonic times (Baumgartel 1955, p. 122; Hayes 1965, p. 129; Rothenberg 1970). More likely Ma'adi was an important entrepôt handling trade between the Nile Valley, the Sinai peninsula and Palestine. Gerzean pottery and stone artifacts occur at Ma'adi and have been interpreted as evidence of increasing cultural influence from the south, which can already be noted at El-Omari. On the other hand, in historic times the main road from Egypt to Palestine passed by Ma'adi, before crossing the eastern Delta. Kantor (1965, p. 9) has established the existence at Ma'adi of a 'considerable body' of imported pottery from the Early Bronze Age I culture of Palestine, which is coeval with the late Predynastic Period. It is therefore possible that copper was being imported from the east at this time, rather than that the Egyptians were going to the Sinai peninsula to mine it themselves. While these alternative explanations must be considered further, it is possible that the Upper Egyptian influences in the north came about as a result of long-distance trade in which, at least during early Gerzean times, the people of Ma'adi and other sites in north-eastern Egypt were playing a key role.

Although the Predynastic cultural sequence in northern Egypt remains poorly defined, the sites in this area are distinguished from those of Upper Egypt by their monochrome, mainly undecorated, pottery and by a greater scarcity of jewellery, sculpture and decoration. On the other hand, the suggestions that pigs, either wild or tame, were eaten in northern Egypt but not in the south; that in the north people were buried inside their settlements rather than in cemeteries; and that settlements in northern Egypt are substantially larger than in Upper Egypt are all dubious distinctions between the two areas. The sequence of sites known at present suggests that, as the Early Dynastic Period was approached, there was progressively less reliance on hunting and an increasing emphasis on crops and herding. It is possible, however, that because of the rich natural resources of the Delta, the transition there was slower than it was in Upper Egypt. While communities such as Ma'adi appear to have played an important role as entrepôts through which goods and ideas from south-western Asia filtered into the Nile Valley in late prehistoric times, the main cultural and political tradition that gave rise to the cultural pattern of Early Dynastic Egypt is to be found not in the north but in the south. To understand why this was so, we must examine the cultural development of Upper Egypt.

## The Upper Egyptian Predynastic Sequence

Cemeteries of the Badarian culture have been excavated along the eastern flank of the Nile Valley between El-Matmar and El-Etmanieh. In addition, Badarian habitation sites have been found in the stratified site at El-Hammamiya, at El-Matmar, at El-Mostagedda and at the foot of the cliffs at El-Badari. Few of these sites are more than a few centimetres thick. Although Kaiser believes that the Badarian culture was confined to this area, typical Badarian artifacts have been found at Armant, Hierakonpolis, and in the Wadi Hammamat (Kantor 1965, p. 4; Hayes 1965, p. 147; for Hierakonpolis, W. A. Fairservis, personal communication). It therefore seems likely that more Badarian sites will eventually be found elsewhere in Upper Egypt (fig. 1.2).

The remains of the Badarian culture appear to reflect a simple, semi-sedentary way of life. No certain evidence of house structures has been noted in any of the Badarian settlements, whose inhabitants presumably lived in skin tents or huts made of mats hung on poles. The site at El-Mostagedda consisted of a circle of grain pits, some lined with baskets or matting, which outlined an area of ash and sand. Cemeteries were located in the desert behind the settlements. The typical Badarian grave was an oval or rectangular pit roofed over with sticks or matting. Graves contained one or more bodies, loosely contracted on their left side, head south. The body was covered with mats or hides, and food and other offerings were placed in the graves. The offerings included rectangular stone palettes, ivory spoons, and small ivory or stone vases; all of which appear to have been associated with the grinding and use of green face-paint. These items were to remain a part of the Predynastic burial kit. Fancy ivory combs and ivory and clay human figurines were also placed in graves. Although graves were of different sizes, the absence of obvious distinctions of wealth among them may, but does not necessarily, indicate a lack of social stratification at this time. While

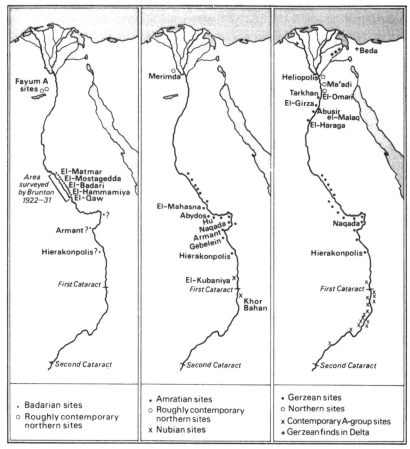

Fig. 1.2   Maps indicating known distributions of Predynastic sites in Egypt and
Lower Nubia at different periods.

it is assumed that all of the people living along the east bank of the river
would have used the cemeteries adjacent to the floodplain, there seems
to be a close connection between the cemeteries and settlements found
along the edge of the desert (O'Connor 1972). This suggests either that
the Badarians only occupied the floodplain seasonally or that the
cemeteries belonging to the population of the valley, as opposed to the
desert margin, have not yet been discovered. Until this problem is
resolved, any interpretation of the Badarian culture will remain
hazardous.

Wheat and barley were grown and traces of bread were found in some graves. Castor seeds, probably wild, were collected for their oil. Clothing was woven out of linen, although skin clothing, with the hair turned inwards, and leather clothes were also worn. The bones of cattle, sheep and goats are listed as occurring on Badarian sites, although they were not studied by experts. A number of animals, some putatively domesticated, were wrapped in mats or cloth and buried in separate graves, like human beings, in the village cemeteries. Flint arrow-heads, throwing-sticks (not boomerangs) and perforated fish-hooks made of ivory and shell reflect the continuing importance of food-collecting, and bones of wild animals, fish and birds are reported from Badarian sites. On the whole, however, the evidence does not seem to indicate as great a dependence on wild game as is found in coeval sites farther north.

Badarian flint-working is not of a high order of expertise. It is primarily a core industry, utilizing nodules found on the surface of the desert. Small push-planes and bifacial sickle-stones are common and arrow-heads were both leaf-shaped and concave-based. The Badarians' failure to use the tabular flint found in nearby cliffs has been interpreted by some as evidence that they did not originate in this part of the valley (because they did not know its resources) and that they came from the south (since flint-bearing limestone ceases south of Esna) (Brunton and Caton Thompson 1928, p. 75). By contrast, the manufacture of Badarian pottery exhibits a high degree of sophistication, although the shapes tend to be simple; semicircular bowls predominate. Ordinary vessels are either smooth or rough brown, but the best quality of pottery is thinner than any other produced in Predynastic times. The surfaces of many vessels were combed and burnished before firing. The fine ware is either polished red or black in colour, but the most distinctive type was red with a black interior and lip formed by removing the pot red-hot from the kiln and placing it upside down in carbonizing material (Lucas and Harris 1962, pp. 377–81).

A small number of awls and pins that were hammered out of copper have been found in Badarian sites, as well as beads made of steatite covered with blue–green glaze. It has been suggested that these objects may have been obtained from itinerant traders coming either from Palestine or across the Red Sea (Arkell and Ucko 1965). In addition to shells from the Red Sea, other supposed evidence of long-distance trade takes the form of turquoise, believed to come from the Sinai peninsula; pine, cedar and other woods thought to come from Syria; and an unusual four-handled vessel similar to some Ghassulian ones (Kantor 1965, p. 6). Since, however, the climate of North Africa was moister then than it is today, the wood may have been indigenous to the Red Sea Hills and better climatic conditions would have made the exploitation of that area easier than it is at present. Copper ores are also found not far to the east of the Nile Valley and it has been suggested that the turquoise may have come from the Libyan massifs. Although it is generally assumed that a knowledge of metallurgy reached Egypt from Palestine, the total absence of copper in sites in northern Egypt prior to late Predynastic times suggests that the use of copper possibly evolved independently in Upper Egypt. The earliest artifacts may have been hammered out of native copper, although this is far from certain. In any case, the well-attested use of copper ore (malachite) for face-paint suggests that conditions were favourable in the Badarian culture for the discovery of how to obtain copper by smelting the ore (Lucas and Harris 1962, pp. 201, 404). Malachite occurs in the eastern desert in sufficient quantities to have supplied the demand for it in Predynastic times. Steatite is also found in Egypt, so that it too may have been glazed locally. This might be interpreted as evidence that the Badarian culture, as it was manifested either elsewhere in Upper Egypt or in sites on the floodplain, was technologically more advanced than is indicated by the marginal sites discovered so far.

Amratian sites generally appear to be larger and more prosperous than the Badarian ones and are found from Deir Tasa as far south as the Nubian border. There is evidence of an Amratian occupation in the town-sites at Hierakonpolis and Naqada, both of which appear to have been key locations in the Predynastic development of Upper Egypt. A concentration of early Amratian sites between Abydos and Naqada also suggests that this stretch of river may have played an important role in the development of the Amratian culture (Kaiser 1957, pp. 74–5). The only house structures definitely identified as Amratian are nine hut ovals at El-Hammamiya, and even these continued to be inhabited into early Gerzean times. The huts were about one to two metres in diameter and, while one had been used to store dung for fuel, at least one other contained a hearth and was clearly a small dwelling. The foundations were built of chips and rough pieces of sandstone set in mud, while the upper parts appear to have been of wattle and daub. As with the huts at Merimda, there were no traces of doorways. The latter were probably set in the walls of the houses some distance above ground level, after the fashion of huts built in parts of the southern Sudan at the present time. Wooden posts in one part of the site have been interpreted as the remains of wind-breaks. Similar wind-breaks are reported from El-

Mahasna and cooking pots were found *in situ* at Armant. While these two settlements appear to have been inhabited in both Amratian and Gerzean times, no more permanent structures were found there. The subsistence economy of the Amratian culture seems to have been much like that of the Badarian. The art of the period demonstrates a continuing familiarity with elephants and giraffes (Vandier 1952, p. 270).

In essential features, cemeteries also appear to be little changed from Badarian times. Headless bodies and extra skulls suggest the possibility of head-hunting at this time, which might betoken the patterns of blood revenge associated with tribal society. It is possible, however, that these finds are related to a more widespread custom of dismembering corpses. There is no archaeological evidence to confirm traditions of cannibalism in Predynastic times (Vandier 1952, p. 248).

A striking improvement can be noted in the manufacture of stone tools, most of which are bifacial. The best flint knives were ground to thin them, prior to being given a final flaking to produce a cutting edge. The most impressive of these tools are the fish-tail artifacts (of uncertain use) and rhomboidal knives. A few basalt vases with a small splayed, or conical, foot have been found and, since somewhat similar vessels are known in Mesopotamia at about the same time, it has been suggested that the Egyptian ones are foreign imports or local imitations of these vessels (Arkell and Ucko 1965, Vandier 1952, pp. 366–8). Crude stone vessels were manufactured in Badarian times, however, and seem to represent the beginning of a tradition of stone-working that was hereafter to be a part of Egyptian culture. The ability of the Egyptians to shape hard stone expertly in Amratian times is proved by the so-called 'disc-shaped' mace-heads. The Amratians also ground rhomboidal palettes out of slate and carried on the Badarian tradition of carving and modelling. Ivory combs have long teeth and their handles are ornamented with human and animal figures. Pairs of ivory hippo-potamus tusks, sometimes ornamented with bearded human heads, may have been of ritual significance. A large number of human figurines, both in ivory and clay, appear to date from this period (Arkell and Ucko 1965, Ucko 1968). Perrot has suggested that the elongated shapes of the ankles and faces, as well as the drill holes found in the ivory statuettes, suggest a cultural affinity with those of the Ghassulian culture (Kantor 1965, pp. 6–7). These similarities are tenuous, however, and the nature of contacts at this period remains to be demonstrated.

While black-topped pottery declined in quality, and rippling died out early in the Amratian period, red wares remained popular. Some of this pottery was painted with white cross-lined designs and later with scenes depicting people and animals in a free and vivid style. Men are frequently shown wearing feathers in their hair, as the Nubians and Libyans did in historic times, as well as penis sheaths, which were worn occasionally into the historic period. Ucko has studied the prehistoric sheaths preserved in the Naga ed-Deir cemetery and offers a provisional classification of them (Ucko 1967). Baumgartel has suggested that the white cross-lined red ware may have been inspired by the painted pottery of Susa I and contemporary Mesopotamian and Iranian cultures. The similarities that Baumgartel has indicated are very general ones, however; hence few scholars are convinced by her arguments (Baumgartel 1955, pp. 54–71; Vandier 1952, pp. 294–6). The absence of similar painted pottery in the Delta is also against an Asian origin for Amratian painted pottery. Metal objects are as rare in Amratian sites as in Badarian ones. Copper pins date from the Amratian period and two gold beads have been tentatively ascribed to it. In general, however, the level of cultural development appears to be little different from what it was in Badarian times. In both periods, the villages of Upper Egypt probably had largely self-sufficient economies, which had as their resource base the Nile Valley and the adjacent eastern desert. It may turn out, however, that the limited evidence now available does not adequately reflect the cultural development of either period.

By contrast, the Gerzean period appears to have been one of rapid change, marked by abundant evidence of contacts with south-western Asia and the evolution of complex social and economic institutions. For the first time, there is positive evidence of south-west Asian influences in Upper Egypt. In the early Gerzean, these influences are limited to the imitation of foreign pottery. The most important of these borrowings were the ledge-handled, or wavy-handled, vessels, which appear to be derived from the Early Bronze Age I culture of Palestine. In Egypt, these vessels have no prototypes, but in Palestine ledge-handles appear in the Early Chalcolithic period (4000 to 3600 BC) and by Early Bronze Age I times they were used on a number of different types of vessels. The type introduced into Upper Egypt gave rise to a whole class of pottery, which henceforth developed along its own lines there. The exact point at which these vessels began to be produced in Upper Egypt remains in doubt, but it is no longer assumed that it was at the very beginning of the Gerzean period (Kantor 1965, pp. 7–8, Ucko 1967). Vessels with tilted spouts and, less certainly, ones with triangular lug handles also appear to be imitations of forms which evolved in

Mesopotamia in the 'Ubaid or early Protoliterate periods. The spouted vessels occur in the 'Amuq area, when that region was a western outpost of Protoliterate influence, and also in the Early Bronze Age I culture of Palestine. These occurrences probably outline the route by which these forms were carried from Mesopotamia to Upper Egypt. Ma'adi was already functioning as an entrepôt between Palestine and Upper Egypt and may have played some role in their transmission. Near the start of the Gerzean period, the pear-shaped mace-head, which was ultimately of south-west Asian origin, appears to have diffused to Upper Egypt from the Delta, where it was already present at Merimda.

Within the Gerzean culture, there is evidence of increasing craft specialization and wider markets. Until this time, all pottery was made of clay deposited by the River Nile, and it is likely that most of this pottery was traded over only a small area. In Gerzean times, however, vessels with a light-coloured fabric began to be made of a mixture of clay and calcium carbonate that is washed out of the limestone hills bordering the Nile Valley. Two areas well known for this clay are Qena and El-Ballas, where deposits have been exploited from an early period; however, other, less important deposits occur in Middle Egypt (Lucas and Harris 1962, pp. 383–4). The ledge-handled jars and another class of pots decorated in red paint with various patterns, and later with representations of sacred boats, trees and files of birds and animals, were made of this same clay type. The standardized forms of these vessels that are found distributed throughout Egypt are evidence not of cultural uniformity but of the mass-production of this ware in one or, at most, only a few centres. The shapes of many red-ware vessels also reflect the impact of mass production during the Gerzean period. While opinions differ, it is possible that a slow, hand-turned wheel was now used to fashion parts of vessels (Baumgartel 1970, p. 488; Lucas and Harris 1962, p. 369). If so, the innovation coincided with the increasing scale of pottery manufacture at this time. The florescence of painted pottery, prior to its decline at the end of the Gerzean period, indicates that, in spite of large-scale production, fancy pottery continued to serve as a vehicle of artistic expression, as it had done in the Amratian period.

Copper artifacts became much more common during the Gerzean and at the beginning of the Early Dynastic Period. Daggers, knives, adzes, axes; spear-heads, harpoons, fish-hooks, needles, finger-rings, small tools and ornaments were now cast, as well as hammered, from this metal and the copper that was used appears to have come from both the eastern desert and the Sinai peninsula where the contemporary, chalcolithic culture of the Nawamis (Petrie 1906, p. 243) has some elements in common with Predynastic Egypt (Lucas and Harris 1962, p. 209).[1] It is possible that the techniques of casting used by the Egyptians owed something to Palestinian metallurgical experience, although the relationship still remains to be worked out (Kantor 1965, p. 7). Gold was also worked at this period and some luxury goods were ornamented with gold foil. Silver objects are described as 'more substantial than one would expect', although the silver is unlikely to have been imported into Egypt as Baumgartel (1960, pp. 6–7) suggests it was. Prior to the Middle Kingdom, 'silver' appears to have been mainly a silver-rich alloy of gold and silver, which is found in the eastern desert. Until the end of the Middle Kingdom, this 'white gold' was valued more highly by the Egyptians than was yellow gold (Lucas and Harris 1962, pp. 246–8).

There was also a marked development in other crafts. Decoration was more finely conceived and formally arranged than ever before and the execution of designs was often of high quality. Flint blades became more common, although the most elaborate flint objects continued to be produced using careful bifacial techniques. Thin, scimitar-like knives manufactured by controlled ripple-flaking were made towards the end of the Gerzean period and bear witness to the skill of certain highly-specialized craftsmen. Slate palettes were manufactured in the shape of fish, birds and animals and zoomorphic vases were ground out of hard stone. Beads and amulets increased in number and quality and were produced in exotic stone, including lapis lazuli, as well as in gold and silver. These objects bear witness not only to artistic and technological advances but also to the emergence of a clientele interested in possessing such luxury goods.

It has been observed that the pottery from the Naqada periods that is found in cemeteries differs considerably from that found in settlements. Much of the fancy pottery as well as many other kinds of luxury goods may have been manufactured specifically for funerary purposes. It is often pointed out that a highly-developed cult emphasizing funerary offerings may greatly stimulate production (e.g. C. Renfrew 1972, pp. 489–94). It is therefore possible to assign a major role to Upper Egyptian funerary customs in increasing the division of labour and generally promoting the development of social complexity from Predynastic times into the historic period.

[1] On the basis of recent work, Bar-Yosef et al. (1977) have been able to cross-date tombs of this type to about Early Bronze Age I of the Palestinian chronology.

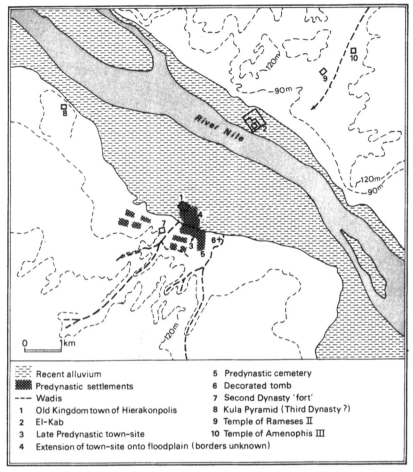

Fig. 1.3  General map of the Hierakonpolis area. (After Butzer 1960.)

While Gerzean sites extend from the borders of the Delta as far south as the Nubian border, the main centres of cultural activity were to the south of Abydos. From its cemeteries, Naqada, the historic Nubet, appears to have been an extremely important centre of population. There was also a major Gerzean settlement, with satellite villages, at Hierakonpolis (fig. 1.3). It is perhaps no coincidence that in historic times these two communities were the respective cult centres of the gods Seth and Horus, who feature so prominently in the Egyptian myths of kingship. While most Egyptians appear to have lived in small communities and been content with reed shelters, even these small settlements had communal kilns for drying grain, in the construction of which brickwork played a part (Baumgartel 1960, pp. 134–5; Vandier 1952, pp. 503–8). At the South Town at Naqada, rectangular brick houses seem to date from this period. Petrie also recorded part of a town wall at Naqada, although its relationship to the houses is unclear. A clay model found in a tomb at Hu shows a portion of the wall surrounding a building or town being guarded by sentinels. A rectangular house model from a grave at El-Amra seems to consist of a single room and an enclosed courtyard, while a house with a similar ground plan was found beneath the temple at El-Badari and is tentatively assigned to the Predynastic or Early Dynastic Periods (Baumgartel 1960, pp. 133–5). It is suggested that these were the houses of the wealthier and more urban classes. Under the historic temple at Hierakonpolis there was an oval retaining wall, built of sandstone blocks laid with a pronounced batter on the outside. This retaining wall was almost fifty metres across and closely resembles the traditional Egyptian hieroglyphic sign for the town. It is suggested that the retaining wall supported a layer of sand on which a temple was erected. As far as can be determined, this structure was built in late Predynastic times. If so, it was the sole trace of monumental architecture surviving from that period (Vandier 1952, pp. 518–25).

Increasing social stratification can be traced in the varied size and design of Gerzean tombs and in the grave-goods being put into them. Some graves were lined with wooden planks and special niches were constructed to receive grave-goods or the bodies of the dead. In Cemetery T at Naqada and at Hierakonpolis, a number of brick burial chambers, each measuring about five by two metres, have been found. These consist either of a courtyard and a single room or a rectangular chamber divided into two rooms. The interior of the tomb at Hierakonpolis had been plastered and was covered with paintings, in which Gerzean motifs appear alongside others that seem to be of south-west Asian origin. It has been suggested that both Cemetery T and the Decorated Tomb at Hierakonpolis were the burial places of Predynastic royalty (Kemp 1973).

In the late Gerzean period, there is evidence of a short period of either direct or indirect contact with the late Protoliterate b and early Protoliterate c cultures of Mesopotamia. A number of vessels and at least some of the Mesopotamian-style cylinder seals found in Egypt appear to be actual imports from Mesopotamia (Kantor 1952, 1965,

p. 10). In addition, a selection of Mesopotamian (and in some cases more particularly Susian) artistic motifs was adopted at this period, particularly for the decoration of fancy stone palettes, ivory knife-handles, and other luxury goods. These motifs include interlacing serpents, serpent-necked panthers, a winged griffin, a carnivore attacking impassive prey, a man dominating two animals, distinctive head-dress and long robes, and possibly a high-hulled ship, although the latter seems to be represented already on a fragment of Amratian pottery (fig. 1.4) (Frankfort 1956, pp. 121–37; Kantor 1965, p. 10; Vandier 1952, pp. 280–1); however, Mesopotamian influences have been discounted by Kelley (1974). While these motifs did not outlast the early years of the First Dynasty, their influence on the elite artistic production of the transitional period appears to have been quite far-reaching and suggests intensive contact with Mesopotamia. The niched brick architecture of tombs and other buildings that appears suddenly at the beginning of the First Dynasty was also probably derived from south-western Asia. Although the Egyptian structures are not exact copies of Mesopotamian originals, the plan and exterior niches of the tombs resemble those of Mesopotamian temples of the early Protoliterate period. In Meso-potamia, however, the prototypes of these buildings are found as early as the 'Ubaid period and the style was an enduring component of the regional architectural tradition; by contrast, in Egypt, niche panelling ceased to be important by the Second Dynasty (Frankfort 1956, pp. 126–9). The Egyptian script can be observed developing locally from very rudimentary beginnings and bears no specific resemblance to that of Mesopotamia; however, general similarities in the two systems of writing have suggested that stimulus diffusion from Meso-potamia may have played a role in the origin of the Egyptian script (Frankfort 1956, pp. 129–32; Pope 1966). It has also been argued that some signs appear to have been invented by Semitic, rather than Egyptian, speakers. This, plus a possible influx of words of Semitic and Sumerian origin and Semitic grammatical forms at this period, suggest the possibility of yet more Near Eastern influence (Baumgartel 1955, p. 48; Meltzer 1970). It is significant that no evidence of reciprocal Egyptian influence has been noted in Mesopotamia at this time.

What is not certain is by what direction these influences reached Upper Egypt. Helck (1962, pp. 6–9) sees no evidence of direct contacts between Egypt and Mesopotamia and believes that Mesopotamian influences reached Upper Egypt by way of the Levant and the Delta. Jar-sealings of Mesopotamian type have been found in the late

Fig. 1.4   Jebel el-Araq ivory knife-handle. Of uncertain provenance, this knife is assigned on stylistic grounds to the late Gerzean period. On the obverse appears a water battle; on the reverse a hero subduing two lions, who resembles the Mesopotamian Gilgamesh 'Lord of the Beasts' motif. This knife has been interpreted as showing evidence of Mesopotamian influence, although Egyptian types of birds and animals are portrayed on it. The 'Gilgamesh' theme also appears in the Decorated Tomb at Hierakonpolis. (Drawing by Susan Weeks.)

Chalcolithic of Palestine and probably indicate trade between these two regions (Kenyon 1960, p. 98). Since there was also trade between Palestine and Egypt at this time, it is not impossible that Palestinians acted as middlemen in the diffusion of ideas from Mesopotamia to Egypt. Others, however, favour a direct sea route around the Arabian peninsula to a point on the Red Sea opposite the Wadi Hammamat. This, it is suggested, would explain why Mesopotamian influences are apparently limited to Upper Egypt and not particularly strong south or west of the 'Amuq and the northern Orontes Valley. It would also explain why these influences reached Egypt over a very short period of time and why many of the design elements appear to be of Susian origin, rather than from Mesopotamia proper. While acknowledging that the imported pottery at Ma'adi provides evidence of contacts and trade with Palestine at this time, Kantor (1965, pp. 11–14) and others argue that independent contact with Mesopotamia is necessary to explain the type of influence that this early phase of Mesopotamian civilization was exerting on the Nile Valley.

It is hazardous, however, to assess the nature of relations between Egypt and south-western Asia at the end of the Gerzean period without considering the motivation for contact. The Protoliterate period is recognized as a vigorous and expansive phase in Mesopotamian history, and large and elaborate ships seem to be portrayed on Mesopotamian seals at this time. This does not, however, explain why the Mesopotamians, or their middlemen, should have been interested in trading, either directly or indirectly, with southern Egypt or why the region between Abydos and Aswan became the economic and political heartland of Pharaonic Egypt (Wilson 1955).

The main product of southern Egypt that would have attracted the interest of foreigners was gold. The gold-bearing region of Egypt lies chiefly between the Nile Valley and the Red Sea, in the part of the eastern desert stretching from the Qena–El-Quseir road south to the Sudan border (Baumgartel 1960, p. 143; Lucas and Harris 1962, p. 244). It is perhaps no accident that Naqada, whose Egyptian name meant literally 'the Golden Town', was located almost opposite Koptos, which stood at the mouth of the Wadi Hammamat and thus controlled access to much of the gold and other mineral wealth of the eastern desert. Indeed, in later times the gold of Egypt was called the 'Gold of the Desert of Koptos' in order to distinguish it from that of Nubia. Hierakonpolis had a similar relationship to El-Kab, its twin city on the east bank of the Nile, which in historic times was dedicated to the tutelary goddess of Upper Egypt. Behind El-Kab, a wadi gave access to gold mines in the eastern desert (Kees 1961, pp. 123–6). Similar routes led into the desert east of Kom Ombo and Edfu, which were also important towns in the historic period.

Perhaps beginning early in the Gerzean period, knowledge of the mineral wealth of the eastern desert induced traders from south-western Asia to establish trading relations with Upper Egypt, in order to obtain gold and other valued minerals. Direct contact may have been established by way of the Red Sea, although it also seems possible that traders entered Egypt through the Delta, but tended to by-pass that area because it did not produce the expensive and easily transportable luxury goods for which they were looking. Efforts to control this trade and to exploit the eastern desert more effectively may have been important factors encouraging the development of greater centralized control and leading to the emergence of small states at key locations in southern Egypt. The nuclei of these states appear to have been communities near to points of easy access to the desert; such cities probably grew into large towns, or small cities, as they became the administrative centres for these states. By the late Gerzean period, the power and wealth of the rulers of Upper Egypt may have made it possible for them to attract Asians to their courts, whose skills were utilized both for administration and to satisfy a growing appetite for luxury goods. Some of these Asians may have been skilled artisans, who continued to utilize west Asian motifs at the same time that they used their skills to turn out works of art modified to suit the taste of their new patrons. On the other hand, architectural forms, or skills such as writing, may have been introduced by adventurers or traders who had only a very imperfect acquaintance with these arts as they were practised in Mesopotamia. This influx of foreign specialists appears to have been short-lived and the Egyptian canons of court art which emerged early in the First Dynasty rejected most of the foreign influences they had introduced.

*Prehistoric Nubia*

At Jebel Silsila, near Aswan, the limestone formations of Egypt give way to Nubian sandstone. To the south, the Nile has cut more easily into the rock and, as a result, the floodplain becomes much narrower and discontinuous. The River Nile is also disrupted as an artery of communication by a series of cataracts which continue as far south as Sabaloka, near Khartoum. While precipitation appears to have been higher in late prehistoric times, especially in the southern part of this area, than it is now, Nubia has been able to sustain only a low population by comparison with Egypt.

The oldest sites in Lower Nubia that appear to contain pottery belong to the Shamarkian industry. These sites occur along the Nile near Wadi Halfa and have been dated to approximately 4000 to 4500 BC. They have yielded only minute quantities of pottery. Later 'Post-Shamarkian' sites in the same area are much larger and also contain pottery. It has been suggested that these may be 'neolithic' sites; however, there is no direct evidence of a farming or herding economy for these sites, hence their food-producing status remains in doubt. The Post-Shamarkian sites contain considerable amounts of imported Egyptian flint and have been dated to between approximately 3600 and 3000 radiocarbon years BC (Schild, Chmielewska and Wieckowska 1968).

The earliest direct evidence of food production comes from the Khartoum Neolithic culture, whose type-site, Esh-Shaheinab, is located on the west bank of the Nile about 48 km north of Omdurman. To date, this culture appears to be confined to the Nile Valley and the adjacent steppeland. The pottery, which was burnished and decorated with shallow punctate patterns, has clearly developed from that of the Khartoum Mesolithic. At Esh-Shaheinab, stone celts suggest a new emphasis on wood-working and bone harpoons, fish-hooks and the use of mussels indicate possibly even more utilization of riverine resources than in earlier times. There is also evidence that a wide range of animals, including giraffe, were being hunted. While no evidence of agriculture was found at Esh-Shaheinab, 2% of the animal bones in the site were those of sheep and goats. The site is radiocarbon-dated 3100 to 3500 BC which, however these dates are calibrated, would make it approximately coeval with the Gerzean culture. It appears that both sheep and goats and a kind of black-topped pottery had spread south from Egypt and been adopted by the local population. More recently impressions of domesticated cereals, in particular *Sorghum vulgare* and various millets, have been reported on Khartoum Neolithic-like pottery from the settlement at Kadero, dated to about 4000 BC (Arkell 1953, 1972, Klichowska 1978, Otto 1963).

Pottery resembling that of the Khartoum Neolithic has been found in sites in the Dongola region (the Karat Group) and also in the southern part of Lower Nubia (the Khartoum Variant) (Marks 1968, Wendorf 1968, vol. II, pp. 1053–4). On the other hand, the lithics associated with the pottery in each of these three areas differ widely, suggesting a diffusion of Khartoum Neolithic-type pottery among groups living in the north. Although no direct evidence of food production has been obtained for the two northern cultures, the dominance of small sites in the Khartoum Variant, both along the river and for at least 20 km west of the Nile, has been interpreted as evidence of a pastoral economy. All of these sites have been tentatively dated to the end of the fourth millennium BC.

Another possibly food-producing culture is the Abkan, which occurs on both sides of the Nile in the vicinity of the Second Cataract. The Abkan lithic assemblage appears to have developed from the Terminal Palaeolithic Qadan Industry. Abkan pottery takes the form of plain, clay-tempered, reddish-brown, open bowls. Multiple occupation sites cover sizeable areas and suggest a larger population than in earlier times. Hunting seems to have been of little importance, but no other evidence concerning the subsistence pattern is available. The presence of small numbers of Khartoum Variant sherds in Abkan sites, and of Abkan sherds in Khartoum Variant sites, suggests that these two cultures must have been at least partly contemporary. It is unclear to what degree Abkan pottery may be related to that of the prehistoric Tergis and El-Melik groups from the Dongola area, both of which have red-slipped pottery with decoration limited to a few incised lines (Marks 1968, Wendorf 1968, vol. II, p. 1053). Further investigations may also reveal whether or not there is any historical connection between Abkan pottery and that of the Northern Predynastic Sequence. It is not impossible that, prior to the beginning of the Badarian culture, a plain red pottery tradition extended from the Delta south into Nubia, of which no trace has yet been identified in Upper Egypt.

The most important cultural development in Lower Nubia during the latter part of the fourth millennium was the formulation of the A-group culture, which persisted into the Early Dynastic Period (Nordström 1972, pp. 17–32). The Abkan and Khartoum Variant cultures appear to have played an important role in the development of the A-group, and pottery derived from both appears in A-group sites, especially in southern Lower Nubia. More striking, however, is the gradual penetration of Lower Nubia by cultural traits of the Upper Egyptian Predynastic Sequence. The earliest evidence of this penetration is the pottery of late Amratian and early Gerzean date found at Khor Bahan, just south of Aswan. During the Gerzean period, pottery of the Upper Egyptian Sequence gradually spread southward along the Nile. Some of this pottery has distinctive features which, already in the early A-group, distinguish it from Egyptian pottery. One example is the so-called black-mouthed variant of Petrie's black-topped ware. This was manufactured in open bowl-shapes which, long before, had gone out of fashion in Egypt. Other forms of pottery, including ledge-handled jars, are clearly imports from Egypt. These jars probably contained cheese, honey, oil and other food products which were sought after by the Nubians. Copper tools, slate palettes and linen cloth also appear to count among the luxury goods that were imported from Egypt at this time (Trigger 1965, pp. 68–73).

It has generally been assumed that at this time the subsistence patterns of Lower Nubia were based on mixed farming, as were those of Upper Egypt; however, Firth has stressed the pastoral aspect of this economy and suggests that the Nubians resembled the Saharan tribes more than they did the Egyptians (Trigger 1965, pp. 67–8). It has been confirmed that wheat, barley and leguminous plants were grown, while cotton seeds (*Gossypium arboreum* or *G. herbaceum*) appear to have been fed to domestic animals (Chowdhury and Buth 1971). The Egyptians listed cattle and goats as booty from Nubia in the Old Kingdom. No traces of house structures have been found in any of the sites of this period, which appear to have been small encampments inhabited by no more than half a dozen families. Each band seems to have occupied its own stretch of arable floodplain. Their camps were probably located by the bank of the river for most of the year, but were moved to the edge of the floodplain during the inundation. Although the A-group people appear to have been physically similar to the Egyptians, their ethnic status remains unknown and there is no basis for suggestions that they were Egyptian, Hamitic, or Eastern Sudanic speaking (Edwards 1971, p. 50). The cultural differences between Lower Nubia and Egypt may be explained largely in terms of the former region's limited agricultural potential, rather than in terms of ethnic differences.

How were the Nubians able to import ever larger amounts of luxury goods from Egypt? It is likely that the growing wealth and prosperity of the Gerzean culture created a market for large amounts of ivory, ebony and other luxury products from sub-Saharan Africa. It may be that the inhabitants of Lower Nubia engaged in small-scale trade in such items and were able to derive a substantial profit from it. It has also been suggested that the Khor Daud site, near the mouth of the Wadi el-Allaqi, was a riverine bartering place for cattle pastoralists living in the eastern desert (Nordström 1972, p. 26); whether such a cattle trade could have supported a significant amount of exchange with the Egyptians is another matter. Alternatively, many of the Egyptian items found in Lower Nubia may have been supplied to the Nubians as goodwill presents by Egyptian traders seeking rights-of-way to travel to and from the south. It is also possible that, as has happened in recent centuries, Nubians might have earned these goods as labour migrants in the north. In particular, they may have been given in payment to detachments of Nubians who served in the Egyptian armies in late Gerzean times.

## EARLY DYNASTIC EGYPT

### The Development of the Egyptian State

Unfortunately, current archaeological evidence sheds little light on the political history of Egypt in prehistoric times. On the Palermo Stone, a year-by-year record of the Egyptian kings that was compiled in the Fifth Dynasty, a series of Predynastic rulers is shown wearing the Red Crown of Lower Egypt, followed by others wearing the Double Crown (*shmty*, 'the two powerful ones') of a united country; however, only the names of these Predynastic kings are recorded, whereas, beginning with the First Dynasty, the Palermo Stone chronicles each year of a king's reign separately, noting appropriate information concerning it. Although there is no evidence that the Double Crown existed prior to the middle of the First Dynasty, Kaiser has shown that these early kings and the prehistoric rulers alluded to in the Turin papyrus and Manetho's history are all variants of a single tradition (Edwards 1971, p. 26; Kaiser 1964). This evidence was once viewed as providing support for Sethe's theory about the emergence, in Predynastic times, of a Deltaic Kingdom which conquered the whole of Egypt. Now, however, Egyptologists tend to view these Predynastic kings, as later the Egyptians themselves did, as demigods who ruled Egypt between the time of the gods and the first human kings. As such, they may have lacked an historical existence. This has encouraged the majority of Egyptologists to assume that the first political unification of Egypt took place at about the beginning of the First Dynasty. Scenes depicted on some elaborately decorated late Gerzean palettes (fig. 1.5) and on the votive mace-heads and palettes of Kings Scorpion and Narmer have thus been interpreted as a record of the conquest of the northern part of the country by kings originating in Upper Egypt. Not long ago, the major disagreement about this period was focused on the debate as to whether King Narmer, or his presumed predecessor, the Scorpion king, was the first monarch to rule over the whole of Egypt (Arkell 1963). It has often been suggested that the canons of art which developed at this time, and which show the king as a figure increasingly aloof from his followers, are a faithful reflection of the growing power of the king.

It has also frequently been assumed that the original Egyptian states were small units equivalent to the nomes or districts which served as administrative divisions of the country in historic times. Out of the union of these tiny states, two coherent, independent kingdoms were

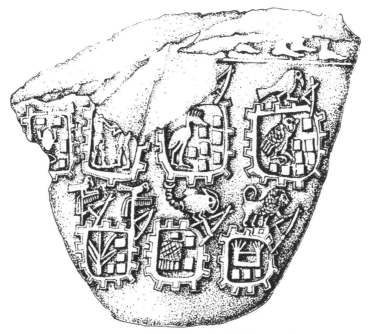

Fig. 1.5   The obverse side of the so-called 'Libyan palette'. This and similar stone palettes have been assigned on stylistic grounds to the late Gerzean period and are often interpreted as illustrating steps in the unification of Predynastic Egypt; however, the precise significance of the walls and the birds and animals hacking away at them are unknown. The former have been interpreted as forts, towns, or as synonyms for a single fort or town. The figures have been interpreted as representing a confederacy of clans or districts, gods helping the king to victory, or the king himself. If Egyptologists disagree concerning the meaning of such key elements, it is clear that the overall significance of the palettes must remain uncertain. (Drawing by Susan Weeks.)

thought to have emerged; one centred in the Delta, the other in Upper Egypt. Between them, these two kingdoms are supposed to have controlled the whole of the Nile Valley north of Aswan. Only after these states were in existence was the unification of Egypt brought about as a result of the conquest of Lower Egypt by Upper Egypt (Edwards 1971, p. 1). Against this interpretation, Frankfort has argued that the idea of a northern kingdom was created as a symbolic counterpart to the southern one after the piecemeal conquest of a series of small states by kings from Upper Egypt. According to Frankfort, the idea of two kingdoms reflects the Egyptian view of a totality as being comprised of opposites in balanced opposition (Frankfort 1948, pp. 15–23). Whatever kind of polity, or polities, existed in the north, the rigorous parallelism in the institutions and symbols ascribed to the two kingdoms supports Frankfort's view that these kingdoms were the creation of political–theological dogma rather than historical realities. While not attempting to underestimate the contribution that Deltaic political and religious institutions made to those of a united Egypt, many Egyptologists now discount the idea that a united prehistoric kingdom of Lower Egypt ever existed.

It has also been generally assumed that the cultural florescence that took place at the beginning of the First Dynasty was a consequence of the political unification of Egypt. Recently, however, Kaiser has challenged this view. He interprets the tradition of kings of a united Egypt before the First Dynasty as evidence that the conquest of the Delta by Upper Egypt took place considerably prior to the First Dynasty. The victory commemorated on the celebrated Narmer palette would thus be related to a reconquest of a northern region, or the crushing of a rebellion there, rather than to the original annexation of that area. In Kaiser's opinion, such an early union would account for the dispersal of various items of Upper Egyptian culture throughout the Delta in late Gerzean times. Large pottery vessels, found not only at Tura and Abusir el-Malaq, near Cairo, but also at Beda, in the north-east Delta, bear *serekhs* that appear to give the Horus-names of kings who ruled prior to those attested in the royal cemeteries at Abydos. Comparing the size of the Predynastic cemetery at Tura with the sections dating from the Early Dynastic Period, Kaiser (1964, p. 114) estimates that the unification of Egypt may have taken place 100 to 150 years prior to King Narmer.

Kaiser's theory has given rise to much interesting speculation. Naqada was clearly an important centre in prehistoric times and it has long been suggested that the legend of Horus and Seth may refer to a political crisis in Upper Egypt in which the rulers of this town were conquered by the followers of the god Horus (Baumgartel 1955, p. 47). It might be that the elaborate brick tombs in Cemetery T at Naqada are the graves of the first kings of a united Egypt, prior to their being supplanted by the rulers of Hierakonpolis, the town sacred to the god Horus (Kemp 1973). The last king of the Hierakonpolitan Dynasty may have been Scorpion, whose monuments are known from that place but not from Abydos (Kaiser 1964, pp. 102–5). On stylistic grounds, Scorpion appears to have preceded by only a little time Ka (or Sekhen) and Narmer, the earliest kings so far attested in the First Dynasty royal cemetery at Abydos. This interpretation would make the kings of the First Dynasty heirs of political traditions that had developed during the course of the previous century. Kaiser also views the political unity of Egypt in the late Predynastic Period as laying the groundwork for the cultural unity of Early Dynastic times. It must be noted, however, that political unity does not inevitably give rise to cultural unity and that at the site of Ma'adi, the Northern Egyptian cultural tradition appears to have survived, in spite of southern influence, until the Early Dynastic Period.

Egypt may have been politically united in late Predynastic times, even though this unity did not express itself in monumental art or architecture, or in any form of literacy; in short, in the formation of a Great Tradition, such as distinguished the civilizations of antiquity. 'Primitive kingdoms' of this sort are well known in sub-Saharan Africa: the Zulu empire and Buganda providing two examples from the last century. By their very nature, however, polities of this sort are difficult to trace in the archaeological record and, at present, the evidence for a single government for the whole of Egypt prior to the First Dynasty must be judged insufficient. The context in which most Gerzean artifacts have been discovered in the Delta is unknown and, in any case, it is possible that all of this material reached Lower Egypt as trade goods rather than as a result of the spread of Upper Egyptian political influence. Pottery bearing royal inscriptions often travelled outside Egypt in the historic period; thus the vessels found in the presumed store-house at Beda do not prove that this site was under Upper Egyptian control or that a united Egypt existed in Predynastic times. It is uncertain to what extent the north-eastern Delta was incorporated into the Egyptian state even as late as the Old Kingdom (Goedicke 1969–70). It is possible that the Predynastic kings whose *serekhs* appear on these pottery vessels were the rulers of small states who were trading with the Delta and, either directly or indirectly, with south-western Asia. It must also be noted that Baumgartel interprets the rosette and scorpion on the largest of the Hierakonpolis mace-heads as a title, rather than the name of a monarch, and thus denies the existence of a King Scorpion (Baumgartel 1960, p. 103, 1966). Until more definite evidence is forthcoming, the very existence of the only pre-Abydene king to whom substantial monuments have been attributed must remain in doubt.

Recent studies of the political development of Egypt in Predynastic times thus have not so much discredited older interpretations as they have raised new alternatives. In the absence of substantial fresh evidence, it is scarcely surprising that this is so. Under the circumstances, it is only possible to outline what appears to be theoretically the most satisfactory sequence of events; at the same time stressing the paucity of data on which any interpretation of this period must be based.

It has been suggested that in early Predynastic times each village was autonomous and had a headman whose power rested on his reputation as a 'rainmaker king'; who was presumably able to control the Nile flood (Frankfort 1948, pp. 18, 33–5). Such rainmakers have been found among African tribes, such as the Dinka, Ngonde and Jukun, in recent times and, in some tribes, they were slain once their magical powers were believed to have begun to wane. Egyptologists saw a manifestation of similar ideas in the Sed festival of the historic period, during which the powers of a reigning king were rejuvenated by rites in which he symbolically died and was reborn. Those who read Seligman's accounts of the Sudan saw in this rite a prototype of the ritual regicide reportedly practised among the Shilluk. The validity of such analogies rests largely on the assumption that Predynastic practices diffused to the upper reaches of the Nile and survived there, or that Egyptian and Nilotic cultures both developed from a common cultural substratum (Seligman and Murray 1911). Interesting as such ideas are, they remain unproved and it seems best to state categorically that nothing is known in detail about the specific social or political institutions of Predynastic Egypt.

Future discoveries may compel us to modify the idea that, in early Predynastic times, the social structure of Egypt was simple and relatively unstratified. It is not unlikely that the rise of monarchical institutions preceeded the development of the iconography by which these institutions were recognized in later times. At present, however, evidence of a high degree of craft specialization, of long-distance trade within Egypt and of sustained contacts with south-western Asia becomes visible only in the early phases of the Gerzean culture. The need to integrate and manage this new economy probably contributed to the breakdown of the relatively egalitarian tribal structures that had hitherto regulated life in the Nile Valley, and encouraged the development of a more hierarchical society, as well as of towns which served as nodal points in the economic organization and as centres of political control. The deities and cults associated with these central places probably played a major role in validating their growing importance and mediating their relationships with smaller subordinate communities. It may be possible, therefore, to describe these communities as cult centres, in the sense in which Wheatley (1971) uses this term. In later times, these cults provided one of the principal sources of identity for such communities and were an important mechanism by which local interests could express themselves vis-à-vis the central government. Up to this point, social development in Egypt seems to have followed essentially the same path as it had done in Mesopotamia. In the latter culture, this pattern gave rise, in early historic times, to a pattern of warring city states.

While northern communities, such as Ma'adi, may have flourished as entrepôts trading with both Palestine and Upper Egypt, the area chiefly affected by these new developments was the southern part of Egypt, where the Nile River approached nearest to the Red Sea Hills. There, the procurement of minerals from the eastern desert and, in particular, the organization of gold mining seems to have provided an especially powerful stimulus to the development of local, or city, states. The rulers of Naqada and Hierakonpolis were probably buried in the so-called royal tombs in the Predynastic cemeteries associated with these town-sites.

As trade with south-western Asia increased, all these local rulers must have been anxious to control this trade and to monopolize the profits derived from it. This would have led to increasing competition and conflict, as the principal rulers of Upper Egypt strove for hegemony over the whole area. The desire to protect trade routes and to eliminate intermediaries in Lower Egypt may also have encouraged these rulers to try to extend their power northward. In the course of these conflicts, the rulers of Naqada appear to have lost their independence, although their aristocratic descendants may have been buried in the very large 'royal' tombs erected there early in the First Dynasty (Kemp 1967, 1973). While it has been suggested that the rulers of Hierakonpolis may have moved their capital down river to Abydos in the course of their conquest of northern Egypt (Vandier 1952, pp. 613–14), this does not explain the importance that the kings of the First Dynasty attached to Abydos as a place of royal burial. It seems more likely that the rulers of Hierakonpolis also became clients of the kings who founded the First Dynasty and that these kings were descended from local rulers whose tombs have gone unrecorded or unrecognized at Abydos (on the other brick-lined tombs in the royal cemetery see Kemp (1966)).

Whether rulers other than those at Abydos extended their power northward remains an open question, although it is not impossible that there were dramatic shifts in the balance of power in Upper Egypt in late Gerzean times. The respect shown for the gods Seth and Horus by the Early Dynastic kings and the lavish gifts that the early kings of the First Dynasty made to the shrine at Hierakonpolis suggest that these kings were anxious to honour the gods of important rival centres and thus to bind these centres into a coalition that would facilitate an extension of royal power northward. The forging of alliances with the rulers of the various city states of Upper Egypt may have played as important a role as military conquest in establishing a basis of power in southern Egypt which allowed the conquest of the whole country.

It is unclear whether King Scorpion (if he existed) ruled from Hierakonpolis or merely left votive offerings there, as did other rulers from Abydos. As we have noted, however, if Arkell is right in reading Scorpion's name on a much-damaged mace-head showing a king wearing the Red Crown of Lower Egypt, Scorpion may already have claimed to be the ruler of a united Egypt. He appears to have been followed by Ka, and then by Narmer and Aha, all three of whom were buried in the royal cemetery at Abydos. The last two clearly claimed kingship over a united Egyptian state, although it is not agreed which, or if any of them, is to be identified as Menes, the traditional founder of the First Dynasty (Emery 1961, pp. 32–7).

These kings, whose reigns follow not long after the phase of furtive Mesopotamian influence noted at the end of the Gerzean period, not only established a royal administration capable of holding together the Nile Valley north of Aswan, but also made this administration the chief patron under which the elite culture of Egypt was to develop in the centuries that followed. It is highly significant that a coherent Great Tradition had not developed prior to the unification of Egypt. Moreover, urban institutions and civic patriotism, which were such vital features of Mesopotamian culture and were to outlive the development of empires in that part of the world, do not appear to have developed to nearly the same degree in Egypt prior to the First Dynasty. With the emergence of a strong centralized government, all of the country's nascent economic and political institutions became subjected to royal authority and control. The central government, either directly or through major officials, became the employer of soldiers, retainers, bureaucrats and craftsmen, whose goods and services benefited the upper classes and the state gods. The large mud-brick enclosure walls that already seem to have surrounded the principal buildings at Hierakonpolis (Fairservis, Weeks and Hoffman 1971–2) and elsewhere served to demarcate and shelter the nodal points in this royal administration.

In the course of the Early Dynastic Period, artisans and civil servants working for the central government were to fashion the highly sophisticated traditions of art and learning that thereafter were to constitute the basic pattern of Pharaonic civilization. In turn, this cultural pattern became a major factor in promoting the stability of the new political order. It is uncertain to what degree cultural know-how from south-western Asia played a role in the fashioning of Early Dynastic culture, but it cannot be doubted that it was one of the factors that helped the First Dynasty state resulting from the conquest to produce an enduring high culture. The highly distinctive style of this civilization and the rapid disappearance of all evidence of Mesopotamian influence is indicative, however, of the internal dynamism of Egyptian society at this time.

Equally striking are the structural differences between Early Dynastic and south-west Asian social organization after this time. The fruits of Mesopotamian civilization were divided among a number of city states and among various interest groups within each of these urban centres. By contrast, the fruits of Egyptian civilization were expended on a royal court and, to a striking degree, as the emphasis on royal mortuary complexes demonstrates, on the person of the king. While Mesopotamia was to create nothing on the scale of the Old Kingdom pyramids, a greater number of Mesopotamians probably benefited from, and participated in, the Great Tradition of their society than did their Egyptian counterparts. The achievement of a stable, centralized government in Egypt also removed some of the insecurity which in Mesopotamia encouraged the rapid growth of fortified urban centres (R. M. Adams 1972, Frankfort 1956). This helped to perpetuate a pattern of dispersed villages and only relatively small regional administrative centres. Such a development may also explain the preoccupation with rural, as opposed to urban, life that was a distinctive feature of the elite culture of Egypt.

After unification, most Egyptians must have found daily life in their villages little changed from what it had been before. More taxes in kind were probably collected and additional demands made for *corvée* labour. In return, peace and greater security against famine provided the average Egyptian with increased prosperity, while agricultural development must have both encouraged and kept abreast of a growing population throughout this period. While the population of Egypt has been estimated to have been as low as 100000 to 200000 inhabitants in late Predynastic times (Butzer 1966), a reference to 120000 men, as either prisoners or part of a grant to a temple, on a mace-head of King Narmer suggests a considerably larger population at the beginning of the Early Dynastic Period (Emery 1961, pp. 44–5). A population of two million or more is not an unreasonable guess for this period.

## Political Organization

According to Manetho, the kings of the first two dynasties originated in the Thinite nome of Upper Egypt. The tombs of the First Dynasty kings are located in the Umm el-Qaab area of the Abydos cemeteries, about 2 km west of the limit of cultivation (fig. 1.6). These tombs, the largest of which had a floor area of about 340 sq. m, consisted of subterranean brick chambers lined with wooden panelling. Each tomb seems to have been covered by a low mound of sand or gravel held inside a brick retaining wall. Here too were erected twin stone stelae bearing the Horus-name of the dead king. While the earliest tombs consisted of one or more single rooms, later ones had a central chamber surrounded by store-rooms. Beginning in the reign of King Den, a stairway gave access to the burial chamber. In Den's tomb, the burial chamber was also paved with blocks of Aswan granite. The relatively small size of these tombs and their proximity to one another suggests that Umm el-Qaab was a location of special sanctity to the kings of the First Dynasty. Perhaps, like the cemetery of the much later Nubian kings at Kurru, it was revered as the burial place of their ancestors. Nearer the cultivated land, and just behind the Early Dynastic town at Abydos, each king also erected a large rectangular brick enclosure, which Kemp (1966, 1967) suggests were intended as funerary palaces. Both the funerary palaces and the royal tombs were surrounded by rows of smaller graves, blocks of which appear to have shared a common roof. The stelae accompanying the graves around the royal tombs indicate that they contained members of the royal entourage. Many are of women, presumably members of the royal harem, while others belonged to minor palace functionaries, court dwarfs, or even favourite dogs. On the other hand, at least some of the graves surrounding the funerary palaces seem to have belonged to artisans. While there is no direct evidence how these retainers died, at least some did so just prior to when a royal burial was closed. This suggests that these retainers were killed so they might continue to serve the king after death. The custom seems to have reached its peak in the reign of King Djer, who was accompanied by over 580 retainers, but persisted at a reduced level in royal burials throughout the Early Dynastic Period.

Aside from the enigmatic Merneith (Kaplan 1979), who may have been a regnant queen, there is no indication that other members of the royal family, or high-ranking officials, were buried at Abydos. Two sets of underground galleries, about 1 km south of the main Early Dynastic

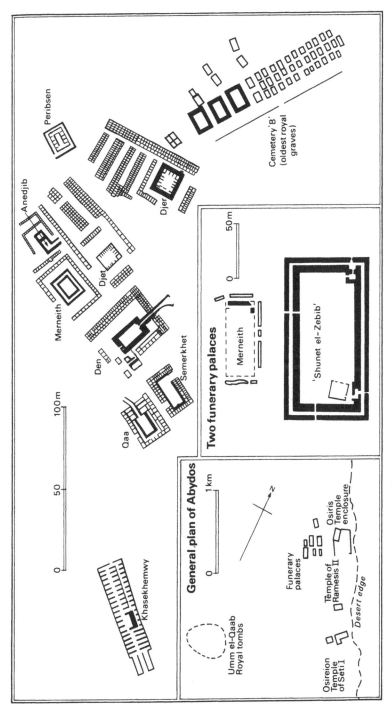

Peribsen

Anedjib

Merneith

Djet

Den

Qaa

Semerkhet

Djer

Cemetery 'B'
(oldest royal
graves)

100m

50

0

Khasekhemwy

**Two funerary palaces**

Merneith

'Shunet el-Zebib'

0          50 m

**General plan of Abydos**

0        1 km

N

Osiris
Temple
enclosure

Funerary
palaces

Temple of
Ramesis II

*Desert edge*

Umm el-Qaab
Royal tombs

Osireion
Temple
of Seti I

Fig. 1.6   The royal tombs and funerary palaces at Abydos.

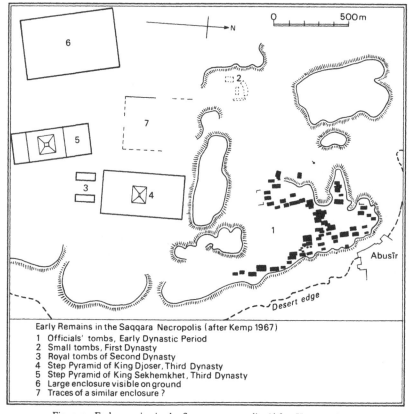

Fig. 1.7   Early remains in the Saqqara necropolis. (After Kemp 1967.)

cemetery at Saqqara, appear to be royal graves of the Second Dynasty (fig. 1.7) (Kemp 1967). Unlike the rulers of the First Dynasty, these kings chose to be buried near Memphis, rather than at their home town of Abydos. The dissension which seems to have divided Egypt late in the Second Dynasty led kings Peribsen and Khasekhemwy to build their tombs at Abydos, while the so-called 'fort' at Hierakonpolis also may have been erected as a funerary palace at about this time (Kaiser 1964, p. 104, n. 4).

According to Herodotus, Menes, the founder of the First Dynasty, constructed dykes to divert the Nile River and, on the land thus protected, he built the city of Memphis and its main temple, which was dedicated to the god Ptah. Whether or not this story is true, Memphis was an important administrative centre from early in the First Dynasty and the palace and temple of Ptah were later regarded as closely connected with the unification of Egypt (Kees 1961, p. 148). Although this part of the Nile Valley was not a particularly rich agricultural area, it was located near the branching of the Nile and was thus strategically placed in terms of riverine communication (Wilson 1955). On the northern spur of the Saqqara plateau behind Memphis, a cemetery was established in the reign of Aha, which eventually contained the tombs of many important officials of the Early Dynastic Period. These so-called mastaba tombs were equipped with rectangular brick superstructures, either filled with gravel or containing storage chambers. Their internal arrangements became increasingly elaborate, as did those of the royal tombs, as storage rooms multiplied, and by the end of the period subterranean chambers were being excavated out of solid rock (Vandier 1952, pp. 644–72). Although the largest of these tombs were bigger than the royal tombs at Abydos, they did not exceed in size the royal funerary palaces. Tumuli found hidden inside the superstructures of some of the Saqqara tombs suggest that they sought to combine the elements of both a tomb and a funerary palace within a single structure (Kemp 1966).

A small number of other very large mastaba tombs have been reported from Naqada, Tarkhan, Giza and Abu Rawash. Some, but not all, of these large tombs were accompanied by subsidiary burials; over sixty have been reported for one such tomb, although the number is usually much smaller. This custom seems to have died out by the end of the First Dynasty, in line with a marked curtailment of retainer sacrifice, in royal burials. Over 10000 graves have been excavated in the Early Dynastic (largely First Dynasty) cemetery at Helwan, on the east bank of the Nile opposite Memphis. While most of these are humble graves, the cemetery also contained the tombs of numerous officials. Although smaller than the graves at Saqqara, these too belonged to people who had easy access to skilled craftsmen and luxury goods. Burial chambers built of large blocks of reasonably well-cut limestone were constructed at Helwan in the First Dynasty, but do not appear in the royal tombs until the end of the Second Dynasty (Saad 1969, pp. 36–7). While the graves of ordinary Egyptians differed little from those of late Predynastic times, the more prosperous provincial cemeteries contained a number of smaller and simpler versions of the mastaba tombs of the upper classes. These tombs appear to have belonged to the headmen of these communities (Reisner 1932, pp. 185–92).

The funerary customs of the Early Dynastic Period suggest a hierarchy of king; great nobles or high officials (including other members of the royal family); lesser officials (including local headmen); craftsmen and retainers; and peasantry, the latter making up the bulk of the population. While the mortuary structures of the king in size considerably outstripped those of the great officials and were surrounded by many more retainer burials, the differences between these two categories of burial are far less marked than they were during the Old Kingdom. This suggests either that the power of the kings to appropriate resources for their own use was more limited in the Early Dynastic Period than it was later on, or that the kings of this period did not choose to emphasize the differences between themselves and other leading men in this fashion. The clustering of the largest tombs of officials around the pyramid of the reigning pharaoh in the Old Kingdom is generally interpreted as indicating the strength of royal authority at that time; hence, it might be argued that the burial of high officials, not only in their own necropolis at Saqqara but also in other cemeteries throughout Egypt, is a sign of greater independence of royal control at this time. On the other hand, the way in which the tombs of even the high nobility were kept away from the Early Dynastic royal cemeteries, both at Abydos and Saqqara, may indicate that kings were accorded a sanctity in Early Dynastic times which did not permit other tombs to encroach upon their burial places (Kemp 1967).[1]

Unfortunately, knowledge of the dynastic history and administrative organization of Egypt during the Early Dynastic Period is extremely limited. Information about the government is derived largely from seals, seal impressions, and inscribed wooden and ivory labels. This material naturally emphasizes ownership of goods and provisioning, and thus gives a far from balanced picture of the government of Egypt at this time. Finally, the archaic form of the Egyptian script with which this material is inscribed presents numerous problems for the translator. In spite of the extremely valuable work that Kaplony (1963) has done in interpreting these early documents, no systematic analysis of the political organization of the Early Dynastic Period has yet been attempted.

There is, however, little doubt that, from the beginning, the kings of Egypt claimed divine status. Through their Horus-names, which were the ones regularly used in contemporary inscriptions, they

---

[1] Note, however, that in the Old Kingdom cemetery at Naga ed-Deir, headmen's tombs were located away from other contemporary ones.

proclaimed themselves to be the earthly embodiment of that deity. Peribsen deviated from this custom only in identifying himself with Seth in place of Horus (Edwards 1971, p. 35). The paramount role of the monarch was emphasized by portraying him as the sole force holding together an otherwise separate Upper and Lower Egypt. This was emphasized by the king wearing distinct regalia to symbolize each realm and by his *nebty*-name, which stressed his dual relationship to the vulture goddess Nekhbet of Upper Egypt and the cobra goddess Uadjyt of Lower Egypt. It was once believed that this name indicated that El-Kab and Buto, the respective towns of these goddesses, had been the capitals of Upper and Lower Egypt. Wilson argues, however, that the goddesses of these two cities were selected as symbols of Upper and Lower Egypt because their cult centres best embodied the extreme contrasts between the arid far south of Egypt and the marshes of the Delta (Wilson 1955). The king's third or *insibya*- name, which is first attested in the reign of King Den, gives his style as king of Upper and Lower Egypt, and thus, like the *nebty*-name, is a dual title. The latter part appears to be connected with the worship of Neith, the goddess of Sais in the western Delta (Edwards 1971, p. 53). A number of Sed festivals are recorded for this period, testifying to the antiquity of this ritual. Little can be said about either the structure of the royal family or the rules governing succession to the throne. The lengths assigned to reigns of this period suggest, however, that the throne was normally passed from generation to generation, and probably from father to son, as it was in later times.

The titles of the Early Dynastic period overwhelmingly refer to positions in an administrative hierarchy, rather than to hereditary rank. Royal children are seldom explicitly identified as such, but, if Kaplony is right in identifying the names of seal-bearers, when juxtaposed with those of kings, as expressing filiation, many high officials may have been members of the royal family. Many offices appear to have been passed from father to son, although it is unclear whether this happened by right, or whether each transfer had to receive royal approbation separately. Officials served under successive kings and had estates whose produce constituted a significant portion of the grave-goods that were deposited in their tombs (Kaplony 1963, pp. 25, 58–9, 71). Whether all of these estates were granted to officials by the king to sustain and reward them for their services, or whether some of them had been hereditary in particular families prior to the First Dynasty, is unknown. It seems likely, however, that, whatever nominal claim the king may have made to pre-eminent domain, older patterns of land-holding at the village level, and possibly among the upper classes also, were not unduly interfered with by the king. In spite of the controls exerted over the Egyptian economy by the central government, these controls could not have developed in an economic vacuum; it is therefore mistaken to underestimate the complexity of land-holding patterns and of economic activities in Egypt at this period.

Only a few titles have been preserved that refer specifically to the regional administration of Egypt at this time. It would be interesting to know if important provincial officials enjoyed hereditary rights in particular areas or if they were transferred from district to district in the course of their career as was done during the Old Kingdom. The general restriction of very large tombs at Naqada, and elsewhere outside Memphis, to a relatively early date, suggests the possible suppression of any tendency towards a feudal-style decentralization of power. While the shifting of officials from district to district might have lessened the efficiency of administration, it would have helped to protect the authority of the central government and thus have laid the basis for the spectacular exercise of this authority early in the Old Kingdom.

More is known about the administration of the palace and of the royal estates, including the vineyards in the western Delta. There was also a large, well-organized bureaucracy which collected taxes in kind throughout the country, stored these goods in government warehouses and supervised their distribution to those who were privileged to receive royal largess. The height of the Nile flood was carefully recorded each year and probably served as the basis for computing annual rates of taxation on crops, while a biennial royal tour of inspection allowed for a general census of taxable resources. Whether or not the king personally took part in this tour, it was known as the 'Following of Horus' (*šmsw Ḥr*) and, along with flood heights, it was faithfully recorded on the Palermo Stone (Edwards 1971, p. 38).

The need for book-keeping, supplemented by a desire to record royal exploits, appears to have been mainly responsible for the development of writing in Egypt. No inscribed papyri have survived from the Early Dynastic Period, so that the early history of Egyptian writing must be derived mainly from jar-sealings, labels and inscriptions on monumental objects (fig. 1.8). These indicate that the evolution of writing was closely associated with the royal court. Until the reign of Den, seals generally recorded only the names of kings and officials; while afterwards titles and other bureaucratic designations became increasingly common (Kaplony 1963, p. xxxii). At the same time, hieroglyphs ceased to serve

Fig. 1.8 Reverse side of the slate palette of King Narmer. Here appears for the first time the classic motif of the monarch dominating a conquered enemy. Hieroglyphs, some obscure because of the early stage in the development of the writing system, identify the figures. Narmer's name is written within the royal *serekh* that appears top centre. (After Gardiner 1927.)

only as legends to pictorial representations and dockets covered largely or wholly with writing began to appear. By the end of the First Dynasty, whole sentences were being conveyed by sequences of signs (Gardiner 1961, p. 415; Vandier 1952, p. 859). Significantly, however, no evidence of the use of writing was found to occur prior to the Fifth Dynasty in the small cemetery at Naga ed-Deir (Reisner 1932).

The central government used some of the food surpluses and manufactured goods that it had at its disposal to engage in foreign trade. While there is no evidence that the king claimed a monopoly over this trade, the needs and wealth of the court encouraged the palace to trade on a scale that greatly exceeded that of any other individual or institution in the country. It therefore seems likely that it was through the court that most foreign goods made their way into Egypt, prior to being distributed as royal bounty. Masses of pottery vessels from the Early Bronze Age II culture of Palestine and coastal Syria have been found in royal tombs of the First Dynasty, as well as in those of high officials. Conversely, pottery of the First Dynasty has been found in sites such as Tell Gath in southern Palestine, which has yielded a jar inscribed with the name of King Narmer. In addition to importing jars of olive oil from southern Palestine, the kings of Egypt obtained large amounts of timber, suitable for building boats, lining tombs and fashioning coffins and household furniture, from Syria and Lebanon; while other exotic items, which came from farther to the north or west, such as obsidian and lapis lazuli, must have entered Egypt along the same routes. This trade appears to have been carried on by both sea and land and to have continued through the Second Dynasty and into the Old Kingdom (Kantor 1965, pp. 16–17). There is no evidence that contacts with Mesopotamia were still maintained at this time; instead, Egyptian trade seems to have been limited to areas of south-western Asia that were economically and culturally less developed than Egypt was. The Egyptian kings also sent expeditions into the eastern desert to exploit the mineral resources of that area. An inscription of Narmer in the Wadi el-Qash and another of Djet in the Wadi Mia, 24 km east of Edfu, appear to commemorate expeditions of a commercial or punitive nature (Edwards, 1971, pp. 22, 24–5; Emery 1961, pp. 47, 49). Copper was used in abundance in the Early Dynastic period, as was turquoise, but there is no proof that the Egyptians had begun to send expeditions to the Sinai peninsula at this time.

The royal court appears to have employed large numbers of artists and craftsmen, who were capable of turning out a wide variety of luxury goods. These craftsmen, most of whom probably worked in the vicinity of Memphis, evolved a coherent style and established artistic canons that were to remain an integral part of the elite culture of ancient Egypt. Some of the jewellery, furniture and other luxury goods produced by these artisans were distributed among the officials who served the king to reward them and retain their loyalty. Donations to temples also reinforced the ties between the king and the locality or region the temple served. It is uncertain whether most temples were still the shrines of light construction that seem to be depicted in representations of the Early Dynastic Period or whether these had been generally superseded by larger and more substantial buildings.[1] The royal administration no doubt played a direct role in the maintenance of the chief temples, and royal visits to the shrines of important deities and the fashioning of cult

[1] On the function and date of the so-called Temple of Khenty-amentiu at Abydos see Kemp (1968b).

statues of the gods are noted on the Palermo Stone as matters of great importance (Gardiner 1961, p. 414). While craftsmen were normally buried only with food, drink and some of the tools of their trade, there can be little doubt that they participated, at least to a limited degree, in the bounty of the king and his officials. Even the peasantry probably received boons in the form of meat and drink on festive occasions, although there is no direct evidence of this for the Early Dynastic Period. If less that was tangible was returned to these classes than was demanded of them in taxes and services, such devices would nevertheless have kept alive older ideas of reciprocity and helped to maintain the goodwill of the masses, in addition to their obedience and reverence. It is also possible that at this period a man of ability could reasonably hope to climb in the administrative hierarchy (Frankfort 1956, pp. 107–8). This was particularly likely if the population was expanding and new positions were developing in an increasingly complex society.

## Foreign Relations

Although the military organization at this period is obscure, force must have played a role in maintaining the unity of the Egyptian state and regulating its relations with its neighbours. References to the suppression of 'northern enemies' on monuments of King Khasekhem suggest the crushing of a rebellion, or a counter-dynasty, in northern Egypt towards the end of the Second Dynasty (Edwards 1971, p. 33), although others interpret this as a campaign against the Libyans, who lived along the borders of Lower Egypt and against whom the kings of Egypt had waged war at an early period (Gardiner 1961, p. 418). Both Kings Djer and Den claim to have engaged in combat with enemies living to the east of Egypt, but neither the eastern border nor the identity of these enemies is certain and suggestions of military intervention into Palestine at this period lack confirmation (Yadin 1955).

More is known about relations with Nubia. With the development of the Early Dynastic court culture, the demand for products from sub-Saharan Africa, particularly ebony and ivory, appears to have increased sharply. In addition, the Egyptian kings may have been concerned about securing their southern border at the First Cataract, up river from Jebel Silsila. It has been suggested that a smiting of Nubia reported for the reign of Aha commemorates the incorporation of this stretch of river into the Egyptian state (Säve-Söderbergh 1941, p. 7). About the beginning of the First Dynasty, an Egyptian expedition probably made its way as far south as Wadi Halfa and, on Jebel Sheikh Suliman, carved a scene claiming a victory over two villages or local groups of Nubians (Arkell 1950).[1] This is the most southerly evidence of Egyptian penetration during the Early Dynastic Period found to date.

A-group communities continued to flourish into the early part of the First Dynasty, particularly in the southern half of Lower Nubia. Large quantities of Egyptian pottery, including wine jars, as well as copper tools, jewellery, pendants, and amulets indicate that the Nubians continued to have access to Egyptian goods at this period, as they had done in late Predynastic times. Rectangular houses with rough stone walls in a village site at Afyeh indicate more sedentarism than before (Lal 1963), while handsomely slipped and painted conical bowls of local manufacture suggest new levels of cultural achievement. One of the most remarkable finds from this period is the grave of a Nubian headman from a cemetery near Sayala, which dates from the early part of the First Dynasty. Among the imported goods found in this grave were a number of large copper axes, bar ingots, and chisels, a dipper of banded slate and several stone vessels, two immense double-bird shaped palettes and two maces with gold handles, one decorated with a series of animals worked in low relief (Kantor 1944). The source of such wealth is uncertain, although the Nubians were probably less able to act as middlemen or to charge tolls in the Early Dynastic Period than they had been in late Predynastic times. Possibly, such goods were rewards given to a headman who had servd as a mercenary in the Egyptian army. Even more elaborate graves dated to the early First Dynasty have been found in Cemetery L at Qustul, near the Egyptian–Sudanese border. This period appears to be the cultural climax of the A-group in Lower Nubia, although the population probably still amounted to only a few thousand people, organized on a tribal basis.

In the course of the First Dynasty, the flow of Egyptian trade goods into Nubia came to an end and the A-group culture began to break down. It is reasonable to assume that this process was related to the growth of the Egyptian monarchy and the centralization of the Egyptian economy. Instead of using the A-group as intermediaries in its trade with sub-Saharan Africa, the Egyptian court now may have sought to carry on this trade directly. The repeated Egyptian invasions of Lower Nubia seem to have been part of this process and no doubt

[1] While the scene clearly dates from about the beginning of the First Dynasty its unity and attribution to Djer are not undisputed: see Helck (1970).

account for the eventual disappearance of a sedentary population in Lower Nubia before the end of the First Dynasty (Nordström 1972, pp. 29–32).

The oldest known Egyptian settlement in Lower Nubia was at Buhen, near the Second Cataract. The large bricks used to construct the lowest levels of the town suggest that it may have been founded as early as the Second Dynasty, although this early date is far from certain (Trigger 1965, p. 79–80). The purpose of this settlement is not clear, but it may have served as a jumping-off point for an overland trade route that ran around the Second Cataract and southward to Dongola. H. S. Smith (1966) has demonstrated that the graves Reisner assigned to his B-group, supposedly equivalent in age to the Old Kingdom, are, in fact, poorer or badly plundered graves of the A-group.

Almost nothing is known about the Sudan at this time. Some pottery from the Omdurman Bridge site resembles that of the A-group, while other pottery, decorated with incisions filled with white pigment, is similar to both Predynastic Egyptian N-ware and some of the later C-group pottery (Arkell 1949, pp. 99–107). Small agricultural communities and pastoralist groups probably occupied the Sudanese Nile Valley and the adjacent steppes at this time. If Egyptian trading expeditions were already reaching the Dongola area, it is possible that the need to collect raw materials from the south in order to trade them with the Egyptians was encouraging greater social complexity in that area, in a manner analogous to what had happened in Egypt in the early Gerzean period (Trigger 1965, pp. 81–3).

## Arts and Crafts

Some of the important changes that came about in Egyptian society at the beginning of the Early Dynastic Period found expression in new patterns of material culture, particularly as these were related to mass-produced goods and products manufactured specifically for the upper classes. Material of both kinds is abundantly represented in cemetery sites, where vast quantities, and many different varieties, of goods were buried in the wealthier graves. The allocation of such large quantities of luxury goods to these tombs must have increased sharply the demand for raw materials and for the services of skilled craftsmen.

Pottery continued to be mass-produced as it had been in the Gerzean period. Vessels with the same pot-marks, apparently indicating the team or workshop that made them, are found throughout the country (Emery

1961, p. 203). The black-topped and painted pottery of Predynastic times did not, however, survive into the Early Dynastic Period; at which time the pottery is well formed, but strictly utilitarian. This does not indicate a decline in cultural or aesthetic standards. Instead, it suggests that pottery no longer served as a medium of artistic expression, as it had done formerly. Pottery jars were used to store wine and foodstuffs, including cheese, while bowls, cups and dishes were used as eating vessels. Most pottery was a reddish-brown ware, manufactured from Nile mud (Emery 1961, pp. 206–14). Although many copper tools were now available for craftsmen who were in the employ of the wealthy, flint was still widely used to manufacture knives, scrapers, arrow- and spear-heads, sickle blades, drills and other implements. Magnificent scimitar-like flint knives continued to be manufactured well into the First Dynasty. Although possibly made for ritualistic purposes, these knives sustained some of the expertise in working flint that had developed during the Gerzean period (Emery 1961, p. 233; Saad 1969, pls. 40–2).

In other spheres, the Early Dynastic culture was markedly in advance of that of Predynastic times. Carpentry appears to have developed very rapidly at the start of the First Dynasty, no doubt aided by the proliferation of copper tools. In particular, the techniques of joining, carving and inlay all manifest a sophistication not attested for the Predynastic Period. The furnishings of wealthier houses now included beds, chairs, stools and numerous chests and boxes, sometimes embellished with ivory or copper fittings. Legs of furniture were frequently carved to represent the limbs of cattle. Near life-size wooden statues were also produced, at least as early as the reign of Djer (Emery 1961, pp. 170–1). Metal ewers, bowls, dishes and other vessels, as well as mirrors, were hammered, and later cast, from copper. Spouts were riveted onto these vessels and handles were sometimes bound on with copper wire. In general, copper vessels reproduced the forms of stone ones. Although no copper statues have survived, one of Khasekhemwy is reported to have been made in the fifteenth year of his reign (Edwards 1971, p. 34). Jewellery was made out of gold, turquoise, lapis lazuli and other semi-precious stones. Engraved and embossed sheets of gold were used to cover the handles of weapons and to adorn other objects. The central chamber of one tomb at Saqqara was inlaid from floor to ceiling with strips of sheet gold; its employment giving some idea of the amounts of this metal available at this time (Emery 1961, p. 228). Bone and ivory were used for inlays, jewellery, arrow-heads, spoons, gaming pieces and statuettes. The modelling and delineation of details on some of the best ivory objects is of very high quality. Beads, pendants, amulets and inlays were also made out of faience, in a wide variety of different shapes (Emery 1961, pp. 228–31).

The most distinctive products of the Early Dynastic Period were a vast number of vessels made of steatite, schist, alabaster, marble, quartz, basalt, diorite and many other types of stone. While carrying on a tradition of stone-working of long standing in Upper Egypt, the aesthetic standards achieved in the manufacture of these vessels were not matched either before or after this time. The softer stones, particularly schist and alabaster, were worked into vessels of exceedingly plastic design, while harder stone was used to fashion simpler-shaped vessels. Sometimes, stone of one kind was inlaid with stone of another. Many of the thousands of stone vessels that were buried in the Step Pyramid at the beginning of the Third Dynasty were made in the Early Dynastic Period (Emery 1961, pp. 214–17).

While the late Gerzean votive mace-heads and palettes bear witness to the development of bas-relief sculpture prior to the First Dynasty, these particular forms of artistic expression did not persist for long afterwards. That bas-relief continued is demonstrated, however, by the funerary stelae from Abydos and a frieze of lions on a limestone lintel from the tomb of Queen Herneith. The royal stelae display erratic variations in design and execution, some being primitive on both counts, others well carved but lacking in balance of design. On the other hand, the stela of King Djet is ranked among the great artistic achievements of ancient Egyptian culture. Later in the Early Dynastic Period, rectangular stelae from both Saqqara and Helwan portray the deceased seated before a table surrounded by funerary offerings (Vandier 1952, pp. 724–74). An inscribed granite door-jamb of Khasekhemwy is described as displaying all of the design and symmetry of the Old Kingdom, in spite of the hard stone from which it was fashioned (Emery 1961, p. 169).

Stone sculpture also developed during the Early Dynastic Period. Animal representations include an alabaster baboon, inscribed with the name of Narmer, and a granite lion. The famous pottery lion from Hierakonpolis may also date from this period, although the Third Dynasty has also been suggested (Vandier 1952, p. 977). A number of human figures, carved out of limestone and granite and smaller than life-size, appear to belong to the Second Dynasty. These portray kneeling officials or seated figures. From the end of the period are two statuettes of Khasekhem, one in schist, the other in limestone; in style these foreshadow the classic art of the Old Kingdom. In its clean lines, increasing symmetry and striving after a monumental effect regardless of size, the sculpture of the Early Dynastic Period represents the formative stage in the development of a major component of classical Egyptian art.

We have already discussed the development of funerary architecture during this period. If the so-called forts of the Second Dynasty are, in fact, all royal funerary palaces, little in the way of non-funerary architecture survives. It is reasonable to believe, however, that brick niching was also used in non-funerary contexts. A niched wall recently uncovered at the Early Dynastic town-site of Hierakonpolis may have been part of some First Dynasty royal construction (Fairservis *et al.* 1971–2). The Palermo Stone records the erection of a stone temple at the end of the Second Dynasty (Edwards 1971, p. 66).

There is little direct evidence concerning the intellectual achievements of the Early Dynastic Period. Records were evidently kept of the sort which could later be used to compile the text of the Palermo Stone. Two treatises are also claimed, on the basis of internal evidence, to·date from this period. One, the so-called Memphite theology, ascribes the creation of the world to Ptah, the patron deity of Memphis. The other is a surprisingly empirical work dealing with medical procedures (Aldred 1965, pp. 63–4).

The Early Dynastic Period appears to have been a time of great creativity and inventiveness, in the course of which the elite culture of Pharaonic Egypt can be seen taking shape. While this creativity was to continue into the Third Dynasty, by the end of the Early Dynastic Period most of the principal elements of the court culture of the Old Kingdom were already well established. The development of new skills and the flowering of so many arts and crafts at the beginning of the First Dynasty have been interpreted by some Egyptologists as 'overwhelming evidence' of an incursion into the Nile Valley, which brought with it the culture of Early Dynastic times (Emery 1961, p. 165). While we have noted evidence of Mesopotamian influence, this influence was only transitory and was replaced by stylistic conventions that were of indigenous origin and which characterized Egyptian culture in later times. The continuities between the Predynastic and Early Dynastic cultures are so numerous as to suggest that some explanation, other than migration or cultural diffusion, is needed to account for the differences between these two periods.

The crucial factor in the emergence of new traditions of craftsmanship seems to be that it was at the beginning of the Early Dynastic Period, or slightly before, that certain craftsmen came under the patronage and control of the royal court. Hitherto, craftsmen had existed in Egypt whose work was clearly of a high order. It would appear, however, that these craftsmen looked to their community, region, or to Egypt as a whole, rather than to a particular class in Egyptian society, as a market for their goods. While some of the goods they turned out may have been for the temples or for the wealthier and more powerful members of the community, these were only some among a broad range of clients. In early times, rulers probably were content to avail themselves of the services of these general craftsmen.

Around the beginning of the First Dynasty, however, the kings of Egypt started to provide work for an increasing number of specialists on a full-time basis. As the Egyptian state grew, the court and the official hierarchy expanded, providing a larger market for specialized goods and services and this, in turn, facilitated a high degree of specialization within particular lines of work. One result of this specialization was a marked increase in the quality of what was being produced. Artisans developed whose work was solely to provide luxury goods for the upper classes. The need to co-ordinate the activities of groups of specialists also encouraged the development of writing and of numerous administrative skills connected with royal government. Within the overall system, craftsmen were subject to control by scribes and bureaucrats, who were charged with supplying them and co-ordinating their activities. One effect of this control of production by accountants and administrators must have been to discourage innovations, once acceptable modes of production had been worked out. The effect of this has been noted by Aldred when he states that, in spite of bold experimentations during the Early Dynastic Period, once a solution had been evolved, development ceased and a new convention was added to a stockpile of existing traditions (Aldred 1965, p. 53).

Because the whole of Egypt was united under a single government, at least by the First Dynasty, a common network of highly specialized craftsmen came to serve a group of patrons on such a scale as was not to be found among the city states of Mesopotamia, even if individual Mesopotamian cities enjoyed hegemony over the rest from time to time. Because of this, it is not surprising that, in the Old Kingdom, building projects could be undertaken on a scale that was impossible in Mesopotamia and that in specific crafts, such as those related to stone-working, the skills of Egyptian workmen greatly outstripped those of their Mesopotamian counterparts. On the other hand, in Egypt basic technological innovation tended to lag behind that of south-western Asia; as evidenced by the late introduction of both bronze and iron. The luxurious products of the court-sponsored culture of Egypt were meant, however, for the use of an elite and stood as material symbols of the superordinate position of these people in Egyptian society. Occasionally, the minor works of highly skilled artisans may have made their way further down the redistributive network or been purchased by an exceptionally prosperous villager. Simplified and cheaper versions of court fashions also seem to have diffused gradually down to the level of ordinary people. On the whole, however, local production and local trade must have continued to supply the needs of the vast majority of Egyptians, as they had done in Predynastic times.

## CONCLUSIONS

While the possibility that certain plants and animals may have been domesticated locally cannot be ruled out, food production in Egypt, from Predynastic times on, was clearly an extension of the south-west Asian pattern. North of the First Cataract, the Nile Valley embraced a floodplain that was larger and easier to cultivate than any in south-western Asia. The abundance of game and natural plant foods initially may have inhibited the spread of food production, and it was perhaps only towards the end of the Predynastic Period that the population became almost totally reliant on agriculture and herding. Moreover, the especially rich natural resources of the Delta may have resulted in an even slower realization of the full potential of a food-producing economy than took place in Upper Egypt. Both in Upper and Lower Egypt, however, the floodplain had the potential for supporting a dramatic increase in population and for the development of a more complex society, as a result of the greater productivity inherent in an agricultural economy. Farther south, in Nubia, the narrow and discontinuous floodplain did not hold out such promise. In that area, food production appears mainly to have compensated for declining natural food sources. The population of this region remained small and at a tribal level.

The development of a complex society in Egypt was further encouraged by the proximity of the southern part of Upper Egypt to the mineral resources of the eastern desert. It has been suggested that gold became an important item of trade with south-western Asia, probably by the early Gerzean period. This trade enhanced the regulatory power of those headmen whose communities were well situated to exploit these resources and may have been a major factor promoting the emergence of these communities as important economic and political centres. Competition over trade may also have led to political struggles among the emerging polities of southern Egypt and the desire to protect trade with Palestine and the rest of south-western Asia, or to eliminate middlemen, may have led to the conquest of northern Egypt, either at the beginning of the First Dynasty or sometime earlier.

The consolidation of the Egyptian state was ensured by the development of a centralized administrative system and of a court-centred Great Tradition predicated on a united Egypt, which thereafter, even in times of political crises, was to dominate the thinking of the Egyptian elite. The early development of a strong central government eliminated many of the factors that in south-western Asia led to the development of urban centres for defensive purposes. In Egypt, regional administrative centres were not necessarily marked by large clusters of population, and the peasantry remained scattered in small villages. The royal court set the cultural standards for the entire country; making the king the fountainhead not only of power and preferment but also of a way of life that the elite, and to some extent all Egyptians, wished to share. The absence of powerful enemies on its peripheries was in early times a source of stability for Egyptian society by comparison with the situation prevailing in Mesopotamia; however, the elite traditions, combined with the scale of Egyptian society, later proved strong enough to survive periods of internal instability and foreign conquest for over three thousand years. The forging of an elite tradition on this vast scale was clearly the greatest achievement of the Early Dynastic Period.

# APPENDIX

## CHRONOLOGY OF THE EARLY DYNASTIC PERIOD

### PREDYNASTIC KINGS

Palermo Stone – top register has seven names fully preserved, two partially; all wear the crown of Lower Egypt. There are traces of more determinatives

69

at either end. The main Cairo fragment has ten determinatives; six wear the Double Crown of a united Egypt.

The Scorpion king (?)
Ka (Sekhen)

FIRST DYNASTY

FROM 3000 ± 100 TO *C.* 2890 BC

Narmer
Aha
Djer (Zer, Sekhty)
Djet (Zet, Uadji, Edjo)
Den (Udimu)
Anedjib (Andjyeb, Enezib)
Semerkhet
Qaa (Ka'a)
(Merneith may have been a regnant queen in the early part of the dynasty)

SECOND DYNASTY

*C.* 2890 TO 2686 BC

Hetepsekhemwy
Reneb
Nynetjer (Nutjeren)
—         Weneg[a]
—         Sened[a]
Sekhemib ⎱
Peribsen[b] ⎰   same ruler?
Khasekhem ⎱
Khasekhemwy[c] ⎰   same ruler?

   [a] Personal name, Horus-name unknown
   [b] Seth-name
   [c] Horus- and Seth-name

(Spelling and order based on *Cambridge Ancient History*, 3rd edn, vol. I, pt. 2, p. 994. For correlations of Horus and personal names see *ibid.*, and for other interpretations of the chronology of this period Gardiner (1961, pp. 429–32).)

# CHAPTER 2

# OLD KINGDOM, MIDDLE KINGDOM AND SECOND INTERMEDIATE PERIOD
## *c.* 2686–1552 BC

The Old and Middle Kingdoms together represent an important unitary phase in Egypt's political and cultural development. The Early Dynastic Period had seen the creation and consolidation of a type of government and court culture which, with the Third Dynasty, now reached levels of scale and competence marking the beginning of the plateau of achievement for ancient Egypt. After five centuries and following the end of the Sixth Dynasty (*c.* 2181 BC) the system appears to have faltered, and there seems to have ensued a century and a half of provincial assertion and civil war, the First Intermediate Period. But the re-establishment of powerful central government which followed, *c.* 2040 BC, seems to have been, with certain changes of nuance, the re-establishment of the patterns of the Old Kingdom. There is thus much to be said for treating certain important aspects of the Old and Middle Kingdoms together.

## DIVINE KINGSHIP

Divine kingship is the most striking feature of Egypt in these periods. In the form of great religious complexes centred on the pyramid tombs its cult was given monumental expression of a grandeur unsurpassed anywhere in the ancient Near East. Yet despite its all-pervading influence in Egyptian civilization it is not easy to present a coherent account of its doctrines, especially one which avoids mixing material from widely separated periods. One good reason for this is the Egyptian mode of communication, presenting doctrine not in the form of cogently argued treatises intended to persuade, but as series of concisely worded assertions which to us often take on a deeply cryptic appearance. The basic assertions are that the king is the holder of an office which is divine, he is 'the good god'; that he is a particular incarnation of Horus, an ancient sky and falcon god who became closely linked with the sun cult of Ra; that he is a son of Ra, the sun god, something incorporated into royal titulary from the Fourth Dynasty onwards. In the latter part of the Old Kingdom the deceased king became identified with Osiris, a god of the dead standing in a special relationship to the kingship.

For the periods under consideration three important texts, or groups of texts, deal with divine kingship. One is the Memphite Theology, known from an eighth-century BC copy of a document composed much earlier, possibly in the Old Kingdom or even before, although this is a disputed matter. It attempts to explain the geographical duality of Egyptian kingship, the positions of the gods Horus and Seth, and the supremacy of the capital city of Memphis and ultimately of its creator god, Ptah. Horus is presented as the first king of Upper and Lower Egypt, acquiring this position, having been earlier only the king of Lower Egypt, after the god Geb had given him also the kingship of Upper Egypt, hitherto held by Seth. The mythically aetiological element is so manifest that it is pointless to search for strictly historical features, particularly since the picture it suggests is at variance with the archaeological record. The second is the Ramesseum Dramatic Papyrus, dating to the reign of Senusret I (c. 1971 BC). It contains forty-six scenes, illustrated by thirty-one drawings, and includes instructions for the performance of ritual acts. The rituals, accompanied by notes on their mystic significance, seem intended for the king's accession or for his jubilee ceremony, and we may presume, therefore, that with this text we are confronted with ideas at the very heart of the Egyptians' concept of kingship. We find that it is concerned primarily with the king's relationship to Horus, Osiris, and Seth, to the very situation for which the Memphite Theology offers its 'historical' explanation. The Pyramid Texts, inscribed in the subterranean parts of the pyramids of kings from Unas to Pepy II, and Aba of the Eighth Dynasty, and of three late Sixth Dynasty queens form the third main source. Although their language is seemingly an archaic one, those who edited the texts for a particular pyramid would seem to have had sufficient working knowledge of it to adapt them to changing revelations, and even perhaps to compose. The increase and change in nature of allusions to Osiris and to Seth is one demonstration that they represent a living tradition. Their purpose is to assert the king's supremacy as a god, after rebirth, in a many-sided afterlife. Although the Horus–Osiris aspect occurs throughout, the climax of the texts is the king's identification with Ra and a cosmic life in heaven.

Because the aetiological element in Egyptian thought, which sought to explain the present by creating historical myths, was so strong, and because of the nature of Egyptian thought which did not demand that the connection between assertions be made explicit, it is difficult both to reconstruct from any text an earlier stage of development and in the end to escape from simply describing the various theological facets of kingship in the Egyptians' own terms. It is, nevertheless, evident that any functional explanation must begin with the Osiris–Horus–Seth motif which, as it were, underpinned kingship and one of whose main themes was to relate the person of the living king in the closest possible way to his country's royal ancestors, and thus to ensure that the historical process of royal succession remained always embraced within a central and authoritative body of myth. The relationship to Ra, the sun god, was presumably more of an abstract compliment to the majesty and power of the living king. Ultimately, the dogmas served to reinforce the historical process by which a central authority had come to exercise its control over a long-established network of community politics, and were themselves continually reinforced in provincial association by ritual and by the iconography of ritual which, for example, made the king responsible for the ceremonies of provincial temples.

The prominence and consistency with which the theology of divine kingship was proclaimed inhibits an understanding of the office of king as a political one, and hence the writing of history, of which we know remarkably little for the Old and Middle Kingdoms. The source material is so slight that narrative history may be considered an inappropriate literary form, particularly if one begins to suspect that the impressive facade of uniformity and continuity presented by inscriptions and monuments designed to propound the theology of divine kingship hides a complex and changing political scene.

The realities of earthly power – the usurpations and complex family relationships, of which one well-studied example is known from the Fourth Dynasty (Goedicke 1954, 1955; Reisner and Smith 1955, pp. 1–12) – imply that kingship must have been perceived on more than one level, and that some form of rationalization was necessary. It has been argued (Goedicke 1954) that this can be observed in the various terms used to refer to the king, distinguishing the human individual and the holder of divine office (the ancient justifications for the royal succession are discussed by Brunner (1955), Otto (1969) and Tanner (1974)). It is just such a varied presentation of kingship as a factor in the lives of men that is found in a body of literary texts from the Middle Kingdom and the period immediately preceding. In some of them the political nature of kingship is freely admitted, particularly in two which claim to be treatises of guidance issued by a king for his son and successor, and, in an introspective mood, contain advice on the maintenance of power and regret at the treachery to which the office is exposed. One of these texts is the Instruction of King Amenemhat (see Lichtheim 1973, pp. 135–9; Pritchard 1969, pp. 418–19; Simpson 1973, pp. 193–7). The earlier text, the Instruction to Merikara (Lichtheim 1973, pp. 97–109; Pritchard 1969, pp. 414–18; Simpson 1973, pp. 180–92), is particularly remarkable for its humanity, for its rational view of kingship, and for its emphasis on royal responsibility:

Well tended are men, the cattle of god.
He made heaven and earth according to their desire,
and repelled the demon of the waters.
He made the breath of life for their nostrils.
They who have issued from his body are his images.
He arises in heaven according to their desire.
He made for them plants, animals, fowl and fish to feed them. . .
He made for them rulers (even) in the egg,
a supporter to support the back of the disabled.
He made for them magic as a weapon to ward off what might happen.

(Lines 130–7.)[1]

The position of the king from this point of view is well summed up in a more formal text of King Senusret I:

He (the god Hor-akhty) created me as one who should do that which he had done, and to carry out that which he commanded should be done. He appointed me herdsman of this land, for he knew who would keep it in order for him.[2]

Central to the Egyptians' views of kingship was the concept of *ma'at* which, whilst sometimes translatable as 'justice' or 'truth', is a term whose meaning goes far beyond legal fairness or factual accuracy. It was used to refer to the ideal state of the universe and society, and was personified as the goddess Ma'at. Although of eternal existence its operation in the world of men was the responsibility of the king, and as such must have acted as a constraint on the arbitrary exercise of power: a 'natural' morality in the place of institutional checks.

In the Middle Kingdom this was taken as a theme suitable for

[1] A related notion of mankind's equality is expressed in a contemporary Coffin Text, spell 1130 (*CT* VII, 461ff); see the literature cited in Grieshammer (1974, p. 167), also Lichtheim (1973, pp. 131–2) and Pritchard (1969, pp. 7–8).
[2] The so-called Berlin Leather Roll (P. Berlin 3029); see Goedicke (1974), Lichtheim (1973, pp. 115–18). For the metaphor 'herdsman' of mankind, applied to gods as much as to the king, see Blumenthal (1970, pp. 27–37), D. Müller (1961).

exposition. The Prophecy of the lector–priest Neferty (Neferyt) (Helck 1970, Pritchard 1969, pp. 444–6; Simpson 1973, pp. 234–40) does this with a simple literary device: a picture of chaos is sketched, calamities of nature and anarchy in society. Then the coming of a king who is probably Amenemhat I is described, in the form of an age when all will be healed: 'Right (*ma'at*) shall come again to its place, and iniquity/chaos, it is cast out.' (Lines 68–9.)[1] The theme of the chaotic society – characterized by social upheaval, the perversion of justice, lack of security against foreign interference, natural calamities, god's abandonment of man, personal alienation from the world – seems at this period to have become something of a literary preoccupation.[2] Nowhere is it explored with more flourish, detail and sense of immediacy than in the Admonitions of the sage, Ipuwer, which presents a carefully-studied negative image of the ideal society, one in which, presumably, *ma'at* was no longer operative (Helck and Otto 1972, cols. 65–6; Lichtheim 1973, pp. 149–63; Pritchard 1969, pp. 441–4; Simpson 1973, pp. 210–29). Indeed, the imaginative powers of its author have repeatedly beguiled people into regarding it as a piece of reporting, and thus descriptive of a period of political and social breakdown at the end of either the Old or Middle Kingdom.[3] The lamentations are apparently being addressed by Ipuwer to a king who is held responsible for what is described: 'Authority, knowledge, and truth are yours, yet confusion is what you set throughout the land.' (Lines 12, 12–12, 13.) The beginning of the text is lost, but the setting is perhaps best imagined as the court of a long-dead king, as with the Prophecy of Neferty, or the scandalous story of Neferkara and the general Sasenet (Posener 1957a). One section is, however, positive in its content, and, by extolling the pious duties of kings, seems to reflect the widespread ancient belief that piety and successful rule go together (Lines 10, 12–11, 10).

This philosophical literature is something peculiar to the Middle Kingdom and First Intermediate Period, and it has been pointed out that it contains an element of propaganda on behalf of kingship and the established order of society, disseminated via scribal schools. It must

---

[1] The close and illuminating parallelism between Neferty and the much later Potter's Oracle is explored by Koenen (1970); Goedicke (1977) follows a somewhat different line of interpretation.

[2] Another important text is the fragmentary lamentation of Khakheperra-senb, whose name, compounded from the prenomen of Senusret II, helps to date it; see Kadish (1973), Lichtheim (1973), pp. 145–9), Simpson (1973, pp. 230–3).

[3] For the later dating see van Seters (1964, 1966, pp. 103–20). A complicated history of redaction is suggested in Barta (1974) and Fecht (1972, 1973); these studies also assume that the key speeches are all addressed to the creator god, with none addressed to a king. A number of scholars have expressed in recent years considerable reservations about the detailed historicity of the text.

also reflect that the relationship between the humanity and divinity of kings was a major intellectual problem for the Egyptians, though with their natural mode of thought and expression being particular rather than abstract the form which their discussions took may now seem unfamiliar and be easily misunderstood. Nor, because of the absence of a comparable body of texts, is it easy to make a balanced assessment of the degree to which the character of kingship at this time differed from that of the Old Kingdom, though in an impressionistic way this latter may appear as an heroic age of absolute royal power untempered by the doubts and cares expressed in these later texts. Yet the concept of *ma'at* was certainly present then, as the force which ensures an orderly universe (for example Pyramid Texts §§ 1582, 1774–6), and as something whose performance was the responsibility of kings (Pyramid Texts §§ 265, 1774–6; the Horus-names of kings Sneferu and Userkaf were, respectively, 'Lord of *ma'at*' and 'Performer of *ma'at*'). Furthermore, the association between *ma'at* and the just society finds expression in the Instructions of the vizier Ptah-hetep of the Fifth Dynasty: ' Justice (*ma'at*) is great, its value enduring. It has not been disturbed since the days of him who created it. He who transgresses the laws is punished.' (Lines 88–90.)[1] The main concepts were thus present in this earlier time, even if some of their wider implications did not find the literary expression that has survived. Yet some measure of the greater variety with which kingship was perceived in the Middle Kingdom is manifest in the royal statues of the period, some of which portray aspects of kingship which certainly represent, whatever else, something more complex and intellectual than the positive idealism of the Old Kingdom. It is hard to avoid the conclusion that the intervening First Intermediate Period and its civil war had a disturbing intellectual effect.

## THE ROYAL FAMILY

So little is known of the history of these periods that in many cases even the reason for dynastic change is unknown. Nevertheless, it is clear that, with the exception of the Palestinian Hyksos kings of the Second Intermediate Period, this was throughout these periods primarily a matter of internal politics and largely localized around the court. Usurpation is one obvious cause, as with Amenemhat I, founder of the

---

[1] The alternative text reads 'since the time of Osiris'. The full text is translated in Lichtheim (1973, pp. 61–80), Pritchard (1969, pp. 412–18) and Simpson (1973, pp. 159–76). Compare also the short text of the vizier Nefersehemra in Lichtheim (1973, p. 17) and Sethe (1932–3, p. 198).

Twelfth Dynasty, who has plausibly been identified with a vizier of the same name in the court of the preceding king. But the circumstances surrounding such an event invariably escape us. Detailed study of the great necropolis at Giza has provided one sketchy case history of the complex family relationships which could lie behind a succession of kings, in this instance those of the Fourth Dynasty and perhaps those of the early Fifth as well (see Goedicke 1954, 1955; Helck 1968; Pirenne 1932–5, vol. II, pp. 14–23, vol. III, ii, pp. 401–2; Reisner and Smith 1955, pp. 1–12). A literary text of the late Middle Kingdom, the Westcar Papyrus, purports to cover some of the same ground and to narrate the circumstances surrounding the origin of the Fifth Dynasty, whose first three kings are here presented as being all sons of the sun god and of the wife of one of his priests (Lichtheim 1973, pp. 215–22; Simpson 1973, pp. 15–30). The prophecy of their accession and of the piety of their future rule is made before King Khufu, builder of the Great Pyramid, who appears in ancient times to have acquired a reputation for both impiety and cruelty. In this tale his impiety is characterized by a search for sacred information (precisely what is still not clear; see Hornung (1973)) which he can use in the construction of his own tomb. The story, which might be termed 'The doom of the house of Khufu', may perhaps further exemplify the theme that piety and impiety have historical consequences and thus serve to illustrate the gulf between ancient and modern historiography.

The Fourth Dynasty is virtually the only period in the Old and Middle Kingdoms where it is possible to learn much about the royal family at all, particularly on the male side. The prominence of the royal family in the great Giza necropolis in large tombs close to the pyramid of Khufu is matched by a prominence of royal sons in the administration. Spanning the entire Fourth Dynasty is a line of viziers, most of them also in charge of the king's building projects, who are kings' sons, though not destined to succeed to the throne. The last one, Sekhemkara, a son of King Khafra, probably served into the reign of Sahura of the Fifth Dynasty, but henceforth (with one exception) no vizier bears the title 'king's son', though he might be married to a princess (Pirenne 1932–5, vol. II, pp. 106–8, vol. III, i, pp. 58–65; Weil 1908).[1] Indeed, it now becomes difficult to discover much at all about royal sons, the

[1] An example of princesses married to other high officials is cited by Yoyotte (1950); also Pirenne (1932–5, vol. III, ii, p. 497). A further example of a vizier who was also a 'king's son' is the Teti buried near the pyramid of Pepy II, but it is very possible that he should be placed after the end of the Sixth Dynasty (Kees 1940, pp. 48–9).

problem being complicated by the occasional use of the term to cover a royal grandson, and its eventual use as a rank indicator (Baer 1960, p. 45; von Beckerath 1964, pp. 100–1; Nims 1938). Five tombs of princes of the Fifth and Sixth Dynasties appear to be known at Saqqara. Neither in size nor by position in the necropolis do they appear to differ from the vast mass of officials' tombs, and inasmuch as tombs were symbols of status give no indication that their owners had a distinctive standard of living. The titles held by this group place them in the administration, but not consistently high in the hierarchy. One, Nefer-seshem-seshat (Baer 1960, no. 275; Gauthier 1907, p. 198), was vizier and overseer of the king's works, two (Isesi-ankh: Baer 1960, no. 64; Gauthier 1907, p. 138; Ka-em-tjenent: Baer 1960, no. 530; Gauthier 1907, p. 197) were overseers of the king's works and commanders of the army, the remaining two (Ra-em-ka: Baer 1960, no. 303; Gauthier 1907, p. 197; Satju: Baer 1960, no. 419; Gauthier 1907, p. 198) had minor posts, one of a priestly nature. A sixth prince (Khesu: Baer 1960, no. 395; Gauthier 1907, p. 168), the location of whose tomb is uncertain, was an 'inspector of priests' at one of the pyramid temples, and a late Fourth or early Fifth Dynasty prince with non-executive titles was probably buried at Abu Rawash (Fischer 1961a). The relative insignificance of princes in the administration of the later Old Kingdom, a period of about three centuries, is also borne out by their general absence in texts referring to the administration, and by the surviving court lists which occur in the reliefs of the later Old Kingdom pyramid temples. Although princes are here put in a place of honour, they are given either no further title, or a priestly one: 'priest of Min' or 'lector–priest'.

In the Middle Kingdom they are even more inconspicuous. If, as seems likely from the negative results of examinations within royal pyramid enclosures, their tombs followed the same pattern and were spread out amongst the tombs of officials then the great destruction which has overtaken these necropolises helps to explain this. A re-used stele of prince Amenemhat-ankh from Dashur lists a number of titles, but all are priestly (de Morgan 1903, figs. 111, 128).[1] Again, their absence is notable from administrative records, including a lengthy fragment of a court journal (Papyrus Bulaq 18; Scharff 1920), where the royal family seems to consist of one prince, one queen, three princesses and no fewer than nine 'royal sisters'.

---

[1] Note also the apparently still unpublished stele of prince Hepu from el-Lisht referred to in Gauthier (1907, vol. II, p. 130, n. 25).

The small role which princes were allowed doubtless contributed to the stability of government, particularly at the sensitive moment of succession. In the Twelfth Dynasty this process was rendered more secure by the expedient of overlapping reigns, or co-regency, in which the heir was made king whilst his father was still alive and dated his reign from this moment. The co-regency of Amenemhat I and Senusret I, for example, lasted ten years. Yet, even so, a popular romance set in this period, the Story of Sinuhe, depicts the moment of Amenemhat's death as one of instability (lines R 17–24, translated in Lichtheim (1973, p. 224), Pritchard (1969, pp. 18–19) and Simpson (1973, pp. 58–9)).

The status of princes as reflected in funerary practices contrasts sharply with that of princesses, queens and royal mothers. Whilst the monumental tomb at Giza belonging to Queen Khentkawes, an ancestral figure for the Fifth Dynasty, is exceptional, substantial tombs for royal ladies immediately adjacent to the king's pyramid are a regular feature of the Old and Middle Kingdoms, sometimes, in the former period, being themselves pyramidal in form. Despite the use of titles such as 'king's daughter' or 'king's wife' it is not always clear whether their owners were queens, daughters, concubines or sisters of the king. At the pyramid of Senusret III at Dashur the tombs of royal ladies formed a carefully planned catacomb with four chapels above ground conforming to the overall design of the pyramid complex, suggesting that their burial arrangements had been made irrespective of their marriage prospects. The prominence of royal ladies in the funerary cult is also borne out by statue cults for some of them carried out by priests attached to some of the royal pyramids. The administrative archives from the pyramids of Neferirkara of the Fifth Dynasty at Abusir and of Senusret II of the Twelfth at El-Lahun attest cults for, in the former case, Queen Khentkawes (Posener-Kriéger and de Cenival (1968, pls. III, LXV); these texts are translated in Posener-Kriéger (1976)), and in the latter, for a predominantly female royal household (Borchardt 1899, Kaplony-Heckel 1971, nos. 3, 42, 73, 81, 107, 271, 287, 307, 311, 421).

The political implications of whom the king married must have been considerable, although for the Old and Middle Kingdoms there is no evidence of the later custom of the king accepting in marriage the daughter of a foreign, or at least western Asiatic, king as part of a diplomatic alignment. It used to be claimed that Nubian blood ran in the early Twelfth Dynasty kings, but this deduction is no longer necessary (Posener 1956, pp. 47–8). A somewhat similar misreading of slender evidence gave rise to a Libyan origin for one of the principal queens of King Khufu (Reisner and Smith 1955, p. 7). It is, in fact, difficult to discover much at all about the backgrounds of queens. Consequently it is hard to judge how singular is the case of two wives of Pepy I of the Sixth Dynasty, the mothers of the future kings Merenra and Pepy II. Both were daughters of a court lady married to a commoner, Khui. One of their brothers, Djau, became vizier, and one of his sons succeeded to a provincial governorship (Gardiner 1954, Goedicke 1955). But whether, as has been claimed, this marked an important historical stage in the weakening of kingship *vis-à-vis* provincial governors or whether it is merely a well-recorded example of how power was kept out of the hands of princes and courtiers is difficult to tell.[1]

## THE CENTRAL ADMINISTRATION

Throughout the Old Kingdom Egypt's capital remained at Memphis. Although some (though possibly not much) of the ancient town mound and an adjacent cemetery still survive at Mit Rahina no serious fieldwork has been done here, so that there is little with which to clothe this fact (Kemp 1976b, Montet 1957, pp. 27–34). In particular, we have no idea of the appearance, or even of the size, of the royal palace. In the Twelfth and Thirteenth Dynasties a new term for the capital is found, 'Amenemhat-ith-tawy' ('King Amenemhat (I) seizes the two lands'), often abbreviated to Ith-tawy, and written inside a symbol representing a fortified enclosure. Over a thousand years later a town of this name was still in existence, situated somewhere in the 50 km between Medum and Memphis, and providing the one specific piece of evidence that Ith-tawy may have lain separately from Memphis, even if only as a southerly suburb, or perhaps closer to El-Lisht. It has otherwise been lost.

Very few administrative documents have survived from the Old and Middle Kingdoms, too few to reveal the full structure of government at any one time, let alone to enable its historical development to be traced in any detail. In their place we must rely heavily on the very numerous titles born by officials. A major difficulty here is that titles were not necessarily descriptive of jobs, but could serve to place a man in the hierarchy of power and thus indicate his rank relative to his fellows. What, if any, duties were performed by, or expected of, a 'mouth of Nekhen' (Hierakonpolis) or an 'elder of the portal' quite escape us. On

[1] Pepy I's mother, Iuput, had a statue cult at Coptos, but whether this implies a provincial origin for her is not clear (Goedicke 1967, pp. 41–54). Another case of provincial royal connections is dealt with in Habachi (1958).

the parallels of better-documented cultures one might expect that the court did indeed contain courtiers, whose role in the decision-making and administrative process was not clearly defined though it might be considerable. The Old Kingdom court lists seem to contain many who might be in this category. One must also allow for the administrative versatility which, with organizational expertise, was a prized quality and could, in turn, place an able man in charge of armies fighting abroad, quarrying expeditions, or legal proceedings at court. At the same time one should not automatically regard holders of titles as full-time civil servants. Egyptian society, insofar as it expressed itself in inscriptions, fell into three groups: literate men wielding authority derived from the king, those subordinate to them (doorkeepers, soldiers, quarrymen, and so on), and the illiterate peasantry. Titles essentially put a man on the right side of society, the one of privilege and authority, something of which literary compositions (especially the Satire of the Trades) provide self-conscious expression. But how much of his life would be occupied by administrative tasks is often not clear. Naturally, government service was a major source of income for such a person, extending beyond daily necessities to gifts of land and to equipment (even architectural elements) for his tomb, although independent provision of such things was also boasted about (Helck 1956a, 1975, chs. 7 and 8). Further information on private wealth is, however, somewhat ambiguous, for private commercial activity is something which finds no place in the formal inscriptions which are our major source of information. Yet private ownership of land is well documented for the Old and Middle Kingdoms, often made into a trust, or pious foundation, and sometimes on a scale which would have put the owner at the centre of a major agricultural concern with substantial marketing implications. Further-more, the archaeological record suggests a complex and extensive marketing system, occasionally even satisfying a local taste for exotic imports by producing imitations, and makes it hard to accept that this was entirely, or even largely, the responsibility of a closed government redistributive system.

One document unique in its class is a long fragment of a court journal (Papyrus Bulaq 18) from the reign of a king of the early Thirteenth Dynasty (B. Adams 1956, pp. 76–88; Scharff 1920). Partly it consists of the court accounts, and partly of summaries of official business: the arrival of parties of desert people (Medja) presumably to parley with the king; the fetching of cult images from a local temple for a festival; the suppression of some form of insurrection in a town accompanied by executions. It covers a period whilst a section of the court was residing at Thebes, so should not be taken as a guide to the normal scale of court activity at the capital. Of the royal family one queen was present, one prince, three king's daughters and nine king's sisters, some of whom probably had their own households. This preponderance of female relatives of the king compares interestingly with the funerary evidence discussed above. A 'house of nurses' is also listed, containing nineteen persons and groups of children. Of officials, a central group of between eight and thirteen is regularly listed, but others make temporary appearances, boosting those on the court books by up to sixty-five extra persons on a feast day, including the vizier. These personnel-lists are primarily daily records of commodities issued, mainly bread and beer, but also meat, vegetables and date-cakes. Commodities (livestock and incense) were also supplied by the court for the cult of the god Menthu at nearby Medamud, whose statue, with that of 'Horus protector of his father', was actually brought into the palace at the time of a festival. The sources of court revenue are unfortunately given only in general terms, basically three administrative divisions: 'the department of the Head of the South',[1] 'the office of government labour', and 'the Treasury'. Consequently it is not clear whether, in this case, taxation or state-owned sources was the principal provider. A further source was the temple of Amen at Thebes.

One important function of government was the location and collection of the resources necessary for the support of the court and its projects. The agricultural resources of Egypt seem to have been divided amongst three classes of estate: owned directly by the crown; belonging to pious foundations whose relationship to the crown was a subtle one; in the hands of private individuals and liable to taxation. The most important event in revenue administration was the assessment of the country's wealth. The Palermo Stone (the main fragment is published, with commentary, in Schäfer (1902)), which covers most of the Old Kingdom, makes a generally biennial census of cattle one of the key events for describing any particular regnal year, and the very term translated as 'regnal year' (ḥsbt) probably derives from this event (von Beckerath 1969). A number of Old Kingdom decrees of exemption show, however, that the demands of the state left little untouched, so that revenue could be assessed even on the basis of the 'canals, lakes, wells, waterbags and trees' of an estate (Goedicke 1967, pp. 56, 72).

[1] An expression for the more southerly part of the Egyptian Nile Valley which possessed a notable degree of political coherence (see pp. 177–8, also Gardiner 1957).

Persons could also be obliged to work for the government, and possibly perform military service (Goedicke 1967, pp. 48–54; Helck 1975, ch. 21). From the Middle Kingdom information on taxation is very slight and relates partly to cattle and partly to land and crops, and includes a fragment of a journal recording the progress of a team measuring plots of land for an assessment involving the treasury (Helck 1975, ch. 25; Simpson 1965, p. 18; Smither 1941). Some Kahun papyri could be interpreted as household census lists, and others as detailed inventories of personal possessions, where the purpose would have been assessment for labour obligations or tax, and which would in any case have put into government hands a formidable amount of personal information. Another papyrus (Hayes 1955), of the Thirteenth Dynasty, has extracts from a prison register listing Egyptians who, having failed to meet their obligations to labour for the government, had been consigned to government farms and labour camps, so augmenting the direct resources of the crown.

One must imagine a network of government agencies spread throughout the country, attempting by bureaucratic methods total assessment and management of resources, and overlying to varying degrees the semi-autonomous functioning of pious foundations and private estates whose own 'officials' would have had as their principal concern not the facilitating of the transfer of wealth to the crown, but rather the effective operation of the foundation or estate of which they themselves were the chief beneficiaries. The resulting tension, or division of loyalty, which will become clearer when provincial government is discussed, and which may, in the Old Kingdom, have found some release in the charters of immunity, is not made explicit in formal texts because these conform to a particular view of the ideal society, where loyal service to the king was paramount.

A second major area of government was the administration of law and justice, an obligation for which justification was found in the Egyptians' concept of *ma'at*, to the extent that some high officials bore amongst their titles that of 'priest of Ma'at'. The very limited documentation that has survived is concerned very much with property, its ownership and transference to others. But it again seems typical of the Egyptian system that the judicial function was not the prerogative of a professional, specialist body reflected in a clearly defined category of official titles. It is true that the titles of certain officers and bodies, such as the 'overseer of the six great mansions', are suspected to relate entirely to the judiciary, but the basic capacity of making accepted judgements seem also to have extended generally to men in a position of authority, even where their titles seem primarily administrative.[1] Decisions both judicial and administrative (a distinction which is a modern and not an ancient one) were also made collectively, by councils or committees, sometimes possibly set up on an *ad hoc* basis (S. Gabra 1929, Goedicke 1967, pp. 133, 170; Hayes 1955, pp. 45–6). The settlement of disputes, with all that this implied in terms of favouritism, must have been a major component in the authority of provincial men of power, and the extent to which they were, in times of weak central government, answerable to no higher authority is closely tied up with the important matter of provincial autonomy of which more will be said below. It remains uncertain, however, how far there was a central body of law or precedent governing the conduct of life generally, a criminal code. The most important document is probably the same late Middle Kingdom papyrus with the prison register mentioned above which deals with the operation of criminal processes against people who have sought to avoid government-imposed labour obligations. In referring to 'laws' it cites precise variations of the general offence, and in so doing implies the existence of a very detailed code of law which has otherwise not survived.

The precise ways in which the various agencies of the central government operated varied with the course of time, and the names given to posts and departments in the Old Kingdom differ appreciably from those of the Middle Kingdom. The most important constant feature was the vizier. The principal source for this office is a set of 'instructions' which, although known only from a number of Theban tombs of the Eighteenth Dynasty, is nevertheless couched in the administrative terminology of the late Middle Kingdom. It shows that, next to the king, his was the ultimate responsibility for fiscal, administrative and judicial affairs. This all-embracing responsibility is also exemplified by surviving letters sent to and from his office at various times during the periods under review.[2] There is no really firm

[1] Note the boasts of impartial judgements made by various officials, e.g. Anthes (1928, no. 14, ll. 9–10; Sethe 1932–3, vol. I, p. 133, ll. 4, 5). Ptah-hetep lines 264–76 seems to be advice on conduct with petitioners for officials generally, 'to whom petitions are made'. The peasant in the story of the Eloquent Peasant addresses his loquacious petitions to a 'chief steward', at the 'gateway' (*'rryt*) and at the 'entrance (*sbз*) to the temple'. A useful note on *'rryt* is given by Gardiner (1925, p. 65). The Eloquent Peasant story is translated in Lichtheim (1973, pp. 169–84), Pritchard (1969, pp. 407–10) and Simpson (1973, pp. 31–49).

[2] See Hayes (1955, pp. 71–85), Simpson (1965, pp. 20–3) and Théodoridès (1960, pp. 108–16). A verbal order is recorded in the stele of Amenysenb (Breasted 1906, pp. 342–3). For bureaucratic reaction to one such letter see Smither (1948), Théodoridès (1959); a hostile response to another is published by Gardiner (1929) and Grdseloff (1948).

evidence for the existence, as in later times, of two viziers each responsible for only one part of the country.

## PIOUS FOUNDATIONS

These were a fundamental part of ancient Egyptian society, and were intended ostensibly to ensure the perpetual maintenance of the cults of statues: of gods, of kings and of private individuals. They took the form of a fund, established by an initial donation of property, or by contracts securing income from elsewhere, often from sources belonging already to another foundation. This fund had to be kept intact as a single unit, unless modified by a specific legal agreement, and was in theory for perpetuity. The income was assigned to those who maintained the cult and to specified supporting personnel, but could, by legal agreement, also be diverted elsewhere. The basic idea behind this type of organization, which sought to bestow on sources of wealth, or trusts, a permanence and inviolability greater than mortal law could provide, has a long history in the Near East, occurring in Muslim law as the *waqf*. Like the *waqf* it was the object of a secondary show of piety: tax exemption.

In the short term, at least, the most important pious foundations in the Old and Middle Kingdoms were the pyramid temples for the royal statue cult. Whilst it is common to emphasize the mortuary character of pyramids and to see them primarily as tombs with temples ancillary to them, the way in which they were in fact organized and referred to suggests that the emphasis should be reversed, and they be regarded first and foremost as temples for the royal statues with a royal tomb attached to each, which, acting as a huge reliquary, gave enormous authority to what was, in essence, an ancestor cult and an important factor in the stability of government. This was a phenomenon repeated on differing scales throughout Egyptian society in the form of private funerary cults. Pious foundations were also, however, the basis of support for provincial temples, and, by involving locally based administrators, became another important component in provincial authority. They will therefore be discussed both in the ensuing section on pyramid temples, and in the subsequent section on provincial government.

## THE MEMPHITE COURT CEMETERIES

For the Old Kingdom the court cemeteries, particularly the royal pyramid complexes, are responsible for much of our impression of the period, and had more survived from those of the Middle Kingdom the same might be true here also. Indeed, it seems impossible to write of the Old Kingdom without in some way using the court cemeteries as an index of royal power. This is certainly a valid attitude from the point of view of the ancients themselves since the hierarchic scaling of tomb size symbolized and reinforced the existing patterns of leadership: 'the very existence of impressive sepulchres in which selected individuals were buried probably validated the power of living leaders, at any rate if their claim to power was based on a relationship with the dead enshrined in the tomb' (Fleming 1973), as could be said to be so in Egypt through the Horus–Osiris myth. Furthermore, inasmuch as their construction and furnishing was the court's principal economic 'output', pyramid cemeteries provide us with the only constant and measurable index of economic activity available.

The channelling of so much of the country's resources into the building and equipping of funerary monuments, which must have represented the single largest industry running more or less continuously through the Old Kingdom and then after a break, and perhaps somewhat less so, through the Middle Kingdom, may seem unproductive on a modern scale of values, and was doubtless regulated by a mixture of ambition and a recognition of the king's role in society. Yet pyramid-building must have been essential for the growth and continued existence of Pharaonic civilization. In ancient societies innovations in technology and in other forms of practical knowledge (particularly administrative control of resources), as well as improvements in the levels of existing skills, arose not so much from deliberate research as from the 'spin-off' consequent upon developing the means to accomplish lavish court projects. The assembling of so much labour, the training of so many artists and craftsmen to mass-produce at a near-optimum standard (a striking feature of Egyptian civilization), the preferment and material rewards given to those who could accomplish these ends, all must have been responsible for much more than the enormous scale of the result. Quarrying and stone-working techniques had to be made sufficient, transport rendered adequate, a body of knowledge developed for the final handling and siting of materials and for the accurate laying out of the building, and, perhaps most important of all, an administrative apparatus created capable of directing manpower, skill and resources to a single undertaking, identified with the pinnacle of the country's power structure: the king. But equally important, the continued consumption of so great a quantity of wealth and the products of craftsmanship, both in the course of building and in the subsequent equipping of the burials, must have had only the effect of sustaining further the machinery which produced them by creating fresh demand as reign succeeded reign, an economic stimulus broadly equivalent to 'built-in obsolescence' in modern technological societies. Indeed, since trade with the outside world in ancient times was primarily a matter of securing imports rather than a search for export markets, home consumption must have assumed an equivalently greater importance in a country's economy. But whilst pyramid-building may be seen now as a vital element in Egypt's prosperity, it would be a serious mistake to introduce altruism as a motive, and to think that positive economic or social effects were intended, or even dimly perceived. Theology and the display of power were justifications enough.

Throughout the Old Kingdom the court cemeteries were constructed at sites along a 35-km stretch of the western desert edge (with an outlier at Medum), the centre of concentration being slightly to the north of Memphis. It has occasionally been suggested that the changing location really represents a regular resiting and rebuilding of the royal palace, but it seems more reasonable to see it simply as the result each time of a search for a suitably flat, firm and unencumbered site. In the Middle Kingdom new sites further to the south were chosen, as well as the old one at Dashur. Inevitably this has influenced discussion on the location of the contemporary Residence at Amenemhat-ith-tawy (see p. 80).

The relative sizes of the royal pyramids, expressed as volumes, are given in fig. 2.1. Even as a rough index to a major economic activity a number of complicating factors must be noted. The Fourth Dynasty pyramids are of massive masonry blocks throughout, originally with a carefully smoothed casing of fine limestone and sometimes of granite as well. But from the reign of Sahura of the Fifth Dynasty the core behind the facing was of smaller and looser stone rubble and even gravel. In the Twelfth Dynasty, from the reign of Senusret I, the core was constructed as a series of limestone casemates filled with mud bricks, an interesting method of reinforced construction which produced a satisfactory scale, finish and stability for a lesser expenditure. The movement away from a megalithic core is in one sense a decline in standards, but when set against the history of more recent building

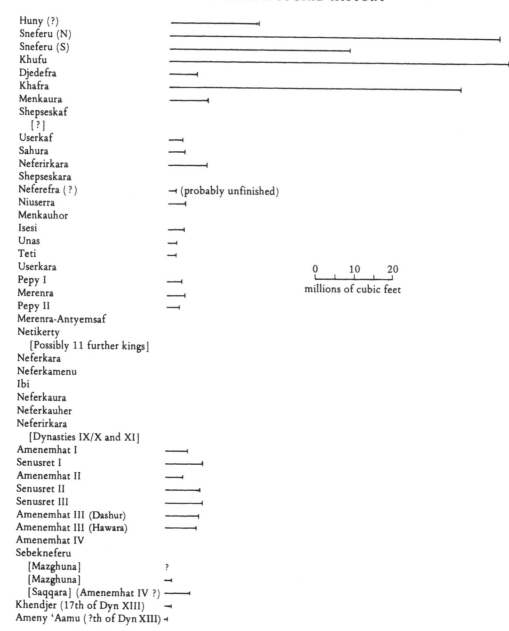

Fig. 2.1 Volumes of pyramids from the Fourth to the Thirteenth Dynasties. (Dimensions based on Edwards 1961a; the remains of the pyramid of Ameny 'Aamu at Dashur are published in Maragioglio and Rinaldi 1968.) A standard angle of 52° was assumed, but in practice the angle varied between about 49° and 57° although the consequences would be scarcely noticeable at this scale (see Lauer 1974, pp. 342–3).

technology with its constant search for more economic means of achieving a given result, has an undeniably rational basis. Each pyramid was also part of a building complex, which might represent a considerable volume of masonry, but one more difficult to measure, and with much of its inner wall surfaces decorated with painted low-relief carving. Consideration of the Fifth Dynasty pyramids must also include the solar temple which seems to have been a further extension of each pyramid complex and emphasizes that pyramid temples were intended as major cult establishments in their own right. The temples and other surrounding structures of the Middle Kingdom pyramids have been almost completely obliterated, but their scant traces do not suggest in most cases a decline of scale. Indeed, the vast building which the Classical world knew as the Egyptian Labyrinth seems to have been nothing else than the mortuary temple of Amenemhat III's pyramid at Hawara. But when all these factors are considered one is still left with the dramatic difference in the scale of the resources deployed on the Fourth Dynasty pyramids, for when size is doubled volume is increased ninefold, with the result that the Great Pyramid of Khufu contains nearly thirty times the bulk of the pyramid of Userkaf, for example. The background to the scaling-down of pyramids after the reign of Khafra is unknown and probably unknowable, but the consequences cannot be observed to have been adverse for the country, possibly because the surplus capacity for organization and for the utilization of resources was absorbed by the provinces, whose level of prosperity and local identity seem to have risen in the later Old Kingdom. In a sense, the continued history of Old and Middle Kingdom civilization contained an important element of freewheeling on the apparatus created through the building of the early pyramids, enabling skills and administrative machinery to be more widely and variably diffused.

The cults at pyramid temples were maintained by pious foundations. Two sets of documents have survived dealing with the daily administration of two of them: of King Neferirkara of the Fifth Dynasty at Abusir (Posener-Kriéger 1976, Posener-Kriéger and de Cenival 1968), and of King Senusret II of the Twelfth at El-Lahun (Borchardt 1899, Kaplony-Heckel 1971a), and in both cases belonging to a period when the cults had already been in existence for some time. The Neferirkara archive reveals a world of detailed and very professional administration. Elaborate tables provide monthly rosters of duty: for guarding the temple, for fetching the daily income (or 'offerings') and for performing ceremonies including those on the statues, with a special roster for the important Feast of Seker. Similar tables list the temple equipment, item by item and grouped by materials, with details of damage noted at a monthly inspection. Other records of inspection relate to doors and rooms in the temple building. The presentation of monthly income is broken down by substance, source and daily amount. The commodities are chiefly types of bread and beer, meat and fowl, corn and fruit. The sources are listed as: *r-š*-estates of Neferirkara and of the long-dead King Khufu,[1] *pr*-estates of the deceased Queen Khentkawes and a princess Irenra, possibly some establishments of Kings Neferefra and Djedefra (Posener-Kriéger and de Cenival 1968, pl. 45), the palace, the nearby solar temple of Neferirkara, and the towns of Iushedefwi and Djed-Sneferu (Maragioglio and Rinaldi 1971). This multiplicity of elements in the supporting pious foundation, involving sharing with other establishments, seems typical of Egypt at this and other periods. In the formal decorative scheme of pyramid temples the grants of land or funerary domains included in the foundation are personified as offering-bearers and preserve some idea of the numbers of units involved. The most complete comes from the valley temple of Sneferu at Dashur where they are grouped also into nomes, or administrative districts. In Upper Egypt thirty-four estates are distributed amongst ten nomes (with the record for eight nomes missing); in Lower Egypt the record is fully preserved for only a single nome and numbers four estates (fig. 2.2). Only rarely are the sizes given, and they vary from 2 arouras (about 0.5 hectare[2]) to $110\frac{1}{3}$ arouras (about 28 hectares) (Goedicke 1976a, pp. 351–69; Helck 1975, pp. 42–4; Jacquet-Gordon 1962, pp. 3, n. 2, 151).

The sharing of revenue extended to private funerary cults, some of which, in the Old Kingdom, enumerate royal domains amongst the sources for their own foundations. One sheet from the Neferirkara archive contains a list of such deceased beneficiaries, headed by Queen Khentkawes, but otherwise belonging to officials whose cults receive portions of meat (Helck 1974a, p. 85; Posener-Kriéger and de Cenival 1968, pls. 45B, 65). The palace is listed as another recipient, albeit a nominal one, as also is the solar temple. Otherwise the income was disposed of on a daily accounted basis to the temple staff as their salary, in the form of bread, beer, meat, cloth, and so on.

The El-Lahun archive remains are, unfortunately, published only par-

---

[1] The technical definition of this type of estate remains unclear; see Goedicke (1967, pp. 69–72), Helck (1974a, p. 66), Kaplony (1972, pp. 56–7).

[2] It should be noted that Baer (1956) has proposed much larger units of land measurement, with an aroura of 8.2 hectares.

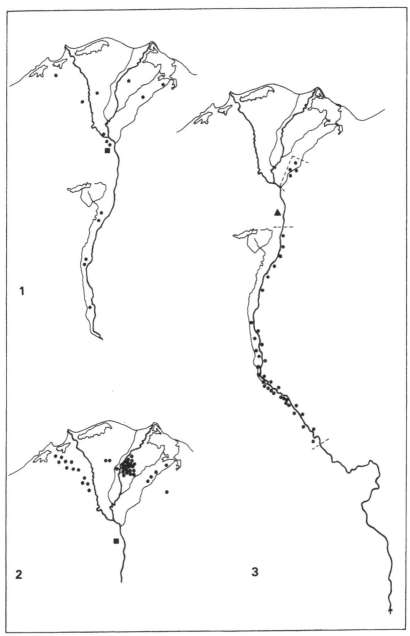

Fig. 2.2   Three examples of the distribution, by nomes, of estates in pious foundations for the mortuary cults of: (1) Khnumenty, an official of the Fifth Dynasty with tomb at Giza, one of whose titles was 'overseer of all the works of the king'; (2) Mehu, an official of the early Sixth Dynasty with tomb at Saqqara, whose titles included those of 'vizier' and 'governor of Upper Egypt', despite the striking concentration of estates in the delta; (3) King Sneferu, first king of the Fourth Dynasty. The list derives from his southern pyramid at Dashur, and is incomplete, see p. 90, also p. 110. (Examples from Jacquet-Gordon 1962, pp. 310–12, 419–26.)

tially, but the available information indicates a broadly similar type of administration and record-keeping, with monthly schedules of personnel on duty, of male and female musicians and singers and of slaves, lists of temple equipment grouped by material with notes of inspection, and accounts of temple income. Of note are fragmentary lists of statues which include not only the king for whom the temple was made (Senusret II) and mainly female members of his family, but also other kings, private individuals, and the reigning king (Senusret III) and his family too (Borchardt 1899, Kaplony-Heckel 1971a, nos. 3, 42, 73, 81, 107, 108, 271, 287, 307, 311, 421), a multiplicity of recipients which is found duplicated in provincial temples. Archaeology has provided the setting for the very substantial community involved in the El-Lahun archive, in the form of the mud-brick town commonly called Kahun, which does, however, appear to have been atypically large, and should probably be seen as part of an ancient conurbation which centred around the site of the modern town of El-Lahun in the cultivation. Other known pyramid towns seem to have been a lot smaller.

The size and monumentality of pyramid complexes proved to be no guarantee for the permanence of their cults. Two examples will illustrate their later history, and the curiously casual way in which the formal layouts of the complexes could be treated.

## Menkaura of the Fourth Dynasty at Giza[1]

It had evidently been planned that the pyramid and valley temples be built in the prevailing megalithic tradition, and their completion in mud brick was presumably a consequence of the king's premature death. Modern excavation of the pyramid temple was not extensive enough to determine if an area of living-quarters accompanied it. Nevertheless, fragments from two inscriptions, probably decrees, bearing the Horus-name of King Merenra of the Sixth Dynasty indicate that the temple was in use late in the Old Kingdom. The valley temple, although mostly of mud brick, had remained remarkably well-preserved, and presents a strange history which says much for the gap that could develop between plans and practice, and between the products of superlative craftsmanship and the way they were treated (fig. 2.3). Outside the

[1] See Hassan (1943, pp. 53–62), Reisner (1931) and Wildung (1969a, pp. 213–17). The relationship to Menkaura's pyramid of the apparently large settlement lying to the south of its causeway is not clear (A.-A. Saleh 1974). See also Goedicke (1967, pp. 16–21, 78–80) and Helck (1957, p. 108).

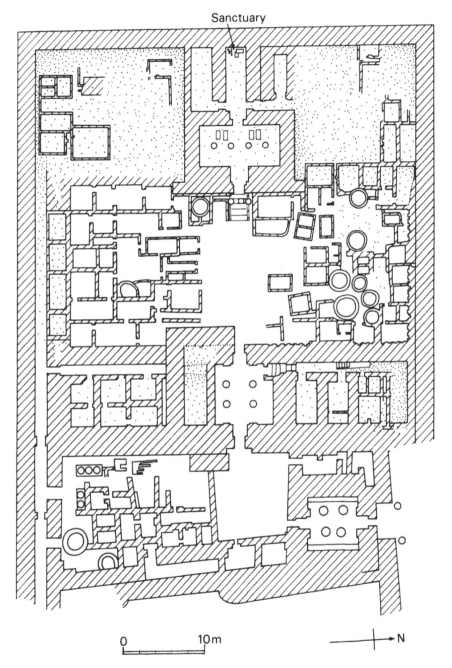

Sanctuary

0          10m          ⊢—→N

Fig. 2.3. The Valley Temple of King Menkaura's pyramid complex in its final phase towards the end of the Old Kingdom. The stippled areas are those whose floor levels had probably risen significantly through the accumulation of rubbish.

front of this temple an annexe had been built, part of which had been occupied by an irregular group of houses. Not long afterwards, these houses spread within the great open court of the temple itself. From then onwards most of the temple except for the sanctuary was allowed to decay, and in places was demolished to make room for the expanding village which gradually buried the lower parts of the temple. A good deal of temple equipment was found by the excavators still in the original storerooms, buried in this dust and rubble. Amongst it were the slate triads which represent some of the finest work of Old Kingdom sculptors. Much of this equipment had been subject to careless treatment amounting to vandalism. Many statues had been smashed up to provide material for the manufacture of model vessels which were a standard part of Old Kingdom burial equipment in the Memphite area, something suggestive of a minor industry to supplement the community's income. The process of decay had been hastened by a flood from a sudden storm. An attempt at renovation was made, but only on top of all this rubbish. This recognized the existence of the village, surrounded it with a new wall, and built a new sanctuary and gatehouse on the sites of the original ones. One still entered the sanctuary, therefore, immediately after having walked from the gatehouse along a path between the two groups of irregular cottages. On the mud floor of the antechamber to the new sanctuary four beautiful life-size statues of Menkaura were resited. The offering-place was found more or less intact. It consisted of an altar about 50 cm high made from a worn slab of alabaster resting on two rough upright stones with a crude libation basin beside it. Nearby were four unfinished diorite statuettes of the king lying on their side, having originally perhaps stood on the altar and thus been the object of the cult in this last phase of the temple's existence.

The date and circumstances of this rough-and-ready cult being carried on in a dingy chamber at the back of a tightly packed mud village are clear both from the associated archaeological material, which seems not to extend beyond the end of the Old Kingdom, and from a decree of King Pepy II of the Sixth Dynasty, found in the floor debris of the gateway, exempting the pyramid town from certain obligations and appointing an official to it. It thus demonstrates official recognition of this site as being part of the pyramid town at a date very close to the end of the Old Kingdom.

After the end of the Old Kingdom the site appears to have been abandoned and the cult of King Menkaura to have ceased entirely.

## Sneferu of the Fourth Dynasty at Dashur

King Sneferu appears to have possessed two pyramids at Dashur, served by more than one community (Fakhry 1959, 1961; Helck 1957, pp. 106–7; Wildung 1969a, pp. 105–52). The only one of these so far documented by excavation was attached to the valley temple of the southern, or 'bent' pyramid. As at the Menkaura valley temple a part, at least, of the town had been constructed within the main enclosure wall, in this case huddled in the space between the wall and the temple itself. Its pottery is primarily Old Kingdom, though some may have been later. Members of the priesthood of Sneferu are attested to the end of the Old Kingdom, buried mostly at Giza and at Dashur itself. Unlike Menkaura, however, King Sneferu went on to become a minor member of the wider Egyptian pantheon, even given a cult at the Sinai turquoise-mines. At Dashur his name began to be invoked in funerary prayers on private objects, and at least ten individuals are known to have held an office in his cult during the Middle Kingdom. One of them, Teti-em-saf, also held offices in the cults of Kings Pepy II and Teti of the Old Kingdom, as well as Amenemhat I and Senusret I of the Twelfth Dynasty, and belonged to an apparently affluent family buried adjacent to the pyramid of Teti at Saqqara. The nature of the cult's income at this time is not known, but it was presumably much reduced from the extensive estates which the Sneferu foundation had owned at the beginning.

This later cult of Sneferu continued to be celebrated in the offering-chapel in front of the pyramid, apparently without statues at all. Although decay and modification had produced a confused layout, the little chapel remained intact, and was discovered still with a pair of roughly cut stone offering-stands bearing the names and titles of Middle Kingdom priests, and a Middle Kingdom pottery dish still containing charcoal. The cult at Dashur did not apparently survive longer.

A further interesting case history is provided by the cult of Teti of the Sixth Dynasty (Firth and Gunn 1926; Helck 1957, p. 110; Porter and Moss 1927, vol. III, pp. 129–46; Quibell 1907). A sequence of priests – men whose small tombs show them to have been of modest means – spans the First Intermediate Period.[1] Early in the Twelfth Dynasty the interests of the more affluent Teti-em-saf family mentioned above and buried beside Teti's pyramid at Saqqara extended for a time

---

[1] There is considerable difficulty in dating many of the stelae, though it is probably too negative to follow the view of Schenkel (1965, p. 91). A note on the dating of the tomb of Ihy and Hetep, of the Teti-em-saf family, is provided by Simpson (1963a).

to include the priesthoods of other surviving Old Kingdom cults as well. As a minor deity (in the form Teti-Merenptah) this king is known from a votive stele and a statue of the Ramesside period over a thousand years after his death.

There are other case histories which could be written, and this is, indeed, a subject on which relatively little research has been done although it provides an important reflection on the capacities and priorities of the central government. Their histories evidently varied considerably from case to case, with accidents of local popularity playing a not insignificant role. At various times their stonework was used as quarries. The pyramid enclosure of Amenemhat I is known to have contained re-used blocks from certain Old Kingdom pyramid complexes, specifically of Khufu, Khafra, Unas and possibly Pepy II (Goedicke 1971). The end of the Old Kingdom marked an important terminal stage, as did the end of the Middle Kingdom in respect of the Twelfth Dynasty pyramids, though their later histories are far less well documented. The temptation for weak governments lacking the authority for large-scale provincial revenue collection to fall back on using the accumulated treasures of court cemeteries as a means of supplementing their income is obvious, although this cannot be documented.[1]

## PROVINCIAL EGYPT

The archaeological evidence for the nature and distribution of early settlements in Egypt is sparse and unsatisfactory, particularly as it concerns those which were not, like the pyramid towns, artificial developments; although it is likely, to judge from textual sources, that Egyptian administrative policies had an important influence generally on the shape, size and location of settlements, even if it cannot be judged whether, say, the groupings of estates in the larger pious foundations were built around existing settlement patterns or, alternatively, interfered with them. At four sites in Upper Egypt the evidence concerning towns of regional importance is reasonably clear, in each case at an important cult centre with a long subsequent history, though one of them, Abydos, was not a nome capital.

---

[1] According to the testimony of an official inspection carried out in the reign of Ramesses IX (c. 1103 BC), two Eleventh Dynasty royal tombs at Thebes were still, after nine centuries, intact. If this is to be believed, it must also be remembered that Thebes probably saw a degree of administrative continuity denied to the Memphite area (Peet 1930, pp. 28–45). In particular, the tomb of Nebhepetra Menthuhetep II, one of the two in question, became a cult centre of some importance (Arnold 1974a, pp. 92–5).

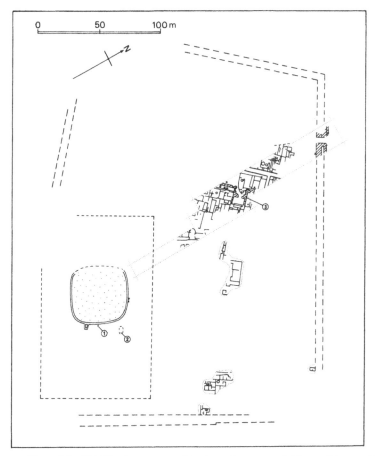

Fig. 2.4  Plan of the Old Kingdom town at Hierakonpolis, as revealed by partial excavation.

1  Part of a granite doorway of King Khasekhemwy of the end of the Second Dynasty

2  Site of the 'Main Deposit' of discarded temple equipment

3  Mud-brick gateway from the Early Dynastic palace incorporated into the later houses

(1) *Hierakonpolis*. Almost immediately beneath the broken modern ground level an Early Dynastic and Old Kingdom town has been located over an area of at least 200 by 300 m (fig. 2.4), apparently reaching its maximum extent during the Old Kingdom (Kemp 1977b). It consists of a tightly packed mass of mud-brick housing crossed by narrow streets, and protected by a heavy town wall, 9.5 m thick in its final stage, following an irregular rectilinear course. Towards the southern corner stood a mound of sand behind a rough stone revetment, and this probably served as the foundation for the temple. This latter

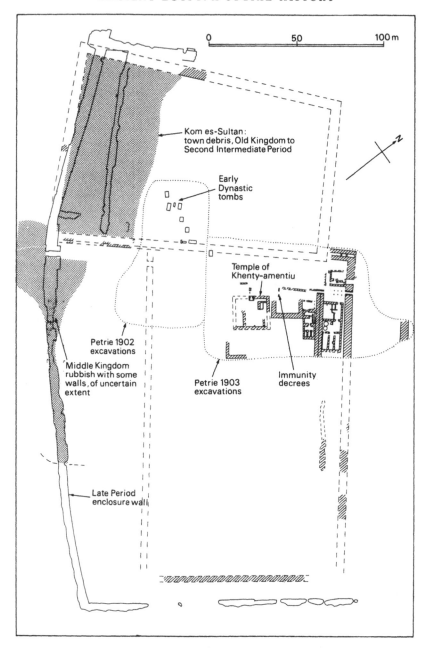

Fig. 2.5  Plan of the town and temple enclosure remains at Abydos.

had been removed in later rebuildings, but part of a granite doorway of King Khasekhemwy of the end of the Second Dynasty, statues and votive objects were found buried in nearby caches, particularly the ' Main Deposit'. Some of the houses towards the centre had incorporated the standing remains of a great brick gateway of the Early Dynastic Period which, to judge from its decorative niched style, had been a palace.

(2) *Abydos*. The earliest strata go back to the Early Dynastic Period. But, as at Hierakonpolis, the Old Kingdom saw rapid expansion and the building of heavily walled enclosures, in this case numbering two: one for the temple (dedicated to the local god Khenty-amentiu), which was made up of a complex of small brick buildings, and an adjoining one for the town which gradually, through to the end of the Middle Kingdom, grew into a stratified mound (fig. 2.5).

(3) *Elephantine*. This had a special role as a frontier town and trading centre, and stood at the southern tip of the most northerly of the granite islands which form the First Cataract.[1] Partly it was built over and around a series of irregular granite ridges which raised it high above the river, and gave it an irregular oval plan (fig. 2.6). It had a mud-brick wall and at least one gateway lined with stone. To the west lay what appears to have been a separate unwalled extramural settlement. Subsequent to this first Old Kingdom phase the town steadily expanded and fresh encircling walls were built, possibly now incorporating the northern part as well. In addition to at least one temple of modest proportions, which began in the Early Dynastic Period as a cleft between boulders, and is later found dedicated to the goddess Satet, a popular shrine existed dedicated to a deceased local dignitary of the late Old Kingdom called Heka-ib. The main necropolis from Elephantine lay in the cliffs of the western bank, the Qubbet el-Hawa, but some Middle Kingdom graves have been found on the island.

(4) *Tell Edfu*. The record here is more difficult to follow, although, as the town is built on a low hill of rock, the base of the stratigraphic sequence is readily accessible (fig. 2.7). The earliest remains visible are a part of the Old Kingdom town and its enclosure wall lying not far to the west of the great Ptolemaic temple which perhaps now covers the earliest site. Subsequently the town expanded, and a fresh wall was laid out on a complicated plan using curved sections, part of which ran over the Old Kingdom cemetery. This was subsequently doubled,

---

[1] As the 'doorway to the foreign lands' where tribute from Nubia was collected, Elephantine is discussed by Edel (1962, 1971, p. 11).

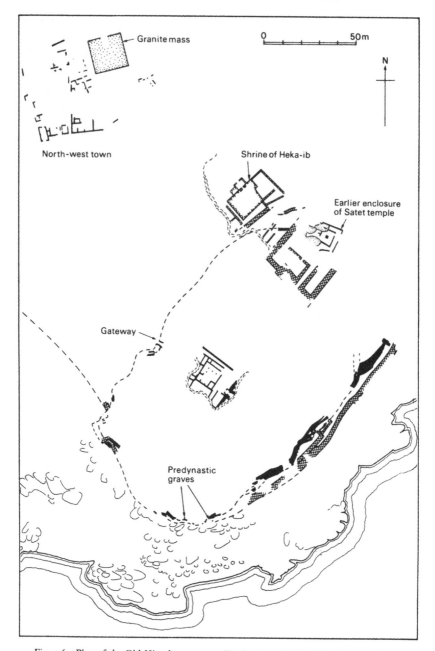

Fig. 2.6 Plan of the Old Kingdom town at Elephantine. Much of the interior of the walled enclosure is still covered with later debris.

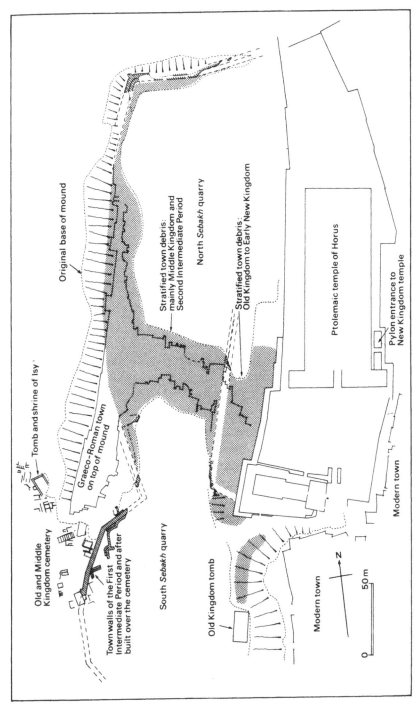

Tomb and shrine of Isy

Original base of mound

Stratified town debris:
mainly Middle Kingdom and
Second Intermediate Period

North Sebakh quarry

Stratified town debris:
Old Kingdom to Early New Kingdom

Graeco-Roman town
on top of mound

Ptolemaic temple of Horus

Old and Middle
Kingdom cemetery

Town walls of the First
Intermediate Period and after
built over the cemetery

South Sebakh quarry

Pylon entrance to
New Kingdom temple

Modern town

Old Kingdom tomb

N

Modern town

0    50 m

Fig. 2.7  The remains of Tell Edfu, partly buried beneath the modern town and partly destroyed by quarrying for *sebakh* (fertilizer). A small section of the early cemetery and town wall complex has been exposed.

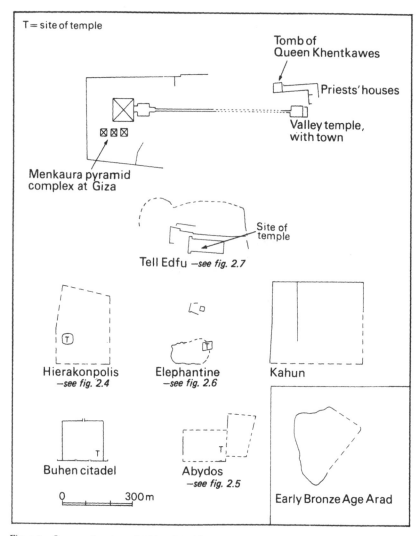

Fig. 2.8 Comparative sizes of Old and Middle Kingdom settlements, with inset of the outline of Early Bronze Age Arad in southern Palestine for comparison with Palestinian urbanism. T, site of temple.

but on a less tortuous course. Within the walls a stratified mound accumulated to the early New Kingdom. Edfu also possessed its own equivalent to the Heka-ib shrine based on a tomb of the vizier Isi of the early Sixth Dynasty (Alliot 1937–8, Edel 1954, Yoyotte 1952).

In the Nile Delta the record is even poorer, but sufficient has been ound at widely scattered sites (principally Abu Ghalib, Mendes, Tell

Basta and Ezbet Rushdi) to show that it possessed settlements and a culture of an entirely Egyptian character.

All of these towns appear somewhat small on an absolute scale which takes into consideration the urbanism of Classical and modern times (fig. 2.8). But when set against a total population for Egypt which has been estimated to have fluctuated during the Old and Middle Kingdoms at around one and one and a half million (Butzer 1976, pp. 81–5), their absolute sizes seem to call for little special comment, except perhaps for the relative magnitude of the government-created town of Kahun, which itself contrasts with other known pyramid communities. It is a not uncommon pattern in non-industrial societies for much of the population to be divided (though not equally) between one very large city and numerous small rural villages. Although the size of ancient Memphis at any one period is very difficult to ascertain at present, such evidence as exists suggests for ancient Egypt a much more even distribution for the population, who would have lived in settlements ranked hierarchically in size down from the main provincial towns such as those described above which seem to have been spaced fairly evenly along the Nile Valley. It is likely, however, that this pattern was itself a development of the Old Kingdom when in Upper Egypt, at least, towns seem to have gone through a dynamic expansive phase which presumably corresponded with the growth of local autonomy which is separately documented (see pp. 107–10). By contrast, the Predynastic period may have been characterized by a primate distribution based, in Upper Egypt, on a very few towns (e.g. Naqada and Hierakonpolis).

In some other countries where civilization developed in a floodplain provincial autonomy was the principal political development, giving rise to a civilization of city states. In Egypt provincial aspirations were normally contained within a system centred on a single royal government, whose paramount authority was expressed through the doctrines of divine kingship, containing theological elements derived from various parts of the country, through monumental building and through statue cults at provincial temples. As the local representative centres of court culture and authority, as well as being the centres of pious foundations and thus of locally important economic cycles, provincial temples were elements of great importance in the towns. Yet there is a striking contrast between the size and monumentality of pyramid temples and these temples for provincial cults, something which was probably not altered until New Kingdom times. This was to some extent apparent from the towns discussed above, especially

Abydos and Elephantine, and can be seen elsewhere, too. At Tell Basta and Ezbet Rushdi in the Nile Delta relatively modest mud-brick temples have been found dating respectively to Pepy I of the Sixth Dynasty and Amenemhat I of the Twelfth. In the former building limestone pillars had supported the roof. Beneath the Middle Kingdom level at Medamud the remains have been found of a bizarre shrine consisting partly of walls and doorways of mud brick and partly of two earthen mounds each covering a chamber and a winding corridor.[1] Furthermore, the re-used stonework in later temples seems to confirm this picture: of essentially mud-brick structures employing stone only for columns, doorways, stelae and statues. Their most impressive aspect was probably their massive brick enclosure walls, containing monumental stone gateways, a persistent feature of Egyptian temple design given theological significance (Reymond 1969, pp. 239–40, 280–1, 326).[2] An early Middle Kingdom papyrus containing building accounts from a provincial temple seems to bear this out (Simpson 1963b, ch. 5). Three exceptions may be noted: a kiosk of Senusret I at Karnak (Porter and Moss 1972, vol. II, pp. 61–3), a shrine of Sankhkara Menthuhetep on the mountains of western Thebes (Porter and Moss 1972, vol. II, p. 340; Vandersleyen 1975, pp. 155–6), and the late Twelfth Dynasty temple at Medinet Ma'adi in the Fayum (Naumann 1939, Vandersleyen 1975, pp. 159–60). But these, whilst built of stone throughout, are quite small.[3]

On the establishment or enrichment of the estates which made up the pious foundations for the local deities there is little inscriptional record, possibly because much of this had been done in very early periods. The Palermo Stone does record, however, amidst substantial donations of land to the cult of Ra in the Fifth Dynasty, also donations to the cults of Ptah, Nekhbet, Uadjyt and Hathor. It also makes a noteworthy event of the fashioning of divine images, and the curious dearth of statues of gods to have survived from pre-New Kingdom times suggests that they were normally of precious materials, though possibly quite small.[4] Far more prominent is the evidence for pious

---

[1] Robichon and Varille (1940); the associated objects seem to date to between the late Old Kingdom and the early Middle Kingdom. On the early forms of temples see also Reymond (1969, pp. 264–6).

[2] A Middle Kingdom commemoration of the building of a large enclosure wall at El-Kab, recorded as a deed of royal piety, is published by Legrain (1905). The strange royal name is evidently a mistaken transformation of the Horus-name of Senusret I into a prenomen. See also n. 1 on p. 128.

[3] The uninscribed stone temple at Qasr el-Sagha, which can also be attributed to the Middle Kingdom (see Vandersleyen 1975, p. 160), being near a quarry site, must be counted a special case.

[4] Possible exceptions are recorded in Ertman (1972), H. W. Müller (1960) and Wildung (1972), but these may come from pyramid temples. A possible Middle Kingdom example is given in Evers

foundations for statues of kings and private individuals. When housed in the local temple they might have their own little shrine, or they might be in a specially built temple of their own, in either case called a *ḥwt-kꜣ* ('soul house') (Goedicke 1967, p. 44; Helck 1975, pp. 46–7; Fischer 1964, pp. 21–2). The small temple of Pepy I at Tell Basta is designated thus (Fischer 1968, Habachi 1957); another example was found at Dendera (Daressy 1917). Numerous statues of kings are known to have existed in provincial temples,[1] and the arrangements of which they were the centre are exemplified by a decree of Pepy II establishing a pious foundation for a copper statue of himself in the temple of Min at Coptos. A financial arrangement of a different sort – a reciprocal one between temple and central government – is attested for the temple of Amen at Thebes in the Thirteenth Dynasty (Scharff 1920), but how normal this was cannot be ascertained.

The nature and operation of pious foundations in the provinces is made fairly explicit in a number of texts, mostly from private tombs, which also show the intimate link that could exist between a local temple and statue cults based on tombs. It would have been highly advantageous for the control of and for the benefits from such foundations to remain in a local family as a virtually hereditary matter, and this was evidently very often the case. Indeed, as will be outlined below, for much of the time considered in this chapter it was probably difficult to be a man of much importance in the provinces unless associated with the local temple in some way. A good example of family involvement is provided by Nika-ankh at Tehneh in the Fifth Dynasty, a man who combined service for the central government with the office of chief priest in the local temple of Hathor (Breasted 1906, pp. 99–107; Goedicke 1970, pp. 131–48; Helck 1974a, pp. 31–4; Mrsich 1968, pp. 70–85; Pirenne 1932–5, vol. II, pp. 372–8; Pirenne and Stracmans 1954). He had been made chief priest by a decree of King Userkaf and placed in charge of the income of the temple's own foundation. A table lists twelve of his sons, his wife, and a period of time (mostly of one month) when each would serve in the temple, and presumably thereby become entitled to a share of the income, as well as the division amongst them of a piece

(1929, fig. 26), but this may be a statue of Amenemhat III himself. For the use of precious materials in divine images see the inscription of Ikhernefret (Breasted 1906, p. 299) and the golden Horus Image from Hierakonpolis (Quibell 1900, pls. XLI–XLIII; Quibell and Green 1902, p. 27, pl. XLVII).

[1] Examples in stone and copper were found at Hierakonpolis (Quibell 1900, pls. XXXIX–XLI; Quibell and Green 1902, pls. L–LVI). Other examples are from Dendera (Daumas 1973) and a dyad of Sahura possibly from Coptos (Hayes 1953a, pp. 70–1, fig. 46). The inscriptional evidence is presented in Goedicke (1967, pp. 81–6), Helck (1978) and Petrie (1903, pl. XXIV). The cult of early kings at Karnak recorded by the king-list there may perhaps have involved individual statues (Bothmer 1974, Wildung 1969b, 1974).

of land (roughly 16.5 hectares) given by King Menkaura some 25 years earlier for the specific support of this temple's priests. A second table allots the same sons a month's service in a separate private foundation as well, made for a deceased local man called Khenuka, possibly one of Nika-ankh's forbears, and some further sons are depicted as being in charge of Nika-ankh's own foundation. Extracts from the deeds of the mortuary foundations place his eldest son in charge, make the arrangements hereditary, prohibit the foundations from being divided up, and exempt these sons from any obligations beyond the provision of offerings.

A second highly informative set of documents is preserved in the tomb of Hapdjefa (I) at Asyut, from the reign of Senusret I (Goedicke 1971–2, Reisner 1918, Théodoridès 1968–72, 1971a). Hapdjefa was both a 'town governor' (ḥ3ty-ʿ) and chief priest of the local temple of Wepwawet. He draws a careful distinction between his property from this dual position: that which came with the office of governor, and that which he had inherited from his father. The latter included the office of chief priest, in charge of temple revenue, but already Hapdjefa had arranged a pious bequest to the temple of part of the annual harvest tax from the rented lands belonging to his governorship, following a local practice of the common people. By means of ten legal contracts he created a pious foundation centred on one or more statues of himself housed, at least for part of the time, in the temple, but also involving his tomb. In return for performing ceremonies on various feast days and making offerings (which augmented temple income) certain specified persons received payments in the form of gifts of land from his paternal estate, various forms of temple income, and some of the diverted harvest tax. The documents explain how people who had a period of service in the temple received a regular income from it: each day's service in the year entitled one to $\frac{1}{360}$ of each day's income (exemplified also in the Kahun papyri; see Helck (1975, pp. 164–5)). Hapdjefa had included a batch of twenty-seven 'temple days' in the foundation. The beneficiaries were primarily the temple staff, including the chief priest, which office, as the sequence of tombs at Asyut shows, remained in Hapdjefa's own family for several generations. One might further anticipate that most of these persons were members of Hapdjefa's family or household. But even if not, they were certainly recipients of his patronage, and the prospect of this must have added to his authority during his life.

As with the sizes of estates making up royal mortuary foundations so the land components of private pious foundations could vary greatly in size, from 4 or 5 arouras to more than 200 (i.e. from 1 to over 50 hectares). All such resources seem to have been at the ultimate disposal of the central government. This led to a second-stage act of piety: the granting of a royal charter of immunity from all kinds of imposition. All examples come from the Old Kingdom, from which one might deduce that this was, in later times, regarded as an unnecessary source of abuse or conflict. The surviving examples concern the temple of Khenty-amentiu at Abydos, a statue cult of the king's mother Iuput at Coptos, the pyramid temple of Sneferu at Dashur, the valley temple of Menkaura, and statue cults of Queens Meryra-ankhnes and Neit. But before concluding that in this way kings were cutting themselves off from their own revenues, one might consider the effectiveness of these charters in the light of a letter purporting to have been written by King Pepy II in which an order for the procurement of supplies for a returning trade mission from Nubia is applied, amongst several establishments, to 'every temple – without making an exception amongst them'.[1] Similarly the great national army raised by Uni in the reign of Pepy I included contingents under the commands of chief priests of the temples of Upper and Lower Egypt. The relationship between these foundations and the central government must have been a very delicate one.

One is left with the impression that an interlocking network of pious foundations for local deities, for statues of kings at pyramids and in local temples, and for statues of private individuals must have played a major role in the economic life of ancient Egypt, involving the families of a great many people. They naturally made the temple an important centre of economic activity and of administration, particularly in view of the close ties which grew up between the temple and local men of power and influence. It is interesting to note that those decrees from Coptos which are concerned exclusively with civil appointments were found in a cache of decrees some of which carry the explicit instruction for erection at the temple gateway. Understandably, provincial temples were the subject of central government decrees concerning their condition and maintenance.

It has long been recognized that behind changes in titles relating to provincial administration in Upper Egypt lie important historical

---

[1] Breasted (1906, p. 161). Lichtheim (1973, p. 27) translates: 'every temple that has not been exempted', but this is difficult to support grammatically; see Edel (1964, p. 457). The possibility that exemption decrees may not always have been entirely binding seems to be reflected in a Coptos decree of Pepy II; see Goedicke (1967, pp. 88, 107 (n. 59) and 246), who cites the passage that has been quoted, which comes from the biography of Harkhuf (see p. 126).

developments. The common interpretation is that for the earlier part of the Old Kingdom different branches of provincial administration were run by different central government officials in such a way that the administration of one whole governorate (or nome) did not fall to one man. These men were sometimes buried in the court cemetery, and must inevitably have been caught up in the pyramid-building industry which, with its great demands on labour, must have spread its influence throughout the country. An example would be a Fourth Dynasty priest of Sneferu's southern pyramid temple at Dashur, Netjer-aperef, who had also held the offices of 'overseer of commissions in the nomes of Coptos, Hu and Dendera' (Fischer 1968, pp. 8–9). But during the Fifth and Sixth Dynasties this central responsibility for all provincial government was gradually diluted by the appearance of true provincial governors or nomarchs, whose position was formalized by the appearance of a new title, 'great chief of a nome'. The title is first attested at Edfu in the reign of King Teti at the beginning of the Sixth Dynasty (Alliot 1937–8, Edel 1954, Yoyotte 1952), and in the course of this dynasty it appeared throughout most of Upper Egypt. The development appears to coincide more or less with the appearance in certain suitable localities of finely decorated rock tombs, often for the burial of these local magnates.

This very fact, however, points to one source of imbalance in the data. Provincial mud-brick mastaba tombs are known from the earlier Old Kingdom, being occasionally quite large (Arnold 1973, Garstang 1902, 1904), but being more vulnerable the inscriptional evidence for the position of their owners has but rarely survived. Yet some may well have formed a complement to the great court cemeteries at Giza which have been recognized as being not able to account for sufficient of the high administrative officials who must thus have been buried elsewhere. Two significant exceptions to the usual anonymity of these provincial mastaba tombs may be quoted. One occurs at Dendera where, amongst a group of mastaba tombs of the Fourth and Fifth Dynasties, the only identifiable one belonged to a priest of the local Hathor cult, one Ni-ibu-nisut, apparently with no civil titles (Fischer 1968, pp. 14–21). The other concerns El-Kab, where, in a similar situation, the only identifiable mastaba tombs belonged to an 'inspector of priests' Nefer-shemen, and a 'chief priest', Kameni, both of the local Nekhbet cult (Fischer 1968, pp. 18–19 (n. 82); Quibell 1898). Their statues have been dated on stylistic ground to the Fourth Dynasty (Stevenson Smith 1946, p. 45; Vandier 1958, pp. 56–7). Neither bore strictly administrative titles. The priesthood of a separate desert temple at El-Kab is also known from groups of graffiti belonging to people whose names show that the group must extend well into the Sixth Dynasty.[1] Part of their interest lies in the predominantly priestly nature of their titles. Amongst their other titles, even in the case of the chief priest, are very few which one can feel were strictly functional, or of importance in the civil administration, as distinct from honorary titles and rank indicators.

But elsewhere, though in a somewhat spasmodic way, the title 'chief priest' was already being born by men who were also 'nomarch' or its equivalent. Such men are known from provincial tombs of the Sixth Dynasty at several Upper Egyptian sites. Two such men from the nome containing Abydos were buried in the court cemetery at Saqqara, whilst a third may have been buried at his home town (Fischer 1954, 1962). From what has been said already about the economic role of temples and of pious foundations this combination seems very logical. Whether one interprets this as evidence for Egypt's having been ruled by priests or for the priesthood having been essentially part of the apparatus of government is a matter of modern nuance. Certainly at no point here or in the Middle Kingdom can men of obviously outstanding authority and power be found whose titles are strictly or even primarily priestly. The history of the title of the chief priest of Ra at Heliopolis seems to confirm this view, being held for the most part by courtiers, princes or high officials as one amongst several titles.

The evidence surrounding the provincial priests of the Fourth and Fifth Dynasties mentioned above is too slight to acquaint us with the part they played in the life of their communities. Equally obscure is the important question of the family origin of the Sixth Dynasty nomarchs: did they originate from local families whose influence had hitherto been confined largely to the priesthood, or were they men whose background had been the court-centred civil administration and who manoeuvred themselves into control of the local temples? The case of the twelfth nome, whose nomarch, appointed by the king, was a member of the influential family of the vizier Djau from Abydos in the eighth nome, is perhaps exceptional, but does illustrate the way in which high officials in the central government retained provincial links, Djau possessing a pious foundation for his statue in the temple of Khenty-amentiu at Abydos. Nika-ankh, discussed above, must represent another tran-

---

[1] Porter and Moss (1927, vol. v, p. 190) give the references. For the title 'inspector of Nekhbet', the goddess of El-Kab, on mud seals from the town site, see *Fouilles de El Kab* (1954).

sitional stage. The unevenness of the evidence and our difficulties in following the backgrounds of individual officials should introduce considerable caution into the drawing of conclusions. But it can at least be recognized that, by the end of the Sixth Dynasty, province-centred government had become an important part of Egyptian society, and it is tempting to link its evolution with the scaling-down of pyramid-building.

The evidence discussed so far relates entirely to Upper Egypt. Old Kingdom material from the Nile Delta is so slight that few conclusions are possible. A late Old Kingdom cemetery has been discovered from the important town site of Mendes, and the offices of the people buried there call for little special comment, although two chief priests of the local temple without important civil titles may be mentioned. Nowhere are nomarchs for Lower Egypt attested; likewise the title 'governor of Upper Egypt', an attempt from the mid Fifth Dynasty onwards to co-ordinate nome affairs, has (with one possible exception)[1] no equivalent for Lower Egypt until the Middle Kingdom. One might consequently conclude that the nomarch phenomenon of the late Old Kingdom was essentially Upper Egyptian. Some support for the idea that Upper Egypt, particularly the more southerly part, was generally less closely associated with the court circle than Lower Egypt comes from the distribution of estates making up the pious foundations of private funerary cults in the Memphite necropolis. Only a very small number of tombs took up the custom of enumerating estates by nome, but of those that did most display a preponderance in Lower Egypt, and in Upper Egypt there are few indeed further south than the fifteenth nome, thus in the true nomarch territory (fig. 2.2). Even allowing for the possibility that there may have been more natural agricultural potential for creating new estates in the north, it seems to imply that the court drew fairly heavily on men whose connections were more with the more northerly parts of the country, especially the delta.

The First Intermediate Period saw variations in provincial government which belong to the disturbed local history of the period and will be mentioned below on pp. 112–16. Significantly, this type of dual-role provincial governor, in charge of the local temple as well as civil affairs, survived to become ubiquitous in the Middle Kingdom. The standard combination becomes 'chief priest' and ḥȝty-ʿ, originally an exalted court title, but now regularly applied to a man governing a town and

---

[1] The official is Userkaf-ankh, and the title probably 'overseer of the nomes of Lower Egypt' (Pirenne 1932–5, vol. II, p. 470 and n. 1).

in charge of its order and responsible for delivering its taxes to the vizier. The translation 'town governor' often seems the most appropriate. Their holders are known throughout Upper Egypt and now in Lower Egypt as well. Many were owners of large and richly decorated rock tombs, and those at Qau el-Kebir, with temples modelled on the royal pyramid layout, were probably the largest provincial tombs to be constructed in Egypt until the Twenty-fifth Dynasty. Their owners are often called 'nomarchs' by modern writers, but the title which is most aptly translated thus is in most cases either not used by them at all, or in an apparently spasmodic way. The principal exception is at Beni Hasan where the tomb-owners appear to be true nomarchs, on the whole without connection with the local temple. A general appreciation of the position of 'town governors', including the fact that places which were not nome capitals, like Abydos, Armant and Kahun, had them, might lead to the conclusion that, by the Middle Kingdom, provincial authority and its rewards was following the 'natural' pattern of urban development in the Nile Valley. The more artificial division of the country into nomes may well have come to exist only as a formal overlay whose offices were primarily honorary, held either by a town governor or, in an exceptional case as at Beni Hasan, by aristocratic families lying somewhat outside the more common pattern of provincial authority.

Much has been made by historians of the fact that after the reign of Senusret III there are no more large provincial tombs (with the exception of one at Qau el-Kebir of the reign of Amenemhat III). The interpretation has been offered that the power of provincial men was curbed in an administrative reform which brought the country wholly under a centralized bureaucracy. This needs to be seen in careful perspective, however. In the first place, the degree of independence implied in a display of local grandeur is not necessarily directly proportional to the scale of that display. For example, at the height of this phase of local government prosperity, in year 38 of Senusret I, twenty town governors, including those from the southernmost part of Egypt, were obliged to take part in a colossal quarrying expedition for the king to the Wadi Hammamat, under the authority of a 'herald', their presence being presumably required by virtue of their obligations to supply people in their area for the royal *corvée*. This has the appearance of a massive exercise in royal control of provincial government. Secondly, whilst changes in local government may well have taken place in the late Twelfth Dynasty, nevertheless men with the titles 'town

governor' and 'chief priest' are known from the late Twelfth and
Thirteenth Dynasties. Thus, late in the reign of Amenemhat III Kahun
was being governed by one such title-holder; at El-Kab these offices ran
in a family who were descended from a vizier of the Thirteenth Dynasty
and who held this position until late in the Seventeenth Dynasty when
one of them, Sebek-nakht, had a decorated rock tomb made. A similar
sequence is visible at Edfu, and the daughter of a town governor of
Armant appears in an administrative papyrus of the early Thirteenth
Dynasty (Scharff 1920). What must be granted is a break in the sequence
of large provincial tombs, but that the economic factor was one inflicted
by the king is entirely a matter of modern inference. Within a generation
the size of royal tombs also went into a sharp decline, evidently
associated with instability within the kingship. But unlike in the history
of the late Old Kingdom this was not accompanied by a transfer of
wealth to the Upper Egyptian provinces.

### THE FIRST INTERMEDIATE PERIOD

With the reign of Pepy II, alleged by ancient sources to have been over
90 years long, the Old Kingdom effectively ended. The outward
manifestation of this is the fact that his was the last in the sequence of
massive pyramid complexes, although it was also surrounded by a
cemetery of his courtiers in the form of curiously impoverished
provincial-like tombs of mud brick which speak eloquently of the
decline in wealth of those most closely associated with the king. At this
modest level the Memphite cemeteries continued in use, as is shown
by a sequence of tombs of priests of King Teti's cult at Saqqara which
probably spans the whole period. But the ability of the court to build
on a truly monumental scale seems to have gone altogether. The country
was not left, however, without kings. These are known from the
king-lists of Turin and Abydos which between them suggest eighteen
kings, and possibly one queen, ruling for a period of perhaps about
20 years, implying an instability of rule which must go far towards
explaining the absence of large pyramids. It is convenient to equate them
with Manetho's Eighth Dynasty, there being no evidence to support
the existence of an intervening Seventh Dynasty, whilst the Turin list
marks no break in continuity of royal succession between the Sixth
Dynasty and the last of this group. A pyramid tomb of very modest
proportions indeed (see fig. 2.1) has been found at Saqqara belonging
to one of them, a King Aba, who had a reign of either two or four years
in which to accomplish it.

At Coptos in Upper Egypt a series of fourteen decrees issued by some of them mostly appoint members of a prominent local family to positions in the provincial and temple administration. In so doing they create the impression of the continued functioning of the Old Kingdom apparatus of government, suggesting that although the power of these kings to determine events may have been small, their role continued to bestow authority, general approval and status on the careers of provincial men of power.

The Memphite kingship next passed to a line of eighteen kings who seem to have originated from the provincial town of Herakleopolis and who are occasionally referred to in contemporary inscriptions as the 'House of Khety', after the first of the line. Whether they took over the Memphite court or continued to rule from Herakleopolis is, like practically everything about them, unknown. They form Manetho's duplicated Ninth/Tenth Dynasty (von Beckerath 1966, Goedicke 1969, Schenkel 1962, pp. 139–45). Its most famous surviving product is the literary text, the Instruction to Merikara (see p. 74), but because of lacunae in the text, many uncertainties in translation, and more particularly its didactic tone, it requires considerable caution to use it as an historical source.[1]

Our ignorance of royal succession and court affairs at this time is basically a reflection of how important a part pyramid cemeteries play in our view of Egypt in these earlier periods. When they are large and well preserved we feel that we know something of their creators; when they disappear the illusion is created of a 'Dark Age'. Yet as far as events in Upper Egypt are concerned, we know far more at this time than during the heyday of the Old Kingdom. Provincial fortunes become evident from a close study of certain cemeteries. Thus at Mo'alla, on the northern frontier of the nome of Hierakonpolis, the tomb of Ankhtyfy contains important biographical texts. Like his father Hetep, Ankhtyfy bore, amongst others, the twin titles 'nomarch' and 'chief priest', and lived probably in the early to middle part of the Ninth/Tenth Dynasty. He records his takeover of the adjoining nome of Edfu, hitherto under the 'House of Khuu', an important nomarch family itself, and there is a hint that a third nome, presumably Elephantine, for a time was associated with his ambitions. But to his north, similar aspirations had produced a hostile alliance between the nomes of Thebes and Coptos, bringing about mutual attacks on fortresses. Subsequently the whole of the southern part of Upper Egypt fell under the control of Thebes. At Mo'alla this is presumably marked by Ankhtyfy's two

---

[1] Contrast the historical value placed on the text by Ward (1971) and by Björkman (1964).

known successors bearing only the single title 'leader of Hierakonpolis'. At Dendera, there is a long sequence of tombs covering virtually the whole period. From between the end of the Sixth Dynasty and a point more or less contemporary with Ankhtyfy are two belonging to men with the same two offices of 'nomarch' and 'chief priest', and one evidently with the same sort of ambitions as Ankhtyfy, being nomarch of the three nomes of Thinis, Diospolis and Dendera. Their relative independence was again curbed by Thebes. This is marked by one official from Dendera who records serving the 'governor of Upper Egypt, Intef the Great', a Theban. Henceforth the tombs at Dendera belong only to 'chief priests'.

This is the period when for the first time Thebes came into prominence. The late Old Kingdom is represented here by a group of five rock tombs (M. Saleh 1977), two belonging to nomarchs, and from the following period the names of three 'town governors' and 'chief priests' are recorded in inscriptions (Björkman 1964; Schenkel 1965, pp. 29–32, esp. no. 19; Winlock 1947, pp. 5–6), but their connection, if any, to the immediately succeeding Intef family is unknown. Of this last family, who were ultimately to emerge as the Eleventh Dynasty, the two earliest figures are a 'nomarch' and 'chief priest' Intef (Cairo stele 2009; see Fischer 1968, pp. 200, 203; Schenkel 1965, pp. 64–5), and Intef the Great, referred to above.[1] The success of this family in curbing the ambitions of provincial governors to their north and south led them to proclaim themselves kings, and to construct far more imposing tombs in the El-Tarif area of western Thebes. Bearing the names Intef and Menthuhetep they form Manetho's Eleventh Dynasty, and were subsequently thought to comprise seven kings ruling for 143 years. Contemporary sources, however – especially the biography of Hetepi from El-Kab (Gabra 1976)[2] – show that the territorial foundation of real Theban power did not occur until the reign of the third, Wahankh Intef, and must raise some doubts as to whether kingship was not later ascribed to the first two from motives of piety. Their position led to a civil war with the kings of the Ninth/Tenth Dynasty in the north. References to this come both from Thebes, and from tombs at Deir Rifeh, near Asyut, which belong again to 'town governors' or 'nomarchs' and 'chief priests'. Two (belonging to It-ibi and Khety II)

[1] See this page and Schenkel (1965, p. 66, no. 46, also perhaps no. 45). It is possible that this Intef and the previously mentioned one, as well as the 'Intef the Great, the son of Ikui' of later records, are all really the same person; cf. Schenkel (1961, pp. 145–9).

[2] It dates to the reign of Wahankh Intef and seems to suggest that not until his reign were the most southerly nomes brought under full Theban control. It also describes the great famine.

contain narrative inscriptions recording the part played by their owners in the civil war, fighting on behalf of the Ninth/Tenth Dynasty.

Both groups of inscriptions, from Thebes and Deir Rifeh, agree in making the area of conflict lie between Thinis and various points further to the north.[1] No inscription mentions ultimate victory, but it seems certain that it was gained by Nebhepetra Menthuhetep II, not least from the fact that two of his officials served in Herakleopolis itself (Fischer 1959a, 1960, Helck 1955, Schenkel 1965). Nebhepetra's reign also marks an astonishingly successful attempt at creating, at Deir el-Bahari, a monumental funerary complex richly decorated in a style which, though based on Old Kingdom models, possessed a great vigour of its own. With this monument the Middle Kingdom may be said to have commenced.

The First Intermediate Period seems essentially to represent a loss of equilibrium between a powerful court and provincial aspirations, and in itself points to where a major source of power had come to reside. The cemeteries of Upper Egypt show that the people of this area who benefited most from the end of the court's ability to collect and to consume a large part of the country's resources were the provincial governors whose identity had become increasingly clear during the Sixth Dynasty. Civil war there was, but only among men whose aspirations, as far as they can be seen, were of a thoroughly traditional nature, and who recognized the role of traditional kingship even if they permitted it to be only a minor influence in their conduct of their own affairs. As for the north of the country, reliable historical evidence is wholly lacking, although reflections of events are probably present in the Instruction to Merikara, and, as will be documented on pp. 137-8, an Asiatic threat of probably low magnitude existed for a time in the eastern Delta.

One aspect of the First Intermediate Period which has held a particular fascination for historians is the possibility that it witnessed something in the nature of a social revolution. To believe this one must accept that behind the philosophical queryings of the literature of this period and of the Middle Kingdom discussed on pp. 74-5, especially the text of the Admonitions of Ipuwer, there lies some historical actuality which took a dramatic, even revolutionary form. There is, in fact, evidence that in funerary religion certain concepts and symbols devised originally for the exclusive use of kings became more widely

---

[1] It is possible that graffito no. 3 of the Abisko Graffiti in Nubia may refer to an extension of the conflict into the Fayum area; see Brovarski and Murnane (1969) and cf. Posener (1952).

adopted (Fischer 1963), and this has been interpreted by some as evidence for a 'democratization of the afterlife', and a counterpart of what was actually happening in the society of the living. Furthermore, the tone of the philosophical literature itself implies a new awareness by the authors concerned of the fragility of the state, and, especially in the Instruction to Merikara (see p. 74) and in another literary work of this time, the Tale of the Eloquent Peasant, the need to ensure that the state accommodated the hopes of the ordinary man. But to assume that such developments could only be expressed in revolutionary action is to take too simplistic a view of historical processes, and tends to deny the Egyptians the capacity of speculating on and questioning rationally the nature of their society, even if their mode of thought and communication tended to be vividly concrete.

As to what brought about the First Intermediate Period, several possibilities will be discussed in the final section of this chapter, on explanations for historical change in Egypt.

## THE AFRICAN HINTERLAND

An important phenomenon to be observed in the ancient cultures of north-east Africa is a process of cultural separation whereby a people settled in some part of the Nile Valley could become involved, for reasons still not properly understood, in a largely spontaneous and self-multiplying course of cultural enrichment and diversity which separated them from their desert background. In particular, settled life in the Nile Valley seems to have encouraged the appearance both of leaders anxious to extend their control over neighbouring valley groups, and of an elaborate cemetery culture. In Egypt proper this process had given birth to the Predynastic culture from which Pharaonic civilization had grown. But in Nubia the far smaller natural potential of this part of the valley and the aggressive policies adopted by Egypt meant that the process had a limited future and was liable to be arrested while still in an incipient phase, and even reversed.

By its very nature this phenomenon obscures the external affinities of Nile Valley groups. On present evidence, which is still very sparse, one should probably see the deserts surrounding Egypt as having supported a 'pool' of widely and thinly dispersed groups of people in whose lives nomadism played a part of varying importance, and whose simple material cultures frequently show broad overall similarities both to each other and to those of the Nile Valley, but which possessed their own very long histories, probably complicated ones when examined in detail and on a regional basis.[1] Distinctive in their later phases are their ceramic products, chiefly hand-made bowls, whose features include burnished black interiors, black-topped red exteriors often burnished, unburnished dark exteriors decorated with various simple incised or impressed patterns, and occasionally ripple-burnished exteriors. Grinding-stones are also prominent. When resemblances to Nubian cultures seem particularly close some relationship between the peoples concerned may be considered, but until a great deal more information is derived from the deserts, and until more is understood of the process of cultural development in the Nile Valley itself, considerable caution should be exercised in identifying desert homelands for the various valley groups. The temptation for sweeping association from the existence of broad similarities over a wide geographical area is particularly evident in the applications of the term 'C-group' (see below, pp. 126–7), to cultures of the western desert whose total features do not amount to the true C-group, which appears to have been a specialized development of Lower Nubia only. Furthermore, recent evaluation of both the archaeological and physical anthropological material of Lower Nubia has tended to favour the idea of, instead of repeated waves of immigration, a basic continuity of culture and ethnic stock from early times onwards.

The rock pictures which occur both along the Nile Valley and in the deserts on either side are a further important product of these peoples, but the problems of dating make them difficult to use historically. There seems to be widespread agreement, nevertheless, that a large proportion of the cattle drawings, which predominate in the rock art of Nubia and the eastern desert and are found widely spread in the deserts to the west as well, are contemporary with the periods under consideration and attest the existence of a widespread cattle-orientated culture to which the Nubian C-group would presumably have belonged. Beyond such a generalized conclusion, however, it seems scarcely possible to proceed at present, though one might note that both the ancient Egyptian ethnic terminology and the first anthropological results from a Pan-grave cemetery of people believed associated with the Medja nomads of the eastern desert (see below, p. 170), suggest that more than one distinct group of peoples were involved. An ancient cattle cemetery is known

---

[1] The references are very scattered, but include: Bagnold *et al.* (1939), Caton-Thompson (1952), Hays (1975a, b), Hester and Hobler (1969), Hobler and Hester (1968), Hölscher (1955), Huard (1965, 1967–8), Huard and Allard (1970), Huard and Leclant (1972), McHugh (1974a, b, 1975), Shaw (1936a, b).

to lie to the north-east of the Wadi el-Allaqi (Murray 1962), and cattle skulls have come from a Lower Nubian site (Hall 1962).

One might expect that contact between desert and valley was always, if only sporadically maintained, and mainly in the form of short-lived desert-edge encampments of semi-nomads, perhaps entering into a symbiotic relationship with the settled valley-dwellers, based on cattle exchange. Virtually the only investigated record of this type of activity comes from the desert edge to the west of Armant in Upper Egypt, where the following groups were found after very careful examination of the desert surface:[1] (1) a cemetery of seventy-six graves, whose Egyptian pottery dates them to the Early Dynastic Period. Other vessels were of a ripple-burnished ware, some with incised chevron pattern beneath the rim. Of the burials, twenty were of oxen. A cemetery like this may imply something more permanent than a seasonal camp; (2) several small camps ('Saharan Sites') represented by scatters of flint tools and sherds with various incised and impressed patterns. At one of them (Saharan Site 15) were also found seven sherds from Old Kingdom orange-burnished bowls, and part of a vessel which resembles a common Middle Kingdom form; (3) a Pan-grave cemetery, and thus possibly for people of eastern-desert origin (see below, pp. 169–70). An accompanying survey located further Saharan Sites all the way south to Edfu, but none further north, at least as far as Farshut. The practice by nomadic groups of camping on the desert edge, leading sometimes to permanent settlement, has been continued into recent times in this general area.[2] The overall cultural impact of this process has been little investigated.

It is surprisingly difficult to trace, in areas further south still, such ephemeral camp-sites of people contemporary with the well-established Nubian groups. One may wonder if the priorities of the earlier archaeological surveys, carried out for rescue purposes, and the tendency for a unilinear view of cultural development to prevail, have not led to the Saharan Site type being overlooked, especially since the

---

[1] The main results remain unpublished. Myers's records are in the archives of the Egypt Exploration Society, and were in an advanced state of preparation at his death. Permission to quote here some of this material was kindly granted by the Egypt Exploration Society. Preliminary discussions can also be found in Bagnold *et al.* (1939) and Mond and Myers (1937).

[2] The modern village of Naga el-Arab on the desert side of the Birket Habu in western Thebes houses the descendants of a nomadic group who were settled here earlier this century. A photograph of one of their original tented camps appears in Borchardt and Ricke (1930, p. 191). Some of these people, or their neighbours, were reputed to have come from Kharga Oasis (Bonomi 1906).

pottery might bear some resemblances to Nubian valley domestic wares (see p. 124).

## The western desert and oases

Archaeological material has been reported from numerous localities in the western desert, but rarely investigated on a scientific basis. As far away as the Gilf el-Kebir pottery has been found which is said to resemble some of the Nubian valley cultures (specifically C-group). The most detailed published fieldwork has been carried out in the vicinity of the Dunqul and Kurkur Oases, no longer permanently inhabited (Hester and Hobler 1969, Hobler and Hester 1968). A series of occupation sites was discovered, most near the Dunqul and Dineigil Oases, but a few at Kurkur, Nakhlai, Taklis and Sheb. The most important were clustered around water sources which still exist today, but even so represented probably not a single occupation but a number of reoccupations by people with essentially the same material culture, though displaying slight variations from site to site. Two near Dunqul consisted of groups of rooms of rough stone masonry construction, many so small as to suggest storage spaces or animal pens. Of apparently the same age were a number of stone game-traps thrown across shallow valleys at Dunqul and Kurkur, intended perhaps for gazelle and ostrich. The occupants of these sites seem to have herded domesticated sheep and possibly goats, and to have either herded or hunted cattle (*Bos* sp.). Their material culture consisted of a chert artifact assemblage, stone grinders, and sherds primarily from bowls and jars principally of the following wares: thin burnished black-topped, with black interior and red exterior; thin unburnished grey with simple incised or impressed decoration on the outside; thin red–brown undecorated; at one Kurkur site four ripple-burnished sherds were present as well. No cemeteries were found at any of the sites, an important feature which distinguishes them (and probably most other desert sites) from those in the Nile Valley.[1] From one site comes a [14]C date of 1690 ± 180 BC (MASCA[2] correction would be c. 2050 BC (Butzer and Hansen 1968, p. 390, Hobler

[1] Although in the Wadi Howar some hundreds of grave cairns have been noted, but apparently for burials without or with very few grave-goods (Shaw 1936a, b). In this latter case it is somewhat misleading to attach the term Badarian to these graves in view of the incomplete history of the various cultural groups of the deserts, who resorted from time to time to the manufacture of ripple-burnished ware.

[2] MASCA corrections, from one of several schemes for calibrating raw radiocarbon dates, are published by the Museums Applied Science Center for Archaeology in Ralph, Michael and Han (1973).

and Hester 1968)), which would place the survival of these cultures well into the periods considered in these chapters.

When the Egyptians encountered these peoples of the western desert, not surprisingly, they ignored whatever groupings they formed and applied to them a very imprecise terminology. A general term was Tjemehu of the land of Tjemeh, and they or their land are mentioned as the object of raiding parties of both the Egyptians and the Nubian valley dwellers in latitudes as far apart as probably 30° and 20° N. A much later reference (Yoyotte 1951), from the reign of Ramesses II in the early thirteenth century BC, speaks of Tjemehu captured for the building of the rock temple of Wadi es-Sebua which, significantly, lies on the Nile bank to the east and south-east of the Dunqul–Nakhlai area. It has been suggested that on clear ethnic grounds the Egyptians distinguished between them and the Tjehenu, among whom the Egyptians recognized princes or leaders, and whose lands may have lain more towards the Mediterranean, west of the Nile Delta, on the edge of a coastal region which was also, but in periods much later than those considered in this chapter, to experience cultural separation from the desert hinterland.

The most important centres of settlement in the west were presumably the larger oases, although as yet there has been little excavation to substantiate this for the periods under consideration. Kharga and Bahriya provided wine for the Egyptian court (Helck 1975, p. 180), and three Middle Kingdom graffiti have been reported from near mine-workings at Bahriya (Fakhry 1973), but probably a more important interest in them was the strategic one of safeguarding the various desert routes which provide alternatives for trade and other contacts with Nubia and lands lying further to the south. Two sources illustrate the use of such routes. One is the biography of Harkhuf of the Sixth Dynasty which concerns donkey caravans being used for the trade with Upper Nubia, and in one case taking 'the oasis road', and the Second Kamose Stele of the Seventeenth Dynasty where the concern is with diplomatic correspondence being carried south to the same area (Habachi 1972, p. 39; Pritchard 1969, p. 555; Säve-Söderbergh 1956; H. S. Smith and A. Smith 1976). Both most likely involved use of the Darb el-Arba'in caravan route (fig. 2.14) and a northward extension through the Bahriya Oasis. In the same stele Kamose actually records the capture of this oasis, and the strategic value of controlling these routes is presumably reflected in the linking of the conquest of 'the oasis' (probably Kharga and Dakhla regarded as a unit) and of Lower

Nubia in the Ballas inscription of Nebhepetra Menthuhetep of the Eleventh Dynasty (Fischer 1964, pp. 112–18, no. 45; Schenkel 1965, pp. 214–16) (see p. 130).

At least as early as the Sixth Dynasty, when Harkhuf was making his journeys, some of the oases had Egyptian or Egyptianized officials stationed there, presumably with some military support. At Dakhla (at the site of Balat), an extensive Egyptian settlement of the Old Kingdom has been discovered (Vercoutter 1977a), associated with mastaba tombs belonging to men with the title 'governor of the oasis' (Fakhry 1973, Leclant 1974, pl. xxxiv) one of them claiming to be a son of Pepy II and buried with some gold artifacts; and from about the Fifth Dynasty comes a statue of an Egyptian who bore the title 'governor of the land of cattle' (Edel 1956), an evocative name which is elsewhere known to have been used for the Farafra Oasis. From the Middle Kingdom various officials are attested with titles concerned with the western desert generally and with the Kharga and Dakhla Oases in particular, including an 'overseer of the oasis army', probably referring to mercenaries from here (Fischer 1957). A Middle Kingdom stele of an official has been found at the watering place of Bir Nekheila, south-east of Kharga (Fakhry 1973).

### The eastern desert

The special feature of this area is the line of broken hills and mountains separating the Nile Valley from the Red Sea. These hills induce a slight annual rainfall, the extent and regularity of which increase southwards. In the extensive wadi systems it supplies wells, maintains vegetation, and even, in the higher reaches of some of the larger wadis, allows irregular cultivation to take place (Gleichen 1905, pp. 86–8). This area provides a home for nomadic and semi-nomadic pastoralist peoples, the more southerly called the Beja, who, from antiquity, have been regarded by outsiders as comprising a number of distinct and relatively important groups, more so than those of the western desert. The ancient Egyptians mounted regular mining expeditions to exploit the mineral resources of these hills, and, by concentrating in some of the same wadi systems, must have come into repeated contact with the local people.[1]

The consequent need to find in Egyptian texts references to the

---

[1] They were occasionally referred to as 'Asiatics', whose origin, if the term was always correctly used by the Egyptians, may have been the people of Palestinian culture in south Sinai in Chalcolithic and Early Bronze Age times (see pp. 139–42). The modern Beja are not Semites, in contrast to those people who inhabit the Red Sea Hills further to the north.

peoples of this important area leads, without a serious alternative, to an identification with the Medja-people. In the Middle Kingdom, when Egyptian activity in the eastern hills probably grew more intensive, Medja-people appear in texts as essentially desert-dwellers, but connected with the Nile, and the object both of Egyptian surveillance and aggression. They also entered Egyptian service. The early Thirteenth Dynasty papyrus referred to above (see p. 81) records the arrival and stay at court of a delegation of eight Medja men and women, and later of a Medja prince. In this reference, as in the Execration Texts (see below p. 134), Medja-people are subdivided into groups. The names used are written as if of places but, as in mediaeval sources, the Egyptians may be transferring the terminology of a settled people to names which were really of tribes who ranged over extensive territories. To this general argument of likelihood for the location of the Medja homeland in the hillier parts of the eastern desert of Nubia should be added the specific information provided by a stele from the Wadi el-Hudi which appears to place this particular region in Medja territory (Bietak 1966, pp. 77–8). Unfortunately, the whole area remains, archaeologically, a virtual blank.

## The Egyptian interest

The Lower Nubian valley acted as a transport corridor giving access to important mining and quarrying areas in the deserts to east and west. These were principally (and in addition to those east of Egypt proper):

(1) Wadi el-Allaqi–Wadi Gabgaba, an extensive network of broad flat wadis which in ancient, as well as in mediaeval, times were important sources of gold obtained from shallow surface workings; also probably copper, to which large slag-heaps reported near the ancient fort of Kubban were presumably connected. Two Sixth Dynasty graffiti have been found 60 km from the Nile along the Wadi el-Allaqi (Piotrovsky 1966, 1967),[1] and possibly three from the Middle Kingdom further on (Černy 1947). One must also presume that this would have been the principal area of contact with the Medja-people.

(2) Wadi el-Hudi, a source of amethyst, and possibly of gold as well. Inscriptions found here mention Kings Nebtawyra Menthuhetep IV (last king of the Eleventh Dynasty), Senusret I, Senusret III, Amenemhat III, all of the Twelfth, and Khaneferra Sebekhetep of the Thirteenth.

---

[1] There is no need to assume that the Uni of one of these graffiti is the same as the famous Uni of the Abydos inscription. Their titles are not the same.

A neatly laid out fortified stone village has been tentatively dated to the Middle Kingdom.

(3) Quarries in the western desert, north-west of Toshka, exploited for diorite gneiss and possibly carnelian.[1] Royal names found here are: Khufu and Djedefra of the Fourth Dynasty, Sahura and Djedkara Isesi of the Fifth, Senusret I, Amenemhat I/Senusret I co-regency, Amenemhat II, and Amenemhat III of the Twelfth. One quarrying record claimed that 1000 donkeys and over 1000 men were involved.

Gold was also available from riverine and riverside deposits between Buhen and Kerma and three Old Kingdom graffiti belonging to a class of officials apparently concerned particularly with the import of minerals have been found at Kulb, near Dal (Hintze 1965). Pharaonic riverside mines have been located at Saras and Duweishat, the former apparently of the Twelfth Dynasty. It has also been suggested that wood from both Upper and Lower Nubia was taken to supplement Egypt's modest reserves.

Provision had also to be made for trading with regions lying even further to the south which could provide the Egyptians with exotic goods. One Sixth Dynasty source (Harkhuf) lists as the products of such trade: 'incense, ebony, *ḥknw*-oil..., panther skins, elephants' tusks, and throwing-sticks'. Since the sources of some of these items would have lain beyond the reach of direct Egyptian penetration by river or by caravan, it was necessary to come to some sort of arrangement with Nubian middlemen, as well as to safeguard the routes themselves. This, as noted above, involved control of the western oases.

From time to time checks were felt to be necessary on political developments amongst the riverine peoples. The process of cultural separation from the desert hinterland and the appearance of ambitious leaders was always liable to take place, more successfully in Upper Nubia where the resources were much greater. Since the imbalance in population between Egypt and her African neighbours must have been much less great in antiquity than in modern times such political developments must have been viewed with an equivalently greater urgency. The expressed Egyptian policy was always one of aggression, but this, especially as it concerns Upper Nubia, contains the ambiguity that amongst these peoples the Egyptians also had to find trading partners. Although it is always possible that they entertained the hope of being able, ultimately, to break through by river or by land to the

---

[1] The second commodity sought was called *mḥnt*, a mineral substance for which the translation 'carnelian' (or 'jasper') has been suggested (Simpson 1963c, pp. 50–1).

true sources of exotic goods and further gold which they were otherwise able to reach directly only by the coastal voyage to Punt (see pp. 136–7).

### The Nubian Nile Valley

The demise of the Nubian A-group culture during the first part of the First Dynasty seems to have marked the beginning of a hiatus in the Lower Nubian cultural record of perhaps as much as five centuries. For some time archaeologists filled this gap with a B-group culture, principally material from very impoverished graves. But a close analysis of the evidence shows that there are no grounds for recognizing in any of the Lower Nubian cemeteries a homogenous phase to be fitted into this period, which in Egypt represents a major part of the Old Kingdom. The most plausible interpretation is that as a result of Egyptian harassment, including perhaps the taking of prisoners, and possibly the exclusion from a hitherto close trading relationship with Egypt, the inhabitants sought refuge in a semi-nomadic way of life between the Nile Valley and the wells and oases of the adjacent deserts.

One feature of the desert cultures discussed above is the rarity of well-defined cemeteries. If the temporary and perhaps seasonal presence of these people in Lower Nubia had been marked by nothing more substantial than camps of the Saharan Site type identified at Armant then it becomes understandable how the methods and standpoints of some of the principal Nubian surveys could have overlooked or undervalued such insubstantial surface sites, particularly since the pottery may well have born superficial resemblances to C-group domestic wares. One of the most exhaustive of the more recent surveys, however, has located some sites of just this nature, though in the ecologically more marginal area of the Second Cataract. One of them, at Saras East, in addition to sherds of types related to both A-group and C-group cultures yielded an Old Kingdom orange-burnished bowl sherd, reminiscent, therefore, of Saharan Site 15 at Armant (Mills and Nordström 1966).[1] The necessity for seeking some such explanation is heightened by Egyptian inscriptions claiming the capture of substantial numbers of men and animals from Nubia (Breasted 1906, p. 66; Helck 1974c, Schäfer 1902, p. 30).

One of the most important discoveries of the Nubian excavations of

[1] Gratien (1978, p. 134) claims that outliers of her Early Kerma phase ('Kerma ancien') occur at Aniba, Serra, Faras and Saras in Lower Nubia, as well as at Akasha, Dal, Sai and Kerma in Upper Nubia. See also Nordström (1966).

the 1960s was that as early as the Old Kingdom there had been an Egyptian attempt to control Lower Nubia by means of centres of permanent occupation. This was established by the excavation of Buhen North. Here, not far from the northern end of the Second Cataract, was a settlement, defined by a rough stone wall, whose material culture was almost exclusively Egyptian. In the best-preserved area the crushing and smelting of what was claimed to be copper ore had been carried on, derived from a source as yet unlocated. Royal names, especially on mud-seal impressions, were of Kings Khafra and Menkaura of the Fourth Dynasty, and Userkaf, Sahura, Neferirkara and Djedkara Isesi of the Fifth. Earlier levels, however, were tentatively ascribed to possibly as early as the Second Dynasty on the basis of mud-brick sizes and much decayed jar seals. Such an early date receives some support from $^{14}$C dates,[1] and a graffito on a nearby hill has also been given an Early Dynastic date (H. S. Smith 1972). Buhen North represents a policy of Egyptian settlement now exemplified at Balat in the Dakhla Oasis (see p. 121), and throws a welcome light on the much earlier discovery of a few Old Kingdom sherds at Kubban, the site subsequently of a large Middle Kingdom fort strategically situated opposite the entrance to the Wadi el-Allaqi (Emery and Kirwan 1935). The apparent lack of a settled population in Lower Nubia may have rendered unnecessary the creation of a chain of garrison forts on the later Middle Kingdom pattern, but the Kubban sherds contain the hint that Buhen North was not alone in Lower Nubia. Buhen North also gave the Egyptians the potential, as in the Middle Kingdom, for striking into Upper Nubia where the pickings must always have been much greater, and this introduces a note of geographical uncertainty into the Fourth Dynasty record of King Sneferu's capture of booty during a raid on Nubia. Buhen North would likewise have been well placed for trade with Upper Nubia, replacing Lower Nubian middlemen.

At Buhen, as in the diorite quarries, the inscriptional sequence ends

---

[1] The various radiocarbon dates are published in *Radiocarbon*, 1963, 5, 21, 288–9; 1965, 7, 352; 1966, 8, 3–4; 1968, 10, 1. Seven of the eight Arizona dates give a reasonably consistent picture when subject to half-life correction and to calibration (e.g. by the MASCA scale, see n. 2 on p. 119), with two samples from below the Old Kingdom floor (A-333, 334) of 2920 ± 60 BC and 2830–2700 ± 50 BC. The five California dates (three of them from samples also used by Arizona) and the one British Museum date are somewhat less consistent, tending to give dates for the upper level a lot earlier than one would expect, although a key sample from a trial trench across the centre of the site (UCLA-247) yielded a date of 2910 ± 60 BC. H. S. Smith (1964) echoed by Säve-Söderbergh and Olsson (1970) has seen in the internal inconsistencies a reason for suspecting the correct interpretation of the stratigraphy. The degree of inconsistency, however, is probably no greater than that, for example, which is apparent amongst radiocarbon dates from the Aegean Bronze Age.

with the Fifth Dynasty, to be resumed at each site only at the beginning
of the Twelfth. For the Sixth Dynasty, however, there are important
inscriptions left behind by Egyptian expeditions to Nubia, often led by
officials called 'overseers of foreign troops' (L. Bell 1973, Edel 1971b,
1973, Fischer 1964, pp. 29–30; Goedicke 1966a). Such expeditions are
recorded in the Wadi el-Allaqi, and by the Nile in the Tomas–Toshka
area. In two graffiti at Tomas the leaders bore also the interesting titles
'overseer of the army of Satju' and 'overseer of the foreign troops of
Satju', referring to a local Nubian riverine community which was
presumably supplying mercenary troops. The longest inscription is the
biography of Harkhuf in his tomb at Aswan. This records three
expeditions, apparently with trade as their prime object, commencing
at Memphis and taking a route either along the river valley, or across
the western desert via the oases. One important feature of the narrative
is the references to apparently well-established Nubian groups in Lower
Nubia, the most important in territories called Satju, Irtjet and Wawat,
apparently in this south-to-north order and covering much of this part
of the Nile Valley. On Harkhuf's second journey Irtjet and Satju were
under the leadership of one man, and by the third journey Wawat had
been joined to them. It is tempting to see this as an actual record of
the process of political concentration accompanying permanent settlement which in this case would have produced, near the end of the Old
Kingdom, a veritable king of Lower Nubia. The archaeological
component to this process is presumably to be found in the earliest phase
of C-group culture, the next major episode of settled life in Lower
Nubia. Occurring in a small number of cemeteries on the west bank,
mainly in the central part of Lower Nubia, a few graves of the earliest
phase contained imported Egyptian 'button seals' which, in Egypt,
were in fashion during the late Old Kingdom. Whether the appearance
of C-group culture was a cause or a result of the apparent abandonment
of Egyptian settlement in Nubia after the Fifth Dynasty cannot be
determined. At this time the governors of Elephantine bear the title
'overseer of foreign lands', in one case 'overseer of the foreign lands
of his lord: Yam, Irtjet and Wawat', and this, together with the strong
mercenary soldier element mentioned above, might suggest some
political agreement to Egypt's advantage with these Nubian groups.

C-group (or Middle Nubian) culture persisted in Lower Nubia until
the early Eighteenth Dynasty, passing through a number of phases
which are essentially modifications and elaborations of the basic pattern.
Since riverside settlement was itself an important stimulus to cultural

development and diversity involving the appearance of an elaborate cemetery culture there is probably little point in looking for fully-fledged C-group culture outside Lower Nubia, and as mentioned above, continuity and migration offer two opposing interpretational positions from which to view C-group beginnings. Until the penultimate phase (IIb) in the Second Intermediate Period the only C-group occupation sites known are small collections of huts, either of wooden posts possibly covered with skins, or more commonly of low walls of upright stone slabs with pitched roofs supported on timbers. The cemeteries were elaborate affairs, sometimes containing free-standing stone slabs occasionally decorated with pictures of cattle. Each tomb possessed a well-built circular superstructure of dry stone masonry, and sometimes the burial lay inside a stone cyst or beneath a mud-brick barrel vault. But again, until the penultimate phase, there is no very obvious scaling of tomb size to reflect social or political standing, a negative feature possessed also in general by the earlier A-group culture.

In material culture, much of it derived from cemeteries, pottery is the most readily distinguishable feature, particularly a varied class of hand-made black bowls with elaborate incised geometric patterns; also polished black-topped red bowls, a variety of coarser domestic wares, and imported Egyptian jars, possibly for storing water. In general, the numbers of Egyptian objects acquired seem to have been relatively limited, and the development of C-group culture appears to have progressed independently of the Egyptian reconquest of Lower Nubia in the Middle Kingdom. The reconquest, however, must have frustrated whatever political ambitions had been nascent during the Sixth Dynasty and First Intermediate Period, but apart from this, C-group people seem to have been able to continue their way of life in which, to judge from their limited artistic repertoire, cattle played an important part. It also involved a modest exchange of goods between individuals, families and villages, but insufficient to create obvious concentrations of wealth.

C-group culture has been found at numerous sites in Lower Nubia, with particular concentrations in the fertile areas around Faras, Aniba and Dakka, and with one outlier in Egypt itself, at Kubaniya, 13 km north of Aswan. At this last site the C-group elements appear to belong to an early phase, presumably of the First Intermediate Period. During the Middle Kingdom the descendants of this community adopted Egyptian culture and burial practices. Southwards, it has been found no further upstream than at Semna at the head of the Second Cataract. Further south again stretches the southern continuation of the Batn el-Hagar, a particularly barren part of the Nile Valley which careful survey has shown was virtually without a settled population in ancient times (Geus and Labre 1974, Vila 1975). Further south still, beyond Dal, the archaeology of Upper Nubia is still only provisionally documented.

The site of the greatest interest here is Kerma, on the east bank above the Third Cataract (W. Y. Adams 1977a, Hintze 1964, O'Connor 1974, el-Rayah 1974, Reisner 1923, Säve-Söderbergh 1941, pp. 103–16; Trigger 1976a).[1] As will be discussed below (pp. 144–5, 162–7), the most striking of the remains – the brick castle and the great tumuli – almost certainly represent the seat of the Kings of Kush ruling much of Nubia during the late seventeenth and early sixteenth centuries BC. Their taste for Egyptian products, extending to pieces of antique inscription and statuary, has led to some confusion in modern interpretations. In the initial analysis of the cemetery, then regarded as for the burial of Egyptian trading officials, a relative chronology was established, with the great tumuli at the southern end representing the earliest classic stage. As with all relative sequences of this nature, however, it is, in theory, reversible, and the modern realization that the great tumuli must be the latest implies that the northern part of the cemetery contains the burials and culture of Kerma extending back in time from the Second Intermediate Period, presumably through the Middle Kingdom. Unfortunately, the small excavated areas of this part remain unpublished, although a few general remarks by the excavator suggest, as might be expected, features common also to the C-group of Lower Nubia, and perhaps to the A-group as well. This alternative view of the Kerma necropolis would seem to receive support from excavations on the island of Sai, which is reported to contain cemeteries as large as those at Kerma itself, though with no tombs to rival in size the royal tumuli.

A provisional scheme of archaeological classification for Upper Nubia has been proposed on the basis of the Sai cemeteries (Gratien 1978). The Classic Kerma phase of the latter part of the Second Intermediate Period, i.e. Hyksos Period in northern Egypt, is here preceded by two others: a Middle Kerma phase which displays certain burial customs common also to Classic Kerma and whose tombs contained, amongst other material, copper daggers presumably from Egypt; an Early Kerma apparently in succession to an Upper Nubian

---

[1] The stele of Intef, a key document in the interpretation of Kerma, has a remarkably close parallel in a stele from El-Kab (see n. 2 on p. 104), which adds weight to the idea that the Intef stele is not describing some sort of fortified structure built locally at Kerma. Note also that a statue claimed to have belonged to a man with the name Hapdjefa has been found at Tell Ḥizzin, in the Lebanon.

version of the A-group of Lower Nubia. Both Middle and Early Kerma are probably to be equated with parts of the northern sector of the great Kerma necropolis itself, and Middle Kerma is presumably the local equivalent of the Lower Nubian C-group, and thus largely contemporary with the Middle Kingdom. Upper Nubia may thus, to judge from the preliminary results so far published, offer a much more continuous cultural record than Lower Nubia, without the major hiatus between A- and C-groups.

Whilst Kerma can no longer be regarded as an Egyptian 'trading colony' of the Middle Kingdom, not all of the Egyptian material need be dismissed as of later importation. This applies particularly to a cache of broken stone vases from the castle courtyard and adjacent rooms, probably from beneath the level of their floors, which bore the names of Pepy I and II of the Sixth Dynasty, and of Amenemhat I and Senusret I of the Twelfth (Reisner 1923, pts. I–III, pp. 30–2, pts IV–V, pp. 507–10).[1] In some respects Kerma in the Second Intermediate Period came to be an African counterpart of Byblos: an independent state beyond Egypt's political frontiers, with a court looking to Egypt as a source of sophisticated court fashion. In the case of Byblos the connection owed much to trade with Egypt. With Kerma the mechanism of contact is more obscure, although the site lies not far from a short-cut across the desert to the great Darb el-Arba'in caravan route. But it is in the light of this subsequent history that one should view Harkhuf's accounts of his trading expeditions. Their goal was the kingdom of Yam. The internal evidence of Harkhuf's narrative is, despite much debate, too insubstantial for locating this place, other than that it lay further from Egypt than the Lower Nubian kingdoms mentioned above. But the Sixth Dynasty vases from Kerma, which have their exact counterparts at Byblos, as well as the later patterns of contact and political growth give priority to the Kerma area as the site of Yam. Furthermore, in the Egyptian spelling of Yam an equation has been sought with Irem, a later name for a country in this very region (Priese 1974, Zibelius 1972, pp. 78–81).[2] It is interesting to note that Yam was already in Harkhuf's

[1] Vercoutter (1967), reviewing Trigger (1965), cites an Old Kingdom vase with the cartouche of Pepy II from a tomb at Mirgissa of the Second Intermediate Period by way of casting doubt on the significance of the Kerma find. Nevertheless, an isolated specimen like this is hardly in the same category as a cache of the size of the one at Kerma, which included, according to Reisner, at least twenty-five different vases with the name of Pepy I. The Mirgissa vase is published in Vercoutter (1975a, p. 98, fig. 31).

[2] The fact that to the west of Yam lay an area occupied by Tjemehu people is of less help than might at first sight seem to be the case, in view of the archaeological evidence for a considerably greater spread of people in the western deserts in ancient times than is probable today (see Strouhal

time regarded as being under the patronage of the Egyptian goddess Hathor (Lichtheim 1973, p. 26),[1] who, like Horus, was to assume in the Middle Kingdom this role in several places in Nubia, including the diorite quarries of the western desert, as well as the mines in Sinai and the port of Byblos.

The reconquest of Lower Nubia seems to have begun with the reign of Nebhepetra Menthuhetep II (c. 2010 BC). A fragmentary inscription from El-Ballas in Upper Egypt, dated to his reign on epigraphic grounds, contains an account of conquest which includes the words: 'Wawat (Lower Nubia) and the Oasis, I annexed them to Upper Egypt' (Fischer 1964, pp. 112–18; Schenkel 1965, pp. 214–16). From the phraseology of a group of graffiti of his reign at Abisko, 10 km south of Aswan, it seems likely that Buhen was reached on a proper campaign.[2] No archaeological material certainly dated to his reign has been encountered in Nubia to show if a policy of settlement had been begun, but the difficulties of precise reign-by-reign dating of Egyptian artifacts should deter one from giving too firm a denial. The same is true also for the reign of Amenemhat I, first king of the Twelfth Dynasty, to whose year 29 a graffito of conquest in Wawat exists at Korosko.

By contrast, beginning with the reign of Senusret I we possess massive archaeological evidence for an Egyptian presence in Lower Nubia in the form of heavily fortified towns. These fall roughly into two groups, representing partly two different types of terrain and partly two major building phases. The first group may be termed the 'plains type', and were constructed on the flat or shelving banks of the Lower Nubian Nile north of the Second Cataract. The most southerly, Buhen, seems to have been in existence by year 5 of Senusret I, and shares sufficient architectural features in common with others at Aniba (stage II) and Kubban (stage II) to provide a similar date for them; although when examined in detail it is also clear that each fort had its own history and may have followed a more continuous process of independent improvement and modification. Unfortunately, precise dating evidence for most of the forts is lacking, but it should be noted that stage I at Aniba and Kubban should, for architectural reasons, strictly be dated

and Jungwirth 1971). As regards proximity to the Darb el-Arba'in caravan route, Sai Island is better placed than Kerma. In the sixteenth century AD the King of Sai collected customs dues from caravans taking this route, but a hundred years later this was being done at Argo, near Kerma, on behalf of the King of Dongola (Crawford 1951, pp. 140–1, 197).

[1] The precise title is 'Hathor, lady of Imaau', perhaps a part of Yam (Zibelius 1972, p. 81).

[2] See n. 1 on p. 115 and Zibelius (1972, pp 11–12). H. S. Smith (1976, p. 63) doubts this.

to before the Buhen of Senusret I, as should also the stage I at Ikkur. These early stages at these sites might just conceivably, therefore, belong to the conquests of Nebhepetra Menthuhetep and Amenemhat I.

These forts were each defended by a massive mud-brick wall, with external towers on all sides and at the corners. On the landward side they overlooked a ditch, at Buhen with counterscarp and glacis. Their most distinctive feature was a secondary defensive line at the base of the wall, between it and the ditch. A low parapet with downward-pointing loopholes ran along the inner edge of the ditch, interrupted at intervals by semicircular bastions. It seems intended to thwart a fairly sophisticated type of siege, and thus raises the possibility that it represents a form of urban fortification developed in Egypt perhaps during the civil wars of the First Intermediate Period. Each of the forts also possessed a river frontage with quays, whilst at Serra East, a later fort where the secondary line of defence had been thought unnecessary, a small harbour was constructed actually within the walls. At Buhen and Aniba (and possibly Kubban, too) these forts became citadels within a much larger fortified area, though little is known about how much of this outer part was built up. Exceptionally at Buhen the foundations of a massive, rectangular, multi-storeyed block were found immediately north of the citadel wall.

Apart from knowing that each contained a garrison of uncertain but possibly modest size (Vila 1970), possessed an administration which was apparently a specialized variant of that operating in Egypt and presumably provided a haven for Egyptian river traffic, we know very little about who lived in these forts, how many they comprised and what they did. It is likely that their roles varied one from another. Thus, at Buhen and Kubban, and possibly at Mirgissa, copper-working seems to have been carried on,[1] whilst some were involved in local trade, the evidence for which will be discussed below. A group of stelae from Buhen have been ascribed to people who came from the El-Rizeikat neighbourhood of Upper Egypt, perhaps as settlers, though this is by no means certain.

The second group of forts resulted from an Egyptian annexation of the entire Second Cataract area in the reign of Senusret III, for which the inscriptional and archaeological evidence is specific. In the rugged terrain each of the new forts took the form of an irregular polygonal

---

[1] For Buhen see Emery (1961) and Lucas and Harris (1962, pp. 207–9); the available evidence on Mirgissa is a reference to a seal of a 'supervisor of copper workers' cited by Hesse (1971); cf. Vercoutter (1977b).

figure tailored to fit over an irregular natural prominence. Narrow ridges were covered with spur walls, and in most places the terrain rendered a ditch unnecessary. Care was taken to ensure a supply of fresh water by the construction of a stone passageway down to the river's edge, a feature present also in some of the Lower Nubian forts. Apart from the island fort of Askut midway in the Second Cataract area (and possible intermediate signalling posts) these forts cluster around the southern part and form an obvious defensive grouping across the narrow Semna Gorge (fig. 2.9). Two inscriptions of the reign of Senusret III from Semna confirm that this was indeed intended as a true frontier. One describes its purpose as: 'to prevent any Nubian from passing it when faring northwards, whether on foot or by boat, as well as any cattle of the Nubians, except for a Nubian who shall come to trade at Iqen, or as an envoy'. Iqen is now known to have been the great fort at Mirgissa which in its position, history and design is intermediate between the two main groups of forts. The reference to envoys is reminiscent of the entertaining at court of the Medja groups referred to in Papyrus Bulaq 18 (see p. 81) and is a useful reminder of the fact that, notwithstanding the consistently aggressive tone of official texts, it was necessary, on commercial and political grounds, for the Egyptians to come to some sort of understanding with their southern neighbours. Two private stelae suggest a reciprocal operation, with Egyptians venturing south into Kush on official missions of some sort.[1]

The Egyptian defensive measures were not limited to walls and battlements. Observation posts on rocky eminences in the Second Cataract area were manned, recourse was had to magical practices to thwart enemy intentions (Reisner, Wheeler and Dunham 1967, pls. 31, 32; Vila 1963, 1973) and, as copies of a group of despatches sent to Thebes (the Semna Despatches) reveal, a detailed surveillance system attempted to gather intelligence in a comprehensive way. One recurrent topic in these despatches is the activities of the Medja-people, some of whom appear at the same time in Egyptian service. In one despatch a track has been followed, three Medja-people found and questioned on their origin; in another the following of a track of thirty-two men and three donkeys is reported; in a third (from the fort at Elephantine) a small party of Medja-people has descended from the desert to request service with the Egyptians, claiming that 'the desert is dying of hunger'.

[1] Cairo 20086, Berlin 19500. The term 'commissions' (*wpwt*) in the latter would be particularly appropriate to diplomatic contact.

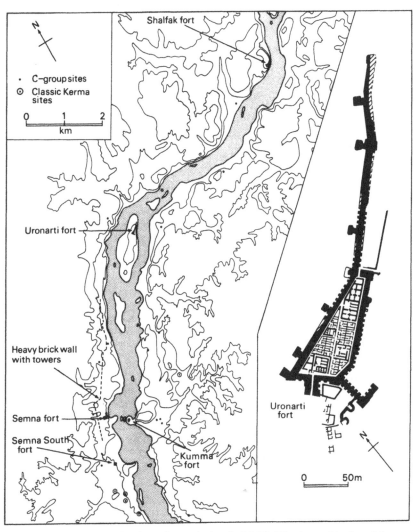

Fig. 2.9 The Egyptian frontier at Semna during the Middle Kingdom, with plan of the fortress of Uronarti inset.

If Medja-people were regarded as a threat, this may have been a factor in the general preference shown by the Egyptians for siting the forts on the opposite bank, with significant exceptions at Kubban and Serra East, respectively opposite the entrances to the Wadi el-Allaqi and Wadi Hagar Shams, both leading to gold-mining regions.

Concern over the eastern-desert nomads does not, however, explain the southward-facing disposition of the Semna group of forts (fig. 2.9). That these looked southwards to potentially hostile riverine kingdoms beyond the Batn el-Hagar, in Upper Nubia, becomes evident from other inscriptional sources. Between the reigns of Senusret I and Senusret III the principal target of Nubian campaigns is said to be Kush. This is a geographical term with two levels of application: as a general geographical term for Upper Nubia, and one which remained as such throughout the New Kingdom, and as the name of a particular kingdom there, presumably the most powerful since the Egyptians used its name to characterize a much larger area, something which might also suggest a locally recognized political supremacy. The references to campaigns against Kush contain very little that is episodic, although one of them, of year 19 of Senusret III recording the return of an expedition against Kush and the difficulty of bringing boats back through the cataracts, by its position at Uronarti shows that in this case a riverine expedition south of the Semna Gorge had been undertaken. Related to these records is a graffito of Senusret III reported from Dal (B. Bell 1975, p. 238; Leclant 1969, p. 282). Kush in the more limited sense as the name of a kingdom appears at or near the head of lists of conquered and hostile places in Nubia, a sign probably of its importance rather than of its geographical proximity to Egypt. With one exception these lists belong to a class of document called Execration Texts.[1] Written on pottery jars or on statuettes of captive figures, and intended for a magical rite to thwart the operation of evil forces, they list people and things of a potentially hostile nature, including foreign kings and their subjects. An early example of the Sixth Dynasty includes the Nubian countries of Irtjet, Wawat, Yam, Medja and Satju (Abu Bakr and Osing 1973, Posener 1971), and for the Middle Kingdom, at least four groups cover Nubia. Few of the places can be localized, though from the fact that in two of the groups at least, Lower Nubia (Wawat) does not occur, one might deduce that Upper Nubia is the prime concern. Furthermore, although the relationship between archaeology and political structure is always a delicate one, it would seem somewhat unlikely on the basis of the nature of the country and of the negative archaeological record that the area between Semna and Ukma – the southern part of the Batn el-Hagar – could have become of much importance. In the New Kingdom, the temple towns founded by the Egyptians in Upper Nubia, probably following the existing political pattern, began only at Amara,

---

[1] The exception is the stele of Menthuhetep from Buhen (Bosticco 1959, no. 29; H. S. Smith 1976, pp. 39–41).

about 10 km downstream from Sai. Sai Island has been identified as the kingdom of Shaat, which also tends to occur towards the head of the lists. If one were to follow fairly strictly the order in which the places are enumerated the Amara–Ukma area might, in view of these limiting factors, seem the most likely original site for Kush. But if one considers the historical developments in Nubia in the Second Intermediate Period and the possibility that the position of Kush in the lists is a tribute to its political importance, then one might conclude that Kush was, from the outset, centred at Kerma. Some other names in the lists appear to be compounds containing the old name Yam, and Medja kingdoms are also included, one of them being Aushek which sent the envoys recorded in Papyrus Bulaq 18.

There remains to be considered the question of Egyptian participation in trade. One might envisage that, apart from Iqen, each fort engaged in small-scale local transactions, particularly to acquire cattle from both C-group and, in the case of Kubban in particular, Medja-people as well, though no inscriptional evidence has survived for this. It is known that cattle in Egypt fetched high prices. Some of the Semna Despatches record the arrivals of parties of Nubians (six in one case) to trade in unspecified commodities at the forts. In return they were given bread and beer, but whether as part of the transaction or as a gift is not made clear. A point at the First Cataract which possessed its own fort, called Senmet, was used as a place for trading for gold with Medja-people under the ultimate supervision of the governor of Elephantine (Edel 1962, 1971a, p. 11). Also important was the acquisition of products from further south for transfer to Egypt, including incense for which a considerable market must have existed in Egypt in view of its ubiquitous use in offering-ceremonies at statue cults in temples and tombs. It is nowhere apparent, however, if the Upper Nubian kingdoms acted as middlemen themselves or merely exacted revenues from caravans passing through their territory. The Semna stele quoted above directed Nubians from the south to the special trading post at Iqen (Mirgissa), but for caravans coming from further afield it would have made more sense to use the Darb el-Arbaʿin, perhaps leaving the Nile at Sai, and making contact with the Egyptians, perhaps to pick up an escort, at one of the oases. Equally conjectural is what the Nubians for their part gained from trade. Such evidence as is available from the earlier phases at Kerma and Sai does not support the idea that, as in the Second Intermediate Period, finished products played a large part, though if their value was kept high by the Egyptians, the Nubians may have netted less for their trade than they did later when the initiative passed more to them. It is also not yet possible to judge if perishable commodities such as corn and cloth were significantly involved, though one might note from Mirgissa and Uronarti thousands of mud seals originating from sacks (Reisner 1955, Vercoutter 1970, pp. 171–2).

The inevitably conjectural nature of discussions on the pattern of Nubian trade should not be allowed to detract from the fair certainty that it was of considerable importance, the Egyptian demand for gold and incense being the counterpart in the south to the demand for timber obtained via Byblos in the north. It should be regarded as a major factor in the political developments of Upper Nubia in the Second Intermediate Period.

### The land of Punt

The significance of the land of Punt appears to lie in the fact that it was the one place where the Egyptians could trade direct with an area producing certain valuable commodities (principally 'ntyw: myrrh or frankincense, or both) which was at the same time too remote to be politically dangerous to them. The kingdoms of Upper Nubia and of the Medja-people must have effectively blocked direct Egyptian contact by land and river, but a coastal journey along the Red Sea eventually brought them to the desired area, perhaps to an established emporium. The precise point of contact has not yet been determined, but the possibilities are limited by the likely ancient distribution of the various characteristics of Punt described and portrayed by the Egyptians. On the assumption that the Egyptians minimized their journey, the most likely area is the Sudan–Eritrea border zone, rather than further along the coast and even through the straits of Bab el-Mandeb. An established emporium, wherever located, could also have drawn on the incense trees native to southern Arabia.

The earliest definite record of contact is an entry on the Palermo Stone of the reign of Sahura of the Fifth Dynasty: the receipt in one year from Punt of 80000 units of 'ntyw, and quantities of electrum and two commodities whose reading is uncertain. There are two indirect references to contact, or attempted contact, with Punt in private biographical inscriptions: one an allusion to a dwarf brought thence in the reign of King Djedkara Isesi, the other to an ill-fated attempt to build a boat on the Red Sea coast for the trip there in the reign of Pepy II. A Sixth Dynasty man claims to have followed his master, a governor of Elephantine, both to Punt and to Byblos. Then from the Eleventh and Twelfth Dynasties come several more records, found actually on the desert road linking Coptos with the Red Sea, and at Wadi Gasus, close to the Red Sea. Recent fieldwork seems to have discovered the site of the Middle Kingdom port itself, at Mersa Gawasis (Sayed 1977).

## EGYPT AND THE MEDITERRANEAN WORLD

Egypt's relations with Palestine and Syria have to be set carefully against the cultural history of this area. Archaeological research is pointing increasingly to the conclusion that urban civilization accompanied by a relatively sophisticated social order was the normal condition not only for Syria but also for much of Palestine during the greater part of the time considered in this chapter, and at times spread into desert areas where urbanized life could hardly have been sustained without careful organization. These areas naturally have their own schemes of chronology. In Palestine the transition from the Chalcolithic to the Early Bronze Age seems to have occurred at a time equivalent to the latter part of the Gerzean (Naqada II) phase in Egypt, with Early Bronze Age I and II extending from here through the Early Dynastic Period. For the Old Kingdom down to some point in the late Fifth or Sixth Dynasty the Palestinian urban equivalent is the Early Bronze Age III culture, and for the Middle Kingdom and Second Intermediate Period it is the Middle Bronze Age (probably beginning with Middle Bronze Age IIA of Albright = Middle Bronze Age of Kenyon). The intervening period, which corresponds more or less to the First Intermediate Period in Egypt, is evidently one of considerable complexity and probably regional variation, something reflected in the still fluid nature of the terminology used, though the term Intermediate Early/Middle Bronze Age seems a good way of resolving the problem (Callaway and Weinstein 1977, Dever 1973, de Geus 1971, Oren 1973a, Prag 1974, Thompson 1978). It is characterized by a widespread decline in urban life, often attributed to the destruction or disruption of immigrants. The new, though only temporary, pattern was a mixture of villages, possibly insubstantial occupation of some of the older cities, and the camp-sites of nomadic or partly nomadic groups. For a time their villages and camp-sites spread westwards across the Sinai peninsula as far at least as the line of the modern Suez Canal. It must have been these people of the Intermediate Early/Middle Bronze Age sites who formed the Asiatic menace considered in the Instruction to Merikara of the Herakleopolitan Dynasty. Although there are no archaeological sites in the eastern delta (as there are for the Second Intermediate Period) to provide the basis for some objective judgement on the seriousness of any Asiatic incursion at this time, it must be emphasized that the cultural background to these people is a complete contrast to that of the Hyksos kings and their followers of the Second Intermediate Period. As will be discussed below (pp. 156–8) these latter came from the highly developed urban culture and society of the late Middle Bronze Age whose transference to Egypt seems to have taken place without the establishment of intervening settlements.

The idea has sometimes been advanced that the eastern Nile Delta itself was not incorporated into the Egyptian state until, say, the Middle Kingdom. This is, however, difficult to reconcile with the archaeological evidence, both the presence of Egyptian material from the late Predynastic Period onwards, and the equivalent absence so far of Palestinian Chalcolithic and Early Bronze Age material despite its abundance in central and southern Sinai (see fig. 2.10). Indeed, one would be obliged by the textual evidence used to support this theory to assume the existence by the Sixth Dynasty of fortified Early Bronze Age cities in the eastern Delta, and these are known to have been very substantial structures. By contrast, recent fieldwork has led to the discovery of numerous camp-sites along the whole north Sinai coastal strip, stretching east from near the Nile Delta margins, where Egyptian objects of the late Predynastic and First Dynasty are mixed with Chalcolithic and Early Bronze Age I and II material, apparently in a ratio of 5 : 1 in favour of the Egyptian (Oren 1973b, Thompson 1975, pp. 9–13). When added to the widespread distribution of imported Egyptian pottery and other objects in Palestinian sites of these same periods as far north as the 'Amuq plain, the point can even be argued that as early as the beginning of the First Dynasty the Egyptians had begun a serious attempt at large-scale conquest in western Asia. A further element in the argument is the existence of large stone gazelle-traps, the so-called 'desert kites', distributed widely in Sinai, Jordan and Syria. It has been suggested that one such is depicted on the Narmer Palette, and that this implies a First Dynasty campaign, at least to Sinai. But since these traps were in use in recent times, more definite dating evidence is required before their relevance to much earlier periods is accepted, and in any case the Narmer Palette depiction is capable of other interpretations (Helms 1975a, Meshel 1974).

An instructive parallel can, however, be drawn with the not dissimilar history of Lower Nubia at this time. On this basis the ready flow of

Egyptian goods eastwards and then north-eastwards would be a sign of trade's being carried out on a local basis, largely free from a centrally directed political framework. The Nubian A-group can be explained as a product of a situation like this, with Egyptian aggressive policies having cultural repercussions only at the end, with the complete demise of settled life and cultural activity in Lower Nubia. The similar apparent disappearance of settlements along the north Sinai coast during or after the Early Dynastic Period could be regarded as an equivalent phenomenon, and more the result of a hard political frontier policy than an attempt at anything more ambitious.

The Sinai peninsula has been, over most of historical time, a wedge of nomadic tribal life separating two urban civilizations: Egypt and Palestine. In the second and third millennia BC the essential difference between the two was that between a centralized government channelling national resources to a single pool of talent, wealth, power and ambition, and, on the other hand, a collection of city states whose resources remained more dispersed and were, so one might imagine, partly consumed by the constant struggle to remain independent. It is an unfortunate consequence of the non-literate nature of this latter society that we know virtually nothing of its political development and, in particular, the extent to which policies were co-ordinated either by means of alliances or through the imposition of the will of one ruler of greater power. It is now known that the network of Palestinian towns and cities in the Early and Middle Bronze Ages spread southwards to terminate in a line running between Tell el-'Ajjul in the west and Tell Arad in the east, forming a frontier zone from which Sinai lay at a distance not much greater than it did from Egypt. Furthermore, recent fieldwork suggests that central and southern Sinai, in contrast to the coastal strip, was an extension of the southern Palestinian culture zone in the Chalcolithic and Early Bronze Age I and II periods, and that already its turquoise and copper deposits were being worked (fig. 2.10) (Amiran, Beit Arieh and Glass 1973, Beit Arieh 1974, Beit Arieh and Gophna 1976, Gophna 1976a, Rothenberg 1969, 1970–1, 1972, 1972–3). The evidence consists of a surprising number of settlements and cemeteries, including some stone-built villages (e.g. site 688 south of Aïn Fogeiya, and Sheikh Nabi Salah). Egyptian objects are said to have been present in only very slight quantities, but it might still be reasonable to see the Egyptians obtaining turquoise and copper by trading, for example, through the site of Ma'adi, near modern Cairo. There is the implication, too, that when the Egyptians eventually gained

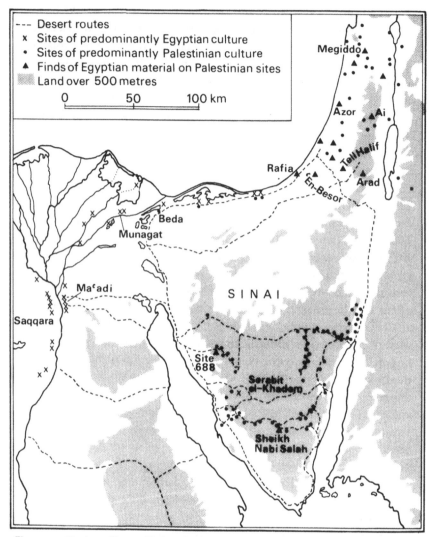

Fig. 2.10 Northern Egypt, Sinai and Palestine in Chalcolithic, Early Bronze Age, late Predynastic and Early Dynastic times. Some clusters of sites have been simplified; others, along the north Sinai coast and between El-Thamad and Jebel el-'Igma, are schematically plotted on account of the brevity of the published preliminary reports.

sole control over Sinai it was at the expense of this Palestinian cultural outlier. It may be significant that, unless the archaeological record differs locally from that in Palestine proper, these widely spread settlements seem not to have survived beyond the Early Bronze Age II period, except for a brief reoccupation in the Intermediate Early/Middle Bronze

Age period when the Egyptians were involved in a civil war. Again, as with the record in Lower Nubia, a considerable destructive power seems to be implied for the Egyptian state of the Early Dynastic Period. Indeed, the complete clearance of settlements in both border zones and beyond is remarkable.

Inscriptions found *in situ* in Sinai recording an Egyptian presence cover the periods between Kings Sanakht of the Third Dynasty and Pepy II of the Sixth, and then between Senusret I and Amenemhat IV of the Twelfth, although a late Eleventh Dynasty inscription from Thebes almost certainly describes an expedition to this region (see p. 142). With one exception these inscriptions make turquoise the object of the expeditions, apparently centred around three areas: Wadi Maghara, Serabit el-Khadem and Wadi Kharit, but the very same part of south Sinai also contains copper, widely exploited by the previous inhabitants. Surveys have located one Egyptian copper-smelting site, at Bir Naṣb, with copper deposits nearby and in the Wadi Baʻaba, but even this may be no earlier than the New Kingdom. Small-scale copper-working was, however, carried on in the Egyptian miners' camp in Wadi Maghara. During the Middle Kingdom the Egyptians built, on a hill-top site called Serabit el-Khadem, a small shrine dedicated to Hathor, Lady of Turquoise. Hathor was evidently felt by Egyptians sent abroad to have both a character which was beneficent towards ordinary Egyptians and the universal immanence necessary for localization at foreign places, such as at Byblos and the diorite quarries in the western Nubian desert and the Wadi el-Hudi. Votive objects from Serabit el-Khadem include a rich and informative collection of Middle Kingdom inscriptions, as well as a small number of private and royal statues.

In the Middle Kingdom, although only Egyptian sites have been located in Sinai, inscriptions indicate, with none of the usual hostility of tone, contact with 'Asiatics' of more than a passing nature. Some of these references are to Asiatics included amongst the personnel of the Egyptian expeditions to Sinai, in one case a party of twenty from Hamy or Harim, a place included in the Execration Texts under the rule of a prince with a Semitic name and to be identified probably with Tell el-Milh, or possibly with Khirbet el-Mshash, both Middle Bronze Age towns along the Tell el-ʻAjjul–Tell Arad line mentioned above. There is also a group of four stelae from the Serabit el-Khadem temple featuring a man riding a donkey, identified on one as the 'brother of the prince of Retenu (Palestine), Khebded', a man known from three other Sinai inscriptions where he appears to have been part of Egyptian expeditions dated to the period between years 4 and 13 of Amenemhat III. The distinctive manner in which he is portrayed on the stelae implies a considerable impact on the Egyptians. This apparently symbiotic relationship between Egyptians and Asiatics at the Sinai mines might be interpreted as a sign that the Egyptians had found it necessary to come to some sort of agreement with whatever political leadership was behind the cities of southern Palestine and which was sufficently strong to influence the conduct of Egyptian expeditions, and perhaps to share in the mined products.

That Palestinian princes appreciated the Egyptian demand for minerals sufficiently to involve themselves in it is suggested by the scene in the tomb of the nomarch Khnumhetep at Beni Hasan of the arrival, at an unfortunately unspecified locality in year 6 of Senusret II, of a colourful Palestinian group under a 'foreign prince' Abisha, bringing galena, a substance widely used in Middle Kingdom Egypt as an eye cosmetic. Their homeland, Shuwet, which also appears in the Execration Texts, has been tentatively localized in Moab. Galena was also included amongst the minerals and stones brought back from an expedition to Sinai and other adjacent lands by the overseer of quarry-work, Khety, in the later Eleventh Dynasty (Helck 1955, 1975, pp. 179–80; Schenkel 1965, pp. 283–4; Ward 1971, p. 59). Amongst other substances were not only turquoise and copper, but also lapis lazuli, something not found naturally in this part of the Near East at all, and thus available only from a transaction with or an attack on an existing trading centre. A term 'Asiatic copper' is seemingly attested in the late Old Kingdom (Posener-Kriéger 1969).

Except for Sinai, Egyptian sources for relations with Palestine and with Syria are meagre in the extreme, and often do not in their terminology enable a distinction to be made between the Sinai nomadic wedge and the settled hinterland.[1] There are, however, a few exceptions which suggest attacks on urbanized Palestine, some of whose cities are now known to have possessed substantial fortifications of the type depicted in the ancient illustrations.

The earliest and most detailed is the biography of Uni from the reign of Pepy I, describing how he led a national army, reinforced with Nubian mercenaries, against the settled population of an unspecified part of Palestine on five separate campaigns, followed by a land and sea

[1] The term 'Aamu, 'Asiatics', was extended to peoples of the eastern desert. This is evident not only from the well-known inscription of Pepy-nakht, but also from a graffito in the Wadi el-Hudi (Fakhry 1952, p. 46, no. 31; also Brovarski and Murnane 1969, no. 1). Helck's suggestion (1971, p. 21) that Pepy-nakht's expedition was to Syria is thus gratuitous. See also Couroyer (1971).

attack in the vicinity of a place called 'Nose of the Gazelle', sometimes, though on purely picturesque grounds, identified with Mount Carmel. From roughly this same period come scenes of attacks on fortifications manned by Asiatics in the tombs of Inti at Deshasha (Sixth Dynasty) and Kaiemhesit at Saqqara (early Sixth Dynasty), probably in the mortuary temple of Nebhepetra Menthuhetep II; and in the tomb of Intef, of the late Eleventh Dynasty (Arnold and Settgast 1965, fig. 2; W. S. Smith 1965, pp. 148–9; Ward 1971, pp. 59–60, n. 227). From the Middle Kingdom there are only the stele of the general Nesu-menthu of the reign of Senusret I, which refers to hostilities against Asiatics in which fortresses were destroyed, and the stele of Sebek-khu, recounting a campaign conducted by Senusret III to the country of Sekmem, identified by some with the city state of Shechem.

The archaeological record of southern Palestine and of Sinai, as well as the advanced state which defensive military architecture had reached in Egypt by the early Middle Kingdom, should leave little doubt that when the Egyptians refer to or depict foreign fortresses we should understand nothing less than the fortified cities of Early and Middle Bronze Age Palestine.

Of a somewhat different character is the Story of Sinuhe, a literary romance in which the hero, exiling himself from Egypt in the reign of Senusret I, achieves fame and wealth in a Palestinian kingdom. The avoidance of references to cities has been variously interpreted, but the practice of sending envoys from the Egyptian court to local rulers is given a prominent place in the narrative. This is something supported by a few brief references in other texts, and fully in keeping with not only the well-documented diplomatic practices of the ancient Near East, but also with the contact via envoys which the Egyptians maintained with their Nubian neighbours (see p. 132). Information gained by this type of contact would be one way by which the Egyptians were furnished with the necessary details for the Asiatic sections of the Middle Kingdom Execration Texts. Listed there are rulers and peoples of towns, cities and regions over most of the area of Middle Bronze Age Palestine, from Moab and the Negev in the south to beyond Kadesh in the north, and then over a separate area even further north lying behind Byblos and Ullaza to Upe.

Diplomacy has as its purpose the influencing of events as well as the collection of information. By analogy with the New Kingdom pattern one might suspect that attacks on fortified towns were the shock tactics intended to force favourable alliances or even vassalage which would then be maintained or extended by diplomatic activity. Such a policy might, in southern Palestine, have had some urgency if, as suggested above, some of the city states in the area had an interest in Sinai and in the supply of minerals and precious stones to Egypt. But as to whether this was followed by the posting of Egyptian officials charged with administrative, as distinct from representative, duties cannot be determined on present evidence, although it is presumably at this point that the term 'empire' becomes justified. One source with considerable implications here is the title sequence of a scribe, Ka-aper of the early Fifth Dynasty, which includes that of 'army scribe of the king' in a number of named places which seem, from the way they are written, to have been some of these Palestinian fortified cities (Fischer 1959b).

Of much greater ambiguity are the Egyptian objects discovered on eastern Mediterranean sites which, with the exception of the material from Byblos, occur in significant numbers only from the Middle Kingdom onwards, although the recent excavations at Ebla (Tell Mardikh) have already produced two diorite bowl fragments with the name of Khafra of the Fourth Dynasty, and part of an alabaster lid of Pepy I of the Sixth Dynasty (Matthiae 1978). This general paucity of Old Kingdom artifacts is true for Nubia and Serabit el-Khadem also. Most striking are the sphinxes of Amenemhat III and IV, and of a queen of Amenemhat II, which have been found at several Syrian sites: Beirut, Qatna, Ugarit and Neirab; also a statuette of Khaneferra Sebekhetep of the Thirteenth Dynasty from Tell Hizzin. Statuettes of private individuals have been found at Tell el-'Ajjul, Gezer (which has also yielded a statuette of a princess), Megiddo, Ugarit, Ji'ara, Atchana and Kürigen Kale in Turkey and Knossos in Crete, the last three from places beyond the confines of the Execration Texts. The sphinxes from Syria might be regarded as diplomatic gifts, but for the statuettes, which would normally have been made to stand in proximity to a cult place from which they could benefit, two quite contrary parallels can be cited. On the one hand there is the Middle Kingdom temple at Serabit el-Khadem in Sinai (or even better, the Late Bronze Age temple at Beth-Shan in Palestine) where inscribed Egyptian objects, including statuettes, commemorate the temporary presence of the owner in a foreign land and his attempt to gain the favour of a local deity, whether that deity was Egyptian or not. On this parallel they would be an indication of the extent of Egyptian postings abroad, though not of the scope of the responsibilities involved. On the other hand, one can use the parallel of Kerma in Nubia (see pp. 128, 166–7), where Egyptian statues and statuettes, some of them quite old by the time in question, had an intrinsic value of their own, helping to endow their new owners with some of the dignity and sophistication of the country that had produced them. On this parallel it can be suggested that some of these statuettes in western Asia reached their destinations quite late in the Middle Bronze Age, during the Hyksos period in Egypt. It is unfortunate that in most cases the context is equivocal, even with excavated examples which in no case would seem to come from a clear early Middle Bronze Age context (i.e. Albright's Middle Bronze Age IIA). This is true, for example, for the statuette of Djehuty-hetep found at Megiddo with three other Middle Kingdom statuettes built into the structure of a temple probably not erected until at least the end of the Middle Bronze Age (Dunayevsky and Kempinski 1973, Kenyon 1969, pp. 49–53).

Although the evidence from Palestine and Syria is ambiguous, the overall effectiveness of Egyptian activity ought to be apparent, so one might imagine, from areas even further afield, whose own rulers would naturally feel jealous of or threatened by a successful Egyptian axis established in Palestine and who would, at the least, seek diplomatic contact. The New Kingdom would provide the appropriate parallel to this situation. Thus the lack of any reference in Egyptian texts to contact with kingdoms even further to the north in Syria and beyond may have some positive significance. There is, too, the archive of the important city of Mari on the Upper Euphrates. Diplomatic contact by means of letters written on clay tablets was maintained with places as far south as Hazor and Byblos, but Egypt is nowhere even mentioned. The period of the letters is not, however, that of the powerful Twelfth Dynasty in Egypt, but the Thirteenth, and more specifically the period of Neferhetep I whose rule began about 45 years after the end of the Twelfth Dynasty, but whose name was, nevertheless, still commemorated at Byblos by one of the local rulers.

Byblos had a very special relationship with Egypt, and the archaeological record is unique as far as Egyptian contact in the eastern Mediterranean is concerned. As the principal centre for the trade which provided the Egyptians with badly-needed timber from the coniferous forests of the Lebanon, as well as resin, a by-product early in demand for mummification, it became a focus for Egyptian cultural influence. Partly this is visible in the form of votive objects from the local temples, where one of the deities was a further form of Hathor: 'Lady of Byblos', though some ambiguity must surround the identity of who was responsible for donating them, and under what circumstances. Amongst the Egyptian objects from the temples and adjacent areas are pieces bearing the names of kings Khasehkemwy of the Second Dynasty, Khufu, Khafra, Menkaura of the Fourth Dynasty, Sahura (?), Neferir-kara, Djedkara Isesi (?), Neuserra and Unas of the Fifth Dyasty, Teti, Pepy I, Merenra and Pepy II of the Sixth Dynasty, and Amenemhat III of the Twelfth Dynasty. There are also a part of a statue ascribed on stylistic grounds to King Neuserra (Bothmer 1971) and a fragment of a sphinx of a Middle Kingdom princess. Amongst the uninscribed objects in Egyptian style are numerous faience animal figurines and a hoard of scarabs, beads and trinkets. During the Middle Bronze Age one of the temples was furnished with small, locally-made obelisks, one with a hieroglyphic inscription made for a prince of Byblos. These princes, who can be traced into the Second Intermediate Period, also had their own scarabs manufactured, as well as hieroglyphic funerary or votive stelae, one of which records building work in a temple dedicated to the goddess Nut, presumably a rendering, by the use of an Egyptian equivalent, of the name of a local goddess, perhaps Anath.

Egyptian influence is even more strikingly evident in the funerary equipment of some of these princes or kings of Byblos contemporary with the later part of the Twelfth Dynasty. It takes the form of Egyptian-made objects equivalent in their artistic standard to objects from Egyptian court burials (e.g. the gold-bound obsidian casket, the obsidian ointment jar decorated with gold, the silver mirror; two pectorals with the names of Amenemhat III and IV from somewhere in the Lebanon may also derive from here); local imitations of Egyptian objects (gold and inlaid pectorals, an elaborate pendant with the name of prince Yapa-shemu-abi in a cartouche, bronze uraeus figures with silver inlays in niello technique); and non-Egyptian-style objects given hieroglyphic inscriptions (the scimitar). Taken together, the cartouches, Egyptian epithets, uraei and jewellery suggest a pastiche of Egyptian royalty at the Byblite court. On their scarabs the princes call themselves simply 'governor of Byblos', and if these were used for sealing items sent to Egypt they may reflect a wish to conform in this one instance to an Egyptian view of their status, whereas their Pharaonic pretensions were for a local context. Even so, this would seem to represent a unique compromise arrangement which involved recognition by the Egyptians that Byblos was an extension of their urban world. The same equivocal status *vis-à-vis* the king of Egypt is apparent from a block showing another one of these princes, Inten, seated, offering a prayer to the Egyptian god Ra-Horakhty, with the cartouche of Neferhetep I also present; also just possibly in the inscription on a lapis lazuli cylinder seal from the early Thirteenth Dynasty. Furthermore, although essentially a Middle Kingdom phenomenon, one should note an Old Kingdom cylinder seal with similar cultural implications (Goedicke 1966b, 1976b, du Mesnil du Buisson 1970, pp. 76–88).

By contrast, records from Egypt of contact with Byblos are very slight for these periods (Horn 1963, Leclant 1954). The name 'Byblos' first occurs in a Fourth Dynasty mastaba at Giza; on the Palermo Stone an entry from the reign of King Sneferu records the acquisition of forty shiploads of timber, and it is assumed that their origin was Byblos; the same official at Aswan who recorded visiting Punt with the governor of Elephantine included Byblos as well; 'Byblos-ships' were thought suitable for the journey to Punt. For the Middle Kingdom references to Byblos are confined to a few naming 'Hathor, Lady of Byblos'.

Overall, the evidence for the nature and extent of Egyptian influence or control in western Asia is highly unsatisfactory, and in this situation it is presumably better to err on the side of caution, and to limit the sphere of direct Egyptian interference to the cities of southern Palestine, the motive being that of securing an extensive border zone. It should be noted, however, that the imperialist phraseology of the New Kingdom can, in essence, be found already in the Middle Kingdom, if not before (Blumenthal 1970, pp. 189–201; Goedicke 1969–70).[1]

## The Aegean

The only part of the Aegean region which received Egyptian goods in any quantity and whose own goods in turn reached Egypt was Crete. A surprising number of Egyptian stone vessels of types dated between the late Predynastic Period and the early Middle Kingdom have been found on Crete, and gave rise to local imitations. But whilst a few come from Early Minoan II or Early Minoan II–Middle Minoan IB/II contexts, many were still apparently in circulation in the Late Minoan periods, thus contemporary with the Hyksos period and New Kingdom in Egypt. To this material should be added some twenty Middle Kingdom scarabs, and a solitary Middle Kingdom statuette from Knossos. The converse situation is represented by small quantities of imported Middle Minoan pottery at Egyptian sites. This consists of two or three Middle Minoan I sherds from El-Lisht, sherds from thirteen and twenty-one Middle Minoan II vessels respectively from Kahun and

[1] Cf. also the title of Pepy I or II on an alabaster vase from Byblos: 'Ra of the foreign lands' (Chéhab 1969, p. 18).

El-Haraga, from a Middle Minoan II vase found in a tomb at Abydos, and a complete vessel from a tomb at Elephantine (Kemp and Merrillees 1980). At Kahun Minoan pottery was imitated, and local potters also produced small amounts of polychrome pottery evidently under its stimulus. Kahun has also yielded a Minoan stone vase lid.

The probable Egyptian name for Crete, Keftiu, whilst it may have been known to Egyptians in the Middle Kingdom, does not occur in any context which suggests direct contact. But it must be admitted that there is a serious paucity of documents which might be expected to have contained such records, such as the decorative schemes of royal and court tombs. Direct contact is not particularly difficult from a seafaring point of view, involving a relatively short open-sea crossing to Cyrenaica, followed by a coastal voyage eastwards to the Nile Delta. Minoan contact with the North African coast during the early New Kingdom seems to be implied by the miniature marine painting from Thera. But it is equally possible for the exchange of goods to have been indirectly carried out via Byblos or Ugarit, both of which sites have also produced Minoan pottery.

A very small number of inscribed Egyptian objects have been found even further afield: a small vase bearing the name of the funerary temple of King Userkaf of the Fifth Dynasty from the island of Kythera, lying between Crete and the Peloponnese; fragments of a gold-plated chair with the name of King Sahura said to come from a tomb at Dorak in north-western Anatolia, about 200 km east from the Aegean coast; and a gold cylinder-seal of an official of the Fifth Dynasty, possibly also from Anatolia (Vermeule and Vermeule 1970, Young 1972). Even if the last two should receive further verification as to provenance, it need not imply a direct link with Egypt. One way by which valuable objects were distributed in the ancient world was as gifts from one ruler to another, in the course of which gifts were made from those already received from some other head of state, or other source. A mixed provenance of this nature can be seen in one hoard of precious objects found in Egypt: the Tod treasure. Apart from Babylonian seals the precise source of the objects, mainly silver vessels, is hard to determine, though Minoan influence is probably visible. Although found in bronze chests of Amenemhat II there is no necessity to assume that the treasure was originally associated with them, and it is clear from the excavation report that, because work on the temple foundations in which the treasure was found was being done as late as the Thirtieth Dynasty, the treasure cannot be regarded as a sealed deposit of the Middle Kingdom.

In general, much more needs to be understood about the mechanisms of ancient trade and other forms of contact before objects found far distant from their homeland can be written into a history of foreign policies pursued by different countries.

## THE SECOND INTERMEDIATE PERIOD IN EGYPT

All the indications are that in Upper Egypt the administrative and cultural patterns of the Twelfth Dynasty continued well into the Thirteenth, with a degree of continuity which might justify extending the term Middle Kingdom to cover this as well as the Twelfth Dynasty. The town of Kahun which housed the community administering the mortuary estate of the nearby pyramid of Senusret II exemplifies this, for it continued to function probably into the latter part of the Thirteenth Dynasty, the last royal name from here being Wahibra Ibiyau (Petrie 1890, p. 31, pl. x. 72; the name is only partially preserved and some doubt must remain over it), whilst administrative papyri from the first two reigns of the Thirteenth Dynasty illustrate the continued operation of the late Twelfth Dynasty administrative system here. Not very far distant, the middle-class cemetery at El-Haraga displays a homogeneity in material culture extending from some point in the Twelfth until probably well into the Thirteenth Dynasty.

At least six tombs of kings of this period have been discovered in the Memphite area: two at Saqqara (one of them belonging to King Khendjer), two at Mazghuna, two at Dashur (Ameny 'Aamu and Awibra Hor). Five are pyramids, small in size but complex in internal design. Another, that of Awibra Hor at Dashur, in some ways epitomizes this period. Built modestly within the pyramid enclosure of Amenemhat III but with funeral trappings very similar to those of the court burials of the Twelfth Dynasty, it displays a basic continuity from the past with an inability to promote the construction of a monumental court cemetery, something inevitably bound up with a general brevity of reign, in this case a mere seven months according to the Turin king-list. Inscriptions from provincial sites further south in Upper Egypt imply a recognition both of kings ruling from (Amenemhat-) Ith-tawy in the north and of an administrative system apparently identical to that of the late Twelfth Dynasty. This material includes the stele of Horem-khauef (stylistically dated to the very end of the Thirteenth Dynasty and probably very close to the beginning of the Seventeenth (Hayes 1947, Vandersleyen 1971, p. 208)) which describes a visit made to the court

TABLE 2.1  *Royal names from statues, stelae, offering-tables and building blocks found at temple sites in Upper Egypt, and on small objects and papyri from Kahun*

| Years BC | Kahun | Abydos | Coptos | Medamud | Karnak | Deir el-Bahari | Tod | Gebelein | Elephantine/Sehel |
|---|---|---|---|---|---|---|---|---|---|
| 1782 | XIII.3 XIII.4 | XIII.3 | | XIII.1 | XIII.1 | | XIII.2 | | XIII.4? |
| | | XIII.C XIII.12 | | XIII.15 XIII.16 | XIII.7 | XIII.12 | | | |
| | | | | | | XIII.16 | | | |
| | | XIII.17 | XIII.21 | XIII.21 | XIII.21? XIII.22 XIII.24 | XIII.24 | XIII.21 | | XIII.21 XIII.22 |
| | | XIII.22 XIII.24 | | | | | | | |
| | XIII.26 | XIII.28 | | | XIII.27 XIII.28 | | XIII.31 | | |
| c. 1680 | | | | | XIII.32 XIII.F XIII.G | XIII.37 XIII.41 | XIII.F | XIII.37 XIII.41 XIII.J | |
| | | | | | XIII.J XIII.K | XIII.44 XIII.L | | | |

TABLE 2.1 (*cont.*)

| Years BC | Kahun | Abydos | Coptos | Medamud | Karnak | Deir el-Bahari | Tod | Gebelein | Elephantine/Schel |
|---|---|---|---|---|---|---|---|---|---|
| | | XIII.M | | | | | | | |
| | | XIII.N | | | | | | | |
| *c.* 1650 | | XVII.1 | XVII.1 | | XVII.1 | | | | |
| | | XVII.2 | XVII.2 | | | | | [XV.4] | |
| | | XVII.3 | | XVII.3 | XVII.3 | XVII.3 | | [XV.5] | |
| | | | | | XVII.6 | | | | XVII.3 |
| | | | | XVII.9? | | | | | |
| *c.* 1560 | | XVII.10 | | | XVII.10 | | | | |
| | | | | | XVII.15 | | | | |

*Note:* The numbers are those of von Beckerath (1964) the Roman numerals indicating the dynasty. The table stresses the continuity of government between the Thirteenth and Seventeenth Dynasties in Upper Egypt.

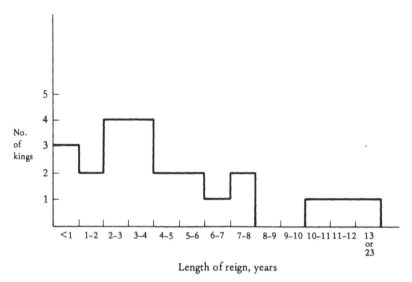

Fig. 2.11 Length of reign from amongst the first fifty kings in succession to the Twelfth Dynasty. (After Kitchen 1967a and von Beckerath 1964.) King Sekhemkara is given between 7 and 8 years on the basis of the Semna inscription reported by B. Bell (1975).

at the old capital of Ith-tawy. The names of many of the kings are attested on statues, stelae, offering-tables and building blocks at a number of temple sites (see table 2.1).

Of the Turin king-list no less than six of its eleven columns are devoted to the period between the end of the Twelfth and the beginning of the Eighteenth Dynasty, representing some 175 reigns for a period of perhaps 220 or 230 years. Current estimates of how many of these names should be ascribed to Manetho's Thirteenth Dynasty vary between the first fifty and the first ninety of those following the last ruler of the Twelfth Dynasty, Sebek-neferu (Manetho himself allotted sixty kings to it). Where the length of reign is preserved in the fragmentary king-list it is often of the brevity to be expected of the situation, as can be seen from fig. 2.11.

Nevertheless, these twenty-three kings represent about a century of rule, a period not much less than the maximum which can be allotted to the Thirteenth Dynasty as a whole, between about 110 and 125 years. This raises the question of how far this group of kings really represents a single line ruling successively from the vicinity of Memphis. The inscribed capstone from the pyramid tomb of one of them, Merneferra Ay, whose reign of 13/23 years and 8 months is the longest known of this group, has been found, not in the Memphite area at all, but in the eastern Delta, near Faqus, from an area sufficiently rich in remains of this and later periods to suggest the existence of a city of some importance. Barring the distant possibility that it was transported there at a later date, it might be taken as a hint of a degree of fragmentation of rule in northern Egypt, although the authority of this man was sufficient for his commemoration in the temple at Karnak. Objects probably from a temple in this same area also record the piety of a King Nehesy, who occupies a position about twenty-three places further on in the Turin list. Acceptance of the idea of a fragmentation of northern Egypt into city states with some rulers writing their names in cartouches becomes a necessity in dealing with the continuation of the Turin list, which gave to six 'foreign kings' (Hyksos) a total reign of 108 years, so covering the remainder of the Second Intermediate Period whilst still leaving at least 79 and possibly as many as 119 kings to be accounted for. Of these, 15 can be set aside as kings of Upper Egypt ruling from Thebes contemporaneously with the Hyksos and in succession to the Thirteenth Dynasty. But this still leaves a great many, whose numbers may even have to be augmented by kings whose names appear on objects, principally scarabs, and cannot be identified with any in the Turin list.

Manetho ignored altogether the possibility of contemporaneous rule, and divided these various kings after the Thirteenth Dynasty into four more dynasties. But in doing this he was, like the king-list compilers before him, working to a preconceived idea: a unitary succession of kings, whose reigns could be added together when necessary to produce extended periods of rule, and who, in Manetho's work, could also be neatly grouped into dynasties ascribed to a city of origin. It is not an attack on the basic veracity of the king-list compilers to say that they sometimes brought a spurious tidiness to periods of history where a degree of complexity, even of disorder, prevailed. Their interest in the past was essentially confined to numbers, names, pious deeds and scraps of legend. The neatness of Manetho's scheme is not in itself necessarily a viable starting-point for historical study, and for this period may be largely unhistorical. Indeed, all that one may in the end be entitled to see in this period as far as kingship goes is that there was a proliferation of kings who can be divided into four groups:

(1) kings following the Twelfth Dynasty whose authority was, for political reasons which may at times have been quite complex, recognized in Upper Egypt and who continued for the most part, but not

necessarily in every case, to rule from and be buried near Memphis, and who may have also exercised a general overlordship, if not total rule, over parts or all of northern Egypt;

(2) a line of kings ruling Upper Egypt in succession to them, but now centred at Thebes, and buried there;

(3) six 'foreign kings', i.e. Hyksos, who replaced group (1) in the north and who ruled at the same time as group (2);

(4) an uncertain number of client kings, presumably of city states, mostly in the north of Egypt and including some with the title 'foreign king', distributed uncertainly in time *vis-à-vis* the other groups.

Purely for convenience the following equations can be made with Manetho: (1) = XIII, (2) = XVII, (3) = XV, (4) = XIV and XVI. With groups (1) and (4) it can become needlessly pedantic to argue as to which dynasty a particular king belonged since the ancient thinking behind the grouping of kings proceeded from a view very different from our own as to what the past was about. There are strong grounds for regarding the hereditary principle of royal succession as having thoroughly broken down during the Thirteenth Dynasty, with continuity of government vested, for at least part of the time, in a family of viziers (von Beckerath 1951, Berlev 1974). Only in the sub-dynasty of Neferhetep I and his successors is any direct family continuity visible (Dewachter 1976, Simpson 1969a).[1] In this essentially non-dynastic situation, implying the existence of several families whose relatives had at some not too distant point in the past been kings, the question of legitimacy must have become so clouded that the appearance of contemporaneous kings in the north is more easily understandable. There is no need to attribute it to foreign influence and to see it as a post-Hyksos development.

As noted, the eventual fate of the northern part of the country is not in doubt. Tentatively placed in the penultimate column of the Turin list is a fragment summarizing the 108-year rule of six 'foreign kings'. The term used ([ḥḳ3w] ḫ3swt, literally 'rulers of foreign lands') contains the true etymology of Manetho's term 'Hyksos'. Manetho, as quoted by Josephus, told a story of how, in the reign of a King Tutimaeus, Egypt had been seized by 'invaders of obscure race/ignoble birth' who 'burned our cities ruthlessly, razed to the ground the temples of the gods and treated all the natives with a cruel hostility'. Although ruling at first from Memphis, they subsequently built a great fortified

[1] For the family background of another king of this time see Macadam (1951).

stronghold on the site of Avaris in the eastern delta. Finally they were attacked by kings from Thebes, confined to Avaris, and allowed to leave Egypt in peace. This view of the Hyksos, as an essentially destructive interlude in Egyptian history, has in the past exercised considerable influence on the writing of the history of the period. It is a view which can be found expressed even more anciently, in Papyrus Sallier I of the reign of Merenptah (1224–1214 BC), a popular tale in which the Hyksos king Apepy (Apophis) in Avaris appears as an archetypal villain; and in the Speos Artemidos inscription of Queen Hatshepsut, where the supposed disorder of the Hyksos period becomes, on a purely un-historical plane, the target for the deliverance from evil which was a fundamental role of kings in Egyptian theology, Hatshepsut claiming to have restored the land to order after their rule. The tradition of the Hyksos was evidently not an entirely uniform one, however. A remarkable genealogy which once probably adorned the walls of a tomb of a priest of Memphis of the Twenty-second Dynasty traces his ancestors back to the Eleventh Dynasty. In listing some of the kings under whom they are supposed to have served, two or three Hyksos kings are given (including Apepy) in place of the Theban Seventeenth Dynasty kings whom one might have expected if the document had been drawn up in Upper Egypt (von Beckerath 1964, pp. 27–8).

What few material remains the Hyksos kings themselves have left behind lend little support to the more lurid views of their rule. For, like later foreign overlords of Egypt, whether Libyan, Sudanese, Persian or Roman, they chose both to present themselves as Pharaohs, complete with traditional titulary employing names compounded with the name of the sun god, Ra, and to indulge in or to encourage a little embellishment of temples, by additions to the fabric, as at Bubastis and Gebelein, or by dedicating an offering-table, or by having their names added to the statues and sphinxes of earlier kings.

Already in the later Middle Kingdom there is evidence for surprisingly large numbers of 'Asiatics' present in Egyptian society, apparently more or less assimilated. An extensive list can be compiled of those in domestic service, the most striking example being Brooklyn Papyrus 35.1446 of the Thirteenth Dynasty from Thebes, where 45 amongst a total of 79 domestic staff are identified as Asiatic. Documents from Kahun refer to the 'officer in charge of the Asiatic troops' and to the 'scribe of the Asiatics', suggesting an interesting counterpart to the position of Nubians in the Old Kingdom (Kaplony-Heckel 1971a, pp. 3, 5–6). A few can be traced in administrative positions, and by their names one or more of the Thirteenth Dynasty kings identify themselves as having possible Asiatic origin.[1] It may, however, despite the formal presentation of themselves by the Hyksos as traditional kings, be misleading to place too much emphasis on this process of immigration as an antecedent to Hyksos rule. For the foreignness of the Hyksos was evidently something which left a deep impression on some Egyptians. Most notably, apart from the literary tradition, the Turin king-list distinguished them uniquely by writing their names without a cartouche and with a hieroglyphic sign added which designates them as foreign, and by using the term 'foreign kings' to describe them. They appear to have represented something more than assimilated Asiatics who had gained the throne through the normal processes of internal politics of this period.

It is at this point that the evidence of archaeology becomes important. In Upper Egypt cemeteries at widely separated places (such as Hager Esna, Abydos, and Qau) show, during this whole period, nothing more than slow changes of fashion which appear to be internally derived. This is not in itself a sign of political stability since the same was broadly true for the First Intermediate Period, but it at least limits the extent of a foreign cultural element present in Egypt at this time. Moving further north, in the El-Lahun area there appears to be a considerable cultural hiatus corresponding to the Hyksos period, and affecting both Kahun and El-Haraga, as well as Medinet el-Ghurab. If the life of the El-Lahun area depended heavily on association with government activity, as it may well have done, then this may perhaps reflect a serious interference with established administration under Hyksos rule.

But it is in the Delta itself, and more particularly its eastern border area, that archaeology makes a vital contribution to our knowledge of the period. At several sites on the east side of the ancient Pelusiac branch of the Nile (principally at Tell el-Yahudiya and Tell ed-Dab'a, see fig. 2.13), a culture heavily influenced by that of contemporary Middle Bronze Age II Palestine has been encountered in tombs and settlement strata (Bietak 1968a, 1970, 1975a, pp. 165, 167; Petrie 1906, chs. 1 and 2).[2] The main elements are: domestic pottery of Egyptian type; jugs

---

[1] Khendjer and Ameny 'Aamu; note also Hetepibra Hornedjheritef son of 'Aamu. However, the name 'Aamu (= 'Asiatic') can be given the alternative reading Kemau, 'landworker', 'winnower' (von Beckerath 1964, pp. 40–2; Posener 1957b).

[2] Attention should also be drawn to a remarkable jewellery hoard, which includes a golden circlet ornamented with stags' heads, and thought to be possibly of the Hyksos period, which is said to have come from El-Salhiya, 16.5 km east of Tell ed-Dab'a, and is now in the

and juglets, bronze axe-heads and toggle-pins of Palestinian inspiration or origin; a small amount of Cypriote pottery; donkeys accompanying human burials (Boessneck 1970, Stiebing 1971); scarabs of designs common to both Egypt and Palestine at this period, and clearly produced in large quantities in the latter area. At Tell el-Yahudiya, as well as at Heliopolis, a large earthen embankment has been compared to the plastered slopes beneath the cities of Middle Bronze Age Palestine, but the comparison probably has no historical validity (Parr 1968, Seger 1975, G. R. H. Wright 1968). The finds from Tell ed-Dab'a, a site with an area at this period of about half a square kilometre, gain greatly in significance from the likelihood that the Hyksos city of Avaris is to be located here (Bietak 1975b). Amongst buildings excavated, there is a complex of temples of probably Palestinian type.

This marked Palestinian influence, however, seems to have been fairly limited in extent, for it has not been encountered at sites lying further to the west,[1] nor in the cemeteries of the Memphite area. It would be interesting to know how much Palestinian influence was present in the eastern Delta in earlier periods, but the evidence is very limited and fragmentary, though where it exists it is consistently without Palestinian features, and includes the lowest strata at Tell ed-Dab'a itself, apparently of the later Middle Kingdom. Tell ed-Dab'a has also yielded an important collection of anthropological material, from 134 bodies of the Hyksos-period cemeteries (Jungwirth 1970). Preliminary reports describe the population as distinctly different from the usual west Semitic type, more akin, indeed, to types from cemeteries of similar date in north and central Europe. But the real meaning of such comparisons, in this case very tentatively made, is by no means obvious and no far-reaching conclusions should be drawn, particularly in view of the lack of comparative material from the eastern Delta from earlier periods. The proximity to Asia, however, may explain the prominence in this area of a cult of the god Seth, who could serve as a manifestation of the alien nature of the country beyond Egypt's borders. It may have been established as early as the late Old Kingdom, and seems certainly to have been in existence before the Hyksos Dynasty. The local

Metropolitan Museum of Art, New York (Aldred 1971, pp. 204-5, pl. 89; Gómez-Moreno 1972-3; Vandersleyen 1975, p. 390. pl. 395a).

[1] Although the amount of excavation done further to the west is very slight indeed. On the western edge of the delta the cemetery of Kom el-Hisn seems to provide negative evidence in that in four seasons of excavations in burials dating from the First Intermediate Period to the New Kingdom the only possible Palestinian material was a single Middle Bronze Age II painted juglet (Hamada and Farid 1947).

importance and character of this god may sufficiently explain why the Hyksos associated themselves with him, though in no instance did one of them employ the name Seth in forming his cartouche.

When seen in the perspective of Palestinian cultural history, this period takes on a particular significance. In Palestine this was a period of great fortified cities and military camps, and, it has been said, 'of the greatest prosperity that the country had seen to that time, or would see again before the Roman peace' (G. E. Wright 1971). Although the absence of written records from Palestine inevitably tends to an undervaluation of its historical role and leaves us ignorant of the doubtlessly complex political background to the striking urban achievement of the Middle Bronze Age II period, it is possible to see in the situation a temporary reversal of the roles between Egypt and Palestine, with north-eastern Egypt falling under the aegis of an emergent Palestinian civilization, receiving increased immigration and accelerated cultural contact, as well as a royal house.

Contemporary finds in Egypt record the names of far more than six kings of this period. Some, like Joam, Jakbaal and Anath-her, display Semitic names, others use the title 'foreign king'. These, together with others with Egyptian names, presumably make up Manetho's Sixteenth Dynasty of 'lesser' Hyksos, and can only represent vassal rulers of city states especially in the northern part of Egypt.

The beginning of the Hyksos period in the north may perhaps be imagined as a combination of various Palestinian groups migrating direct from southern Palestine into the eastern Delta, intent upon settlement, and more mobile fighting groups, perhaps centred on or in loose federation with a main army making for Memphis, fanning out and taking over various delta cities, though also leaving others still in the charge of their Egyptian rulers, perhaps by prior agreement. Destruction levels noted at some eastern delta sites, including Tell ed-Dab'a (Bietak 1968a, pp. 84, 89; 1975a, p. 194), may record some of the more serious conflicts. (The date of the installation of the first Hyksos king is apparently to be placed between about 1672 and 1649 BC.)[1]

It has been claimed that the pattern of overlord and vassal was something introduced from western Asia where it was a recognized part

[1] By adding the 108 years of the Turin king-list fragment to a date for somewhere around year 10 of Ahmose I of the Eighteenth Dynasty. Unfortunately, it remains difficult to be precise with New Kingdom chronology (Redford 1970, Wente 1975). The relative date of the fall of Avaris is discussed in Vandersleyen (1971, pp. 33–40); an even later date is suggested in Hodjache and Berlev (1977).

of the political scene. But even if true, this may simply have been a matter of bringing a formally recognized scheme to an existing situation in view of the possibility that northern Egypt had begun to fragment politically during the Thirteenth Dynasty.

Some objects bearing the name of the Hyksos king Seuserenra Khyan have been found outside Egypt, but so far outside as to make any political deduction from them very hazardous. They comprise: a small lion statuette bought in Baghdad, the lid of an alabaster vase from Knossos and a fragment of an obsidian vase from Boghazköi; also a seal impression from southern Palestine. In view of the likely origin of the Hyksos it would not be surprising to find that a part of southern Palestine remained under their hegemony. But possible direct references to this seem limited to the second Kamose stele, and even these are ambiguous.[1]

The most important of those ruling a part of Egypt simultaneously with the Hyksos was a line of kings of Thebes who form Manetho's Seventeenth Dynasty. They perhaps numbered as many as fifteen, and are best known from objects from their small pyramidal tombs in the Dira Abu el-Naga necropolis of western Thebes. Within the southern part of Egypt, perhaps southwards from the Abydos area, they appear to have been able to exercise some of the traditional functions of kingship, notably by making additions and donations to temples, including those at Abydos, Coptos, Deir el-Ballas, Medamud and Edfu (see table 2.1). The temple of Abydos, in particular, furnishes a record of royal patronage between the end of the Twelfth and the beginning of the Eighteenth Dynasties which leaves the Hyksos very conspicuous by their absence. Only at Gebelein, upstream from Thebes, have the names of Hyksos kings been recovered on monumental blocks, apparently from the temple of Hathor there, the kings being Seuserenra Khyan and Aaweserra Apepy.[2] But to these can be added a few other signs that in the minds of some people in Upper Egypt the Hyksos claim to kingship was legitimate.[3] Two further inscriptions illustrate aspects

---

[1] Second Kamose stele, line 4: Apepy is addressed as 'prince of Retenu (= Palestine)', but this may signify his origin; lines 13–15 list commodities captured from ships, summarized as 'the produce/tribute of Retenu', the word *inw* being somewhat ambiguous in its implications. Cf. also Giveon (1974a), who argues that scarabs from Canaan also support Hyksos rule over Palestine.

[2] Note also a sistrum from Dendera with the name Apepy (von Beckerath 1964, p. 148); an adze-blade with the name 'Aaweserra, beloved of Sebek, lord of Sumenu', to the south of Thebes (James 1961). Von Beckerath (1964, pp. 148–9) doubts whether the Gebelein blocks came originally from this site, but it is difficult to imagine why they would have been imported from much further north to an area so close to stone quarries.

[3] Principally the dating of the Rhind mathematical papyrus to year 33 of Aaweserra Apepy. It is said to have come from Thebes.

of government operating under the authority of these Theban kings without reference to the Hyksos. In one, King Nubkheperra Intef orders the expulsion from his office in the temple of Min at Coptos of a priest accused of an act of sacrilege; in the other, the transference of a civil office, that of 'governor of el-Kab', was conducted under the aegis of King Sewadjenra Nebiryaw and a copy on stone of the deed displayed in the temple at Thebes by the king's favour. This document is also one source which enables the history of this governorship to be traced with an important degree of continuity through much of the Second Intermediate Period.

If the Hyksos kings tacitly accepted these Theban kings governing this, from their point of view, most distant part of the country, it may have been because it seemed neither rich nor important enough to warrant serious interference.

### THE SECOND INTERMEDIATE PERIOD IN NUBIA

As in Egypt, the transition from the Twelfth to the Thirteenth Dynasty has left no immediately obvious trace of discontinuity. The names of various kings from the first part of the Thirteenth Dynasty have been recovered from the Egyptian fortresses in Lower Nubia, amongst them a sealing of Sekhemra-khutawy Amenemhat Sebekhetep from Mirgissa, a statue and stele of Khutawyra Ugaf from Semna and Mirgissa, and a plaquette of Khasekhemra Neferhetep from Buhen.[1] At the Semna Gorge (and at Askut Island) a series of graffiti recording, presumably with some concern, unusually high flood levels spans the period between year 2 of Amenemhat III to year 1 of Sedjefakara (probably the fifteenth king of the Thirteenth Dynasty), a period of some 70 years of which about the last 18 belong to the Thirteenth Dynasty (B. Bell 1975). However, from the absence of names of later Thirteenth Dynasty and Seventeenth Dynasty kings prior to Kamose, as well as from the state of political affairs made very explicit in the Kamose stelae (see below), it has to be assumed that Egyptian government control over Nubia was eventually lost or relinquished. Some of the fortresses show signs of conflagration, but whether from the attacks of hostile Nubians, from local warfare in a confused situation following the withdrawal of Egyptian control, or from the invading Egyptian armies of the New

---

[1] For the Ugaf stele from Mirgissa see Vercoutter (1975b). Note also a statue of Khaneferra Sebekhetep from Argo Island, but this is not far from Kerma so the same doubt attaches to it as to the statuary from Kerma itself.

Kingdom is difficult to say.[1] All of these choices are feasible because of evidence that some of these fortresses remained occupied during parts at least of the ensuing periods.

Thus, at Aniba, the main cemetery of family vaults with brick superstructures displays a probable continuity of Egyptian-style burial from the late Middle Kingdom to the New Kingdom.[2] The occurrence of true Tell el-Yahudiya juglets,[3] a product of the Hyksos period in Egypt, is to be noted (Steindorff 1937). In the fortress some restoration of the defences was carried out at a time when the ditches were about one-third filled with sand and rubble. The dry-stone masonry used in the reconstruction has been plausibly seen as a sign of the influence of the local C-group tradition of building, an influence which would be less likely at other periods.

The preliminary statements published so far concerning the site of Mirgissa date the principal surviving building phase in the upper fort to the Thirteenth Dynasty, and the corresponding Egyptian-type cemeteries to both this and the Hyksos period.

At Uronarti the evidence is to be found in a large group of mud sealings (about 4500) from letters, sacks and boxes bearing the impressions of stamp seals and scarabs. Most were found in the 'commandant's house', and amongst them was one, a 'sample-sealing', bearing the name of the Hyksos king Maatibra (Lawrence 1965, p. 86, n. 1, Tufnell 1975). A few impressions carry designs from scarabs which in style might also belong to the period of Hyksos rule. It seems impossible to isolate any other material in the fort which could be ascribed to this period, but neither is there a trace of an alien cultural presence, suggesting that whoever was handling these seals was essentially Egyptian in culture.

The most explicit record, however, comes from Buhen, where a cemetery sequence similar to that at Aniba exists, again including true Tell el-Yahudiya juglets (Randall-MacIver and Woolley 1911, pls. 49, 92). But the fortress itself has yielded a group of stelae which, on grounds of style, epigraphy and content must be ascribed to the period of the Hyksos and Seventeenth Dynasty in Egypt (Barns 1954, Säve-Söderbergh 1949).[4] The owner of one (named Sepedher) states:

---

[1] The evidence from Buhen now seems to favour the first explanation (H. S. Smith 1976, pp. 80–2).

[2] Note that these are mainly family vaults covering perhaps several generations, in some cases running into the New Kingdom.

[3] On the distinction between true Tell el-Yahudiya ware and El-Lisht ware, see n. 1 on p. 167.

[4] More of these, covering several generations, are published in H. S. Smith (1976, pp. 72–6, 80–5); cf. also Vandersleyen (1971, pp. 56–61).

'I was a valiant commander of Buhen, and never had any commander done what I did. I built the temple of Horus, lord of Buhen, in the days of the King of Kush.' The owner of another (named Ka) also records service with the King of Kush, whose name is given as Nedjeh. Another possible record of mercenary service (not from Buhen) is that of a soldier, Ha-ankhef, who after six years' service in Kush returned home to Edfu in Upper Egypt with enough gold to buy himself land.

The recognition by these men of the rule of this king is but a hint of the power which this Nubian ruler had come to acquire. On the pair of stelae set up at Karnak by Kamose, last king of the Seventeenth Dynasty, describing the early stages of the civil war between Thebes and Avaris, Kamose makes a speech: 'Give me to understand what this strength of mine is for. A king is in Avaris, another is in Kush, and so I sit alongside an Asiatic and a Nubian. Each one has his slice of this Egypt, dividing up the land with me.' The expression 'this Egypt' reflects a claim that Nubia was a part of Egypt (Vandersleyen 1971, pp. 53–6; Vercoutter 1970, pp. 184–6). His courtiers, in a diffident reply, confirm this situation: 'Behold, it is Asiatic territory as far as Cusae...Elephantine is strong. [Thus] the middle part of the land is ours, as far as Cusae.' During the ensuing invasion of Hyksos territory Kamose's army intercepts a letter being conveyed, apparently via the Darb el-Arba'in route, from the Hyksos king Aaweserra Apepy to a king of Kush, newly in office. The text of the letter, quoted in full on the stelae, contains nothing less than an invitation by Apepy for the king of Kush to invade Kamose's kingdom from the south: 'Come, journey downstream! Fear not! He is here with me, and there is no-one [else] who will stand up against you in that part of Egypt. Behold, I will allow him no road until you have arrived. Then shall we divide up the towns of that part of Egypt, and (our lands) shall thrive in joy.' (Habachi 1972 (note that Habachi restores 'Khent-hen-nefer' a term for Nubia, instead of 'our lands'), Säve-Söderbergh 1956, H. S. Smith and A. Smith 1976.)

The implication is that Kush had emerged as a kingdom of considerable strength and importance, a counterpart to the Hyksos kingdom of the north. Yet although both here and in the Buhen stelae Lower Nubia appears to be under the control of these kings, both in the Middle Kingdom and in the New Kingdom Kush as a geographical entity seems to have been regarded as typically Upper Nubian. And it is in Upper Nubia that excavation has revealed, at Kerma, the site which seems, in all respects, to invite identification as the capital of these kings.[1] As already noted (p. 128), the site stands at the beginning of the fertile Dongola Reach, just above the Third Cataract. It consists of two parts.

Close to the river stood the town. Current excavations are revealing a spread of small brick houses of more than one occupational phase, with traces on the southern edge of what may be a substantial system of fortifications to surround the town, employing a ditch and walls of stone and brick (Bonnet 1978a, 1979). But the dominant feature in the town was a massive brick building, the 'Western Deffufa', an early and very impressive form of castle. Traces of earlier architectural phases have recently been revealed, but in its final form it consisted of an L-shaped block (fig. 2.12), preserved up to 18 m high, and for the most part of solid mud brick. A single broad staircase rose up through the interior, doubtless to the apartments which must have been built on the top. In the latest phase the great staircase rose from a courtyard, on whose opposite side was a building wing representing one of the earliest known uses in the Nile Valley of baked brick.

Amidst the debris which had collapsed into a group of cellars were numerous mud-seal impressions, mostly from the sealing of pots, baskets and other receptacles. The repertoire of designs contrasts sharply with that from Uronarti. Entirely absent are those with the names and titles of administrators. The only names were those of Hyksos kings (Jakeb-her, Sheshi, Maatibra, also Queen Ineni), occurring just once or twice in each case. Two-thirds of the sealings had been done with five scarab seals carrying designs which are probably in all, and certainly in three cases stylistically of the Hyksos period (Reisner 1923, pts. I–III, pp. 38–9, pts. IV–V, p. 81). The implication, an important one, must be that most of the sealing was done at Kerma itself, presumably on the receipt of goods sent or brought in from outside, thus employing an administrative practice derived from Egypt. The local origin of some of the sealed receptacles is further confirmed by the incised patterns from Nubian pots faithfully impressed on the backs of some of the sealings.

The debris from buildings surrounding the castle contained industrial waste from the manufacture of the distinctive local pottery, of objects glazed in the Egyptian fashion, of beads, and of mica ornaments.

On the desert plateau behind lay the cemetery of tumulus graves, only

[1] The picture of Kerma may need some modification from the current excavations of the Henry M. Blackmer Foundation; for preliminary reports see Bonnet 1978a, 1979.

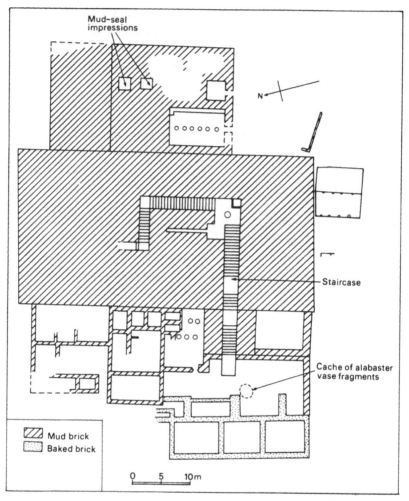

Fig. 2.12 Castle at Kerma (Western Duffufa, KI), contemporary with the Hyksos period in Egypt. The plan of the outer walls is a slightly simplified rendering of the latest of several superimposed phases.

partially excavated and published. The southern part was most likely the latest, and was dominated by three exceptionally large tumuli (KIII, IV, and X) (fig. 2.13) possessing internal structures of mud brick which included a central burial chamber and containing as well numerous separately-made subsidiary graves. Burial was on a bed, in one case of glazed quartz, surrounded by personal effects and pottery, and accompanied by the bodies of up to a dozen humans, mostly females, and also

164

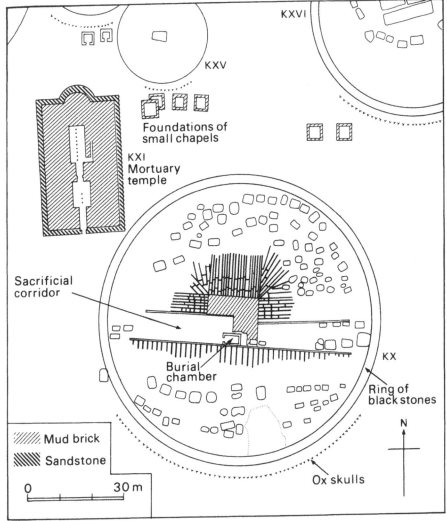

Fig. 2.13  Part of the royal cemetery at Kerma, contemporary with the Hyksos period in Egypt.

of rams. The human burials around the main one seem to have been sacrificial, and were in addition to the mass of sacrificial victims found in the central part of the great tumuli, over 300 in one case.

By their size and complexity, and by the evidence they give of the power over the lives of others which is so vividly demonstrated by the sacrificial bodies, these tumuli leave little doubt that they were the tombs of powerful kings of Nubia. Indeed, a record of the burial practices for Sudanese kings of the Middle Ages contains some remarkably close parallels (Vycichl 1959). Furthermore, that their date was one contemporary with the Hyksos and Seventeenth Dynasty should not be in doubt. The scarabs found in them are, when not of local design and manufacture, primarily of this period (including one of the chancellor Har); so also are the datable contexts in which the distinctive Classic Kerma pottery is found, sometimes as imports, in Lower Nubia and Egypt (Bietak 1968b, pp. 123–7, 180).[1] Other tumuli in this part of the cemetery would have belonged, so one imagines, to members of an extensive royal family and court, but to the north the largely unexcavated portions probably continue the burial record back into the Middle Kingdom and perhaps beyond. Recent excavations have now uncovered a group of large stone-lined structures, possibly elaborate tombs of a quite different type, in an area lying to the south of the Western Deffufa (Bonnet 1978b).

The court at Kerma must have been both rich and colourful, with reminders of Pharaonic Egypt to set the tone for civilized life (as it had done at Byblos) and to supply symbols of dignity, sometimes in the form of second-hand statuary. Although in the badly plundered tumuli little gold was left, it occurred in places – heavy plate on wooden bed legs, a rim on a pottery cup – suggesting an abundant supply. Court ladies wore leather or cloth cylindrical caps on which were stitched pieces of mica cut in various shapes, including some derived from Egyptian symbolism. One lady had worn a crown of thin silver. Egyptian influence can be seen in the handful of burials employing wooden coffins, and more particularly in the introduction into the cemetery of mortuary temples. Two large brick examples were built,[2] one of them (KXI) encased in sandstone blocks. The other (KII) had been given an external frieze of lions in Egyptian style composed of faience tiles, and possessed a granite door lintel decorated with a carved winged-disc, an Egyptian motif found painted also on a wall of the burial chamber of one of the royal tumuli, KIII. Inside, the walls of both mortuary temples had been painted with scenes in Egyptian style, depicting fleets of sailing ships, and giraffes and other animals. Although points of contact with

[1] Supposed Kerma beakers found in a tomb at Saqqara (Mastaba 3507, no. 10) and now in the British Museum, London, resemble only superficially Classic Kerma beakers, being much coarser, and should not be identified as such. The group is listed in Merrillees (1968, pp. 27–8). For dating, note the scarab of Nubkheperra Intef from the Mirgissa cemetery (Vercoutter 1970, pl. XXVI), and the scarab of Maatibra from the Akasha cemetery (Maystre 1975).

[2] The basic design, in which rooms occupy only a relatively small part of the otherwise solid brickwork, can be paralleled in the Middle Kingdom temple at Ezbet Rushdi in the Nile Delta (Adam 1959), but this may be just a common feature of the times. Some of the faience tiles from KII are illustrated in W. S. Smith (1962, 1965, fig. 60).

Egypt are essentially influences on an overwhelmingly indigenous culture, and although no fully Egyptian-style tombs have been found, one must accept the presence at Kerma of a number of Egyptians, both artisans directing mud-brick building and various industrial processes (glazing, joinery, metal-casting), and perhaps advisors or administrators responsible for the sealings found in the castle, and for doing the secretarial work necessary for maintaining the diplomatic contact with Egypt exemplified by the letter captured by Kamose's army.

One important question which has to receive a somewhat imprecise and speculative answer is the source of Kerma's wealth. As noted above, Upper Nubia must have been actively involved in trade with Egypt during the Middle Kingdom, but to what local economic benefit is not clear. The rich, Classic phase of Kerma culture seems primarily to have coincided with Hyksos rule in the north of Egypt, and during this time the kings of Kush may have had ample opportunity to acquire a virtual monopoly of Nubian gold. By having gold to offer for services they may have had no difficulty in attracting Egyptian craftsmen and soldiers, like the man from Edfu mentioned above. As a trading partner Kush must have grown even more important than hitherto, but since the Darb el-Arba'in caravan route could put Kush into direct contact with Hyksos-held territory, by-passing the kingdom of the Theban Seventeenth Dynasty altogether, it is particularly difficult to estimate what the arrangement might have been, though the modesty of the Seventeenth Dynasty royal burials at Thebes compared to their counterparts at Kerma might be an indication that they were, in fact, being passed by in whatever trade was being conducted with the south. Some of the second-hand statuary may have come from Upper Egypt (O'Connor 1969, pp. 31–2) but otherwise the Egyptian material from Kerma itself is of little help in determining its ultimate origin, though one can imagine that analysis of the composition of the bronzes might yield important clues. An interesting negative feature is the absence so far of true Tell el-Yahudiya pottery juglets,[1] contrasting with the numerous examples from Egyptian-style graves at Buhen and Aniba.

The culture of Kerma is that of a court, and in this respect remains unique. Naturally, the political influence of its rulers cannot be measured accurately by archaeology, and so the fate of the other Nubian kingdoms of the Middle Kingdom lists is not known. Classic Kerma material has been found as far south as Bugdumbush, and on sites

[1] True Tell el-Yahudiya juglets should be carefully distinguished from the El-Lisht type which appeared during the late Middle Kingdom (Merrillees 1974, 1978).

northwards to just beyond the Dal Cataract, of which the most important are claimed to be Sai Island, Akasha and Ukma West (Geus and Labre 1974; Giorgini 1971, ch. 2, pl. 4; Gratien 1973, 1974, 1975, 1978; Macadam 1955, p. 160, no. 0919; Maystre 1975; *Report of the Antiquities Service and Museums in the Anglo-Egyptian Sudan* 1946, p. 10, 1947, pp. 5, 9; Vila 1975). Further north still, in Lower Nubia, Classic Kerma forms a distinctive component of the culture contemporary with the Hyksos and Seventeenth Dynasties. In widely scattered localities individual or small groups of burials with features characteristic of Kerma culture, including the distinctive pottery, have been found, suggestive of immigrants from the south forming a numerically very small but widely dispersed element in the population. Not surprisingly, the largest of these cemeteries (twenty-three graves) occurs in the most southerly part of Lower Nubia, at Mirgissa. Kerma pottery has also been noted in the debris of two forts, Mirgissa (Hesse 1971, Vercoutter 1970, pp. 13, 22–3, 183, n. 125) and Buhen (Egypt Exploration Society 1963, Randall-MacIver and Woolley 1911, p. 239, pl. 50; H. S. Smith 1976, p. 81), in both cases apparently associated, in very limited quarters, with a level of destruction or decay. Kerma pottery has also been found in tombs in Upper Egypt, but, with the exception of two adjacent graves at Abydos containing contracted burials, the style of burial and of other grave goods is wholly Egyptian, suggesting that the Kerma pots are either trade goods themselves, or perhaps even souvenirs from a period of mercenary service.

The knowledge that at Buhen and Aniba (and apparently Mirgissa as well) there were Egyptians who continued to live and be buried after the severing of Egypt's political control provides an acceptable historical context for understanding the significance of groups of graffiti at various Lower Nubian localities, containing one or two somewhat eccentrically written royal names not attested elsewhere: Ii-ib-khent-ra and Kakara In. Although normally ascribed to the First Intermediate Period, they are accompanied by names and titles of officials which, as a group, are essentially Middle Kingdom.[1] One interpretation which can be placed on them is that they derive from an attempt at establishing an independent kingdom by Egyptians who had once belonged to the garrisons of the Egyptian forts, engineered during the later Thirteenth Dynasty. It would have been of relatively limited duration since, by

[1] The two most important are: *imy-r '-ḥnwty* (Gauthier 1918, Helck 1958, p. 12, n. 9) and *ḥrp skw* (Gardiner *et al.* 1955, vol. II, p. 97, n. c). These titles accompany the Abu Hor graffito. Accompanying the Medik graffito is one of 'the prophet Khnum-hetep'; an identically written graffito also occurs at Semna (Reisner, Dunham and Janssen 1960, p. 133, pl. 94A).

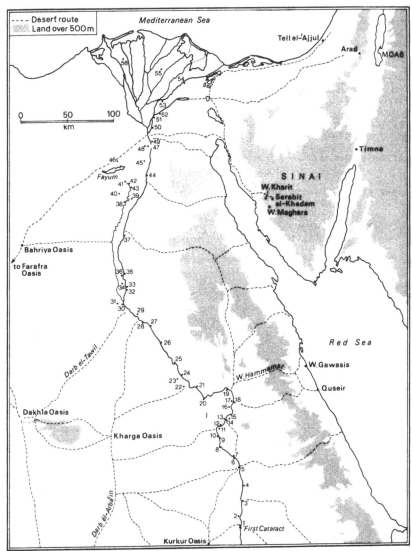

Fig. 2.14  Map of Egypt for the Old and Middle Kingdoms. The Delta branches are after Bietak (1975a, Abb. 23); ancient desert routes can only be inferred from more recent patterns, one useful source for the western desert being the map at the rear of Bates (1970). (See p. 182 for explanation of numbers.)

Kamose's time, Lower Nubia seems to have been a vassal of the kings of Kush.

To a complex situation in Lower Nubia, as well as in Egypt, must be added a further element: the immigration and settlement of desert peoples whose culture passes under the term 'Pan-grave'. The cemeteries are often small, but reached at least the total of 49 burials at Balabish and 107 at Mostagedda in Upper Egypt, and occur on both banks of the Nile between Deir Rifeh in Upper Egypt and Toshka in Lower Nubia (with possible Pan-grave influence in the Second Cataract area), a sign that some of these immigrant groups crossed the river. Related material which may or may not be real Pan-grave has been found even further north (Kemp 1977a, Menghin and Bittel 1934). Distinctive features of the culture are its pottery (bowls, often with indented or emphasized rim, either black-topped red or dark with roughly incised patterns), bracelets made of mother-of-pearl strips, and bucrania (sometimes painted) buried in the cemeteries. Small camp sites have been found on the desert margins in the El-Badari area, and incised sherds of pottery of apparent Pan-grave character have been found on the surface of Egyptian town sites at Kahun, Abydos, Ballas, Hierakonpolis, Edfu, Qasr es-Sagha, Karnak (*Bulletin de Liaison du Groupe Internationale d'Etude de la Céramique Egyptienne* 1977) and El-Kab, and at the Nubian forts of Kubban and Mirgissa.

Although it cannot be substantiated by particularly convincing evidence, there is a strong suspicion, which must at present rest largely on the greater dissimilarity between Pan-grave and western desert material than between the latter and C-group culture, that these newcomers originated in the eastern desert, being thus Medja-people. Comparisons have been made with material from distant parts of the eastern Sudan (Kassala) and northern Ethiopia (Agordat) (Arkell 1954, Bietak 1966, p. 70), but the similarity is not apparently one of total culture, only of selected individual traits in pottery decoration, and thus not necessarily of immediate relevance in view of the widely dispersed and long-lasting pottery traditions of north-east Africa. A preliminary statement on the physical anthropology of a Pan-grave group from Sayala in Lower Nubia contrasts them strongly with C-group people (and with Kerma people, too) (Strouhal and Jungwirth 1971), and finds similarity with a much more ancient stratum of population encountered in the Wadi Halfa area in Late Palaeolithic (Mesolithic) times.[1] But as with the Hyksos material from Tell ed-Dab'a there is insufficient comparative material to know what is really implied by this observation.

The historical inscriptions of Kamose's attack on the Hyksos record that his army contained units of Medja troops, and the suggestion that

---

[1] Statements on the significance of anthropological data should be considered in conjunction with van Gerven, Carlson and Armelagos (1973).

Pan-grave culture belonged to the same people is quite an old one.[1] But whilst it still seems perfectly feasible to regard Kamose's Medja mercenaries as drawn from these immigrants, their number and ubiquity suggests a much more important movement of people affecting Lower Nubia as well as southern Egypt. Indeed, if they are to be identified with Medja-people they would have to be regarded as more than disjointed groups for, as Papyrus Bulaq 18 shows for the Thirteenth Dynasty (see pp. 81, 122), the Medja-people possessed leaders sufficiently identifiable to receive an invitation to the Egyptian court at Thebes. The reasons for this migration, which became a unique cultural intrusion in Upper Egypt in the Pharaonic period, remain wholly obscure, as does the long-term effect. As with the Palestinian Middle Bronze Age II culture in the eastern Delta, Pan-grave culture failed to retain its identity beyond the beginning of the New Kingdom, but there is no evidence to suggest that its bearers were subject to Upper Egyptian hostility. It is just possible that the prominent Ahmose–Paheri family at El-Kab in the early Eighteenth Dynasty was descended from such people.[2]

In Lower Nubia, alongside the various newcomers and remaining Egyptians, C-group culture continued to exist, and in fact passed through its most developed phase (IIb), though towards the end of the period exhibiting (in its phase III) a degree of local variation and influence from the immigrant groups as well as a possible overall decline in its affluence. The most striking feature of phase IIb is the appearance of a greater variation in tomb size, the larger tumuli sometimes coming to possess small mortuary chapels of mud brick or stone and suggestive, perhaps, of a greater degree of social stratification. This also coincided with the emergence of larger C-group settlements, in the form of fortified stone villages well exemplified at Areika and Wadi es-Sebua. These were evidently designed as places of refuge in troubled times.

It becomes evident that in the late Thirteenth Dynasty and Hyksos period Lower Nubia passed through a complex and eventful period of history which has more than a few echoes of events in northern Egypt:

---

[1] Note also the soldier's archery case reported in Shore (1973), an object of the Seventeenth or early Eighteenth Dynasty from Upper Egypt, where the owner is depicted attended by a Nubian soldier.

[2] The foreignness of some of the names in this family has been commented on by others, e.g. Helck (1971, p. 101) and Vandersleyen (1971, pp. 24–5), with the assumption of Asiatic origin. But another relative actually bore the name *Mdзy-s*, 'Medja-man' (Tylor and Griffith 1894, pl. VII). The *ru* element in two other family names, Itruri and Ruru, also occurs in Nubian names, e.g. *Rwiw* and *Rwnз* (Säve-Söderbergh 1963), *R-kз* and *Rwiw/Rwiз* (Steindorff 1937, p. 250).

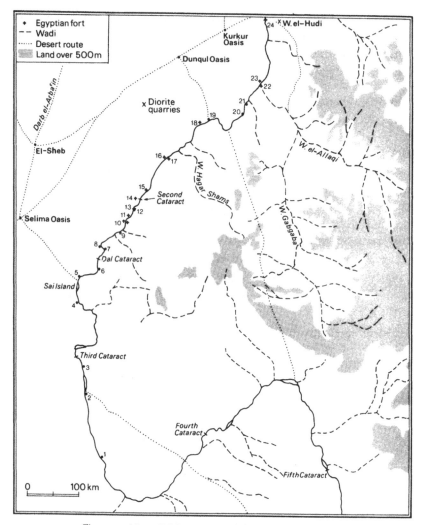

Fig. 2.15   Map of Nubia in the Old and Middle Kingdoms.
(See p. 182 for explanation of numbers.)

a fragmentation of society, exacerbated by immigration, with ultimate authority eventually passing to a dominant power from outside, the kingdom of Kush, whose court looked to Egypt for symbols of authority and employed Egyptians in its service. Thus the Second Intermediate Period emerges as one of great significance in the history of Egypt's relationships with her neighbours. A time of internal governmental weakness coincided with a period of prosperity and political growth in Palestine and Nubia so that, for once, the Egyptians found themselves the victims of both the political initiative and cultural momentum of others.

## THE THEBAN DEFEAT OF THE HYKSOS AND OF KUSH

Both kingdoms were simultaneously destroyed in a period of warfare probably initiated by Kamose, the last king of the Seventeenth Dynasty, and continued by his immediate successors of the Eighteenth Dynasty. The evidence for hostilities prior to Kamose is somewhat ambiguous, though it has been strengthened by the demonstration that Kamose's predecessor, Sekenenra Ta'a II, died a violent death from weapons, one of which had the distinctive shape of a Syro-Palestinian axe-head of a type found in the eastern Delta at this time (Bietak 1974). A conflict between this king and the Hyksos king Apepy is narrated in Papyrus Sallier I, a much later popular tale, but this may have been of the 'out-witting' type, although it correctly presupposes in its setting the opposed interests of the two kingdoms. The main source for the Theban revolt is a pair of stelae (and a scribal copy of one of them) erected in Karnak temple by Kamose and dated to his year 3 (Habachi 1972, p. 39; Pritchard 1969, pp. 554–5; Säve-Söderbergh 1956; H. S. Smith and A. Smith 1976). In a council of war the scene is initially set as a stable tripartite division of Egypt: the Hyksos kingdom ruled by Aaweserra Apepy, who is known to have reigned for at least 40 years, Thebes and Kush. This is used as a contrasting literary device to emphasize Kamose's personal responsibility for making the winning aggressive move of a northward attack, commencing with the town of Nefrusy, 'a nest for Asiatics', ruled by one Teti son of Pepy, presumably an Egyptian vassal of the Hyksos. The difficult language of the text, which mixes narrative with rhetoric, leaves one in doubt as to with what success Kamose penetrated the Delta.[1] The text ends abruptly, not with the defeat of the Hyksos in battle or siege, but with a triumphal return to Thebes at the onset of the inundation season. The last engagement mentioned is described thus: 'I sent a strong troop overland to destroy the Bahriya Oasis – whilst I was in Sako – in order to prevent rebels from being behind me.' Sako is still about 70 km south of Herakleopolis, and the action was presumably designed to sever communications between the Hyksos kingdom and Kush. It was at this point that the famous letter from Apepy was captured.

[1] The stele of Emheb, a man who seems to have belonged to Kamose's force, also refers to reaching Avaris in this same year 3 (Černý 1969).

This letter from Apepy has already been mentioned. Before inviting the King of Kush to invade southern Egypt, Apepy sets the scene: 'Do you see what Egypt has done to me? The king of the place, Kamose (given life!), is attacking me on my ground. I had not assailed him in the manner of all that he has done to you. He chooses to plague these two lands, mine and yours. He has ravaged them.' The allusion to a prior attack on Kush was probably no rhetoric. A building inscription of this same year 3 of Kamose at Buhen (H. S. Smith 1976, p. 8, pls. II, I and LVIII. I, no. 488) suggests an almost simultaneous conquest of the whole of Lower Nubia, borne out by two graffiti of his reign at Arminna commemorating possibly the earliest holders of the New Kingdom office of Viceroy of Kush (Simpson 1963c, p. 34).[1]

The ultimate success of the Theban revolt had to await the early reigns of the New Kingdom. It was not limited to regaining control of the territory ruled by the Middle Kingdom, but became, in the end, the conquest and the attempt to control the lands whence the kings of Kush and the 'foreign kings' from the north-east had originated.

## EXPLANATIONS OF HISTORICAL CHANGE IN THE OLD AND MIDDLE KINGDOMS

The presentation of ancient Egyptian history in narrative form inevitably draws particular attention to change and development, but, for the laudable purpose of making narrative lively, tends in practice to an overdramatization which the sources often do not warrant. In the sections on Egyptian internal history in this chapter the narrative element has consciously been played down. But the alternative of presenting the historical basis of the Old and Middle Kingdoms in the form of a governmental system, with each part – the king, his officers, provincial governors, and temple staff – playing its role without unduly disturbing others can easily lead too far in the opposite direction, and by presenting the system as so harmoniously balanced make it hard to comprehend how, in particular, the upsets of the First Intermediate Period came about. With the exception of the Hyksos Dynasty the roots of historical change seem to lie within Egypt, and, at the political level, particularly in the relationships between the king, the officers of his

---

[1] Vandersleyen (1971, pp. 61–3) discusses a further possible source. The stele of Emheb (see previous note) couples the reaching of Avaris with a Nubian locality called Miu. Historical circumstances demand that this cannot be identical with the Miu of the Armant stele of Tuthmosis III, evidently a far-distant place, but was perhaps related to the *tp* ('head of') Miu in the Pennut tomb at Aniba.

court, and provincial men of ambition. But the lack of documentation often makes it difficult to discover if the development of some institution or facet of society, other than the kingship itself, is an indication of a weakening of royal control or a sign of the ability of the office of king to adapt to and perhaps bring about change. It is only, for example, the need of modern historians to find some reason for the First Intermediate Period which sees the emphasis on solar worship in the Fifth Dynasty as a sign of diminishing royal authority rather than as an interesting development in the cults patronized by the court which in no way detracted from the king's dominance in government, and may just as easily have added to it. The resort to *post hoc, ergo propter hoc* reasoning is often the only alternative if comprehensive explanation for events is regarded as essential.

It may be, however, that an *ad hoc* historical approach, concentrating on just one specific situation at a time, places too great an emphasis on the more superficial aspects. There is the alternative of beginning from a more theoretical, determinist position, and of arguing that the bureaucratic state possesses certain basic structural properties, some of them weaknesses, and that in the case of early floodplain civilizations, they took a particular common form.[1] If one wished to consider Egypt from this point of view, several closely interrelated aspects of society require attention.

In the first place, although the Nile has a regimen somewhat different from, say, the Tigris–Euphrates system, with irrigation remaining at the elementary level of basin irrigation not requiring elaborate central control (Butzer 1976, pp. 42–3), it would still have possessed, with other major floodplains, the capacity for producing an agricultural surplus beyond the immediate needs of its overall initial population. However, although subsequent population increase was probably never on a scale to constitute a problem in the periods under consideration,[2] rising demand stimulated by the conspicuous consumption of the court may have eventually led to the extension of agriculture to less productive lands with consequent diminishing returns.

Bureaucracy is a central feature of the early major civilizations, and

---

[1] An important phase of discussion began with Wittfogel's 'hydraulic hypothesis' (Wittfogel 1955, 1957). This has provoked much critical comment, some of it of considerable value, e.g. Friedman (1974), Kappel (1974), Lees (1974) and Mitchell (1973).

[2] A valuable review of recent discussions of this topic is in Cowgill (1975). Helck (1974c, 1975, pp. 98–100) has postulated that the growth of bureaucracy and demand for labourers and craftsmen in the Old Kingdom created a demand for increased population, to be met by raids on neighbouring countries.

in Egypt probably arose primarily to serve the ambitions of the early kings. When seen in operation through surviving administrative texts, it seems to have been concerned mainly with facilitating the transfer of produce to the various centres which made up the 'court' and to its provincial outliers and with supervising constructional work, rather than with the maintenance of the agricultural system. It would be in this group that a proliferation of numbers and rise in material expectations would produce serious pressures on the agricultural surplus.

Pious foundations occupied a key place in the Egyptian economy. Those which were mainly or exclusively for the benefit of private individuals, and were then most effectively operated in the provinces, offered one way through which people living off surplus could safeguard their economic positions and perhaps satisfy growing expectations, but this would ultimately have been something in competition with the court. The economic behaviour of these foundations probably had an important role in the history of the early periods, but the terrible dearth of quantifiable data would make a more detailed assessment very difficult.

Finally, although monumental tomb construction and burial of riches is an obvious feature of ancient Egypt, its effects are still not properly understood. Explanation for the First Intermediate Period has sometimes been sought in the idea that continued pyramid-building exhausted the country. However, this may have been true only in so far as it stood in the way of growing demand amongst the official class, bearing in mind the finite limits of agricultural surplus. Irrespective of whether this private demand, channelled through pious foundations, was instrumental in creating a weak and unstable court, the latter's inability to continue massive court cemetery construction would have been a most damaging failure for the long-term continuation of what we recognize as 'civilization' in Egypt and to the prosperity of those very people who may have been competing with it. For in this form of monumental construction the authority of the king and all that this implied politically was finalized, ambitious men found a prestigious and rewarding outlet within a controlled framework, and the country's material and intellectual resources were stretched to a greater degree within a centralized programme. The role of strong central government in raising the general level of prosperity is shown by the way in which, during the First Intermediate Period, and even probably during the late Old Kingdom, the level of consumption of men of power, as indexed by their tomb sizes, seems to have declined. Yet they were now no longer in competition with a lavishly endowed court.

This type of formal approach implies a degree of inevitability, particularly if the bureaucratic state is regarded as, in the long term, an unstable phenomenon. But even if one allows this, it does not deprive the historian of the opportunity of explaining why, at one moment rather than another, history took a particular course. The political element is not readily absorbed into a determinist framework of explanation. Thus the re-establishment of a single strong kingship in the Middle Kingdom which allowed, or was forced to accept, the continued existence of provincial governors of considerable pretensions is not an obvious product of a determinist explanation of why the Old Kingdom had come to an end. Furthermore, this provincial aspect of Egypt's system of government was no longer in existence at the end of the Twelfth Dynasty, so that the second period of short reigns and downturn in the scale of court activity which followed cannot be explained in quite the same way as the first, and is, indeed, difficult to explain adequately on either political or determinist grounds.

The notion that explanation is possible at all also depends on the assumption that the evidence and the factors at work were distributed fairly evenly around the country, so that what is encountered in one area can be regarded as nationally typical. But the possibility must be considered that, because accidents of preservation have greatly favoured Upper Egypt, our attention is focused too much on a part of the country whose involvement in Memphite court politics was often less than the more northerly regions, and which does not therefore always offer a particularly reliable guide to those factors which most seriously affected the fortunes of the ruling house at Memphis. An examination of the broad sweep of ancient Egyptian history (including the later periods not considered in this chapter) might suggest that a political dichotomy can be seen emerging in those times when a strongly centralized and centralizing government was absent. In such periods, the country tended to divide, as a first stage, into two parts: the delta and the seven or eight most northerly nomes of Upper Egypt on the one hand, and the rest of Upper Egypt south of, say, El-Minya or Asyut on the other (see Wainwright 1927). The next step in the north was for continued fragmentation into city states to produce eventually a pattern known elsewhere in the ancient Near East, with complex ties recognizing a hierarchy of authority amongst them which included a nominal capital at Memphis or somewhere else in the north. The more southerly part of Upper Egypt was, however, more readily kept together as one unit, ruled from a single place whose pre-eminence received justification through theology, whereby a local cult was paid special attention and its deity given a central place in the theology of divine kingship. The gods Seth and Horus represent the legacy of prehistoric periods when respectively Naqada and Hierakonpolis were in turn centres of importance in Upper Egypt. Thebes was to fill this role from the Eleventh Dynasty onwards, with its temple eventually becoming the principal cult centre in Upper Egypt and its god Amen/Amen-Ra, gaining a dominant position in the theology of kingship. Memphis also had this symbolic role, justified in the Memphite Theology, but it acted less effectively in the north in times of weak central government.

This geographical factor is useful as a possible overall perspective to prevent irregularities in the preservation of evidence from having too great an influence in the writing of history. But from period to period modification is obviously necessary in the light of what is known of the complexities of situations which are bound to be, in detail, unique every time. Thus the short-lived fragmentation of Upper Egypt under nomarchs in the Eighth and perhaps early Ninth/Tenth Dynasties was an exceptional occurrence which happened at a time when no one place in Upper Egypt had yet emerged with pre-eminent regional authority since at least the Early Dynastic Period. This vacuum was shortly filled by Thebes. Then again, the Thirteenth Dynasty seems to have been able to continue to rule Upper Egypt, including the Thebaid, at a time when the fragmentation of the delta may already have been beginning. This last possibility leads to an interesting argument (though one for which supporting evidence is conspicuously lacking): whilst in the late Old Kingdom it was the provincial governors of Upper Egypt who began competing for resources with the court, in the late Middle Kingdom this role was taken over by incipient city states in the Delta. It does not seem unreasonable to consider that the rash of client kings who must have ruled the northern part of Egypt under the Hyksos overlordship had come into possession of a system which had some historical and economic background.

### Climatic variation

The interaction of political, economic and social factors should not be considered against an entirely stable climatic background. Evidence of a rather scattered kind has been used to suggest certain important variations both in seasonal rainfall over Egypt and in Nile flood levels (the two should be very carefully distinguished) for the Old and Middle Kingdoms. The evidence stems either from interpretations placed on ancient written and pictorial sources, or from field observations in areas geographically marginal to the Egyptian Nile Valley.

Representations of desert fauna and trees in tombs suggest that by the end of the Old Kingdom both had been depleted, presumably by the onset of more arid conditions, though in view of changes in the fashions of subject matter and the very selective nature of the Egyptian representations of their world the evidence should be treated cautiously. The archaeological evidence for herding and hunting communities in the western desert mentioned above (pp. 119–20), ought to be crucial, but the dating evidence is as yet highly unsatisfactory. The appearance of C-group culture in Lower Nubia has been seen as an effect of deteriorating conditions of life in the desert, but the really widespread immigration of desert peoples into the Nile Valley represented by the Pan-grave people did not take place until significantly later. Whether ecological change in the neighbouring deserts had any significant effect on the Egyptian economy is hard to tell. In southern Upper Egypt and Lower Nubia greater wadi activity in the period c. 4000–3000 BC is apparently to be attributed to winter rains. This did not recur in Pharaonic times (Butzer 1975, Butzer and Hansen 1968, ch. 3), and the evidence obviously supports the idea of increasing aridity in the early centuries of Egyptian history.

A little futher south, careful investigation into the relationship between geology and late Neolithic settlements in Sudanese Nubia (especially at Debeira West and Ashkeit) has pointed to a major decline in Nile flood levels during the later prehistoric phases (Butzer and Hansen 1968, pp. 277–8; de Heinzelin 1968). By the late fourth millennium BC areas of the river bed had been permanently exposed. It would seem that this degradation phase must have ended somewhere around the beginning of the dynastic period, when deposition of silt began again, but with the Nile now flowing permanently in a somewhat lower floodplain. There appears to be some correlation actually within the summer monsoonal rainfall belt whence the Nile waters originate (Butzer 1976, pp. 30–3; Grove, Street and Goudie 1975). Connected with this are ancient Nile flood levels, recorded on the Palermo Stone, which appear to show a decline of average flood levels of a little over a metre during the First Dynasty, but to maintain themselves thereafter into the Fifth Dynasty, when the record ceases (B. Bell 1970). In the Fayum, the maximum extent (at 22–24 m above sea level) of Lake

Moeris seems to have persisted into Old Kingdom times, covering the greater part of this depression (B. Bell 1975, Said *et al.* 1972a, b). But, by the mid Twelfth Dynasty the level had dropped to below 18 m, possibly to below 15 m, thus exposing a substantial area of land for cultivation. On it were built the temples of Medinet Ma'adi and Kiman Faris, and the colossi of Biyahmu. This was presumably a delayed consequence of declining Nile flood levels, the crucial regulating factor being the state of the Hawara channel at any particular time, something still not properly documented. This newly exposed land would have been a major addition to the agricultural resources of the Nile Valley.

From the period following the end of the Old Kingdom comes a remarkably large number of the ancient references to famine in Upper Egypt, some explicitly linked with low Nile levels. By contrast, as noted on p. 160, a series of Nile flood-level records from Nubia covering the late Twelfth and early Thirteenth Dynasties document an intermittent series of high flood levels averaging about 7.3 m above their modern counterparts. A Thirteenth Dynasty stele from Karnak records the flooding of the temple of Amen, but since the chronological position of the king named is not certain, this particular flooding need not belong to the same series recorded at Semna.[1] Finally, it should be noted that a completely different type of source, the Admonitions of Ipuwer, has been used as an eye-witness account not only of historical events but also of natural disasters, including famines from low Niles. But as noted above (pp. 74–6), its date and nature are open to such widely varying interpretations, some of which lift it right out of the category of eye-witness reporting, that it is dangerous to use it as a source for the events of any one period.

Human society must inevitably be sensitive to ecological change, yet one must also allow a margin of adjustment and ability to overcome calamity and adverse circumstances. In some of the texts of the early First Intermediate Period the great famine is presented not as something which reduces man to helplessness and despair but as an illustration of the writer's authority and capacity to administer relief, sometimes over a wide area. As far as provincial cemetery culture in Upper Egypt south of the Fayum is concerned, no breaks of more than local significance can be observed over the entire period considered in this chapter, even

---

[1] Baines (1974, 1976), Habachi (1974). The practice of recording individual levels in Egypt itself similar to the Semna levels is attested by an inscribed block found loose at Naga ed-Deir dated to year 23 of Amenemhat III (Robert H. Lowie Museum of Anthropology 1966, p. 64). A startling alternative theory that the Semna levels are evidence for an ancient barrage at Semna has been advanced by Vercoutter (1976a).

when accompanied by variations in burial rate. Furthermore, the blossoming of court culture in the Middle and New Kingdoms is itself a sign that whatever changes in environment (and society) did occur, they were not of a permanently damaging nature.

The only climatic change of any dimensions that has been deduced is the ending of the Neolithic subpluvial late in the Old Kingdom, which seems to have affected the desert fauna. But as noted above, the Pan-grave movement into the Nile Valley some three or four centuries later is perhaps a sign that its consequences were more long-drawn-out or regionally variable. The cry 'the desert is dying of hunger' comes not from the late Old Kingdom, but from a small party of Medja-people in the reign of Amenemhat III (see p. 132).

In the case of the river Nile, once the major adjustment of the floodplain had taken place in the Early Dynastic Period, one would expect, from the records of more recent periods, both an annual variation of a few metres (3.8 m in modern times), and cyclic overall changes of level and volume, operating generally within reasonable limits but occasionally producing critical effects on the communities living on its floodplain. Of these, high floods, although they damage property and food stores, may be counted somewhat less serious in their consequences than very low floods which endanger the whole basis of agriculture. The famine records of the First Intermediate Period are evidently to be understood, from their phraseology, as the result of an extreme trough in the cyclic pattern of Nile variation.

It can scarcely go unnoticed that the decline of court culture after the Sixth and Twelfth Dynasties occurred close in time to freak Nile levels: the famine-creating lows of the early First Intermediate Period and the highs of the Semna levels. Although neither seems to have interfered appreciably with the development of riverine culture in Nubia, an area which one might have supposed to be even more exposed to ecological change than Egypt, they can scarcely be ignored in attempting to understand the historical processes at work at these times. It involves far too simplistic a view of society to see governmental decline as a direct and inevitable consequence of ecological adversity. Its most likely contribution would have been to impose a further strain on the balance between competing demands for surplus, particularly if it also came at a time of diminishing returns from a period of increasingly intense agricultural exploitation. But the way in which this aggravated situation was resolved would depend very much on the relative strengths of the competing groups. The way in which a period of governmental weakness seems to have followed these two periods of eccentric Nile behaviour may itself be evidence for the existence of groups of people before whose power kings had to give way.

---

*Explanation of numbers for figs. 2.14 and 2.15*

**Fig. 2.14**

| | | | |
|---|---|---|---|
| 1 | Elephantine | 29 | Dier el-Gabrawi |
| 2 | Kubaniya | 30 | Cusae |
| 3 | Kom Ombo | 31 | Meir |
| 4 | Gebel es-Silsila | 32 | Deir el-Bersha |
| 5 | Edfu | 33 | Sheikh Said |
| 6 | Hierakonpolis | 34 | Hermopolis |
| 7 | El-Kab | 35 | Beni Hasan |
| 8 | Esna | 36 | Nefrusy |
| 9 | Mo'alla | 37 | Cynopolis |
| 10 | Gebelein | 38 | Deshasha |
| 11 | Tod | 39 | Herakleopolis |
| 12 | Armant | 40 | Medinet Ma'adi |
| 13 | Theban necropolis | 41 | Medinet el-Fayum |
| 14 | Thebes | 42 | Hawara |
| 15 | Medamud | 43 | El-Lahun |
| 16 | Naqada | 44 | Atfih |
| 17 | Ballas | 45 | El-Lisht |
| 18 | Coptos | 46 | Kasr es-Sagha |
| 19 | Dendera | 47 | Memphis |
| 20 | Diospolis Parva | 48 | Saqqara |
| 21 | Balabish | 49 | Tura |
| 22 | Abydos | 50 | Heliopolis |
| 23 | Bet Khallaf | 51 | Tell el-Yahudiya |
| 24 | Naga ed-Deir | 52 | Inshas |
| 25 | Akhmim | 53 | Tell Basta |
| 26 | Qau el-Kebir | 54 | Tell ed-Dab'a |
| 27 | Deir Rifeh | 55 | Mendes |
| 28 | Asyut | 56 | Buto |

**Fig. 2.15**

| | | | |
|---|---|---|---|
| 1 | Bugdumbush | 13 | Askut |
| 2 | Kawa | 14 | Mirgissa |
| 3 | Kerma | 15 | Buhen |
| 4 | Soleb | 16 | Faras |
| 5 | Amara | 17 | Serra |
| 6 | Firka | 18 | Aniba |
| 7 | Akasha | 19 | Tumas |
| 8 | Ukma | 20 | Wadi es-Sebua |
| 9 | Duweishat | 21 | Sayala |
| 10 | Semna | 22 | Kubban |
| 11 | Shalfak | 23 | Dakka |
| 12 | Saras | 24 | Biga (Senmet) |

# CHAPTER 3

# NEW KINGDOM AND THIRD INTERMEDIATE PERIOD, 1552–664 BC

## PROLEGOMENA

### Chronology

The history of Egypt between 1552 and 664 BC, as for earlier periods, is conventionally divided up into usually sequential, numbered dynasties (table 3.1). These are derived from later 'Epitomes' of Manetho's history of Egypt (late fourth century BC) and usually do in fact coincide with real breaks, alterations or divisions in the line of dynastic succession.

The absolute chronology of these dynasties has been reconstructed with a high degree of reliability. It is true that two chronologies can be postulated for the Eighteenth to Twentieth dynasties (1552–1069 BC), because it is uncertain whether several dynastically-dated astronomical observations – vital for chronological reconstruction – were made near Memphis ('high' chronology) or near Thebes ('low' chronology). On the whole, the 'low' chronology fits the available evidence better, and is followed in the chronological table; nevertheless, neither the 'high' nor 'low' chronologies can yet be shown to be unquestionably correct. For the period between 945 and 330 BC there are an increasing number of reliable synchronisms, another dated astronomical observation, and some chronologically exceptionally well-documented dynasties (Twenty-sixth and Twenty-seventh), and the degree of disagreement amongst scholars is correspondingly smaller. In fact, disagreement about the absolute chronology of the entire period 1552–664 BC is quite small; significant developments within Egypt and the ever-changing pattern of its contacts with other areas can be dated with considerable if not complete precision.

Egyptian absolute chronology should prove a most important complement to radiocarbon and other dating methods in the reconstruction of the ancient history of north-east and east Africa as a whole. Egyptian contacts with these regions were extensive (see pp. 252–78); the absolute chronology of the comparatively well-known Nubian cultures is based upon datable Egyptian contacts and, as the indigenous cultures of Punt and Libya become better known, Egyptian contact

TABLE 3.1 *Names and dates of the kings of Egypt from 1552 to 664* BC

**NEW KINGDOM**

| Eighteenth Dynasty | Regnal dates | Nineteenth Dynasty | Regnal dates |
|---|---|---|---|
| Ahmose | 1552–1527 | Ramesses I | 1305–1303 |
| Amenhotep I | 1527–1506 | Seti I | 1303–1289 |
| Tuthmosis I | 1506–1494 | Ramesses II | 1289–1224 |
| Tuthmosis II | 1494–1490 | Merenptah | 1224–1204 |
| Hatshepsut | 1490–1468 | Amenmesses | 1204–1200 |
| Tuthmosis III | 1490–1436 | Seti II | 1200–1194 |
| Amenhotep II | 1438–1412 | Siptah | 1194–1188 |
| Tuthmosis IV | 1412–1402 | Twosret | 1194–1186 |
| Amenhotep III | 1402–1364 | | |
| Amenhotep IV ⎫ Akhenaten ⎭ | 1364–1347 | Twentieth Dynasty | |
| Smenkhare | 1351–1348 | Sethnakht | 1186–1184 |
| Tutankhamen | 1347–1337 | Ramesses III | 1184–1153 |
| Ay | 1337–1333 | Ramesses IV | 1153–1146 |
| Horemheb | 1333–1305 | Ramesses V | 1146–1142 |
| | | Ramesses VI | 1142–1135 |
| | | Ramesses VII | 1135–1129 |
| | | Ramesses VIII | 1129–1127 |
| | | Ramesses IX | 1127–1109 |
| | | Ramesses X | 1109–1099 |
| | | Ramesses XI | 1099–1069 |

**THIRD INTERMEDIATE PERIOD**

| Twenty-first Dynasty | | Twenty-third Dynasty | |
|---|---|---|---|
| Smendes I | 1069–1043 | Pedubast I | 818–793 |
| Amenemnisu | 1043–1039 | Iuput I | 804–783 |
| Psusennes I | 1039–991 | Shoshenq IV | 783–777 |
| Amenemope | 993–984 | Osorkon III | 777–749 |
| Osochor | 984–978 | Takeloth III | 754–734 |
| Siamun | 978–959 | Rudamun | 734–731 |
| Psusennes II | 959–945 | Iuput II | 731–720 |
| | | Shoshenq VI | 720–715 |
| Twenty-second Dynasty | | | |
| Shoshenq I | 945–924 | Twenty-fourth Dynasty | |
| Osorkon I | 924–889 | Tefnakhte I | 727–720 |
| Shoshenq II | c. 890 | Bakenranef | 720–715 |
| Takeloth I | 889–874 | | |
| Osorkon II | 874–850 | Twenty-fifth (Kushite) Dynasty | |
| Takeloth II | 850–825 | Alara | c. 780–760 |
| Shoshenq III | 825–773 | Kashta | c. 760–747 |
| Pimay | 773–767 | Piankhy | 747–716 |
| Shoshenq V | 767–730 | Shabako | 716–702 |
| Osorkon IV | 730–715 | Shebitku | 702–690 |
| | | Taharqa | 690–664 |
| | | Tanwetamani | 664–656 |

should prove chronologically important to their study. Moreover, it seems likely that the cultures of the contact areas will prove to have had interconnections with more remote and as yet unknown African cultures, which will thus be linked indirectly to Egyptian chronology.

Radiocarbon, thermoluminescence and similar dating methods (with their still considerable and perhaps irreducible margins of error) cannot contribute significantly to Egyptian dynastic chronology. However, they are most important for the absolute chronology of Egyptian archaeological data, i.e. for establishing dates for many structures, occupation strata and graves associated with sites in Egypt or Egyptian settlements abroad, and for the absolute time-ranges of the specific types and techniques of Egyptian artifacts of all kinds. Political, social and economic changes within Egypt and the chronology and nature of its continually changing foreign contacts are strongly reflected in the archaeological record, which often reveals aspects of these historical phenomena that the written sources either never did or no longer do preserve.

## The data

During the period 1552–664 BC Egypt generated a great mass of richly varied data suitable for analysis by historians. Archaeologically, there is a variety of settlement types, including extensive urban complexes, palaces and fortresses, as well as smaller rural or more specialized villages. Temples of varying sizes were frequent, either as parts of larger units or as centres of settlement complexes. And the dead, of all social strata, were habitually buried in cemeteries. To a degree these types of archaeological data overlap. A wide range of socio-economic status and of profession is reflected in the remains of large towns; palaces and temples had significant resemblances in appearance and function; and the cemeteries yield many decorated chapel walls depicting the social types and characteristic occupations of the population, as well as numerous artifacts of secular as well as specifically funerary use. Despite this overlapping, however, the total complexity of Egyptian society and history cannot be appreciated without fully representative samples of all the types of archaeological data.

In the apparently abundant textual data a most important distinction should be made between *archival* material and the *monumental* texts. The archival texts – usually on fragile papyrus or small ostraca (pottery or limestone fragments) include the varied records of government at all levels (e.g. official reports, court proceedings, land registers) and the mass of letters, memoranda, agreements and wills generated by the population as a whole. A related category of more specialized texts includes literary works, religious material, mathematical and medical records and the like. The monumental texts are those carved or painted upon the walls of temples and tombs or upon artifacts designed for these contexts, such as statuary, offering-tables and coffins.

The complementary character of the two main sets of textual data is vital for the reconstruction of Egyptian history. Despite frequent and useful inclusion of historical and biographical information, the fundamental purposes of most monumental texts are limited and religious. They are not concerned with the details of civil and religious government or of the ordering of social relationships (all of which are richly represented in papyri and ostraca). Addressed primarily to the gods, the monumental texts present a highly idealized version of Egyptian history and life.

In Egyptian belief both the formal appearance and essential natures of their political, social and economic systems had been fixed by a creator god aeons earlier. The network of relationships which linked the members of the Egyptian community to each other and to foreign political and cultural units were part of an immutable world order (see pp. 196–7). This idealism which dominates the monumental texts is historically significant since a continuous interaction between the ideal and the real, between ideology and practice, was important in policy-making and in political and social relationships. However, in order not to offend the gods, important but deviant events and practices had to be ignored or at best referred to in oblique terms. They must often be inferred from changes in the pattern of political or ritual activity, unusual combinations of titles and offices or the desecration of royal and private monuments, and are only revealed in detail in archival and similar records.

Thus any significant political or religious act – conservative, reformative or innovative – was invariably presented to the gods as being in accordance with a long-established, universal order. Akhenaten, a religious innovator, claimed to 'live upon' Ma'at (Wilson 1969, p. 370), the ancient personification of that order (pp. 196–7), but his successor Tutankhamen abolished that innovation with the claim that 'Ma'at is established, she causes falsehood to be the abomination of the land, as in (the land's) first time' (Bennett 1939). Akhenaten himself is never referred to in subsequent monumental texts, but his true status in later times is expressed unambiguously in the archival record, where he had to be referred to for dating purposes; there he is identified as 'the Enemy' (Gardiner 1905, pp. 11, 23). Offences against Ma'at, frequently referred to in the archives, were ignored in the monumental record. An assassination attempt upon Ramesses III is described in great detail in papyri generated by the subsequent state trial but is nowhere referred to in the extensive texts in his temples or tomb.

Given the potential richness and variety of the data, and the essential complementary interrelationships of the different types, it is, therefore, disappointing to record that the modern scholar has a most disproportionate representation at his disposal. Information derived from inevitably biased textual and archaeological data from temples and cemeteries far outweighs that from settlement remains and archival or functionally short-lived texts.

Several factors are responsible for this imbalance and, of these, cultural ones are the least significant. Admittedly, politically unstable, economically depressed periods (especially the Third Intermediate Period) produce fewer major monumental buildings and elaborate tombs, and customs can change in important ways. Scenes of daily life on tomb walls and the funerary deposition of artifacts of secular use, for example, are much less frequent after the New Kingdom. Nevertheless, throughout the entire period there was always considerable building activity in the towns and villages, and large quantities of archival and similar material were produced.

Preservation is a more critical factor. Throughout Egypt most of the mud-brick palaces and settlements, with their invaluable, archival and other textual material, were located in the alluvial plain of the Nile, as were perforce many of the Delta cemeteries. These remains therefore were particularly susceptible to damage from the annual inundation, the rising level of the plain and the water table and the activities of a dense rural population. Many temples of the New Kingdom and after, however, were built of stone and, whatever their location, either have survived largely intact or at least have yielded many inscribed elements. Moreover, in Middle and Upper Egypt cemeteries were usually located in the low desert or valley cliffs flanking the alluvial plain and, apart from the ravages of plundering, are relatively well preserved.

Most critical of all, however, are systematic exploration and recovery, for without these, we cannot estimate the degree to which information has been genuinely and irretrievably lost through damage. For reasons of traditional interests and convenience, Egyptologists have tended to concentrate on material from cemeteries of Upper and Middle Egypt and from temple sites; there are few excavated settlement sites for any period, although many certainly exist, and both earlier and recent work has shown that Delta sites in general are better preserved than might be expected. Moreover, certain areas and, to a degree, certain periods have been traditional foci for scholarly attention, especially the cemeteries of Memphis and Thebes, and the temples of the latter, in the New Kingdom. This means that our knowledge of provincial history is extremely patchy and that many major sites in the Delta, which was a particularly important area after the New Kingdom, have not been adequately explored.

The inadequacies of the data explain the inevitably conjectural or indecisive character of many conclusions about specific events or general patterns within Egyptian history, and exacerbate the normal problems of historical interpretation created by the assumptions and values of individual historians. For example, one scholar notes the 'absolute power' of the Eighteenth Dynasty kings in all spheres, while another claims that they 'relinquished [their] religious [and military] authority to others' (compare Hayes (1973, p. 313) with Wilson (1974, p. 401)). The usurpation of monuments and a contemporary, archival reference to conflict during the Twentieth Dynasty suggest to one historian a civil war, with all its political and social implications, but to another, merely customary activity and an 'obscure local conflict' (compare Černý (1975, pp. 612–13) with Kitchen (1972)).

## THE EGYPTIAN WORLD-VIEW, 1552–664 BC

The world-view of a society is here defined as a set of concepts, held by all or most of its members, about the natural, human and supernatural worlds of which that society is a part; and about the interrelationships which link these worlds into a meaningful, intelligible whole. In this sense a world-view is not an intellectual abstraction but rather an historically important phenomenon which plays a major part in shaping the political, social, and economic life of the society. Since a specific and identifiable world-view dominated Egyptian thought, attitudes, and actions throughout the period discussed here a preliminary discussion of it renders material later in this chapter more readily intelligible and eliminates repetitious commentary.

At the outset it can be said that throughout the period 1552–664 BC, there was no basic change in the fundamentals of the Egyptian world-view, although there were important shifts of emphasis, particularly in the Third Intermediate Period. Moreover, the world-view described below was shared by all strata of society, albeit with inevitable variations in sophistication.

Several major factors contributed to the shaping, sustaining, and social pervasiveness of the Egyptian world-view. Tradition was an extremely important one. New Kingdom and later Egypt enjoyed an unbroken linguistic and cultural unity with its past, accessible through rich and intelligible textual and iconographic records, and the world-view of earlier periods continued to be a most potent model for contemporary thought and action. Its potency derived from a characteristic Egyptian religious belief. Through both their ritual and social activity men had a vital role to play in ensuring the continuity and survival of an ideal universal order – *ma'at* (p. 196) – established by a creator god aeons earlier. Conformity to earlier patterns of political and religious life was therefore encouraged, and innovations – if they were to be successful – had to adapt but not radically alter the supernaturally sanctioned formal structure.

The influence of the earlier world-view was then not dependent solely on an unconscious process of cultural transmission. Rather, ancient precepts and beliefs were deliberately sought out as guides for current policies and behaviour, while increasingly in the Third Intermediate Period there were also copies and adaptations of earlier attempts at rendering the Egyptian world-view in visual terms – in painting, reliefs, statuary and even architecture. Archaism was partly a style, partly manipulative propaganda; but it was also a process of ritual and religious significance. When there were significant changes in historical circumstances their effect was to *reinforce* the traditional world-view; partly this was due to the quality of these changes (pp. 194–6), but also to the inherent flexibility of the world-view and the supernatural strength it embodied. By repeating ancient formulations of the early world-view, reviving the names of famous kings and individuals and by copying the style and content of earlier art-forms, the Egyptians believed they created channels along which the supernatural potency of the past flowed into the present ensuring the success of the attitudes being emulated.

Particularly important for the sustaining of a similar world-view over time were basic continuities in the natural and human environment. There was no major climatic change, although periodic changes in the volume of the annual inundation had economic repercussions. The floral and faunal repertoire remained essentially unchanged throughout the period except for the introduction of the horse from Asia (*c.* 1600 BC), an innovation which enhanced both warfare and communications (giving rise to chariotry and, perhaps as early as 930 BC, cavalry).

The size, density and ethnolinguistic homogeneity of the population was another important factor. No doubt the absolute population size fluctuated as it did in mediaeval and recent times, but its general parameters are indicated by estimates of a population of 2 900 000 to 4 500 000 for the late New Kingdom and by explicit references to a figure of 7 000 000 to 7 500 000 for Hellenistic and Roman Egypt. These last two figures are unlikely to have been reached in pre-Hellenistic times. Assuming that some 6 000 000 arouras (about 1 500 000 hectares) were cultivated in pre-Hellenistic times, the average density was fairly high, and, in fact, there was a higher density in the more fertile and 'urbanized' regions (p. 213). Over the entire 1200 years substantial groups of foreigners were absorbed, but they never appeared in overwhelming numbers, and despite the 'official' prominence of Aramaic under the Persians, the Egyptian language and its characteristic writing systems survived far beyond the period discussed here.

Essentially, then, the population provided a strong and concentrated resource base, without being so large as to create administrative and social problems unprecedented in earlier times. Largely sedentary and agricultural, the population remained amenable to centralized control, and its density created a favourable environment for the communication of uniform ideas and attitudes, both geographically and across socio-economic divisions. It was characterized by a set of social interactions and conflicts similar to those of earlier periods and therefore requiring no basic change in attitudes or governmental policies.

The governmental system enjoyed great authority because of its antiquity and supernatural implications. It was adequate to meet the perennial social and economic needs of the population and it was adept at reinforcing and enhancing its own political power. The form of this government was a unique, quasi-divine kingship, the desirability of which to the Egyptians is evident from its perpetuation throughout the period and later. It is true that its partial disintegration in the Third Intermediate Period (pp. 232ff.) led to a shift of emphasis, then and in the Late Period, whereby the personal political initiative of the king was minimized in the monumental record (p. 186) and his role as an 'instrument' of the gods emphasized (Otto 1954); but the king remained potentially and usually in reality the most powerful figure in government. Strong centralization, combined with a comprehensive concept of government's functions, encouraged the maintenance of a departmentalized and hierarchical structure.

The functions of government, as conceived by the Egyptians, are identified explicitly in various texts and implicitly by actual policies. Always vigorously stressed was a religious function reflecting the supernatural basis of the governmental system, the provision of ritual attention and economic benefits to the kings' 'fathers, all the gods, in the desire to placate them by doing that which their kas [spirits] love, so that they may protect [Egypt]' (Bennett 1939).

Externally the government was expected to maintain Egypt's territorial integrity and, under the auspices of the gods, extend its frontiers. Internally, its functions were more varied. These included maintaining and enhancing the agricultural economy upon which depended Egypt's ability to produce the surplus needed to support the governmental superstructure. They also included the development and maintenance of the regulating and arbitrating mechanisms that would control the entropy that threatens any society.

The imperative to create civic and individual security led to a continuous stress upon the necessity for efficient, impartial and incorruptible administration. These maxims recur throughout the period, but are most concisely summarized in the formulaic verbal instructions issued by the kings in the New Kingdom during the installation of their viziers (p. 208). 'Law' and the 'regulations' must be adhered to throughout the bureaucracy, 'for what is required is the doing of justice by the fiat of the vizier... [for] he has been its rightful guardian since [the time of the creator] God' (Faulkner 1955). The persistence of this ideal as an integral element of the Egyptian world-view is more important than the frequent trangressions against it, for it reflects that national consensus without which no system of government can long exist. We cannot pose as an absolute the question as to 'whether these ideals were obligations or façade' (Helck 1958, p. 543) and suggest a dichotomy between ideal and actual motives in the activities of government, for motivation was complex, involving both self-interest and altruism.

The principal divisions of the society whose world-view we are discussing were the vertical ones of the occupations – this form of social classification was a bureaucratic commonplace – and, cutting across these horizontally, broad socio-economic divisions. The persistence and nature of the chief activities of the population can be appreciated by comparing those listed in a rental record of 1143 BC (the Wilbour

TABLE 3.2    *Small-scale farm-holders recorded in the Wilbour Papyrus (see pp. 227–8 and Helck (1961, p. 260))*

| Plot size in aroura | Priests, % | Citizenesses, % | Soldiers, % | Stable-masters, % | Herdsmen, % |
|---|---|---|---|---|---|
| 2 | 2.91 | 2.63 | — | — | — |
| 3 | 16.50 | 23.16 | 93.22 | 2.89 | — |
| 5 | 62.14 | 59.47 | 5.08 | 92.13 | 80.67 |
| 10 | 17.48 | 10.53 | 1.69 | 3.94 | 13.45 |
| 20 | 0.97 | 4.21 | — | 1.05 | 5.88 |
| Total each occupation | 103 | 190 | 236 | 119 | 381 |

Papyrus) with those enumerated by the historian Herodotus some 700 years later. The earlier document reveals a typical cross-section of contemporary society, a small group of high-ranking and wealthy officials and a much larger group of scribes (i.e. bureaucrats), priests, soldiers (military colonists) stable-masters (concerned with chariotry horses), 'citizenesses', cultivators and herdsmen. Artisans were another important group, not frequent in this particular document because their income came not directly from land but as payment for their products or as government rations. Later, Herodotus (II. 164) describes the principal occupations as those of 'priests, warriors, cowherds, swine-herds, tradesmen, interpreters and pilots'; the obvious omission here is that of 'cultivators'.

The Wilbour Papyrus provides rare specific evidence on the wide range of economic resources to be found in Egyptian society (table 3.2), while broader socio-economic divisions are strongly reflected in textual and archaeological data (fig. 3.1). The elite – the royal dynasty in its fullest sense (pp. 207–9) and the high-ranking officials of government – enjoyed high status, substantial economic benefits and considerable potential for significant activity within the confines of the traditional political system. Of lesser status and economic importance (except in periods of political fragmentation) were the provincial nobilities, also based upon government service but perhaps more secure in the hereditary possession of their offices. A group of lesser bureaucrats, priests, military officers, wealthy farmers and artisans probably had a distinct enough intermediate socio-economic position to be identified as a 'middle class', while the 'lower class', by far the largest segment of the population, had great diversity of occupation (soldiers, minor

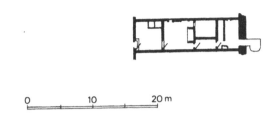

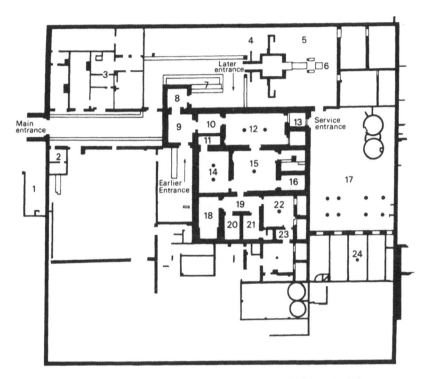

Fig. 3.1    Plans of a nobleman's villa at Tell el-Amarna and of an artisan's house at
Deir el-Medineh. Both New Kingdom.

| | |
|---|---|
| 1 Chariot house | 13 Ante (*sic*) |
| 2 Gatekeeper | 14 West Loggia |
| 3 Servants' quarters | 15 Central room |
| 4 The chapel | 16 Store |
| 5 Chapel garden | 17 Kitchen court |
| 6 Altars | 18 Master's bedroom |
| 7 Flower bed | 19 Vestibule |
| 8 Later porch | 20 Guest's room |
| 9 Earlier porch | 21 Anointing room |
| 10 Vestibule | 22 Inner sitting room |
| 11 Store | 23 Ante |
| 12 North Loggia | 24 Magazines |

officials and priests, tenant-farmers, peasants of virtually serf status and slaves), and also of income and quality of subsistence.

The political influence of the middle and lower classes was extremely limited, and was most evident in times of general disorder and disunity. Nevertheless, their indirect political significance was considerable. The elite, while exploitative, were conscious of the necessity of providing certain basic services and recognizing particular rights in order to ensure social stability. The gods explicitly sanctioned attention to the problems of the less fortunate, and government was aware of the importance of both the appearance and reality of correct behaviour. 'As for a magistrate who judges in public', the Instructions to the Vizier (p. 191) noted, 'wind and water make report of all that he does.' (Faulkner 1955.) Periodic reforms of abuses are well documented, and officials' biographies frequently refer to their aid to the disadvantaged. Indeed, the severe and socially disturbing problems of the Third Intermediate Period appear to have accentuated this aspect of the Egyptian world-view. Thereafter officials felt that the ethical performance of their duties had an intrinsic value, separate from the utilitarian one of making them acceptable to the gods of the afterlife.

Another important continuity was the Egyptian attitude to foreigners. By the New Kingdom centuries of successful military and quasi-military commercial activities in neighbouring regions had established an Egyptian self-image as a culturally superior group whose foreign activities were encouraged by their gods. Despite the shock of the Hyksos invasion (see chapter 2), this image was reinforced by the general success of New Kingdom expansionist policies and the failure of any comparably strong political unit to develop in immediately adjacent areas (except, later, to the south, in Kush). Subsequently, this concept of the nature of the appropriate relationship between Egypt and foreign states had to be adjusted in the face of serious vicissitudes, but it was done without changing its fundamental nature. The Libyans and Kushites who invaded and infiltrated Egypt at various times from the later New Kingdom on were partially and increasingly acculturated, and while conflict later on with 'superpowers' evidently more powerful than Egypt (Assyria, Babylonia and Persia) was psychologically disturbing, several periods of foreign occupation did not in fact substantially alter the traditional governmental and social structure or its supporting religious ideology. A potent factor in sustaining the sense of Egyptian superiority was its supernatural validity, which made reverses abroad, however serious, mere incidents in a cosmic drama in which Egypt and its gods would ultimately triumph. Mythic and real struggles were inextricably fused; the state, personified by the king, ritually aided the gods in their implicitly always successful struggle against supernatural enemies and disorder, while the gods promised the state ultimate victory over its foreign enemies, who were themselves part of that threatening chaos.

It has been argued that changes in internal and external historical circumstances were so great that by the Late Period there was a fundamental change in the Egyptian world-view. In this interpretation Late Period Egypt was afflicted by a 'Janusgesicht' (Janus head) (Kienitz 1967), a national schizophrenia characteristic of a culture in a state of advanced decay. In this view, Archaism reflected a deliberate effort to expunge the memories of the Third Intermediate Period; society was static and rigid; and extreme tension was generated by the contrast between traditional concepts of foreign relations and the reverses suffered by Egypt abroad. Moreover, traditional, often meaningless religious beliefs and practices were out of keeping with a strong, if largely subterranean, belief in ethically-based behaviour. At least partially, 'this culture was dying away from within' (Otto 1951).

The present writer, however, sees the Third Intermediate and Late Periods as representing complex and subtle responses by a flexible political and ideological system to greatly changed circumstances, but not a fundamental reordering or internal disintegration. Egypt did not need to, and apparently did not, perceive itself as in decline; despite periods of foreign occupation, it remained relatively prosperous for most of the Late Period and was often successful in its foreign-policy aims. It did finally collapse before the innovative military machine of the Macedonians (323 BC), but so did the other Near Eastern powers. And if national resistance to the Macedonian Ptolemies was less successful than that against the Persians (343 BC), this was partly due to the differing attitudes of the new conquerors, which were more in keeping with the traditional Egyptian world-view. The Ptolemies treated Egypt as their territorial centre, not as a province; they exploited traditional religious beliefs to their own advantage and encouraged an at least partially successful Egypto-Greek symbiosis which eased the problems of internal cultural heterogeneity.

The social pervasiveness of the Egyptian world-view – allowing for the varying degrees of sophistication to be expected in a social spectrum ranging from a literate court and bureaucracy to a mass of illiterate peasants of narrow horizons – was due to several factors. The state itself encouraged the acceptance of a world-view in which the existing political system had an integral position and the world-view of the elite maintained a sustaining contact with the attitudes and needs of Egyptian society as a whole. Another important mediating agency was the middle class, to some degree socially mobile and linked to both the elite and the lower classes. Another was the occupational categories, which formed important chains of contact and communication running through all three classes.

Also significant was the deep involvement of government and all segments of the population in agricultural life and in the values, priorities and religious activities naturally associated with it. Most administrative activity was concerned with enhancing and exploiting the agricultural economy; much state and private religious activity was directed towards ensuring agricultural fertility; and land and its products were the chief sources of wealth and status. The elite owned substantial estates and expressed a strong and genuine appreciation of the amenities of rural life, while urbanism never became strong enough to generate a clear dichotomy between city and rural life.

Finally, a potent source of the world-view's tenacity and pervasiveness was the religious system and its characteristic myths and rituals, which were shared by all classes of society. Modern scholarly reaction to the rich complexities of Egyptian religion is diverse. It has been variously described as 'vast accumulations of mythological rubbish' (Gardiner 1961) and as 'the ever growing and creative thought of an intelligent polytheism' susceptible to a 'subtle and profound syncretism' (Redford 1976). The latter attitude is more historically accurate, recognizing the utility and flexibility of the system. Certainly the course of Egyptian history cannot be understood without continual reference to the intricate interrelations between religious and secular life.

Historically of great importance was the concept of *ma'at* – the appropriate arrangement of the universe and of human affairs – an effort to summarize the Egyptian world-view in coherent, mythic form. Centuries old by the time of the New Kingdom, the concept of *ma'at* was a crystallization of a myriad of religious and secular ideas, and its continuity depended upon *their* continuity; nevertheless, its very existence as a formalized statement of Egyptian beliefs helped to perpetuate the ideas and attitudes upon which it was based.

The clearest expression of the significance of *ma'at* is found in several creation myths. The identity of the creator god and the mechanism of creation vary (compare the masturbation of Atum with the intellectual and emotional acts of Ptah), but the basic theme is identical: a unique creator god emerges from primeval chaos, sets the creative process in operation by creating the other gods, fashions the universe with those astronomical and seasonal rhythms and geographic circumstances characteristic of the Egyptian environment and, finally, establishes the bases of social life and technological organization as understood by the Egyptians.

(Thus justice was given to) him who does what is liked (and injustice to) him who does what is disliked. Thus life was given to him who has peace and death was given to him who has sin. Thus were made all work and all crafts, the movement of the legs, and the activity of every member – [Ptah] had formed the gods, he had made cities, he had founded nomes [provinces], he had put the gods in their shrines.... (Wilson 1969, p. 5.)

The world-view expressed through the myths was not complacent and self-satisfied. The Egyptians had a keen sense of the tension and conflicts which threatened political and social stability and of vicissitudes in the natural environment which could create acute personal or national distress. These fears were extended into the supernatural world, being embodied in a number of ambiguous or clearly malevolent figures and most specifically in Seth, a powerful god associated with disorder, sterility, sexual aberration, the desert and thunder, and the Egyptians felt themselves deeply involved in the continuous efforts of the gods to stave off a threatening chaos. Nevertheless, the forces of disorder were felt to be under the control of the creator god; 'Reharakte (king of the gods) says: "Let Seth...be given to me (as son). And he shall speak out of the sky, and men shall be afraid of him."' (Wilson 1969, p. 17.)

There were many gods with different personalities and functions, each having one or more main cult centres. This regional diversity was further complicated in that some, probably many, communities had distinctive pantheons dominated by a local form of the chief regional god but incorporating others selected by criteria which varied according to the nature of the community. Despite this variety, however, the various personalities and functions of individual gods interlocked to form the very substance of the universe, while theological synthesis, mythic marriages and other relationships created many additional links amongst them. Besides the gods, certain genii and spirits and the dead formed other significant supernatural communities, but the ritual needs of all three groups were very similar, creating great uniformity in both cult activity and in the structures which were the scenes of this activity.

All classes of supernatural beings were potent, even the dead, to whom letters were sometimes addressed accusing them of harming the

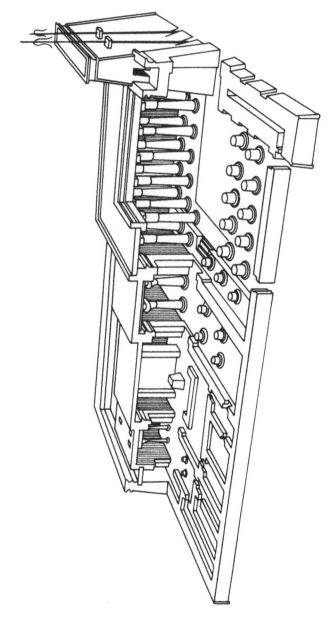

Fig. 3.2 Sectional view of a typical New Kingdom temple. Its form reflects the processional character of the rituals followed, while its rich relief decoration moved from the 'public' acts of the reigning king (e.g. victory in battle, prowess in the hunt) on the pylons and sometimes in the first columned hall, to a depiction of the king's intimate relations with the gods and of his performance of the cult.

living, or appealing to them to bring good fortune. The gods, however, were the most powerful figures and communication with them was of greatest concern. Their desires and wishes might be indirectly expressed, as when a low Nile or a major political disturbance implied divine anger, but they were frequently sought out explicitly by means of an oracle, a practice first seen in the New Kingdom and persisting thereafter. Oracles were employed at high levels of government in the New Kingdom to ratify important decisions, but later, as royal authority lessened, they were resorted to for relatively minor administrative and judicial decisions. Government appeals to the oracle were merged with a more generalized function of oracles which affected all levels of society. Oracles, which were always delivered by a specific god but variously in his 'national' or local form, were a source of reassurance and guidance for individuals and an important social mechanism easing the tensions and conflicts inherent in closely-knit and largely self-regulating town and village communities. The local kenbet-councils (p. 214) were clearly unable or unwilling to solve many disputes involving ownership or rights and cases of theft or other crimes, and these were therefore submitted to a god as a neutral arbitrator of unimpeachable authority. While some manipulation was involved, there is good evidence that the process was carried out in good faith under the influence of 'suggestion and autosuggestion' (fig. 3.3) (Černý 1957, p. 76).

Myths provide us important insights to the world-view, but ritual and not myth or theology dominated Egyptian religious life. The religious experiences and perceptions of the individual were insignificant compared to the ritual activity of the community which, through cult and festival, hoped to effect 'the renewal and rejuvenation of the life of the cosmos, of the community and the individual' (Bleeker 1967, p. 22). Primary foci for the rites were of course the temples, which ranged from the great national shrines to hundreds of smaller, local ones and which followed a uniform plan and decorative system (fig. 3.2). Temples had a cosmological symbolism: each represented a universe, the roof being the sky and the sanctuary the horizon where the sun rose and set, symbolizing an eternal cycle or renewal, decline and rebirth in the universe. At least once the royal city itself became subsumed into this concept; Tell el-Amarna (p. 220) was conceived of as set totally within a natural temple, defined by the real sky and horizons of the valley. In both the houses of the nobility and of the middle and lower classes there was considerable domestic cult activity directed towards

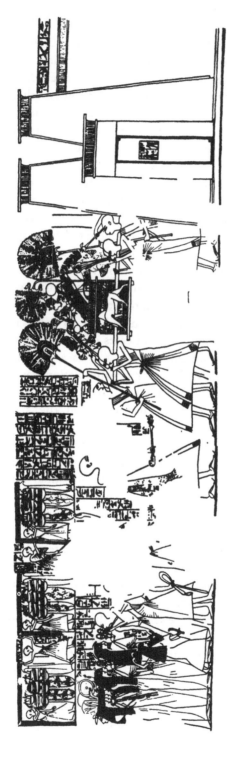

Fig. 3.3   An oracle is sought from a New Kingdom local god, the deified King Amenhotep I, whose image has just been carried on a litter out of its temple (right). The god's High Priest, Amenmose, stands before the litter holding an incense burner and wearing a leopard skin, and asks the god to judge which of two men (bowing and partially obliterated behind the high priest) is 'right' in some unspecified dispute. The god explicitly finds one of the men 'right', probably by 'forcing' his bearers to approach the favoured disputant. (See Černý 1962, pp. 42–5 and fig. 9.)

the same gods, while the cemeteries, both royal and non-royal, were other centres of fundamentally similar rituals.

Turning to the main political and economic effects of the religious system, we note first that while it contributed to the dominant position of the king, it also subtly qualified his apparently absolute power. Dogmatically, the survival of the kingship was vital; the formal relationship between Egypt and its gods, which symbolized its integral position within a divinely-created universal order, depended upon the king, who was the chief channel of divine power and guidance. To maintain the order established by the gods the king was given supreme political authority, while he sustained a fruitful reciprocal relationship between men and gods through his unique ritual role. All the priests serving the myriad cults were merely his delegates, temple iconography depicting *only* the king performing the ritual. Yet the king's dogmatic position was not unambiguous. He enjoyed the powers of and reverence due to the gods, but he was implicitly and sometimes explicitly subordinate to them; even the powerful kings of the New Kingdom sometimes sought 'a command... from the great throne [of a god], an oracle of the god himself' (Breasted 1906, II s. 285). Moreover, kings did not have the *specific* wonder-working powers of the gods. The royal temple built by each king was for his funerary cult for, after death, kings no longer remained 'on earth' but, like the gods, dwelt in some celestial realm.

This dogmatic ambiguity had its effects in the political sphere. The king's ritual and dogmatic position enhanced his political authority and motivation. The altruistic performance of his duties was identical with his self-interest in maintaining his political supremacy and that of his dynasty. Yet the existence of *ma'at* set up a kind of formal standard against which the king's ability, and the degree of divine approval he enjoyed, could be measured. Weakness, inability or inefficiency on the part of the king could create persistent maladministration in Egypt or losses abroad, all evidence of the disintegration of *ma'at*. That such an attitude was inherent in Egyptian thought is clearly revealed in the Demotic Chronicle (Ptolemaic period), which attributes the fall of several Late Period kings to their failure to satisfy the gods, and is seen earlier in the destruction of monuments that had been set up by certain kings later deemed offensive to *ma'at* and in the common vernacular identification of Akhenaten (in the Nineteenth Dynasty) as 'the Enemy'.

Every Egyptian god was supplied with a temple to house his cult-image, a staff of priests and servants, and estates and other gifts to support his establishment. The chief gods (and amongst these Amen, in various forms, was the most important in the New Kingdom and held a more qualified dominance for the remainder of the period) had special functions and status, reflected in the size and elaboration of their temples, the great number and variety of their personnel, and their extensive and diverse possessions (lands, mines, quarries, ships, and even villages and towns). In about 1153 BC the temples as a whole owned about one-third of Egypt's cultivable land and about one-fifth of its inhabitants, although, on the broader time-scale, the size of the temple holdings doubtless fluctuated considerably.

However, while the high priests of the main cults, and especially the High Priest of Amen of Thebes, were undoubtedly high-ranking and influential figures, we must not exaggerate their political importance. Theologically, they were subordinate to the king, high priest of all the gods, and the nature of the religious system was such that the priests (literally, 'the god's servants') could undertake no politically disturbing theological initiative; influential 'prophets', in the Hebrew sense, were unknown. All religious appointments and promotions were theoretically subject to royal approval and, while hereditary rights to certain positions did become firmly established, so did they in all other branches of government as well. The administration of religious establishments was essentially part of the civil government, and although the temples were income-generating (through renting land and trading), the collection and control of this income appears to have been, at least partially, subject to the civil government. Substantial amounts of royal income, in the form of booty, land and other gifts, were transferred to the temples, but royal relatives and loyal officials were also appointed to many of the resulting religious sinecures. Most significantly of all, the temple establishments had neither the necessity nor the occasion of developing substantial military or police powers, coercive resources which were intimately linked to political power in ancient Egypt. Temple establishments were, therefore, on the whole more subject to political manipulation and exploitation, rather than initiators of such activity.

## INTERNAL HISTORY

The period between 1552 and 664 BC is conventionally divided into two main phases, the New Kingdom (1552–1069 BC) and the Third Intermediate Period (1069–664 BC). The New Kingdom was a period of extraordinary Egyptian expansion abroad and of strong centralization and considerable stability internally. During the Third Intermediate Period Egypt's foreign contacts contracted sharply and foreign policy was with rare exceptions defensive and unaggressive until the Twenty-fifth Dynasty (747–656 BC). These characteristics of Third Intermediate Period foreign relations directly reflect a high degree of internal decentralization and indeed at times disintegration of government, breaking out sporadically into civil war.

Despite their strong differences the two periods are of course intimately related; the Third Intermediate Period was the direct result of political, social and economic processes which came into being in the New Kingdom. The exact natures and interactions of these processes are – and will long remain – matters of debate; but a description and analysis of them, however qualified, must be the substance of any historical discussion of the New Kingdom and Third Intermediate Period. The details of Egyptian relations with other parts of the ancient world are not of prime interest in this book.[1]

In the following sections, emphasis will be placed upon the *internal* effects of foreign affairs; variations in the formal structure and in the tone and character of government, and the political implications of these variations; the interplay of competition and conflict within the political system; and the effect of all these factors upon the relations between government and governed and upon the social and economic condition of the population as a whole.

## THE NEW KINGDOM (1552–1069 BC)

For the New Kingdom especially a brief description of the general pattern of Egypt's foreign affairs and certain key events within them is essential for the understanding of internal history. During this period Egypt maintained control over extensive foreign conquests and sustained its Levantine position successfully against the pressure of the other two dominant powers in the region, the Mittanians and their successors, the Hittites. Extensive political–commercial contacts were developed with a number of other states and groups in the Aegean, the Near East and East Africa. During the reign of Ramesses III, in the twelfth century BC, two critical events occurred: the Asiatic conquests were apparently lost and the political and ethnic structure of Syria, Palestine and Anatolia was drastically altered as the result of a mysterious population movement, that of the 'Sea-Peoples', who surged along the eastern Mediterranean and had to be repulsed at the seaward and eastern frontiers of Egypt itself. At the same time, perhaps

---

[1] For the latter, reference should be made to the *Cambridge Ancient History*, 3rd ed, vol. II, and to Kitchen's *The Third Intermediate Period in Egypt*.

not coincidentally, Libyan pressure, which had been building up for forty years, reached a climax in two abortive invasions of the western Delta.

To a degree, these developments were uncontrollable; neither the Hittites nor any other state in the region had been able to resist the 'Sea-Peoples', while the Libyans had never before demonstrated the strength they showed from the reign of Ramesses II onward. But it is significant that Egyptian reaction was comparatively weak. After the time of Ramesses II Egypt was unable to regain its position in the Levant, now broken up into a number of comparatively small kingdoms with no dominant 'great power'; it could not prevent massive and continuing Libyan infiltration; and, only about eighty years after Ramesses III's death, Egypt also lost its African conquests after a struggle that was more of a civil war than a foreign conflict. Clearly the reverses of the late New Kingdom must have had serious internal repercussions, some of which will be discussed below; but are they sufficient in themselves to account for the deteriorating situation in foreign affairs, let alone the internal political problems of the Third Intermediate Period that followed?

## The structure of government

To attempt to answer that question we must turn to the internal history of the New Kingdom, and in particular to an important historical problem that is epitomized in two quotations. The first is of a type repeated continuously in royal texts: the god Amen declares to King Tuthmosis III 'I cause your victories to circulate in all lands. The gleaming [serpent], she who is upon my brow, is your servant, [so that] there shall arise none rebellious to you as far as that which heaven encircles.' (Wilson 1969, p. 374.) The second is an extremely rare type: Piankh, High Priest of Amen and generalissimo of southern Egypt – hence one who owed his position theoretically to royal appointment and favour – writes contemptuously of Ramesses XI in a letter: 'Of whom is Pharaoh superior still?' (Wente 1967, p. 53.) This apparent contradiction cannot be interpreted too arbitrarily. It is only partly a matter of chronology, for although Piankh's question reflects a real decline in royal power and authority towards the end of the New Kingdom, the supremacy of the king was still formally stated in the monumental record. It is therefore also a problem of sources, for the paucity of those letters, memoranda and private reports against which we can check the validity of the picture of royal power presented in the monumental texts makes it extremely difficult at any time to assess the degree to which the king's political independence was circumscribed by the system of which he was part.

Piankh's attitude, although extreme as a result of specific historical circumstances, reflected a fundamental characteristic of the political system. An inherent problem of a comparatively highly centralized system based on a single individual, the king, is that whatever the king's theoretical powers may be, his political effectiveness depends upon the support and co-operation of others. Inevitably they will attempt to exploit this situation to their own advantage. Beyond this particular problem is a more general one, the development of a concentration of power elsewhere within the system which will create the potential for an individual or group to usurp important functions nominally reserved for the king and his chief executive officials, and perhaps to replace the latter and even usurp the kingship.

In general the reality of royal power through most of the New Kingdom seems confirmed by the admittedly largely inferential evidence. This includes the explicitly acknowledged role of the king in administrative and military affairs, the long-sustained and successful policy of Egyptian expansion, the executive and economic strength indicated by the extensive temple-building programmes undertaken by most of the kings, and the development of a luxuriant mythology concerning the quasi-divine aspects of the kingship. More specific events are also revealing, particularly those connected with Akhenaten (pp. 219–22). A significant but gradual change in the nature and strength of royal power seems to become evident first in the late Nineteenth Dynasty and increasingly in the Twentieth. Prior to this time, favourable circumstances abroad, the structure of the political system itself and the supervisory and manipulative abilities of the kings appear to have rendered the royal power, so frequently celebrated in the monumental record, a reality.

Throughout the New Kingdom, the Levant and north-east Africa were the foreign areas of greatest Egyptian interest. Egypt had already been active in these income-producing regions for one and a half millennia, and the traditional stimuli to renewed contact and expansion were reinforced in the early Eighteenth Dynasty by the presence in both regions of powerful forces which had been sources of great humiliation and danger to Egypt in the Second Intermediate Period (see chapter 2).

The effect of foreign affairs was certainly significant internally. The expulsion of the Hyksos and of the Kushites in c. 1555–1540 BC (see chapter 2), the expansion, which was a logistical necessity to prevent further invasion, and the conflict which this expansion generated with Mittanians and the Hittites, meant that Egypt was on a permanent war-footing. The early Eighteenth Dynasty kings were true war-leaders, directing and often personally participating in major campaigns, establishing a tradition that continued to be an ideologically potent convention and often a reality for the rest of the New Kingdom. However, the kings were not preoccupied with campaigning and in fact devoted most of their reigns to internal affairs. Apart from those of the atypical Tuthmosis III, campaigns were usually restricted to the early years of each reign, partly perhaps because actual or incipient revolts tended to occur at a reign-change, but probably also to demonstrate the military abilities of the new king and the divine approval he enjoyed.

These periodic campaigns, the need to control the conquered lands and the necessity for rapid military action in external emergencies, led to the development of a permanent, professional army. Its professionalism lay in a permanent military administration, headed by a 'great army general', standing garrisons abroad and in Egypt, and a continuous levying and training programme which created a large, experienced reserve which could be rapidly mobilized. In addition, many veterans were settled on farms in Egypt which were inherited by their families so long as the male descendants remained available for military training and service. The army was professional also in its organization, being divided up into various units, primarily infantry and chariotry but also more specialized units, each with its own hierarchy of officers. There was thus created a most significant element in the political structure, highly organized and with a potential for great coercive force, which was also thoroughly integrated into the fabric of society because of its dependence on military colonists and general levies. Its functional and ideological links with the kingship were strong, and were enhanced by royal policies described below.

Expansion and conquest also augmented royal income and increased the manipulative capabilities of the kings. To the traditional income from taxes, the personal possessions of the dynasty, and a monopolistic position in foreign trade were now added sporadic but often large amounts of booty, regularly delivered foreign tribute, and expanded, quasi-political trading opportunities. As war-leader and sole delegate of the gods, the king naturally received much of this additional income himself, and had firm control over the distribution of the remainder. He was able to emphasize the status of the royal family by the scale and embellishments of its palaces and estates, demonstrate his ideological authority by lavishly endowing the major temples and reinforce this political power by judiciously rewarding loyal bureaucrats and officers.

The exigencies of foreign affairs and the military experiences of the kings and of many important officials also strongly affected the structure of government. This was based on a Middle Kingdom prototype and, like it, responded efficiently to certain perennial social and economic needs of the population, but the New Kingdom structure was less complex and thus more rapidly responsive to royal command, mobilization and the need for creating war-materials and supplies. From the point of view of internal politics, the most interesting aspect of government is that its very structure reinforced the dominant position of the kings and enhanced their manipulative abilities, but at the same time presented them with serious supervisory problems and created the potential for other competitive and divisive power centres to develop.

The governmental structure is well documented and is summarized on fig. 3.4. This schematic version of course ignores some known changes in administrative organization and does not reflect the fluctuations of power throughout the system which are, in any case, rarely recorded explicitly in the textual record. But its general outline seems to be valid for the entire New Kingdom. The structure was shaped to a large degree by functional efficiency and geographical circumstances, but these contributed also to royal supremacy, as did a sometimes clearly evidenced manipulation of the system. Thus government was broken into three major units, of which two, internal government and the administration of the conquests, make sense functionally; the third, the dynasty proper, on the other hand had a very limited political role. While it undoubtedly must have been a large and complex group, most of its members were excluded from major political or military office and normally also from the succession, unless they belonged to a certain segment of the direct line. This effectively restrained any individual who might have had some not too remote claim to the supernatural authority emanating from the kingship. Only those dynasty members with a vested interest in maintaining loyalty to the reigning king received important posts: the crown prince – the designated heir – was frequently 'great army general', controlling the military in the king's name; and the king's chief wife, the 'great royal wife' (or, alternatively, her eldest daughter) was appointed 'God's wife of Amen'. This mythologically justifiable role for the chief queen (the New Kingdom kings believed that their mothers had been impregnated by Amen) also

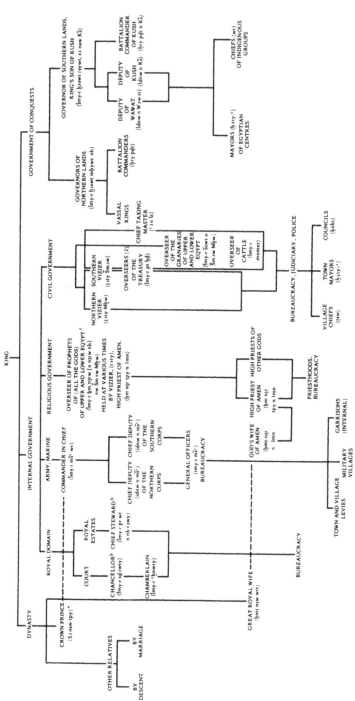

Fig. 3.4  Schematic outline of the developed structure of government in the New Kingdom. The fragility of much of the evidence on which this diagram is based must be emphasized, as must its inability adequately to illustrate significant changes in the structure (for some indication of these, see notes b and c). Nevertheless, the writer believes that the diagram gives a reasonable approximation of the divisions of functions and powers within New Kingdom government.

(a) On the sometimes ambiguous terms used to designate the crown prince, see Kitchen (1972).

(b) On the rise of the 'chief steward' at the expense of the 'chamberlain', see Helck (1958, pp. 80–2).

(c) Held at various times by the vizier, the High Priest of Amen (frequently) and others.

(d) On the office of 'high taxing master', the importance of which is still in dispute and which is as yet dated no earlier than Akhenaten, see especially Gardiner (1948, pp. 10, 110, 161, 206), Helck (1958, pp. 143–5) and Seele (1959, p. 9).

208

brought a substantial portion of Amen's temporal possessions under direct royal control.

Since the king normally spent most of his reign in Egypt, the government of the conquered lands was internally significant to the degree that it might provide a power-base for an individual or group who could then usurp royal functions and perhaps the throne itself. In fact, the richest and politically most sophisticated of the conquests, the 'North lands' along the Mediterranean coast of Asia (fig. 3.5), were unlikely to do so. They were, for topographical and administrative reasons, divided ultimately into three provinces, each with its own governor, usually an Egyptian but sometimes an Asiatic. These governors in practice shared political power with a number of vassal kings and were not militarily strong. The garrisons of Egyptian (and Kushite) troops in the 'Northlands' were small, scattered and under the direct control of several 'battalion-commanders' and not of the governors. For perennial, but small-scale, police and military activities considerable use was made of the forces of the local city states and, in major campaigns, the large armies sent from Egypt were under the command of the king or the 'great army general'. The 'Southlands' (Wawat and Kush), with their Nubian population, were potentially much more significant. The region was ruled by a single governor, who shared no important administrative power with the local chieftains; its military forces were centralized under a single 'battalion-commander'; and it had a geographical unity combined with easy and rapid access to Egypt proper. The power of the Viceroy of Kush was to be important internally at the end of the Twentieth Dynasty.

The internal government of Egypt was divided for functional reasons, into four major units (fig. 3.4) and these were sometimes further divided geographically, in the interests of efficiency and perhaps also of the stability of royal power. Centralized control was maintained by means of the small group of powerful officials who headed each department, who reported directly to the king, and who were appointed and removed by him. It was amongst these that the politically most influential and potentially most divisive individuals within the system were normally to be found. Within the general system, the disposition of coercive power was particularly significant. The military had a minimal role to play in the normal operations of government, being concerned primarily with registering and training those liable for military service, administering the small standing garrisons in Egypt and abroad, stock-piling and dispatching supplies, and mobilizing on a large scale when necessary.

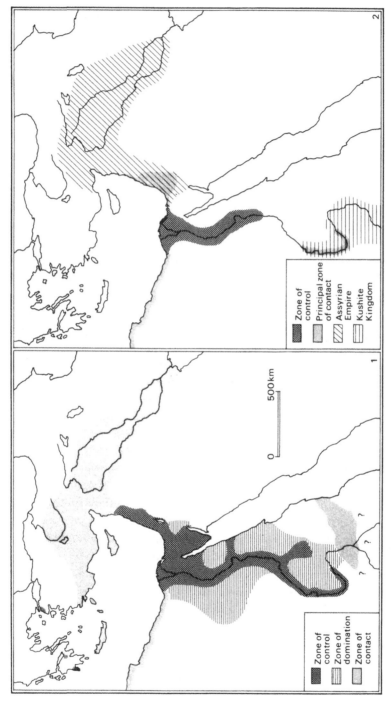

Fig. 3.5    The changing pattern of Egyptian foreign relations. 1, New Kingdom; 2, Third Intermediate Period.

Zone of
control

Principal zone
of contact

Assyrian
Empire

Kushite
Kingdom

500 km

Zone of
control

Zone of
domination

Zone of
contact

The civil government was concerned primarily with regulating agriculture, collecting taxes, administering justice and maintaining civic order and its orders were enforced by a relatively weak police force, the Medjayu.

The personal possessions of the king and the royal family were extensive and formed virtually a separate branch of government which we may call the 'royal domain', while another substantial mass of land and other income-generating assets accumulated under the religious government, a fact that was politically useful to the kings (p. 202). The administration of the religious establishment was particularly fragmentary and the degree to which it came under a centralized control is uncertain; the High Priest of Amen was certainly the most powerful individual within this governmental unit, and he often (although not always) held a post entitled 'overseer of all the priesthoods of Upper and Lower Egypt'. The real, as compared to the titular, importance of this office has not, however, been documented but it was presumably in the royal interest to keep this supernaturally charged and economically wealthy section of the government politically weak. It is interesting in this connection to note that in two New Kingdom depictions of high officials processing in hierarchical order, the sequence is crown prince, viziers, stewards of the royal estate and court, high-ranking military and civil officials and finally important high priests, who are followed by a provincial official in one instance and by lower ranks of priests in the other (Hayes 1973, p. 362).

Dominant as the royal position was, however, each branch of government exercised some degree of effective power. To appreciate better the interplay of power and influence, and the peculiar problems of royal power, we must examine also the political geography of Egypt and the tone and character of government. For the New Kingdom these aspects are comparatively well documented.

Two factors of fundamental importance for the stability of government were the effectiveness of the links between the central and provincial governments and the pervasiveness of royal authority and supervision. Facilitating these was the concentration of population upon the alluvial plain and the usefulness of the Nile as an administrative artery (fig. 3.6), but problems were created by the extreme length of the country, the highly personal character of government and the comparative inefficiency of communication.

The structure of provincial government is poorly documented and the following sketch highly tentative. There was a distinct hierarchy of

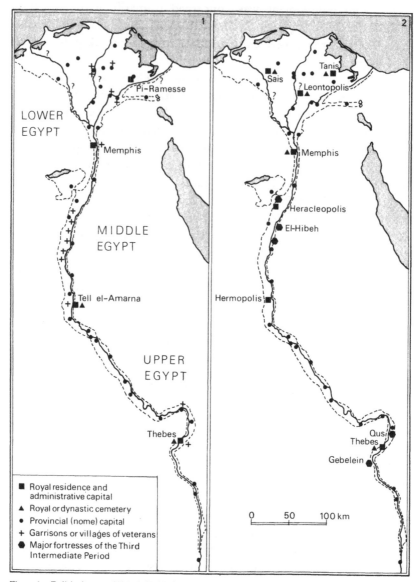

Fig. 3.6    Political map of Egypt in (1) the New Kingdom and (2) the Third Intermediate Period. For garrisons and villages of veterans see Helck (1939, pp. 17–20); those immediately south of Herakleopolis represent a zone of such settlements rather than specific sites (O'Connor 1972a), and the military settlements of the Delta aᵢe inferred from the later importance of Mendes, Sebennytos, Busiris, Bubastis and Pi-Soped as centres for Mashwash soldiery.

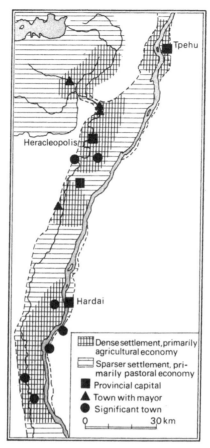

Fig. 3.7  Reconstruction of typical New Kingdom provincial settlement pattern.

settlements. *The* cities were Memphis, Thebes and (later) Pi-Ramesse. Elsewhere, in any given region, the provincial capital was usually the most important administratively and probably the largest in population. It was surrounded by a zone of fairly large and densely concentrated villages (interspersed by rare towns intermediate in administrative function (and size?) between the villages and the capital), which thinned away to smaller, scattered settlements (fig. 3.7). Unfortunately, it is impossible to equate this hierarchy with any certainty to Egyptian nomenclature; 'cities', 'towns' and 'villages' (respectively *niwt*, *dmi* and *whyt*) were distinguished from each other, but the terms appear to be used with great looseness. Slightly less ambiguous are smaller units, such as 'nobleman's estate' (*bḫn*) and 'house (hamlet?) of X' (*'t n x*).

The key units in the administration of these varied settlements were the mayors (ḥȝty-ʿ) and kenbet-councils (ḳnbt) (see fig. 3.4); for both categories there was internal hierarchization and differences in function. National and provincial capitals each had a mayor, as did some (perhaps all) of the 'intermediate' towns. Village (wḥyt) mayors are sometimes referred to in general terms, but more precisely village leaders were ṭsw (literally 'commanders') and perhaps often simply the functionally and socio-economically dominant figures in the community. The degree to which the major provincial mayors had authority over the agricultural hinterlands and over the 'lesser' mayors remains uncertain, but the functions of mayors in general were clear; they were responsible for collecting taxes, facilitating the work of representatives of the central government, and implementing orders received from them.

The New Kingdom kenbet-councils were primarily judicial but they were also quasi-administrative, since they were often concerned with property rights. The two 'great kenbet-councils' of Thebes and Memphis were each headed by a vizier and were concerned with civil cases. Throughout Egypt were many lesser kenbet-councils, a more widespread mechanism than that of the mayors, and their primary functions were to prosecute criminal activity (excepting that involving capital punishment, which was referred to the vizier) and to resolve countless cases of property rights and disputes. Holding 'court in the towns according to the excellent plans' (Pflüger 1946) of the king, these councils were an important source of civic order. The 'great kenbet-councils' consisted of high-ranking priests, bureaucrats and soldiers; the provincial ones, certainly subject to government approval, were made up of people of high *local* socio-economic status.

The provincial centres were of course widely dispersed (fig. 3.6), while the offices and archives of the central government had to be physically concentrated. As a partial solution to the problems of administration, the New Kingdom continued the traditional practice of dividing Egypt up into two (rather than, as earlier, three) major units, one governed from Thebes and the other from Memphis. Important offices were divided, if their responsibilities were sufficiently complex and extensive. This was true of the vizierate (that is, there was a northern and a southern vizier) responsible for the efficient functioning of the civil government as a whole, of the Treasury and of the two military 'deputies'. At times the office of 'great steward of the royal domain' was also divided. Other important offices with more limited responsibilities remained unitary, such as those of the 'overseer of granaries' and the 'overseer of cattle', both concerned with regulating economic life and storing or securing the taxes owed to the state. The chief agents of communication between the centres and the provinces were the viziers' 'messengers' and the representatives of other departments who frequently visited provincial towns to carry out specific tasks and check the conduct of local officials.

The national capitals were also the chief royal residences, enabling the king to enhance his control over administration through a variety of formal and informal personal contacts. Since there were two and, after Ramesses II founded another at Pi-Ramesse, three such capitals, the king clearly had to divide his time between them. In fact, since each was also a major religious centre celebrating annual festivals in which the king took a leading part, the royal circuit often served as a provincial tour of inspection by the king. In this way the king was not dependent solely on his chief officials for knowledge of provincial affairs and the population as a whole was reminded of the king's primary role in politics.

The potential (although, in the New Kingdom, rarely used) coercive power of the kingship, derived from its close links with the army, was enhanced also by the undefended character of Egyptian towns and the reliance of civil government on police rather than military power. This potential was, probably deliberately, further improved by the disposition of military forces within Egypt (fig. 3.6). Perhaps only the capitals or royal residences had garrisons of any significant size while the military colonists, the most rapidly mobilized and efficient of the reserve troops, were located, in general, in areas close to the capitals. The colonists were not armed, and when mobilized they and other levies were equipped at arsenals in the residence cities where, as one text significantly puts it, they were armed 'in the presence of Pharaoh' (Edgerton and Wilson 1936, p. 36).

The tone of government life in the capitals is well documented textually, in art and to a certain degree by architectural remains. Texts and scenes convey a vivid impression of elaborate court ceremonies such as the presentation of taxes (by the mayors and others responsible, under the supervision of the appropriate central officials) and of the more intimate life of the court; of the mixture of dignity and excitement at the regular hearings presided over by the vizier, with petitioners ranked before him in order of precedence; and of the king's personal involvement in administration, as in the vignette of the vizier and treasurer meeting every morning in the palace gateway, comparing notes after the vizier had reported to the king. The structure of the royal

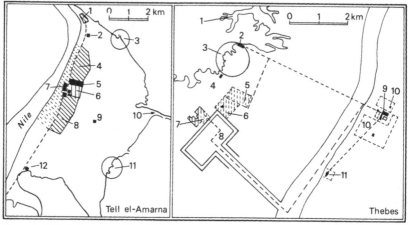

Fig. 3.8   Tell el-Amarna and its chief elements

1  Royal residence complex
2  North (ceremonial) palace
3  Cemetery of officials of the court and priests of the Aten cult
4  North residential zone
5  Great Aten temple
6  Official city
7  Ceremonial palace and annexe

8  South residential zone (government officials, high-ranking priests)
9  Village of artisans of the royal tomb
10  Royal tomb (up wadi)
11  Cemetery of chief officials of the central government and the city, with some cult officials
12  Maru-Aten

(The broken line represents the main north–south road.)

Thebes under Amenhotep III: tentative reconstruction

1  Tombs of the kings
2  Deir el-Bahari, funerary temples of Hatshepsut and Tuthmosis III and Hathor chapel
3  Cemetery of court and government officials
4  Village of artisans of the royal tomb
5  Funerary temple of Amenhotep III (approximate)
6  Residential area (?) in the time of Amenhotep III

7  Royal residence complex of Amenhotep III at Malkata
8  Modern Birket Habu = Maru-Amen (?)
9  Karnak temple of Amen: with hypothetical adjoining 'official city' and ceremonial palace, the latter possibly 'Amenhotep III is the shining sun-disc'
10  Hypothetical residence zones for officials
11  Luxor temple of Amen (of Amenhotep III), with hypothetical residential zone

(The broken lines represent the main processional routes linking the various parts of the city which, as reconstructed here, is much more diffuse and less continuous than Tell el-Amarna.)

cities is documented only for Akhenaten's capital at Tell el-Amarna, although one can reasonably conjecture that Thebes, under his father, Amenhotep III, may have been similar in important ways. Tell el-Amarna was not very rigorously planned, but certain structural differentiations were deliberate (fig. 3.8). The royal residential palace-complex was located in the north, with nearby settlements probably occupied by court officials and servants (as indicated by the burials in the adjacent cemetery). A ceremonial palace marked the transition to a residental zone, which was succeeded by the official quarter, containing the main Aten temple and a large ceremonial palace which, with its annexe, was the setting for the ceremonial public activities of the king. Immediately adjacent were the offices of the government and the police headquarters. A smaller temple, surrounded by a pseudo-fortified wall, indicated a transition to a less sacred, more supernaturally vulnerable area, in fact the chief residential city, where resided the vizier, high priest, police chief, mayor, and other chief officials of the government and the city. Providing a structural backbone was a broad avenue, running from the northern royal complex to a 'Maru-Aten' a southern complex combining shrines, pavilions and artificial lakes.

The sequestered character of the royal residence and the splendid settings designed for the ceremonial and ritual acts of the king in the official quarter aptly indicate the high status of the kingship in the late Eighteenth Dynasty. Simultaneously however, the clustering of royal residence, government centre and officials' residences within a single city reflects the close personal supervision the king exercised over the central government. Thebes under Amenhotep III was perhaps similarly differentiated (fig. 3.8), but whether this urban pattern existed earlier and continued after the Eighteenth Dynasty, is as yet unknown.

The sources also illustrate other methods whereby the kings maintained politically useful personal contacts with their chief subordinates. The true dynasty was excluded from power (p. 207) but a number of high officials enjoyed a kind of quasi-dynastic status as the sons or husbands of royal wet-nurses and harem women; this custom is well attested in the Eighteenth Dynasty and occurs as late as the Twenty-first. Gift-giving was another important relationship; the kings regularly rewarded deserving officials in public ceremonies and, in turn, received New Year gifts from officials and institutions. There is also evidence suggesting that the king banqueted regularly with groups of officers and soldiers, and he certainly rewarded retired officers with posts on the royal estates.

The obligations of the population in terms of taxes, compulsory labour levies and the like are well known but it is evident that, in return, conditions of security and relative prosperity prevailed for much of the New Kingdom. Relationships between government and the governed showed a mixture of bureaucratic sophistication and other mechanisms emphasizing more personal, direct and, in a sense, 'primitive' means of inquiry and decision-making.

At the provincial level the varied conflicts and tensions typical of village communities are well documented at the artisans' village of Deir el-Medineh. Here the local kenbet-council usually settled disputes or accusations without reference to a higher, outside authority; the mechanisms used included reference to written documents, personal judgement and, frequently, recourse to an oracle (p. 199) delivered publicly by the local god and clearly expressing the general feeling and judgement of the community.

Relationships between central and provincial governments and individuals are documented by a court case (of the time of Ramesses II) about a perennial problem, disputes within an extended family concerning hereditary rights to the ownership and income of an estate. The comparatively small scale at which government worked is seen in the involvement of the vizier's 'great kenbet-council' of northern Egypt in current and earlier disputes about the estate, which was substantial (about 5 or 6 hectares) but not huge, and the owners of which were of comparatively low status. The disputants regularly resorted to petition and officials cited, from records, earlier decisions about the estate over the previous eighty years as well as its original foundation 300 years earlier! However, records were not relied on exclusively and with reason: forged documents had been inserted, even into the vital land-registers of the treasurer and 'overseer of granaries' in the capital. The local Memphite kenbet-council, with its better knowledge of local affairs, was involved; a representative of the 'great council' several times visited the village and took (sometimes perjured) oral depositions; and the final decision was based on oral testimony of members of the community who were not involved in the dispute.

In microcosm, therefore, we see a system which, despite the abuses of inefficiency and corruption, appears to have fundamentally satisfied the need of the population for arbitration and control.

### The royal succession

The basic form and character of the political system just described evolved throughout the early Eighteenth Dynasty, but there is very little data on specific, internally significant events until c. 1490 BC. (Foreign affairs are, from the outset, comparatively better documented because of the nature of the surviving evidence.) The first apparent crisis is suggested by the atypical, officially recognized co-reign (22 years) of Tuthmosis III and 'king' Hatshepsut, by the latter's sex and by the defacement of her monuments by Tuthmosis after her peaceful (?) death. These peculiarities and the apparent bitterness of Tuthmosis have, to some scholars, reflected the clash of powerful institutions, perhaps a coterie of civil officials supporting Hatshepsut against the army, with the Amen priesthood supporting Tuthmosis. Yet the evidence (defaced tombs and monuments) on the fall of Hatshepsut's supporters is ambiguous, and during her lifetime Tuthmosis was allotted considerable civil and, more significantly, military power, which he did not turn against her.

That an unusual manipulation of the succession system was involved has long been evident and a recent suggestion is that, while the succession was patrilineal (i.e. father–son), royal mothers and wives had a symbolically critical matriarchal role which Hatshepsut attempted to turn into real power. However, other factors may also have been significant. In the New Kingdom, succession was rapid and automatic, and practice reveals a general agreement that the heir, in order of preference, should be son of the chief queen, or of a lesser queen, or husband of a chief queen's daughter. The last procedure eased a critical situation when there was no direct male heir, and was used, for example, to legitimize the transfer of kingship between the Eighteenth, Nineteenth, Twentieth and Twenty-first Dynasties.

If the new king was a minor, a regent (preferably a *female* relative) had to be appointed (as had been done for Ahmosis?), and Tuthmosis III was unusually young. At accession he was a stripling and, despite his 54-year-long reign (1490–1436 BC) his mummy shows little sign of ageing. Hatshepsut's accession, within a few years of his, may have been as much a dynastic defence-mechanism as an act of personal ambition. The co-reign no doubt generated tension, but it appears to have been fundamentally amicable, and the destruction of Hatshepsut's monuments is partly explicable as the expunging of a politically necessary reign which was offensive to the concept of *ma'at* (p. 201).

The next important set of events – those surrounding Akhenaten's reign (1364–1347 BC) – are better documented. Although his reign was politically significant, its precise implications remain controversial. Akhenaten is no longer seen as a social reformer or international pacifist, although it is still generally agreed that his explicit physical peculiarities were reflected in mental ones which affected his actions. To some, the unique features of Akhenaten's reign suggest a conflict between the king and other powerful sections of government, specifically the civil bureaucracy and the Amen priesthood. More probably, however, they were extreme examples of a tendency to royal absolutism which was inherent in the political system.

Akhenaten was both offensively innovative and politically strong. He promoted a monotheistic form of religion based on the Aten (sun-disc); he excluded the traditional pantheon from the new capital he began at Tell el-Amarna; and he tried to eradicate their cults elsewhere in Egypt. (It is uncertain how comprehensive this effort was except so far as the dominant state god, Amen, was concerned).

Akhenaten's strength arose partly from skilful manipulation of the traditional resources of kingship. He maintained the image of a war-leader; he initiated one campaign in Nubia; and in the Levant he responded to the collapse of the Mittanians before the Hittites with a mixture of diplomacy and military action. If on the one hand formal adulation of the monarch reached new heights, on the other there was increased elaboration in ceremonial gift-giving to bureaucrats and soldiers. The Aten-cult itself had strong traditional elements and art continued to emphasize the high status of king and dynasty, and their intimate links to the supernatural.

Akhenaten's other source of strength was a contemporary process (begun before his time and persisting long after it) of enhancing royal authority by emphasizing its quasi-divine aspects and yet avoiding the rigid, politically debilitating role of uncompromising deification. Increasing stability abroad since Amenhotep II's time (1438–1412 BC), internal tranquillity and growing royal wealth had created exceptionally favourable circumstances for this.

The increased importance of the Aten-cult was one aspect of the process; although a symbol of imperial power the sun-disc was mythically colourless and a more suitable manifestation of the kings' immanent divinity than was the already strongly defined Amen. The identification of king and disc had become more explicit in the reign of Tuthmosis IV (1412–1402) and was to continue until Ramesses II (1289–1224) and the cult itself survived, despite its associations with obnoxious innovations. Characteristic also of the later Eighteenth Dynasty were the 'purification' of royal rituals and strong interest in the kingship's antiquity. At Abydos at this time, a tomb of a First Dynasty king was indentified as that of Osiris, long since a symbol of all deceased kings, while early Nineteenth Dynasty kings built vast temples at Abydos celebrating their co-equal status with the chief gods. Prominence was given to king-lists implicitly (and, in the Turin Canon, in the time of Ramesses II, explicitly) linking the contemporary incumbents to the divine dynasty which originally ruled Egypt.

Akhenaten's father, Amenhotep III, was particularly significant in this process, and provided a model for cultic activity concerning the kingship in the Nineteenth and, less directly, the Twentieth Dynasties. Under him, the creation of dramatic functional and symbolic expressions of ideas about the kingship accelerated. A new royal residence city at Malkata (fig. 3.8), western Thebes, was associated with a more 'pristine' version of the ancient royal site of the Sed festival and some functionally absurd elements of the site, such as its excessively large harbour, reflect its ritual and symbolic, as well as utilitarian, roles. The royal residence for the first time was dominated by the royal funerary temple, not that of a national god (Amen or Ptah); an innovation not perhaps continued later. The colossal scale of Amenhotep's temple architecture and particularly of his funerary temple was also emulated by later kings (Ramesses III in fact attempted *no* major construction except for his funerary temple) and the production of large numbers of huge royal colossi (some explicitly and probably all implicitly hypostases of a divine Amenhotep and cult-statues in their own right) were also paralleled later, sometimes in a directly imitative way, especially by Ramesses II.

Akhenaten's innovations are explicable in the context of this process. His general relationship to it is indicated by his devotion to the Aten and the cult of kingship, and the colossal scale of his temple-buildings. These included hundreds of royal colossi, whose at times hermaphroditic form reveals not so much Akhenaten's personal abnormalities as 'an extreme symbolism which, since he was "in the likeness of Aten" depicted him as having all the attributes of the major godhead, the "father and mother" of all creation' (Yoyotte 1966, p. 250). Akhenaten's unique monotheism was itself, in part, an abortive offshoot of royal absolutism; the old gods were gone, but (to his own political benefit) the king maintained his traditional role as mediator between men and the wishes of the new, unhistorical god, inscrutable to all but Akhenaten.

Perhaps most importantly, the cessation of the festivals which were the main focus of Egyptian religious life must have profoundly disturbed the population,[1] while Akhenaten's religious innovations were equally repugnant to the educated elite. His son-in-law and successor, Tutankhamen, acting on the advice and, as a minor, the compulsion of

---

[1] See Wente 1976, pp. 23–4.

officials who had also been prominent in Akhenaten's government, restored the traditional religious system and abandoned Amarna. But, continuing bitterness surfaced some fifty years later, when Akhenaten's mummy was probably destroyed and the official denigration of his memory began. It was, however, symptomatic of the kingship's power that there was no overt opposition during Akhenaten's reign and that the execration of his memory, long delayed, was released only on *royal* (Nineteenth Dynasty) initiative. Contemporary texts depict Akhenaten as an effective ruler, promoting innovations from a vulnerable, unwalled city and securely in control of the military structure. We are uncertain about the degree to which his policies were economically disruptive, created excessive administrative centralization leading to abuses, replaced professional bureaucrats with less efficient new men and thus indirectly led to the loss of substantial parts of the Asiatic conquests.

Akhenaten's immediate (to Horemheb) successors coped successfully with serious internal and external problems, and consequently the early Nineteenth Dynasty kings were able to function as traditionally successful rulers, enjoying great internal authority and reacting strongly to recurrent emergencies abroad. However, after Merenptah (1224–1204 BC) the succession was clearly irregular for several reigns and there may have been a partial breakdown of political and social stability. Order was restored by Sethnakht (1186–1184 BC), first ruler of the Twentieth Dynasty, and the regime of his successor, Ramesses III (1184–1153 BC), was sufficiently stable to respond effectively to strong pressures from Asia and Libya.

From the reign of Ramesses III on, there are clear indications of growing internal problems. Contraction, not expansion, characterized the foreign policy while the disintegration of government became evident in the unprecedented events which closed the period of the New Kingdom, as we shall see.

Efforts to identify the ultimate causes of this disintegration need considerable qualification. The conservative reaction after Akhenaten, it has been suggested, so strengthened the Amen establishment in its inherent conflict with other political elements that 'the history of the Ramesside period is that of the conflict' (Helck 1968, p. 183). But the political weakness of the religious system should be noted (p. 202) and *military* officers, not priests, were responsible for the final division of New Kingdom Egypt into two units. The idea that Akhenaten destroyed a professional, idealistic bureaucracy which was thereafter staffed increasingly by deracinated men, frequently of foreign origin and military background, and characterized by inefficiency and corruption, must be set against the continuation of effective centralized government for a further 250 years and the disproportionate amount of surviving Nineteenth and Twentieth Dynasty archival material, always more revealing on abuses than the monumental record. The concept of increasing tension between an innovative, sophisticated northern world-view and that of a conservative south, exacerbated by later New Kingdom rulers' preference for a northern residence, is suggestive, but the north–south division was *always* a feature of the administrative structure (p. 214).

The fundamental problem was the decline in royal religious authority, military prestige and political power, factors upon which the integrity of the state depended. This decline cannot be traced in detail, but important contributing factors and symptoms are evident. Particularly significant in this highly personal form of government were problems inherent in the succession system and overt challenges to it. The latter disturbed the dynastic integrity necessary for royal stability, while both impaired the effectiveness of royal political manipulation, either by lessening the king's personal efficiency or by creating dynastic factions competing for the support of various segments of government. Both also depreciated royal prestige and authority by offending, sometimes subtly, against *ma'at*.

While the succession system functioned effectively during the difficult transition period after Akhenaten (all kings between Tutankhamen and Ramesses I were heirs by marriage, not direct descent (p. 219) it is certain that Seti II was usurped (temporarily, and only in Upper Egypt?) by a 'king' Amenmesses. If the latter was indeed *both* a royal relative and Viceroy of Kush the event demonstrates the wisdom of the usual divisive and dynastically exclusionary policies of the kings (p. 207). This was followed by further irregularities, in particular the accession of another female 'king', Twosret (as co-regent, ultimately successor of a short-lived minor, Siptah). Equally revealing was the plot to assassinate Ramesses III in favour of a 'lesser' son, far removed from the chance of direct succession. The plot involved harem and court members and important government officials, including high military officers; their failure, despite some close family links, was due probably to the absence of any institutional means of bringing these forces effectively together.

Peculiar features of the succession during the Twentieth Dynasty surely contributed to its political problems. These features were the unusually large number of short reigns and elderly kings (table 3.3),

TABLE 3.3  *Comparative regnal lengths in the New Kingdom. Particularly short reigns (8 years or less) are in bold type; it is noteworthy that they tend to cluster in the late Nineteenth and earlier Twentieth Dynasties*

| Eighteenth Dynasty | | Nineteenth Dynasty | | Twentieth Dynasty | |
|---|---|---|---|---|---|
| Name | Regnal length | Name | Regnal length | Name | Regnal length |
| Ahmose | 25 years | Ramesses I | **2 years** | Sethnakht | **2 years** |
| Amenhotep I | 21 years | Seti I | 14 years | Ramesses III | 31 years |
| Tuthmosis I | 12 years | Ramesses II | 65 years | Ramesses IV | **7 years** |
| Tuthmosis II | **4 years** | Merenptah | 20 years | Ramesses V | **4 years** |
| Hatshepsut | 22 years | Amenmesses | **4 years** | Ramesses VI | **7 years** |
| Tuthmosis III | 54 years | Seti II | **6 years** | Ramesses VII | **6 years** |
| Amenhotep II | 26 years | Siptah | **6 years** | Ramesses VIII | **2 years** |
| Tuthmosis IV | 10 years | Twosret | **8 years** | Ramesses IX | 18 years |
| Amenhotep III | 38 years | | | Ramesses X | 10 years |
| Amenhotep IV ⎫ Ahkenaten  ⎭ | 17 years | | | Ramesses XI | 30 years |
| Smenkhare | **3 years** | | | | |
| Tutankhamen | 10 years | | | | |
| Ay | **4 years** | | | | |
| Horemheb | 28 years | | | | |
| Average regnal length | 19.56 years | | 15.63 years | | 11.70 years |

generated by inherent weaknesses in the royal succession system itself, in this case by the survival of several inevitably elderly heirs of the long-lived Ramesses III combined with the premature deaths of younger kings (Ramesses V, VII), who would have generated the usual father–son, relatively long-reigned succession pattern (fig. 3.9). These events were both psychologically and administratively disturbing. The concept of *ma'at* accommodated the limitations of humanity within royal quasi-divinity but in the context of a natural progression in the ruler's life from early maturity to a substantially later death. The comparatively rapid succession of elderly or dramatically mortal rulers stressed the ambiguous character of the kings' relationship to the supernatural (pp. 199–201). Moreover, the political system depended upon the personal energy and flexibility of the ruler and had developed in the context of relatively young accession ages which now, for a period, were no longer the norm.

One of the two main rhythms of Egyptian official life was now disconcertingly discontinuous. The normal routine of the bureaucracy (now largely hereditary, even in its upper echelons; see p. 229), based largely on the agricultural year, continued uninterruptedly. But each

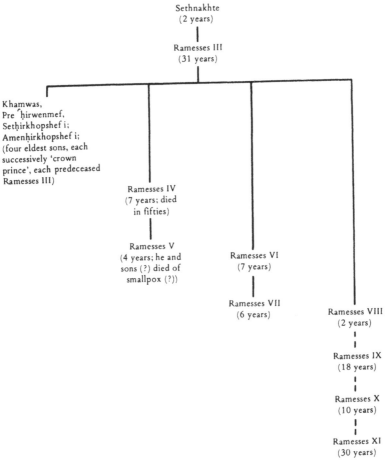

Fig. 3.9  Genealogy of Twentieth Dynasty; regnal lengths are given, and a broken line represents an assumed relationship. (See Kitchen 1972.)

king at accession normally entered upon a characteristic programme, generally similar but different in important details and based upon the expectation of a long reign (Ramesses IV made a request of Osiris for a 134-year reign!). Sometimes important administrative or foreign-policy initiatives were involved, and always the symbolically important features of a potentially substantial temple-building programme and the development of the royal incumbent's funerary establishment. Short reigns and probably a degree of personal remoteness (p. 231) would have contributed to the aborted building programmes, subdued foreign policy and reduced political flexibility evident for the Twentieth Dynasty kings.

## Economic problems and their significance

Although there was probably a weakening of royal economic power – a potent source of political influence and prestige – in the Twentieth Dynasty, its full nature and intensity remain uncertain. Marked diminution in temple-building or expansion even during longer reigns (Ramesses III, IX, XI) is the best proof, but is ambiguous in its implications. The king initiated and to a degree funded temple-building, but the state levied the large labour forces and collected the food and building supplies required. Was there a *quantitative* decrease in the economic resources available to the king and his officials, or was there a *qualitative* decline in the efficient manipulation of these resources?

The elaborate annual ceremonies of presenting taxes and tribute to the king symbolized the fact that in general little distinction was made between royal and state income. However, certain resources were more immediately accessible to the king's manipulation than others; tribute, booty and much foreign trade were his prerogatives as war-leader and the dynasty's estates were administered by his personal stewards. By contrast, state income from taxes (one-tenth of grain crops and animals?), dues, government lands, monopolies and requisitioning powers, had to support the civil, religious and military establishments and passed through a complex structure of administrative intermediaries who, to some degree, were capable of manipulating the economic system. Decrease in *any* of the resources was politically significant, especially those most accessible to the king, but so was a decline in the quality of administration.

It may, in fact, be reasonably presumed that tribute, booty and foreign trade declined after Ramesses III (p. 204), while royal copper-mining expeditions to Sinai and the Arabeh ceased after Ramesses V and VI respectively. However, the decrease in the wealth of the kingship should not be exaggerated. Sudanese gold was accessible until the end of the dynasty; Ramesses XI at one time gave gifts worth 50 deben of silver (equivalent to a year's food for 470 people) to a high priest; and Smendes, as *de facto* (soon to be *de jure*) king, imported Lebanese cedar.

It has been argued that the amount of cultivable land effectively controlled by the king and his government shrank seriously during the later New Kingdom. Although in theory the king owned all land and merely delegated its use to others, some scholars believe that, by the end of the Twentieth Dynasty, temples and private individuals, by a gradual process of alienation, in effect 'owned' most land. Given good administration, this development would still have provided the government with income from taxes and dues, and it is in any case not provable. The Harris Papyrus (Ramesses IV) shows that the temples then owned one-third of Egypt's arable land, but the status of the remaining two-thirds remains unknown, as does the degree to which the kings were able to tax and manipulate the use of temple lands. In a survey of temple, royal and government lands within a specific region (Wilbour Papyrus; Ramesses V), the temples appear as by far the greatest landowners, but the statistical significance of this is unknown, for the document is concerned with only a small proportion of the arable land actually available within the region.

In fact, the Wilbour Papyrus – our chief source on New Kingdom land tenure – seems to reveal an interpenetration of civil and temple administration which would make it unlikely that the temples could become effective economic and political counterweights to the kingship. Here, as in other documents, secular officials are shown as having responsibility for and some power over temple lands (unless these were specifically exempted). The land surveyed was divided partly into large estates and partly into much smaller farms. The owning institutions perhaps rented out the estates for half their annual yield and paid a tax on this income. The investors – wealthy officials and priests – expected a profit from the remainder, even though it was shared with the agents and cultivators who actually supervised and worked the land.

The small farms were primarily for the subsistence of the family of each individual who held a farm and paid a small part (much less then half) of the yield to the owning institution. Rather than reflecting a deliberate government policy of systematically dividing up arable land amongst all but the lowest levels of Egyptian society, these small-scale tenants were probably created in two independent ways. One large group – priests, scribes, herdsmen, cultivators and (rarely) artisans – presumably worked for the owning institution and each was also allotted a dues-paying farm for his subsistence (cf. the manors of early mediaeval Europe). The other large group, functionally unconnected with the temples, consisted of military personnel whose subsistence was a particular government concern (p. 206), here apparently settled on primarily temple lands – another index of secular power! The great uniformity of farm size was not so much 'planned' as a spontaneous response to subsistence needs (a phenomenon again paralleled in mediaeval European manors); the normal farm occupied five arouras (about 1.25 hectares), sufficient for a family of eight or so, while

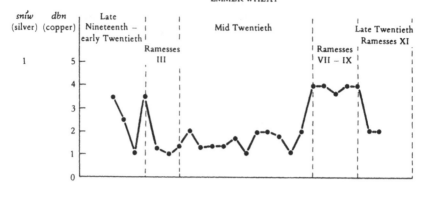

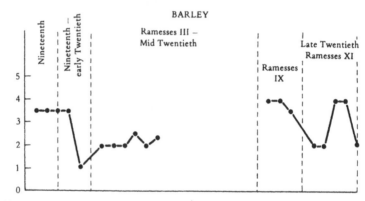

Fig. 3.10 The fluctuating values of emmer wheat and barley in the Nineteenth and Twentieth Dynasties: although the *general* chronological variation is valid, it must be noted that many of the instances are dated only approximately and that the figure represents chronological 'blocks' of instances, not a precise chronological progression. The data are taken from J. J. Janssen (1975, pp. 112–16, 119–22). Certain doubtfully dated examples, or atypically high values, have been omitted. The unit of measurement is 1 *ḫȝr* (76.48 l), the values are expressed in the *sniw* of silver (5 *dbn* copper) and the *dbn* of copper (91 g).

'soldiers' (although not other military personnel such as stable-masters) and their families habitually occupied only three arouras (about 0.75 hectare), perhaps because some family members were permanently or periodically on duty elsewhere.

Another economic phenomenon, the rising inflation of the later Twentieth Dynasty, may have been politically significant but, again, its causes and effects remain uncertain. After Ramesses VI grains, and perhaps other produce, increased sharply in value (fig. 3.10), but the prices of cattle, donkeys and manufactured items did not rise, partly because of the strong traditionalism of the Egyptian barter economy, partly because the cost-factors of raising animals or making artifacts were not reckoned as part of their value. Deliberate manipulation was most unlikely to have been involved in the rising value of grains and perhaps of produce. Recurrently inadequate inundations of the Nile or a declining labour force could have created an absolute decrease in available foodstuffs, but there is little evidence for these during the 60-year period (compare the frequent references to famine during the first hundred years of the First Intermediate Period (see chapter 2) with the single reference under Ramesses XI).

Administrative inefficiency was a more likely cause of economic problems. Abuses in the collection and distribution of food are documented (peculation of temple grain, Ramesses III, IV and V, and artisans' strikes provoked by *arrears*, not formally decreased rations, Ramesses III to Ramesses X). The robbery of royal and private tombs in the Theban area at the time was linked to these abuses as well as to the deteriorating integrity of local administration. Only the lower echelons of government were directly involved in these events, but the resulting scandals created intrigues and declining morale amongst higher officials.

### The weakening of the kingship

Probably the most important contributors to the weakening integrity of the kingship were the changing relationships between king, civil government and army. Governmental structure did not collapse in the late New Kingdom – it survived to provide a foundation for the revised political system of the Third Intermediate Period – but it was characterized by the growing strength of hereditary office, a tendency that is analysed in detail in a recent study (Bierbrier 1975). Related to this was the growth of family ramifications linking the powerful upper levels of institutionally separate branches of government, vividly epitomized by the Merybast family which held several vital offices from the reign of Ramesses III to Ramesses XI (fig. 3.11). Particularly noteworthy was their substantial control of major economic resources of the state, the dynasty and the religious establishment but, at the same time, their *dependence* upon the traditional diffusion of powers. As the deposition of Amenhotep, the High Priest of Amen, showed, the family had no significant military strength.

In any case, the civil government became less susceptible to roya

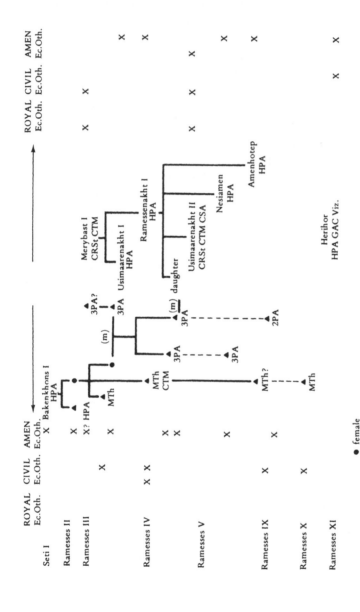

Fig. 3.11 Diagram illustrating the history of the Merybast family and their relations with two other powerful families of the Twentieth Dynasty; particularly noteworthy are the hereditary character of the offices and the family relationships linking institutionally separate branches of government. (Adapted, with changes, from Bierbrier (1975), pp. 2–13).)

Ec., economically significant. Oth., other. HPA, High Priest of Amen. 2PA, 3PA, second and third prophets of Amen (next in hierarchy after High Priest). CRSt, chief royal steward. CTM, chief taxing master. CSA, chief steward of Amen. MTh, mayor (h3ty-ꜥ) of Thebes. GAC, great army commander. Viz., vizier. (For most of these titles see fig. 3.4.) (m), marriage link.

control. The kings reduced their travels and became more remote from immediate administration; their personal influence decreased and they lost a degree of informed knowledge. Possibly the need to defend the north against the Libyans and to re-establish commerce with the Levant were sufficiently important to reinforce an already evident royal preference for northern residences (cf. Pi-Ramesse) and the age and physical strength of several kings may also have been significant.

As the kings' supervisory tours became less frequent, royal princes and other deputies carried out major religious rites formerly performed by the kings; and butlers of the royal court played a prominent role in important administrative acts, as if checking upon the highest officials of civil government. These butlers, however, lacked the expertise of the bureaucrats and were themselves not necessarily reliable, as evidenced by the involvement of some in the assassination attempt upon Ramesses III.

The assigning to the High Priest of Amen of certain functions that would normally have been performed by civilian officials (as, for instance, paying the artisans of the royal tomb, securing building materials for Karnak) may also have been administratively convenient but the price was a further loss of royal prestige. The High Priest Amenhotep had had himself depicted as equal in stature to the king – iconographic *lèse-majesté*!

The coercive resources of the kingship also declined. Despite the Libyan victories of Ramesses III, the threat of violence from Libyan infiltrators continued to disturb the work routines of the local inhabitants, as far south as Thebes and as late as the time of Ramesses IX and X, a fact suggesting a militarily weak situation in the primary infiltration areas of the Delta and Middle Egypt. After Amenhotep's deposition by a local faction, Ramesses XI restored order by requesting Penehasy, Viceroy of Kush, to take control of Upper Egypt in direct command of his own forces – two unprecedented steps – instead of himself dispatching troops from the northern garrisons. Penehasy's regime in Middle and Upper Egypt, using substantial numbers of Nubian troops (the *z ͨͨw*, literally 'jabberers'; see Bell 1973, Wente 1966), was sufficiently akin to a foreign invasion to act eventually as a catalyst for internal mobilization. After perhaps seven years of rule Penehasy retreated into Kush, presumably under pressure from the newly emerged, politically dominant and essentially military figures of the Theban Herihor and his son (?) Smendes. Piankh, Herihor's son and successor in the south, continued to campaign against Penehasy in Lower Nubia.

The discipline of the Egyptian armed forces, therefore, continued to be a politically stabilizing resource, as it had been earlier when Horemheb staffed with the 'finest of the army' the depleted and demoralized priesthoods left by Akhenaten's innovations (Gardiner 1953). But, in contrast to the fruitful relationship between king and army which had eased the transition from the Eighteenth to the Nineteenth Dynasties, Herihor and Smendes imposed upon Ramesses XI, their titular monarch, a territorial division of Egypt which was plainly opposed to the integrity of New Kingdom government and kingship. Ramesses XI survived as titular head of both divisions until his death; Smendes then became king of 'all' Egypt, but effectively only of the north, while the descendants of Herihor controlled Middle and Upper Egypt. Ramesses IX's appeal to Penehasy reflected the fact that only in Kush did the exigencies of control and defence still permit a substantial and responsive standing army, but the king's surrender of war-making prerogatives to the viceroy set a precedent followed by subsequent military leaders such as Herihor.

A final index to the disintegration of traditional government was the granting of extraordinary combined powers to individuals. These were not unprecedented in times of crisis, but there were now significant differences. Formerly the grants were less extensive, were held by formally proclaimed (if not birthright) crown princes and were a temporary expedient. But Penehasy, a commoner, was simultaneously Viceroy of Kush, an army-leader and overseer of granaries, while Herihor was vizier, High Priest of Amen and generalissimo, the last two titles to be inherited by his successors in perpetuity.

## THE THIRD INTERMEDIATE PERIOD

The ensuing Third Intermediate Period was characterized by virtually continuous tension, only rarely flaring into open conflict, between centralizing and centrifugal forces. The interaction of these forces led to extreme political fragmentation in the last century of the period. They also, however, sustained a striving towards stability that resulted in rapid and effective recentralization under the Twenty-sixth Dynasty. For the first 124 years of the Third Intermediate Period (Twenty-first Dynasty) government was relatively stable, despite the deep fissure in the state's integrity created by the concordat whereby a unique royal dynasty (of Smendes) received formal recognition throughout Egypt, in return for ceding effective control of Middle and Upper Egypt to a line (descended from Herihor) of 'great army commanders' who were

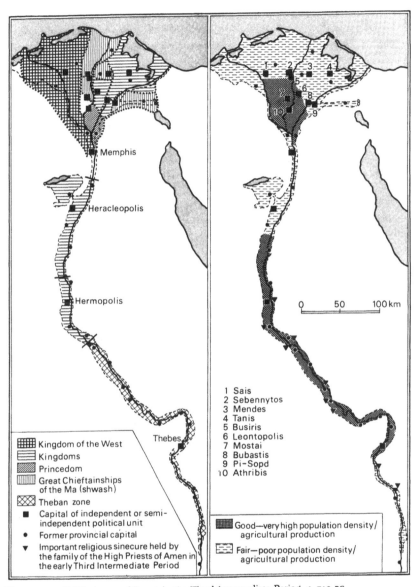

Fig. 3.12  1 Political map of Egypt in the Third Intermediate Period, *c.* 730 BC.
 2 The recent pattern of population density and agricultural yield superimposed on the political
map (see Wilson 1955).

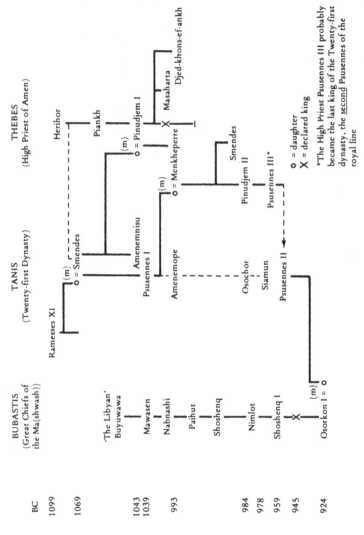

Fig. 3.13  Genealogies and interrelationships of the Twenty-first Dynasty, and the two contemporary families of the High Priest of Amen, 'great army commanders' of Thebes and the 'great chiefs of the Ma(shwash)' at Bubastis.

simultaneously High Priests of Amen at Karnak. Potential conflict was avoided because the two lines were branches of the same family (fig. 3.13) and had different preoccupations. The Twenty-first Dynasty, residing at Tanis, the former port of Pi-Ramesse, was more internally secure than the Herihor lineage and, as a result, was comparatively expansive (though usually pacific) in its relations with the Levant. The 'great army commanders' had more pressing internal problems; they resided, for strategic reasons, at El-Hibeh, not at the old centres of Memphis or Thebes (fig. 3.6), and made no serious effort to penetrate Kush, their logical area of expansion and the region they explicitly desired to control.

Power was apparently amicably transferred from the Twenty-first to the Twenty-second Dynasty, whose members were descended from hereditary Libyan 'chiefs of the Ma' at Bubastis but resided at Tanis. This dynasty attempted to enhance royal power by ending the hereditary principle in the rule of Middle and Upper Egypt, but they did not alter the basic administrative methods of the Twenty-first Dynasty nor its reliance upon royal relatives in government. The foreign policies of Shoshenq I and Osorkon I in the Levant were unusually aggressive but, thereafter, foreign policy became more subdued as internal dynastic tensions and powerful elements amongst the Egyptian provincial nobility became more pressing. In response, the dynasty entered upon a *formal* bifurcation of the state. It installed a royal co-dynasty at Leontopolis (the Twenty-third; fig. 3.14) which was, in effect, charged with reasserting dynastic control of the south while the Twenty-second concentrated upon the Delta.

The effort was a failure and contributed to further disintegration. As a result the Twenty-second/Twenty-third Dynasties were unable to display the major military initiative needed in the Levant, where the expansion of Assyria was threatening Egypt's commercial interests. Internally, other royal relatives at Herakleopolis and Hermopolis followed the example already set and declared themselves kings, while in the Delta several 'great chiefdoms of the Ma' became increasingly independent. One, based on Sais, was particularly expansive, and under Tefnakhte (Twenty-fourth Dynasty) it gained control of the western Delta from Memphis to the sea. In the extreme west, a further divisive unit was a 'great chiefdom' of the Libu, caused by continuing immigration from Libya. In the south, a Kushite kingdom was extending its control over Middle and Upper Egypt.

Throughout the Third Intermediate Period there was increasing

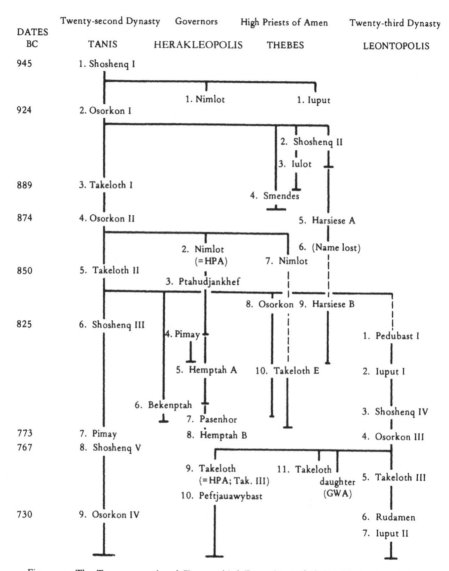

Fig. 3.14  The Twenty-second and Twenty-third Dynasties, and their relationships with the
High Priests of Amen of Thebes and the governors of Herakleopolis. HPA, High Priest of Amen.
GWA, god's wife of Amen. (See Kitchen 1973.)

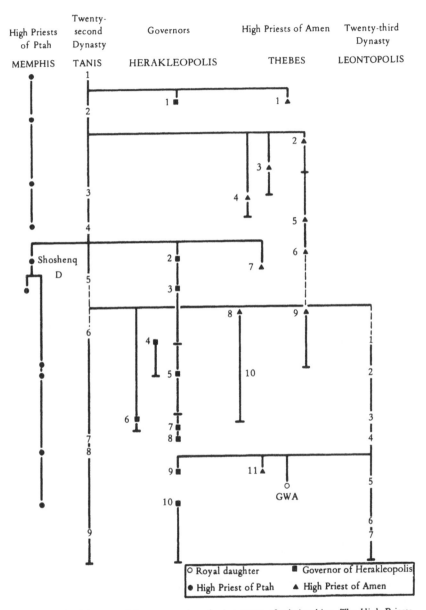

Fig. 3.15 Simplification of fig. 3.14 to show basic pattern of relationships. The High Priests of Ptah have been added. GWA, god's wife of Amen. (See Kitchen 1973.)

Fig. 3.16  A passage from the Amada stela of Merenptah describing the impalement of Libyans (captured in the campaign of regnal year 5) in the vicinity of Memphis. The determinative (arrowed) makes the sense of the text quite unambiguous. (After a hand-copy, Kitchen 1968.)

tension over the degree of regional or provincial independence which could be tolerated or secured, and over the control of vital economic resources. The competing elements arose from the political and social structure of the late New Kingdom and represent, in significantly altered form, potentially divisive elements which New Kingdom government had been designed to keep subordinate. Royal relatives were now assigned unprecedented administrative power, collateral dynasties were inadvertently or deliberately created by royal policies and a variety of local hereditary bureaucrats, priests and military chieftains of provincial origin became more firmly entrenched in their positions. High officials of central government (e.g. the viziers), formerly influential and powerful, were now, in the case of Tanis (fig. 3.6), effective only within the immediate territory of their residence city; at Thebes, the descendants of the agents of centralized government and of the Amen establishment continued to hold the appropriate titles but became themselves a very powerful provincial nobility. Glimpses of other provincial nobilities can be caught elsewhere: at Memphis one lineage monopolized the high priesthood of Ptah until c. 870 BC and continued to hold valuable benefices there subsequently, while at Thinis, the local nobility secured valuable administrative and economic monopolies which lasted well into the Twenty-sixth Dynasty.

In the north, 'chieftains of the Ma' were particularly important. They were descended from the Libyan chiefs of Mashwash military settlements attached to some central and eastern Delta towns after the Libyan victories of the Nineteenth and Twentieth Dynasties. Foreign prisoners of war and foreign levies by that time were a regular constituent of the Egyptian army in the field, but the Libyan prisoners were unprecedented *within* Egypt and not easily subject to selective weeding-out. Exemplary cruelty was tolerated (fig. 3.16), but not extermination; expulsion to Libya (not controlled by Egypt) was strategically undesirable; and Libyan fighting ability was needed to enhance the power of the kings (now usually resident in the Delta) and to strengthen the eastern frontier, hence, the settlements. Originally subordinate to Egyptian officers, some Ma chiefs came to dominate certain towns and their territories, aided by the weakness of the central government but also by their own military resources and a degree of ethnic solidarity evident, despite strong Egyptianization, in personal names, dress and, occasionally, in political action (cf. Twenty-second Dynasty, p. 236).

In the Twenty-first to the Twenty-third Dynasties, the primary royal response to the problem of controlling a fragmenting political system was to assign extraordinary combined civil, religious and military powers to royal relatives, install them in strategic regional and provincial commands throughout the country and explicitly recognize military force, not bureaucratic control and police power, as the basis of government's authority. Dynasty members functionally displaced the officials of centralized government, hence the latter's decline. The new policy was opposed to normal New Kingdom practice (p. 207) but, given the greatly changed historical circumstances, had significant antecedents in that period.

Supreme power had *always* been reserved for dynasty members (king, chief queen, crown prince); government's personal character was such that high officials regularly received quasi-dynastic status; and royal relatives, politically ineffective, nevertheless held high rank in military and religious establishments. The combined powers now held by royal relatives were anticipated by those of 'adoptive' New Kingdom crown princes in times of political crisis (p. 232), an endemic situation in the Third Intermediate Period.

Earlier foreign policy was also relevant. Large areas of Egypt, because of the independent, sporadically aggressive attitudes of their inhabitants, were analogous to New Kingdom foreign conquests, and dynasty members were akin to the earlier governors of foreign lands, maintaining control through garrisons and fortified towns at internally strategic points. Regionally diffused members and branches of the royal family (and leading members of the provincial nobilities) took on some of the character of independent rulers and a complex, politically motivated network of intermarriages developed between these elements and the theoretically dominant royal line. This practice had been important in earlier foreign (not internal) policy, although now royal daughters were married *into* the other power-groups while, earlier, the reverse was usual.

The new policy sustained dynastic power and the formal appearance of a united kingship, but at considerable cost to royal manipulative and coercive resources. The governing royal relatives were habitually 'great army commanders' or 'army-leaders' controlling their own forces and residing in heavily fortified provincial centres hard to reduce militarily (Breasted 1906, IV, ss. 857–65). Dynastic integrity was strained, since these relatives naturally tended to establish semi-independent, provincially-based collateral dynasties, sometimes even claiming royal status. The Twenty-first Dynasty solution was to recognize frankly the dynastic status of the south's 'great army commanders' and High Priests of Amen. The inherent tension caused by the latter's sporadic claims to royal titles was eased by close family links. Pinudjem I (fig. 3.13), son-in-law (and nephew?) of Smendes, became a 'co-king' at Tanis and, when the royal line died out, the incumbent 'commander' naturally became king (Psusennes II; fig. 3.13).

The Twenty-second and Twenty-third Dynasties tried to strengthen royal control by restricting regional commands to sons of the reigning king rather than to more remote relatives, thus preventing collateral dynasties. This policy, initially successful, within eighty years generated problems which caused Osorkon II to petition Amen to 'establish my children in the [posts which] I have given them, so that brother is not jealous [?] of brothe[r]' (Kitchen 1973, s. 276).

In the south, which was now divided into two units, one governed from Herakleopolis and one from Thebes, deviations from desired practice were soon evident (figs. 3.14–15). The Theban High Priest, Shoshenq (2) generated a collateral dynasty, being succeeded by his two brothers (3 and 4) who were markedly independent of their nominal king, Takeloth I; and by a son, who declared himself 'king' (5), and a grandson (6). King Osorkon II rectified the situation, appointing as governor of Herakleopolis *and* Thebes his son Nimlot (Herakleopolis 2, Thebes 7), who was appropriately succeeded at Thebes by Osorkon (8), crown prince of King Takeloth II. High Priest Osorkon's rule, however, was sporadic and contested by descendants of Shoshenq (see Thebes 2–9) and Nimlot (see Thebes 10) and by other grandees as far north as Hermopolis (Kitchen 1973, ss. 293–4; see also Caminos 1958, pp. 29 and 153, 111 and 164, 88 and 161, 105 and 163). The result was widespread, ten-year-long civil war. Herakleopolis itself was ruled by a rarely interrupted collateral dynasty descended from Osorkon II via Nimlot (2–8), while the (?) crown prince of Osorkon II, installed as the Memphite High Priest, founded yet another dynasty (figs. 3.14–15).

This disintegration, combined with the independence of provincial elements, prompted the division of power between the Twenty-second and Twenty-third Dynasties. King Shoshenq III (825–773 BC) asserted his control of the Delta, establishing a hereditary fiefdom for Twenty-second Dynasty crown princes at Athribis–Heliopolis, and installing other sons at provincial centres (Sais?, Busiris). In the south, the Twenty-third Dynasty had to dispute for control at Thebes and Herakleopolis with descendants of the collateral dynasties of the Twenty-second, but Osorkon III (777–749 BC) succeeded in installing his crown prince at both centres. When the latter became co-regent, another royal relative was appointed to Herakleopolis (10), while the 'Theban problem' was solved by an ingenious adaptation of New Kingdom practice: the office of 'god's wife of Amen' (p. 207) had survived. The High Priesthood was now left in abeyance; the 'god's wife' became dominant and was always a royal daughter, installed by the incumbent king. Now required to be a virgin, the 'god's wife' could not generate a collateral dynasty!

While the central bureaucracy of the north was absorbed into the residence city at Tanis and continued to be under the traditional direct supervision of the kings, the descendants of central government administrators at Thebes were only sporadically in direct contact with their overlords, usually (Twenty-first Dynasty) 'Commanders' or sometimes (Twenty-second Dynasty) residents at El-Hibeh or Herakleopolis. The Theban nobility characteristically conflicted with the (broad) dynasties over access to important and lucrative Theban religous sinecures. The family of Herihor attempted to monopolize these, as later did royal sons and Libyan allies of the Twenty-second Dynasty and, in each case, Theban resistance forced a compromise, whose ill-effects for the dynasties were eased by intermarriage with the Thebans. Not surprisingly, the Thebans supported semi-independent, locally-based collateral dynasties such as that of Shoshenq, and refused even formal co-recognition to the Twenty-second Dynasty after the Twenty-third was established. The transfer of political dominance at Thebes to a woman, initiated by Osorkon II and continuing after, further strengthened in a male-oriented society the Theban bureaucrats who were nominally her agents.

Another royal response to contemporary internal problems was to revive the expansionist foreign policy which had, in the past, benefited royal power (pp. 205–7). However, internal weakness forced tactics far different from earlier ones. Emphasis was now upon maintaining commercial and diplomatic relations with the Levant (cemented by marrying Egyptian princesses to foreign rulers, the reverse of earlier practice) rather than on military aggression, and in both cases the geographical extent of Egyptian activity was much less than before (fig. 3.5). The Palestinian military campaigns of Siamun and Shoshenq I were isolated instances. Although the later Twenty-second Dynasty intrigued against Assyrian expansion, its kings were reduced to 'buying off' any Assyrian army which threatened the Egyptian frontier.

Shoshenq's scribes chose New Kingdom literary models (from Amenhotep III; see p. 221) to celebrate his victories, a reminder that foreign campaigning had religious and propagandistic as well as practical ends. Throughout the Twenty-first to Twenty-third Dynasties the kings tried to maintain authority by persistently summoning up the supernatural potency of the politically stable past. Royal names and epithets identical with, or similiar to, those of New Kingdom rulers were frequently assumed and, of at least two Sed festivals (symbolic celebrations of the kingships' political and religious role) documented, one was based on a New Kingdom version of the 'absolutist' Amenhotep III. Paradoxically, the ideal of a royal political structure conformable to *ma'at* made it the model for the indigenous (and intrusive Kushite) elements competing with the dynasties.

## The rise of the Kushites and Saites

Weak royal government and a concentration upon Levantine and internal relationships were responsible for the expansion of Sais and the Kushites, which changed the situation. The development of a Kushite kingdom and its invasion of Upper Egypt was facilitated by a comparative lack of Egyptian royal interest in Kush, by the condition of Lower Nubia (formerly a buffer zone and now an uninhabited corridor) and by the relative decline of Aswan (p. 247). The north-west and western Delta, agriculturally poor and commercially insignificant, were also of peripheral interest to the Twenty-first and Twenty-second Dynasties. Tefnakhte of Sais and his father, among the 'great chiefdoms of the Ma', were able gradually to expand their control in these regions, eclipsing the Libu 'great chiefdom' until they forged the vital strategic link with Memphis and gained access to Middle Egypt (fig. 3.12).

By this time, Egypt was divided into eleven major and virtually independent political units governed by a bewildering variety of rulers (fig. 3.12). They consisted of five formally proclaimed kings whose very contemporaneity was an extraordinary offence to the earlier concept of *ma'at* (pp. 196–7); a crown prince and another royal son;

Tefnakhte, prince of the western Delta and now (?) 'great chief of the Libu and Ma' (the two major Libyan groups deeply involved in Egyptian history since the Nineteenth Dynasty); and four 'great chiefs of the Ma'. Some lower-ranking rulers also had a degree of independence, including 'chiefs of the Ma', a local high priest, and several *ḥ3ty-'*, the latter more akin to the similarly titled, independent, magisterial governors of 1400 years earlier, than to the New Kingdom mayors. Under Piankhy (Twenty-fifth Dynasty) in 728 BC, the Kushites halted Tefnakhte's expansion southwards (but not eastward) into the home territories of Tanis and Leontopolis, where the Twenty-second/Twenty-third Dynasties continued to rule. In 715 BC, Piankhy's successor Shabako conquered the Delta, making the Twenty-fifth Dynasty recognized overlords of all Egypt, but the fragmented political structure survived their half-century of rule unchanged. Most of the same political units continued to exist for another sixty years, their rulers often the lineal descendants of those of Piankhy's time and bearing identical titles, including 'king'.

The Twenty-fifth (Kushite) Dynasty failed to generate internal reunification, even during its first relatively peaceful forty years. Ruling two kingdoms may have made reunification impossible to achieve but, more likely, it was realized that a strong Egypt could not be controlled by the smaller Kushite state. Kushite rule was based on military strength, and local civil government was left largely to the Egyptian dynasts. Nevertheless, Kushite contributions to *future* unity were significant. At Thebes, the Kushites continued the politically useful office of 'god's wife'; the High Priesthood, held by a Kushite prince and his son, was revived but stripped of military and civil authority. The former was surely exercised by Kushite commanders, the latter first by Kushite governors, and later by Theban bureaucrats. A distribution of powers strongly reminiscent of the stable New Kingdom was emerging.

Psychologically important was the subtle Kushite exploitation of traditional religious ideas concerning the kingship. Stressing symbolic unity and recalling the form if not actuality of the great periods of centralization, the Kushites were genuinely devoted to *maʿat*. Their devotion, they argued, generated supernatural aid and demonstrated the legitimacy of Kushite accession. They preferred the Old and Middle Kingdoms to the New Kingdom as models. A sophisticated, pseudo-Old-Kingdom creation myth was developed; Memphis (the Old Kingdom capital) became the preferred royal residence, and the royal tombs

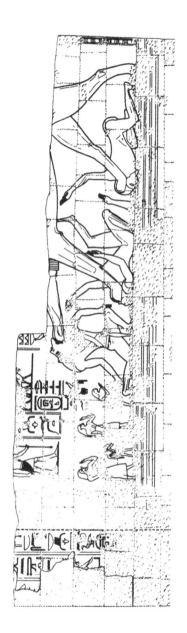
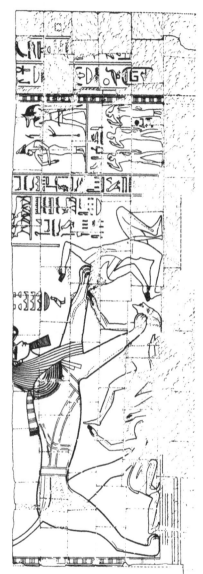

Fig. 3.17 Scenes carved upon the walls of a temple built by Taharqa (Twenty-fifth Dynasty) at Kawa. Depicting the king as a sphinx trampling Libyan opponents, the scenes are based closely upon Old Kingdom prototypes, clearly copied directly from still standing monuments at Saqqara and Abusir. (After Macadam 1955.)

at Napata in the Sudan were modelled on the Old Kingdom royal pyramids (*not* the New Kingdom pyramidal tombs, known since the mid-eighth century but not copied). With a subtle selectivity, scenes from Old Kingdom royal funerary temples were reproduced to embellish contemporary gods' temples; not accidentally, they included an Old Kingdom depiction of victory over the Libyans (fig. 3.17).

Superficially, the main political emphasis thereafter was upon the struggle between Kush and Assyria for the control of Egypt. The Twenty-fifth Dynasty aggressively opposed Assyria in the Levant, mounting a major campaign there in 701 BC and repulsing an Assyrian invasion of Egypt in 674 BC. Assyria conquered the Delta in 671, lost it to King Taharqa in 668/7, gained control of *all* Egypt in 667/6, and regained it in 664/3 after being temporarily driven out by a campaign of King Tanwetamani. However, on another, less obvious, level these events gave a major impetus to Egyptian reunification, an outcome desired neither by Kush nor Assyria. Their policies, combined with fortuitous circumstances, eventually created a context in which the most expansive of the Egyptian dynasts, Psammetichus I (Twenty-sixth Dynasty) of Sais and the 'Kingdom of the West' was able rapidly to restore unity to the Egyptian state.

Kushite and Assyrian policies inadvertently had a decisive effect upon this process. Kushite emphasis upon the ideological and ritual unity of the state prepared Egypt psychologically for a return to centralized rule; while the active Kushite opposition to Assyria required an unprecedented degree of military and political co-ordination amongst the Egyptian dynasts. Subsequently, the Assyrian conquerors, reluctant to assume total control, tried to create a system of Egyptian vassal states that would be too disunited to threaten Assyria's position in the Levant but strong enough to resist (with Assyrian aid) a successful reinvasion by the Kushites. Kushite desire to maintain fragmentation had ensured the survival of the Saite kingdom, and Assyria now assigned it a major although not uniquely dominant position in its vassal system.

Despite Assyrian insensitivity to Egyptian susceptibilities – Egypt sent regular offerings to Assyrian gods without apparent reciprocity – reality compelled a relatively benevolent regime in Egypt. The Egyptian dynasts' relationship with Assyria was complex; as vassals and compelled to offer tribute, they escaped total Assyrian rule by protecting the true area of Assyrian interest, the Levant, against Kushite attack. Assyrian military officials resident in Egypt supervised tribute collection and military preparedness but the highest ranks of Assyrian military and civil officials were not installed there. Civil government and a degree of military power was left to the dynasts aided by indigenous Egyptian tax-collectors and 'chiefs' who bore Assyrian titles.

The only dynasts to enter (as inferiors) into treaty alliances with Assyria and consequently to receive special attention, were Necho of Sais and the Ma chief Pekrur of Pi-Soped. The former had territorial strength (the west and Memphis, and Athribis–Heliopolis under Necho's crown prince, Psammetichus). The Ma chief had a strategic location (Pi-Soped) which dominated the convergence of the invasion routes linking Palestine and Memphis. Thus, both were essential to the buffer system and politically useful counterweights to each other. In any event, Sais proved loyal to the Assyrians during King Tanwetamani's campaign, while Pi-Soped eventually led the submission to him. As a result, Assyrian reconquest led to Pi-Soped's eclipse and ensured the dominance of Sais.

The final assertion of Saite rule occurred when Kush was militarily exhausted and Assyria distracted elsewhere; Assyrian hegemony had enhanced Sais' opportunities for foreign contact and enabled it to recruit foreign mercenaries from Anatolia who tipped the internal military balance in its favour; and its chief Egyptian rival, Pi-Soped, was weak. Psammetichus I showed great skill not only in exploiting these circumstances but in enhancing the internal trend towards a stable, ideologically acceptable kingship. Within a ten-year period (664–654 BC) he had effectively reunited the country and, by the time of his death in 610 BC had largely, if not entirely, consolidated this unity.

### New patterns of settlement

Throughout the Third Intermediate Period, the map of real and symbolic power altered as it reflected changing political circumstances and their cultural effects; and there was probably an important change in the general pattern of settlement, responding to a new political system, the altered relations between government and the governed, and a prevailing civic insecurity. Ultimately, these alterations reflected important changes in the character of Egyptian life.

Particularly striking was the changing pattern of 'royal cities' i.e. towns which were royal residences and administrative centres (cf. figs. 3.6, 3.12). Pi-Ramesse was eclipsed by Tanis, a port-town more easily defensible than the former capital and vital for maintaining profitable sea-links with the Levantine trade. Memphis and Thebes also declined, because of internal strategic considerations which had not been relevant in the New Kingdom political structure (see below). Thebes enjoyed only sporadic royal status and Memphis was not again 'the city of kingship' until the Twenty-fifth Dynasty. Some other claims to royal status (Herakleopolis, Hermopolis) were late and ephemeral, reflecting the acute stage of fragmentation. The rise of Leontopolis and Sais was also linked to the problem of controlling and exploiting two vital regions, the Delta apex and the valley from Hardai to Gebelein (fig. 3.6).

According to recent analogy these regions would have been particularly fertile and densely populated (fig. 3.12) and as prime surplus-producing areas they would not only have provided the subsistence basis for most of the population and the superstructure of government, but also supported the personal estates and religious benefices of royal and collateral dynasty members and their provincial rivals. The estates of Amen of Tanis and associated cults presumably lay in the Delta, while the strings of benefices occasionally listed for dynasty members in the south demonstrably lay mainly between Hardai and Gebelein.

The importance of the Delta apex is further indicated by the exclusion of Mashwash and Libu settlements from it since the late New Kingdom; by the royal (Twenty-third Dynasty) status of Leontopolis and the crown prince's fief Athribis–Heliopolis, both of which enhanced dynastic access to the Delta apex and to the routes linking it to Tanis; and by the assumption of royal status by Sais after it had secured control over the western edge of the apex. The significance of the Hardai–Gebelein zone (fig. 3.6) was marked by the fortification of its northern (El-Hibeh, and nearby Shurafa) and southern ends (Gebelein) early in the rule of the Twenty-first Dynasty 'army commanders', and by the relative decline of Aswan, located in an infertile area and of lessened strategic and commercial importance after the loss of Kush at the end of the Twentieth Dynasty. El-Hibeh and Herakleopolis owed their importance at this time to the fact that they were better able than Thebes to maintain the vital dynastic intercommunications with Tanis and yet were more convenient for the control of the southern fertile zone than Memphis. Moreover, the many villages with military traditions in the immediate area were an important resource (fig. 3.6).

Significant changes in symbolic topography are evident in royal and dynastic cemeteries (fig. 3.6), which reflect shifting political power, insecurity and the strong regional and local character of politico-religious attitudes. In the New Kingdom, kings and royal relatives were always buried at Thebes, but it was notoriously susceptible to cemetery-plundering after the Twentieth Dynasty. Thenceforth, relatively secure Tanis housed the tombs of the Twenty-first and Twenty-second Dynasties (in the very heart of the temple and administrative quarter, i.e. *within* the city) but the Twenty-third to Twenty-fourth and the Twenty-sixth Dynasties preferred Leontopolis and Sais respectively, and the Twenty-fifth distant Napata, its ancestral centre. High Priests of Amen and Twenty-second Dynasty High Priests of Ptah (both royal relatives) were buried at Thebes (in 'secret' tombs) and Memphis (within the city) respectively. The relative stability of Tanis was further reflected by its being chosen as the site of comparatively continuous major temple-building and additions, although Thebes's traditional importance stimulated sporadic building activities when economic circumstances permitted.

The proliferation of walled, fortified cities made a striking contrast to the New Kingdom. The process began as early as the late New Kingdom when the massive fortifications of Ramesses III's Theban funerary temple-'town' must have been paralleled elsewhere. By the late eighth century, the process had reached an advanced stage. Piankhy's stele, commemorating his defeat of Tefnakhte in 728 BC, refers to nineteen fortified towns along a 266-km stretch of the river in Middle Egypt (and average of one for every 14 km!) and, in general terms, to the 'walled towns' of the Delta, whose appearance is documented both archaeologically and iconographically. Fortified towns responded to insecurity, civil war and invasion, but also reflected the fragmentation of administration and the reliance upon armed force in government. Major administrative changes were usually accompanied by the building of supporting fortresses.

Data also suggest that the fairly extensive settlement pattern of the New Kingdom (p. 213) had become more concentrated and that more people than formerly lived in urban or semi-urban contexts. For example, in the late Twentieth Dynasty some 86% of the population within a 7-km zone between the funerary temples of Seti I and Ramesses III at Thebes lived within a densely packed town within the latter's walls. Later, at El-Matmar in Middle Egypt a local population, earlier spread over a wider area, now lived within the walls of a provincial temple. Insecurity, particularly in the outlying villages, contributed to this process (cf. Piankhy's orders about a besieged town: 'Let not the peasants go to the field, let not the plowman plow.' (Breasted 1906, IV, s. 821, cf. s. 833)). This uneasiness, together with the difficulties of trading in bulky grains in the context of a fragmented political structure, underlay the depressed land values of the period. More positive factors also promoted concentration. Local markets were now prime outlets for surplus, and access to local government, the chief source of arbitration, was more important. Contemporary funeral inscriptions reveal that the local town-gods had increased in status as mediators and centres of cult activity.

## THE ONSET OF THE LATE PERIOD

Throughout the Late Period, Egypt made a sustained and largely successful effort to maintain an effectively centralized state which, except for the two periods of Persian occupation (Twenty-seventh and Thirty-first Dynasties) was based upon earlier indigenous models. However, despite its strong, deliberately cultivated affinities with the stable political systems of the New Kingdom and earlier periods, Late Period Egypt displayed certain unique features which were caused by the effects of the Third Intermediate Period and by factors which had been less significant or non-existent before.

The traits inherited from the Third Intermediate Period were not purely negative. They provided important mechanisms for the transition to centralized government under Psammetichus I, and archaism became a useful ideological and administrative tool in the Twenty-sixth Dynasty. Less beneficial was the kingship's decreased sanctity (but not political power!) and its increased susceptibility to usurpation. The periodic re-emergence of regionally-based politico-military units whose importance ultimately derived from the Third Intermediate Period (Sais, Sebennytos, Mendes) was complex in its effects. It contributed significantly to the revolts against Persian occupation, but also to the recurrent internal crises of the Twenty-eighth to Thirtieth Dynasties.

The most important new factors were the restricted access to traditional sources of royal income in the Levant and in the Sudan, and (particularly after the end of the first Persian occupation) persistent pressure upon Egypt's own territorial integrity. As a result, while Egypt was on a more or less permanent war-footing, its foreign policy was more defensive than in the New Kingdom and involved contacts and alliances with a new group of foreign states (fig. 3.5). In addition, the use of foreign soldiers (and mariners) was much more important than before both in foreign and internal affairs.

The career of Psammetichus I typifies the often subtle mixture of the old, recent and new characteristics of Late Period policies and society. At the outset (664 BC) he was a vassal of the Assyrians like the eleven other rulers (each residing in a fortified town and commanding an army) with whom he shared control of Egypt. Already king of the largest single unit (p. 246) Psammetichus arranged for a Memphite oracle, strongly reminiscent of the type issued by 'national' gods in the New Kingdom, proclaiming his right to sole rule. Another oracle, of a more local and recent character, at Buto, near the coast of his kingdom, legitimized his use of Ionian and Carian mercenaries (the latter from Asia Minor) who had arrived there possibly at Psammetichus's invitation. The special abilities and equipment of these mercenaries gave Psammetichus an advantage over the indigenous troops of his rivals. He probably used both military and political strategy in the Delta, which came quickly under his control (by 657 BC), and the long, exposed internal frontiers both compelled and facilitated an at least partially military solution.

The military reduction of the less exposed, strategically stronger centres of Middle and Upper Egypt was likely to be undesirably protracted. The threat of foreign intervention, for which this would be an excellent opportunity, was omnipresent. Psammetichus's unification policy was specifically noted by the Assyrians as a violation of his treaty with them and he also had to reckon with the Kushite king, now residing at Napata, whose adherents at Thebes still recognized him as late as 657 BC.

Political action alone, backed by the *threat* of superior force, was, therefore, desirable south of Memphis. In this process the appointment of loyal northerners to strategic southern posts was certainly important, but less so than the exploitation of Third Intermediate Period mechanisms which made such appointments possible without military activity. For example, Herakleopolis had apparently been in eclipse since Memphis became a quasi-national capital in the Twenty-fifth Dynasty, and it did not appear in an Assyrian list of major and minor Egyptian 'kingdoms' of 667–666 BC. By 661 BC, however, it had regained its earlier status as the residence and centre of royal relatives governing Middle and Upper Egypt. Psammetichus's first such official, Pediese, was either from the Saite region or was an incumbent Herakleopolitan governor, deliberately linked by marriage to the king.

Pediese and his son and successor, Somtutefnakht, had, in fact, limited *territorial* control, but they effectively exercised the unique office of 'overseer of the (river) harbours' of Middle and Upper Egypt. This ensured royal control of the main communication artery, generated an increasing revenue from dues (within four years a 50%, within fifteen a 100%, increase) and secured some kind of hold over the provincial harbours, weak links in the cities' defences. Father and son were essentially royal officials, not semi-independent rulers; they generated no collateral dynasty and their most powerful functions had been eliminated by the end of the reign.

In general, Psammetichus left local rulers in office if they abandoned such 'independent' titles as 'king', 'great chief' and 'army-leader' and became incorporated into a centralized form of royal government. This process, apparently rapid in the Delta, was undertaken cautiously in less readily accessible regions. The admittedly royal, but uniquely powerful, office of 'overseer of harbours' survived to at least Psammetichus's year 34, while relations with Thebes, the major southern centre, were typically complex.

Thebes still controlled the six southernmost Egyptian provinces when it reached a political settlement with Psammetichus in 656 BC. The chief office-holders of the region (including two descendants of Kushite kings) were *confirmed* in office, and the royal government was inserted in typical Third Intermediate Period fashion by the adoption of Psammetichus's daughter as heir to the 'god's wife of Amen' (p. 241). Thereafter, this office continued to be held by a Twenty-sixth Dynasty princess. During Psammetichus's reign a royal governor was placed over the second and third Upper Egyptian provinces, and a royal garrison installed at Aswan, effectively ending Theban–Kushite contact. However, the assimilation of the Theban administration was still continuing some seventeen years after the settlement, when much of the power formerly held by the Theban mayor cum governor of the south was transferred to the steward of the 'god's wife'. Either during Psammetichus's reign or later (by year 1 of Psammetichus II) the office of High Priest of Amen was combined with that of 'god's wife' and remained so to the end of the dynasty.

In 655/4 BC a major crisis permitted Psammetichus to demonstrate (and perhaps increase) his already considerable power. At this time much of western Egypt from Oxyrhynchus to the sea – almost one-third of Egypt's length – was invaded by Libyans, who may have been in collaboration with dispossessed Egyptian dynasts. Psammetichus took the initiative of driving them out in good New Kingdom style, ordering 'the mayors (ḥȝty-ʿ) of *all* the towns' of Egypt to send their troops to join his army (Spalinger 1976).

Despite recentralization, the effects of the Third Intermediate Period probably persisted through the following three centuries. Massive Persian intervention and pressure was a major new feature but the periodic instability experienced by the independent Egyptian dynasties reflected continuing internal as well as external problems.

## EGYPT'S RELATIONS WITH AFRICA

Throughout the nine centuries covered in this chapter, contacts between Egypt and other African regions were active and varied and must now be surveyed in detail; the Sudan after the rise of the Twenty-fifth Dynasty is excluded.

The 'Africa' known directly or indirectly to the Egyptians was comparatively small in area and restricted to regions adjoining Egypt, the sole exception being an ephemeral expansion of knowledge in the Late Period under Necho. Little evidence supports claims for widespread Egyptian influence throughout the continent, from western to southern Africa; rather, we still await better documentation of the available facts (see Leclant 1972). Even if some claims eventually are proven, cultural diffusion via partly Egyptianized Kushites and Libyans is likely to have been a more important mechanism than direct contact.

Egyptian contact with and knowledge of Africa was relatively shallow, partly because of severe natural restrictions on access such as the Sahara and the difficulty of movement along the upper Nile. A related and equally important factor was the comparatively unsophisticated Egyptian political and military organization, which never created an 'imperial' hegemony like that of the Assyrians, the Persians or, even earlier, the Hittites. Once territorial integrity was assured and control over or access to relatively close trade routes and sources of raw materials was established the Egyptians seem to have had little impetus to advance further. Changing historical circumstances were also significant. Contacts and knowledge gained in the expansive New Kingdom dwindled in the contracting Third Intermediate Period, and were hindered in the re-expansive Late Period by a strong Kushite state in the south. The extraordinary circumnavigation of Africa sponsored by Necho failed to discover any major new sources of income and its time-span (over two years) must have confirmed the primacy of the short-run Red Sea and Mediterranean routes.

To the Egyptians 'Libya', the northernmost contact area, probably stretched no further west than Cyrenaica (fig. 3.18). Libya, in the New

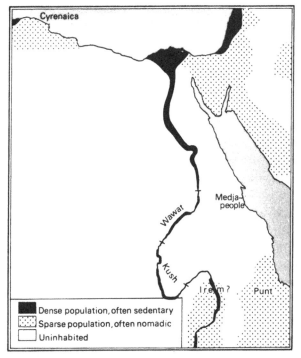

Fig. 3.18  Schematic version of the modern population pattern of north-east Africa, probably approximating to that of the second and first millennia BC.

Kingdom and later, was frequently called Tjehenu or Tjemeh, archaic and loosely applied terms; the former tended to refer to a peripheral zone of Libyan settlement along the western Delta and the latter to more remote areas. It is unfortunately impossible to match with certainty two sets of Libyan tribal names, the first supplied by New Kingdom sources, the other 600 years later by Herodotus. The dominant tribes during the New Kingdom were the Libu and the Mashwash, both probably located in Cyrenaica. Their sustained interaction with Egypt and their contacts with the 'Sea-Peoples' of the eastern Mediterranean makes it unlikely that either was based at Tripolitania, an important area of coastal occupation but some 2500 km west of Egypt. Their substantial animal holdings and relative independence strongly suggests that the well-watered Cyrenaican plain and massif was their homeland and not the harsh coastal plain to the east.

South of the Libyan coastal region, population rapidly fell to virtually nil, as it did throughout most of the deserts flanking the relatively densely settled Nile Valley, until there began a gradually increasing density, part of a broad arc sweeping from the western coast of the Red Sea across central Africa (fig. 3.18). The arc marked the beginning of the semidesert, shading eventually into savanna, created by the northern edge of the east and central African rainfall belt which, in antiquity, corresponded roughly to the modern limits between latitudes 20° and 14–16° N.

The deserts themselves were not entirely devoid of population. The western Egyptian oases supported populations and linked the desert routes, running north and south, which were of economic and strategic interest to Egypt. Consequently, throughout the entire 900 years covered here, at least some, and sometimes all, of the oases were under Egyptian control. To the east, the relatively better watered Red Sea Hills supported an appreciable nomadic population persisting perhaps as far north as latitude 27° N (cf. the distribution of intrusive Pan-grave/Medja sites; see chapter 2). These eastern nomads were, in the New Kingdom at least, still called Medja-people and, because of their dispersed character, were not easy to bring under control.

The New Kingdom conquest of 'Kush', comprising the riverine zones of Wawat (Lower Nubia, First to Second Cataracts; previously occupied by Egypt in the Middle Kingdom) and Kush proper (Upper Nubia, Second to Fourth (?) Cataracts), gave Egypt intimate knowledge of its Nehasyu ('southerner, Nubian') population. Egyptians also penetrated the area south of the Fifth Cataract but to a depth which remains uncertain. New Kingdom Egypt was also regularly in direct contact with the country of Punt, a region which can now be approximately defined (O'Connor 1982, pp. 926, 935) and, on at least one occasion, penetrated its interior perhaps to a depth of 250 km. Although Egyptian contacts re-expanded after the Third Intermediate Period contraction, Kush proper remained under indigenous control from the Kushite capital at Napata, with Wawat a virtually uninhabited and contested area between the two powers. No definite recontact with Punt is recorded but, during the Twenty-sixth Dynasty and the period of Persian occupation, Egyptian shipping was active in the Red Sea and, in view of the strong maritime emphasis of the Late Period, may have anticipated the Ptolemaic pattern of contact which ran as far south as the Bab el-Mandeb and Cape Guardafui.

The location of some of the African toponyms referred to by the Egyptians is of great importance for the reconstruction of Egyptian activity in Kush, Punt and contiguous regions. Unfortunately, the locations of most of the toponyms – even the most important – remains a matter of debate. The writer follows in this chapter the conclusions published in O'Connor 1982 (pp. 925–40).

The changing pattern of relations between Egypt and other African regions was shaped by several factors. These included the aims of Egyptian policy, which varied from region to region; the logistics imposed by specific topographies; the characteristics of the indigenous cultures and their reactions to contact with Egypt; and the vicissitudes of Egypt's own internal stability. Policies followed by Egypt in the Levant and Africa were closely linked. Successful expansion into the Levant depended upon there being no threat of a substantial distraction created by rebellion in Kush, and the gold which became a major element in Egyptian Levantine policy was derived from Kush.

The conquest of Kush created new contacts and conflicts with more remote Nubian groups, while the increasing importance of Nubian gold in Egypt's diplomatic relations with Asiatic states led to significant policy shifts in the regions to the south of Egypt. By contrast, Libya lacked desirable resources and only became a matter of acute concern when its threat to Egyptian security increased (p. 203). Punt, chief source of the highly desired incense used in religious ritual, was somewhat remote and was probably not contacted again directly until Hatshepsut's reign. Thereafter its products and the access it provided to inland regions ensured that Egyptian contacts with it were maintained to the end of the New Kingdom.

### RELATIONS WITH KUSH AND THE EASTERN DESERT

Expansion southward (fig. 3.19.1) was, therefore, intimately linked to relations with the Levant and to internal events which either inhibited or enhanced Egyptian activity abroad. Kamose (Seventeenth Dynasty) and Ahmose (Eighteenth Dynasty) had simultaneously to deal with the Hyksos and the Kushites, who were politically and strategically linked, expelling them respectively from Egypt and Wawat and creating buffer zones in southern Palestine and the Second Cataract region. Internal rebellions late in Ahmosis' reign showed that the Egyptian political situation itself was not completely stable and, not surprisingly, his successor, Amenhotep I, seems to have advanced southward no further than Sai and to have attempted no Asiatic campaigns. Tuthmosis I, however, did secure the whole Third Cataract region, consolidating his hold by building a fortress at Tombos, and traversed Kush itself, setting

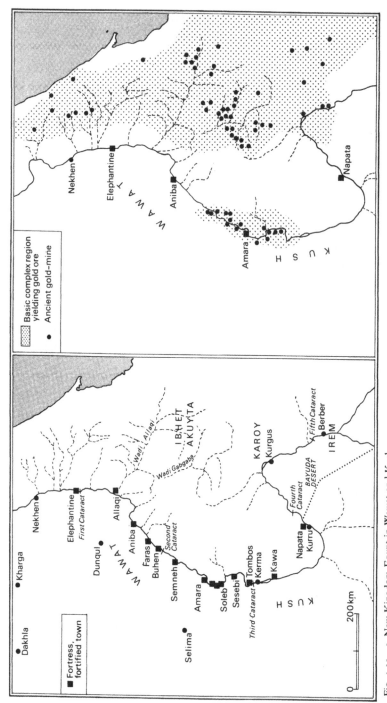

Fig. 3.19  1 New Kingdom Egypt in Wawat and Kush
2 Gold-bearing areas of Wawat and Kush (after Vercoutter 1959).
The dotted line across the Bayuda desert indicates the route formed by a series of water holes (see Chittick 1955).

up an at least symbolically significant frontier stele at Kurgus (just as, shortly after, he set up another on the Euphrates). Nevertheless, stubborn resistance to the Egyptian advance continued. That against Amenhotep I and Tuthmosis I was almost certainly led by unique political and military leaders descended from the 'rulers of Kush' (based at Kerma) who had dominated much of Upper Nubia and Wawat during the later Second Intermediate Period; the Kushite 'royal family', with allies from further south in Upper Nubia, appears to have made its final resistance against Tuthmosis II.

Even so, the Third Cataract region remained unstable until Hatshepsut and Tuthmosis III not only finally reduced it but extended full Egyptian control as far south as the Fourth Cataract. Although the evidence is slight, it is sufficient to show that the atypically intense and sustained Levantine campaigning of Tuthmosis III's sole reign, which extended permanent Egyptian control over a much expanded area, was preceded by a comparable expansion in Kush during the co-reign of Tuthmosis and Hatshepsut. This campaign was less demanding than the conflict with the urbanized and politically and militarily sophisticated Asiatics, but the final suppression of potentially distracting Kush was a necessary prelude to expansion into the Levant.

If, as was likely, an early Nubian campaign of Hatshepsut was provoked by attacks on Egyptian garrisons it logically would have been in the most recently conquered zone, i.e. the Third Cataract region; and twenty years after her accession, Tuthmosis III, on Hatshepsut's behalf, quelled a rebellion or invasion in Miu, a territory of the same approximate region. The co-rulers were also familiar with regions further south, since Hatshepsut set up a list of toponyms including Irem and others probably located in the Fifth to Sixth Cataract area; further, a strong Egyptian expedition at least once contacted Irem and exacted tribute, reaching the valley from the land of Punt in the east while Tuthmosis III, during Hatshepsut's reign, hunted a rhinoceros in the 'Southlands', which lay south of Upper Nubia, itself environmentally unsuitable for such an animal (O'Connor 1982, appendix).

Thereafter, Tuthmosis was extremely active in the Levant from his years 22 to 42, an indication that Egyptian dominance in Upper Nubia had been securely established under Hatshepsut or in the early sole reign of Tuthmosis III. The significant date may well be Tuthmosis' year 31, the first time the *bȝkw* (revenue) of Wawat *and* Kush was recorded. In year 34, four sons of the chief of Irem were dispatched (as hostages, prisoners?) to Egypt; and it was probably the next year that Tuthmosis set up a duplicate of Tuthmosis I's frontier stele at Kurgus, just as he had two years earlier on the Euphrates. Napata was certainly a permanent Egyptian centre by year 47.

The Third Cataract region, now under close Egyptian control, remained peculiarly important throughout the New Kingdom despite its agricultural poverty and relatively low population. Several major fortress (or temple) towns developed here, continuing to flourish even after the more fertile remainder of Kush was finally conquered and one – Amara – was the preferred administrative centre for Kush, despite its non-central position. This continuing importance reflects the area's early role as a base of operations, its reduced exposure to external attack, and its economic value, for the chief riverine gold sources were precisely in this zone (fig. 3.19.2). It also has been argued that this area was an important focus for desert trade routes linking Upper Nubia and the northern Butana.

Thereafter, with Kush secured, the foci of Egyptian military activity moved, in partially interrelated ways, both east and south. Throughout the New Kingdom Napata and Karoy (the riverine zone between the Fourth and Fifth Cataracts) are consistently referred to as the southern limit of full Egyptian control; but the development of a looser form of control in the Fifth and Sixth Cataract regions, and even further, was imperative. The uninhabited nature of Karoy and the difficulties of riverine movement through it, as well as the aridity of the Bayuda desert, made this a natural frontier zone; while the diffused pastoral populations of the regions beyond Karoy would have exacerbated the normal problems of full control. But these same populations, if left completely unhampered, could monopolize access to desirable products (e.g. gold) and raid the tempting targets provided by Egyptian centres and a pacified population in adjoining Kush. Eventually, the Egyptians seem to have established a system of control in Irem and adjoining regions based not on permanent centres, but on patrols, interspersed, when necessary, with campaigns (cf. the similar situation between Sixth Dynasty Egypt and Wawat, and – to a degree – Middle Kingdom Wawat and Kush; see chapter 2).

The eastern Nubian desert, accessible primarily from Wawat via the Wadis el-Allaqi and Gabgaba, contained valuable gold resources (fig. 3.19.2); Wawat sometimes yielded twenty times more gold than Kush. The Egyptians were again exploiting these resources in the early Eighteenth Dynasty; but the area increased in importance when gold became a major source of Egyptian influence in the Levant (as campaigning was largely replaced by alliances and quasi-diplomatic commercial relationships in the later Eighteenth Dynasty and, after a renewal of major campaigning, in the Nineteenth Dynasty).

Aridity created logistical problems in eastern Nubia but equally significant was the presence of a nomadic or semi-nomadic population (in broad terms, the Medja-people) who interfered with Egyptian exploitation. The eastern deserts were related to Irem and contiguous regions in several ways: all contained significant gold deposits (fig. 3.19.2); their populations were probably in contact; and the Medja-people were directly – and the Irem and nearby peoples indirectly – linked to the Red Sea coast. Certainly Egyptian activities in both regions seem at times to have been linked together.

Given the policy aims suggested above, a consistent pattern for later Eighteenth Dynasty activity in the south can tentatively be suggested. Tuthmosis IV campaigned in the deserts east of Wawat and perhaps in Irem and two other toponyms in its vicinity; if so, he anticipated the better documented activity of his successor, Amenhotep III, presumably for the same reasons. In the reign of Amenhotep III, a comprehensive plan to expand and improve the exploitation of the gold-mining areas as a whole can be discerned. At about this time the authority of the Viceroy of Kush was extended to include the southern Egyptian gold-mines and, in fact, the name of Amenhotep's viceroy, Merymose, has been found in southern Egypt at Reddesiyeh, an area which had become an important gold producer by the early Nineteenth Dynasty. Ibhet, a region in the gold-bearing desert east of Wawat, was invaded by the same Merymose, moving from the valley along the Wadi el-Allaqi, probably in conjunction with other campaigns which date to Amenhotep's fifth regnal year.

During this year an army sailed along the Red Sea coast, opposite Wawat and Kush, and harassed the Nehasyu inhabitants of the region; these were presumably nomads based on the coastal plain or hills who had been penetrating inland and hindering an expanded exploitation of the gold-mines. The area affected was called *Wrš[k]*, probably the same toponym as the eastern-desert toponym *ʒwšk*, dominated by the Medja-people in the Middle Kingdom. Amenhotep also indicated that Irem and a nearby toponym *Twrk* were invaded by another army; this would have improved security on the frontier and enhanced access to the gold-mines of *ʿmw* – along latitude 19° N (O'Connor 1982, p. 939) – from which came the gold of Karoy specifically referred to in connection with this campaign.

The depth of the penetration of Amenhotep III into the eastern desert is marked by the appearance of a new toponym, Akuyta, first attested in the toponymical lists of his reign, and certainly to be located in this region. Akuyta's continuing importance is reflected by its reappearance in lists of Akhenaten (Amenhotep IV), Horemheb, Ramesses II and Ramesses III and was based upon the continuous effort to maintain the enhanced gold supply created by Amenhotep III. Akhenaten punished the Akuyta people for threatening the food supplies of the gold-miners, while Seti I and Ramesses II were much concerned about the water supply of their gold miners in Akuyta. A viceroy of Ramesses II recorded the submission of Akuyta's chief, although Ramesses' successor Merenptah may have had further trouble in the east; how else to explain a campaign of his in year 4 connected with long stabilized and acculturated Wawat? Thereafter perhaps Akuyta was more submissive to Egypt; the 'deputy of Wawat' was active in Akuyta as late as the reign of Ramesses VI while under Ramesses IX Nehasyu from Akuyta assisted the Egyptians by repelling nomadic attack upon the gold-mines of the Wadis Hammamat or el-Allaqi.

Activity in the area of the Fifth and Sixth Cataracts was also maintained. The locations of the Nubian campaigns of Tutankhamen(?) and Horemheb are unknown. However, once Seti I had concluded his vigorous campaigning in Asia with diplomatic accord the need for diplomatically potent gold was reinforced. In year 9 Seti began the further development of the southern Egyptian gold-mines and at the same time attacked Irem. Ramesses II also campaigned in Irem and recorded tribute from thence and Ramesses III probably also engaged in hostilities against Irem. Captive chiefs of Kush, of an obliterated toponym perhaps to be restored as Irem, and of two other toponyms in Irem's vicinity were depicted at Medinet Habu, and Irem people were compelled to serve at the royal court in Egypt. Significantly, Ramesses III also exploited the gold-mines of '$mw$, access to which depended upon the acquiescence of Irem.

The long Egyptian occupation of Kush and Wawat (to the end of the Twentieth Dynasty) generated an intense and sustained interaction between Egyptians and indigenes which had results of the greatest interest. The more important aspects of that interaction are epitomized in the wall scenes of the tomb of Huy, Viceroy of Kush under Tutankhamen (fig. 3.20). Textual commentary is minimal but the content and symbolically varying scales of the iconography reflect the basic Egyptian interests in the region; the administrative structure

Fig. 3.20 Officials of the administration of Nubia under Tutankhamen, bringing gifts to the viceroy Huy. They are: upper register, left to right, the deputy of Wawat (destroyed), the deputy of Kush, the mayor of Soleb, and an overseer of cattle; lower register, left to right, the high priest of Tutankhamen at Faras, the 'deputy' of the fortress of Faras and the mayor of Faras. (After Davies and Gardiner 1926.)

that satisfied them; and, partially, the nature of the relations between Egyptians and indigenes.

The depiction of Huy's investiture emphasized both the importance of the viceroy and his close personal relationship with the king. The data on the viceregal office shows that it was intimately related to the expansion into Wawat and Kush, a phenomenon strongly linked to the actual power and the mystique of the kingship. The first viceroy was installed perhaps by Kamose but certainly by Ahmose, and thirty have now been documented, succeeding each other until the end of the reign of Ramesses XI; few, if any, are yet to be discovered. The earliest viceroys were perhaps, like Ahmose Turo (Ahmosis–Tuthmosis I), drawn from the administration set up to control the expanding conquest territory, but thereafter they were drawn from the administration within Egypt, except for the relatively rare cases when a son succeeded his father as viceroy. The chief responsibilities of the viceroy were to collect and deliver tribute and taxes (given pride of place in Huy's tomb), to exploit efficiently the gold-bearing regions, and to oversee the civil government of the province. Although the viceroys rarely bore military titles contemporary with their incumbency and although formal military command was vested in the 'battalion-commander of Kush', in practice, they could assume direct military command of the province's forces (e.g. Merymose under Amenhotep III and Panehesy under Ramesses XI). Moreover, at least a third of the viceroys between the later Eighteenth and earlier Twentieth Dynasties were drawn from the royal chariotry or royal stable-administration, a fact that probably reflects their role in the desert campaigning typical of that period (pp. 258ff.).

The viceroys' close links with the king were emphasized by their titles, administrative habits and origins. The viceroys were functionally equivalent to (although inherently more powerful than) the Levantine 'overseers of northern lands', and enjoyed a unique quasi-dynastic status as 'king's son' or 'king's son of Kush' (p. 209). Appointed by the king and reporting directly to him, many (nearly 50%) of the viceroys were drawn from the 'royal' sections of the bureaucracy and army, i.e. from the ranks of royal envoys, heralds, scribes, charioteers and stable-overseers. This close connection facilitated royal control over an unusually powerful official governing an extensive territory (from Nekhen in Upper Egypt to Napata), the chief product of which – gold – was peculiarly important to the temporal and supernatural power of the kingship, since king and Amen establishment were the chief beneficiaries. It also however reflected the symbolic importance of Kush, wherein the war-making, divinely-approved abilities of the Egyptian kings were particularly satisfactorily demonstrated.

The administrative structure of Kush, sketched out in Huy's tomb (fig. 3.20) and documented elsewhere, interestingly mimicked centralized royal government in Egypt. The viceroy had his own staff of scribes, envoys and agents, while Wawat and Kush were each directly administered by a 'deputy' (*idnw*). Government was centralized in two provincial capitals, clearly Faras and Soleb (ancient Khaemhet; see fig. 3.20) under Tutankhamen (see the prominence given to the officials of these towns in Huy's tomb) but more usually Aniba and Amara. These and the other towns renovated or founded by the New Kingdom Egyptians throughout the region were each governed by a mayor (*ḥзty-ꜥ*) or, when of a military character, by a military official (*ṯsw*, *ḥry pḏt*, or *imy-r mr ḥtm*), and most of them had a priesthood serving the cults of Egyptian gods.

Throughout the New Kingdom, these ethnically and culturally Egyptian urban centres were surrounded by a substantial population which was un-Egyptian in ethnicity, language(s) and, initially (in Kush if not in Wawat), in material culture. There is no reason to assume a massive displacement of indigenes by incoming Egyptians and the theory that Wawat, and even Kush, became gradually depopulated because of falling river levels or repressive Egyptian policies seems to the writer unlikely. The subordinate roles of the Nubians are emphasized in Huy's tomb, where they are shown apparently delivering tribute to centres in Nubia and certainly accompanying the presentation of the tribute to the king. Nubian chiefs humble themselves before the king, their children appear as hostages or future royal harem members and other Nubians appear as prisoners or slaves (fig. 3.21). Certainly, the basic agricultural and pastoral system of Kush must have been maintained by the indigenes, their services on behalf of the civil, military and religious establishments of the province enforced, and numerous Kushites drafted into the army, frequently as specific segments of the Levantine garrisons.

Two aspects of the indigenes' relations with Egypt were particularly important. First, some southerners were incorporated into the administration of the province, not, as in the Middle Kingdom, excluded from it; secondly, there was, at *all* levels of indigenous society, increasing acculturation to Egyptian norms in material and intellectual culture, eventually complete in Wawat and presumably reaching an advanced

Fig. 3.21   1 Egyptianized Nubians (?) delivering tribute to the viceroy Huy.
   2 Nubians delivering tribute to Tutankhamen. Upper register, right to left: the three chiefs of Wawat, including Hekanefer, followed by a Nubian princess and several princes. Lower register, right to left: three of the six chiefs of Kush depicted in Huy's tomb. (After Davies and Gardiner 1926.)

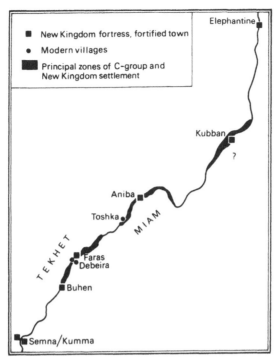

Fig. 3.22 The three (?) chiefdoms of Lower Nubia (Wawat) in the Eighteenth Dynasty. It is assumed that each chiefdom coincides with one of the three principal zones of settlement (cf. Trigger 1965, figs. 2, 3), an assumption supported by the distribution of the tombs and monuments of the chiefs and their relatives (fig. 3.23), and by the three chiefs of Wawat depicted in Huy's tomb (fig. 3.21).

degree in at least some parts of Kush. Given these facts, one may legitimately speculate that the distinctions between resident Egyptians and numerically dominant Nubians became increasingly blurred, with Nubians beginning to move into the upper levels of provincial government and society. Unfortunately, the acculturation process in Wawat makes it impossible to confirm this hypothesis, while data from Kush are as yet inadequate.

The indigenous elite was dominated by paramount 'chiefs' (*wrw*), best documented in the Eighteenth Dynasty but also referred to later. For that period, depictions of Nubian tribute, in which the chiefs are indicated by their activity, large size, and distinctive apparel, suggest there were only a small number of chiefs (between seven and nine) for Kush in its broader sense. In Huy's tomb only three chiefs of Wawat are shown (fig. 3.21), and in fact two principal chiefdoms therein are well documented, leaving room for another in the north. This division corresponds to topographically enforced breaks in the Lower Nubian settlement pattern (fig. 3.22) which had affected indigenous political structures as early as the Old Kingdom. This implies, of course, that the twenty-five toponyms assigned to Wawat in the list of Tuthmosis III (see O'Connor 1982, p. 928) were subsumed into the larger political units of the chiefdoms, and a similar process must be envisaged for Kush proper. Although at least eight or nine toponyms of the Tuthmoside list are to be located in Upper Nubia, only six chiefs of Kush are depicted in Huy's tomb. Earlier, in fact, Tuthmosis II, in apparent reference to Upper Nubia as a whole, specifically describes it as divided into five chieftainships (Breasted 1927, p. 139; see also Gardiner 1961, p. 180).[1] These chiefs were appointed by the Egyptians but were probably drawn from the upper levels of Nubian society, perhaps even from the families of hereditary chiefs of earlier periods.

Two chiefs' 'families' of Eighteenth Dynasty Wawat illustrate the administrative functions of the chiefs and the increased acculturation their role encouraged. The tombs, graffiti, dedicatory statues and stelae of one family are concentrated within the chiefdom of Miam, and the other in that of Tekhet (figs. 3.22–3). Chiefs' sons appear to have been sent to Egypt as hostages, brought up as pages at the Egyptian court (as were many Egyptians, including some viceroys, who later achieved high office) and subsequently incorporated into the bureaucracy of Wawat as 'administrators,' 'scribes' and 'viceregal deputies'. Those who eventually succeeded their fathers or other relatives as chiefs (*wrw*) presumably managed the internal affairs of the Nubian communities, and were the chief liaison between the indigenes and Egyptian officials. Although ethnically non-Egyptian (e.g. Hekanefer, as depicted in Huy's tomb; fig. 3.21), the chiefs were completely acculturated. Their personal names are usually partially or entirely Egyptian, their tombs Egyptian in function, form and decoration; and they appear to have assumed partially indigenous regalia only on such symbolically significant occasions as the presentation of tribute to the king. Iconographic evidence indicated that the Kushite chiefs underwent a similar, although not necessarily identical, process.

Archaeological evidence shows that, with a few exceptions, the indigenes of Wawat at all levels of society acculturated rapidly to Egyptian norms, at least in terms of material culture. Except on the

---

[1] The number of 'chiefs' actually involved in this text is ambiguous, but the reference to a five-fold division is explicit, and is suggestive in the context of the other data cited in this paragraph.

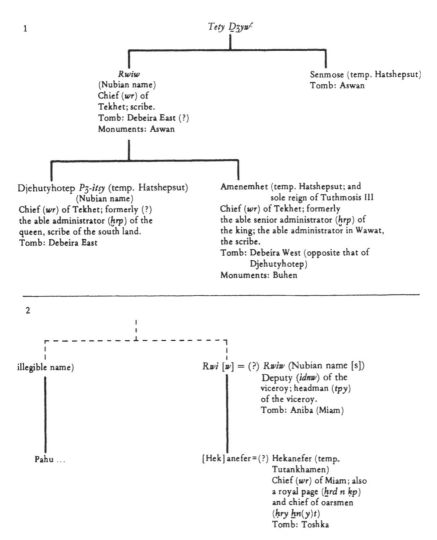

1

Tety Ḏ₃yw⁽

Rwiw
(Nubian name)
Chief (wr) of
Tekhet; scribe.
Tomb: Debeira East (?)
Monuments: Aswan

Senmose (temp. Hatshepsut)
Tomb: Aswan

Djehutyhotep P₃-itsy (temp. Hatshepsut)
(Nubian name)
Chief (wr) of Tekhet; formerly (?)
the able administrator (ḥrp) of the
queen, scribe of the south land.
Tomb: Debeira East

Amenemhet (temp. Hatshepsut; and
sole reign of Tuthmosis III
Chief (wr) of Tekhet; formerly
the able senior administrator (ḥrp) of
the king; the able administrator in Wawat,
the scribe.
Tomb: Debeira West (opposite that of
Djehutyhotep)
Monuments: Buhen

2

illegible name)

Rwi [w] = (?) Rwiw (Nubian name [s])
Deputy (idnw) of the
viceroy; headman (tpy)
of the viceroy.
Tomb: Aniba (Miam)

Pahu ...

[Hek]anefer = (?) Hekanefer (temp.
Tutankhamen)
Chief (wr) of Miam; also
a royal page (ḥrd n ḳp)
and chief of oarsmen
(ḥry ẖn(y)t)
Tomb: Toshka

Fig. 3.23  Genealogies and offices of the 'chieftains' families' of (1) Tekhet and (2) Miam. For the former, see Säve-Söderbergh (1960, 1963) and Edel (1963). As for the individuals from Miam, the identification between Rwi[w] and Rwiw is quite possible (cf. Steindorff 1937, 27; Plates, Taf. 13.56, for Rwi[w] and Text 69–70, 79 for Rwiw). The restoration of the name of Rwi[w]'s son as [Hek]anefer (not suggested by Steindorff, but cf. his Text 37, Plates, Taf, 13.56) is less plausible since, as Lanny Bell pointed out to me, the restoration requires the 'āleph vulture-sign (3) to be written out, which would not normally be the case in the New Kingdom. On Hekanefer, chief of Miam, see Simpson (1963).

southern edge of Wawat, the characteristic C-group culture (see chapter 2) did not survive the Second Intermediate Period. During that time, traditional C-group cemeteries rapidly became 'Egyptian' in tomb types, funerary artifacts and burial customs. The characteristic circular–oval C-group houses of rubble, vegetable materials and leather (?) were also replaced by right-angled structures making considerable use of mud brick. For lack of evidence, changes in contemporary Kushite material culture cannot yet be traced. It is important to note that a thoroughly 'Nubian' archaeological assemblage claimed to postdate and to be descended from the Second Intermediate Period 'Kerma culture' is, in fact, probably the latter's Middle Kingdom predecessor (see chapter 2).

At the end of the New Kingdom, the Kushite viceroy Penehasy, expelled from Egypt, retained control of Lower (and implicitly Upper) Nubia, since he was buried at Aniba (ancient Miam). The Lower Nubian population was markedly heterogeneous, consisting of Egyptians, many settled there for generations, a majority of Egyptianized Nubians and, probably, some Egypto-Nubians, but it maintained its political cohesion. This is indicated by its strong resistance to the sustained Egyptian effort at reconquest under Herihor and his son Piankh (p. 231); by a possible successor to Penehasy, who bore titles somewhat similar to his and whose recognition of the titular authority of Ramesses XI did not preclude continued hostility to Herihor; and by the voluntary and wholesale evacuation of Lower Nubia at about this time, which may initially have been caused by the intensity of Piankh's campaigning. This intensity is demonstrated by the facts that the younger artisans of the royal romb at Thebes were drafted into Piankh's army, and the Theban necropolis scribes were assigned to organizing the production of metal weapons instead of the normal artisans' tools.

The depopulation of Lower Nubia was long sustained, largely because of political circumstances rather than fluctuations in Nile level or in the local agricultural economy. Resettlement was, at first, precluded by Egyptian hostility; as late as Pinudjem II the ruling family of southern Egypt still claimed the title of Viceroy of Kush, and the Nubian campaign of Shoshenq I indicates more explicit conflict. No major resettlement was attempted under the Twenty-fifth (Kushite) Dynasty, and the unprecedented existence of a Kushite state approximately equal to Egypt in military and political strength throughout the Late and Ptolemaic Periods encouraged the maintenance of a mutually advantageous, largely empty, buffer zone, as did periodic open conflicts. Psammetichus II invaded Upper Nubia, and Cambyses and probably

Khababash (*c.* 335 BC?) also campaigned against the southerners. Only the strong expansionist tendencies of the Ptolemaic and Meroitic states (see chapter 4; Shinnie 1981), combined with some form of Egyptian–Meroitic accord under Ptolemy IV, led eventually to the resettlement of Lower Nubia in the first century BC.

The evolution of a Kushite state throughout the Third Intermediate Period is undocumented, except for the tombs of the apparent predecessors of the Twenty-fifth Dynasty at Kurru, near Napata. Going back to about 860 BC, these tombs indicate that the society from which the Twenty-fifth Dynasty arose was Upper Nubian in origin and, in its earlier phase, little affected by Egyptian culture. The circular earthen tumuli covering the simple pit-and-chamber tombs and the non-Egyptian orientation of the latter strongly suggest that, whatever degree of acculturation was reached in the New Kingdom, it had been lost in the intervening two centuries. However, even these earlier graves had assemblages of funerary goods which were dominated by artifacts imported from contemporary Egypt, indigenous culture being represented by stone arrow-heads and certain pottery types. These imports were presumably the result of trade, probably in Nubian gold, which occurred frequently amongst the grave-goods. Quite apart from the internal Egyptian demand for gold, Egypt had become increasingly involved in commercial and diplomatic activities in the Levant since the reign of Siamun (Twenty-first Dynasty). Given Egypt's weak military structure, gold was probably even more important in these activities than it had been in the New Kingdom.

The continual recurrence of Egyptian artifacts in the Kurru tombs shows that trade persisted and other evidence suggests an increasing intensity and variety of contact. During the eighth century BC, square mastabas replaced the tumuli style; stone masonry was used with increasing frequency; a preference for right-angled architectural forms became evident; and the burial-pit orientation conformed to Egyptian practice. These developments imply increased exposure to Egyptian models and techniques, a greater penetration of the Egyptian cultural region (aided certainly by the accelerating political fragmentation within Egypt) and perhaps the importation of Egyptian artisans. Conversely, the growing centrality of the Kushite state, reflected in the increasing size and elaboration of these royal tombs, culminated perhaps under the 'son of Re', 'the chieftain', Alara. His successor, Kashta, controlled Lower Nubia and was in close contact with Egypt. Shortly thereafter, the Kushite Piankhy conquered Middle and Upper Egypt. This led to a period of intense cultural interaction with Egypt which deeply affected the subsequent development of both Napatan and Meroitic culture. These themes are explored elsewhere (Shinnie 1981).

## EGYPT AND PUNT (fig. 3.24)

Punt was an important African contact area for the Egyptians, who probably visited it fairly regularly, but the region is tantalizingly poorly documented. The single *detailed* Egyptian source is the Punt reliefs of Hatshepsut at Deir el-Bahari and the region occupied by Punt has not been explored archaeologically. Within broad limits, the location of Punt is now well established (O'Connor 1982, p. 935) although it is important to note that the savanna animals sometimes ascribed to Punt actually are characteristic of Irem and *Nmȝyw*, adjoining Punt on the western side. Punt included the coastal plain and the hilly country east of it between latitudes 17° and 12°N, but little of the semidesert and savanna lands east of the hills. The characteristic indigenous Puntite products were *cntyw* incense, much desired by the Egyptians for ritual uses, ebony and short-horned cattle. The Puntites also traded in products derived from elsewhere – ivory (elephants are never associated with Punt or Irem and *Nmȝyw*), gold and panther and cheetah skins.

The Puntites are depicted in several Eighteenth Dynasty scenes. Typically, the men have dark reddish skins and fine features; characteristic negroid types are not shown, although they occur amongst depictions of riverine southerners (of Wawat, Kush, Irem, etc.). Other Puntite features are also not found amongst other southerners. Long hairstyles are typical for Puntites until the reign of Amenhotep II; during his reign and earlier, in that of Tuthmosis III, an intermediate 'bobbed' hairstyle appears, and thereafter Puntites have close-cropped hair similar to that of the chief of Punt under Hatshepsut. A long or medium dressed goatee is found at all periods, and decoration and dress are relatively simple; a medium-length or long kilt is the only male garment. Puntite women are rarely depicted and were in some cases steatopygous. Dwellings were beehive-shaped structures on piles.

The Egyptians – so far as we know – always reached Punt by sea, while conversely Puntite raft-like boats sometimes sailed to the Red Sea coast of Egypt in order to trade. Puntites, including the children of chiefs, also came to the Egyptian court and probably Punt acknowledged some kind of Egyptian overlordship. It must however have been very

Fig. 3.24   Merchants from Punt arriving at the Red Sea coast of Egypt and being received by Egyptian officials. Probably reign of Amenhotep III. (After Säve-Söderbergh 1946.)

loose. The fundamental Egyptian–Puntite relationship was one of trade, not political super- and subordination. Warlike activity against Punt is never referred to and indeed Punt would have been logistically very difficult to control. No permanent Egyptian centres were established there. However, sailing conditions in the Red Sea encouraged Egyptian expeditions to spend two or three months in Punt and to penetrate further inland. Archaeological exploration will eventually surely reveal traces of those visits – certainly rock inscriptions and graffiti, and perhaps more. Hatshepsut's expedition, for example, set up a shrine to Amen and the queen in Punt.

Egyptian–Puntite contacts are attested from the reign of Hatshepsut to that of Ramesses III. Thereafter, no reference has survived and probably direct contact with Punt was lost in the contraction of foreign contacts typical of the Third Intermediate Period.

## EGYPT AND LIBYA

New Kingdom and later relations with Libya, the other main African contact area, are one of the most intriguing and least studied aspects of Egyptian foreign relations. Any effort – such as the following – to analyse these relations must necessarily be tentative until further archaeological and epigraphic fieldwork is carried out in the western Delta, the adjacent deserts and Cyrenaica itself.

There are no explicit references to conflict with Libyans in the Eighteenth Dynasty. Intensifying although never specifically characterized contact is indicated by increasing references to Libyans in the later Eighteenth Dynasty. An official of Amenhotep III had Libyan (Mashwash) cattle in his stockyard, though whether these were booty, imports, or simply a type bred in Egypt is unknown; and Libyans (perhaps specifically Libu; see p. 253) are depicted as present at Akhenaten's court. Here they appear as chiefs or ambassadors bringing tribute or witnessing the king's public activities and also as members of the (predominantly Egyptian) military escort of the king.

References in the Nineteenth and Twentieth Dynasties are more frequent and increasingly detailed. Seti I fought a campaign against the chiefs of Tjehenu, the enemy being iconographically identifiable as Mashwash *if* the Egyptians were consistent in their depictions of the apparently slight differences in dress and appearance which distinguished the Mashwash from the Libu. Under Ramesses II, there are generalized references to conflict with the Tjehenu and Tjemehu and once specifically to the Libu, the earliest occurrence of that name. Ramesses II also founded or renovated a series of architectural complexes running along the coastal road to Libya and along the north-western edge of the Delta; the exact nature of these has never been fully investigated, but the exposed positions of some (fig. 3.25) and the military titles of an Egyptian(?) official associated with one, suggests that at least some of them were fortresses.

Both Merenptah (year 5, c. 1220 BC) and Ramesses III (year 5, c. 1180 BC) fought off substantial Libyan invasions, both dominated by the Libu. Merenptah killed over 9300 Libyans and their allies, but the figures of Ramesses III, if taken at their face value, indicate that over 28 000 Libyans were slain! Later, in year 11 (c. 1174 BC) Ramesses III forestalled a Mashwash invasion, killing 2175 and capturing a further 2052. Even if the numbers of Libyans slain during the first campaign of Ramesses III are lowered, they still numbered between 12 000 and 13 000, and the overall figures emphasize the seriousness of these invasions. Egyptian records rarely record the numbers of enemy slain and captives are usually numbered in hundreds or less, not in thousands.

The general level of culture and acculturation reached by the Libyans at this time is difficult to assess. Although they are shown as wearing entirely non-Egyptian dress, this depiction may be misleading, since it is in just such battle and capture scenes that traditional indigenous garb was regarded as symbolically appropriate by Egyptian artists (p. 266).

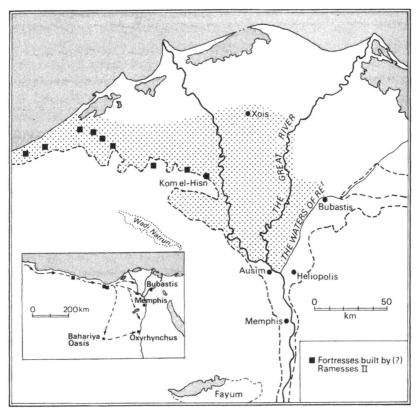

Fig. 3.25 The Libyans and Egypt in the New Kingdom. The broken lines on the smaller map indicate possible lines of Libyan movement, while the stippled area on the larger shows the area apparently affected by Libyan settlement and raiding. For fortresses see Rowe (1954).

That pastoralism was a major element in Libyan economy is suggested by the animals captured by the Egyptians, particularly the very large numbers of cattle, sheep and goats taken from the Mashwash under Ramesses III. Yet reference to the 'town' of the Libu chief Meryey and the 'towns' of the Mashwash indicate that permanent settlements existed, and the gold and silver, the numerous bronze swords and other artifacts, and the (primarily Mashwash) chariots included in the booty from the Libyans suggest that the level of material culture was well above that of a simple pastoral society. Here again, we must wait upon systematic survey and excavation for further data.

Typical of Egyptian–Libyan relations in the later New Kingdom were infiltration and culminating invasion by the latter, although the 'invasions' were, perhaps, actually organized Libyan resistance to periodic Egyptian attempts to exterminate or expel the infiltrators. The details of these processes are only partly reconstructible, largely because the locations of most of the relevant toponyms are unknown. The actual zone of Libyan settlement was only once defined (under Ramesses III) as running along the western Delta frontier from the Memphite province to Karabona, a place of unknown location. Possibly the primary zone of Libyan settlement lay between Kom el-Hisn and Ausîm (fig. 3.25), avoiding the apparently heavily fortified north-west corner of the Delta. Such a pattern would help explain their far-flung depredations in the central Delta and the anxiety with which, according to Merenptah, Memphis and Heliopolis reacted to the news of invasion. The Libyan settlements along the Delta fringe were the bases for extensive raiding, sometimes lasting for months, according to Merenptah, and even for 'many years', according to Ramesses III. Under both kings the raiders reached the Sebennytic branch of the Nile ('the Great River') and threatened the region of Bubastis on the eastern Nile branch ('the waters of Re'), and the raiding of the Xoite region is also noted under Ramesses III.

The Libyan campaign of Merenptah (c. 1220 BC) and the second Libyan campaign of Ramesses III are described in some detail and may have occurred in the same area. In each case the invading Libyans came from abroad, first attacking 'Tjehenu-land', in this context a pacified zone incorporating the northern oases and the home of such subdued groups as the Tjuk–Libyans who served in the Egyptian army in the Twentieth and Twenty-second Dynasties. Merenptah defeated the invaders between a fortress in Pi-yer and a point called 'the beginning of Earth' (*Wpt-t3*), and Ramesses III between a fortress at *Wpt-t3* and another about 16 km away, called the 'House of Sand' (*Hwt šꜥy*). This battle is depicted in a desert landscape (Fig. 3.26). The expression *Wpt—t3* was habitually applied to the furthermost limits of Egyptian dominion, but may not refer to an identical area in the two texts cited here; and the location of the 'House of Sand' remains uncertain, although a Thirtieth Dynasty text indicates that it lay west of the Delta proper. Its strategic importance is suggested by the titles of its tutelary deity, Min of *Hwt šꜥy*, specifically charged in Ptolemaic times with control of the Tjehenu and Tjemehu.

The New Kingdom Egyptians appear never to have attempted to establish permanent control over Cyrenaica (which would have yielded them little desirable income) and perhaps they never penetrated it. The westernmost known point of Egyptian occupation was the Ramesside

Fig. 3.26   Mashwash Libyans fleeing the army of Ramesses III during the Libyan campaign of his year 11. The relevant text reads (above the fortresses in the background): 'The [slaughter which his majesty made among the foe of] the land [of Mash]wash, who had come to Egypt; beginning from [the tow]n of Ramesses III which is upon the [mount]ain of *Wpt-t3* [to] the town *Hwt š῾y*, making 8 *itrw* (i.e. about 84 km) of carnage amongst them.' (See Edgerton and Wilson 1936, p. 61.) (After Nelson *et al.* 1932, pl. 70.)

fortress (?) at Zaouyet um el-Rakham, which is perhaps to be identified with the 'Fortress of the West' under Merenptah, which reported that a defeated Libyan chieftain had fled past it into his homeland, where he was deposed by his own people. Ramesses III did attempt to impose an Egyptian vassal (a youth, perhaps a chief's son and a hostage brought up in Egypt) over the Libu, Mashwash, and others: but the result was a major rebellion, not the acquiescence that would have been anticipated, for example, in contemporary Kush.

What were the causes of this unprecedentedly intense and long-sustained interaction between Libya and Egypt? The westernmost Delta had been periodically penetrated by Libyans for millennia, partly because of its natural proximity but also because of its lightly settled character. Prior to the Hellenistic period, this region was of low agricultural productivity, was given over chiefly to cattle grazing and had an inferior status in the hierarchy of government concerns – facts alluded to under Merenptah. However, while these circumstances facilitated the developments outlined above, they are insufficient as a cause.

There may have been pressure upon Cyrenaica's food supplies, due to climatic change or to a population increasing naturally or by immigration. The texts of Merenptah's reign suggest that the Libyan invasion of his time was caused by famine, and the Mashwash invasion under Ramesses III had the character of a true migration, since substantial numbers of women and enormous numbers of animals accompanied the fighting men. The relatively late appearance of the Mashwash and Libu in Egyptian texts (p. 253) might also suggest the appearance of new immigrant groups in Cyrenaica, but might equally well reflect the informed interest that Egypt was compelled to take as a result of Libyan pressure. Only archaeological fieldwork within Cyrenaica can resolve these questions. Unfortunately, so far, not even tentatively identified indigenous remains have been located prior to the sixth and fifth centuries BC.

Perhaps more significant than population pressure was a growing political cohesion and military strength amongst the Libyans, stimulated partly by the models presented by Egypt but also by other contacts. Surprisingly, non-Libyans made up perhaps a third of the Libyan force defeated by Merenptah, the foreigners consisting of the 'foreign Peoples of the Sea' the Sherden, Shekelesh, and Ekwesh, originating in the Aegean–western Anatolian region; the Teresh, of unknown origin; and the Lukki, from Lycia, also in Asia Minor. These foreigners clearly reached Libya by ship and were, the texts imply, recruited by the Libu chief, presumably because of their superior weaponry and armour. That trading contacts existed even before this time is suggested by the numerous bronze swords of Sherden type (and even armour) owned by (or derived from?) the Mashwash and included amongst the booty recorded by Merenptah. The international implication of these contacts is deepened by the, admittedly highly tentative, identification of the south-western Anatolian kingdom of Aḥhiyawa with the Ekwesh, who made up about two-thirds of the foreign allies of the Libyans. Aḥhiyawa was a powerful coastal state causing much concern to the contemporary Hittite kingdom, with which Merenptah was on good terms and which he may even have actively supported against such enemies as Aḥhiyawa!

A substantial degree of political centralization and military efficiency seems to have existed amongst the Libyans. It is true that the Libu and the Mashwash, the two most important groups, must be distinguished from each other. Although both probably included both dark-skinned, brunette types and fair-skinned, blue-eyed 'Berbers', they differed in dress and general appearance and in resources, the Mashwash having a much greater number of horses as well as apparently better links with the trading network of the eastern Mediterranean. The dichotomies suggest that the Mashwash were coastal and the Libu lived in the hinterland, or that the Mashwash were east of the Libu and better located for contact with Egypt and the Levantine seas.

Despite these differences, the two groups acted in concert, the Mashwash participating under Libu leadership in the battles against Merenptah and Ramesses III (year 5); and, if the Mashwash alone faced Ramesses III in year 11, they explicitly did so at the urging of the Libu. The dominant figure in each Libyan invasion was a single chief (*wr*), representing hereditary dynasties which respectively ruled the Libu and the Mashwash. For the former, the succession of the chiefs Ded, his son (?) Meshken, and *his* son Meryey is documented. Meryey, after his defeat by Merenptah, was deposed in favour of one of his 'brothers', and one of Meryey's descendants was, perhaps, the Libu chief opposing Ramesses III. For the Mashwash, we know that the chief Meshesher led the Libyan forces against Ramesses III, and that his still-living father, Kheper, also had great political authority. The military strength of the Libyans is indicated by the great relief the Egyptians expressed at their defeat, and, more explicitly, by the bowmen, swordsmen and foreign troops used by the Libu against Merenptah, as well as by the substantial number of chariots, bowmen and swordsmen found in the Mashwash army, defeated by Ramesses III.

The Libyan 'invasions' appear to have been the culmination of substantial, relatively long-term Libyan infiltration and settlement in the western Delta, which continued even after the great defeats described above. This movement was facilitated by internal political disintegration within Egypt, the relatively unimportant status of the western Delta in Egyptian eyes, and the rise of dynasties of Libyan origin (Twenty-second, Twenty-third, Twenty-fourth) in the Third Intermediate Period. Even in the later Twentieth Dynasty the roving bands of 'desert-dwellers' (*ḫ3styw*; sometimes specifically identified as Libu and Mashwash) which disturbed the Theban area may have been infiltrators as much as unruly soldiery. The importance of the Mashwash centres of the Delta during the Third Intermediate Period was partially derived from the military colonies of freed(?) Libyan prisoners of war set up in the Twentieth and perhaps Nineteenth dynasties but probably also from continuing immigration. The western Delta appears to have sustained a fresh wave of Libu immigration during the latter part of this period. The military clash between Psammetichus I and the Tjehenu (*c.* 654 BC) who occupied the western edge of the Nile Valley from Oxyrhynchus to the sea, while stated to have been caused by a Libyan invasion, is highly reminiscent of New Kingdom efforts to remove long-established infiltrators in that zone.

# CHAPTER 4

# THE LATE PERIOD, 664–323 BC

The years between the beginning of the Twenty-sixth Dynasty in 664 and the death of Alexander the Great in 323 are an age of unique interest in the history of Pharaonic Egypt. In the first place, they include the last periods during which it functioned as an independent political entity; secondly, since the source material is often unusually varied, both in origin and in character, this era yields insights into historical events and the nature of Egyptian society which would be difficult to parallel in earlier times; finally, and most intriguing of all, we are presented during these years with the spectacle of Egyptian culture under pressure from major civilizations of the Eastern Mediterranean and the Near East and are able to study in some depth the adaptations which it made in ideology, institutions, and technological apparatus in order to counter recurrent challenges to its cultural identity. In the present chapter an attempt will be made, in the first instance, to define the political and military context within which these developments unfolded; we shall then proceed to a detailed analysis of the socio-economic system whose vigour, efficiency, and flexibility ultimately determined the success and even survival of the nation during these years of intermittent triumph and disaster.

PROLEGOMENA

## *Chronology*

To the Egyptologist chronology is a recurrent problem, and the period covered by this chapter is no exception. Indeed, the difficulties are particularly acute; for not only is it necessary to deal with no fewer than three oriental systems of dating – Egyptian, Babylonian and Jewish – but the historian is also required to master Greek and Roman chronological techniques as well.

Egyptian, Babylonian and Jewish chronologies are all based on the regnal years of kings, that is, an event is said to take place in regnal year $x$ of king $y$. Theoretically, converting such dates into dates BC is a simple matter: all we need to do is to establish the sequence of kings and the length of each reign and then identify one fixed point which can be tied into our own chronological scheme. Unfortunately, it is impossible to realize these preconditions fully in the period under discussion for a variety of reasons. To begin with, it is sometimes impossible to establish the sequence of kings or their reign-lengths – sometimes both. Regnal dates for the Saite period present no problem, since the reign-lengths of all its kings are known, and we have fixed points convertible into our dating system in the form of an astronomical date and the date of the Persian invasion of Egypt at the end of the Saite Dynasty. The regnal dates of the Persian kings of the Twenty-seventh and Thirty-first Dynasties are equally trouble-free since they can be determined from unimpeachable Babylonian and related sources. On the other hand, those for the Twenty-eighth, Twenty-ninth, and Thirtieth Dynasties are more problematic since the fragments of the Egyptian historian Manetho, on which they must be based, present serious problems of interpretation: his *History of Egypt* survives only in later quotations of dubious accuracy, and the chronological data given in the quotations relating to our period are contradictory. This situation, combined with the paucity of contemporary Egyptian sources, means that some uncertainty remains on reign-lengths and even the order of succession of some Pharaohs of the period. The beginning of the reign of Nectanebo II is fixed by astronomical evidence at 359/8, and, if Manetho is used in conjunction with all available data, a workable chronological scheme can be constructed, but regnal dates should in general be regarded with a measure of circumspection.

Even if these difficulties did not exist, there are still pitfalls awaiting the unwary chronographer. In the first place, establishing the reign-length of an Egyptian king is not as straightforward as it might seem. To the Egyptians, unlike the Babylonians, a king's first regnal year began as soon as he came to the throne and ended with the end of that calendar year. This was regarded as regnal year 1, irrespective of the length of time involved. However, it also counted as the last regnal year of his predecessor. We must always make allowance for these conventions in any attempt to establish the actual length of a Pharaoh's reign. Difficulties can also arise when attempting to fix dates given in the Egyptian scheme within a particular reign. It is easy to forget that, when converting a date expressed in regnal years, we need to count inclusively, for example regnal year 3 of Amasis is 570 – 2, not 570 – 3. There is another less obvious, but much more insidious danger. It can happen that, with the increase in our knowledge, the date for the

TABLE 4.1  *Names and dates of the kings of Egypt from 664 to 323 BC*

| SAITE PERIOD | | FIRST PERSIAN PERIOD | |
|---|---|---|---|
| Twenty-sixth (Saite) Dynasty | | Twenty-seventh Dynasty | |
| | Regnal Dates | | Regnal Dates |
| Psammetichus I | 664–610 | Cambyses | 525–521 |
| Necho II | 610–595 | Darius I | 521–485 |
| Psammetichus II | 595–589 | Xerxes | 485–464 |
| Apries | 589–570[a] | Artaxerxes I | 464–423 |
| Amasis (Ahmose II) | 570–526 | Darius II | 423–404 |
| Psammetichus III | 526–525 | | |

| EGYPTIAN INDEPENDENCE | | | |
|---|---|---|---|
| Twenty-eighth (Saite) Dynasty | | Thirtieth (Sebennyte) Dynasty | |
| Amyrtaeus | c. 404/3–398/7 | Nectanebo I | c. 379/8–361/0 |
| Nepherites I | c. 398/7–392/1 | Tachos/Teos | c. 361/0–359/8 |
| Achoris | c. 392/1–379/8 | Nectanebo II | c. 359/8–342/1 |
| Psammuthis | (?)[b] | | |
| Nepherites II | c. 379/8 | Ochus | 342–337 |

| SECOND PERSIAN PERIOD | |
|---|---|
| Thirty-first Dynasty | |
| | Regnal Dates |
| Artaxerxes III (Ochus) | 341/0–337 |
| Arses | 337–335 |
| Darius III (Codomannus) | 335–332 |
| Alexander III of Macedon | 332–323 |

[a] Deposed 570, killed 567 (Edel 1978, pp. 13ff).

[b] Regnal year, undatable, but probably contemporaneous with one of the earlier regnal years of Achoris.

accession of a ruler will be altered, as has happened in recent years in the case of the kings of the Twenty-sixth Dynasty. This means that all dates for events within the reign, if they are based on regnal years, will also need to be revised to keep in step. A classic example of the consequences of failing to do this is provided by the current confusion over the dating of the Nubian campaign of Psammetichus II which is still often given as 591. The date in the Egyptian chronological scheme is regnal year 3, which was originally converted using one of the older dates for Psammetichus' accession, viz. 593: subtract 2, answer 591. Unfortunately the accession date has now been raised to 595; subtract 2, answer 593.[1]

Dates given in the Classical writers who are so important for our

[1] For detailed discussions of the Egyptian chronology of this period see Kienitz (1953, pp. 153ff); Drioton and Vandier (1962, pp. 621ff); Lloyd (1975a, pp. 191ff); for Jewish chronology see Finegan (1964); for Babylonian chronology see Parker and Dubberstein (1956).

period employ several systems. Herodotus' Saite chronology consists simply of giving reign-lengths which are evidently based on Egyptian sources. The systems used by Diodorus Siculus (first century BC), our main authority for fourth-century Egyptian history, are Greek or Roman, being based on annual magistracies in Athens or Rome and Olympiad dates.[1] The conversion of such dates into years BC presents no difficulty, but the results are often startlingly confused: for instance at xv, 29, Achoris is described as making hostile moves against Persia in 377, which was after the end of his reign; at xvi, 40, Artaxerxes III's attack on Egypt is dated to the archonship of Thessalus (actually Theellus), which fell in 351, and the consulship of Marcus Fabius and Titus Quinctius, which fell in 354. Since these cases are far from isolated, it is impossible to place any confidence in his chronological precision, and dates for fourth-century Egyptian history emanating from his work should be regarded as tentative only, even if they are not contradicted by internal or external evidence.

## Political and military history

The Twenty-sixth Dynasty represents the last great age of pharaonic civilization. Its political basis was created by Psammetichus I of Sais. When he succeeded his father Necho I as ruler of Sais in 664 he controlled a small kingdom comprising the western Delta and the Memphite area under the nominal suzerainty of the Assyrians. On his death in 610 he had made Egypt a powerful and unified kingdom able once more to take its place amongst the great nations of the Orient. This transformation was not achieved without difficulty. The unification of the country and the consolidation of the kingdom were a matter of decades of judicious and sometimes ruthless effort in the face of major obstacles. Within the country he had to cope with rival princes, the ambitions of the priesthood of Amen-Ra at Thebes, and, initially, his own economic and military weakness. Externally, Assyrians, Ethiopians and Libyans all posed a constant threat to Egyptian security and even independence.

Psammetichus' first problem was inevitably that of providing himself with the economic and military means necessary for the fulfilment of his ambitions. According to our Greek sources he satisfied the first requirement by embarking on a large-scale policy of establishing

---

[1] Tables of Athenian archons and Roman consuls will be found in Bickerman (1968, pp. 168ff). For dating by Olympiads see *ibid.*, pp. 75ff.

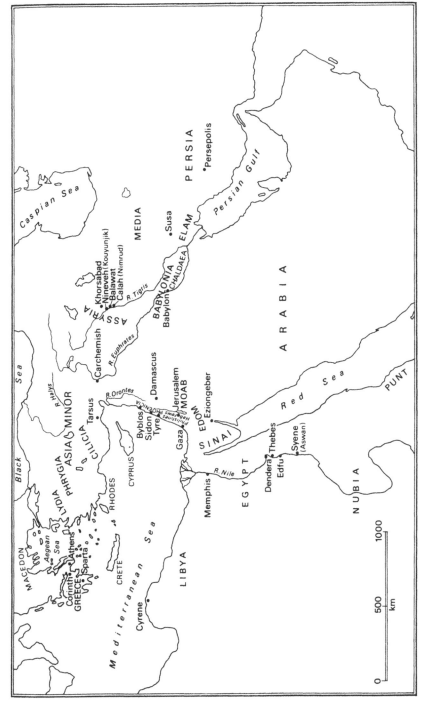

Fig. 4.1   Egypt, the eastern Mediterranean and the Near East in the first millennium BC.

trade-relations with Greeks and Phoenicians. Foreigners also played an important role in meeting his military needs. No doubt many of his troops derived from the native Egyptian warrior class, but our sources make it clear that the cutting-edge of his army was made up, in the main, of mercenary troops, particularly Carians and Ionian Greeks. Having established his power on this basis of economic and military strength, Psammetichus rapidly conquered the rival princes of the Delta to achieve total domination of the northern part of the kingdom.

In Middle and Upper Egypt more subtle methods were employed. The Petition of Petiese[1] reveals that, at an early period in his reign, Psammetichus was able to neutralize his rivals in Middle Egypt by exploiting his close relationship with Petiese and Somtutefnakht, 'Shipmasters' of Herakleopolis, the most important city in that area. To the south diplomacy proved equally effective in dealing with the power of the Theban temple state (see below p. 303) which was brought firmly, if deftly, under his control in 656. However, gentle though these measures both in Upper and Middle Egypt may have been, it would be unwise to ignore the fact that the velvet glove concealed a mailed fist. As in Lower Egypt, the ultimate sanction and guarantee of Psammetichus' power was military force, particularly his tough foreign mercenaries who would be even less likely than Egyptian troops to be troubled by scruples in discharging any instructions issued by their paymaster.

All in all, we may say that after 656 the policies pursued by Psammetichus I operated more and more efficiently and that a steady integration of the kingdom ensued, accompanied by a growing sense of national unity and power. This was evidently expressed by the resumption of interest in all the traditional spheres of activity, particularly in the resuscitation of a nation-wide programme of building on a monumental scale, and was complemented by carefully orchestrated and highly successful military and political activity abroad.

The half century of Psammetichus I's reign clearly achieved such success in the resurgence of the country that his son Necho II (610–595) was able to commit a high proportion of his resources and energies to a policy of expansion abroad. Not surprisingly, therefore, these activities dominate our tradition. Trade with the Red Sea coast was pursued with

---

[1] Recorded in P. *Rylands* IX, published by Griffith (1909). It dates to the reign of Darius and records the fortunes of a priestly family at El-Hibeh from the time of Psammetichus I down to the early years of the reign of Darius. This text is our most important source for the social history of the period which it covers and has been heavily used in the following discussion.

enthusiasm, and he is even alleged to have dispatched an expedition to circumnavigate Africa.

To the east Egyptian military control of the Levant was pushed for a short while as far as the Euphrates but maintaining these Asiatic possessions proved, in the long term, beyond Necho's capabilities, and all was lost after his defeat by the Chaldaeans at Carchemish in 605. Nevertheless he did succeed in thwarting all efforts of this aggressive and ruthless enemy to follow up his success by invading Egypt itself.

Necho's activities in Asia had their African counterpart in the short reign of Psammetichus II (595–589) when a great military expedition was dispatched into Nubia in 593. This certainly penetrated beyond the Third Cataract but did not lead to the resumption of Egyptian control over the area. Psammetichus also attempted to reaffirm Egyptian authority in Philistia by conducting a ceremonial progress there in 592.

The reign of Apries (589–570), despite its concluding disasters, left an impression in later traditions of considerable success and prosperity. Again, however, it is foreign relations which loom largest in the record. The spectre of the north-east frontier haunted Apries as much as it did his predecessors and led to large-scale military and naval operations in Phoenicia, Palestine and Cyprus to check the ambitions of Chaldaea. The western frontier also posed problems in the form of the rising power of the Greek city of Cyrene. Here Apries most unwisely resolved upon a military solution and dispatched a large force of native Egyptian troops to deal with the threat. The disastrous defeat of this army led to a mutiny which was fanned to white heat by nationalist resentment against the privileged position of the foreign mercenaries favoured by Apries. The mutineers set up a courtier of Apries called Amasis as a rival Pharaoh, defeated Apries, and forced him to flee the country (570). He then took refuge with the Chaldaean king Nebuchadrezzar II who, in 567, dispatched an army to Egypt to reinstate him as a pro-Chaldaean puppet. This force was met in the Delta by Amasis and crushingly defeated in an action during which Apries himself was killed.

Amasis (570–526) was, beyond doubt, the last great Pharaoh of Egypt. Herodotus speaks in fulsome terms of the immense prosperity of the country under his rule, and this is confirmed both by the substantial body of documents surviving from this time and by the large amount of building, some of it on a colossal scale, which he was able to carry through. It is clear that his reign saw the consummation of the process of unification initiated by Psammetichus I, but, prosperous though the country might have been, it was in continual danger of attack, first from the Chaldaeans and later from the Persians, and Amasis clearly devoted much thought and energy to the problem. An army of Egyptian troops and mercenaries was maintained, financed, in the main, by commercial dealings with foreign states. Alliances were also concluded against Chaldaea and later against Persia, which were cemented in some cases by intermarriage and in the others by a calculated generosity which was spectacularly successful in winning him good will. In all these activities one detects the workings of a mind keenly aware of the international political scene and capable of the shrewdest appraisal of political and strategic realities. It would appear that he was not even above exploring the advantages of marrying off an Egyptian princess into the Persian royal family.[1]

With the reign of Amasis' son Psammetichus III (526/5) the Saite period comes to an end. Even in Amasis' time the steady rise of Persia had caused increasing anxiety, and in 525, after prodigious preparations, the Persian king Cambyses invaded the country. He quickly overran it, deposed Psammetichus, and eventually executed him.

Persian control of Egypt fell into two periods separated by an interval of independence under native Egyptian rule. The first and most successful phase began in 525 with the conquest of the country by Cambyses and ended in 404. Cambyses himself gained a grim reputation in Egypt for impiety and cruelty, but there is good evidence that this was largely unjustified. In some cases, he certainly took a stringent view of temple privilege, but, in general, his policy was characterized by forbearance and conciliation. This was also the attitude of Darius (521–485), whose regard for Egyptian religious sentiment and concern for the general well-being of the country won him the respect and, sometimes, the devotion of the native Egyptian population. The honeymoon was, however, brief, and was succeeded by a series of revolts. The first began in 486 at the end of the reign of Darius in the wake of the Persian defeat at Marathon in 490. It was put down by the beginning of 484, but it had the most serious consequences in that it led to a much more repressive attitude on the part of the Persian administration which all but guaranteed the resumption of hostilities. The second revolt, the famous rebellion of Inarus, began c. 463/2 and

---

[1] According to Herodotus (III, 1–2) there was a tradition that Amasis had given an Egyptian princess in marriage to Cyrus or Cambyses. This narrative undoubtedly owes much to Egyptian nationalist propaganda (Lloyd 1982b, p. 175), but it is at least possible that it is based on an historical attempt of Amasis to establish close links with the Persian royal house.

simmered on until *c.* 449; the third broke out in 414/13 and ended with the liberation of the country by Amyrtaeus of Sais in 404. The roots of this instability lay in two factors: the inveterate hostility of a small number of high-ranking Egyptian and Egypto-Libyan families to Persian domination, and the fact that Egypt was quite simply too far away from the heart of the Empire to be held securely for more than a few decades.

The independence won in 404 lasted until 343. The history of these years is dominated by two factors: in foreign relations the spectre of resumed Persian intervention was an overwhelming consideration which found expression sometimes in covert support, sometimes in active alliance with rebellious Persian vassals or satraps in the western provinces of the Persian Empire, and in particular, a close, if pragmatic, relationship with the Greek state of Sparta whose generally anti-Persian stance created a strong community of interest with Egypt and made her a ready collaborator in Egypt's foreign policy; internally, stability was continually threatened by squabbling between the feudal princes and families of the great cities of the Delta, in particular Sais, Mendes and Sebennytus, a situation which could not but weaken the military strength of the kingdom. In general, however, it could be said that it was Egypt's distance from the heart of the Empire and, therefore, its relatively low priority in the scale of imperial preoccupations which saved it from renewed subjection to Persian power until the second half of the fourth century.

The second and final period of Persian domination began with the reconquest of the country by Artaxerxes III in 343, after an earlier unsuccessful attempt, apparently in 351, and lasted until the Macedonian conquest in 332. Source material is far from plentiful for this decade, but the documentation available creates a strong impression that rapacity and avarice were conspicuous features of Persian administration. Indeed, there is a distinct possibility that armed rebellion once more raised its head in the form of the revolt of the enigmatic Khabbash, perhaps about 338, but the precise date of this event remains uncertain. It is, however, beyond dispute that Alexander the Great, who arrived in the last months of 332, was welcomed with open arms by the indigenous population for whom the presence of yet another foreigner on the throne of Egypt was of much less importance than the definitive expulsion of the hated Mede. Unfortunately for the Egyptians, the misrule of the conqueror's minions over the next ten years was to prove such jubilation premature, and it was not until the country passed into the hands of Ptolemy, son of Lagus, after Alexander's death at Babylon in 323, that sound government was re-established in the country.

## ORGANIZATION

The political and military achievements described in the preceding summary were expressions of a specific socio-economic structure. It is the main purpose of the remainder of this chapter to define that structure as precisely as possible within the limits of the space available. Any such discussion is inevitably dominated by the issue of kingship since Pharaoh provided nothing less than the theoretical and institutional basis of the entire system, and the first part of this section will be devoted to an analysis of that office. We shall then proceed to describe social stratification in the Late Period, settlement patterns, economic structure, and internal administration.

### The king

According to traditional concepts Pharaoh was a god incarnate, the earthly embodiment of the god Horus and, as such, the champion of the cosmic order (*mȝʿt*). To fulfil this role he disposed of three main qualities: *siȝ*, 'perception', *ḥw*, 'authoritative utterance', and military prowess. He discharged this cosmicizing function in three main capacities: as priest of all the deities of Egypt he maintained the power of the gods and, with it, the very fabric of the universe; as administrator he was responsible for the economic well-being and ordered life of the Egyptian people; as soldier he repelled the enemies of Egypt and guaranteed, by main force, the continuance of ordered life.

If we consider the concept of kingship which prevailed in the Late Period, we find much that fits perfectly into these age-old patterns of thought. The five-fold titulary used since the Old Kingdom as a dogmatic statement of the functions of an Egyptian king was still *de rigueur*, and the vocabulary applied to Pharaoh and the language of royal documents present an equally familiar picture: he is designated by the traditional terms *ḥm·f*, 'His Majesty', *nb tȝwy*, 'Lord of the Two Lands', *ḥkȝ ʿȝ n Kmt*, 'Great Ruler of Egypt', and his actions are described using the time-honoured terminology which evoked his divine function as a source of order. There are, however, significant variations: in the Saite period the royal titulary can be written in ways which recall features characteristic of Old Kingdom inscriptions. Similarly, the Apries stele at Mit Rahina imitates the language and structure of Old Kingdom decrees and even the very shape of Old Kingdom stelae (Gunn 1927, pp. 211ff). There can be no doubt that these and similar traits are considerably more than an antiquarian fancy and that they reveal an important aspect of the way in which these kings conceived of the royal office; their role was not simply to embody the ideal of kingship, but to restore Egypt to the pinnacles of its ancient glory.

The iconography of kingship shows a similar pattern of traditional motifs interspersed with significant variations or points of emphasis. Ancient forms of head-dress, such as the crowns of Upper and Lower Egypt, the blue crown, and the *nemes*, retain their popularity, as do the royal kilt, the bull's tail and the royal beard. Occasionally, however, the material shows an unusual and highly revealing interest in a particular motif: during the Saite period the blue crown was particularly popular, probably for two reasons: in the first place, since it was never worn by the Nubian conquerors of Egypt, whose vestigial power in Upper Egypt had been destroyed by Psammetichus I, its use in the Saite period was probably tantamount to a forceful affirmation of the Egyptian origin of the Saite Dynasty itself; secondly, inasmuch as the use of this crown seems always to have expressed a claim to legitimacy (Davies 1982, pp. 71ff), its insistent employment by Saite kings amounted to nothing less than an assertion of their right to rule. The prevalence of the sphinx in the royal iconography of the Late Period may have served a similar propagandist function. At all periods such sculptures usually, if not always, represented the king with a lion's body and clearly symbolized his role as a powerful and invincible protector of the people against Typhonic forces. Amasis seems to have had a marked taste for depicting himself in this form, and the granite lions of Nectanebo I in the Vatican representing the king as a recumbent lion are patently no more than variations on the same theme which have their antecedents in the New Kingdom. It need hardly be said that a symbol of the king as guardian and protector of his people was more than marginally relevant in the perilous world within which Egypt was striving to maintain its unity, independence, and cultural integrity in the years between 664 and 323.

The examination of the facial expressions of royal statues can often yield insights into contemporary concepts of the role of the kingly office, the classic case being the royal statues of the late Twelfth Dynasty. Saite sculptures were not as brutal or as strident in conveying their message, but were, nevertheless, capable of portraying significant variations from one reign to another. Representations attributed to Psammetichus I

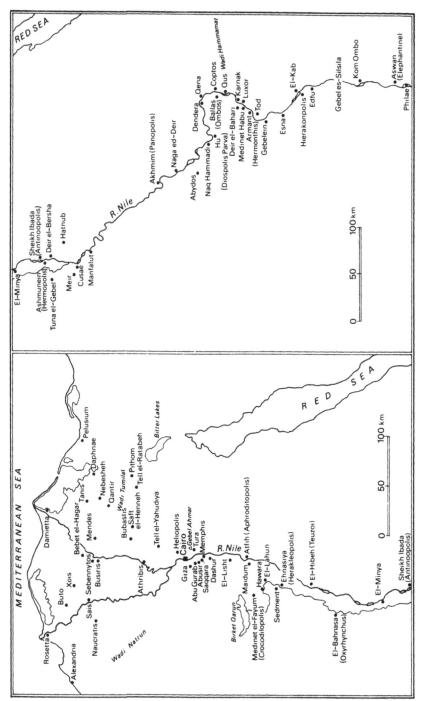

Fig. 4.2 Egypt in the first millennium BC.

show a face which is rather grim and determined, no doubt accurately reflecting a reaction to the formidable problems with which that king was confronted. On the other hand, the statues of later Saite rulers display a mixture of benevolence and god-like detachment quite at variance with those of the dynasty's founders. Again, we can be sure that the features in question are a reflection of historical circumstances: the struggles of Psammetichus' reign had given way to a quiet confidence in Egypt's ability to maintain its unity and security. In none of this, however, can one detect fundamental changes from traditional modes of royal iconography. This last remark cannot, however, be made of a group of statues of Nectanebo II, the last native Egyptian Pharaoh, which show him under the protection of a god represented as an animal. In the green schist example from Heliopolis, for instance, the king is shown under the protection of Horus who is depicted as a huge falcon towering above the minuscule figure of the king. This statue has, of course, conceptual affinities with the well-known Old Kingdom seated statue of Khafra in which the latter is represented with a hawk at his head, but the difference of scale between animal-god and king in the two statues speaks volumes for the evolution of concepts of kingship. Khafra, whilst acknowledging his role as the incarnation of Horus, confidently asserts his individual majesty and power; Nectanebo, on the other hand, confesses his total dependence on the beneficence of the god for his continued enjoyment of the kingly office. It might be argued that this is not particularly novel since the Instruction to Merikara (Simpson 1973, pp. 180ff) written at the end of the First Intermediate Period also insists on the dependence of kings on the will of the gods, but the evidence of the Demotic Chronicle (see below, pp. 299ff) suggests that these Thirtieth Dynasty statues reflect an acknowledgement of royal dependence upon divine help which passes beyond anything previously identifiable.

The continued vitality of the traditional concept of kingship exemplified by the material already discussed is also reflected in the survival and enthusiastic exploitation of traditional genres in literary and epigraphic descriptions of royal action. There is still a taste for the *Königsnovelle* ('tale of royal deeds') in which the king is first of all represented in council with his courtiers about him who are completely at a loss as to how to deal with a particular problem; the king then provides the answer, and the courtiers respond with encomia in honour of their omniscient ruler. There are two excellent examples of this motif from the Saite period: the Nitocris Adoption Stele, which refers to the installation of Psammetichus I's daughter as prospective High Priestess of Amen-Ra in 656, is quite clearly cast in this mould, and the Amasis Stele describing the conflict between Amasis and Apries also exploits this motif (Caminos 1964, pp. 71ff; Edel 1978, pp. 13ff). Another genre which continues to enjoy popularity is the biographical inscription describing royal commissions discharged by officials. Examples of the Saite period are plentiful: in the biographical inscription of Peftjuaneith we are informed that the owner was sent by Amasis to Abydos where he conducted the reconstruction of the sanctuary and the reorganisation of its revenues; Neferibranefer in the reign of Psammetichus II describes how he was sent by the king to save the sanctuaries of the gods of Sais; Nakhthorheb narrates his achievements when he was placed in charge of ensuring the offerings of temples in the reign of Amasis; and Psamtjeksineith boasts in the same reign that he was chosen by the king to make monuments in Sais (Lloyd 1982b, p. 167, n. 4). Such texts, at all periods, give expression to the canonical doctrine that power and initiative are the preserve of the king, and that officials of all ranks function as no more than his deputies.

The concept of the king preserved in Egyptian popular tradition of the Late Period was very different from that described above but is, in its way, equally traditional. It is characterized by a marked irreverence for the royal office. Readers of Herodotus will be familiar with his picture of the bibulous and iconoclastic Amasis (II, 173–4), and there can be no doubt that, despite some crude retouching, this tradition derives from Egyptian sources. It surfaces again in the third century BC tale of Amasis and the Skipper written on the back of the Demotic Chronicle. In this tale we read how the king took rather too much to drink while on a boating picnic with his harem and was afflicted on the following morning with so severe a hangover that he was quite incapable even of standing up. In this parlous state he made a request to be entertained by a story and was told a tale of a boatman, his wife, and a Pharaoh, the details of which are unfortunately lost since the end of the papyrus is destroyed (see Spiegelberg 1914, pp. 26ff). Such light-hearted tales of royal self-indulgence, and sometimes discomfiture, were clearly part of the stock-in-trade of Egyptian tradition. In the Middle Kingdom Westcar Papyrus we are presented with the spectacle of the bored king Khufu needing amusement and being entertained with stories, not to speak of a salacious account of his father's relaxation on the palace-lake with the ladies of the harem! In the New Kingdom tale of Neferkara and Sasenet the conduct of the Pharaoh Neferkara is not only described as being distinctly unroyal but as following a pattern which spectacularly violated Egyptian moral sentiment! In the demotic tale of the Setem-priest Khaemwese we are treated to a scene depicting the humiliation of the great Pharaoh Tuthmosis III.[1] In all these cases the motivation behind such caricatures was, in the main, the need to provide comic relief as a counterweight to the aura of omnipotence and ineffable majesty surrounding the god-king.

Let us now consider the question of the extent to which Late Period Pharaohs followed the traditional programme of action characteristic of the royal office. This involves the study of the king's actions in three areas: the cult, defence, and administration, though it should be emphasized that these categories are simply a matter of convenience for the modern scholar and that, to the Egyptian, they were far from mutually exclusive.

The religious role of Pharaoh was central to his office and entailed nothing less that his functioning as the link between the divine order and human beings. As such, he was the channel through which the life-giving power of the gods was bestowed upon men and the agent through whom the resources of men could be conferred upon the gods to maintain them at a maximum level of potency. Without Pharaoh both gods and men were lost. Pharaohs of the Late Period discharged their obligations in this respect to the letter. In the first place, the building, maintenance and endowment of temples, which had always formed an essential part of Pharaoh's priestly duties, were vigorously pursued whenever circumstances and resources permitted. Psammetichus I did much work at Memphis where he built a pylon on the south side of the Temple of Ptah and also a court for the Apis Bull (Herodotus, II, 153); the Mit Rahina Stele of Apries refers to donations to the same temple. The Nitocris Adoption Stele lists many endowments settled on Nitocris as the presumptive High Priestess of Amen-Ra at Thebes. Amasis was a prodigious builder and was active at many sites including Sais (where architectural and sculptural work is known which shows a marked taste for gigantism), Karnak, Edfu, Philae, Elephantine, and Memphis. In Memphis Herodotus mentions a colossus of his which suggests that he may even have been attempting to emulate Ramesses II's achievements in this respect in the same city (II, 176, 1). Such an ambition would have been very much of a piece with Amasis' work on the temple of Wadjet at Nebesheh where he clearly attempted to associate his activities with those of Ramesses II and Senusret III.

The Persian rulers of Egypt initially adopted this priestly aspect of

---

[1] For the Westcar Papyrus see Simpson (1973, pp. 15ff); for Neferkara and Sasenet see Posener (1957, pp. 119ff); for the demotic tale of Tuthmosis III see Griffith (1900, pp. 173ff).

the Pharaonic role with enthusiasm. The inscription of Udjahorresnet of the early Persian period speaks in glowing terms of the services to the temple of Neith at Sais of Cambyses and Darius.[1] Darius was also largely responsible for the construction of a temple in honour of Amen-Ra at Hibis in the Kharga Oasis, was active in the temple of Kasr el-Ghoueita in the same area, worked at Abusir, and made dedications at Edfu. The care shown by these rulers in this respect forcefully demonstrates the continued importance of this aspect of the Pharaonic office in that it implies a recognition on their part that the discharge of such duties was a prerequisite to their being accepted in the fullest sense as legitimate rulers of Egypt. The period of Egyptian independence from 404 to 343 provides further illustrations of this point. The Naucratis Stele of Nectanebo I describes elaborate measures on behalf of the finances of the temple of Neith at Sais (Gunn 1943, pp. 55ff; Posener 1947, pp. 117ff), and the last native Pharaoh Nectanebo II constructed a massive temple in honour of Isis at Behbet el-Hagar.

It is evident, therefore, that the basic principles determining the relationship of Pharaoh to the temples show no significant modification in our period. There are, however, some changes in the deities receiving attention which are very much a sign of the times. Isis features prominently: Amasis built a temple for her at Memphis, which is the first substantial temple known to have been constructed in her honour anywhere in the country, and another at Philae; Nectanebo II's huge granite temple at Behbet el-Hagar, probably the goddess' place of origin, still provides one of the most impressive ruins in Egypt. This sudden efflorescence of her cult as a major feature of state concern is not, however, difficult to explain: her worship was associated closely with kingship, and in the Late Period the concept of kingship needed all the support it could get; the cult of Isis was Lower Egyptian in origin, and all the native dynasties of the Late Period derived from Lower Egypt; since Isis had become increasingly popular amongst the Egyptian people at large, royal patronage of the goddess would yield an obvious political dividend by establishing a close bond of religious sympathy between the crown and the populace at large. Animal cults also received much more royal attention than previously: Nectanebo I was active at Hermopolis on behalf of Thoth the Ibis, at Saft el-Henna for Horus, and at Mendes on behalf of the sacred ram, to name only three; Nectanebo II worked at Saqqara both in the Serapeum (the burial place

---

[1] A modern English translation will be found in Lichtheim (1980, pp. 36ff). For a detailed discussion with full bibliography see Lloyd (1982b).

of the Apis Bulls) and in the complex of the Mother of the Apis to the north; he also showed an interest in other centres of animal worship such as Armant and Bubastis. The royal predilection for these cults is again not difficult to explain. They were uniquely Egyptian, and by supporting them these kings were, at one level, asserting the distinctive nature of Egyptian civilization in the face of growing pressure from foreign culture. Furthermore, like the cult of Isis, animal worship was immensely popular, and royal support of such cults inevitably served to encourage a sense of national identity.

The relationship of Pharaoh to the temples was not, however, confined to ensuring their material well-being. He was also, in theory, the priest of all the deities of Egypt, a role which is copiously illustrated in earlier times both by written sources and on temple walls and lesser monuments. Counterparts in the era under discussion have not survived in large numbers, but the tradition evidently continued intact: reliefs in the temples of ᶜAin el-Muftella in the Bahriya Oasis depict Amasis engaged in the cult in classic fashion; the inscription of Udjahorresnet insists relentlessly on the central importance of this aspect of the king's duties in the early Persian period; and the unimpaired relevance of this concept to the very end of our period is demonstrated unequivocally by the Demotic Chronicle.

The second traditional aspect of Pharaoh's activities requiring discussion is his role as protector of his people. This he was expected in earlier times to discharge in two senses: first, he was to guarantee security within the country by adequate policing, and, if necessary, formal military operations; secondly, he was expected to defend Egypt from its foreign enemies. These ideas are amply illustrated by such texts as the Twelfth Dynasty hymns in honour of Senusret III from Kahun. It is clear from epithets and attributes borne by kings throughout our period as well as from the measures taken to ensure internal security and the defence of the kingdom from foreign attack (see below pp. 333, 337ff) that these aspects of Pharaoh's responsibilities were as important in the Late Period as they had ever been.

The third major aspect of Pharaoh's office was the administration of the kingdom. It was a central dogma of the Egyptian state that all power derived ultimately from Pharaoh, and all aspects of government were under his control. In practice, of course, delegation of authority was essential and far-reaching. Here again, the Late Period shows no difference in principle from earlier practice (see below, pp. 331ff).

Up to this point, the burden of our discussion of kingship during the

Late Period has been that, except at the end of this epoch, there does not seem to have been any change in the ideological underpinning of this institution. This may seem a strange conclusion in the light of some recent writing on the subject which has made much of Herodotus' depiction of Amasis as a drunkard and an iconoclast. One author (Spalinger 1978a, p. 26) has written:

The Greek tales surrounding Amasis also indicate that the Pharaoh was far from being a regal personage. Quite to the contrary, Amasis is depicted as a common man, fond of drinking. In fact, he seems not to have been immediately approved by all Egyptians after the conclusion of the civil war. The fragmentary Demotic story woven around Amasis' noted drunken behavior fully supports the traditions recounted by Diodorus and Herodotus. Amasis, in the tale 'Amasis and the Skipper', pales in comparison to P. Berlin 13598 wherein the death of Psammetichus I is recounted in so formal a fashion as to make one wonder if Amasis could ever have been regarded by his subjects as divine.

This judgement is quite unsound. Apart from the fact that it is uncertain how much of this material is Greek and how much Egyptian, there is nothing in the least untraditional in representing Pharaoh in so light-hearted a vein. It might be countered that Herodotus does not tell the same tale about other Saite kings and that this must be significant. Significant indeed it is, but what it signifies is that Amasis, through his apparently philhellenic policy, had made a profound impression on Greek historical consciousness which, therefore, assimilated and embroidered more material concerning that king than any other. The character of this material provides no evidence of any change of attitudes to kingship as such during the Saite period. However, a careful reading of Egyptian texts over the entire time-span of Pharaonic history reveals that acceptance of the dogmas of divine kingship did not preclude a wide divergence in personal attitudes to the crown and individual relationships to it, and that these attitudes can be ascribed to contemporary circumstances when it is possible to ascribe them an origin at all. Old Kingdom tomb inscriptions, composed at a time of strong central government, insist on the deceased's dependence on royal favour; Ankhtyfy, in the late Herakleopolitan period (c. 2200), an age of weak central government, never mentions the king in his great biographical inscription and leaves us with the impression of a man exulting in his independence and de facto autonomy, though there are good reasons for believing that he acknowledged, at least formally, the suzerainty of Herakleopolis (Schenkel 1965; pp. 45ff); Tjetji, at the beginning of the Eleventh Dynasty, in the centralized, if relatively small, Theban state, is abject in his confessions of reliance on royal patronage (Lichtheim 1975, pp. 90ff). It is not surprising, therefore, that certain features are detectable in Late Period attitudes to kingship which quite clearly reflect contemporary conditions without, in any way, compromising ancient dogmas.

In the first place, the Egyptians were faced with the problem of reconciling their ancient concept of kingship with the fact of foreign domination, initially Persian, then Macedonian. Pharaoh was the champion of order; foreign rulers, by definition, were traditionally regarded as Typhonic beings, the agents of destruction and chaos. The Egyptian reaction to this dilemma was typically pragmatic: if the foreign ruler was prepared to accept fully the role of Pharaoh, with all its obligations, the Egyptians were prepared to accept him. For some Egyptians, at any rate, Cambyses fell into this category. The inscription of Udjahorresnet informs us that he had accepted the Pharaonic titulary and other forms, had shown particular respect to the royal city of Sais and its cults, had assumed the priestly office there, and had carried it through with particular fervour and close attention to ancient practice. Given Cambyses' studied orthodoxy, the author of the inscription has no difficulty in speaking of the Persian's conduct in precisely the same terms as those used of a native Egyptian king. If someone acts like Pharaoh, he *is* Pharaoh! Darius' conduct was equally exemplary in that he restored the House of Life at Sais, was active in temples at Abusir and possible El-Kab, and devoted much attention to the temples of the Kharga Oasis. All these actions are classic Pharaonic actions and led to his full acceptance by the Egyptians as a legitimate Pharaoh. Alexander the Great sacrificed to the gods at Memphis, was crowned there, with all traditional pomp, as Pharaoh, and then visited Siwa where he not only honoured Amen-Ra but was actually greeted by the priests as the son of the god himself. Not surprisingly, the Egyptians had no difficulty in accepting him as Pharaoh in the fullest sense. Indeed they even invoked the ancient doctrine of the theogamy to sanction their acquiescence. According to this dogma, which dated back at least to the Old Kingdom, the king was the physical son of the sun-god who was supposed to have visited the queen incarnated as the king. It is likely that this doctrine was applied to Cambyses since Herodotus records (III, 2) an Egyptian story that Cambyses was the son of Cyrus and an Egyptian princess called Nitetis, a claim which may well reflect a theogamy in which Cyrus was represented as Amen-Ra, but there is no doubt at all in the case of Alexander; for the Alexander Romance contains the explicit tradition that he was the physical son of the last native Egyptian Pharaoh Nectanebo II and Olympias, the wife of Philip II of Macedon.

It hardly needs saying that by no means every foreign ruler was as successful as these in winning Egyptian acceptance. Such rejections were caused quite simply by their failure to integrate with the ideal of kingship. When this happened the Egyptians would invariably have recourse to the traditional stereotype of foreign rulers as Typhonic beings. Their reigns meant the absence of Pharaoh, the absence of order, and the irruption of chaotic forces into the land. Xerxes fell firmly into this category. In the Satrap Stele of 311 he is described as an enemy of order who had deprived the gods of Buto of a large tract of land in violation of ancestral custom. This ungodly act, we are told, was punished by the gods with the deposition of Xerxes. Artaxerxes III is a similar case. According to Classical sources, his invasion of Egypt in 343 was accompanied, amongst other things, by gross abuse of Egyptian temples, disasters which are ascribed to divine abandonment of Egypt in the biographical inscription of Somtutefnakht, a contemporary of these events. At no time in any text is the perpetrator of these abominations assimilated to the Pharaonic ideal (Lloyd 1982b, pp. 175ff).

A second characteristic of Late Period attitudes to kingship is the marked determination of officials to emphasize their independence of royal control or, at least, their insistence on their own responsibility for a particular achievement. For instance, officials frequently underline their own role in guaranteeing the well-being of their cities. Intriguingly enough, in doing this they will often use of themselves terminology drawn from royal inscriptions and from the texts of the First Intermediate Period. Some inscriptions even go so far as to claim that Pharaoh was actually dependent upon the owner or, at the very least, they allow the royal role in a particular situation to slip into the background and assign the centre of the stage to the non-royal subject of the inscription; in the reign of Apries Nesuhor emphasizes that it was he who got the king out of difficulties with his mercenaries; Udjahorresnet asserts continually that he was responsible for directing Cambyses' activities at Sais; and Peftjuaneith gives scant space to his royal master when describing his personal achievements at Abydos. These traits all reflect ultimately the consequences of the greater need for self-reliance and independence of action created by the uncertainties of life and uneven effectiveness of royal authority in Egypt in post-New Kingdom times.

This greater independence of officials from the king is part of another tendency apparent at this time: the determination to diminish Pharaoh's own independence. We can see this in the recurrent willingness to concede the king's reliance on the gods. This is certainly not new and can be exemplified in earlier periods of internal weakness, but now it led to a startling and distinctive development: the concept of royal dependence evolved into the notion that the king might fail in the sight of heaven itself. The concept of royal fallibility emerges occasionally in older texts, e.g. the Instruction to Merikara in the First Intermediate Period (see p. 74), and the inscription of Mes in the New Kingdom, but now the Egyptians go much further in that this notion is established as a major principle of historical causation. The Demotic Chronicle of the early Ptolemaic period, which consists of a series of oracles with their interpretations relating to kings of Egypt from Amyrtaeus (*c.* 404–399) to Nectanebo II (*c.* 358–41), preaches the doctrine that only those kings who live in accordance with the will of the gods will prosper and explains recent disasters in Egyptian history as illustrations of this principle. Earlier texts normally assume that the king is, *ex officio*, in harmony with the divine will whereas this text insists that many were not. What seems to have happened is that the disruption and fragmentation of central authority has demolished the aura of godhead surrounding Pharaoh. He has been brought nearer mortals, and the moral code which applies to them is now applied to him. Men can violate the divine order, incur divine wrath, and be punished; so can the king (see further Lloyd 1982a, pp. 41ff). Although these attitudes receive their clearest statement in a text composed after our period, there can be no doubt that they existed earlier; for in the biographical inscription of Somtutefnakht, whose official career began in the Thirtieth Dynasty, there is a definite implication that the defeat of Nectanebo II by the Persians was the result of divine hostility, and that, in turn, must mean that Nectanebo himself was considered to have fallen from divine grace.

## Social stratification

The population of Egypt during our period is stated in no extant source. Diodorus Siculus claims (I, 31, 7–8) that during the first century BC it was not less than three millions, and that it had been about seven millions 'in antiquity'. The precise point of reference of the second figure is unclear, but, since it corresponds approximately to that which Lane calculated to be the absolute maximum supportable in the agricultural conditions of the early nineteenth century (Lane 1966, pp. 23ff), it is a reasonable guess that it related to the early Ptolemaic period when technological innovations in agriculture, combined with a ruthless and totalitarian efficiency, must have raised the population as close to the maximum as it ever reached in antiquity. The pre-Ptolemaic figure must have been lower. A peak was certainly attained during the Saite Dynasty; for Herodotus himself insists on the unusually high population in the time of Amasis (II, 177, 1), but a precise figure is largely a matter of speculation. Herodotus' statements on the maximum size of the two groups within the warrior class are the only guide-lines available. Unfortunately, these totals are not related to any specific period, but they can hardly refer to any time-range earlier than the beginning of the Saite Dynasty. If, therefore, we accept that the maximum totals for the two groups were reached at the same time, we can interpret Herodotus' comments as implying that, at some time between the beginning of the Saite Dynasty and his visit to Egypt in the middle of the fifth century, the total number of warriors was *c.* 410000. If we then allow for each warrior household a total of four persons, which Lane considered reasonable for the provinces in his own time, we get a total for warriors and dependants of *c.* 1640000. Confidence in this figure is strengthened by the fact that it is confirmed by another method. According to Herodotus every warrior was given a fief of 12 arouras of land (see below, p. 310). If Baer is right in claiming that the carrying capacity of Egyptian agriculture was a little less than one person per 2 arouras (Butzer 1976, pp. 76ff), a warrior's plot would have supported a maximum of five, and the average would certainly have been lower. There is, then, some justification for accepting that, when the warrior class was at its most numerous, they and their families did indeed amount to a total of *c.* 1640000. Now the warriors held over half the agricultural land of Egypt (see below, p. 310), and, if we assume a similar density of settlement for the rest, we get a total population of *c.* 3000000. This figure is entirely compatible with estimated figures for the New Kingdom (see p. 190); it also has the considerable merit of fitting a figure known to Diodorus for the Hellenistic period and is well within the bounds of the feasible. It should, however, be remembered that it is being suggested as a *maximum for the Saite period only*, and that population figures must have fluctuated sharply in the turbulent centuries preceding the Macedonian conquest.

When we come to consider the way in which this population was stratified we are on much firmer ground. Four major groups of free men are detectable, none of them a novelty: administrative officials, priests, *machimoi* (warriors), and commoners, a term of convenience which we use to cover peasants, craftsmen, and comparable elements. The privileged position of the first three classes is amply demonstrated by Egyptian and Classical sources, but there was, at all periods, a certain amount of overlap between them. Indeed, the upper strata of the higher social groupings tended to merge, and it can become very difficult at that level to assign an individual to one or other of these groups: a high-ranking soldier could be, or become, a priest or official and sometimes all at once. Nevertheless, the rank-and-file will have preserved their sense of corporate identity and communal interest, and, with them, the capacity to bring corporate pressure to bear and the potential to express corporate resentment. In addition to free men there were also serfs and slaves in Egyptian society during the Late Period. Their numbers are impossible to establish, but the documentation, for all its deficiencies, leaves the impression that serfs, at any rate, formed a significant element in the population. We must also make allowance for a substantial foreign population.

### Administrative officials

During the Saite and Persian periods, government officials constituted an extremely important and numerous social grouping whose activities penetrated almost every aspect of Egyptian life. They ranged from the humblest of scribes toiling with the minutiae of local government to functionaries of national importance based in the capital whose competence ranged over issues of national and even international importance. We shall, however, postpone the detailed discussion of their organization for our section on internal administration (see below, p. 331ff).

### Priests

In Ptolemaic times the priests were one of the three main land-owning bodies of Egypt, alongside the Crown and the warrior class (Diodorus Siculus, 1, 73). It is impossible, with the available evidence, to gain a precise estimate of their economic power during the Late Period, but some pointers do exist: Herodotus leaves us in no doubt that they were a highly privileged group during the First Persian Occupation and speaks of them in much the same breath as the warriors, who, to judge from his data, held over half the cultivable land in the country (see below, p. 310); when Psammetichus I installed his daughter Nitocris as prospective High Priestess in the temple of Amen at Thebes in 656, she was given an endowment of no less than 2230 acres, apart from revenues in kind such as bread, milk, cake, herbs, emmer, oxen, geese and beer, some offered daily, some on a monthly basis; Apries' Mit Rahina Stele describes the dedication to the temple of Ptah at Memphis of a perpetual endowment, tax-free, consisting of a neighbouring district and all marsh and arable land adjacent to it, including serfs, large and small cattle, produce in town and country, and the farmlands of gods and goddesses located there, the whole clearly amounting to a very sizeable donation; the Petition of Petiese of the Persian period speaks of the tax-free temple estates of Amen of Teuzoi (El-Hibeh) and mentions herds of cattle belonging to Amen-Ra as far north as the Oxyrhynchite Nome (XIXth of Upper Egypt); according to the Satrap Stele of 311 the temples of Buto had held during the Persian period a prodigious estate called 'the Land of Wadjet' bounded by the Mediterranean to the north, the Saite Nome to the south, the Canopic Branch of the Nile to the west, and the Sebennytic Nome to the east. These and other references leave the strong impression that a very high proportion of the wealth of the nation must have been locked up in temple estates even if the proportion was not as high as the figure given by Diodorus for later times. Such a situation would not, of course, be any great novelty. The Great Harris Papyrus of Ramesses III reveals that the temples held about a third of the cultivable land and about one-fifth of its inhabitants in the early Twentieth Dynasty, whilst the Wilbour Papyrus of Ramesses V informs us that a high proportion of the land in the part of Middle Egypt covered by the text was held by the temples (see above, p. 227).

It is hardly surprising that the temples were not always left in undisturbed tenure of such wealth, and during our period we encounter several references to royal interference in their economic power: a decree of Cambyses recorded on the back of the Demotic Chronicle describes the curtailment of temple incomes, though he is careful to exclude the great temple of Ptah at Memphis from these measures; Xerxes confiscated the estate of Buto described above, and it was only restored in the time of the mysterious Pharaoh Khabbash; a passage in the pseudo-Aristotelian *Oeconomica* (1350b–51a) describes the severe demands made on temple exchequers by Tachos in order to finance his Persian war; and, according to Diodorus (XVI, 51), Artaxerxes III confiscated sacred treasures after the conquest of the country in 343.

It is, however, significant that three out of the four were Persians and that even Tachos took his dubious measures only *in extremis*. All four were visited with an uncompromising *damnatio memoriae* for their impiety!

The power and prestige of the temples meant that priestly offices were highly coveted positions, but appointment was no easy matter. The theoretical basis of the Egyptian priesthood remained constant throughout the Pharaonic period: Pharaoh himself was the High Priest of all the gods of Egypt and the sole officiant entitled to celebrate the main rituals in the holy of holies at the rear of the temple within which the divine statue stood. The priests who attended him, whatever their rank, were simply assistants appointed by him to discharge essential but subordinate functions. In practice it was impossible for Pharaoh to carry out his priestly duties in every temple in the land, and it was necessary for him to appoint proxies who were generally known simply as 'the first god's servants', that is, High Priests, though in some shrines they were given a distinctive title. Dogmatic orthodoxy was ensured by the ritual conversion of the High Priest into Pharaoh before he began the daily cult. Whether we consider this priest or his subordinates, however, their positions all had the same basis *de jure*: they were all royal appointments. In practice, inevitably, the situation was more complicated. We find at all periods that there was a tension between the right of the king to appoint, on the one hand, and the hereditary principle on the other. Appointments to the lower ranks of the priesthood were presumably made by the High Priest or his immediate subordinates and at best ratified by Pharaoh. The office of High Priest was another matter. When the central government was strong, Pharaoh himself made the appointment; when it was weak, the hereditary principle was often the more important criterion.

In our period examples of royal appointment are not lacking. We have already mentioned that in 656 Psammetichus exercised his prerogative in this respect and dispatched his daughter Nitocris to Thebes to become 'god's wife' of Amen-Ra and eventually High Priestess. This precedent was followed by Psammetichus II who used his daughter ᶜAnkhenesneferibra in precisely the same way. The purpose of these actions is quite transparent: at this period the most important politico-economic unit in Upper Egypt was the Thebaid which was ruled as a priest-state by Amen-Ra of Thebes; the most powerful sacerdotal office was that of High Priestess of Amen-Ra; royal control of that office, therefore, gave the crown control of the Theban temple-state itself. This

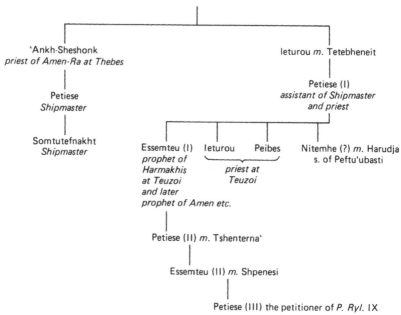

Fig. 4.3  The genealogy of Petiese III.

policy, which followed the example set by the Nubian Twenty-fifth Dynasty, was pursued with the utmost tact, but nevertheless provides a striking example of the way in which a powerful Pharaoh could exercise his prerogative of appointment to his own political advantage.

The Petition of Petiese provides another example of Psammetichus I's exercising this right. We are informed (8, 14–20) that Pharaoh appointed Petiese I as priest of Amen-Ra, Harsaphes, Osiris, Onuris, Min, and Sobk. Again there may have been a political dimension to these appointments, but it is interesting to observe that the argument used by Petiese to persuade Pharaoh of the justice of his claim was that his own father Ieturou had already held the offices in question. The binding force of this assertion was doubtless more moral than legal, but it clearly carried weight. The same hereditary principle also emerges at 14, 9–16, where we are informed that Petiese was succeeded as High Priest of Amen-Ra at Teuzoi by Essemteu and that he, in turn, was succeeded by his son Petiese (II). The wording of this passage suggests that, if royal ratification were necessary *de jure*, it was of no great significance *de facto*, and that the hereditary principle had simply taken its natural course.

The hereditary principle is equally in evidence at 8, 8–14, where we are informed that, in the reign of Psammetichus I, a priest of Amen-Ra at Thebes called Harudja had asked Petiese (I) for a priestly appointment at Teuzoi and supported his request with the claim that his father had been a priest there. Here also the argument may not be based upon legal right, but it was strong enough for Petiese to accede to Harudja's request without more ado. Interestingly enough, Herodotus claims that the hereditary principle was absolute during the Persian period (II, 37, 5). In this he is certainly incorrect, since priestly birth did not become an absolute prerequisite for the priesthood until Graeco-Roman times, but the very fact that this assertion could be made at all implies that it had already become almost universal practice.

The Petition of Petiese suggests, however, that the claims of kinship could be even more far-reaching and effective than those already described: at 15, 11ff, we are informed that Petiese II, High Priest of Amen-Ra at Teuzoi, had relatives who were priests of the same god at Thebes, and that in times of difficulty he used to go to them for assistance. This passage speaks volumes for the workings of Ancient Egyptian society: kinship in primitive and ancient communities usually, if not always, implies a powerful nexus of mutual obligation and support much greater than anything with which most modern European societies are familiar.[1] It is quite evident that Petiese's appeal for help exemplifies precisely this principle, and that the existence of these family ties created a strong sense of sympathy and solidarity between the two priesthoods which could express itself, amongst other things, in a keen regard for their mutual self-interest. It is, therefore, not at all impossible that the Harudja discussed above was actually a relative of Petiese I himself, and that this factor exercised a powerful, if covert, effect on his successful request for the priesthood at Teuzoi. The existence and ramifications of such family groupings are rarely as easy to detect as in this instance, but we can be sure that they were to be found throughout the country, and that they were a major factor in the creation and expression of priestly power in all its aspects. If this was indeed the case, then we have an example, rare in extant sources, of the operation of a factor which must have been a major element in the institutional structure of Egypt throughout antiquity: the exploitation of kinship as a major integrating mechanism in the social, economic, and political life of the country. To compare great things with small, we might invoke as a parallel the manipulation of kinship ties by the

---

[1] Useful introductions to the study of this issue are Bohannan (1969, parts 2–4); Mair (1977), Index, s.v. Kin; Goody (1971).

nomarchs of Middle Egypt during the early Twelfth Dynasty as a means of creating feudal power-blocks (cf. *BAR* I, §622ff).

In most respects no significant changes were introduced into the organization of the priesthood and the temple staff during the period under discussion. In the Old and New Kingdoms we encounter officials who were responsible for overseeing the administration of temples throughout the country. In the earlier period they bore the title 'controller of every divine office', in the New Kingdom 'chief of temples and of all the prophets of the entire country'. They were evidently intended by the central government to keep a tight rein on the undue exercise of the economic power of the temples. Both offices were essentially secular in character, but we find that the latter position could be held by the High Priest of Amen-Ra at Karnak during the New Kingdom. At the beginning of the Twenty-sixth Dynasty it still occurs, but then it lay in the hands of the great Theban baron Montuemhet who, amongst other things, held the relatively humble office of 'fourth god's servant' of Amen. After his death the office seems to disappear and no equivalent is identifiable. On the other hand, we do encounter priests who functioned as the head of all the priests of a particular deity, e.g. Somtutefnakht was the 'overseer of all the *wēb*-priests of Sekhmet in the entire land' in the late fourth century. The precise implications of such titles are unknown, but it is at least possible that they reflect rather the same governmental attitude as the offices previously discussed. Similar suspicions also arise in connection with the office of *lesonis* (*imy-r šnw*) which appears frequently in our period, though it goes back at least as far as the Eighteenth Dynasty. The *lesonis* functioned as a temple president, and was, in essence, a secular official concerned with financial administration. Inevitably, however, we find instances where priests were appointed, such as Petosiris of Hermopolis, who held this office alongside numerous priestly titles including that of High Priest of Hermopolis.[1] During the first Persian period and possibly throughout the Late Period, these officials were appointed, and on occasion deposed, by the central government.

In earlier times the priestly staff of a major temple could be very large and was made up of several categories. At the top of the hierarchy were the 'god's servants' (*ḥmw nṯr*), the 'first god's servant' being the High Priest. At Karnak we also hear of a 'second', 'third', and 'fourth god's

---

[1] For the *lesonis* in general see Zauzich (1980, 1008ff). A translation of Petosiris' biographical texts will be found in Lefebre (1924, vol. 1). See also Otto (1954, pp. 174ff); Lichtheim (1980, vol. III, pp. 44ff).

servant'. The rest of this class was divided into four groups called 'watches' (*sзw*, Greek *phylae*) each of which served in the temple for one month and was then off-duty for three. The upper reaches of the hierarchy also included the prestigious, if problematic 'god's fathers' (*itw nṯr*). Below these came two important classes: *wēb*-priests (*wˁbw*), undoubtedly the most numerous group in the temple, and lector-priests (*ḫryw-ḥbt*, lit. 'scroll-carriers'). Both categories were divided into 'watches' or *phylae* which functioned on the same basis as those of the 'god's servants'. The *wēb*-priests were ritual assistants whose prime duty was to maintain the maximum state of purity to enable them to handle cult objects such as statues and ritual instruments whilst the lector-priests were experts in sacred texts who ensured that the rites were carried out in all respects according to the strict letter of the law. Priestesses were also an important part of the staff, their role being to act as singers and dancers in the cult. We hear, in addition, of less important officiants, often called simply the *wnwt*, who are best described as lay-priests, and of individuals described as *wnw*, 'shrine-openers(?)' (Gk. *pastophoroi*) whose precise status is debatable but who certainly included amongst their functions the execution of minor cultic duties in relation to divine images.

A host of inscriptions ranging from the biographical texts of Montuemhet at the beginning of our period to those of Petosiris at the end, make it quite clear that the system just described remained unimpaired throughout the Late Period in major shrines. Smaller temples, of course, had to rest content with a smaller staff: a medium-sized temple at Teuzoi described in the Petition of Petiese had a staff consisting of one 'god's servant' who functioned as the High Priest and four 'watches' of *wēb*-priests, each with twenty members. Finally, it should be remembered that, in addition to the priesthoods connected with the temples of the gods, there were also many professional mortuary priests and priestesses in the Late Period who were very similar to the old *ḥmw kз*, 'soul-servants'. They were called *wзḥw-mw*, '*choachytae*, water-pourers', and usually held office on a hereditary basis.

The payment of priests was liberal and made in kind. Many, if not all, were given land-allotments on temple estates, though legal texts make it clear that they normally leased them out instead of working them in person. Priests also received a proportion of the temple's income: at Teuzoi, for instance, the temple's income in emmer wheat was divided into 100 stipends one-fifth of which were paid to the 'god's servant', and one-fifth to each of the four 'watches' of *wēb*-priests. Other similar items of revenue were doubtless administered on the same principle. In addition to all this, the priest's income also included a daily ration which, according to Herodotus, consisted of bread, beef, geese, wine and beer. Substantial though these rewards were, every priest had the opportunity to increase his remuneration by pluralism, and many availed themselves of it to the full. We have already indicated that Petiese I of Teuzoi held priesthoods in several parts of the country and that Harudja of Thebes felt no qualms about holding priesthoods in Thebes and Teuzoi. Similarly, Somtutefnakht could describe himself as 'the god's servant of Horus, Lord of Hebu, the god's servant of the gods of the Sixteenth Nome, the god's servant of the god Smatawy (Somtus) of Iat-hehu...the overseer of the *wēb*-priests of Sekhmet in the entire land'. Indeed, the financial advantages of priestly offices emerge in a particularly striking form in the passage in the Petition of Petiese where a priestly stipend is actually used as a bribe to a high official at court (*P. Rylands* IX, 3, 8ff).

Thanks to Herodotus we are well informed on the priests' mode of life during the mid fifth century BC, and we need not doubt that his comments held true for the entire period under discussion. Not surprisingly, he lays great stress on their obligation to maintain a high level of ritual purity: they shaved their bodies every other day, had to be circumcised, wore only linen garments and sandals of papyrus, and washed twice a day and twice a night. They were also forbidden to eat fish or beans. Whether these regulations applied throughout their career is uncertain, but it seems likely that they were only compulsory during the months when the priest was actually officiating within the temple. It would, however, be a mistake to assume that prescriptions of ritual purity were a guarantee of an upright and sober life. The invaluable Petition of Petiese paints a grim picture of standards of probity at Teuzoi where priests of the early Saite period did not stop short of murder to preserve their economic interests. This crime met its due reward when the culprits were arrested, taken before Pharaoh, and punished, probably by death, but, given the financial rewards involved, it is hardly surprising that such unsavoury episodes should occur from time to time, and that priestly morality sometimes fell far short of the ideal, a situation for which the history of the mediaeval church in Europe provides an instructive parallel. Nevertheless, we should not allow such lapses to induce too baleful a view of Late Period priests; Somtutefnakht, addressing the god Harsaphes, claims: 'I am thy servant, my heart is devoted to thee; my heart is filled with nothing but thee...my heart sought truth in thy house day and night'.[1] Where such ideals exist, there will always be many who devote their energies to realizing them, however far short they may fall in the attempt.

## Machimoi (warriors)

The high standing of this group is clearly demonstrated by the Darius Decree of 495/4 BC preserved on the back of the Demotic Chronicle. At the beginning of this text three groups are mentioned as people to be consulted when new laws were to be framed: warriors, priests, and scribes, and it is the warriors who are listed first.

Most, if not all, of the warrior class originated from Libyan mercenaries who had settled in Egypt during the New Kingdom or had subsequently infiltrated the country where they were probably permitted to take up residence on condition that they provided military service to the Crown when called upon to do so. They were concentrated mainly in the Delta where they grew into a numerous and powerful element in the population. They were divided into a series of principalities which were virtually autonomous under rulers called 'Great Chiefs of the Mashwash (Ma)' and which survived in some cases into the reign of Psammetichus I to be absorbed in the early phase of his expansion. This change of political status did not impair their military value, and they continued to play a major role as militia down to the end of the Pharaonic period. In Saite times they were used as general infantry, certainly by land and probably also as marines, and they also provided Pharaoh with the Egyptian equivalent of the Roman imperial Praetorian Guard; during the Persian period they featured prominently as marines; and subsequently they played an important role in the campaigns of Tachos and Nectanebo II. In these fourth-century operations they were still predominantly infantry, but it is intriguing that Diodorus mentions the use of cavalry in the Egyptian army (XV, 42), in a context where Egyptian troops alone seem to have been involved.

It is claimed by Herodotus that the maximum population of the warrior class had been 410000, a figure which probably refers to the Saite–Persian period (see above p. 300). He also asserts that they were divided into two groups, the Kalasiries and the Hermotybies. The former were concentrated in the southern and eastern Delta, though some were settled in the Theban Nome; the Hermotybies, on the other

---

[1] For a translation consult Lichtheim (1980, vol. III, pp. 41ff); see also Lloyd (1982b, pp. 178ff).

hand, occupied a solid block of nomes in the western and central Delta. Each warrior is alleged to have received from the Crown a tax-free fief of 12 *stȝt* of land (*c.* 8 acres or 3.2 hectares), which was perfectly adequate for the maintenance of a household of five persons, but officers must have received more on a scale graded by rank, though we have no information on what this scale may have been. If all these figures are correct, the sum total of the land allotted to the warriors amounts to two-thirds of the available agricultural land in the Delta and over half the cultivable land of Egypt as a whole. This compares with the proportion of about one-third held by the temples during the Twentieth Dynasty and does not seem implausible. How the warriors organized the working of their land is a matter of speculation. If we discount the obvious tendency in Classical sources to confuse the warriors with the Spartan military elite, and make our guesses on the basis of standard Egyptian practice, it may be suggested that, since they functioned as a militia, not as a standing army, the majority would have lived most of their lives as peasants, but that plots could also be leased out on a share-cropping basis wherever this was economically feasible. At all events, the prominence of soldiers, Egyptian and mercenary, in the agricultural life of the country, is far from novel: The Wilbour Papyrus, for instance, demonstrates that they were amongst the most important land-exploiting groups in the country at least as early as the Twentieth Dynasty.

## Commoners

In his survey of Egyptian society of the Persian period Herodotus mentions several social groups in addition to the priests and warriors: cowherds, swineherds, merchants, interpreters, and steersmen (boatmen), by which he presumably means all those who earned their livelihood on the water whether they captained freighters and ferries or punted papyrus rafts about the marshes as fishermen and fowlers. He might also have listed a wide range of craftsmen and other specialists, both industrial and agricultural, who played a crucial role in the socio-economic life of the country. Interestingly enough, he makes no reference to free-men farmers in this list, presumably because he believed that agricultural land was concentrated in the hands of priests and warriors and that the farm labour described at II, 14, 2 was either carried out by them or by serfs who could not be included in a list of the classes into which free men were divided. Nevertheless, it is quite clear that agricultural land was often rented by ordinary citizens during our period, though this system certainly has an earlier origin. In the Wilbour Papyrus we find that, although most of the land was actually owned by the Crown or temples, it was worked by, or on behalf of, a variety of individuals including not only priests and soldiers but also 'cultivators', 'ladies', herdsmen, scribes and stablemasters. The Saite period presents us with the earliest known contracts for letting such land. Dating from the reign of Amasis, they all refer to priests who are concerned to lease out their plots in the temple-domain of Amen-Ra and mention lessees who include herdsmen, beekeepers, and other priests. The plots probably did not exceed $3\frac{1}{2}$ acres and the lessee was required to provide everything for cultivation himself. He evidently did not expect to do the work in person, but either used slaves or hired labourers to farm the plot for him.

All the social groups discussed up to this point consisted of free men. They differed from one another in many important respects, but they all shared the same institutional foundation: the family. Before considering other social categories it is, therefore, fitting to give some attention to the nature of this institution in the Late Period.

To the Ancient Egyptians the family did not simply consist of its living members but was regarded as a corporation of the living and the dead. Traditionally this attitude expressed itself through the mortuary cult, and this practice lost none of its prominence in the Late Period. On the contrary, we detect at that time an even stronger sense of this relationship than emerges in earlier texts; there is evidence that it was the custom in the fifth century to retain the mummified body of deceased members of the family in a vault within the house itself (Herodotus, II, 86, 7; Diodorus Siculus, I, 91, 7), and we also find a greater tendency for individuals to assert their ancestry by recording their genealogies in inscriptional form.[1]

The basis of the family in our period was monogamous marriage. There is no evidence of polygamy, though the maintenance of concubines was not uncommon. Close consanguineous marriages are certainly exemplified between half-brother and half-sister, but full brother–sister marriage does not seem to have been acceptable outside the royal house. The traditional concept of marriage shows no change: marriage was still a private act in which the law was not interested per se. As in earlier times, we encounter documents which, for sake of

---

[1] The problems of Herodotus, II, 86, 7, are discussed in Lloyd (1976, pp. 363ff), where I deny the connection with Diodorus' comments. I now believe this view to be mistaken.

convenience, are called by scholars 'marriage contracts', but they are concerned essentially with the financial arrangements attendant upon the marriage and do not constitute a legal prerequisite. Examples from our period indicate that marriage might be patrilocal (wife moves to husband) or, very rarely, matrilocal (husband moves to wife), and they strikingly illustrate one of the more unexpected features of Egyptian social life throughout Pharaonic times: the very high degree of independence enjoyed by women. In law women were able to function on very much the same terms as men, one of the few distinctions being that they do not seem to have had the right to appear as witnesses in legal transactions. Several types of late contract illustrate this point by demonstrating the freedom of the woman to own property, retain it on marriage, and dispose of it exactly as she chose. What is more, these contracts are arrangements between equals, and sometimes push the principle of reciprocal obligations to remarkable lengths: in one contract (P. Chicago 17481) a woman hands over a large sum of money to the bridegroom as payment for all the rights and privileges which he will grant in the course of the marriage; the woman is empowered to collect any arrears in her dues; the children of the marriage are to receive everything which the father has or will have; and the husband has no right to break the agreement unilaterally. By no means all marriage contracts were as detailed as this – the *sẖ n sꜥnẖ*, 'maintenance document', which this text exemplifies is, in fact, an invention of the fourth century – and a wide degree of latitude was observed in dealing with the various problems which it attempts to solve, but the principles and attitudes which it presupposes were of general validity.

Since marriage was a private act, the same held true of divorce: one party simply repudiated the other. In practice, however, social pressures must have restricted considerably the abuse of such freedom, and these pressures were often powerfully reinforced by the marriage contract itself in that it could make divorce as difficult as possible by ensuring that the financial penalties were severe and sometimes crippling. No doubt such measures were often successful, but, since we possess many late documents relating to divorce, it was clearly a common phenomenon.

The relationship between fathers and their children was determined not only by social attitudes but also in law. It is evident that the father had considerable rights even over the property of grown sons and also had a right to their labour. It is equally clear that, in cases of debt, the creditor could proceed legally against the children as well as the slaves of any defaulter. Adoption was also a possibility, but operated in such a way that the adopted child did not necessarily lose its right to the property of the natural father. Filial piety was a potent force in Egyptian life, and sons were considered to be under a strong moral obligation to maintain their parents during old age, though they were absolved of this responsibility if the parents themselves had failed in *their* duties. On the other hand, it would appear that daughters were bound by law to support their parents.

The continued viability of any family was dependent upon the maintenance of a satisfactory economic base, which might consist of real or movable property, and was also considered to include any offices held by one or more of its members. Establishing a legal title to all this was of central importance, and the transactions by which any major item came into the family's possession or 'user' were normally recorded carefully in writing in the proper legal form. Acts of sale and purchase assumed particular prominence here, and the texts show some intriguing features. It is evident that, in earlier times, no act of sale was valid unless the principle of balanced reciprocity had been observed: the vendor must receive an acceptable exchange for the item being sold. The principle of balanced reciprocity was, and is, a fundamental element in the socio-economic life of primitive and early societies, and certainly played a major role in the institutional machinery of Ancient Egypt.[1] However, in the demotic texts of our period we find a new and interesting modification of the principle. Previously, and in the old-fashioned abnormal-hieratic texts used in Upper Egypt until the latter part of the reign of Amasis, we find that it was obligatory to state precisely what both parties received in carrying through the process of reciprocity; in demotic deeds of sale, on the other hand, we are given information on what was sold, but nothing on what the vendor himself received. We are simply told that the latter was 'satisfied' with what he had been given. Certainly, the insistence on satisfaction is not in itself a novelty. In older contracts detailed accounts of the items exchanged are accompanied as a matter of course with an explicit statement that the parties in question were satisfied with the exchange. However, it is clear that the demotic practice implies a considerable advance in legal thinking. Previously, the law had placed the main emphasis on the mechanical process of reciprocity; now it was insisting that the crucial

---

[1] On reciprocity in primitive and peasant societies see Bohannan (1969, pp. 229ff); Mair (1977), Index, s.v. Reciprocity. Théodoridès (1975, pp. 87ff) offers some stimulating remarks on reciprocity in Egyptian foreign relations.

factor in the contract was the attitude of the participants to the transaction.

Where family property is so important, inheritance must be an issue of major significance. In earlier times in Egypt we find that the problem was often solved by using a document called an *imt-pr*, 'deed of conveyance', which was the standard deed employed for transference of property of all kinds. When made in anticipation of death, it functioned as a will. The term *imt-pr* seems to have been obsolete in the Late Period, but a similar document was still often used to ensure a smooth transference of property after, or in anticipation of, death. Not infrequently, however, a man would die intestate, and in such cases the eldest son occupied a privileged position in the disposal of the deceased's property. Nevertheless, every child, male or female, had a legal claim on the estate.

It will be evident from what has already been said that the life of the Ancient Egyptian was document-ridden in the extreme. This situation was aggravated by the fact that, when any transaction of sale or purchase took place, *all* the documentation relating to the relevant item *which had ever existed* and was still extant had also to be transferred to the purchaser. Most families, therefore, kept their own archives where such texts could be safely stored. Since these were periodically sorted out and obsolete material thrown away, a number of family archives, or portions of them, have survived to yield fascinating glimpses into the basics of social life in Late Period Egypt.

### Serfs and slaves

The question of serfdom and slavery in Ancient Egypt has given rise to considerable debate, and some commentators have gone so far as to doubt the very existence of slavery in the Late Period. Essentially the problem is that of correlating the institutional structure and vocabulary of one society with that of another. In such operations it is sometimes possible to achieve an exact correspondence, but all too often we have to rest content with approximate equivalents. This is the situation when we consider the status of the 'unfree' in Ancient Egypt. It may well be that there were no individuals in the Late Period who satisfied in all respects the definition of a slave in Roman or Athenian law, but it is certain that there were individuals whose degree of 'unfreedom' was so great that there is much more truth than falsehood in using the term 'slave' to describe them. The topic will, therefore, be discussed on the basis of the following principle: serfdom will be regarded as a specific form of slavery in which individuals are bound to the land and required to work for the owner or his tenant. Anyone else who is owned by another will be called simply a 'slave'.

Serfs were a common feature of Egyptian life in earlier times when they appear as workers on the domains of Pharaoh, the temples, and the wealthier members of the community. They acquired their status in a variety of ways: they might be born to it, they could be prisoners of war, or they might have been condemned to serfdom for criminal offences. Evidence for the institution in our period is not plentiful, but it is sufficient to prove that serfs continued to form an important element in the population: they are included in the donations assigned to Nitocris by Psammetichus I in 656 (Adoption Stele, l. 31); the Apries Stele from Mit Rahina informs us that serfs (*mrt*) were included in the king's endowment to Ptah (see above, p. 289); and in the stele of Peftjuaneith they are given to the temple of Osiris at Abydos (see above, p. 292). In the first two cases there is no clear indication of their origin, though we are left with the impression that they comprised the entire population of the areas in question; in the third instance, however, some of them are specifically stated to have been prisoners-of-war.

Slavery was recognized by law in the Late Period and is well illustrated by surviving contracts of sale. Legally the slave (*bзk*) owned nothing at all. He was a living chattel who could be bought and sold at will. Nevertheless, it was certainly possible for him to dispute his status if he so wished. Many slaves would have been foreigners who owed their position to such factors as war, foreign trade, or both, but it was undoubtedly possible for Egyptians themselves to sink to this level – indeed, at Elephantine during the Persian period we find Egyptians even functioning as slaves of Jewish mercenaries. Recently discovered evidence from an unpublished demotic ostracon unearthed at Saqqara also attests to the existence of voluntary serfdom to temples at this period. What circumstances gave rise to the enslavement of Egyptians at any period is an open question, but debt or a desperate desire to secure the means of basic sustenance would both be obvious possibilities. However, whether the slave was foreign or Egyptian, the overwhelming impression created by the documents is that the relationship between slave and master was often very good and was essentially paternalistic in character.

*Foreigners*

Foreigners must have accounted for a sizeable proportion of the population of Egypt during the Late Period. They came in a variety of guises and from many different quarters. Merchants, mercenaries, travellers, students, allies and conquerors are all abundantly exemplified, and few of the major ethnic groups of the Eastern Mediterranean, Near East, and North Africa fail to appear at some time or another. The Egyptian reaction to their presence was far from uniform, being marked by a complex interplay of prejudice, ideology, pride and self-interest. More often than not, it is the last of these attitudes which gained the ascendancy, but the others are rarely inoperative.

Herodotus gives us clear indications of the basis of the Egyptian's perception of national identity during the fifth century. According to him, the oracle of Amen-Ra at Siwa had declared that Egypt included everything which was covered by the waters of the inundation, and that everyone was an Egyptian who lived north of Elephantine and drank the waters of the Nile; later we are told that the Egyptians considered everyone a foreigner who did not speak Egyptian (II, 18; 158, 5). Nowhere does Herodotus give any indication that racial considerations were an issue of any importance; domicile and culture, not physical characteristics, were the key criteria. In other statements he gives an equally clear picture of Egyptian attitudes towards those who failed to satisfy these conditions: eating habits which did not conform to good Egyptian practice were considered disgraceful (II, 36, 2); the Egyptian method of writing from right to left was the correct one, not that of the Greeks (II, 36, 4); the heads of sacrificed cattle which had been heaped with curses might be thrown into the river – or sold to Greeks; Egyptians refused to kiss Greek men or women on the mouth and would not use their knives, spits, or cooking pots, nor would they touch any meat cut with Greek knives because all of these items might have been contaminated by contact with slain cows (II, 39; 41, 2–3); at II, 110, the priests of Memphis are represented as comparing the achievements of Darius with those of the legendary Egyptian king Sesostris to the considerable disadvantage of the former. It is evident from all this that Herodotus found the Egyptian attitude to foreigners a mixture of cultural superiority and distaste, a distaste, moreover, which was not infrequently powerfully reinforced by religious taboos.

In view of these attitudes it is hardly surprising that we should encounter outbursts of hostility towards foreigners from time to time, but it would be a mistake to interpret these events simply as the result of an aversion to non-Egyptians. The nationalist revolt of the *machimoi* against Apries (see above p. 285) must have owed something to xenophobia, but we can be sure that at least as potent a force was the sense of injured pride felt by the Egyptian troops at the privileged position allotted to foreign mercenaries within the Egyptian army. Similarly, the series of revolts against the Persians during the First Occupation were not merely expressions of a hatred for foreigners, but the products partly of the political and economic aspirations of power-groups within the Egyptian population and partly the legacy of the repressive measures employed by the Persians after the reign of Darius.

A particularly interesting example of the enmity which could arise between Egyptians and foreigners is provided by events at Elephantine in the year 410. Here the hostility between the priests of the Egyptian god Khnum and the Jewish mercenary community reached such a pitch that the Egyptian priests prevailed on the Persian officer commanding the area to destroy the temple of Jahweh, the centre of Jewish worship in the town. Why this antipathy arose is never explicitly stated, but it is quite evident that it sprang from something more potent than an Egyptian distaste for aliens. The most plausible explanation by far is that the venom was injected into the situation by religious fervour. If, as is highly likely, the Jews had been in the habit of sacrificing lambs in their temple, they would have given grave offence to the religious susceptibilities of the priests of Khnum who was believed to be incarnated in a ram.

One important corollary of these Egyptian attitudes is that foreigners could become Egyptians simply by accepting Egypt as their home and by adopting Egyptian culture in all its aspects. The importance of this point in relation to kingship has already been discussed (see above, p. 293), but its relevance is much broader than that. The very real attractions of Egyptian civilization, particularly from the religious point of view, ensured that many immigrants at all levels were prepared to go a long way in adapting to local ways. Carian immigrants from Asia Minor and their descendants showed a marked capacity for cultural assimilation and embraced Egyptian names and Egyptian religion with particular enthusiasm; the progressive Egyptianization of the Persian conquerors is strikingly illustrated by such texts as the inscriptions of the brothers Atiyawahy and Ariyawrata in the Wadi Hammamat (476–449); the tomb of Si-amen in the oasis of Siwa, which belongs somewhere in our period, demonstrates that Greeks too were far from proof against the influence of Pharaonic culture; even the Jewish mercenaries at Elephantine were affected by the indigenous civilization, though here the influence was less profound than in many other cases.[1] This tendency to cultural integration was particularly promoted by the widespread practice of intermarriage between Egyptians and foreigners at this time.

## ECONOMIC STRUCTURE

### Settlements

There is no reason to believe that there was ever any fundamental change in settlement patterns during Pharaonic times, and we can be confident that the Late Period population described above was distributed over the classic Egyptian range of sites stretching from individual farms and hamlets through villages and local towns to great capital cities. The majority will have lived in relatively small settlements like those frequently mentioned in the Wilbour Papyrus (see above, p. 227), but the centres best documented for our period are large conurbations. As always in Egypt, the archaeological record for such sites is entirely unsatisfactory, but there is a surprising amount of written evidence, both Egyptian and Classical, and a clear picture can be gained of the character of these towns even if, in most cases, we cannot draw on an accurate ground-plan.

Towns on the alluvium fell into three main groups: national capitals, such as Memphis and Sais; the administrative centres of the provinces, or nomes, into which Egypt was divided, such as Bubastis and Mendes; and smaller local towns such as Nebesheh.[2] To obviate the effects of flooding, they were invariably constructed on the highest ground available. In their lower reaches the sites were usually based on natural deposits such as old river banks or, in the Delta, the sandy elevations known as 'turtle-backs', but, in a settlement of any age, these natural raised areas were considerably heightened by the débris of generations of inhabitants; most buildings were made of sun-dried mud brick, and, when they collapsed, the surface was subjected to the minimum of levelling and a new structure erected on top. These city mounds were

---

[1] For Carian reactions to Egyptian cultural influence see Lloyd (1978, pp. 107ff); for Atiyawahy and Ariyawrata see Posener (1936, pp. 117ff); for Si-amen see Boardman (1980, p. 159); for Jewish mercenaries and Egyptians see Porten (1968, pp. 151ff).

[2] Nebesheh was the old capital of the Nineteenth Nome of Lower Egypt but had been supplanted by Tanis before the beginning of our period (Helck 1974, pp. 195ff).

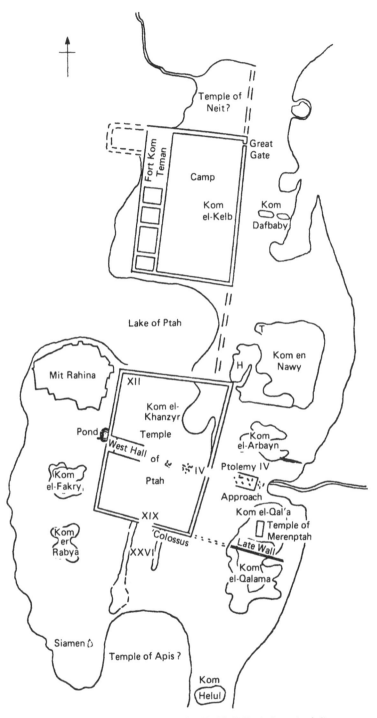

Fig. 4.4. The site of Memphis (after W. M. F. Petrie (1909a), pl. I).

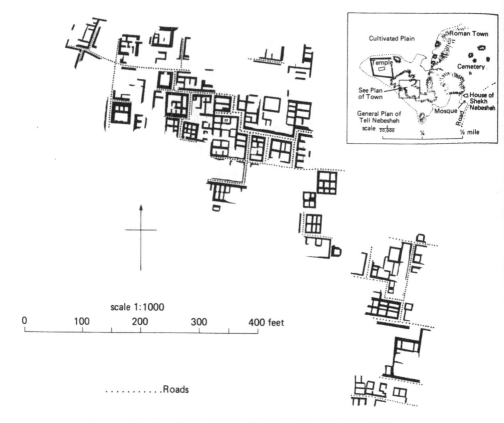

Fig. 4.5 The site of Nebesheh (after W. M. F. Petrie (1888), pl. XVII).

everywhere to be seen in the Late Period and made a great impression upon Herodotus (II, 97, 137); he gives a particularly vivid description in his account of Bubastis of one of the effects of the progressive rise of the mound itself when he informs us that the temple of the goddess Bastet stood in his time in a hollow surrounded by houses built on mounds. Clearly, the mounds on which the mud-brick houses were built had gradually increased in height with successive reconstruction whereas the temple, being of stone, had been proof against collapse and had remained at its original level.

The physical layout of such towns is easily established. All had at least one nodal point; great cities such as Memphis had several. These might consist of temples or administrative centres such as palaces and mayoral offices. Late Period temples were of the classic type. That of Bastet at Bubastis was constructed of granite and limestone, and appears to have

been surrounded by an enclosure wall of black basalt about 228.6 m by
176.78 m in size and carved with relief sculpture. Between this and the
temple building proper stood a sacred grove, probably of palm trees,
symbolizing the protective and life-giving presence of the goddess.
Access to the temple was gained by a processional way about 685.8 m
long, traces of which survived into modern times. The temple enclosure
was encircled by a horseshoe-shaped lake or *iśrw* comparable to that
surrounding the temple of Mut at Karnak. The temple complex of Neith
at Sais was particularly splendid; not only did it contain the shrines of
Neith and other major Saite deities such as Osiris Hemag, but also the
tombs of the kings of the Twenty-sixth Dynasty. These apparently stood
in the courtyard preceding the hypostyle hall of the shrine of Neith
herself and exemplified a characteristic type of late royal tomb, namely
the temple-court burial found earlier at Medinet Habu and Tanis. Each
of these tombs comprised a superstructure, consisting of a cult-chapel
which was entered through a portico supported by palm-tree columns,
and a substructure immediately below which took the form of a burial
vault which would have contained the body of the king enclosed in a
coffin of precious metal, as at Tanis. Tombs of this type were also used
later at Mendes during the Twenty-ninth Dynasty and seem to have been
imitations of the mortuary installations associated with the prehistoric
kings of Egypt, but they were not simply inspired by conservative
sentiment: they had, in addition, the merit of conferring greater security
on the burial than the New Kingdom practice of interment in the Valley
of the Kings, and also satisfied the kings' desire to be protected in death
by the divinities of their native city.

In a great national metropolis, the splendour of the city's temples was
matched by that of the palace. Though no trace of the one in Sais has
been identified, we are informed that it was both large and spectacular.
Memphis, on the other hand, provides us with the ruins of a Twenty-sixth
Dynasty example in the form of the Palace of Apries. This stood in the
north-west angle of a great enclosure, clearly military in character,
which was surrounded by a battered mud-brick wall 10 m thick at the
base. The palace itself was constructed on an artificial mud-brick mound
of a type characteristic of the Late Period which may have been as high
as 13.66 m and was constructed on the honeycomb principle: a grid of
mud-brick walls was erected creating a large number of boxes or
casemates, and these were subsequently filled with earth or mud brick.
Access to the top was gained from the south by way of a great ramp
about 87 m wide. Once the upper surface of the platform had been

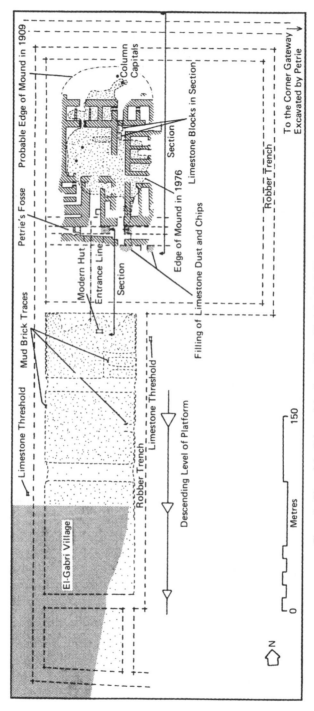

Fig. 4.6  Plan of the Palace of Apries at Memphis (after B. J. Kemp (1977b), Fig. 1).

prepared, the palace was constructed on its northern section. In this operation an unusual quantity of stone was used, and this feature, combined with its spectacular position, must have created an overwhelming impression of power and magnificence.

Around the focal point provided by such buildings were constructed the houses of the populace. Excavations at Nebesheh and Elephantine have demonstrated that street-planning in a normal Egyptian town was as rudimentary as ever, and, wherever it occurred, we can be confident that it was quickly broken down by the organic expansion of the settlement, particularly through the untrammelled house extensions characteristic even now in Egyptian rural areas. Houses were usually of mud brick, but there is some evidence that a large amount of stone could be used for the dwellings of the wealthy (see *P. Rylands*, IX, 20, 12–15). This fits our data from the Palace of Apries and may reflect a growing tendency in the Late Period. In congested areas high-rise building was the order of the day. At Elephantine houses were usually of two storeys, but there is evidence that they could reach at least three storeys at Memphis. Local differences there certainly were. At Elephantine, for instance, brick barrel-vaults were the rule for roofing purposes; further north, on the other hand, in the southern dependencies at North Saqqara we find the builders employing bundles of bound reeds laid upon wooden beams and coated with a heavy layer of mud. The overall impression gained from the study of domestic architecture of this period is that it continued traditional techniques and designs, and that these traditions have remained the basis of mud-brick architecture in the country down to modern times.

On the whole, the Late Period was an age of insecurity, and it comes as no surprise to find that most, if not all, substantial settlements were surrounded by fortifications. There are few remains, but the formidable ruins of the fort at Tell Defenneh (Daphnae), as well as those of the camp within which the Palace of Apries stands, give some idea of what they must have been like. That they were highly effective is indisputable. The Egyptians had long experience of military engineering, and there is ample evidence that they had lost none of their ancient mastery. During the revolt of Inarus (*c.* 462–455) the citadel of Memphis held out successfully against the best efforts of the Athenians, the acknowledged Greek experts in siege warfare; the engineering works employed for the defence of the country during the fourth century show consummate skill (cf. Diodorus, XV, 42); and Artaxerxes III, after his conquest of the country in 343, paid Egyptian military architects the

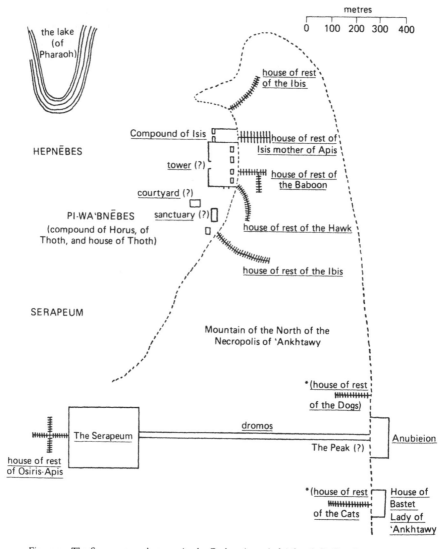

Fig. 4.7 The Saqqara temple town in the Ptolemaic period (after J. D. Ray (1976), 153).

dubious compliment of demolishing the walls of the most important cities of Egypt. Circuit walls were not, however, the limit of a town's defences at this time. Citadels were also constructed within the walls rather like the keeps of medieval castles. The palace of Apries was obviously part of some such installation at Memphis, and Diodorus Siculus mentions a fourth-century example in the north-eastern Delta which was certainly not unique (XV, 42).

Since water-transport was the standard means of communication, all towns on the alluvium must have had harbours of some kind. We know that towards the end of the fifth century a naval arsenal was located at Memphis and may guess that it functioned as the headquarters of the Egyptian fleet in rather the same way as the New Kingdom *Prw nfr* (Bowman 1941, pp. 302ff; Lloyd 1980, pp. 196ff). Cemeteries were another essential adjunct of Egyptian towns. In the Delta they were contiguous with the settlements themselves, a good example being the one at Nebesheh which was established just to the east of the city on a sandy hillock where the tombs were laid out quite unsystematically with the graves of foreigners intermingled with those of Egyptians. In the valley, on the other hand, the dead were normally, though far from invariably, interred in the western desert. In some cases this practice led to a dramatic expansion of the urban complex itself. The most arresting example of this trend is provided by Memphis itself where the development of the western desert as an extension of the city proper was immensely encouraged by the fact that the area was not simply the burial place of the bodies of ordinary mortals but also the place of interment for important Memphite sacred animals like the Apis Bull and the Mother of the Apis. We find, therefore, that temple towns grew up in the desert to serve the mortuary cult of these gods at least as early as the Thirtieth Dynasty, forming a large complex closely linked to the city of Memphis itself. However, novel though these towns may seem, they have an obvious parallel in the pyramid towns of the Old and Middle Kingdoms and in the temple towns of the New Kingdom, such as those of Medinet Habu and the Ramesseum.

### The economy

The sophisticated social and settlement structure described in the previous sections could only have existed on a complex and efficient economic base. A wealth of evidence demonstrates that the economic system of Egypt before the Late Period was a classic example of the storage and redistribution type. The palace was, amongst other things, an institution responsible for organizing the entire economy, collecting and storing wealth produced inside the country, acquiring foreign produce, and then filtering it back through the system as it was required. The assignment of substantial estates to temples and officials created secondary storage and redistribution centres, but these were always closely enmeshed with that of the palace and formed an integral part of it. Although the evidence for our period is not particularly full, it leaves us in no doubt that this machinery continued to function and flourish. It would, however, be a mistake to assume that all circulation of goods was dependent upon a storage and redistribution system. Indeed, it is questionable whether that held true for any period of Egyptian history. Day-to-day exchange of commodities was certainly facilitated in the Late Period by the exchange of goods in town and village market-places where surplus from the domestic economy could be bartered by members of the household for items which they needed and where professional merchants were also active (cf. Herodotus, II, 35, 39, 138, 141, 164).

The basis of the economy, as earlier, was agriculture in the form of crop-cultivation and animal husbandry. How much land was available for this purpose is not known with any precision. According to Schlott's interpretation of a text in the temple at Edfu, the amount available in the Ptolemaic period was $c.$ 24808 sq. km, a figure which is compatible with the modern situation whereby 35000 sq. km are available and 24982 sq. km are used. The same text also indicates that there was about three times as much usable land in the Delta as there was in Upper Egypt. Ptolemaic agriculture was certainly more efficient than anything known in Pharaonic times, and the Edfu figures must be too high for our period. Nevertheless, they give some idea of the agricultural potential of the country in times of high prosperity and can perhaps be taken as a very rough guide to the situation which obtained at least at the height of the Saite period when the population seems to have been relatively high (see above, p. 300), and attempts were apparently made to increase the area of land previously exploited in the Delta by a policy of progressive colonization (Butzer 1976, pp. 95ff).

Large-scale crop-cultivation relied at all periods upon the relatively primitive but efficient basin system of irrigation. This was organized at a local rather than a national level, but the ease and success of the process was always dependent upon the volume of the Nile which varied considerably in antiquity. There is good evidence that irrigation was greatly facilitated in our period by unusually high floods, a factor which, in turn, encourages confidence in the tradition that the reign of Amasis was one of unparalleled prosperity. The engineering feats involved in constructing and maintaining this system made a great impression on Herodotus who speaks in awed tones of a dyke maintained by the Persians in his own time in the vicinity of Memphis (II, 99, 3) and finds no difficulty in believing the mistaken tradition that Lake Moeris and

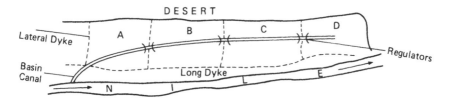

Fig. 4.8  Schematized drawing to illustrate the principles of the basin system of irrigation. A–D are basins formed by the long dyke, lateral dykes and the western cliff. When the Nile flooded, it was held back by the long dyke until sufficient pressure had built up. The dyke was then cut and water admitted into the basins via the basin canal. Depth of flood was controlled by the regulators. When the water had stood on the field for the requisite time (*c.* 40 days in modern times), it was released and the seed was then sown (after Lloyd (1976), 75).

the Bahr Yusuf were both excavated by the Egyptians themselves (II, 149–50); at II, 108, he describes the complex network of canals to be found in Egypt in the fifth century; even the tomb-chamber of Khufu was fed with water from a canal (II, 124, 4)! On the other hand, he was astonished at the ease with which the processes of agriculture proper were conducted as compared with the situation in Greece: he observed farmers for whom ploughing and hoeing were quite unnecessary. They simply waited for the river to flood, and, when the waters receded, they sowed their seed and then let pigs loose on the land to tread it in. Once the harvest had been gathered, the corn was simply threshed by letting pigs trample upon it.

The main food crop during the Late Period was emmer or hulled wheat (*bdt*) which gained an ascendancy over barley at the end of the New Kingdom despite its inferior nutritional value. Barley and naked wheat (*swt*) were also grown. Flax continued to be cultivated on a wide scale together with other industrial crops and a wide range of fruit and vegetables. As for animal husbandry, Herodotus and the reliefs in the fourth-century tomb of Petosiris at Tuna el-Gebel leave us in no doubt of its continued importance.

It is generally assumed that, in theory, all land belonged to the crown. This view is certainly consistent with available evidence, and there is good reason to believe that it held true in the Late Period. In practice, however, there were three main land-exploiting entities: the crown, the priests, and the *machimoi*. The economic position of the priests and the *machimoi* has already been discussed (see above pp. 301ff, 309ff). As for crown lands, they do not figure prominently in surviving texts but are clearly mentioned in the Nitocris Adoption Stele as the source of some of the land given to Nitocris as part of her endowment (ll. 17–20), and we may have another reference to such land in Herodotus' description of Amasis' reorganization of Naucratis (II, 178). Some crown land will have been worked directly by the palace, but substantial amounts must have been handed over to royal officials as estates by way of payment for services rendered, in which case the land would not have become absolute property but was only held as long as the office itself. Such estates could be worked directly by the official or by leasing out in whole or in part on a share-cropping basis. It is, however, a reasonable guess that the crown would also have leased out land directly on the same terms (cf. p. 307).

Within any economic system the circulation of wealth is fundamental. In the Late Period this problem continued to be solved, in the main, by payments in kind through such transactions as purchase, the payment of taxes and wages, and the delivery of dowries and gifts.[1] As earlier, however, it was found necessary to employ media of exchange, and emmer wheat and silver were both used for the purpose. The latter was particularly favoured, but it was normally treated by weight, being measured in kite (9.53 g) and deben (10 kite) in purely Egyptian contexts, though foreigners such as the Jewish mercenaries at Elephantine could use their own metrological systems. Silver was certainly available in the form of Greek and Persian coins, but since in commercial transactions they were weighed like silver in any other form, and not accepted at face value, we cannot speak of the existence of a money economy in the strict sense. Nevertheless, there are indications of moves in that direction. From time to time we encounter references to payments in the form of pieces of silver where no indications of weight are given (e.g. P. Rylands, IX, 15, 15–19); yet the weight would hardly have been different from one piece to another nor would it have been irrelevant, and in these cases we can only assume that pieces of silver of a standard weight were employed. In many commercial dealings they would doubtless have been weighed, but where the exact value was not crucial such pieces could have been taken at face value. This policy would have been particularly easy to follow in the case of the Athenian tetradrachms which were so common in the country; for the quality and weight of these coins was absolutely consistent. The advantages of such a system had evidently become clear to the Egyptians themselves towards the end of our period when we occasionally meet with Egyptian silver coins stamped with hieroglyphic and

---

[1] For economic exchange at an earlier date see, in particular, Janssen (1975a, *passim*).

demotic signs, a development which provides us with a particularly clear example of foreign influence on Egyptian civilization during the Late Period.

Many desirable commodities were not available within Egypt proper, for instance good quality timber, silver, and magically or religiously potent substances such as myrrh, not to speak of a wide range of luxury items. The palace had always played the chief role in meeting these requirements, and in the Late Period this situation did not change. Various methods were employed to ensure supplies. In the first place, foreign traders were encouraged to come to Egypt and establish commercial links. According to Diodorus, Psammetichus I opened up the country to Greek and Phoenician traders at the very beginning of his reign and profited very considerably by his enterprise (I, 66, 8; 67, 9). Subsequently, *c.* 620 at the latest, he encouraged the settlement of the Greek trading post of Naucratis in the western Delta, and there is good evidence of other Greek trading stations within the country, though their scale is impossible to determine. Not the least important economic feature of the settlement at Naucratis is the fact that this site provides the first evidence of iron smelting in Pharaonic Egypt, and the possibility, therefore, arises that it played an important role in the introduction of this technology into the country. However that may be, the existence of such bases in Egypt itself is a distinct novelty and constitutes a strikingly original response to contemporary conditions. Some time about 570 Amasis concentrated all Greek import and export trade at Naucratis which thereby assumed a status comparable to that of Mirgissa in Nubia during the Middle Kingdom.[1] The palace certainly derived an immense profit from this measure in the form of customs dues, as emerges from the fiscal arrangements described in the Naucratis Stele of Nectanebo I. Probably the most valuable item in this Greek trade from the Egyptian point of view was silver, but Greek wine was also imported on a large scale.

Another time-honoured technique for acquiring produce or raw materials from foreign parts was the royal expedition whereby the king dispatched officials to sources of supply such as the Wadi Hammamat, Sinai, Byblos or Punt. Here again precedent was observed. Expeditions were sent into the Wadi Hammamat by Psammetichus I, Necho II, Psammetichus II and Amasis, as well as by the agents of the Persian government of Egypt and by later Egyptian Pharaohs. A determined

[1] The privileged position of Mirgissa (Iqen) is described in the first Semna Stele of Senusret III (*BAR* I, §652).

attempt seems to have been made by Necho II to resume commercial contacts with the land of Punt both by sweeping pirates from the Red Sea and by undertaking the abortive construction of a great canal from the Pelusiac Branch of the Nile via the Wadi Tumilat to the Gulf of Suez. This enterprise provides an interesting example of the combination of the new and the old in Saite policy: the exploitation of Red Sea commerce features prominently in earlier Egyptian history; on the other hand, the excavation of a great canal to facilitate such operations seems entirely novel, though waterways were certainly cut for other purposes in this area in earlier times. Another region to which royal expeditions were possibly sent is Phoenicia. Several passages in Saite texts refer to the use of ʿš-wood, 'pine', which traditionally derived from the Lebanon through the port of Byblos. It is, of course, possible that this got to Egypt in the vessels of enterprising Phoenician traders or even as the result of Saite military operations in the Levant, but it could well be that it was obtained by trade missions of the ancient type.

Another means of supply which requires serious consideration is warfare which often proved an extremely lucrative economic activity in the ancient world and was frequently regarded in precisely these terms. It emerges from such texts as Tuthmosis III's description of the Battle of Megiddo (Pritchard, 1969, p. 234ff) that the Egyptians themselves were perfectly well aware of this dimension, though the question of how far economics constituted a primary motive in Egyptian imperialism is probably unanswerable. However, there can be no doubt that the domination exercised for most of the Saite period over Philistia brought considerable economic rewards, particularly since it gave control of one of the northern points of exit for trade routes from Arabia and also for the southern end of the grand trunk road from the north, and the situation is similar in relation to the Saite conquest of Cyprus and, to some extent, Saite activities in Libya (see below, pp. 337ff).

One final possible source of foreign goods needs consideration. In his account of the reign of Amasis Herodotus frequently mentions gifts given by the king to states within the Greek world: Delphi, Cyrene, Lindus (on Rhodes), Samos, and Sparta all benefited from his largesse. These activities undoubtedly had a strategic dimension (see below, pp. 342ff), but it would surely be a mistake to ignore other possible aspects. Gift-giving in primitive and early societies is a primary mechanism for establishing socio-economic relations which can be exploited within the entire range of human contacts since it establishes a context within which reciprocal exchanges of all kinds are expected, and indeed obligatory.[1] It seems, therefore, justifiable to suspect that Amasis' gifts had economic as well as strategic motives and that he envisaged these donations as favours which could be repaid in economic as well as military assistance.

The foregoing analysis has been mainly concerned with the days of Egypt's autonomy. What, however, were the effects of the Persian occupation in 525? It is indisputable that it brought no significant change in the internal economic structure of the country, but in foreign relations the situation was inevitably different. The Achaemenid conquest made Egypt part of a great world empire which stretched from the Aegean to Afghanistan, and the Persians attempted, as far as possible, to integrate the country into the economic machinery of the empire as a whole. The most obvious link was fiscal: Egypt had to pay an annual tribute of 700 talents into the imperial treasury, by no means a princely sum for so rich a province, and was also required to provide the Great King's table with salt and Nile water, again no heavy burden, which presumably acted as little more than a symbol of subservience; we are also informed that the city of Anthylla had to provide the Persian queen with money for needles, shoes, and belts! Apart from all this, an effort was also made to tie Egypt into the empire's economic life in a physical sense by means of the great canal of Darius which ran from the Pelusiac Branch of the Nile to the Red Sea. This was opened in 497, and was evidently intended to function as a maritime counterpart to the Persian road system, as a component in a vast communications network devised to tie together the major sections of the widely scattered empire (Hinz 1975, pp. 115ff). The practical economic effects of this policy upon the Egyptians are lost upon us for lack of evidence, but it seems improbable that it led to a major increase in imports or exports and in any case the instability of the country after the reign of Darius must have ensured that any such benefits were short-lived.

## GOVERNMENT

The governmental institutions of Egypt were concerned at all periods with the same basic issues: the direction of the economy, the administration of justice, the maintenance of civil order, the defence of the

---

[1] The fundamental anthropological study of gift-giving is that of Mauss (1954). The importance of this practice in Egyptian society is just beginning to be recognized by Egyptologists (cf. Janssen 1982, pp. 253ff). The Greek recipients of Amasis' gifts would have had the same attitude to the reciprocal nature of the transaction as the Egyptians: cf. e.g. Finley (1956), Index, s.v. Gifts; Walcot (1970), Index, s.v. Gift.

realm, and the organization of the divine cult. In the complex machinery devised to satisfy these requirements the king was theoretically the fount of all authority; in principle, officials held power only as his deputies and, whether they functioned in central or provincial government, they were integrated into a coherent hierarchy by this one basic concept. An obvious consequence of this attitude was that the right of appointing all officials lay ultimately with Pharaoh himself, but in practice hereditary claims to office exercised as potent an influence in the Saite period as they had done earlier. Once appointed, officials who gained royal favour could still acquire a bewildering array of functions, combining, at the same time, civilian, military and priestly duties, a custom which exemplifies the profound Egyptian distaste for departmentalizing authority. At the highest level the authority of Pharaoh was all-embracing; consequently, the higher the rank of an official, the more comprehensive his power became.

Saite central administration was certainly based at Memphis in the reign of Amasis and this probably held true for most, if not all, of the Twenty-sixth Dynasty. Within this system the king functioned as much more than a titular head. In P. *Rylands* IX we find him administering justice, vetting a high official who had been a subject of complaint, and rewarding faithful and efficient servants; his active role in making governmental decisions also emerges in other texts of our period. Such personal involvement meant that major issues could often be resolved by gaining personal access to the royal presence which seems to have been surprisingly easy throughout Ancient Egyptian history. Under these circumstances, those who lived in close proximity to the king, whatever their rank, could acquire an inordinate influence on state affairs, and it is hardly surprising to find the continued employment of old court titles, such as 'sole companion' and 'acquaintance of the king', which insist that the officials in question enjoyed a high level of intimacy with the ruler. Royal favourites were a potent force for the same reason.

The hierarchy of civil servants to be found in Saite central government cannot be determined in detail. The old title of 'vizier' (*ṯ3ty*) still occurs, but whether this dignitary continued to function as the head of the administration is questionable, and it may well be significant that he is never mentioned in P. *Rylands* IX. However, there is no difficulty in identifying civil servants who were concerned with all the major preoccupations of central government. We encounter an *imy-r 3ḥ*, 'overseer of farmlands', who was assisted by a body of 'land-measurers' and clearly occupied a position of great importance in the economic administration; the *imy-r šnˁ*, 'overseer of the *šnˁ*', was also a powerful figure in the same sphere and was assisted by an influential subordinate called the *sš iw·f ip*, 'scribe of accounts'. Justice was well served: apart from Pharaoh, who acted as the ultimate court of appeal, we find that high officials, such as 'the overseer of the *šnˁ*', could also act as judges in disputes. In addition there are references to a body of *wpyw*, 'judges', who were associated with the *ˁy n wpyw*, 'House of Judgement', at Memphis. Cases will have been judged by statute or customary law, but our documentation strongly suggests that, wherever possible, judges acted as arbitrators to bring about a reconciliation between dissentient parties, a competence which seems even to have applied to criminal cases. For police duties the central government used army officers; on several occasions in *P. Rylands* IX we find an *imy-r mšˁ*, 'army commander', being employed in this way. These officers were, however, also concerned with the defence of the country as a whole, as were dignitaries like Nesuhor, 'Overseer of the Gate of the Southern Foreign Lands', and Udjahorresnet who was 'Admiral of the Fleet' both under Amasis and Psammetichus III. As for the central government's role in the organization of the cult, this had already been described in an earlier section (see above, p. 303ff).

Whichever field of activity we consider, the effective operation of this elaborate machinery was ultimately dependent on a ubiquitous army of scribes who disposed of one of the few undoubted innovations of the Late Period, i.e. the demotic script. This system of writing, invented in Lower Egypt, is first exemplified in *P. Rylands* I of 643/2, and became universal for ordinary purposes in the second half of the reign of Amasis, a status which it was to retain until the demise of Pharaonic civilization during the Roman period.

The Persian conquest brought no change in the theory of government as far as the indigenous population was concerned: the Egyptian Pharaoh was simply replaced by a Persian Pharaoh. In central administration the Persian imperial system was, as far as possible, simply superimposed on the Egyptian organization with the minimum of disruption. The head was the governor or satrap based at Memphis who was chosen from the cream of the Persian aristocracy, and was very often a royal kinsman. His major obligation was to guarantee taxes and any *ad hoc* imposts which the imperial government might require. Despite his birth, he was always kept under close surveillance: members of the imperial intelligence service (the 'King's Ears') were always in attendance; annual inspections were held by the 'King's Eye'; and the satrap was compelled to share the functions of government with colleagues who acted as an effective control on his activities. Amongst these officers may be mentioned the 'inquisitor' (*patifrasa/frasaka*) who participated in the legal functions of government, and the chancellor who directed a chancellery modelled on that of the Persian emperor. This official was assisted by the 'scribe' and a corps of 'royal scribes', but Egyptians were also to be found in his office, many of them presumably concerned with translating documents drawn up in Aramaic which served as the official language of the Persian Empire. As in earlier times, the state treasury continued to play a crucial role. It was located at Memphis, and it is interesting to note that in the fifth century the important office of 'Overseer of the Treasury' was actually held by an Egyptian.

On the whole, it seems to have been Persian policy to adopt a *laissez-faire* attitude where possible, and this was made all the easier by the fact that there were close similarities in principle between Achaemenid and Egyptian systems of administration. Indeed, it is likely that there were no significant changes in the lower echelons of the central administration, and that even those in the upper reaches did not involve a startling break with Egyptian tradition and were therefore perfectly acceptable. If so, the expulsion of the Persians in 404 would not have caused major administrative problems for the liberators, and it would have been a simple matter to reactivate the Saite machinery of government, though it must be conceded that the paucity of evidence makes it impossible to establish the details of the administrative structure during the final period of Egyptian independence.

The basis of provincial administration during the Saite period was the nome, of which there were probably about forty. Each was governed by a nomarch whose brief was probably to exercise a general supervision over all aspects of local administration, with particular emphasis on economic organization and justice. Detailed evidence is not available, but the economic dimension of his work does emerge in the Nitocris Stele, according to which every nomarch on Nitocris' route south was required to provide her with supplies (l. 10), and also in the biography of Peftjuaneith which refers to a nomarch's role in levying taxes. His legal functions are less easy to identify, but it is at least possible that a nomarch is described as acting in this capacity in P. *Rylands* XI (19, 21). Much judicial business was, of course, dealt with at a lower level by civil servants acting in a legal capacity, by courts of 'judges', by priests, by the consultation of oracles, and doubtless by the rough local justice of the village sheikh. Like the central government the nomarch was assisted by an army of scribes; we hear, in particular, of 'scribes of the nome' who were evidently functionaries of high rank concerned with the nome's administrative archives. As for the maintenance of order, the nomarch could rely on the paramilitary 'chiefs of police' (*ḥryw mḏзy*) who sometimes, at any rate, employed *machimoi* in the execution of their duty. Their sphere of operation was not confined to individual nomes, and, amongst other duties, they could be employed to protect individuals where rights or property were under threat. We also hear of officials called 'commissioners' (*rmt pз sḥn*) who were, on occasion, associated with police work, and 'factors' (*rwdw*), who were used both by officials and private citizens as agents to carry out business which they were unable to execute in person.

Within the nome, towns formed important centres of government. At the beginning of our period we hear of a mayor (*ḥзty-ᶜ*) at Thebes, and some such official evidently existed in all of them. We also encounter 'scribes of the city' who seem to have been particularly concerned with taxation. At town and local level much legal documentation was probably drawn up by the school scribe (*sḥ n ᶜ-sbз*) whose position and functions appear to have been comparable to those of the *fiqy* or 'schoolmaster' in traditional Arabic society.

The reunification of the country under Psammetichus I, *c.* 656, gave rise to a major problem in provincial administration – the maintenance of royal writ over the nomes of Upper Egypt and, in particular, over the temple-state of Amen-Ra in the Thebaid where authority lay *de jure* in the hands of the High Priestess of Amen-Ra at Thebes and *de facto* in those of the great Theban baron Mentuemhet. Psammetichus attempted to solve this difficulty by arranging for his daughter Nitocris to be established in Thebes as the prospective High Priestess and by constituting the area from the Memphite Nome to Assuan (*Ptores*, 'the Southern Land') as a special administrative unit under the 'Shipmasters' of Herakleopolis, who were, however, superimposed upon the nome system in a supervisory capacity without in any way impairing it. They were responsible, in particular, for economic administration and received an annual report on everything produced in the area. The site of Herakleopolis was an ideal base for such operations since it gave easy access both to the Fayum and to Upper Egypt, and the 'Shipmasters' themselves were an excellent choice as agents inasmuch as they had close family ties with the priests of Thebes which would both allay suspicion and doubtless facilitate an accommodation with the political and economic interests in that city. It is worth noting, however, that this administrative device was no novelty; it had an ancient parallel in the 'overseer of Upper Egypt' introduced in the Sixth Dynasty to serve much the same function, and it appears in a new guise in the Ptolemaic *stratēgos tēs Thēbaidos*, 'governor of the Thebaid'. It quickly disappeared in the Twenty-sixth Dynasty, and there is good evidence that by regnal year 22 of Amasis, at the latest, Saite administrative control of the entire country was no longer a matter of dispute.

The provincial system just described was ideally suited to Egyptian conditions and not only the Persians but also the Macedonians took it over with few modifications. The former did, however, find it convenient to divide Upper Egypt into at least two large provinces comparable to the Saite *Ptores*. These were Tshetres, which probably stretched from Hermonthis to Aswan, and No, which was probably the Thebaid. Each had its own governor assisted by a chancellery in which the 'scribes of the prince' played an important role. These functionaries were 'royal scribes' who were responsible in particular for the registration of land and the assessment of taxes. Each province had its own treasury, and garrisons were stationed throughout the country whose commanders were empowered to exercise functions which passed far beyond the military sphere.

Up to this point we have focused attention upon the machinery of government. We must now briefly consider the way in which it worked in practice. In this respect, there was probably little difference from one period to another, and much that we meet in Late Period texts has earlier parallels. That the system had serious demerits is beyond doubt. Its centralized character made it extremely bureaucratic and created endless opportunities for delay and obstruction; it was so paper-ridden that issues must often have disappeared completely beneath mountains of papyrus; maladministration was certainly common, and bribery endemic – indeed, well-placed baksheesh was not infrequently the only means of breaking the inertia or indifference of Egyptian civil servants; physical brutality was still too common a feature of the conduct of Egyptian administrators; control of subordinates was at times totally inadequate, and royal commands could easily be ignored even under powerful rulers (cf. *P. Rylands* IX, 5, 2ff); in official contexts family connections were as important as in other spheres of Egyptian life, and they were exploited quite spontaneously and without compunction. For all this, however, Ancient Egyptian government had great merits, and three of these are particularly easy to detect in our period. In the first place, though bureaucratic, the Egyptian system was not bedevilled with the impersonality of modern bureaucracy. Government was personal even at the highest level; access to authority was not difficult, and the right to make an appeal to Pharaoh in person was taken as much for granted in the Petition of Petiese as it had been in the Middle Kingdom Tale of the Eloquent Peasant. The old paternalistic ideal of the relationship between ruler and ruled was also very much alive and frequently expressed in tomb biographies: the official was the father of his people and obliged by divine command and time-honoured codes of conduct to consult their welfare in all respects. The system also laid emphasis not only on achieving equilibrium in state and society, but also on gaining the willing acquiescence in that system by the subject. These aims are particularly evident in the weight placed upon the principle of reciprocity and reconciliation in legal disputes where the primary intention was not to impose a verdict on the parties, but to get both parties to work out by mutual compromise a solution which satisfied the requirements of each. On balance, one leaves the study of the subject with the firm conviction that there are, and have been, far worse systems of government.

## FOREIGN POLICY

The foregoing discussion has concentrated mainly on conditions within the country. It is, however, impossible to ignore the fact that Egypt formed part of a large and complex Eastern Mediterranean world whose individual elements interacted with one another at many different levels and often with far-reaching consequences. Not surprisingly, therefore, Egypt's relations with her neighbours exerted a powerful and sometimes crucial effect not only on her capacity for political action, but also on her socio-economic development. The effects of Persian domination have already been adequately discussed. In this section it is the policies of the independent Egyptian state between 664 and 332 to which we shall devote our attention.

### Egypt and the Levant

Throughout the Late Period Egypt's foreign policy was dominated by the problem of defining her relationship with a series of great oriental empires, first Assyria, then Chaldaea, and finally Persia. The character and motives of Egypt's policy towards Assyria in the early years of the

Saite Dynasty are still, in some respects, a matter of dispute. It is clear that Psammetichus I, like his father, was initially an Assyrian vassal, but it is probable that this situation changed very quickly in the early years of his reign when he emerged as an ally of Gyges of Lydia in the latter's rebellion against Assyria, and we are forced to assume that, at this stage, Psammetichus was concerned to assert his independence of Assyrian domination. Subsequently, as the tide of Assyrian imperialism in the Levant receded, he readily availed himself of the power vacuum created in that area. His occupation of Philistia at least is certain and was sealed by the capture of Ashdod, probably some time between *c.* 655 and 630 BC. This city was of immense strategic value since it was the northernmost Philistine city and lay on the grand trunk road from Egypt to Damascus and the north. Its conquest, therefore, not only guaranteed control of Philistia itself but also created a barrier to any force advancing from the north. His hold on Ashdod also conferred economic benefits in that this city was commercially extremely rich, controlling, as it did, the north-south and east-west trade routes by land and also the maritime commerce in the area through its port at Tell Mor. Sometime between *c.* 637 and 625 Psammetichus' supremacy in Philistia was temporarily interrupted by a horde invasion from the north by Scythian barbarians, but it is most improbable that this disaster had any serious long-term effects on Egypt's position.

By 616 Psammetichus' relations with Assyria had undergone a startling volte-face. In that year we find the Egyptian army operating on behalf of the Assyrians against the rising imperial power of Chaldaea. There can be no doubt that it was the advent of this young and vigorous force as the new Asiatic super-power which motivated the realignment, and it was against this threat that Necho II immediately had to turn his attention on his accession in 610. Heavy military and naval forces, including a fleet of war-galleys of the most modern Graeco-Phoenician type, were committed in an attempt to halt the advance of Chaldaea at the Euphrates, but this project proved beyond Egypt's capacity; the remnants of her Assyrian allies were conquered in 610/9, and the catastrophic defeat of Necho's forces at Carchemish in 605 placed the entire Levant at the mercy of the Chaldaeans, an opportunity of which they speedily availed themselves. On the credit side, the Egyptians roundly defeated their attempt to invade Egypt in 601–600, and there is some evidence that this success enabled Egyptian forces to counter-attack. It is, however, indisputable that they did their utmost by diplomatic means to disrupt Chaldaean control of Syria and Palestine,

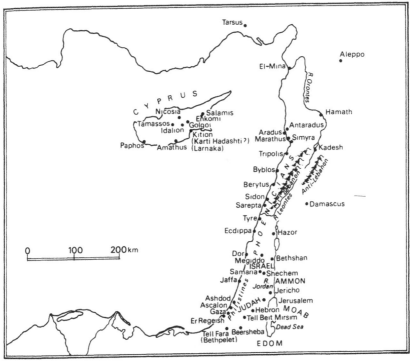

Fig. 4.9   The Levant in the first millennium.

efforts which achieved a signal success *c.* 590 when Zedekiah of Judah embarked on a full-scale rebellion against his Chaldaean overlords. Egypt became actively involved in 589 when Apries attempted un-successfully to relieve Jerusalem. In 582 the Chaldaeans invaded Egypt itself, but we find Apries able to mount a major offensive *c.* 574–70 when he attacked Tyre, Sidon, and Cyprus. These operations were evidently a carefully planned land and sea assault aimed at gaining control of Phoenicia and Cyprus and thereby posing a serious threat to the maintenance of Chaldaean power in the west. If successful, these campaigns would also have conferred considerable economic benefits in the form of raw materials, such as timber and metals, as well as control of maritime trade routes, but, despite conspicuous triumphs, the project ultimately failed, at least as far as Phoenicia was concerned, though it is possible that Cyprus at least was brought under Egyptian domination. The final round in the duel with Chaldaea was fought out in the following reign. In 567 a Chaldaean army invaded Egypt with the purpose of deposing the usurper Amasis and replacing him with the legitimate Pharaoh Apries. The advantages of this scheme from the Chaldaean point of view are self-evident, but the plan foundered when the invaders were disastrously defeated and Apries himself killed.

The rise of Persia under Cyrus the Great soon raised up a new threat to Egyptian security, and rapidly led to a regrouping of forces in the form of an anti-Persian alliance in which Amasis associated himself with the Chaldaeans, Lydians, and Spartans. This confederacy was short-lived: Lydia was conquered in 546, the Chaldaeans in 538, and Amasis was left to find his salvation elsewhere. There is reason to believe that he may have concluded a diplomatic marriage-alliance with the Persians, but he placed his trust mainly in alliances with Greek states (see below pp. 342ff).

When we consider these events as a whole, it is evident that Egypt derived two main benefits from her Asiatic policy during the Saite period. In the first place, dangerous and predatory Asiatic enemies were kept at bay; secondly, her military conquests conferred significant economic benefits. What, however, was the primary motive? The economic returns can hardly be regarded in that light; for the produce in question could easily have been acquired through normal trade-channels without the expensive, exhausting, and occasionally disastrous military operations on which the Saite Pharaohs embarked. Imperialist phantasies may occasionally have played a part, but it is impossible to escape the conviction that their Asiatic policy was essentially defensive in character, however aggressive some of its manifestations may have been, and that they were concerned pre-eminently to maintain the independence of Egypt against Asiatic powers by whatever means came readily to hand. In their efforts to realize this aim they suffered severe setbacks, but they were faced with formidable opponents, and it was no mean achievement to keep the country free of Asiatic domination until Cambyses' invasion in 525.

On turning to the period of independence between 404 and 343 we find that Egyptian foreign policy was essentially a resumption of that of the Saites. The dominant issue was to keep at bay a powerful Asiatic enemy, in this case, Persia. The evidence is often confused and confusing, but it is clear that the basic strategy was no novelty: the enemy was kept from the frontier of Egypt by taking advantage of any disruption in the western provinces of the Persian Empire. In the first half of the fourth century the Egyptians found ready allies in the Spartans whose struggle to maintain their hegemony within the Aegean world often brought them into collision with Persian interests. Several phases in the development of this policy are detectable: initially the Egyptians showed great caution. They kept out of the rebellion of Cyrus which threw the western empire into turmoil in and immediately after 401, and they even executed one of the main insurgents who had fled to Egypt; in the second phase, during the reign of Nepherites I and the early part of that of Achoris, they functioned as the paymasters of disaffected Persian subjects without, however, getting personally involved in military operations; later, if Diodorus' account is to be trusted, Achoris' position changed, and we find him participating actively in the rebellion of Evagoras of Cyprus; with the accession of Tachos we encounter total commitment. About 361 he took advantage of a general revolt in the west of the Persian Empire and, with the assistance of the Spartans, embarked on large-scale military operations on behalf of the rebels. Despite initial success this campaign collapsed into a civil war between Tachos and the usurper Nectanebo (II), which led to the former's deposition. Nectanebo was understandably a great deal more cautious, but we do find him in 351 collaborating with rebellious Levantine states against the Great King.

The ability of the Persians to deal with Egyptian hostility was severely impaired throughout this period by their commitments elsewhere; Egypt was a long way from the heart of the empire and, therefore, despite an awesome capacity for disruption, it inevitably occupied a low level in the scale of imperial priorities. Nevertheless, the Persians made at least three serious attempts to solve the problem: in 374 Artaxerxes II dispatched a large invasion force by land and sea which succeeded in invading the Delta but was ultimately defeated by a combination of Egyptian military skill, geographical circumstances, and jealousies within the Persian high command; in 351 Artaxerxes III made another attempt which also failed, though the details are lost; finally, in 343, he mounted a second assault which brought speedy success and delivered the country once more, and for the last time, into Achaemenid hands.

When we consider these events two questions arise insistently: first, did the Egyptians adopt the best methods for dealing with Persia; secondly, what were the effects of their policy upon Egypt itself? Theoretically, they had two options open to them: they might assume an isolationist position in the hope that the Persians would reciprocate; alternatively, they might pursue a programme of action to prevent a Persian attack upon Egypt. There can be no doubt that the second approach was the only practical solution. Given a chance, the Persians would certainly have returned, and the Egyptians wisely determined that this chance must not be given to them. There were, however, various ways of achieving this. Disruption of the western empire by diplomatic means was one; large-scale military action was another. A keen perception of military realities should have revealed that the first was by far the least dangerous alternative, and some rulers of the period clearly had the good sense to pursue it; the second was certain to excite massive retaliation sooner or later and would, in addition, put strains on Egypt itself which the country could ill withstand. That these strains were severe admits of no doubt. War tests a nation's institutions as no other source of pressure can, and the events of the ambitious Asiatic war of Tachos reveal with startling clarity the instability of the kingdom at the highest level and the ease with which the ambitions of the mighty could be kindled to aspire to the kingly office. Egypt's Asiatic policy could also place a massive strain upon the economy of the country, particularly since a large part of the fighting was done by expensive foreign mercenaries. Nothing illustrates this point more forcefully than the desperate fiscal measures used by Tachos to fill his coffers for the Asiatic war (Ps. Aristotle, *Oeconomica*, 1350b–51a), and we can be sure that the bitterness and hardship created by this policy played a significant part in causing the uprising which led to his deposition.

### Egypt and the north

When we turn to Egypt's foreign policy in the Aegean and Eastern Mediterranean we find that it was, to a large extent, dependent upon her machinations in Asia. About 600 we find Necho II shrewdly dedicating at Branchidae, a major East Greek temple, the very breastplate which he had worn during his victorious campaign against the Chaldaeans in 601/600, doubtless in formal recognition of the importance of Greek mercenaries in these operations. This precedent in calculated generosity was wisely followed by Amasis, who contributed substantially to the rebuilding of the premier Greek shrine at Delphi which had been burnt down in 548/7, and also dedicated two stone statues and a linen breastplate in the temple of Athene at Lindus on the island of Rhodes. Ties with some states, however, were more formal: he entered into an alliance with Polycrates, tyrant of Samos between *c.* 533 and 522 and owner of the most powerful fleet in the Aegean, and he also concluded a defensive alliance with Sparta, in both cases cementing the relationship with well-chosen gifts. The one exception to this generally friendly standpoint towards the Greek world is the island of Cyprus: Apries undoubtedly attacked and possibly took it; Amasis certainly brought it under Egyptian control.

It is not difficult to detect the motives behind all these activities. Although economic considerations clearly played their part, defence was indisputably the crucial consideration. Since Egypt's security was now to a large extent dependent upon ready access to a supply of Greek mercenaries and the support of powerful allies in the Aegean, the maintenance of close and amicable relations with that area was imperative.

For most of the First Persian Occupation we cannot speak of an *Egyptian* Aegean policy. The one clear exception is the revolt of Inarus in the late 460s. At the very beginning of this rebellion Inarus formed an alliance with the Athenians whose anti-Persian stance at this time made them ideal for this purpose. Here he was doing no more than following Saite precedent, and we find the same course of action being pursued in the period of Egyptian independence between 404 and 343 when several alliances were concluded with major Greek powers, particularly Sparta and Evagoras of Cyprus. It is likely enough that there were economic ramifications to all this, but the military aspects dominate our tradition, and we need not question their pre-eminent importance.

### Egypt and Libya

As far as contacts with the west are concerned, two peoples are at issue, the Libyans and the Cyreneans. Relations with the former began on a bad note when Psammetichus I was forced to deal with a Libyan attack on Egypt in 654, but subsequent contacts seem to have been friendly; towards the end of the 570s we find Libyans placing themselves under the protection of Apries, and in the fourth century Nectanebo II is alleged to have had no fewer than 20000 of them in his army, presumably as allies, though they may have been mercenaries. The Greek city of Cyrene posed a less tractable problem. War broke out *c.* 570, sparked off by bad relations between Cyrene and the neighbouring Libyan tribes who had become increasingly disturbed at encroachments on their territory resulting from the expansion of the Greek city and asked Apries for assistance. This he readily gave, though his reasons are a matter of inference only. Economically, Cyrene would certainly have been a rich prize, but the main inducement was probably that the

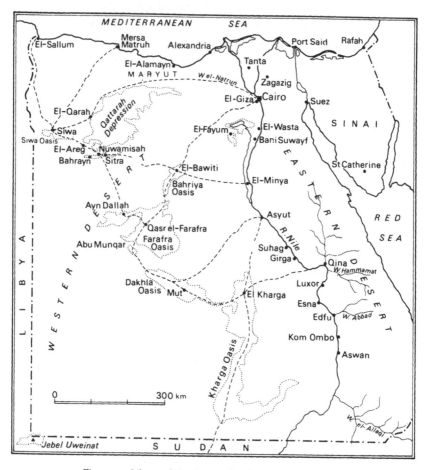

Fig. 4.10   Libya and the Oases (after A. Fakhry (1974), 23).

growing power of Cyrene was regarded as posing a threat to the security of Egypt's western frontier. At all events, a force of *machimoi* was sent to the assistance of the Libyans which was severely defeated. This disaster led to the deposition of Apries and his replacement by Amasis whose approach to the Cyrenean question was altogether different in that he decided to neutralize the threat by diplomatic means. The Cyreneans were certainly his allies in the campaign of 567 against the Chaldaeans, and that alliance is known to have lasted down to the Persian period. Its importance to Amasis is strikingly demonstrated by the fact that he went so far as to cement it by marrying a woman of the Cyrenean royal family.

It is doubtless in the context of these military problems that we must place the attention lavished by Pharaohs of the Late Period on the Libyan oases. From at least the Old Kingdom there is evidence of Egyptian contacts with these areas which reveals that the Egyptians were not only concerned to exploit their economic resources and the lucrative commercial channels which passed through them but had also come to appreciate their strategic value as outposts for defending the western frontier of Egypt itself. It is hardly surprising, therefore, that by the New Kingdom, and probably long before, all the oases running from the Wadi Natrun to Kharga lay under direct Egyptian control and had assumed culturally and administratively the character of provincial offshoots of Egypt comparable to Nubia. Saite Pharaohs followed, and indeed improved upon, this precedent. Not only did they devote themselves enthusiastically to the development of the Bahriya and Kharga Oases and other traditional centres of interest, but we also find them moving even further west and bringing the oasis of Siwa for the first time under Egyptian control. It was Amasis who was responsible for the first temple of the Siwan oracle at Aghurmi and the oldest tombs at Jebel el-Mawta also belong to the Saite period. This extension of Egyptian influence may, of course, have been motivated in part by economic or even religious considerations, but it can hardly be coincidence that the occupation of Siwa took place at the very time that Cyrene began to pose a serious threat to the western frontier of Egypt. This political, economic and strategic integration of the oases with Egypt remained a constant feature of Egyptian policy and attitudes throughout the Late Period. It is this which indubitably explains the desire of Cambyses to bring the entire oasis area under his control, and it is this which motivated the temple-building of Darius at Kharga, Nectanebo II at Umm ʿEbeideh in Siwa, and Alexander the Great at Kasr el-Megysbeh in the Bahriya Oasis.

## Egypt and the south

The history of Egyptian attitudes towards the Nubian kingdom south of the First Cataract shows some similarity to her relations with Asia: at the beginning of the Saite period the Nubians, like the Assyrians, claimed possession of Egypt, and these claims the Saites were determined to thwart. Since Nubia was undoubtedly the more dangerous of the two, it is hardly surprising to find Necho I and Psammetichus I supporting the Assyrians against their African rivals. This alliance was at first unsuccessful; for in 664 the Nubian king Tanwetemani defeated and killed Necho I at Memphis, but this triumph was quickly reversed when Psammetichus crushed Tanwetemani's forces in that area later in the same year. Subsequently Psammetichus' problem was that of breaking the influence of Nubia in Upper Egypt, and this aim was pursued by diplomatic means which proved as effective as they were skilful.

Necho II certainly had an interest in the south. It is probable that his Red Sea canal was intended to facilitate the reopening of trade relations with Punt, and recent work at Elephantine has yielded a fragmentary inscription which refers to activities within Africa, though insufficient is preserved to establish the precise context (Müller 1975, pp. 83ff). Whatever the situation in Necho's reign, however, relations with the south were certainly bad in that of his successor Psammetichus II who dispatched a military expedition into the very heart of the Nubian kingdom in 593. This enterprise undoubtedly brought some economic benefits, but contemporary evidence proves that it was, in essence, a pre-emptive strike designed to forestall a projected attack on Egypt by the Nubian king himself. In this aim the campaign was entirely successful, and it marked the end of any Nubian ambition to recover control of the northern kingdom.

The only other Saite reference to Egyptian involvement with the south occurs in a demotic papyrus dated to regnal year 41 (530) of Amasis (*P. Berlin* 13615), but this expedition does not look like a major military operation, and Erichsen plausibly suggested that it was simply intended as an escort to protect a caravan (Erichsen 1941, pp. 56ff). We hear very little of contacts with Nubia in the final period of Egyptian independence, but the fact that Nectanebo II fled south in 341 suggests that recent relations had been cordial enough to give every hope of a friendly reception.[1]

## CONCLUSIONS

The history of Egypt between 664 and 323 could hardly be described as a series of unalloyed triumphs. It began in the reign of Psammetichus I with Egypt for the last time functioning, if only briefly, as a world power of the first rank, but subsequently her career as an independent

---

[1] In this discussion of Egyptian foreign policy limitations of space have made it impossible to justify every statement made. A fuller treatment will be found in the forthcoming third volume of my commentary on Herodotus Book II and in my chapter on Egypt from 404–332 BC in the third edition of the *Cambridge Ancient History*.

state was at best that of a second-rate political force desperately striving to preserve her autonomy against more powerful oriental neighbours who disposed of economic resources, a stock of manpower, and a degree of military efficiency, prowess, and dynamism with which Egypt was quite unable to compete. This stark decline in her relative position amongst the great nations of the earth is grimly revealed by the ultimate humiliation of two periods of Asiatic domination as a province of the Persian Empire. The means by which Egyptian civilization confronted and adapted to these circumstances present an intriguing blend of pliability and conservatism.

The character of any civilization is determined, in the final analysis, by three factors: its technology, institutions, and ideology. If we consider these aspects of Egyptian culture in the Late Period, we find a varied pattern of response. In technology one observes distinctive features such as the temple- or palace-mound, and the increased use of stone for non-religious buildings, though it is impossible to be confident that these developments did not have their origin before 664. However, the Saites were certainly responsible for introducing into Egypt a revolutionary change in naval architecture in the form of the ramming war-galley which reflects a totally different concept of naval warfare from that which had previously prevailed in the country. This innovation was obviously motivated by the need to combat similar warships in foreign navies, and the expertise which it presupposed was itself acquired from foreign sources. Another important technological development of the period was the introduction of the large-scale use of iron. In the main, however, the technical apparatus of Late Period Egypt shows few departures from older practice, and the rule would seem to be that Egypt changed in this respect when she needed to, but that, in general, her traditional resources were fully capable of meeting the demands placed upon them.

When we turn to institutional structure, we encounter a more complex picture. The basic administrative machinery shows no startling departures, though it is possible to trace a progressive tendency to establish Lower Egyptian norms throughout the country. In other areas, however, significant adaptations are detectable: economically, we observe the introduction of foreign trading stations into Egypt itself, and halting steps were taken in the direction of a money economy; in law the importance of the principle of intention receives greater recognition, at least in the formulation of contracts; militarily, we note a much greater reliance on foreign commanders and much heavier emphasis on alliances with foreign states, whilst we also meet the first evidence of the use of cavalry in the Egyptian army; religion shows no basic change, though some revealing modifications in points of emphasis are detectable: in particular, animal-worship, the cult of Isis, and, probably, the ancestor-cult enjoyed a greater vogue. In the sphere of communication we encounter a particularly striking institutional change in the introduction of the demotic script. It would, however, be a mistake to overrate the effects of these developments. Numerous though they may seem, they cannot be regarded as creating fundamental changes in the institutional structure of the country. The overall impression is of continuity with ancient practice and of undiminished confidence in the relevance and resilience of ancestral ways of doing things. In certain essential areas these might be modified by a process of fine tuning to take full advantage of existing opportunities, to meet a pressing challenge, or to intensify the Egyptians' sense of national identity in the face of pressures from foreign cultural influence, but there is no question of any radical restructuring of Egypt's institutions.

What of ideology? A close and sympathetic reading of contemporary texts yields little which excites surprise. Concepts of the gods and of the nature of man, the perception of nationality, and, for the most part, of the royal office can all be paralleled in earlier sources. However, at the end of the period a crucial change in attitudes to kingship does emerge when the idea becomes firmly implanted that kings are not, *ex officio*, the repositories of righteousness and the allies of the gods, but are all too likely to act in ways of which the gods disapprove. The currency of this conviction was a development of incalculable importance; for it struck a deadly blow at the ideological basis of the royal office which was nothing less than the central concept on which Egyptian civilization as a whole was based.

# BIBLIOGRAPHICAL ESSAYS

## I. THE RISE OF EGYPTIAN CIVILIZATION

The formative periods of Egyptian civilization, although acknowledged to be of major historical interest, have generally been neglected by anthropologists, while Egyptologists have devoted far less attention to them than they have to later periods of Egyptian history. Between the 1930s and the 1960s very few archaeological excavations were carried out that related to the Predynastic Period and most studies published at that time were re-examinations of earlier work. Few general studies, even today, attempt to view the early development of Egyptian civilization in terms of a comprehensive theoretical framework. Petrie's popular but now largely obsolete *The making of Egypt* (1939) was the extreme statement of a diffusionist interpretation of the development of Egypt in Predynastic times. Childe (1934), while not rejecting diffusion, offered a materialist interpretation of the origin of Egyptian civilization which saw surpluses appropriated in a more centralized fashion than in ancient Mesopotamia. Frankfort (1956) also studied, with special reference to their differing world views, the structural contrasts between the mature expressions of these two civilizations and examined their differing developmental sequences. Hoffman (1979) has recently published a comprehensive, semi-popular account of the archaeology and culture historical development of Egypt in prehistoric and Early Dynastic times. His interpretations, which are anthropological in orientation, differ from our own mainly in according Hierakonpolis a pre-eminent role in the developments of the late Predynastic Period and not emphasizing the role possibly played by the gold trade at that time. Fairservis' (1971–2) description of the aims of his work at Hierakonpolis suggests growing interest in the comparative study of the development of Egyptian civilization. Works of this sort reflect a growing rapprochement between Egyptology and anthropology which is also evident elsewhere.

The archaeology of the Predynastic and Early Dynastic Periods and related site reports are discussed in the text. The most comprehensive secondary source for both periods is Vandier (1952). His encyclopaedic work summarizes evidence and interpretations in a generally impartial manner. For briefer and more popular interpretations of both periods, see Aldred (1965) and Hoffman (1979). The most important recent excavations are those carried out in 1979 by the German Archaeological Institute of Cairo at Merimda. According to preliminary reports, five stratigraphic levels have been identified at the site. New correlations have been established between the oldest level and early pottery sites in south-western Asia. The two latest levels are comparable to the Middle Neolithic culture in Palestine and Fayum A in Egypt. Merimda thus appears to be the oldest known Neolithic site in Egypt and may date 1000 years earlier than was hitherto believed (Leclant 1980, p. 350). For recent important finds at Hierakonpolis relating to the Predynastic Period, see Hoffman (1980).

Petrie (1920) remains the basic source of published material for the Amratian and Gerzean Periods and, along with his corpus of prehistoric pottery and palettes (1921) and site reports (1896, 1901b), is still a much used reference work. Needler (1981) has drawn attention to a largely ignored but important rationalization of Petrie's pottery wares developed by Federn in the 1940s. The most important attempt to revise Petrie's chronology is Kaiser's (1957) study of the Predynastic cemetery at Armant; his promised book on the Predynastic Period still has not appeared. Baumgartel (1955, 1960) has published a two-volume report on her studies of the Predynastic cultures of Upper Egypt which contains useful data and interesting, if sometimes speculative, interpretations. She has also produced a reconstitution of gravelots from the Naqada cemeteries and a description of the elite Gerzean Cemetery T there (Baumgartel 1970b). Krzyzaniak (1977) has published an important synthesis of material relating to the Predynastic Period in Upper Egypt, stressing economic and social changes. In recent years there has been growing interest in tracing the development of social stratification in Predynastic and Early Dynastic times, especially using the abundant cemetery data from Upper Egypt. Published examples include Fattovich (1976), Krzyzaniak (1979), and a series of papers by Castillos (1978, 1979, 1981, 1982). More substantial studies of this problem are currently in progress. The best synthesis of archaeological data concerning Predynastic Lower Egypt is the published fragment of Hayes' (1965) unfinished history of Egypt; and the best general interpretation is found in Hoffman (1979). Baumgartel's (1970a) latest summary of the Predynastic Period pays inadequate attention to views other than her own, especially concerning the cultures of northern Egypt. For still-valid critiques of research on Predynastic Egypt, see Arkell and Ucko (1965) and Trigger (1968).

The most popular synthesis of the Early Dynastic Period is Emery (1961), which summarizes much useful factual material, although the concept of a 'Dynastic Race' which he champions is now widely regarded as unacceptable. Edwards (1971) provides a useful summary of information about the dynastic history of this period. Kaplony's (1963) monograph on the difficult-to-read inscriptions of this period is of exceptional importance for understanding its political and economic structures and Kemp (1966, 1967) seems to have resolved the thorny issue of the burial places of the First Dynasty monarchs. Apart from the excavations at Hierakonpolis, little important archaeological work has been done on this period in recent years.

The relative chronology of Predynastic and Early Dynastic times has been examined by Kantor (1965), who stresses particularly connections with south-western Asia. The implications of radiocarbon dates have been discussed by H. S. Smith (1964) and Derricourt (1971). Much current analysis centres on the implications of the bristlecone-pine calibration for radiocarbon time-scales (Suess 1970) and thermoluminescent dates for Upper Egyptian pottery (Caton-Thompson and Whittle 1975). A recent attempt to use radiocarbon dates to push the beginning of the First Dynasty several hundred years earlier in time (Mellaart 1979) has been convincingly refuted (Kemp 1980). Hassan (1980) is currently engaged in a systematic investigation of the radiocarbon chronology of the Predynastic and Early Dynastic Periods.

Work in recent decades has dispelled many entrenched beliefs concerning the origins of the ancient Egyptians. Passarge (1940) and Butzer (1959) had clarified the environmental setting of Predynastic Egypt and, in particular, have rejected the notion that the Nile Valley was a primordial swamp inimical to human settlement. Changes in rainfall patterns (Butzer 1959) and the regime of the Nile River (Bell 1970) have also been investigated for the Predynastic and Early Dynastic Periods. Works by Krzyzaniak (1977), Schenkel (1978), and, above all, Butzer (1976) have sought to define the nature and role played by irrigation during these periods. Theories of the origin of Egyptian food production have been viewed in a broad regional setting by Reed (1966), Clark (1971), McHugh (1974), and Wendorf and Schild (1980). The linguistic status of ancient Egyptian as an Afroasiatic language has been clarified by Greenberg (1955) and Fleming (1969). This and other linguistic problems relating to Egyptian and Afroasiatic are discussed by Vergote (1970) and in Hodge (1971). Although no comprehensive study of the racial characteristics of ancient Egyptians has been published recently, Berry, Berry and Ucko (1967) and Berry and Berry (1973) tend to reject Derry's (1956) concept of a 'Dynastic Race' and to support Batrawi's (1945, 1946) views of continuity in early Egyptian population; see also Trigger (1978).

A traditional summary of Nubian culture history is found in Emery (1966). Excavations begun in Nubia in the early 1960s have greatly extended knowledge of the archaeological sequence in this region prior to 3000 BC (Wendorf 1968). More recent anthropological-style interpretations of Nubian culture history can be found in Trigger (1976) and Adams' (1977) encyclopaedic history of Nubia. Physical anthropological studies increasingly are accounting for morphological changes in terms of local transformations rather than major population shifts (Carlson and Van Gerven 1977). Archaeological research in the Sudan is slowly increasing our knowledge of Arkell's Early Khartoum (1949) and Esh-Shaheinab (1953) cultures. Related cultures have been found to extend over large areas of the Sudan. An important linguistic study by Ehret (1979) sheds important light on the origin and possible high antiquity of food production in Ethiopia and the eastern Sudan and relates these to the spread of the Afroasiatic language family. Excavations near Khartoum indicate that the Sudan was an important centre of innovation with respect to the domestication of sorghum and millet and that cattle, as well as goats, were being herded there prior to 3000 BC (Krzyzaniak 1978; Haaland 1981). H. S. Smith (1966) has convincingly disposed of Reisner's B-Group. Recent work on the A-Group is summarized in Nördstrom (1972). Bruce Williams' (1980) striking claim that there was a late A-Group kingdom in Lower Nubia has not won support.

## 2. OLD KINGDOM, MIDDLE KINGDOM AND SECOND INTERMEDIATE PERIOD C. 2686–1552 BC

The basic framework of dynasties for ancient Egyptian history laid down by the Egyptian priest Manetho in the late fourth or early third century BC is still followed, although there are grounds for doubting the integrity of certain of them in the First and Second Intermediate Periods. The surviving versions of Manetho have been edited by Waddell (1940). It was probably more in the nature of a chronicle than a history properly speaking, but little of it has survived other than summary lists of his kings, dynasties and lengths of reign. These have been the subject of some critical comment by Helck (1956b). The most important earlier chronological source is the Turin Canon or King List. A complete transcription has been published by Gardiner (1959), with further analysis and comment by von Beckerath (1962, 1964, 1966) and Barta (1979, 1981b). Its basic data are conveniently tabulated alongside those from the other king lists (principally from Abydos and Saqqara) in an appendix in Gardiner (1961). The Palermo Stone is now too fragmentary to be of much chronological use, but still contains interesting details of the events that the Egyptians of the Old Kingdom thought to be significant. The basic source here is Schäfer (1902), with the chronological aspects discussed by Kaiser (1961), Helck (1974b) and Barta (1981a).

Absolute calendrical dates have been deduced by combining totals given in the Turin King List with the results of calculations based on ancient astronomical observations, for which the fundamental work is Parker (1950). Debate on the accuracy of these calculations has been continued in articles by Ingham (1969), Read (1970), Parker (1970, 1976), and Long (1974), but with nothing very seriously contradictory emerging. More serious are the discrepancies between these and radiocarbon dates which have been discussed in individual articles, for example by Smith (1964), Quitta (1972), Long (1976), and Mellaart (1979), and in two major symposia, see Michael and Ralph (1970), Säve-Söderbergh and Olsson (1970), and Edwards (1970). The calibrations derived from dendrochronology, however, show increasing signs of resolving the problem (Hassan 1980, Kemp 1980).

The history of these early periods is largely built up from a multiplicity of hieroglyphic sources, mostly very laconic. The collected translations by Breasted (1906) still have no rival for completeness and appear surprisingly good, although naturally there have been improvements in lexicography and grammatical knowledge since they were made. The number of significant historical texts for these periods discovered since Breasted's day is small, the most important being the various Kamose texts relating to the expulsion of the Hyksos edited by Gardiner (1916) and Habachi (1972). A selection of texts relating to Old Testament background has been translated by Wilson in Pritchard (1969); Schenkel (1965) has provided translations of all First Intermediate Period sources; and Goedicke (1967) has done the same for Old Kingdom royal decrees. For literary texts, which sometimes reflect political matters, there are two recent collected editions, by Faulkner,

Wente and Simpson (Simpson, ed. 1973), and Lichtheim (1973). Administrative and economic papyri have not been treated as a body, but may be encountered in individual editions by Griffith (1898), Scharff (1920), Hayes (1955), Simpson (1963b, 1965, 1969b), Posener-Kriéger and de Cenival (1968), and Posener-Kriéger (1976). The second Kahun (Lahun) archive is still available only in summary form, see Borchardt (1899) and Kaplony-Heckel (1971a).

Progress in the study of Egyptian history has been slow since the great pioneering works of Meyer (1887), and Breasted (1906), and others of this period. Petrie (1924) is particularly noteworthy for its documentation. The lack of widespread scepticism as to the testimony of literary sources has been commented on by Björkman (1964). Hornung (1966) and Otto (1964–6) have discussed the merging of myth and history in the Egyptian mind, and the ritualistic conception of history at the level of formal Egyptian monuments. Amongst the histories of Egypt which have appeared in recent decades should be noted those by Gardiner (1961), Drioton and Vandier (1962), Bottéro, Cassin and Vercoutter (1967), Helck (1968) and Hallo and Simpson (1971). The ambitious attempt in the third edition of the *Cambridge Ancient History*, edited by Edwards, Gadd and Hammon (1971), to cover in considerable detail the ancient history of the entire Middle East and surrounding areas naturally includes chapters on Egypt, and these, written in dense narrative style and with a tendency to concentrate on kings and chronology, provide a fundamental reference source for historical detail, though with relatively little attention to African connections. Detailed historical studies of separate periods have not been common, the most valuable being those by Winlock (1947), Schenkel (1962), von Beckerath (1964), van Seters (1966) and Gomaà (1980). Wilson (1951) represents an imaginative attempt at interpreting the dynamics of Egyptian history, and Posener (1956) a study of Middle Kingdom literature as a political vehicle. The more intractable inscriptional material from private tombs offers some promise for regional historical studies, based very much on titles and genealogies, but has been carried out in a serious and consistent manner only by Fischer (1964, 1968) for the areas of Coptos and Dendera. A useful series of detailed coloured maps of Egypt and Nubia at different historical periods is currently being published as the *Tübinger Atlas des Vorderen Orients* (TAVO).

Studies on Egyptian administration and economy tend to suffer from an insensitivity to the idea that rational working systems were involved.

Basic treatments of the source material in this mould are those of Helck (1958, 1975), and to a lesser extent of Pirenne (1932–5). The documentation for more limited periods is analysed by Helck (1954), Adams (1956), Baer (1960), and Zibelius (1978). An important contribution to our understanding of ancient Egypt's geographical background is that by Butzer (1976).

For external relationships Säve-Söderbergh (1941), Arkell (1961), Emery (1965), Trigger (1965, 1976), Hofmann (1967), and Adams (1977) deal with Nubia, in each case attempting to relate inscriptional and archaeological sources. Whereas Egyptologists have tended to dominate the field of Nubian studies and therefore have come to terms with the cultural background, the same is not true for Palestine and Syria. The archaeological record for settlement history tends to feature only peripherally in studies on Egypt's relations with these areas, as is particularly clear in the major documentary study by Helck (1971). Ward (1971) and van Seters (1966) represent limited attempts to create an archaeological context for individual periods; at the level of cultural influence Egypt features prominently in an analysis by Smith (1965) of the cultural interdependence of the ancient Near East. Seyfried (1981) is a recent treatment of eastern desert expeditions in the Middle Kingdom.

One notable aspect of Egyptology is the consistency of its intellectual framework, which is essentially in the Classical mould: textual exegesis dominates history, prosopography and genealogy are the mainsprings in the study of local history, art history is regarded as the major component in evaluating the development of material culture. This results in a marked homogeneity in style and approach, and a considerable versatility amongst Egyptologists. But it also helps to make the subject more resistant to the proper evaluation of archaeological data and to the use, or at least consideration, of alternative frameworks into which existing information can be set. This has the overall effect of probability exaggerating the uniqueness of the essential character of Egyptian culture and society. Nevertheless, some of the issues raised by articles on the character and dynamics of early societies written from a more theoretical point of view are appropriate for discussion in Egyptological terms, and such discussion might be expected both to broaden the intellectual basis on which ancient Egypt is studied, and to make more widely accessible the rich source material which Egypt has to offer on certain aspects of early society. An interesting step in this direction is the collection of conference papers edited by Weeks

(1979), entitled *Egyptology and the Social Sciences*, which includes a section on urbanism by Bietak.

With archaeological data, the careful analysis of cemetery sequences offers one supplementary direction for historical study, though probably a rather limited one, but even here where so much material exists already, only the most tentative beginnings have been made (e.g. O'Connor 1972, 1974; Kemp 1976a, 1982). The excavation and study of settlement sites is still in its infancy in Egypt, and the failure to understand such evidence as exists has led to outright denials that towns were a significant element in Egyptian society (e.g. Helck 1975, chapter 12; cf. Kemp 1977b). The dramatic results from Tell ed-Dabᶜa achieved by Bietak (1968a, 1970, 1975a) are probably exceptional in their historical impact because of the nature of the site itself. For many more town sites it is probably true to say that until a more coherent framework of social and cultural processes is achieved for ancient Egypt it will remain difficult to direct excavation to the best advantage.

Since completing the original text for this chapter several reports on excavations have appeared which bear materially on its content. Bietak (1981a) is a valuable commentary on his Tell ed-Dabᶜa excavations and the Palestinian connections, while Bietak (1981b) adds to the limited documentation on the Hyksos royal family. The *Bulletin de l'Institut français d'Archéologie orientale* has published a number of reports on the work at Dakhla oasis, two dealing with the remarkable Old Kingdom settlement there (Giddy and Jeffreys 1980, 1981). Two more Kerma reports have appeared (Bonnet 1978, 1980) emphasizing the much greater degree of archaeological complexity at the settlement site around the western deffufa, whilst in a separate study (Bonnet 1981) the case is argued for the western deffufa having been a temple. Further work in the northern Fayum has brought a significant revision in the date of the maximum lake level in historic times. Far from having been in the Old Kingdom, it occurred during the Middle Kingdom (Ginter, Heflik, Kozłowski and Śliwa 1980). The meaning of this in terms of other Middle Kingdom sites in the Fayum and the Semna flood level inscriptions has yet to be worked out. In textual matters, the idea that the Memphite Theology is a composition of the Late Period and not just a late copy of a very ancient text is gaining ground (e.g. Lichtheim 1980, p. 5).

## 3. NEW KINGDOM AND THIRD INTERMEDIATE PERIOD, 1552–664 BC

The following bibliography is confined mainly to English language sources; a more detailed bibliography guide is appended to O'Connor (1982b), pp. 966–70.

1. *Histories and historical studies.* A good overview of the entire period is provided in Gardiner (1961; Chapters VIII–XII), while New Kingdom history is reviewed in detail by Hayes (1973), James (1973), Aldred (1975), Černý (1975), and Faulkner (1975) in the new edition of the *Cambridge Ancient History.* The latter also contains valuable chapters on the government of New Kingdom Asiatic conquests by Drower (1973) and Albright (1975), while the New Kingdom history of Steindorff and Seele (1957) also emphasizes foreign relations. The best historical outline of the Third Intermediate Period is found in Part 4 of Kitchen (1973).

More specialized historical studies are Redford's (1967) discussion of individual Eighteenth Dynasty Pharaohs, Kemp's (1978) discussion of New Kingdom imperialism and Bierbrier's (1975) analysis of some of the factors contributing to the collapse of the New Kingdom.

2. *Texts in translation.* Histories and historical studies such as the above should be read in conjunction with translations of the relevant historical, literary, and archival texts, which convey the reality of historical events and processes with a vividness and immediacy that no historical narrative can provide. The best and most comprehensive collection of translated historical texts remains Breasted (1906, vols. II and III); more recent translations of some of these texts are provided by Wilson in Pritchard (1969) and Lichtheim (1976, 1980). Major literary works of the period are translated in Lichtheim (*ibid.*) and Simpson (1973). Caminos (1954) provides a variety of model letters, hymns and the like which illuminate many aspects of contemporary New Kingdom attitudes, while Wente's (1966) translations of later New Kingdom letters provide a unique insight into the realities of Egyptian political and administrative life.

3. *Egyptian society in the New Kingdom and Third Intermediate Period.* The best introduction to the Egyptian environment and related agricultural and demographic factors is Butzer (1976), while Kees (1961) surveys

the interrelationships between environment and society in ancient Egypt and introduces the student to major sites which were important in New Kingdom and Third Intermediate Period history. The raw materials and technology of Egyptian industry is discussed in Lucas and Harris (1962). The best history of Egyptian art and architecture in English remains Smith (1981; Parts 4 and 5 are relevant to this chapter), and Hayes (1959) provides a richly illustrated introduction to the material culture of the New Kingdom, covering both the royal families and the other classes of Egyptian society.

The governmental structure of the period has not yet received the comprehensive analysis it requires; the best source of data on the administrative structure is in German (Helck, 1958), while Edgerton's (1947a) study is a rare attempt to understand the system as distinct from the structural skeleton of government. Faulkner (1953) and Schulman (1964b) provide good surveys of the New Kingdom army. Théodoridès (1971) is a useful introduction to Egyptian law; Wilson (1954b) discusses the relationship between authority and law; and Černý (1962) provides an excellent overview of oracles and their roles in law and general social relationships. An excellent 'case-history' of the New Kingdom legal system in operation is the famous case of Mose, on which see especially Gardiner (1905) and Gaballa (1977). Janssen (1975b) outlines our very limited knowledge of the Egyptian economy and has also published a superlative monograph on prices and wages in Ramesside Egypt (1975a).

Egyptian religion was, as noted above, of great historical significance. Černý (1957) is an excellent introduction to the topic, while Bleeker (1967) discusses the significance of festivals in Egyptian life. Wilson (1954a) provides an interesting introduction to the world view of the Egyptians, but other valuable approaches to aspects of this question are to be found in Posener (1960; in French) and Hornung (1966; in German).

Urbanism is a subject of increasing interest in Egyptological studies, and the richest data come from the New Kingdom. A useful introduction is O'Connor (1982a), while Kemp has published several important reinterpretations of Tell el-Amarna, the best documented urban site (1976, 1977, 1981). Broader patterns of settlement and urbanization in the New Kingdom and later are discussed by Kemp (1972a, b), O'Connor (1972a), and H. S. Smith (1972).

4. *Egypt and Africa.* For the New Kingdom, Säve-Söderbergh (1941;

in German) remains fundamental, but good, more recent general studies covering both the New Kingdom and Third Intermediate Periods are Trigger (1976; Chapters VII and VIII) and W. Y. Adams (1977a; Chapters 9 and 10). Emery (1965; Part 3, Chapters V–VIII) is also useful, as is the well-illustrated Wenig (1978; Chapters 1 and 2); Kitchen (1971) is a brief but excellent discussion on the location of Punt.

5. *Bibliographies and chronology.* Most of the works cited above have extensive bibliographies that will guide the student in further reading and research. There are also available several invaluable bibliographical aids of which the student should be aware. Pratt (1925, 1942) provides an extremely comprehensive if not totally complete bibliography running to 1941, conveniently divided into topics and with an excellent index of authors and topics. Federn (1948–50) covers the years 1939 to 1947 (without topic categorization but with an author index); while the *Annual Egyptological bibliography* (J. M. A. Janssen 1948–63, J. M. A. Janssen and Heerma van Voss 1964, Heerma van Voss 1968–9, Heerma van Voss and J. J. Janssen 1971, J. J. Janssen 1971–6; continuing) is a completely inclusive bibliography covering 1947 to the present and still continuing; it is not categorized, but there is an index of authors, titles and topics for 1947–56. From 1971–1979 Kemp produced *Egyptological titles*, an up-to-date quarterly bibliography conveniently divided into categories. Porter and Moss (1927–74; continuing) and Malek (1974; continuing) provide a detailed guide to all known reliefs, paintings and hieroglyphic texts; there is no guide for hieratic or demotic texts, or to purely architectural and archaeological data.

Convenient recent discussions of *New Kingdom chronology* are Hornung (1964; the 'short' chronology) and Hayes (1970; the 'long' chronology); see also Kitchen (1965). For *Third Intermediate Period chronology* Kitchen (1973) is fundamental. Debate remains lively and more recent studies are found in the bibliographic aids noted above.

## 4. THE LATE PERIOD, 664–323 BC

Written sources include material in hieroglyphic, demotic, cuneiform, Hebrew, Aramaic, Phoenician, Carian, Greek, and Latin. Hieroglyphic texts are far fewer than in the New Kingdom and particularly sparse after the Twenty-sixth Dynasty. English translations of important Saite examples appear in Breasted (1906), though these versions have usually been superseded, whilst the main hieroglyphic texts of the First Persian

Occupation can be found in Posener (1936). Otto's translations and analyses of major biographical inscriptions of the Late Period (1954) are invaluable; Lichtheim (1980) has also translated some of the best-known specimens. Demotic material is of varying character. Literary texts include the immensely important Demotic Chronicle (Spiegelberg 1914; Roeder 1927; Bresciani and Donadoni 1969), and the tales of the Petubastis Cycle also yield valuable information if properly used (Kitchen 1973). Amongst documentary sources *P. Rylands* IX occupies a pre-eminent position (Griffith 1909; Wessetzky 1963). Cuneiform evidence is available in Assyrian, Babylonian, and Persian (Luckenbill 1927; Wiseman 1961; Kent 1953); the most important Hebrew material appears in II Kings, II Chronicles, Jeremiah, Ezekiel, and the derivative account of Josephus' *Antiquities of the Jews*, X (Marcus 1937); the Aramaic material is analysed by Kraeling (1953), Fitzmyer (1965), and Porten (1968). For Phoenician texts Magnanini (1973) and Kornfeld (1978) should be consulted, whilst the Carian material has been discussed by Ray (1982). Amongst the Greek sources Herodotus occupies pride of place (Hude 1927; de Selincourt 1972; Lloyd 1975ff), but Hellenistic writers such as Manetho (Jacoby 1958; Waddell 1940) and Diodorus Siculus (Oldfather et al., 1946ff) are indispensable particularly for the late fifth and fourth centuries BC.

There are several general works covering the political and military history of the period. Wiedemann's account (1880) is still worth consulting and Petrie (1905) is also valuable. Hall's work on the Saite period in the *Cambridge Ancient History* (1925) is obsolete, but discussions of later developments in subsequent volumes can still be read with profit. They are all due to be replaced by new studies in the revised edition. Kienitz (1953) is essential reading, and Gyles (1959) contains some useful material but is unreliable and best avoided by the novice. The same holds true of Pirenne's survey (1963). Drioton and Vandier (1962) is particularly useful for its bibliographical information and its discussions of major problems. On specific periods there is some excellent work, e.g. Posener (1936), De Meulenaere (1951), Kraeling (1953), Bresciani (1958), and Kitchen (1973).

Egyptian kingship in general has been analysed by Moret (1902a), Müller (1938), Jacobsohn (1939), Frankfort (1948, 1961), Vandier (1949), Brunner (1956, 1964), Posener (1960), Derchain (1962), Hornung (1966), Decker (1971), and Bergman (1972), but a modern large-scale synthesis is a pressing need. On Late Period ideas Meyer (1915) is useful and Otto (1954) fundamental. Spalinger's analysis (1978a) cannot withstand close scrutiny, but does provide a handy 'open-sesame' to the material. Kaplony (1971), Johnson (1974), Russmann (1974), Aldred (1980), Davies (1982), and Lloyd (1982a, b) provide food for thought on several important points.

The structure of Late Period society has not failed to attract attention, but much remains to be done even with the limited material available. Meyer (1928) is still the starting-point. Pirenne (1963) should not be ignored, but critical use is obligatory. The Classical traditions on Egyptian society at this period are analysed by Wiedemann (1886) and Froidefond (1971). Much can be learned by a careful comparison with studies of Hellenistic Egypt (e.g. Rostovtzeff 1953) and also from accounts of more modern Egyptian society like those of Lane (1966) and Blackman (1927). Availability of land has been studied by Schlott (1969) and Schwab-Schlott (1972), whilst a judicious assessment of population size will be found in Butzer (1976). The priesthood has been better studied than most elements of the population (Blackman 1918; Bonnet 1952; Kees 1953; Sauneron 1957; de Cenival 1972; De Meulenaere 1975–6; Vittmann 1978). Here too comparative Hellenistic material such as that in Otto (1905–8) should not be ignored. The origins, development and character of the *machimoi* are discussed by Cavaignac (1919), Kees (1926), Meyer (1928), Struve (1932), Kienitz (1953), Bresciani (1958), Gyles (1959), Pirenne (1963), Kitchen (1973, 1977), Gomaà (1974) and Winnicki (1977). Rostovtzeff (1953) and Crawford (1971) provide access to Hellenistic evidence on the class. There is no proper survey of the data for the main body of the population. Hughes (1952) and Seidl (1968) are helpful, but, if the evidence were properly exploited, a much fuller picture could be gained. In the study of the family good work has been done (Černý 1954; Pestman 1961; el-Amir 1964; Seidl 1966; Tanner 1967; Théodoridès 1976; Allam 1977, 1981), but we still have far to go, particularly in the employment of models of family organization based on anthropological research and customs in other oriental societies. Slavery is discussed by Griffith (1909), Bakir (1952), Seidl (1968), and Menu (1977). General comments on race relations in Ancient Egypt will be found in Davis (1951), and Egyptian attitudes to foreigners are analysed by Sauneron (1959) and Helck (1964), but there is much on relations with individual ethnic groups: Greeks, Mallet 1893, 1922; MacFarquhar 1966; Austin 1970; Lloyd 1969, 1972a, b, 1975a, b; Boardman 1980; Davis 1981; Cypriots, Masson 1971; Davis 1979, 1980; Carians, Masson and Yoyotte 1956; Masson

1969; Lloyd 1975a, 1978; Jews and Aramaeans, Kraeling 1953; Porten 1968; Ghali 1969; Porten and Greenfield 1974; Dupont-Sommer 1978; Phoenicians, Leclant 1968.

The study of town sites is one of the black spots of Egyptology, but is beginning to receive the attention which it deserves, e.g. Ucko *et al.* 1972; Smith 1974b, 1976; Butzer 1976; Kemp 1977a; Leahy 1977; Parlebas 1977. Information on specific sites during our period is far from satisfactory: on Memphis see, in particular, Petrie (1909–13) and Kemp (1976, 1977b, 1978b); Sais has yielded little, and the prospects are not good (Champollion 1868; Habachi 1943; Bakry 1968; Wâsif 1974), though much profitable work has been done on the literary evidence for the structure and installations of the city's temple area (Mallet 1888; Matthiae Scandone 1967; Schott 1967; el-Sayed 1974, 1975, 1976; Pernigotti 1978); Bubastis was dug unsatisfactorily by Naville (1891, 1892), better and more recently by Habachi (1957); work is in progress at Mendes (De Meulenaere *et al.* 1976). The situation with Nebesheh is much better since Petrie's work (1888) has provided an enlightening, though far from complete, picture of the site during the Saite and Persian periods. Late temples are discussed by Sauneron (1964), Stadelmann (1971), and Badawy (1975). Smith (1974b) provides a brief summary of work on the desert settlements of North Saqqara, whilst the work of Guilmot (1962) and Ray (1972, 1976) is suggestive.

There is no general discussion of economic organization during the Late Period. The student is compelled to start from general studies, such as those of Hartmann (1923) and Heichelheim (1957), and from works concerned with earlier and better documented periods such as those of Helck (1960–9, 1975) and Janssen (1975a, b) which can be usefully supplemented by Hellenistic material (cf. Schnibel 1925; Rostovtzeff 1953). The workings of the basin system of irrigation have been described by Butzer (1976), and Late Period cereal production is briefly discussed by Griffith (1909) and Porten (1968). Some of the evidence for landownership is analysed by Seidl (1968), but there is more to be said even on the basis of the meagre evidence. Aspects of the circulation of wealth are discussed by Seidl (1968), Porten (1968), and Daumas (1977). The best-documented foreign commerce is that with the Greek world (Austin 1970; Lloyd, 1975a; Boardman, 1980). Necho's commercial interest in the Red Sea and his alleged circumnavigation of Africa have received much attention (Senac 1967; Mauny 1976; Lloyd 1977; Janvier 1978).

Data for the workings of government during our period are highly defective but have been the subject of careful study. Pirenne and Théodoridès (1966) have provided a useful conspectus of older literature. Conditions at the beginning of the Saite Dynasty are examined by De Meulenaere (1964), Kitchen (1973, 1977), and Gomaà (1974). The crucially important Nitocris Stele is published by Caminos (1964). Nitocris' position has recently received the attention of Vittmann (1977, 1978) who has also discussed early Saite officials at Thebes. General information on nomes is available in Brugsch (1879–80), Gauthier (1925–31), Gardiner (1947), Montet (1957–61), Helck (1974), and Bietak (1975), and their distribution in the Late Period has been examined by Gauthier (1935), Ball (1942), and Helck (1974). On Saite internal administration Kees (1934–6) and De Meulenaere (1964) are required reading. Wessetzky (1963) should also be consulted. The alleged reforms of Amasis have been discussed by Tresson (1931), Ranke (1943), Posener (1947), Malinine (1953) and Jelínková-Reymond (1956). Jurisdiction is briefly analysed by Seidl (1968), and the workings of oracles are examined by Blackman (1925, 1926), Roeder (1960), Parker (1962), and Ray (1981). The best description of Persian government in Egypt is still that of Bresciani (1958), and Egyptian collaboration with the Persians is discussed, in particular, by Cooney (1953) and Lloyd (1982a, b).

Late-Period foreign policy should never be treated in isolation; evidence from other periods can be illuminating even if it must be used with caution. Théodoridès (1975) has produced a perceptive discussion of Egyptian attitudes to foreign relations down to the end of the New Kingdom which has much to teach the student of the Late Period. The same holds true of recent work on Egyptian imperialism in pre-Late Period times (Kemp 1978a; Aḥituv 1978). Saite activities in the Levant have received much attention from a variety of points of view (Yoyotte 1951b; Sauneron and Yoyotte 1952b; Dothan and Freedman 1967; Freedy and Redford 1970; Dothan 1971; Lipinski 1972; Spalinger 1974, 1976a, b, 1977b, 1978a, b; Malamat 1950, 1968, 1973, 1974, 1975, 1976; Lindsay 1976). The problem of Saite naval policy has generated a rash of studies (Basch 1969, 1977, 1980; Lloyd 1972a, b, 1975a, b, 1977, 1980) which have led to a clearer understanding of the limitations of the evidence, but large questions still remain unanswered and unanswerable. The analysis of Amasis' relations with Chaldaea has been placed on a completely new footing by Edel (1978). For the Chaldaean view of Egyptian Levantine involvements Wiseman (1961) is essential. Foreign policy during the last years of independence is most conveniently studied through Kienitz (1953) and Olmstead (1959). The evidence for Greek mercenaries is discussed by Petrie (1888), Parke (1933), Austin (1970), Lloyd (1975a), Oren (1977, 1979), and Boardman (1980). Egypt's relations with Samos continue to excite interest (Jantzen 1972; Mitchell 1975). Contacts with Athens are relatively well documented (Meiggs 1963, 1972; Salmon 1965; Libourel 1971) whilst relations with Cyprus are summarized by Hill (1940). For a possible case of a diplomatic marriage cementing relations between Nectanebo I and a Greek state see Kuhlmann (1981). Late Period activities in Libya must be studied against the background of earlier contacts summarized by Gsell (1913ff), Hölscher (1937), Fakhry (1942, 1944, 1950, 1973-4), Redford (1977a), and Gostynski (1975). Psammetichus I's Libyan policy is analysed by Goedicke (1962), and the Cyrene problem is studied by Schaefer (1952), Chamoux (1953), and Mazzarino (1947). On the oases in the Late Period see Fakhry (1973-4). Several articles deal with the Nubian campaign of Psammetichus II (Yoyotte 1951a; Sauneron and Yoyotte 1952a; Bakry 1967; Habachi 1974), and the evidence for Amasis' Nubian expedition is scrutinized by Erichsen (1941).

# BIBLIOGRAPHY

I. THE RISE OF EGYPTIAN CIVILIZATION

Adams, B. (1974). *Ancient Hierakonpolis* (with *Supplement*). Warminster.

Adams, R. M. (1972). Patterns of urbanization in early southern Mesopotamia. In P. J. Ucko, R. Tringham and G. W. Dimbleby (eds.), *Man, settlement and urbanism*, 735–48. London.

Adams, W. Y. (1977). *Nubia: corridor to Africa*. London.

Aldred, C. (1965). *Egypt to the end of the Old Kingdom*. London.

Amélineau, E. (1899–1905). *Les nouvelles fouilles d'Abydos (1895–98)*, 3 vol. Paris.

Arkell, A. J. (1949). *Early Khartoum*. Oxford.

(1950). Varia Sudanica. *J. Egypt. Archaeol.* **36**, 27–30.

(1953). *Shaheinab*. Oxford.

(1963). Was King Scorpion Menes? *Antiquity* **37**, 31–5.

(1972). Dotted wavy-line pottery in African prehistory. *Antiquity* **46**, 221–2.

Arkell, A. J. and P. J. Ucko (1965). Review of Predynastic development in the Nile Valley. *Curr. Anthrop.* **6**, 145–66.

Bar-Yosef, O., A. Belfer, A. Goren and P. Smith (1977). The *nawamis* near Ein Huderah (eastern Sinai). *Israel Exploration J.* **27**, 65–88.

Batrawi, A. (1945). The racial history of Egypt and Nubia. *J. R. anthrop. Inst.* **75**, 81–101.

(1946). The racial history of Egypt and Nubia, *J. R. anthrop. Inst.* **76**, 131–56.

Baumgartel, E. J. (1955). *The cultures of prehistoric Egypt*, vol. I, 2nd edn. Oxford.

(1960). *The cultures of prehistoric Egypt*, vol. II. Oxford.

(1966). Scorpion and rosette and the fragment of the large Hierakonpolis mace head. *Z. ägypt. Sprache Altertumskunde* **92**, 9–14.

(1970a). Predynastic Egypt. In *Cambridge Ancient History*, 3rd edn, vol. I, pt 1, 463–97.

(1970b). *Petrie's Naqada excavation: a supplement*. London.

Bell, B. (1970). The oldest records of the Nile floods. *Geogrl J.* **136**, 569–73.

Berry, A. C. and R. J. Berry (1973). Origins and relations of the ancient Egyptians. In D. R. Brothwell and B. A. Chiarelli (eds.), *Population biology of the Ancient Egyptians*, 200–8. New York.

Berry, A. C., R. J. Berry and P. J. Ucko (1967). Genetical change in ancient Egypt. *Man* N.S. **2**, 551–68.

Brunton, G. and G. Caton Thompson (1928). *The Badarian civilisation*. London.

Butzer, K. W. (1958). *Quaternary stratigraphy and climate in the Near East*. Bonn.

(1959). Studien zum vor- und frühgeschichtlichen Landschaftswandel der Sahara. III. Die Naturlandschaft Ägyptens während der Vorgeschichte und der dynastischen Zeit. *Abh. math.-naturw. Kl. Akad. Wiss. Mainz* **2**, 1–80.

(1960). Archaeology and geology in Ancient Egypt. *Science*, **132**, 1617–24.

(1961). 'Archäologische Fundstellen Ober- und Mittelägyptens in ihrer geologischen Landschaft', *Mitt. dt. archäol. Inst. Abt. Kairo* **17**, 54–68.

(1966). Archaeology and geology in ancient Egypt. In J. R. Caldwell (ed.), *New roads to yesterday*, 210–27. New York.

(1971). *Environment and archaeology: an ecological approach to prehistory*, 2nd ed. Chicago.

(1976). *Early hydraulic civilization in Egypt: a study in cultural ecology*. Chicago.

Butzer, K. W. and C. L. Hansen (1968). *Desert and river in Nubia*. Madison.

Camps, G. (1969). *Amekni: néolithique ancien du Hoggar*. *Mém. CRAPE* **10**.

(1982). Beginnings of pastoralism and cultivation in north-west Africa and the Sahara. In *Cambridge History of Africa*, vol. II, 548–623.

Carlson, D. S. and D. P. Van Gerven (1977). Masticatory function and post-Pleistocene evolution in Nubia. *Am. J. Phys. Anthrop.* **46**, 495–506.

Castillos, J. J. (1978). An analysis of the Predynastic cemeteries E and U and the First Dynasty cemetery S at Abydos. *J. Soc. Stud. Egypt. Antiq.* **8**, 86–98.

(1979). An analysis of the tombs in the Predynastic cemetery N7000 at Naga-ed-Dêr. *J. Soc. Stud. Egypt. Antiq.* **10**, 21–38.

(1981). An analysis of the tombs in the Predynastic cemeteries at Naqada. *J. Soc. Stud. Egypt. Antiq.* **11**, 97–106.

(1982). Analyses of Egyptian Predynastic and Early Dynastic cemeteries: final conclusions. *J. Soc. Stud. Egypt. Antiq.* **12**, 29–53.

Caton-Thompson, G and E. W. Gardner (1934). *The desert Fayum*, 2 vols. London.

Caton-Thompson, G. and E. Whittle (1975). Thermoluminescence dating of the Badarian. *Antiquity* **49**, 89–97.

Childe, V. G. (1934). *New light on the most ancient east*. London.

Chowdhury, K. A. and G. M. Buth (1971). Cotton seeds from the neolithic in Egyptian Nubia and the origin of Old World cotton. *Biol. J. Linn. Soc. Lond.* **3**, 303–12.

Clark, J. D. (1962). Africa south of the Sahara. In R. J. Braidwood and G. R. Willey (eds.), *Courses towards urban life*, Viking Fund Publications in Anthropology, Chicago, **32**, 1–33.

(1971). A re-examination of the evidence for agricultural origins in the Nile Valley. *Proc. prehist. Soc.* **37**, 34–79.

Derricourt, R. M. (1971). Radiocarbon chronology for Egypt and North Africa. *J. Near East. Stud.* **30**, 271–92.

Derry, D. E. (1956). The dynastic race in Egypt. *J. Egypt. Archaeol.* **42**, 80–5.

Dixon, D. M. (1969). A note on cereals in ancient Egypt. In P. J. Ucko and G. W. Dimbleby (eds.), *The domestication and exploitation of plants and animals*, 131–42. London.

Edwards, I. E. S. (1971). The Early Dynastic Period in Egypt. In *Cambridge Ancient History*, 3rd edn, vol. I, pt 2, 1–70.

Ehret, C. (1979). On the antiquity of agriculture in Ethiopia. *J. Afr. Hist.* **20**, 161–77.

Emery, W. B. (1949–58). *Great tombs of the First Dynasty*, 3 vols. Cairo and London.

(1961). *Archaic Egypt*. Harmondsworth.

(1965). *Egypt in Nubia*. London.

Fairservis, W. A. Jr., K. Weeks and M. Hoffman (1971–2). Preliminary report on the first two seasons at Hierakonpolis. *J. Am Res. Cent. Egypt* **9**, 7–68.

Fattovich, R. (1976). Trends in the study of Predynastic social structure. In D. Wildung (ed.), *First International Congress of Egyptology Abstracts of Papers*, 30–1. Munich.

Flannery, K. V. (1972). The origins of the village as a settlement type in Mesoamerica and the Near East: a comparative study. In P. J. Ucko, R. Tringham and G. W. Dimbleby (eds.), *Man, settlement and urbanism*, 23–53. London.

Fleming, H. C. (1969). The classification of West Cushitic within Hamito-Semitic. In D. F. McCall *et al.* (eds.), *East African history*, 3–27. New York.

Frankfort, H. (1948). *Kingship and the gods*. Chicago.

(1956). *The birth of civilization in the Near East*. London.

Frankfort, H., H. A. Frankfort, J. A. Wilson and T. Jacobsen (1949). *Before philosophy*. Harmondsworth.

Gardiner, A. (1927). *Egyptian Grammar*. Oxford.

(1961). *Egypt of the Pharaohs: an introduction*. Oxford.

Goedicke, H. (1969–70). An Egyptian claim to Asia. *J. Am. Res. Cent. Egypt* **8**, 11–27.

Greenberg, J. H. (1955). *Studies in African linguistic classification*. New Haven.

Griffiths, J. (1960). *The conflict of Horus and Seth*. Liverpool.

Haaland, R. (1981). *Migratory herdsmen and cultivating women: the structure of Neolithic seasonal adaptation in the Khartoum Nile environment*. Bergen.

Hassan, F. A. (1980). Radiocarbon chronology of Archaic Egypt. *J. Near East. Stud.* **39**, 203–7.

Hayes, W. C. (1965). *Most ancient Egypt*. Chicago.

(1970). Chronology I. Egypt to the end of the Twentieth Dynasty. In *Cambridge Ancient History*, 3rd edn, vol. I, pt 1, 173–93.

Hays, T. R. (1976). Prehistoric Egypt: recent field research. *Curr. Anthrop.* **17**, 552–4.

Helck, H. W. (1962). *Die Beziehungen Ägyptens zu Vorderasien im 3. und 2. Jahrtausend v. Chr.* Wiesbaden.

(1970). Zwei Einzelprobleme der thinitischen Chronologie. *Mitt. dt. archäol. Inst. Abt. Cairo* **26**, 83–5.

Higgs, E. S. (1967). Domestic animals. In C. B. M. McBurney, (ed.), *The Haua Fteah*, 313–19. Cambridge.

Hobler, P. M. and J. J. Hester (1969). Prehistory and environment in the Libyan Desert. *S. Afr. archaeol. Bull.* **23**, 120–30.

Hodge, C. T. (ed.) (1971). *Afroasiatic: a survey*. The Hague.

Hoffman, M. A. (1979). *Egypt before the Pharaohs: The prehistoric foundations of Egyptian civilization*. New York.

(1980). A rectangular Amratian house from Hierakonpolis. *J. Near East. Stud.* **39**, 119–37.

Hugot, H.-J. (1968). The origins of agriculture: Sahara. *Curr. Anthrop.* **19**, 483–8.

Kaiser, W. (1956). Stand und Probleme der ägyptische Vorgeschichtsforschung. *Z. ägypt. Sprache Altertumskunde* **81**, 87–109.

(1957). Zur Inneren Chronologie der Naqadakultur. *Archaeologia Geographica* **6**, 69–77.

(1964). Einige Bermerkungen zur ägyptische Frühzeit. *Z. ägypt. Sprache Altertumskunde* **91**, 86–125.

Kantor, H. J. (1944). The final phase of Predynastic culture: Gerzean or Semainean? *J. Near East. Stud.* **3**, 110–36.

(1952). Further evidence for early Mesopotamian relations with Egypt. *J. Near East. Stud.* **11**, 239–50.

(1965). The relative chronology of Egypt and its foreign correlations before the Late Bronze Age. In R. W. Ehrich (ed.), *Chronologies in Old World archaeology*, 1–46. Chicago.

Kaplan, H. R. (1979). The problem of the dynastic position of Meryet-nit. *J. Near East. Stud.* **38**, 23–7.

Kaplony, P. (1963). *Die Inschriften der ägyptische Frühzeit.* Wiesbaden.

Kees, H. (1961). *Ancient Egypt: a cultural topography.* ed. T. G. H. James, trans. I. F. D. Morrow. London and Chicago.

Kelley, A. L. (1974). The evidence for Mesopotamian influence in predynastic Egypt. *Newsl. Soc. study Egypt. antiqu.* **4**, 2–11.

Kemp, B. J. (1966). Abydos and the royal tombs of the First Dynasty. *J. Egypt. Archaeol.* **52**, 13–22.

(1967). The Egyptian 1st Dynasty royal cemetery. *Antiquity* **41**, 22–32.

(1968a). Merimda and the theory of house burial in prehistoric Egypt. *Chronique d'Egypte* **43**, 85, 22–33.

(1968b). The Osiris Temple at Abydos. *Mitt. dt. archäol. Inst. Abt. Kairo* **23**, 138–55.

(1973). Photographs of the Decorated Tomb at Hierakonpolis. *J. Egypt. Archaeol.* **59**, 36–43.

(1980). Egyptian radiocarbon dating: a reply to James Mellaart. *Antiquity* **54**, 25–8.

Kendall, D. G. (1969). Some problems and methods in statistical archaeology. *World Archaeol.* **1**, 68–76.

(1971). Seriation from abundance matrices. In F. R. Hodson, D. G. Kendall and P. Tăutu, *Mathematics in the archaeological and historical sciences*, 215–52. Edinburgh.

Kenyon, K. (1960). *Archaeology in the Holy Land.* London.

Klichowska, M. (1978). Preliminary results of palaeo-ethnobotanical studies of plant impressions on potsherds from the Neolithic settlement at Kadero. *Nyame Akuma* **12**, 42–3.

Krzyzaniak, L. (1977). *Early farming cultures on the lower Nile: the Predynastic Period in Egypt.* Warsaw.

(1978). New light on early food-production in the central Sudan. *J. Afr. Hist.* **19**, 159–72.

(1979). Trends in the socio-economic development of Egyptian Predynastic societies. *Acts of the First International Congress of Egyptologists*, 407–12. Cairo.

Lal, B. B. (1963). Work by an Indian mission at Afyeh and Tomas. *Illustrated London News*, 20 April 1963, 579–81.

Leclant, J. (1980). Fouilles et travaux en Egypte et au Soudan, 1978–1979. *Orientalia* 49, 346–420.

Lucas, A. and J. R. Harris (1962). *Ancient Egyptian materials and industries*, 4th ed. London.

McBurney, C. B. M. (1960). *The Stone Age of northern Africa*. Harmondsworth.

McHugh, W. P. (1974). Late prehistoric cultural adaptation in southwest Egypt and the problem of the Nilotic origins of Saharan cattle pastoralism. *J. Am. Res. Cent. Egypt* 11, 2–29.

Marks, A. E. (1968). Survey and excavations in the Dongola Reach, Sudan. *Curr. Anthrop.* 9, 319–23.

Mellaart, J. (1979). Egyptian and Near Eastern chronology: A Dilemma? *Antiquity* 53, 6–18.

Meltzer, E. S. (1970). An observation on the hieroglyph *mr. J. Egypt. Archaeol.* 56, 193–4.

Morant, G. M. (1925). A study of Egyptian craniology from prehistoric to Roman times. *Biometrika* 17, 1–52.

Murray, G. W. (1951). The Egyptian climate: an historical survey. *Geogrl J.* 117, 422–34.

Needler, W. (1981). Federn's revision of Petrie's Predynastic pottery classification. *J. Soc. Stud. Egypt Antiq.* 11, 69–74.

Nims, C. F. (1965). *Thebes of the Pharaohs*. London.

Nordström, H.-Å. (1972). *Neolithic and A-group sites*. Uppsala.

O'Connor, D. (1972). A regional population in Egypt to circa 600 B.C. In B. J. Spooner (ed.), *Population growth: anthropological implications*, 78–100. Cambridge, Mass. and London.

Otto, K. H. (1963). Shaqadud: a new Khartoum Neolithic site outside the Nile Valley. *Kush* 11, 108–15.

Passarge, S. (1940). Die Urlandschaft Ägyptens und die Lokalisierung der Wiege der altägyptischen Kultur. *Nova Acta Leopoldina* 9, 77–152.

Petrie, W. M. F. (1896). *Naqada and Ballas*. London.

(1900). *The Royal Tombs of the First Dynasty*, pt 1. Egypt Exploration Fund Memoir 18. London.

(1901a). *The Royal Tombs of the Earliest Dynasties*, pt 2. Egypt Exploration Fund Memoir 21. London.

(1901b). *Diospolis Parva*. Egypt Exploration Fund Memoir. 20. London.

(1906). *Researches in Sinai*. London.

(1920). *Prehistoric Egypt*. London.

(1921). *Prehistoric Egypt. Corpus*. London.

(1939). *The making of Egypt*. London.

Petrie, W. M. F. and J. E. Quibell (1895). *Naqada and Ballas*. London.

Pope, M. (1966). The origins of writing in the Near East. *Antiquity* 40, 17–23.

Quibell, J. E. (1900). *Hierakonpolis*, pt 1. London.

Quibell, J. E. and F. W. Green (1902). *Hierakonpolis*, pt 2. London.

Reed, C. A. (1966). Animal domestication in the prehistoric Near East. In J. R. Caldwell (ed.), *New roads to yesterday*, 178–209. New York.

Reisner, G. A. (1932). *A provincial cemetery of the Pyramid Age, Naga-ed-Dêr*, vol. II. Oxford.

Renfrew, C. (1972). *The emergence of civilisation*. London.

Renfrew, J. M. (1969). The archaeological evidence for the domestication of plants: methods and problems. In P. J. Ucko and G. W. Dimbleby (eds.), *Domestication and exploitation of plants and animals*, 149–72. London.

Rothenberg, B. (1970). An archaeological survey of south Sinai: first season 1967/1968, preliminary report. *Palestine Exploration Quarterly* **102**, 4–29.

Saad, Z. Y. (1969). *The excavations at Helwan: art and civilization in the First and Second Egyptian Dynasties*. Oklahoma.

Säve-Söderbergh, T. (1941). *Ägypten und Nubien*. Lund.

Schenkel, W. (1978). *Die Bewässerungsrevolution im Alten Ägypten*. Mainz.

Schild, R., M. Chmielewska and H. Wieckowska (1968). The Arkinian and Shamarkian Industries. In F. Wendorf (ed.), *The prehistory of Nubia*, vol. II 651–767. Dallas.

Seligman, C. C. and M. A. Murray (1911). Note upon an early Egyptian standard. *Man* **11**, 165–71.

Sethe, K. (1930). *Urgeschichte und älteste Religion der Ägypter. Abhandlungen für Kunde des Morgenlandes* **18**. Leipzig.

Simoons, F. J. (1965). Some questions on the economic prehistory of Ethiopia. *J. Afr. Hist.* **6**, 1–13.

Smith, H. S. (1964). Egypt and $C_{14}$ dating. *Antiquity* **38**, 32–7.

(1966). The Nubian B-group. *Kush* **14**, 69–124.

Smith, P. E. L. (1976). Early food production in northern Africa as seen from southwestern Asia. In J. R. Harlan, J. M. J. de Wet and A. B. L. Stemler (eds.), *Origins of African Plant Domestication*, 155–86. The Hague.

(1982). The Late Palaeolithic and Epi-Palaeolithic of northern Africa. In *Cambridge History of Africa*, vol. I, 342–409.

Suess, H. E. (1970). Bristlecone pine calibration of the radiocarbon time-scale 5200 B.C. to the present. In I. U. Olsson (ed.), *Radiocarbon variations and absolute chronology, Nobel Symposium 12*, 303–13. New York and Stockholm.

Trigger, B. G. (1965). *History and settlement in Lower Nubia. Yale Univ. Publs Anthrop.* **69**.

(1968). *Beyond history: the methods of prehistory*. New York.

(1976). *Nubia under the Pharaohs*. London.

(1978). Nubian, Negro, Black, Nilotic? In S. Hochfield and E. Riefstahl (eds.), *Africa in antiquity: the arts of ancient Nubia and the Sudan*, Vol. I, *The essays*, 26–35. Brooklyn.

(1982). The late Palaeolithic and Epi-Palaeolithic of northern Africa. In J. D. Clark (ed.), *Cambridge History of Africa*, vol. I, 342–409.

Ucko, P. J. (1967). The Predynastic cemetery N 7000 at Naga-ed-Dêr. *Chronique d'Egypte* **42**, 345–53.

(1968). *Anthropomorphic figurines of Predynastic Egypt and Neolithic Crete. Occ. Pap. R. Anthrop. Inst.* **24**.

Vandier, J. (1952). *Manuel d'archéologie égyptienne*, vol. 1. Paris.

Vergote, J. (1970). Egyptian. In T. A. Sebeok (ed.), *Current trends in linguistics*, vol. VI, 531–57. The Hague.

Weeks, K. (ed.) (1979). *Egyptology and the social sciences: five studies.* Cairo.

Wendorf, F. (ed.) (1968). *The prehistory of Nubia*, 2 vols. Dallas.

Wendorf, F. and R. Schild (1980). *Prehistory of the eastern Sahara.* New York.

Wendorf, F., R. Said and R. Schild (1970). Egyptian prehistory: some new concepts. *Science, N.Y.* **169**, 1161–71.

Wheatley, P. (1971). *The pivot of the Four Quarters.* Edinburgh.

Whittle, E. H. (1975). Thermoluminescent dating of Egyptian Predynastic pottery from Hemamieh and Qurna-Tarif. *Archaeometry* **17**, 119–22.

Williams, Bruce (1980). The lost Pharaohs of Nubia. *Archaeology* **33**, 12–21.

Wilson, J. A. (1955). Buto and Hierakonpolis in the geography of Egypt. *J. Near East. Stud.* **14**, 209–36.

Wright, G. A. (1971). Origins of food production in southwestern Asia: a survey of ideas. *Curr. Anthrop.* **12**, 447–77.

Yadin, Y. (1955). The earliest record of Egypt's military penetration into Asia? *Israel Exploration J.* **5**, 1–16.

Zeuner, F. E. (1963). *A history of domesticated animals.* London.

### 2. OLD KINGDOM, MIDDLE KINGDOM AND SECOND INTERMEDIATE PERIOD

Abu Bakr, A. M. and J. Osing (1973). Ächtungstexte aus dem Alten Reich. *Mitt. dt. archäol. Inst. Abt. Kairo* **29**, 97–133.

(1976). Ächtungstexte aus dem Alten Reich. *Mitt. dt. archäol. Inst. Abt. Kairo* **32**, 133–85.

Adam, S. (1959). Report on the excavations of the Antiquities Department at Ezbet Rushdi. *Ann. Serv. antiquités Égypte* **56**, 207–26.

Adams, B. (1956). *Fragen altägyptischer Finanzverwaltung; nach Urkunden des Alten und Mittleren Reiches.* Munich and Pasing.

(1974). *Ancient Hierakonpolis* (with *supplement*). Warminster.

Adams, W. Y. (1968). Invasion, diffusion, evolution? *Antiquity* **42**, 194–215.

(1970). A re-appraisal of Nubian culture history. *Orientalia* **39**, 269–77.

(1977a). Reflections on the archaeology of Kerma. In E. Endesfelder *et al.* (eds.), *Ägypten und Kusch* (*Schriften zur Geschichte und Kultur des Alten Orients* **13**), 41–51.

(1977b). *Nubia, corridor to Africa.* London.

Adams, W. Y. and H.-Å. Nordström (1963). The archaeological survey on the west bank of the Nile: third season, 1961–62. *Kush* **11**, 10–46.

Aharoni, Y., V. Fritz and A. Kempinski (1974). Excavations at Tel Masos (Khirbet el-Meshâsh). Preliminary report on the first season, 1972. *Tel Aviv* **1**, 64–74.

Albright, W. F. (1959). Dunand's new Byblos volume: a Lycian at the Byblian court. *Bull. Am. Sch. Orient. Res.* **155**, 31–4.

(1964). The eighteenth-century princes of Byblos and the chronology of Middle Bronze. *Bull. Am. Sch. Orient. Res.* **176**, 38–46.

Aldred, C. (1970). Some royal portraits of the Middle Kingdom in ancient Egypt. *Metropolitan Mus. J.* **3**, 27–50.

(1971). *Jewels of the Pharaohs.* London.

Allam, S. (1963). *Beiträge zum Hathorkult (bis zum Ende des Mittleren Reiches).* Munich and Berlin.

Alliot, M. (1937–8). Un nouvel exemple de vizir divinisé dans l'Égypte ancienne. *Bull. Inst. fr. archéol. orient. Caire* **37**, 93–160.

Altenmüller, H. (1974). Zur Vergöttlichung des Königs Unas im Alten Reich. *Stud. altägypt. Kultur* **1**, 1–18.

Aly, M. S. (1970). The tomb of *Wnjs-ʿnḫ* at Qurna (PM-No. 413). *Mitt. dt. archäol. Inst. Abt. Kairo* **26**, 199–206.

Amiran, R. (1974a). An Egyptian jar fragment with the name of Narmer from Arad. *Israel Exploration J.* **24**, 4–12.

(1974b). The painted pottery of the Early Bronze II period in Palestine. *Levant* **6**, 65–8.

Amiran, R., Y. Beit Arieh and J. Glass (1973). The interrelationship between Arad and sites in southern Sinai in the Early Bronze Age II. *Israel Exploration J.* **23**, 193–7.

Anthes, R. (1928). *Die Felseninschriften von Hatnub, nach den Aufnahmen Georg Möllers.* Leipzig.

(1954). Remarks on the Pyramid Texts and the early Egyptian dogma. *J. Am. orient. Soc.* **74**, 35–9.

(1959). Egyptian theology in the third millennium B.C. *J Near East. Stud.* **18**, 169–212.

Arkell, A. J. (1954). Four occupation sites at Agordat. *Kush* **2**, 33–62.

(1961). *A history of the Sudan: from the earliest times to 1821*, 2nd edn. London.

Arnold, D. (1968). Bemerkungen zu den Königsgräbern der frühen II. Dynastie von El-Târif. *Mitt. dt. archäol. Inst. Abt. Kairo* **23**, 26–36.

(1973). Bericht über die vom Deutschen Archäologischen Institut Kairo im Winter 1971–72 in El-Târif durchgeführten Arbeiten. *Mitt. dt. archäol. Inst. Abt. Kairo* **29**, 135–62.

(1974a). *Der Tempel des Königs Mentuhotep von Deir el-Bahari. Vol. I: Architektur und Deutung; vol. II: Die Wandreliefs des Sanktuares.* Mainz.

(1974b). Bericht über die vom Deutschen Archäologischen Institut Kairo im Winter 1972/73 in El-Târif durchgeführten Arbeiten. *Mitt. dt. archäol. Inst. Abt. Kairo* **30**, 155–64.

(1975). Bemerkungen zu den frühen Tempeln von El-Tôd. *Mitt. dt. archäol. Inst. Abt. Kairo* **31**, 175–86.

(1976). *Gräber des Alten und Mittleren Reiches in El-Tarif.* Mainz.

Arnold, D. and J. Settgast (1965). Erster Vorbericht über die vom Deutschen Archäologischen Institut Kairo im Asasif unternommenen Arbeiten. *Mitt. dt. archäol. Inst. Abt. Kairo* **20**, 47–61.

Badawy A. (1967). The civic sense of Pharaoh and urban development in ancient Egypt. *J. Am. Res. Cent. Egypt* **6**, 103–9.

Baer, K. (1956). A note on Egyptian units of area in the Old Kingdom. *J. Near East. Stud.* **15**, 113–17.

(1960). *Rank and title in the Old Kingdom.* Chicago.

(1962). The low price of land in ancient Egypt. *J. Am. Res. Cent. Egypt* **1**, 25–45.

(1963). An Eleventh Dynasty farmer's letters to his family. *J. Am. orient. Soc.* **83**, 1–19.

Bagnold, R. A., O. H. Myers, R. F. Peel and H. A. Winkler (1939). An expedition to the Gilf Kebir and Uweinat, 1938. *Geogr J.* **93**, 281–313.

Baines, J. (1973). The destruction of the pyramid temple of Sahure. *Götting. Misz.* **4**, 9–14.

(1974). The inundation stela of Sebekhotpe VIII. *Acta orient.* **36**, 39–54.

(1976). The Sebekhotpe VIII inundation stela: an additional fragment. *Acta Orient.* **37**, 11–20.

Barns, J. W. B. (1954). Four Khartoum stelae. *Kush* **2**, 19–25.

Barta, W. (1967–8). Zum scheinbaren Bedeutungswandel des Seth in den Pyramidentexten. *Jaarber. Vooraziat-Egypt. Genoot. 'Ex Oriente Lux'*, **7**, 20, 43–9.

(1969). 'Falke des Palastes' als ältester Königstitel. *Mitt. dt. archäol. Inst. Abt. Kairo* **24**, 51–7.

(1974). Das Gespräch des Ipuwer mit dem Schöpfergott. *Stud. altägypt. Kultur* **1**, 19–33

(1974–5). Die Erste Zwischenzeit im Spiegel der pessimistischen Literatur. *Jaarber. Vooraziat.-Egypt. Genoot.* **24**, 50–61.

(1975). *Untersuchungen zur Göttlichkeit des regierenden König.* Munich and Berlin.

(1976). Der dramatische Ramesseumpapyrus als Festrolle beim Hebsed-Ritual. *Stud. altägypt. Kultur* **4**, 31–43.

(1979). Bemerkungen zu den Summenangaben des Turiner Königspapyrus für die Frühzeit und das Alte Reich. *Mitt. dt. archäol. Inst. Abt. Kairo* **35**, 11–14.

(1981a). Die Chronologie der 1. bis 5. Dynastie nach den Angaben des reconstruierten Annalensteins. *Z. ägypt. Sprache Altertumskunde* **108**, 11–23.

(1981b). Bermerkungen zur Chronologie der 6. bis 11. Dynastie. *Z. ägypt. Sprache Altertumskunde* **108**, 23–33.

Bates, O. (1914). *The eastern Libyans.* London. (Reprinted 1970.)

Beckerath, J. von (1951). Notes on the viziers 'Ankhu and Iymeru in the Thirteenth Egyptian Dynasty. *J. Near East. Stud.* **37**, 20–8.

(1962). The date of the end of the Old Kingdom of Egypt. *J. Near East. Stud.* **21**, 140–7.

(1964). *Untersuchungen zur politischen Geschichte der Zweiten Zwischenzeit in Ägypten.* Glückstadt.

(1965). Zur Begründung der 12. Dynastie durch Ammenemes I. *Z. ägypt. Sprache Altertumskunde* **92**, 4–10.

(1966). Die Dynastie der Herakleopoliten (9./10. Dynastie). *Z. ägypt. Sprache Altertumskunde* **93**, 13–20.

(1969). Die Lesung von 'Regierungsjahr': ein neuer Vorschlag. *Z. ägypt. Sprache Altertumskunde* **95**, 88–91.

(1976a). Die Chronologie der XII. Dynastie und das Problem der Behandlung gleichzeitiger Regierungen in der ägyptischen Überlieferung. *Stud. altägypt. Kultur* **4**, 45–57.

(1976b). Die Hyksos in Aegypten. *Antike Welt* **7**, 53–8.

Beit Arieh, Y. (1974). An Early Bronze Age II site at Nabi Salah in southern Sinai. *Tel Aviv* **1**, 144–56.

Beit Arieh, Y. and R. Gophna (1976). Early Bronze Age II sites in Wâdi el-Qudeirât (Kadesh-Barnea). *Tel Aviv* **3**, 142–50.

Bell, B. (1970). The oldest records of the Nile floods. *Geogrl J.* **136**, 569–73.

(1971). The dark ages in ancient history. I. The first dark age in Egypt. *Am. J. Archaeol.* **75**, 1–26.

(1975). Climate and the history of Egypt: the Middle Kingdom. *Am. J. Archaeol.* **79**, 223–69.

Bell, L. (1973). Once more the '*w:* 'interpreters' or 'foreigners'? *News. Am. Res. Cent. Egypt* **87**, 33.

Berlev, O. D. (1966). [The price of a slave in Egypt during the Middle Kingdom.] *Vestnik Drevnei Istorii* pt 1, **92** (sic, read **95**), 28–39. (In Russian.)

(1974). [A Thirteenth Dynasty stela in the Würzburg University Museum.] *Palestinskii Sbornik* **25** (88), 26–31. (In Russian.)

Bernand, É. (1975). *Recueil des inscriptions grecques du Fayoum, vol. I: La 'Méris' d'Hérakleidès.* Leiden.

Berry, B. J. L. (1961). City size distributions and economic development. *Econ. Devel. Cult. Change* **9**, 573–88.

Bietak, M. (1966). *Ausgrabungen in Sayala-Nubien 1961–1965. Denkmäler der C-Gruppe und der Pan-Gräber-Kultur.* Vienna.

(1968a). Vorläufiger Bericht über die erste und zweite Kampagne der österreichischen Ausgrabungen auf Tell ed-Dab'a im Ostdelta Ägyptens (1966, 1967). *Mitt. dt. archäol. Inst. Abt. Kairo* **23**, 79–114.

(1968b). *Studien zur Chronologie der nubischen C-Gruppe.* Vienna.

(1970). Vorläufiger Bericht über die dritte Kampagne der österreichischen ausgrabungen auf Tell ed Dab'a im Ostdelta Ägyptens (1968). *Mitt. dt. archäol. Inst. Abt. Kairo* **26**, 15–42.

(1974). Die Todesumstände des Pharaos Seqenenre (17. Dynastie). *Ann. naturhist. Mus. Vienna* **78**, 29–52.

(1975a). *Tell el-Dab'a* vol. II. Vienna.

(1975b). Die Hauptstadt der Hyksos und die Ramesesstadt. *Antike Welt* **6**, 28–43.

(1981a). *Avaris and Piramesse: archaeological exploration in the eastern Nile Delta* (Mortimer Wheeler Archaeological Lecture 1979.) London and Oxford.

(1981b). Eine Stele des ältesten Königssohnes des Hyksos Chajan, *Mitt. dt. archäol. Inst. Abt. Kairo* **37**, 63–71.

Björkman, G. (1964). Egyptology and historical method. *Orient. Suecana* **13**, 9–33.

Blumenthal, E. (1970). *Untersuchungen zum ägyptischen Königtum des Mittleren Reiches, vol. I: Die Phraseologie* Leipzig.

(1976). Die Datierung der *Nḥri*-Graffiti von Hatnub. Zur Stellung der ägyptischen Gaufürsten im frühen Mittleren Reich. *Altorient. Forsch.* **4**, 35–62.

(1977). Die Koptosstele des Königs Rahotep (London W.C. 14327). In E. Endesfelder *et al.* (eds.), *Ägypten und Kusch (Schriften zur Geschichte und Kultur des Alten Orients* **13**), 63–80.

Boessneck, J. (1970). Die Equidenknochen von Tell ed Dab'a. *Mitt. dt. archäol. Inst. Abt. Kairo* **26**, 42.

Bongrani, L. (1963). I rapporti fra l'Egitto, la Siria el il Sinai durante l'Antico Regno. *Oriens Antiquus* **2**, 171–203.

Bonnet, C. (1978a). Fouilles archéologiques à Kerma (Soudan); rapport préliminaire de la campagne 1977–1978. *Genava* NS **26**, 107–27.

(1978b). Nouveaux travaux archéologiques à Kerma (1973–1975). In *Études nubiennes; colloque de Chantilly 2–6 juillet 1975*, 25–34. Cairo.

(1979). Remarques sur la ville de Kerma. In *Hommages à la mémoire de Serge Sauneron 1927–1976, vol. I: Égypte pharaonique*, 3–10. Cairo.

(1980). Les fouilles archéologiques de Kerma (Soudan), *Genava* NS **28**, 31–72.

(1981). La Deffufa Occidentale à Kerma: essai d'interprétation, *Bull. Inst. fr. Archéol. orient. Caire*, **81** (Supp.), 205–12.

Bonomi, J. (1906). Topographical notes on western Thebes collected in 1830. *Ann. Serv. Antiquités Egypte* **7**, 78–86.

Borchardt, L. (1899). Der zweite Papyrusfund von Kahun und die zeitliche Festlegung des mittleren Reiches der ägyptischen Geschichte. *Z. ägypt. Sprache Altertumskunde* **37**, 89–103.

(1907). *Das Grabdenkmal des Königs Ne-user-Re'*. Leipzig.

(1909). *Das Grabdenkmal des Königs Nefer-ỉr-keȝ-re'*. Leipzig.

(1910–13). *Das Grabdenkmal des Königs Saȝḥu-Re'*, 2 vols. Leipzig.

Borchardt, L. and H. Ricke (1930). *Egypt: architecture, landscape, life of the people*. London.

Bosticco, S. (1959). *Le stele egiziane dall'Antico al Nuovo Regno*. Rome.

Bothmer, B. V. (1971). A bust of Ny-user-ra from Byblos, in Beirut, Lebanon. *Kêmi* **21**, 11–16.

(1974). The Karnak statue of Ny-user-ra. *Mitt. dt. archäol. Inst. Abt. Kairo* **30**, 165–70.

Bottéro, J., E. Cassin and J. Vercoutter (1967). *The Near East: the early civilizations*. Translated by R. F. Tannenbaum. London.

Breasted, J. H. (1905). *A history of Egypt; from the earliest times to the Persian Conquest* New York. (Also London, 1906.)

(1906). *Ancient records of Egypt*, 5 vols. Chicago.

Brovarski, E. (1970). The House of Ḥww. *Serapis* **2**, 39.

Brovarski, E. and W. J. Murnane (1969). Inscriptions from the time of Nebhepetre Mentuhotep II at Abisko. *Serapis* **1**, 11–33.

Brunner, H. (1936). *Die Anlagen der ägyptischen Felsgräber bis zum Mittleren Reich.* Glückstadt.

(1955). Die Lehre vom Königserbe im frühen Mittleren Reich. In O. Firchow (ed.), *Ägyptologische Studien,* 4–11. Berlin.

(1958). Die Zeit des Cheops. *Oriental. Literaturz.* **53,** 293–301.

Brunner-Traut, E. (1974). Noch einmal die Fürstin von Punt. Ihre Rasse, Krankheit und ihre Bedeutung für die Lokalisierung von Punt. In *Festschrift zum 150 jährigen Bestehen des Berliner Ägyptischen Museums,* 71–85. Berlin.

Brunton, G. (1949). The title *Khnumet Nefer-Hezt. Ann. Serv. Antiquités Egypte* **49,** 99–110.

Brunton, G. and R. Engelbach (1927). *Gurob.* London.

Bruyère, B., J. Manteuffel, K. Michałowski, and J. Sainte Fare Garnot (1937). *Tell Edfou 1937. Fouilles franco-polonaises, rapports* 1. Cairo.

Buchholz, H.-G. and V. Karageorghis (1971). *Altägäis und Altkypros.* Tübingen.

*Bulletin de Liaison du Groupe International d'Etude de la Céramique Egyptienne* 2.

Butzer, K. W. (1959). Studien zum vor- und frühgeschichtlichen Landschaftswandel der Sahara. III. Die Naturlandschaft Ägyptens während der Vorgeschichte und der dynastischen Zeit. *Abh. math.-naturw. Kl. Akad. Wiss. Mainz* **2,** 1–80.

(1975). Patterns of environmental change in the Near East during Late Pleistocene and Early Holocene times. In F. Wendorf and A. E. Marks (eds.), *Problems in prehistory: North Africa and the Levant,* 389–410. Dallas.

(1976). *Early hydraulic civilization in Egypt: a study in cultural ecology.* Chicago.

Butzer, K. W. and C. L. Hansen (1968). *Desert and river in Nubia.* Madison.

Callaway, J. A. and J. M. Weinstein (1977). Radiocarbon dating of Palestine in the Early Bronze Age. *Bull. Am. Sch. orient. Res.* **225,** 1–16.

Caton-Thompson, G. (1952). *Kharga Oasis in prehistory.* London.

Černý, J. (1947). Graffiti at the Wādi el-'Allāki. *J. Egypt. Archaeol.* **33,** 52–7.

(1969). Stela of Emhab from Tell Edfu. *Mitt. dt. archäol. Inst. Abt. Kairo* **24,** 87–92.

Červíček, P. (1970–3). Datierung der nordafrikanischen Felsbilder durch die Patina. *IPEK* **23,** 82–7.

(1974). *Felsbilder des Nord-Etbai, Oberägyptens und Unternubien.* Wiesbaden.

Chéhab, M. (1969). Noms de personnalités égyptiennes découvertes au Liban. *Bull. Mus. Beyrouth* **22,** 1–47.

Coldstream, J. N. and G. L. Huxley (eds.) (1972). *Kythera; excavations and studies conducted by The University of Pennsylvania Museum and The British School at Athens.* London.

Couroyer, B. (1971). Ceux-qui-sont-sur-le-sable: les Hériou-Shâ. *Rev. Biblique* **78,** 558–75.

(1973). Pount et la Terre du Dieu. *Rev. Biblique* **80,** 53–74.

Couyat, J. and P. Montet (1912). *Les inscriptions hiéroglyphiques et hiératiques du Ouâdi Hammâmât.* Cairo.

Cowgill, G. L. (1975). On causes and consequences of ancient and modern population changes. *Am. anthrop.* **77**, 505–25.

Crawford, O. G. S. (1951). *The Fung Kingdom of Sennar, with a geographical account of the Middle Nile region.* Gloucester.

Crüsemann, F. (1973). Überlegungen zur Identifikation der Ḥirbet el-Mšāš (*Tel Māšôš*). *Z. dt Palästina-Vereins* **89**, 211–24.

Daressy, G. (1917). Chapelle de Mentouhotep III à Dendérah. *Ann. Serv. Antiquités Égypte* **17**, 226–36.

Daumas, F. (1965). Rapport préliminaire sur les fouilles exécutées par l'Institut Français d'Archéologie Orientale entre Seyala et Ouadi es Sebouâ en avril–mai 1964. *Bull. Inst. fr. Archéol. orient. Caire* **63**, 225–63.

—— (1973). Derechef Pépi I<sup>er</sup> à Dendara. *Rev. Égypt.* **25**, 7–20.

Davies, N. de G. (1943). *The tomb of Rekh-mi-rēʿ at Thebes.* New York.

Davis, E. N. (1974). *The Vapheio Cups and Aegean gold and silver ware.* University Microfilms 74-1869, Ann Arbor.

Dever, W. G. (1973). The EBIV-MBI horizon in Transjordan and southern Palestine. *Bull. Am. Sch. orient. Res.* **210**, 37–63.

Dewachter, M. (1976). Le roi Sahathor et la famille de Neferhotep I. *Rev. Egypt.* **28**, 66–73.

Dixon, D. (1958). The land of Yam. *J. Egypt. Archaeol.* **44**, 40–55.

Drioton, E. (1945). Notes diverses, 2. Une corégence de Pepy I<sup>er</sup> et de Mérenrê (?). *Ann. Serv. Antiquités Égypte* **44**, 55–6.

Drioton, E. and J. Vandier (1962). *Les peuples de l'orient méditerranéen, vol. II: L'Égypte,* 4th ed. Paris.

Dunayevsky, I. and A. Kempinski (1973). The Megiddo temples. *Z. dt. Palästina-Vereins* **89**, 161–87.

Dunbar, J. H. (1941). *The rock pictures of Lower Nubia.* Cairo.

Dunham, D. (1938). The biographical inscriptions of Nekhebu in Boston and Cairo. *J. Egypt. Archaeol.* **24**, 1–8.

Edel, E. (1954). Inschriften des Alten Reichs, I. Die Biographie des Gaufürsten von Edfu. *Z. ägypt. Sprache Altertumskunde* **79**, 11–17.

—— (1955). Inschriften des Alten Reiches. V. Die Reiseberichte des, Ḥrw-ḫwjf (Herchuf). in O. Firchow (ed.), *Agyptologische Studien,* 51–75. Berlin.

—— (1955–64). *Altägyptische Grammatik. Analecta Orientalia* **34–9.** Rome.

—— (1956). Ein 'Vorsteher der Farafra-Oase' im Alten Reich? *Z. ägypt. Sprache Altertumskunde* **81**, 67–8.

—— (1960). Inschriften des Alten Reiches. XI. Nachträge zu den Reiseberichten der Ḥrw-ḫwjf. *Z. ägypt. Sprache Altertumskunde* **85**, 18–23.

—— (1962). Zur Lesung und Bedeutung einiger Stellen in den biographischen Inschrift Sꜣ-rnpwtʾs I. *Z. ägypt. Sprache Altertumskunde* **87**, 96–107.

—— (1967). Die Ländernamen und die Ausbreitung der C-Gruppe nach den Reiseberichten des Ḥrw-ḫwjf. *Orientalia* **36**, 133–58.

—— (1971a). *Beiträge zu den Inschriften des Mittleren Reiches in den Gräbern der Qubbet el Hawa.* Munich and Berlin.

—— (1971b). Zwei neue Felsinschriften aus Tumâs mit nubischen Ländernamen. *Z. ägypt. Sprache Altertumskunde* **97**, 53–63.

(1973). Nachtrag zur Felsinschriften des *Mḫw* und *Sꜣbnj* in Tumâs, ZÄS 97, 1971, 53ff. *Z. ägypt. Sprache Altertumskunde* **100**, 76.

(1975). Der Fund eines Kamaresgefässes in einem Grabe der Qubbet el Hawa bei Assuan. In *Actes XXIX Congr. Int. Orientalistes, Égyptologie*, vol. 1, 38–40. Paris.

Edwards, I. E. S. (1961a). *The pyramids of Egypt*, revised ed. Harmondsworth.

(1961b). Two Egyptian sculptures in relief. *Br. Mus. Quarterly* **23**, 9–11.

(1970). Absolute dating from Egyptian records and comparison with carbon-14 dating. *Phil. Trans. Roy. Soc. Lond.* **269**, 1193, 11–18.

Edwards, I. E. S., C. J. Gadd and N. G. L. Hammond (eds.) (1971). *The Cambridge ancient history*, 3rd ed., vol. 1, pt 2, *Early history of the Middle East*. Cambridge.

Egypt Exploration Society (1963). *Report of the seventy-seventh ordinary general meeting.*

Emery, W. B. (1923). Two Nubian graves of the Middle Kingdom at Abydos. *Ann. Archaeol. Anthrop., Liverpool* **10**, 33–5.

(1961). A preliminary report on the excavations of the Egypt Exploration Society at Buhen, 1959–60. *Kush* **9**, 81–6.

(1963). Egypt Exploration Society. Preliminary report on the excavations at Buhen, 1962. *Kush* **11**, 116–20.

(1965). *Egypt in Nubia* London.

Emery, W. B. and L. P. Kirwan (1935). *The excavations and survey between Wadi es-Sebua and Adindan 1929–1931.* Cairo.

Engelbach, R. (1922). Steles and tables of offerings of the late Middle Kingdom from Tell Edfû. *Ann. Serv. Antiquités Égypte* **22**, 113–38.

(1923). *Harageh*. London.

(1933). The quarries of the western Nubian desert: a preliminary report. *Ann. Serv. Antiquités Égypte* **33**, 65–74.

(1938). The quarries of the western Nubian desert and the ancient road to Tushka. *Ann. Serv. Antiquités Égypte.* **38**, 369–90.

Erman, A. and H. Grapow (1926–31). *Wörterbuch der Ägyptischen Sprache*, 5 vols. Leipzig.

Ertman, E. E. (1972). The earliest known three-dimensional representation of the god Ptah. *J. Near East. Stud.* **31**, 83–6.

Evers, H. G. (1929). *Staat aus dem Stein. Denkmäler Geschichte und Bedeutung der ägyptischen Plastik während des Mittleren Reichs*, 2 vols. Munich.

Fairman, H. W. (1958). The kingship rituals of Egypt. In S. H. Hooke (ed.), *Myth, ritual and kingship*, 74–104. Oxford.

Fairservis, W. A., K. Weeks and M. Hoffman (1971–2). Preliminary report on the first two seasons at Hierakonpolis. *J. Am. Res. Cent. Egypt* **9**, 7–68.

Fakhry, A. (1952). *The inscriptions of the amethyst quarries at Wadi el Hudi.* Cairo.

(1959). *The monuments of Sneferu at Dahshur, vol. I: The Bent Pyramid.* Cairo.

(1961). *The monuments of Sneferu at Dahshur, vol. II: The Valley Temple*, 2 pts. Cairo.

(1973). The search for texts in the western desert. In *Textes et langages de l'Égypte pharaonique, Hommage à Jean-François Champollion*, vol. II, 207–22. Cairo.

Farid, S. (1964). Preliminary report on the excavations of the Antiquities Department at Tell Basta (season 1961). *Ann. Serv. Antiquités Égypte* **58**, 85–98.

Faulkner, R. O. (1969). *The ancient Egyptian pyramid texts*. Oxford.

Fecht, G. (1956). Die Ḥatjw-ʿ in Iḥnw, eine ägyptische Völkerschaft in der Westwüste. *Z. dt. morgenländ. Ges.* **106** (N.S. **31**), 37–60.

(1968). Zu den Inschriften·des ersten Pfeilers im Grab des Anchtifi (Moʿalla). In W. H. Helck (ed.), *Festschrift für Siegfried Schott zu seinem 70. Geburtstag*, 50–60. Wiesbaden.

(1972). *Der Vorwurf an Gott in den 'Mahnworten des Ipu-wer' (Pap. Leiden I 344 recto 11, 11–13, 8; 15, 13–17, 3). Zur geistigen Krise der ersten Zwischenzeit und ihrer Bewältigung*. Heidelberg.

(1973). Ägyptische Zweifel am Sinn des Opfers: Admonitions 5, 7–9. *Z. ägypt. Sprache Altertumskunde* **100**, 6–16.

Firth, C. M. and B. Gunn (1926). *Teti pyramid cemeteries*, 2 vols. Cairo.

Fischer, H. G. (1954). Four provincial administrators at the Memphite cemeteries. *J. Am. orient. Soc.* **74**, 26–34.

(1957). A god and a general of the Oasis on a stela of the late Middle Kingdom. *J. Near East. Stud.* **16**, 223–35.

(1959a). An example of Memphite influence on a Theban stela of the Eleventh Dynasty. *Artibus Asiae* **22**, 240–52.

(1959b). A scribe of the army in a Saqqara mastaba of the early Fifth Dynasty. *J. Near East. Stud.* **18**, 233–72.

(1960). The inscription of *In-it.f*, born of *Tfi. J. Near East. Stud.* **19**, 258–68.

(1961a). Three Old Kingdom palimpsests in the Louvre. *Z. ägypt. Sprache Altertumskunde* **86**, 21–31.

(1961b). Land records on stelae of the Twelfth Dynasty. *Rev. Égypt.* **13**, 107–9.

(1962). A provincial statue of the Egyptian Sixth Dynasty. *Am. J. Archaeol.* **66**, 65–9.

(1963). A stela of the Heracleopolitan Period found at Saqqara: the Osiris *Iti. Z. ägypt. Sprache Altertumskunde* **90**, 35–41.

(1964). *Inscriptions from the Coptite nome; Dynasties VI–XI. Analecta Orientalia* **40**, Rome.

(1968). *Dendera in the third millennium B.C.; down to the Theban domination of Upper Egypt*. New York.

(1974). *Nbty* in Old Kingdom titles and names. *J. Egypt. Archaeol.* **60**, 94–9.

(1975). Two tantalizing biographical fragments of historical interest. *J. Egypt. Archaeol.* **61**, 33–7.

Fleming, A. (1973). Tombs for the living. *Man*, N.S. **8**, 177–93.

*Fouilles de El Kab: documents* (1954). Livraison III. Fondation Égyptologique Reine Elisabeth, Brussels.

Frankfort, H. (1948). *Kingship and the gods*. Chicago.

Friedman, J. (1974). Marxism, structuralism and vulgar materialism. *Man*, N.S. **9**, 444–69.

Gabra, G. (1976). Preliminary report on the stela of ·Ḥtpi from El-Kab from the time of Wahankh Inyôtef II. *Mitt. dt. archäol. Inst. Abt. Kairo* **32**, 45–56.

Gabra, S. (1929). *Les conseils de fonctionnaires dans l'Égypte pharaonique*. Cairo.

Gardiner, A. H. (1916). The defeat of the Hyksos Kamôse; The Carnarvon Tablet no. 1, *J. Egypt. Archaeol.* **3**, 95–110.

(1925). The autobiography of Rekhmerēʿ. *Z. ägypt. Sprache Altertumskunde* **60**, 62–76.

(1929). An administrative letter of protest. *J. Egypt. Archaeol.* **13**, 75–8.

(1947). *Ancient Egyptian Onomastica*, 3 vols. Oxford.

(1954). Was the vizier Djaʿu one of six like-named brothers? *Z. ägypt. Sprache Altertumskunde* **79**, 95–6.

(1957). The reading of the geographical term [tp-rs]. *J. Egypt. Archaeol.* **43**, 6–9.

(1959). *The royal canon of Turin*. Oxford.

(1961). *Egypt of the Pharaohs: an introduction*. Oxford.

Gardiner, A. H., T. E. Peet and J. Černý (1955). *The inscriptions of Sinai. Egypt Exploration Society Memoir* **55**. London.

Garstang, J. (1902). *Maḥâsna and Bêt Khallaf*. London.

(1904). *Tombs of the Third Egyptian Dynasty at Reqâqnah and Bêt Khallaf*. London.

Gauthier, H. (1907). *Le livre des rois d'Égypte, vol. I: Des origines à la fin de la XII<sup>e</sup> dynastie*. Cairo.

(1918). Le titre *imi-ra âkhnouti* et ses acceptions diverses. *Bull. Inst. fr. Archéol. orient. Caire* **15**, 169–206.

(1924). La titulaire des reines des dynasties memphites. *Ann. Serv. Antiquités Égypte* **24**, 198–209.

Gerven, D. P. van, D. S. Carlson and G. J. Armelagos (1973). Racial history and bio-cultural adaptation of Nubian archaeological populations. *J. Afr. Hist.* **14**, 555–64.

Geus, C. H. S. de (1971). The Amorites in the archaeology of Palestine. *Ugarit-Forsch.* **3**, 41–60.

Geus, F. and Y. Labre (1974). La Nubie au sud de Dal: exploration archéologique et problèmes historiques. *Etudes sur l'Égypte et le Soudan anciens (Cahiers de Recherches de l'Institut de Papyrologie et d'Égyptologie de Lille* **2**), 103–23.

Giddy, L. L. and D. G. Jeffreys (1980). Balat: rapport préliminaire des fouilles à ʿAyn Aṣīl, 1979–1980. *Bull. Inst. fr. Archéol. orient. Caire*, **80**, 257–69.

(1981). Balat: rapport préliminaire des fouilles à ʿAyn Aṣīl, 1981. *Bull. Inst. fr. Archéol. orient. Caire*, **81**, 198–205.

Ginter, B., W. Heflik, J. K. Kozłowski and J. Śliwa (1980). Excavations in the region of Qasr el-Sagha, 1979. *Mitt. dt. archäol. Inst. Abt. Kairo* **36**, 105–69.

Giorgini, M. S. (1971). *Soleb, vol. II: les nécropoles*. Florence.

Giveon, R. (1965). A sealing of Khyan from the Shephela of southern Palestine. *J. Egypt. Archaeol.* **51**, 202–4.

(1967). Royal seals of the XIIth Dynasty from Western Asia. *Rev. Égypt.* **19**, 29–37.

(1971). [The temple of Hathor at Serabit el-Khadem.] *Qadmoniot* **4**, 14–18. (In Hebrew.)

(1972). Le temple d'Hathor à Serabit el-Khadem. *Archéologia* **44**, 64–9.

(1974a). Hyksos scarabs with names of kings and officials from Canaan. *Chronique d'Egypte* **49**, 222–33.

(1974b). A second relief of Sekhemkhet in Sinai. *Bull. Am. Sch. orient. Res.* **216**, 17–20.

(1975). [Lady of the turquoise: Hathor at Serabit el-Khadim and Timna.] *Eretz-Israel* **12**, 24–6. (In Hebrew.)

Gleichen, Count Albert E. W. (ed.) (1905). *The Anglo-Egyptian Sudan: a compendium prepared by officers of the Sudan Government*, vol. I. London.

Goedicke, H. (1954). An approximate date for the harem investigation under Pepy I. *J. Am. orient. Soc.* **74**, 88–9.

(1955). The Abydene marriage of Pepi I. *J. Am. orient. Soc.* **75**, 180–3.

(1956). Zu *imj-rз šm'* und *tp šm'* im Alten Reich. *Mitt. Inst. Orientforsch.* **4**, 1–10.

(1957). Bemerkungen zum Alter der Sonnenheiligtümer. *Bull. Inst. fr. Archéol. orient. Caire* **56**, 151–3.

(1960a). *Die Stellung des Königs im Alten Reich*. Wiesbaden.

(1960b). The inscription of *Dmi*. *J. Near East. Stud.* **19**, 288–91.

(1962). Zur Chronologie der sogenannten 'Ersten Zwischenzeit'. *Z. dt. morgenländ. Ges.* **112** (N.S. 37), 239–54.

(1963). The alleged military campaign in southern Palestine in the reign of Pepy I (VIth Dynasty). *Riv. Stud. Orient.* **38**, 187–97.

(1966a). An additional note on 'з 'foreigner.' *J. Egypt. Archaeol.* **52**, 172–4.

(1966b). The cylinder seal of a ruler of Byblos reconsidered. *J. Am. Res. Cent. Egypt* **5**, 19–21.

(1967). *Königliche Dokumente aus dem alten Reich*. Wiesbaden.

(1969). Probleme der Herakleopolitenzeit. *Mitt. dt. archäol. Inst. Abt. Kairo* **24**, 136–43.

(1969–70). An Egyptian claim to Asia. *J. Am. Res. Cent. Egypt* **8**, 11–27.

(1970). *Die privaten Rechtsinschriften aus dem Alten Reich*. Vienna.

(1971). *Re-used blocks from the pyramid of Amenemhet I at Lisht*. New York.

(1971–2). Tax deductions for religious donations. *J. Am. Res. Cent. Egypt* **9**, 73–5.

(1974). The Berlin Leather Roll (P. Berlin 3029). In *Festschrift zum 150jährigen Bestehen des Berliner Ägyptischen Museums*, 87–104. Berlin.

(1976a). Eine Betrachtung des Inschriften des Meten im Rahmen der sozialen und rechtlichen Stellung von Privatleuten im ägyptischen Alten Reich. *Ägyptologische Abhandlungen* **29**. Wiesbaden.

(1976b). Another remark about the Byblos Cylinder Seal. *Syria* **53**, 191–2.

(1977). *The prophecy of Neferyt*. Baltimore.

Gomaà, F. (1980). *Ägypten während der Ersten Zwischenzeit*. (Beihefte zum Tübinger Atlas des Vorderen Orients, Reihe B, 27.) Wiesbaden.

Gómez-Moreno, C. (1972–3). Gold. *Bull. Metropol. Mus. Art* **31**, 69–121.

Gophna, R. (1976a). Excavations at 'En Besor. *'Atiqot* 11, 1–9.

(1976b). Egyptian immigration into southern Canaan during the First Dynasty? *Tel Aviv* 3, 31–7.

Gostynski, T. (1975). La Libye antique et ses relations avec l'Égypte. *Bull IFAN*, B, 37, 473–588.

Goyon, G. (1957). *Nouvelles inscriptions rupestres du Wadi Hammamat.* Paris.

(1969). Le cylindre de l'Ancien Empire du Musée d'Ismailia. *Bull. Inst. fr. Archéol. orient. Caire* 67, 147–57.

Gratien, B. (1973). Les nécropoles Kerma de l'île de Saï. *Études sur l'Egypte et le Soudan anciens (Cahiers de Recherches de l'Institut de Papyrologie et d'Égyptologie de Lille* 1), 143–84.

(1974). Les nécropoles Kerma de l'île de Saï, II. *Études sur l'Égypte et le Soudan anciens (Cahiers de Recherches de l'Institut de Papyrologie et d'Égyptologie de Lille* 2), 51–74.

(1975). Les nécropoles Kerma de l'île de Saï, III. *Études sur l'Égypte et le Soudan anciens (Cahiers de Recherches de l'Institut de Papyrologie et d'Égyptologie de Lille* 3), 43–66.

(1978). *Les cultures Kerma; essai de classification.* Lille.

Grdseloff, B. (1948). Remarques concernant l'opposition à un rescrit du vizir. *Ann. Serv. Antiquités Égypte* 48, 505–12.

Grieshammer, R. (1974). *Die altägyptische Sargtexte in der Forschung seit 1936. Ägyptologische Abhandlungen* 28. Wiesbaden.

Griffith, F. Ll. (1898). *The Petrie Papyri: hieratic papyri from Kahun and Gurob (principally of the Middle Kingdom).* London.

Griffiths, J. G. (1960). *The conflict of Horus and Seth.* Liverpool.

(1966). *The origins of Osiris. Münchner Ägyptologische Studien* 9, Berlin.

Grove, A. T., F. Alayne Street and A. S. Goudie (1975). Former lake levels and climatic change in the rift valley of southern Ethiopia. *Geogrl J.* 141, 177–202.

Guest, E. M. (1926). Women's titles in the Middle Kingdom. *Ancient Egypt* 46–50.

Gunn, B. (1929). A Middle Kingdom stela from Edfu. *Ann. Serv. Antiquités Égypte* 29, 5–14.

Habachi, L. (1957). *Tell Basta.* Cairo.

(1958). God's fathers and the role they played in the history of the First Intermediate Period? *Ann. Serv. Antiquités Égypte* 55, 167–90.

(1972). *The second stela of Kamose, and his struggle against the Hyksos ruler and his capital.* Glückstadt.

(1974). A high inundation in the temple of Amenre at Karnak in the Thirteenth Dynasty. *Stud. altägypt. Kultur* 1, 207–14.

Hall, H. T. B. (1962). A note on the cattle skulls excavated at Faras. *Kush* 10, 58–61.

Hallo, W. W. and Simpson, W. K. (1971). *The ancient Near East: a history.* New York.

Hamada, A. and S. Farid (1947). Excavations at Kôm el-Ḥisn, season 1945. *Ann. Serv. Antiquités Égypte* 46, 195–205.

Hansen, D. P. (1965). Mendes 1964. *J. Am. Res. Cent. Egypt* 4, 31–7.

(1967). Mendes 1965 and 1966, I. The excavations at Tell el Rub'a. *J. Am. Res. Cent. Egypt* 6, 5–16.

Harris, J. R. (1961). *Lexicographical studies in ancient Egyptian minerals.* Berlin.

Hassan, Fekri A. (1980). Radiocarbon chronology of Archaic Egypt. *J. Near East. Stud.*, 39, 203–7.

Hassan, S. (1943). *Excavations at Gîza, vol. IV: 1932–1933.* Cairo.

Hayes, W. C. (1946). Royal decrees from the temple of Min at Coptus. *J. Egypt. Archaeol.* 32, 3–23.

(1947). Horemkha'uef of Nekhen and his trip to It-towe. *J. Egypt. Archaeol.* 33, 3–11.

(1953a). *The scepter of Egypt*, pt I. New York.

(1953b). Notes on the government of Egypt in the late Middle Kingdom. *J. Near East. Stud.* 12, 31–9.

(1955). *A papyrus of the late Middle Kingdom in the Brooklyn Museum* [*Papyrus Brooklyn 35.1446*]. Brooklyn. (Reprinted with an additional page of errata and recent bibliography as *Wilbour Monographs* 5.)

Hays, T. R. (1975a). Neolithic settlement patterns in Saharan Africa. *S. Afr. archaeol. Bull.* 30, 29–33.

(1975b). Neolithic settlement of the Sahara as it relates to the Nile Valley. In F. Wendorf and A. E. Marks (eds.), *Problems in prehistory: North Africa and the Levant*, 193–204. Dallas.

Heinzelin, J. de (1968). Geological history of the Nile Valley in Nubia. In F. Wendorf (ed.), *The prehistory of Nubia*, vol. 1, 19–55. Dallas.

Helck, H. W. (1954). *Untersuchungen zu den Beamtentiteln des ägyptischen Alten Reiches.* Glückstadt.

(1955). Zur Reichseinigung der II. Dynastie. *Z. ägypt. Sprache Altertumskunde* 80, 75–6.

(1956a). Wirtschaftliche Bemerkungen zum privaten Grabbesitz im Alten Reich. *Mitt. dt. archäol. Inst. Abt. Kairo* 14, 63–75.

(1956b). *Untersuchungen zu Manetho und den ägyptischen Königslisten.* Berlin.

(1957). Bemerkungen zu den Pyramidenstädten im Alten Reich. *Mitt. dt. archäol. Inst. Abt. Kairo* 15, 91–111.

(1958). *Zur Verwaltung des Mittleren und Neuen Reichs.* Leiden and Cologne.

(ed.) (1968). *Geschichte des alten Ägypten, Handbuch der Orientalisk,* Abt. 1, Bd. 1, Absch. 3. Leiden and Cologne.

(1969). Eine Stele Sebekhotops IV. aus Karnak. *Mitt. dt. archäol. Inst. Abt. Kairo* 24, 194–200.

(1970). *Die Prophezeiung des Nfr.tj. Textzusammenstellung.* Wiesbaden.

(1971). *Die Beziehungen Ägyptens zu Vorderasien im 3. und 2. Jahrtausend v. Chr.* 2nd edn. Wiesbaden.

(1974a). *Ägyptische Aktenkunde des 3. und 2. Jahrtausends v. Chr.* Munich and Berlin.

(1974b). Bemerkungen zum Annalenstein. *Mitt. dt. archäol. Inst. Abt. Kairo* 30, 31–5.

(1974c). Die Bedeutung der Felsinschriften J. Lopez, Inscripciones Rupestres Nr. 27 und 28. *Stud. altägypt. Kultur* 1, 215–25.

(1975). *Wirtschaftsgeschichte des Alten Ägypten im 3. und 2. Jahrtausend vor Chr.* Leiden.

(1976). Ägyptische Statuen im Ausland – ein chronologisches Problem. *Ugarit-Forsch.* **8**, 101–15.

(1978). Die Weihinschrift Sesostris' I, am Satet-Tempel von Elephantine. *Mitt. dt. archäol. Inst. Abt. Kairo* **34**, 67–78.

Helck, H. W. and E. Otto (eds.) (1972–   ). *Lexikon der Ägyptologie*, vols 1–  . Wiesbaden.

Hellström, P. and H. Langballe (1970). *The rock drawings.* Scandinavian Joint Expedition to Sudanese Nubia. Stockholm and New York.

Helms, S. W. (1975a). Jawa 1973: a preliminary report. *Levant* **7**, 20–38.

(1975b). Posterns in Early Bronze Age fortifications of Palestine. *Palestine Exploration Quarterly* **107**, 133–50.

(1976). Jawa excavations 1974: a preliminary report. *Levant* **8**, 1–23.

Hennessy, J. B. (1967). *The foreign relations of Palestine during the Early Bronze Age.* London.

Hepper, N. (1969). Arabian and African frankincense trees. *J. Egypt. Archaeol.* **55**, 66–72.

Herzog, R. (1968). *Punt.* Glückstadt.

Hesse, A. (1971). Tentative interpretation of the surface distribution of remains on the upper fort of Mirgissa (Sudanese Nubia). In F. R. Hodson, D. G. Kendall and P. Tǎutu (eds.), *Mathematics in the archaeological and historical sciences* 436–44. Edinburgh.

Hester, J. J. and P. M. Hobler (1969). *Prehistoric settlement patterns in the Libyan desert. Anthrop. Pap. Univ. Utah* **92**, Nubian series 4.

Hintze, F. (1964). Das Kerma-Problem. *Z. ägypt. Sprache Altertumskunde* **91**, 79–86.

(1965). Preliminary note on the epigraphic expedition to Sudanese Nubia, 1963. *Kush* **13**, 13–16.

Hobler, P. M. and J. J. Hester (1968). Prehistory and environment in the Libyan desert. *S. Afr. archaeol. Bull.* **23**, 120–30.

Hodjache, S. and O. Berlev (1977). Objets royaux du Musée des Beaux-Arts Pouchkine à Moscou. *Chronique d'Égypte* **52**, 22–39.

Hofmann, I. (1967). *Die Kulturen des Niltals von Aswan bis Sennar; vom Mesolithikum bis zum Ende der christlichen Epoche.* Hamburg.

Hölscher, W. (1955). *Libyer und Ägypter.* Glückstadt.

Horn, S. H. (1963). Byblos in ancient records. *Andrews Univ. Sem. Stud.* **1**, 52–61.

Hornung, E. (1966). *Geschichte als Fest; zwei Vorträge zum Geschichtsbild der frühen Menschzeit.* Darmstadt.

(1973). Die 'Kammern' des Thot-Heiligtumes. *Z. ägypt. Sprache Altertums-kunde* **100**, 33–5.

(1974). Seth. Geschichte und Bedeutung eines ägyptischen Gottes. *Symbolen* **2**, 49–63.

Huard, P. (1965). Recherches sur les traits culturels des chasseurs anciens du Sahara centre-oriental et du Nil. *Rev. Egypt* **17**, 21–80.

(1967–8). Influences culturelles transmises au Sahara tchadien par le Groupe C de Nubie. *Kush* **15**, 84–124.

Huard, P. and L. Allard (1970). Etat des recherches sur les chasseurs anciens du Nil et du Sahara. *Bibliotheca Orient.* **27**, 322–7.

Huard, P. and J. Leclant (1972). *Problèmes archéologiques entre le Nil et le Sahara.* Cairo.

Ingham, M. F. (1969). The length of the Sothic cycle. *J. Egypt. Archaeol.* **55**, 36–40.

Jacquet-Gordon, H. K. (1962). *Les noms des domaines funéraires sous l'Ancien Empire égyptien.* Cairo.

James, T. G. H. (1961). A group of inscribed Egyptian tools. *Br. Mus. Quarterly* **24**, 36–43.

(1962). *The Hekanakhte papers and other early Middle Kingdom documents.* New York.

Janssen, J. J. (1975). *Commodity prices from the Ramessid period.* Leiden.

Jéquier, G. (1929). *Tombeaux de particuliers contemporains de Pepi II.* Cairo.

(1935). *La pyramide d'Aba.* Cairo.

(1938). *Le monument funéraire de Pepi II, vol. II: Le temple.* Cairo.

(1940a). *Le monument funéraire de Pepi II, vol. III: Les approches du temple.* Cairo.

(1940b). *Douze ans de fouilles dans la nécropole memphite 1924–1936. Mém. Univ. Neuchatel* **15**.

Junge, F. (1973). Zur Fehldatierung des sog. Denkmals memphitischer Theologie oder: Der Beitrag der ägyptischen Theologie zur Geistesgeschichte der Spätzeit. *Mitt. dt. archäol. Inst. Abt. Kairo* **29**, 195–204.

Jungwirth, J. (1970). Die anthropologischen Ergebnisse der Grabungskampagne 1969 in Tell ed Dab'a, Unterägypten. *Ann. naturhist. Mus. Vienna* **74**, 659–66.

Junker, H. (1955). *Gîza XII.* Vienna.

Kadish, G. E. (1966). Old Kingdom Egyptian activity in Nubia: some reconsiderations. *J. Egypt. Archaeol.* **52**, 23–33.

(1973). British Museum writing board 5645: The complaints of Kha-kheper-rē'-senebu. *J. Egypt. Archaeol.* **59**, 77–90.

Kaiser, W. (1956). Zu den Sonnenheiligtümern der 5. Dynastie. *Mitt. dt. Archäol. Inst. Abt. Kairo* **14**, 104–16.

(1961). Einige Bemerkungen zur ägyptischen Frühzeit. II. Zur Frage einer über Menes hinausreichenden ägyptischen Geschichtsüberlieferung. *Z. ägypt. Sprache Altertumskunde* **86**, 39–61.

Kaiser, W., P. Grossmann, G. Haeny and H. Jaritz (1974). Stadt und Tempel von Elephantine. Vierter Grabungsbericht. *Mitt. dt. archäol. Inst. Abt. Kairo* **30**, 65–90.

Kanawati, N. (1974). The financial resources of the viziers of the Old Kingdom and the historical implications. *Archaeol. Hist. Stud. Alexandria* **5**, 1–20.

(1976). The mentioning of more than one eldest child in Old Kingdom inscriptions. *Chronique d'Egypte* **51**, 235–51.

(1977). *The Egyptian administration in the Old Kingdom.* Warminster.

Kantor, H. J. (1965). The relative chronology of Egypt and its foreign correlations before the Late Bronze Age. In R. W. Ehrich (ed.), *Chronologies in Old World Archaeology*, 1–46. Chicago.

Kaplony, P. (1965). Die wirtschaftliche Bedeutung des Totenkultes im Alten Ägypten. *Asiat. Stud.* **18–19**, 290–307.

(1968). Neues Material zu einer Prosopographie des Alten Reiches. *Mitt. Inst. Orientforsch.* **14**, 192–205.

(1972). Das Papyrusarchiv von Abusir. *Orientalia* N.S. **41**, 11–79, 180–244.

Kaplony-Heckel, U. (1971a). *Ägyptische Handschriften*, pt 1, ed. E. Lüddeckens. (W. Voigt (ed.), *Verzeichnis der Orientalischen Handschriften in Deutschland*, vol. XIX.) Wiesbaden.

(1971b). Eine hieratische Stela des Mittleren Reichs. *J. Egypt. Archaeol.* **57**, 20–7.

Kappel, W. (1974). Irrigation development and population pressure. In T. E. Downing and M. Gibson (eds.), *Irrigation's impact on society* (*Anthrop. Pap. Univ. Arizona*, **25**), 159–67. Tucson, Arizona.

Kees, H. (1940). Beiträge zur Geschichte des Vezirats im Alten Reich. Die Chronologie der Vezire unter König Chiops II. *Nach. Ges. Wiss. Göttingen, Phil.-hist. Kl.* **4**.

Kemp, B. J. (1968). The Osiris temple at Abydos. *Mitt. dt. archäol Inst. Abt. Kairo* **23**, 138–55.

(1973). The Osiris temple at Abydos. A postscript to *MDAIK* 23 (1968) 138–155. *Götting. Misz.* **8**, 23–5.

(1972). Fortified towns in Nubia. In P. J. Ucko, R. Tringham and G. W. Dimbleby (eds.), *Man, settlement and urbanism*, 651–6. London.

(1976a). Dating Pharaonic cemeteries. Part I: non-mechanical approaches to seriation. *Mitt. dt. archäol. Inst. Abt. Kairo* **31**, 93–116.

(1976b). A note on stratigraphy at Memphis. *J. Am. Res. Cent. Egypt* **13**, 25–9.

(1977a). An incised sherd from Kahun (Egypt). *J. Near East. Stud.* **36**, 289–92.

(1977b). The early development of towns in Egypt. *Antiquity* **51**, 185–200.

(1978). The harim-palace at Medinet el-Ghurab Z.Ä.S. **105**, 122–33.

(1980). Egyptian radiocarbon dating: a reply to James Mellaart. *Antiquity*, **54**, 25–8.

(1982). Automatic analysis of predynastic cemeteries: a new method for an old problem. *J. Egypt. Archaeol.* **68**, 5–15.

Kemp, B. J. and R. S. Merrillees (1980). *Minoan pottery in second millennium Egypt*. Mainz am Rhein.

Kenyon, K. M. (1969). The Middle and Late Bronze Age strata at Megiddo. *Levant* **1**, 25–60.

Kirwan, L. P. (1939). *Oxford University excavations at Firka*. Oxford.

Kitchen, K. A. (1961). An unusual stela from Abydos. *J. Egypt. Archaeol* **47**, 10–18.

(1967a). Byblos, Egypt, and Mari in the early second millennium B.C. *Orientalia* **36**, 39–54.

(1967b). An unusual Egyptian text from Byblos. *Bull. Mus. Beyrouth* **20**, 149–53.

(1971). Punt and how to get there. *Orientalia* **40**, 184–208.

Klasens, A. (1968). A social revolution in ancient Egypt. *Études et Travaux* **2** (*Prace Zakładu Archaeologii Śródziemnomorskiej Polskiej Akademii Nauk* **6**), 6–13.

Knudstad, J. (1966). Serra East and Dorginarti. *Kush* **14**, 165–86.

Koenen, L. (1970). The prophecies of a potter: a prophecy of world renewal becomes an apocalypse. In D. H. Samuel (ed.), *Proc. XII Int. Congr. Papyrology* 249–54. Toronto.

Kuchman, L. (1977). The titles of queenship: part I, the evidence from the Old Kingdom. *Newsl. Soc. Stud. Egypt. antiquities, Toronto* **7**, 9–12.

Lanczkowski, G. (1959). Das Königtum im Mittleren Reich. In *La regalità sacra/The sacral kingship (Studies in the history of religions*, vol. IV). Leiden.

Larsen, H. (1935). Vorbericht über die schwedischen Grabungen in Abu Ghalib 1932–1934. *Mitt. dt. Inst. ägypt. Altertumskunde Kairo* **6**, 41–87.

Lauer, J.-P. (1973). Remarques sur la planification de la construction de la grande pyramide. *Bull. Inst. fr. Archéol. orient. Caire* **73**, 127–42.

(1974). *Le mystère des pyramides* Paris.

(1976). A propos du prétendu désastre de la pyramide de Meïdoum. *Chronique d'Egypte* **51**, 72–89.

Lawrence, A. W. (1965). Ancient Egyptian fortifications. *J. Egypt. Archaeol.* **51**, 69–94.

Leclant, J. (1954). Fouilles et travaux en Égypte, 1952–1953. *Orientalia* **23**, 64–79.

(1969). Fouilles et travaux en Égypte et au Soudan, 1967–1968. *Orientalia* **38**, 240–307.

(1974). Fouilles et travaux en Égypte et au Soudan, 1972–1973. *Orientalia* **43**, 171–227.

Leclant, J. and A. Heyler (1961). Sur l'administration de l'Égypte au Moyen- et Nouvel-Empire. *Orient. Literaturz.* **56**, 118–29.

Lees, S. H. (1974). Hydraulic development as a process of response. *Hum. Ecol.* **2**, 159–75.

Legrain, G. (1905). The king Samou or Seshemou and the enclosures of el-Kab. *Proc. Soc. Bibl. Archaeol.* **27**, 106–11.

Lichtheim, M. (1973). *Ancient Egyptian literature; a book of readings, vol. I: The Old and Middle Kingdoms.* Berkeley.

(1980). *Ancient Egyptian literature: a book of readings, vol. III, The Late Period.* Berkeley.

Limme, L. (1973). Les oases de Khargeh et Dakhleh d'après les documents égyptiens de l'époque pharaonique. *Études sur l'Égypte et le Soudan anciens (Cahiers de Recherches de l'Institut de Papyrologie et d'Égyptologie de Lille* I), 39–58.

Lloyd, A. B. (1970). The Egyptian Labyrinth. *J. Egypt. Archaeol.* **56**, 81–100.

Long, R. D. (1974). A re-examination of the Sothic chronology of Egypt. *Orientalia* **43**, 261–74.

(1976). Ancient Egyptian chronology, radiocarbon dating and calibration. *Z. ägypt. Sprache Altertumskunde* **103**, 30–48.

Lopez, J. (1967). Inscriptions de l'Ancien Empire à Khor el-Aquiba. *Rev. Egypt.* **19**, 57–66.

Lowie, R. H. Museum of Anthropology (1966). *Ancient Egypt.* (Exhibition Catalogue.) Berkeley.

Lucas, A. and J. R. Harris (1962). *Ancient Egyptian materials and industries*, 4th edn. London.

Macadam, M. F. L. (1951). A royal family of the Thirteenth Dynasty. *J. Egypt. Archaeol.* **37**, 20–8.

(1955). *The temples of Kawa*, vol. II. London.

MacDonald, J. (1972). Egyptian interests in Western Asia to the end of the Middle Kingdom: an evaluation. *Austral. J. Bibl. Archaeol.* **2**, 72–98.

McHugh, W. P. (1974a). Cattle pastoralism in Africa – a model for interpreting archaeological evidence from the eastern Sahara desert. *Arctic Anthrop.* **11** (Suppl), 236–44.

(1974b). Late prehistoric cultural adaptation in southwest Egypt and the problem of the Nilotic origins of Saharan cattle pastoralism. *J. Am. Res. Cent. Egypt* **11**, 9–22.

(1975). Some archaeological results of the Bagnold-Mond expedition to the Gilf Kebir and Gebel 'Uweinat, southern Libyan desert. *J. Near East Stud.* **34**, 31–62.

Mace, A. C. (1921). Excavations at Lisht. *Bull. Metropol. Mus. Art* pt 2, 5–19.

(1922). Excavations at Lisht. *Bull Metropol. Mus. Art* pt 2, 4–18.

Maragioglio, V. and C. Rinaldi (1968). Note sulla piramide di Ameny 'Aamu. *Orientalia* **37**, 325–38.

(1971). Considerazioni sulla città *Dd-Snfrw*. *Orientalia* **40**, 67–74.

Marinatos, S. (1974). *Excavations at Thera, vol. VI (1962 season)*. Athens.

Martin, G. T. (1968). A new prince of Byblos. *J. Near East. Stud.* **27**, 141–2.

(1969). A ruler of Byblos of the Second Intermediate Period. *Berytus* **18**, 81–3.

Martin-Parday, E. (1976). *Untersuchungen zur ägyptischen Provinzialverwaltung bis zum Ende des Alten Reiches*. Hildesheim.

Matthews, J. M. (1975). An inscribed sherd from the Palestine Exploration Fund. *Palestine Exploration Quarterly* **107**, 151–3.

Matthiae, M. P. (1978). Recherches archéologiques à Ebla, 1977: le quartier administratif du palais royal G. *C.r. Acad. Inscriptions et Belles-Lettres*, 204–36.

Maystre, C. (1975). Découvertes récentes (1969–1972). près d'Akasha. In K. Michałowski (ed.), *Nubia: récentes recherches. Actes du colloque Nubiologique International au Musée national de Varsovie 19–22 juin 1972*, 88–92. Warsaw.

Mazar, B. (1968). The Middle Bronze Age in Palestine. *Israel Exploration J.* **18**, 65–97.

Mellaart, J. (1959). The royal treasure of Dorak. *Illustrated London News* 28 November 1959, 754.

(1979). Egyptian and Near Eastern chronology: a dilemma? *Antiquity* **53**, 6–18.

Mendelssohn, K. (1974). *The riddle of the pyramids* London.

Menghin, O. and K. Bittel (1934). Kasr el Sagha. *Mitt. dt. Inst. ägypt. Altertumskunde Kairo* **5**, 1–10.

Menu, B. (1970). La gestion du patrimoine foncier d'Hekanakhte. *Rev. Egypt.* **22**, 111–29.

Menu, B. and I. Harari (1974). La notion de propriété privée dans l'Ancien Empire égyptien. *Cahiers de Recherches de l'Institut de Papyrologie et d'Égyptologie de Lille* **2**, 125–54.

Merrillees, R. S. (1968). *The Cypriote Bronze Age pottery found in Egypt. Studies in Mediterranean Archaeology* **18**, Lund.

(1970). Evidence for the bichrome wheel-made ware in Egypt. *Austral. J. Bibl. Archaeol.* **1**, 3–27.

(1974). *Trade and transcendence in the Bronze Age Levant. Studies in Mediterranean Archaeology* **39**, Göteborg.

(1978). El-Lisht and Tell el-Yahudiya Ware in the Archaeological Museum of the American University of Beirut. *Levant* **10**, 75–98.

Meshel, Z. (1974). New data about the 'desert kites'. *Tel Aviv* **1**, 129–43.

Mesnil du Buisson, R. du (1970). *Etudes sur les dieux phéniciens hérités par l'Empire romain.* Leiden.

Meulenaere, H. de (1971). La statue d'un contemporain de Sébekhotep IV. *Bull. Inst. fr. Archéol. orient. Caire* **69**, 61–4.

Meyer, E. (1887). *Geschichte des alten Aegyptens.* Berlin.

(1968). *Einführung in die antike Staatskunde.* Darmstadt.

Michael, H. N. and E. K. Ralph (1970). Correction factors applied to Egyptian radiocarbon dates from the era before Christ. In I. U. Olsson (ed.), *Radiocarbon variations and absolute chronology.* 109–19. New York and Stockholm.

Michałowski, K., J. de Linage, J. Manteuffel and J. Sainte Fare Garnot (1938). *Tell Edfou 1938.* Cairo.

Michałowski, K., Ch. Desroches, J. de Linage, J. Manteuffel and Żejmo-Żejmis (1950). *Tell Edfou 1939.* Cairo.

Mills, A. J. (1965). The reconnaissance and survey from Gemai to Dal: a preliminary report for 1963–64. *Kush* **13**, 1–12.

(1967–8). The archaeological survey from Gemai to Dal – a report on the 1965–1966 season. *Kush* **15**, 200–10.

Mills, A. J. and H.-Å. Nordström (1966). The archaeological survey from Gemai to Dal. Preliminary report on the season 1964–65. *Kush* **14**, 1–15.

Mitchell, W. P. (1963). The hydraulic hypothesis: a reappraisal. *Curr. Anthrop.* **14**, 532–4.

Mond, Sir Robert and O. H. Myers (1937). *Cemeteries of Armant*, 2 vols. London.

Montet, P. (1928). *Byblos et l'Égypte. Quatre campagnes de fouilles à Gebeil 1921–1922–1923–1924.* Paris.

(1936). Les tombeaux de Siout et de Deir Rifeh, 3. *Kêmi* **6**, 131–63.

(1957). *Géographie de l'Égypte ancienne*, vol. 1. Paris.

(1964). Notes et documents pour servir à l'histoire des relations entre l'Égypte et la Syrie. XIII. *Kêmi* **17**, 61–8.

Morenz, S. (1973). *Egyptian religion.* Translated by A. E. Keep. London.

Morgan, J. de (1895). *Fouilles à Dahchour, mars–juin 1894.* Vienna.

(1897). *Carte de la nécropole memphite.* Cairo.

(1903). *Fouilles à Dahchour en 1894–1895.* Vienna.

Moursi, M. I. (1972). *Die Hohenpriester des Sonnengottes von der Frühzeit bis zum Ende des Neuen Reiches.* Munich and Berlin.

Moussa, A. M. (1971). A stela from Saqqara of a family devoted to the cult of King Unis. *Mitt. dt. archäol. Inst. Abt. Kairo* **27**, 81–4.

Mrsich, T. (1968). *Unstersuchungen zur Hausurkunde des Alten Reiches.* Berlin and Munich.

Müller, D. (1961). Der gute Hirte. Ein Beitrag zur Geschichte ägyptischer Bildrede. *Z. ägypt. Sprache Altertumskunde* **85**, 126–44.

Müller, H. W. (1960). Kopf einer Statue des ägyptischen Sonnengottes aus dem Alten Reich. *Pantheon* N.S. **18**, 109–13.

(1964). Der Gute Gott Radjedef, Sohn des Rê. *Z. ägypt. Sprache Altertumskunde* **91**, 129–33.

Murnane, W. J. (1977). *Ancient Egyptian coregencies.* Chicago.

Murray, G. W. (1962). Graves of oxen in the eastern desert of Egypt. *J. Egypt. Archaeol.* **12**, 248–9.

(1965). Harkhuf's third journey. *Geogrl J.* **131**, 72–5.

Naumann, R. (1939). Der Tempel des Mittleren Reiches in Medīnet Mādi. *Mitt. dt. Inst. ägypt. Altertumskunde Kairo* **8**, 185–9.

Needler, W. (1961). Four relief-sculptures from the pyramid of Sesostris I at Lisht. *Annual (Art & Archaeol. Div.), Roy. Ontario Mus.* 15–26.

Newberry, P. E. (1938). Three Old Kingdom travellers to Byblos and Pwenet. *J. Egypt. Archaeol.* **24**, 182–4.

Nims, C. F. (1938). Some notes on the family of Mereruka. *J. Am. orient. Soc.* **58**, 638–47.

Nordström, H.-Å. (1966). A-Group and C-Group in Upper Nubia. *Kush* **14**, 63–8.

el-Nur, O. (1976). [Kerma culture and its origins.] *Vestnik Drevnei Istorii* **1**, 29–51. (In Russian, with English summary.)

O'Connor, D. B. (1971). Ancient Egypt and Black Africa – early contacts. *Expedition* **14**, 2–9.

(1972). A regional population in Egypt to circa 600 B.C. In B. Spooner (ed.), *Population growth: anthropological implications*, 78–100. Cambridge, Mass. and London.

(1974). Political systems and archaeological data in Egypt: 2600–1780 B.C. *World Archaeol.* **6**, 15–38.

Oren, E. D. (1973a). The Early Bronze IV period in northern Palestine and its cultural and chronological setting. *Bull. Am. Sch. orient. Res.* **210**, 20–37.

(1973b). The overland route between Egypt and Canaan in the Early Bronze Age. *Israel Exploration J.* **23**, 198–205.

Osing, J. (1976). Ächtungstexte aus dem Alten Reich (II). *Mitt. dt. archäol. Inst. Abt. Kairo* **32**, 133–85.

Otto, E. (1951). Die Endsituation der ägyptischen Kultur. *Die Welt als geschichte* **114**, 203–13.

(1956). Prolegomena zur Frage der Gesetzgebung und Rechtssprechung in Ägypten. *Mitt. dt. archäol. Inst. Abt. Kairo* **14**, 150–9.

(1964–6). Geschichtsbild und Geschichtsschreibung in Ägypten. *Welt des Orients* **3**, 161–76.

(1969). Legitimation des Herrschens im pharaonischen Ägypten. *Saeculum*, Munich **20**, 385–411.

Parker, R. A. (1950). *The calendars of ancient Egypt.* Chicago.

(1970). The beginning of the lunar month in ancient Egypt. *J. Near East. Stud.* **29**, 217–20.

(1976). The Sothic dating of the Twelfth and Eighteenth Dynasties. *Studies in honor of George R. Hughes* 177–89. Chicago.

Parr, P. J. (1968). The origin of the rampart fortifications of Middle Bronze Age Palestine and Syria. *Z. dt. Palästina-Vereins* **84**, 18–45.

Peet, T. E. (1914). *The cemeteries of Abydos, pt II: 1911–1912. Egypt Exploration Fund Memoir* **34**, London.

(1930). *The great tomb-robberies of the Twentieth Egyptian Dynasty.* Oxford.

Pendlebury, J. D. S. (1930). *Aegyptiaca; a catalogue of Egyptian objects in the Aegean area.* Cambridge.

Peterson, B. J. (1965–6). Two Egyptian stelae. *Orient. Suecana* **14–15**, 3–8.

Petrie, W. M. F. (1890). *Kahun, Gurob, and Hawara.* London.

(1891). *Illahun, Kahun and Gurob.* London.

(1901). *Diospolis Parva. Egypt Exploration Fund, Memoir* **20**. London.

(1902). *Abydos, pt I: 1902. Egypt Exploration Fund Memoir* **22**. London.

(1903). *Abydos pt II: 1903. Egypt Exploration Fund Memoir* **24**. London.

(1906). *Hyksos and Israelite cities.* London.

(1909). *Qurneh.* London.

(1924a). *A history of Egypt, vol. I: from the earliest kings to the XVth Dynasty,* 11th edn, revised. London.

(1924b). *A history of Egypt, vol. II: during the XVIIth and XVIIIth Dynasties,* 7th edn, enlarged. London.

Petrie, W. M. F. and G. Brunton (1924). *Sedment,* vol. 1. London.

Piotrovsky, B. B. (1966). [Two Egyptian inscriptions of the Sixth Dynasty in Wadi Allaki.] *Vestnik Drevnei Istorii* **92** (sic, read **95**), 80–2. (In Russian.)

(1967). The Early Dynastic settlement of Khor-Daoud and Wadi-Allaki: the ancient route to the gold mines. In *Fouilles en Nubie (1961–1963)* (*Campagne Internationale de l'UNESCO pour la sauvegarde des monuments de la Nubie*), 127–40. Cairo.

Pirenne, J. (1932–5). *Histoire des institutions et du droit privé de l'ancienne Égypte.* Brussels.

(1949). Le domaine dans l'ancien Empire égyptien. *Recueils Soc. Jean Bodin* **4**, 5–24.

Pirenne, J. and M. Stracmans (1954). Le testament à l'époque de l'Ancien Empire égyptien. *Rev. Int. Droits Antiquité* **1**, 49–72.

Porter, B. and R. L. B. Moss (1927–51). *Topographical bibliography of ancient Egyptian hieroglyphic texts, reliefs and paintings* 1st edn, 7 vols. Oxford.

(1972). *Topographical bibliography...*, vol. 11 (2nd edn).

Posener, G. (1952). A propos des graffiti d'Abisko. *Archiv Orientální* **20**, 163–6.

(1956). *Littérature et politique dans l'Égypte de la XIIe dynastie.* Paris.

(1957a). Le conte de Néferkarè et du général Siséné (Recherches Littéraires, VI). *Rev. Égypt.* **11**, 119–37.

(1957b). Les Asiatiques en Égypte sous la XIIe et XIIIe dynasties. *Syria* **34**, 145–63.

(1958a). Pour une localisation du pays Koush au Moyen Empire. *Kush* 6, 39–68.

(1958b). [Nehasyu and Medjayu.] *Z. ägypt. Sprache Altertumskunde* 83, 38–43.

(1960). *De la divinité du Pharaon. Cahiers de la société Asiatique* 15). Paris.

(1966). Les textes d'envoûtement de Mirgissa. *Syria* 43, 277–87.

(1969). Sur l'emploi euphémique de ḫftj(w) 'ennemi (s)'. *Z. ägypt Sprache Altertumskunde* 96, 30–5.

(1971). À la recherche de nouveaux textes d'envoûtement. In *Proc. V World Congr. Jewish Studies*, 144–9. Jerusalem.

Posener-Kriéger, P. (1969). Sur un nom de métal égyptien. In *Ugaritica* 6 (*Institut français d'Archéologie de Beyrouth: Bibliothèque archéologique et historique* 81), 419–26. Paris.

(1976). *Les archives du temple funéraire de Néferirkarê-Kakaï, les papyrus d'Abousir; traduction et commentaire*. Cairo and Paris.

Posener-Kriéger, P. and J. L. de Cenival (1968). *Hieratic papyri in the British Museum, Series V: The Abu Sir Papyri*. London.

Pounds, N. J. G. (1969). The urbanization of the Classical world. *Ann. Assoc. Am. Geogr.* 59, 135–57.

Prag, K. (1974). The Intermediate Early Bronze-Middle Bronze Age: an interpretation of the evidence from Transjordan, Syria and Lebanon. *Levant* 6, 69–116.

Priese, K.-H. (1974). *'rm* und *'ʒm*, das Land Irame. Eine Beitrag zur Topographie des Sudan im Altertum. *Altorient. Forsch.* 1, 7–41.

Pritchard, J. B. (ed.) (1969). *Ancient Near Eastern texts relating to the Old Testament*, 3rd edn with supplement. Princeton.

Quibell, J. E. (1898). *El Kab*. London.

(1900). *Hierakonpolis*, pt 1. London.

(1907). *Excavations at Saqqara (1905–1906)*. Cairo.

Quibell, J. E. and F. W. Green (1902). *Hierakonpolis*, pt 2. London.

Quitta, H. (1972). Zu einigen Problemen und Perspektiven der Radiocarbondatierung. *Ausgrabungen und Funde* 17, 99–109.

Rainey, A. F. (1972). The world of Sinuhe. *Israel Orient. Stud.* 2, 369–408.

Ralph, E. K., H. N. Michael and M. C. Han (1973). Radiocarbon dates and reality. *MASCA Newsletter*, 9, no. 1.

Randall-MacIver, D. and C. L. Woolley (1911). *Buhen*. Philadelphia.

el-Rayah, M. B. (1974). The problems of Kerma culture of ancient Sudan re-considered in the light of ancient Sudan civilization as a continuous process. *Ethnogr.-archäol. Z.* 15, 287–304.

Read, J. G. (1970). Early Eighteenth Dynasty chronology. *J. Near East. Stud.* 29, 1–11.

Redford, D. B. (1970). The Hyksos invasion in history and tradition. *Orientalia* 39, 1–51.

(1975). The historiography of ancient Egypt. Unpublished paper, Conference on Ancient Egypt: problems of history, sources and methods. Cairo.

(1977). The oases in Egyptian history to Classical times. *Newsl. Soc. Stud. Egypt. Antiquities* 7, I, 7–10; II, 2–4; III, 2–6.

Reisner, G. A. (1918). The tomb of Hepzefa, nomarch of Siût. *J. Egypt. Archaeol.* **5**, 79–98.

(1923). *Excavations at Kerma*, pts I–III, pts IV–V. Cambridge, Mass.

(1931). *Mycerinus: the temples of the third pyramid at Giza.* Cambridge, Mass.

(1955). Clay sealings of Dynasty XIII from Uronarti Fort. *Kush* **3**, 26–9.

Reisner, G. A. and W. S. Smith (1955). *A history of the Giza necropolis, vol. II: The tomb of Hetep-heres the mother of Cheops.* Cambridge, Mass.

Reisner, G. A., D. Dunham and J. M. A. Janssen (1960). *Semna Kumma. (Second Cataract Forts*, vol. I.) Boston.

Reisner, G. A., N. F. Wheeler and D. Dunham (1967). *Uronarti Shalfak Mirgissa. (Second Cataract Forts*, vol. II.) Boston.

Resch, W. F. E. (1966–9). Das Alter der östägyptischen und nubischen Felsbilder. *IPEK* **22**, 114–22.

(1967a). *Das Rind in den Felsbilddarstellungen Nordafrikas.* Wiesbaden.

(1967b). *Die Felsbilder Nubiens.* Graz.

Reymond, E. A. E. (1969). *The mythical origin of the Egyptian temple.* Manchester.

Riad, H. (1958). Le culte d'Amenemhat III au Fayoum à l'époque ptolémaïque. *Ann. Serv. Antiquités Égypte* **55**, 203–6.

Ricke, H. (1965). *Das Sonnenheiligtum des Königs Userkaf*, vol. I. Cairo.

Riefstahl, E. (1956). Two hairdressers of the Eleventh Dynasty. *J. Near East. Stud.* **15**, 10–17.

Robichon, C. and Varille, A. (1940). *Description sommaire du temple primitif de Médamud.* Cairo.

Rothenberg, B. (1969). An archaeological survey of south Sinai; first season 1967/68, a preliminary report. *Mus. Haaretz Bull.* **11**, 22–38.

(1970–1). An archaeological survey of South Sinai. First season 1967/1968, preliminary report. *Palestine Exploration Quarterly* **102**, 4–29.

(1972). Sinai explorations 1967–1972. *Mus. Haaretz Bull.* **14**, 31–42.

(1972–3). Sinai explorations III. A preliminary report on the sixth season of an archaeological survey of Sinai, February 1973. *Mus. Haaretz Yearb.* **15–16**, 16–34.

Rowe, A. (1930). *The topography and history of Beth-Shan.* Philadelphia.

(1940). *The four Canaanite temples of Beth-shan.* Philadelphia.

Said, R., C. Albritton, F. Wendorf, R. Schild and M. Kobusiewicz (1972a). A preliminary report on the Holocene geology and archaeology of the northern Fayum desert. *Playa Lake Symposium*, 41–61. Texas.

(1972b). Remarks on the Holocene geology and archaeology of northern Fayum desert. *Archaeologia Polona* **13**, 7–22.

Saleh, A.-A. (1972). Some problems relating to the Pwenet reliefs at Deir el-Bahari. *J. Egypt. Archaeol.* **58**, 140–58.

(1974). Excavations around Mycerinus pyramid complex. *Mitt. dt. archäol. Inst. Abt. Kairo* **30**, 131–54.

Saleh, M. (1977). *Three Old-Kingdom tombs at Thebes.* Mainz.

Sanders, J. A. (ed.) (1970). *Near Eastern archaeology in the twentieth century.* New York.

Sauneron, S. (1954). La justice à la porte des temples (à propos du nom égyptien des propylées). *Bull. Inst. Fr. Archéol. orient. Caire* **54**, 117–27.

Säve-Söderbergh, T. (1941). *Ägypten und Nubien: ein Beitrag zur Geschichte altägyptischer Aussenpolitik.* Lund.

(1946). *The navy of the Eighteenth Egyptian Dynasty.* Uppsala and Leipzig.

(1949). A Buhen stela from the Second Intermediate Period (Khartūm no. 18). *J. Egypt. Archaeol.* **35**, 50–8.

(1956). The Nubian Kingdom of the Second Intermediate Period. *Kush* **4**, 54–61.

(1963). The tomb of the Prince of Teh-khet, Amenemhet. *Kush* **11**, 159–74.

(1969). Die Akkulturation der nubischen C-Gruppe im Neuen Reich. *Z. dt. morgenländ. Ges. (Suppl I)*, **17**, 12–20.

Säve-Söderbergh, T. and Olsson, I. U. (1970). C14 dating and Egyptian chronology. In I. U. Olsson (ed.), *Radiocarbon variations and absolute chronology (Proc. XII Nobel Symposium)*, 35–53. New York and Stockholm.

Sayed, A. M. A. H. (1977). Discovery of the site of the 12th Dynasty port at Wadi Gawasis on the Red Sea shore. *Rev. Egypt* **29**, 138–78.

Schachermeyr, F. (1967). *Ägäis und Orient.* Vienna.

Schäfer, H. (1902). *Ein Bruchstück altägyptischer Annalen.* Berlin.

Scharff, A. (1920). Ein Rechnungsbuch des königlichen Hofes aus der 13. Dynastie (Papyrus Boulaq Nr. 18). *Z. ägypt. Sprache Altertumskunde* **56**, 51–68.

Schenkel, W. (1962). *Frühmittelägyptische Studien.* Bonn.

(1965). *Memphis Herakleopolis Theben; die epigraphischen Zeugnisse der 7.–11. Dynastie Agyptens. Ägyptologische Abhandlungen* **12**. Wiesbaden.

(1973). Ein Türsturz von der Grabkapelle des Königs Wзḥ-ʿnḫ Antef. *Mitt. dt. archäol. Inst. Abt. Kairo* **29**, 215–19.

(1978). *Die Bewässerungsrevolution im alten Ägypten.* Mainz. (This important book appeared too late for its conclusions to be considered in the text.)

Schmid, H. H. (1968). *Gerechtigkeit als Weltordnung.* Tübingen.

Schmitz, B. (1976). *Untersuchungen zum Titel Sз-Njswt 'Königssohn'.* Bonn.

Schulman, A. R. (1976). The Egyptian seal impressions from 'En Besor. *'Atiqot* **11**, 16–26.

Seger, J. D. (1975). The MBII fortifications at Shechem and Gezer: a Hyksos retrospective. *Eretz-Israel* **12**, 34*–45*.

Seters, J. van (1964). A date for the 'Admonitions' in the Second Intermediate Period. *J. Egypt. Archaeol.* **50**, 13–23.

(1966). *The Hyksos; a new investigation.* New Haven and London.

Sethe, K. (1932–3). *Urkunden des alten Reichs.* G. Steindorff (ed.), *Urkunden des ägyptischen Altertums*, 2nd edn, vol. 1. Leipzig.

Seyfried, K.-J. (1981). *Beiträge zu den Expeditionen des Mittleren Reiches in die Ost-Wüste* (Hildesheimer Ägyptologische Beiträge, 15.) Hildesheim.

Shaw, W. B. Kennedy (1936a). An expedition in the Southern Libyan desert. *Geogl J.* **87**, 193–221.

(1936b). Two burials from the south Libyan desert. *J. Egypt. Archaeol.* **22**, 47–50.

Shore, A. F. (1973). A soldier's archery case from ancient Egypt. *Brit Mus. Quarterly* **37**, 4–9.

Simpson, W. K. (1954). Two Middle Kingdom personifications of seasons. *J. Near East. Stud.* **13**, 265–8.

(1956). The single-dated monuments of Sesostris I: an aspect of the institution of coregency in the Twelfth Dynasty. *J. Near East. Stud.* **15**, 214–19.

(1957). Sobkemḥēt, a vizier of Sesostris III. *J. Egypt. Archaeol.* **43**, 26–9.

(1959). Historical and lexical notes on the new series of Hammamat inscriptions. *J. Near East. Stud.* **18**, 20–37.

(1963a). Studies in the Twelfth Egyptian Dynasty: I–II. *J. Am. Res. Cent. Egypt* **2**, 53–63.

(1963b). *Papyrus Reisner I: the records of a building project in the reign of Sesostris I.* Boston.

(1963c). *Heka-nefer.* New Haven and Philadelphia.

(1965). *Papyrus Reisner II: accounts of the dockyard workshop at This in the reign of Sesostris I.* Boston.

(1969a). The Dynasty XIII stela from the Wadi Hammamat. *Mitt. dt. archäol. Inst. Abt. Kairo* **25**, 154–8.

(1969b). *Papyrus Reisner III; the records of a building project in the early Twelfth Dynasty.* Boston.

(1972). A tomb chapel relief of the reign of Amunemhet III and some observations on the length of the reign of Sesostris III. *Chronique d'Egypte* **47**, nos. 93–94, 45–54.

(ed.) (1973). *The literature of ancient Egypt; an anthology of stories, instructions, and poetry,* with translations by R. O. Faulkner, E. F. Wente, Jr., and W. K. Simpson. New Haven and London.

Slater, R. A. (1970). Dendereh and the University Museum, 1888–1970. *Expedition* **12**, 15–20.

Smith, H. S. (1964). Egypt and C14 dating. *Antiquity* **38**, 32–7.

(1966a). The Nubian B-Group. *Kush* **14**, 69–124.

(1966b). Preliminary report on the rock inscriptions in the Egypt Exploration Society's concession at Buhen. *Kush* **14**, 330–4.

(1966c). Kor: report on the excavations of the Egypt Exploration Society at Kor, 1965. *Kush* **14**, 187–243.

(1972). The rock inscriptions of Buhen. *J. Egypt. Archaeol.* **58**, 43–61.

(1976). *The fortress of Buhen; the inscriptions. Egypt Exploration Society Memoir* **48**. London.

Smith, H. S. and A. Smith (1976). A reconsideration of the Kamose texts. *Z. ägypt. Sprache Altertumskunde* **103**, 48–76.

Smith, P. E. L. (1968). Problems and possibilities of the prehistoric rock art of northern Africa. *Afr. Hist. Stud.* **1**, 1–39.

Smith, W. S. (1946). *A history of Egyptian sculpture and painting in the Old Kingdom.* Boston and London.

(1957). Fragments of a statuette of Chephren. *Wien. Z. Kunde Morgenlandes* **54**, 186–90.

(1958). *The art and architecture of ancient Egypt.* Harmondsworth.

(1962). Some recent accessions. *Bull. Mus. Fine Arts, Boston* **60**, no. 322, 132–6.

(1965). *Interconnections in the ancient Near East: a study of the relationships between the arts of Egypt, the Aegean, and Western Asia.* New Haven and London.

(1969). Influence of the Middle Kingdom of Egypt in Western Asia, especially in Byblos. *Am. J. Archaeol.* **73**, 277–81.

Smither, P. C. (1941). A tax-assessor's journal of the Middle Kingdom. *J. Egypt. Archaeol.* **27**, 74–6.

(1945). The Semnah Despatches. *J. Egypt. Archaeol.* **31**, 3–10.

(1948). The report concerning the slave-girl Senbet. *J. Egypt. Archaeol.* **34**, 31–4.

Soghor, C. L. (1967). Mendes 1965 and 1966, II. The inscriptions from Tell el Rub'a. *J. Am. Res. Cent. Egypt* **6**, 16–32.

Steckeweh, H. (1936). *Die Fürstengräber von Qaw.* Leipzig.

Steindorff, G. (1937). *Aniba,* vol. II. Glückstadt.

Stiebing, W. H. (1971). Hyksos burials in Palestine: a review of the evidence. *J. Near East. Stud.* **30**, 110–17.

Stracmans, M. (1955). Textes des actes de fondation de l'Ancien Empire. *Rev. Int. Droits Antiquité* **2**, 31–8.

(1958). Le titre de Hatj-â sous l'Ancien Empire égyptien. *Rev. Int. Droits Antiquité* **5**, 21–32.

Strouhal, E. and J. Jungwirth (1971). Anthropological problems of the Middle Empire and Late Roman Sayala. (Preliminary report on the first stage of the elaboration of the Austrian anthropological material from Nubia). *Mitt. anthrop. Ges. Wien* **101**, 10–23.

Tanner, R. (1974). Bemerkungen zur Sukzession der Pharaonen in der 12., 17., und 18. Dynastie. I. *Z. ägypt. Sprache Altertumskunde* **101**, 121–9.

Théodoridès, A. (1959). La procédure dans le *Pap. Berlin 10.470. Rev. Int. Droits Antiquité* **6**, 131–54.

(1960). Du rapport entre les parties du *Pap. Brooklyn 35.1446. Rev. Int. Droits Antiquité* **7**, 55–145.

(1962). Le rôle du Vizir dans la *Stèle Juridique de Karnak. Rev. Int. Droits Antiquité* **9**, 45–135.

(1967). À propos de la loi dans l'Égypte pharaonique. *Rev. Int. Droits Antiquité* **14**, 107–52.

(1968–72). À propos du sixième contrat du gouverneur Hâpidjefa. *Annuaire Inst. Philol. Hist. Orientales et Slaves* **20**, 439–66.

(1970). Le testament dans l'Égypte ancienne. *Rev. Int. Droits Antiquité* **17**, 117–216.

(1971a). Les contrats d'Hâpidjefa. *Rev. Int. Droits Antiquité* **18**, 109–251.

(1971b). The concept of law in ancient Egypt. In J. R. Harris (ed.), *The legacy of Egypt,* 2nd edn, 291–322. Oxford.

(1972). La révocation d'un acte testamentaire dans le *Pap. Kahoun VII.1. Rev. Int. Droits antiquité* **19**, 129–48.

(1973). Les Égyptiens anciens, 'citoyens' ou 'sujets de Pharaon'. *Rev. Int. Droits Antiquité* **20**, 51–112.

(1974). Mise en ordre chronologique des éléments de la Stèle Juridique de Karnak, avec ses influences sur la procédure. *Rev. Int. Droits Antiquité* **21**, 31–74.

Thompson, T. L. (1975). *The settlement of Sinai and the Negev in the Bronze Age.* Wiesbaden.

(1978). The background of the Patriarchs: a reply to William Dever and Malcolm Clark. *J. Stud. Old Testament* **9**, 2–43.

Toynbee, A. (1971). *An ekistical study of the Hellenic city-state.* Athens.

Trigger, B. G. (1965). *History and settlement in Lower Nubia.* New Haven.

(1976a). Kerma: the rise of an African civilization. *Int. J. Afr. hist. stud.* **9**, 1–21.

(1976b). *Nubia under the Pharaohs.* London.

*Tübinger Atlas des Vorderen Orients (TAVO).* Wiesbaden 1977– .

Tufnell, O. (1973). The Middle Bronze Age scarab-seals from burials on the mound at Megiddo. *Levant* **5**, 69–82.

(1975). Seal impressions from Kahûn town and Uronarti fort. *J. Egypt. Archaeol.* **61**, 67–101.

Tufnell, O. and W. A. Ward (1966). Relations between Byblos, Egypt and Mesopotamia at the end of the third millennium B.C. A study of the Montet jar. *Syria* **43**, 165–241.

Tylor, J. J. and F. Ll. Griffith (1894). *The tomb of Paheri at el Kab. Egypt Exploration Fund Memoir* **11**. London.

Valloggia, M. (1962). Amenemhat IV et sa corégence avec Amenemhat III. *Rev. Egypt.* **21**, 107–33.

(1974). Les vizirs des XIᵉ et XIIᵉ dynasties. *Bull Inst. fr. Archéol. orient. Caire* **74**, 123–34.

Vandersleyen, C. (1971). *Les guerres d'Amosis.* Brussels.

(ed.) (1975). *Das Alte Ägypten.* Berlin.

Vandier, J. (1936). *La famine dans l'Égypte ancienne.* Cairo.

(1950). *Moʿalla. La tombe d'Ankhtifi et la tombe de Sébekhotep.* Cairo.

(1958). *Manuel d'archéologie égyptienne vol. III: Les grandes époques, la statuaire.* Paris.

(1968). Une stèle égyptienne portant un nouveau nom royal de la troisième dynastie. *C.r. Acad. Inscriptions et Belles-Lettres,* 16–22.

Velde, H. te (1967). *Seth, god of confusion: a study of his role in Egyptian mythology and religion.* Leiden.

Vercoutter, J. (1956). *L'Egypte et le monde égéen préhellénique: étude critique des sources égyptiennes.* Cairo.

(1957). Upper Egyptian settlers in Middle Kingdom Nubia. *Kush* **5**, 61–9.

(1959). The gold of Kush. *Kush* **7**, 120–53.

(1964). La stèle de Mirgissa IM.209 et la localisation d'Iken (Kor ou Mirgissa?). *Rev. Egypt.* **16**, 179–91.

(1966). Semna South fort and the records of Nile levels at Kumma. *Kush* **14**, 125–64.

(1967). Review of Trigger, B. G. History and settlement in Lower Nubia, *Rev. d'Égyptologie* **19**, 203–12.

(1970). *Mirgissa* vol. 1. Paris.

(1975a). *Mirgissa vol. II: Les nécropoles* pt 1. Paris and Lille.

(1975b). Le roi Ougaf et la XIIIᵉ dynastie sur la IIᵐᵉ cataracte (stèle de Mirgissa IM.375). *Rev. Egypt.* **27**, 222–34.

(1976a). Egyptologie et climatologie. Les crues du Nil à Semneh. *Etudes sur l'Egypte et le Soudan anciens (Cahiers de Recherches de l'Institut de papyrologie et d'Egyptologie de Lille* **4**), 139–72.

(1976b). *Mirgissa, vol. III: Les nécropoles,* pt 2. Paris and Lille.

(1977a). Les travaux de l'Institut français d'Archéologie orientale en 1976–1977. *Bull. Inst. fr. Archéol. orient. Caire* **77**, 271–86.

(1977b). Les poids de Mirgissa et le 'standard-cuivre' au Moyen Empire. *Ägypten und Kusch (Schriften zur Geschichte und Kultur des Alten Orients* **13**), 437–45.

Vermeule, E. and Vermeule C. (1970). Aegean gold hoard and the court of Egypt. *Curator* **13**, 32–42.

Vila, A. (1963). Un dépot de textes d'envoûtement au Moyen Empire. *J. Savants* 135–60.

(1970). L'armement de la forteresse de Mirgissa-Iken. *Rev. Égypt.* **22**, 171–99.

(1973). Un rituel d'envoûtement au Moyen Empire égyptien. In *L'homme, hier et aujourd'hui: recueil d'études en hommage à André Leroi-Gourhan*, 625–39. Paris.

(1975–    ). *La prospection archéologique de la vallée du Nil, au sud de la Cataracte de Dal (Nubie Soudanaise), vols.* 1ff. Paris.

Vycichl, W. (1954–6). Die Fürsten von Libyen. *Ann. Ist. Univ. orient. Naples* **6**, 43–8.

(1959). The burial of the Sudanese kings in the Middle Ages. *Kush* **7**, 221–2.

Waddell, W. G. (1940). *Manetho.* Loeb Classical Library, Cambridge, Mass. and London.

Wainwright, G. A. (1927). El Hibeh and esh Shurafa and their connection with Herakleopolis and Cusae. *Ann. Serv. Antiquités Égypte* **27**, 76–104.

Ward, W. A. (1961). Egypt and the East Mediterranean in the early second millennium B.C. *Orientalia* **30**, 22–45 and 129–55.

(1964). Relations between Egypt and Mesopotamia from prehistoric times to the end of the Middle Kingdom. *J. econ. social Hist. Orient* **7**, 1–45 and 121–35.

(1970). The origin of Egyptian design-amulets ('button seals'). *J. Egypt. Archaeol.* **56**, 65–80.

(1971). *Egypt and the East Mediterranean world 2200–1900 B.C.* Beirut.

(1976). Some personal names of the Hyksos period rulers and notes on the epigraphy of their scarabs. *Ugarit-Forsch.* **8**, 353–69.

Warren, P. (1969). *Minoan stone vases.* Cambridge.

Watermann, U. and R. Watermann (1957). Über die rätselvolle Gestalt der Königin von Punt. *Homo* **8**, 148–54.

Weeks, K. (ed.) 1979. *Egyptology and the social sciences, five studies.* Cairo.

Weigall, A. E. P. (1907). *A report on the antiquities of Lower Nubia.* Oxford.

Weil, A. (1908). *Die Veziere des Pharaonenreiches, pt 1: Die Veziere des Alten Reiches.* Strasbourg.

Weinstein, J. M. (1975). Egyptian relations with Palestine in the Middle Kingdom. *Bull. Am. Sch. orient. Res.* **217**, 1–16.

Wente, E. (1975). Thutmose III's accession and the beginning of the New Kingdom. *J. Near East. Stud.* **34**, 265–72.

Wildung, D. (1969a). *Die Rolle ägyptischer Könige im Bewusstsein ihrer Nachwelt,* pt 1. Munich and Berlin.

(1969b). Zur Frühgeschichte des Amun-Tempels von Karnak. *Mitt. dt. archäol. Inst. Abt. Kairo* **25**, 212–19.

(1972). Two representations of gods from the early Old Kingdom. *Misc. Wilbourana* 1, 145–60.

(1974). Aufbau und Zweckbestimmung der Königsliste von Karnak. *Götting. Misz.* 9, 42–8.

Williams, R. J. (1964). Literature as a medium of political propaganda in ancient Egypt. In W. S. McCullough (ed.), *The seed of wisdom: essays in honour of T. J. Meek*, 14–30. Toronto.

Wilson, J. A. (1951). *The burden of Egypt: an interpretation of ancient Egyptian culture.* Chicago. (Reprinted as *The culture of Ancient Egypt.*)

Winlock, H. E. (1947). *The rise and fall of the Middle Kingdom in Thebes.* New York.

Winter, E. (1957). Zur Deutung der Sonnenheiligtümer der 5. Dynastie. *Wien. Z. Kunde Morgenlandes,* 54, 222–33.

Wittfogel, K. A. (1955). Developmental aspects of hydraulic societies. In J. H. Steward *et al., Irrigation civilizations: a comparative study.* Washington. (Reprinted (1971) in S. Streuver (ed.), *Prehistoric agriculture,* 557–71. New York.)

(1957). *Oriental despotism: a comparative study of total power.* New Haven and London.

Wright, G. E. (1971). The archaeology of Palestine from the Neolithic through the Middle Bronze Age. *J. Am. orient. Soc.* 91, 276–93.

Wright, G. R. H. (1968). Tell el-Yehūdīyah and the glacis. *Z. dt. Palästina-Vereins* 84, 1–17.

Yadin, Y. (1955). The earliest record of Egypt's military penetration into Asia? *Israel Exploration J.* 5, 1–16.

Young, W. J. (1972). The fabulous gold of the Pactolus Valley. *Boston Mus. Bull.* 70, no. 359, 5–13.

Yoyotte, J. (1950). Les filles de Téti et la reine Sheshé du Papyrus Ebers. *Rev. Egypt.* 7, 184–5.

(1951). Un document relatif aux rapports de la Libye et de la Nubie. *Bull. Soc. fr. Egyptol.* 6, 9–14.

(1952). Trois notes pour servir à l'histoire d'Edfou. *Kêmi* 12, 91–2.

(1958). À propos de la parenté féminine du roi Téti (VIᵉ dynastie). *Bull. Inst. fr. Archéol. orient. Caire* 57, 91–8.

(1975). Les *Sementiou* et l'exploitation des régions minières à l'Ancien Empire. *Bull. Soc. fr. Egyptol.* 73, 44–55.

Žaba, Z. (1951). Dating of the social revolution in ancient Egypt. (Summary of a lecture.) *Archiv Orientální* 19, 615.

Zayadine, F. (1973). Recent excavations on the citadel of Amman. (A preliminary report.) *Ann. Dept Antiquities Jordan* 18, 17–35.

Zibelius, K. (1972). *Afrikanische Orts- und Völkernamen in hieroglyphischen und hieratischen Texten.* Wiesbaden.

(1978). *Ägyptische Siedlungen nach Texten des Alten Reiches.* (Beihefte zum Tübinger Atlas des Vorderen Orients, Reihe B, 19.) Weisbaden.

3. NEW KINGDOM AND THIRD INTERMEDIATE PERIOD, 1552–664 BC

Adams, W. A. (1964). Post-pharaonic Nubia in the light of archaeology I. *J. Egypt. Archaeol.* **50**, 102–20.

Adams, W. Y. (1977a). *Nubia: corridor to Africa*. London.

(1977b). Reflections on the archaeology of Kerma. In E. Endesfelter *et al.* (eds.), *Ägypten und Kusch*, 41–51. *Schriften zur Geschichte und Kultur des Alten Orients*. **13**. Berlin.

Aharoni, Y. (1968). *The Land of the Bible: a historical geography*. Translated by A. F. Rainey. London.

Albright, W. F. (1975). The Amarna letters from Palestine. In *Cambridge Ancient History*, 3rd edn, vol. II, pt 2, ch. 20.

Aldred, C. (1968). *Akhenaten, Pharaoh of Egypt: a new study*. London.

(1969). The 'New Year' gifts to the pharaoh. *J. Egypt. Archaeol.* **55**, 73–81.

(1970). The foreign gifts offered to pharaoh. *J. Egypt. Archaeol.* **56**, 105–16.

(1975). Egypt: the Amarna period and the end of the eighteenth dynasty. In *Cambridge Ancient History*, 3rd edn, vol. II, pt 2, ch. 19.

Aldred, C. and A. T. Sandison (1961). The tomb of Akhenaten at Thebes. *J. Egypt. Archaeol.* **47**, 41–65.

(1962). The Pharaoh Akhenaten: a problem in Egyptology and pathology. *Bull. Hist. Med.* **36**, 293–316.

Anthes, R. (1940). Das Bild einer Gerichtsverhandlung und das Grab des Mes aus Sakkara. *Mitt. deutsch. Inst. ägypt. Altertumskunde Kairo* **9**, 93–119.

Arkell, A. J. (1950). Varia Sudanica. *J. Egypt Archaeol.* **36**, 24–40.

(1961). *A History of the Sudan. From the earliest times to 1821*, 2nd edn. London.

Assman, J. (1972). Palast oder Tempel? Überlegungen zur Architektur und Topographie von Amarna. *J. Near East. Stud.* **31**, 143–55.

Astour, M. C. (1963). Place names from the kingdom of Alalakh in the north Syrian list of Thutmose III: a study in historical topography. *J. Near East. Stud.* **22**, 220–41.

Baer, K. (1962). The low price of land in ancient Egypt, *J. Am. Res. Cent. Egypt* **1**, 25–45.

Bakir, Abd el-M. (1952). *Slavery in Pharaonic Egypt*. Supplement to *Annales du Service des Antiquités de l'Egypte Cahier* **18**. Cairo.

Barbour, K. M. (1961). *The Republic of the Sudan. A regional geography*. London.

Barnett, R. D. (1975). The Sea Peoples. In *Cambridge Ancient History*, 3rd edn, vol. II, pt 2, ch. 28.

Bates, O. (1914). *The Eastern Libyans*. London.

Beckerath, J. von (1951). *Tanis und Theben*. Ägyptologische Forschungen **16**. Glückstadt–Hamburg–New York.

Bell, L. (1973). Once more the 'w: 'interpreters' or 'foreigners'?, *Newsl. Am. Res. Cent. Egypt* **87**, 33.

Bennett, J. (1939). The restoration inscription of Tut'ankhamun, *J. Egypt. Archaeol.* **25**, 8–15.

Bierbrier, M. L. (1975). *The Late New Kingdom in Egypt (c. 1300–664 B.C.). A genealogical and chronological investigation*. Warminster.

Bleeker, C. J. (1967). *Egyptian festivals. Enactments of religious renewal*. Leiden.

Bonnet, H. (1952). *Reallexikon der ägyptischen Religiongeschichte*. Berlin.

Breasted, J. H. (1906). *Ancient records of Egypt*, 5 vols. Chicago.

(1927). *A history of Egypt from the earliest times to the Persian conquest*, 2nd edn. London.

Brunner-Traut, E. (1976). Giraffe. In H. W. Helck and W. Westendorf (eds.), *Lexikon der Ägyptologie*, Bd. II Lfg. 4 (Lfg. 12). Wiesbaden.

Bruyère, B. (1924–53). *Rapports sur les fouilles de Deir el Médineh*, 17 vols. Fouilles de l'Institut français d'Archéologie orientale du Caire, Cairo.

(1939). *Rapport sur les fouilles de Deir el Médineh (1934–1935). III. le village, les décharges publiques, la station de repos du col de la vallée des rois*. Fouilles de l'Institut francais d'Archéologie orientale du Caire, Cairo.

Buck, A. de (1937). The judicial papyrus of Turin. *J. Egypt. Archaeol.* **23**, 152–64.

Butzer, K. W. (1959). Studien zum vor- und frühgeschichtlichen Landschaftswandel der Sahara. III. Die Naturlandschaft Ägyptens während der Vorgeschichte und der dynastischen Zeit. *Abh. math.-naturw. Kl. Akad. Wiss. Mainz* **2**, 1–80.

(1970). Physical conditions in eastern Europe, Western Asia and Egypt before the period of agricultural and urban settlement. In *Cambridge Ancient History*, 3rd edn, vol. I, pt 1, ch. 2.

(1976). *Early hydraulic civilization in Egypt: a study in cultural ecology*. Chicago.

Caminos, R. A. (1954). *Late Egyptian miscellanies*. Oxford.

(1958). *The Chronicle of Prince Osorkon. Analecta Orientalia* **37**, Rome.

(1968). *The shrines and rock-inscriptions of Ibrim. Archaeological Survey of Egypt Memoir* **32**, London.

(1974). *The New Kingdom temples of Buhen*. 2 vols. *Archaeological Survey of Egypt Memoirs* **33** and **34**. London.

Caminos, R. A. and T. G. H. James (1963). *Gebel el-Silsilah. I. The shrines. Archaeological Survey of Egypt Memoir* **31**. London.

Černý, J. (1927). Le culte d'Amenophis Ier chez les ouvriers de la Nécropole thébaine. *Bull. Inst. fr. archéol. orient. Caire* **27**, 159–203.

(1931). Les ostraca hiératiques, leur intérêt et la nécessité de leur étude. *Chronique d'Egypte* **6**, 212–24.

(1934). Fluctuations in grain prices during the Twentieth Dynasty. *Archiv Orientalni* **6**, 173–8.

(1954). Prices and wages in Egypt in the Ramesside period. *J. World Hist. Paris* **1**, 903–21.

(1957). *Ancient Egyptian religion*. London.

(1959). Two King's Sons of Kush in the twentieth dynasty. *Kush* **7**, 71–5.

(1962). Egyptian oracles. In R. A. Parker, *A Saite Oracle papyrus from Thebes*, ch. 4. Providence, R.I.

(1966). Das Neue Reich in Ägypten. II. Die Ramessiden (1309–1080). In E. Cassin, J. Bottero and J. Vercoutter (eds.), *Fischer Weltgeschichte, vol. III: Die altorientalischen Reiche II*, ch. 4. Frankfort-am-Main.

(1969). Stela of Emhab from Tell Edfu. *Mitt. dt. Inst. ägypt. Altertumskunde Kairo* **24**, 87–92.

(1973). *A community of workmen at Thebes in the Ramesside period*. Cairo.

(1975). Egypt from the death of Ramesses III to the end of the twenty-first dynasty. In *Cambridge Ancient History*, 3rd edn, vol. II, pt 2, ch. 35.

Černý, J., A. Gardiner and T. E. Peet (1955). *The Inscriptions of Sinai*, vol. II. London and Oxford.

Chittick, H. N. (1955). An exploratory journey in the Bayuda region. *Kush* 3, 86–92.

Daressy, G. (1916). Une inscription d'Achmoun et la géographie du nome libyque. *Ann. Serv. Antiquités Égypte* 16, 221–46.

Davies, N. de G. (1903–8). *The rock tombs of El Amarna*, vols. I–VI. London.
(1943). *The tomb of Rekh-mi-Rēʿ at Thebes*. Publications of the Metropolitan Museum of Art, Egyptian Expedition, vol. XI. New York.

Davies, Nina de G. and A. H. Gardiner (1926). *The tomb of Huy, Viceroy of Nubia in the reign of Tutʿankhamun*. London.

Desroches-Noblecourt, C. (1963). *Tutankhamen: life and death of a pharaoh*. London.

Dixon, D. M. (1964). The origin of the Kingdom of Kush (Napata-Meroe). *J. Egypt. Archaeol.* 50, 121–32.
(1969). A note on cereals in ancient Egypt. In P. J. Ucko and G. W. Dimbleby (eds.), *The domestication and exploitation of plants and animals*, 131–42. London.

Donadoni, S. (ed.) (1963). *Le fonti indirette della storia Egiziana*. Rome.

Drenkhahn, R. (1967). *Darstellungen von Negern in Ägypten*. Hamburg.

Drioton, E. and J. Vandier (1962). *L'Égypte*. 'Clio'. *Introduction aux études historiques. Les peuples de l'orient méditerranéen*, vol. II, 4th edn. Paris.

Drower, M. S. (1973). Syria *c.* 1550–1400 B.C. In *Cambridge Ancient History*, 3rd edn, vol. II, pt 1, ch. 10.

Dunham, D. (1950). *The royal cemeteries of Kush, vol. I: El Kurru*. Boston.

Edel, E. (1963). Zur Familie des Sn-msjj nach seinen Grabinschriften auf der Qubbet el Hawa bei Assuan. *Z. ägypt. Sprache Altertumskunde* 90, 28–31.

Edgerton, W. F. (1947a). The government and the governed in the Egyptian empire. *J. Near East. Stud.* 6, 152–60.
(1947b). The Nauri decree of Seti I. A translation and analysis of the legal portion. *J. Near East. Stud.* 6, 219–30.
(1951). The strikes in Ramses III's twenty-ninth year. *J. Near East. Stud.* 10, 137–45.

Edgerton, W. F. and J. A. Wilson (1936). *Historical records of Ramses III*. Chicago.

*Egyptology Titles* (1971–present). Cambridge.

Emery, W. B. (1965). *Egypt in Nubia*. London.

Erman, A. (1927). *The literature of the ancient Egyptians. Poems, narratives, and manuals of instruction, from the third and second millennia B.C.* Translated by A. M. Blackman. London.

Fairman, H. W. (1939). Preliminary report on the excavations of 'Amara West, Anglo-Egyptian Sudan, 1938–9. *J. Egypt. Archaeol.* 25, 139–44.
(1948). Preliminiary report on the excavations of 'Amara West, Anglo-Egyptian Sudan, 1947–8. *J. Egypt. Archaeol.* 34, 3–11.
(1949). Town planning in Pharaonic Egypt. *Town Planning Rev.* 20, 32–51.

Faulkner, R. O. (1945). Review of The Tomb of Rekhmi-re' at Thebes. *J. Egypt. Archaeol.* **31**, 114–15.

(1947). The wars of Sethos I. *J. Egypt. Archaeol.* **33**, 34–9.

(1953). Egyptian military organisation. *J. Egypt. Archaeol.* **39**, 32–47.

(1955). The installation of the vizier. *J. Egypt. Archaeol.* **41**, 18–29.

(1975). Egypt: from the inception of the nineteenth dynasty to the death of Ramses III. In *Cambridge Ancient History*, 3rd edn, vol. II, pt 2, ch. 23.

Federn, W. (1948). Egyptian bibliography. (1939–  ). *Orientalia* **17**, 467–89.

(1949). Egyptian bibliography. *Orientalia* **18**, 73–99, 206–15, 325–35 and 443–72.

(1950). Egyptian bibliography. *Orientalia* **19**, 40–52, 175–86 and 279–94.

Frankfort, H., J. D. S. Pendlebury *et al.* (1933). *The city of Akhenaten.* pt 2. *Egypt Exploration Society Memoir* **40**. London.

Gaballa, G. A. (1977). *The Memphite tomb-chapel of Mose.* Warminster.

Gabra, S. (1929). *Les conseils de fonctionnaires dans l'Égypte pharonique. Scènes de récompenses royales aux fonctionnaires.* Cairo.

Gardiner, A. H. (1905). *The inscription of Mes. A contribution to the study of Egyptian judicial procedure.* In K. Seth (ed.), *Untersuchungen zur Geschichte und Altertumskunde Ägyptens,* vol. IV. Leipzig.

(1918). The Delta residence of the Ramessides. *J. Egypt. Archaeol.* **5**, 127–38, 179–200 and 242–71.

(1935). *The attitude of the ancient Egyptians to death and the dead.* Cambridge.

(1941–52). *The Wilbour Papyrus,* 4 vols. Oxford.

(1947). *Ancient Egyptian onomastica,* 3 vols. Oxford.

(1953). The coronation of king Haremhab. *J. Egypt. Archaeol.* **39**, 13–31.

(1961). *Egypt of the Pharaohs.* Oxford.

Gardiner, A. H. and K. Sethe (1928). *Egyptian letters to the dead.* London.

Gauthier, H. (1921). Les 'fils royaux de Kouch' et le personnel administratif de l'Éthiopie. *Recl Trav. rel. philol. archéol. égypt. assyr.* **39**, 179–238.

(1922–31). *Dictionnaire des noms géographiques contenus dans les textes hiéroglyphiques,* 7 vols. Cairo.

Giorgini, M. S. (1971). *Soleb, vol. II: les necropoles.* Florence.

Goedicke, H. (1962). Psammetik I. und die Libyer. *Mitt. dt. Inst. ägypt. Altertumskunde Kairo* **18**, 26–49.

(1965). The location of Ḥnt-ḥn-nfr. *Kush* **13**, 102–11.

Goetze, A. (1975a). The struggle for the domination of Syria (1400–1300 B.C.). In *Cambridge Ancient History*, 3rd edn, vol. II, pt 2, ch. 17.

(1975b). Anatolia from Shuppiluliumash to the Egyptian war of Muwatallish. In *Cambridge Ancient History*, 3rd edn, vol. II, pt 2, ch. 21a.

(1975c). The Hittites and Syria (1300–1200 B.C.). In *Cambridge Ancient History*, 3rd edn, vol. II, pt 2, ch. 24.

Goyon, G. (1949). Le papyrus de turin dit 'des mines d'or' et le Wadi Hammamat. *Ann. Serv. Antiquités Égypte* **49**, 357–92.

Gratien, B. (1978). *Les cultures Kerma.* Lille.

Griffith, F. Ll. (1927). The Abydos decree of Seti I at Nauri. *J. Egypt. Archaeol.* **13**, 193–208.

Gunn, B. (1916). The religion of the poor in ancient Egypt. *J. Egypt. Archaeol.* **3**, 81–94.

Habachi, L. (1957). The graffiti and work of the Viceroys of Kush in the region of Aswan. *Kush* 5, 13–36.

(1959). The first two Viceroys of Kush and their family. *Kush* 7, 45–62.

(1961). Four objects belonging to Viceroys of Kush and officials associated with them. *Kush* 9, 210–25.

(1969). *Features of the Deification of Ramesses II. Abhandlungen des deutschen Archäologischen Instituts Kairo, Ägyptische Reihe* 5. Glückstadt.

(1976). Miscellanea on Viceroys of Kush and their assistants buried in Dra' abu El-Naga. *J. Am. Res. Cent. Egypt* 13, 113–16.

Hall, H. R. (1928). *Babylonian and Assyrian Sculpture in the British Museum*. Paris and Brussels.

Hari, R. (1965). *Horemheb et la Reine Moutnedjmet, ou la fin d'une dynastie*. Geneva.

Harris, J. E. and K. R. Weeks (1973). *X-raying the Pharaohs*. New York and London.

Harrison, R. G. (1966). An anatomical examination of the pharaonic remains purported to be Akhenaten. *J. Egypt. Archaeol.* 52, 95–119.

Hartmann, F. (1923). *L'agriculture dans l'ancienne Égypte*. Paris.

Hayes, W. C. (1955). *A papyrus of the late Middle Kingdom in the Brooklyn Museum [Papyrus Brooklyn 35.1446]*. Brooklyn (Reprinted with an additional page of errata and recent bibliography as *Wilbour Monographs* 5.)

(1959). *The Scepter of Egypt* vol. II. Cambridge, Mass.

(1970). Chronology. Egypt – to the end of the. Twentieth Dynasty. In *Cambridge Ancient History*, 3rd edn, vol. I, pt I, ch. 6.

(1973). Egypt: Internal affairs from Tuthmosis I to the death of Amenophis III. In *Cambridge Ancient History*, 3rd edn, vol. II, pt I, ch. 9.

Heerma van Voss, M. S. H. G. (1968–9). *Annual Egyptological Bibliography, 1963–1965*. Leiden.

Heerma van Voss, M. S. H. G. and J. J. Jannsen (1971). *Annual Egyptological Bibliography, 1966*. Leiden.

Helck, H. W. (1939). *Der Einfluss der Militärführer in der 18. ägyptischen Dynastie. Untersuchungen zur Geschichte und altertumskunde Ägyptens* 14. Leipzig.

(1955). Eine Stele des Vicekönigs Wśr-St. t. *J. Near East. Stud.* 14, 22–31.

(ed.) (1957). *Urkunden der 18 Dynastie*, pt 20. Berlin.

(1958). *Zur Verwaltung des mittleren und neuen Reichs*. ed. H. Kees, III; *Probleme der Ägyptologie*, Leiden–Cologne.

(1961–70). *Materialien zur Wirtschaftsgeschichte des Neuen Reiches*, pts I–VI. Weisbaden.

(1961). *Urkunden der 18 dynastie. Übersetzung zu den Heften 17–22*. Berlin.

(1962). *Die Beziehungen Ägyptens zu Vorderasien im 3 und 2 Jahrtausend v. Chr. Ägyptologische Abhandlung* 5, Wiesbaden.

(1967). Eine Briefsammlung aus der verwaltung des Amuntempels. *J. Am. Res. Cent. Egypt* 6, 135–52.

(ed.) (1968). *Geschichte des alten Ägypten, Handbuch der Orientalistik*, I, Bd. 1, Absch. 3. Leiden and Cologne.

(1975). *Wirtschaftsgeschichte des Alten Ägypten, im 3. und 2. Jahrtausend v. Chr.* Leiden and Cologne.

Herodotus, bks I and II. Translated by A. D. Godley. Loeb Classical Library, Cambridge, Mass. and London.

Herzog, R. (1968). *Punt. Abh. dt. archäol. Inst. Kairo, Ägyptologische Reihe*, **6**. Glückstadt.

Hilzheimer, M. (1932). Zur geographischen Lokalisierung von Punt. *Z. ägypt. Sprache Altertumskunde* **68**, 112–14.

Hölscher, W. (1955). *Libyer und Ägypter*. Glückstadt, Hamburg and New York.

Hornung, E. (1956). Chaotische Bereich in der geordneten Welt. *Z. ägypt. Sprache Altertumskunde* **81**, 28–32.

   (1957). Zur geschichtlichen Rolle des Königs in der 18. Dynastie. *Mitt. dt. Inst. ägypt. Altertumskunde Kairo* **15**, 120–33.

   (1964). *Untersuchen zur Chronologie und Geschichte des neuen Reiches. Ägyptologische Abhandlungen* **11**. Weisbaden.

   (1966). *Geschichte als Fest: zwei Vorträge zum Geschichtsbild der frühen Menschzeit*, Darmstadt.

   (1967). Neue Materialien zur ägyptischen Chronologie. *Z. dt. morgenländ. Ges.* **117**, 11–16.

   (1971a). (with Teichmann). *Das Grab des Haremhab im Tal der Könige*. Bern.

   (1971b). Politische Planung und Realität im alten Ägypten. *Saeculum* **22**, 48–58.

James, T. G. H. (1973). Egypt from the explusion of the Hyksos to Amenophis I. In *Cambridge Ancient History*, 3rd edn, vol. II, pt 1, ch. 8.

Janssen, J. J. (1972– ). *Annual Egyptological bibliography, 1967–1972* (Continuing). Leiden.

   (1975a). *Commodity prices from the Ramessid period*. Leiden.

   (1975b). Prolegomena to the study of Egypt's economic history during the New Kingdom. *Stud. altägypt. Kultur* **3**, 127–85.

Janssen, J. M. A. (1948–63). *Annual Egyptological bibliography, 1947–1961*. Leiden.

Janssen, J. M. A. and M. S. H. G. Heerma van Voss (1964). *Annual Egyptological bibliography, 1962*. Leiden.

Johnson, J. H. (1974). The Demotic Chronicle as an historical source. *Enchoria* **4**, 1–17.

Junge, F. (1973). Zur Fehldatierung des sog. Denkmals memphitischer Theologie oder: Der Beitrag der ägyptischen Theologie zur Geistesgeschichte der Spätzeit. *Mitt. dt. archäol. Inst. Abt. Kairo* **29**, 195–204.

Kaplony, P. (1971). Bemerkungen zum ägyptischen Königtum, vor allem in der Spätzeit. *Chronique d'Egypte* **46**, 250–74.

Kees, H. (1936a). Herihor und die Aufrichtung des thebanischen Gottesstaats. *Nachr. Ges. Wiss. Göttingen, Phil.-hist. Kl* 1.

   (1936b). Zur Innenpolitik der Saïtendynastie. *Nachr. Ges. Wiss. Göttingen, Phil.-hist. Kl* 1, 96–106.

   (1953–58). *Das Priestertum im ägyptischen Staat vom neuen Reich bis zur Spätzeit*, 2 vols. *Probleme der Ägyptologie* 1. Leiden and Cologne.

   (1961). *Ancient Egypt. A cultural topography* (ed. T. G. H. James). Translated by I. F. D. Morrow. London and Chicago.

   (1964). *Die Hohenpriester des Amun von Karnak von Herihor bis zum Ende der Änthiopienzeit. Probleme der Ägyptologie* **20**, Leiden.

Kemp, B. J. (1972a). Temple and town in ancient Egypt. In P. J. Ucko, R. Tringham and G. W. Dimbleby (eds.), *Man, settlement and urbanism*, 657–80. London.

(1972b). Fortified towns in Nubia. In P. J. Ucko, R. Tringham and G. W. Dimbleby (eds.), *Man, settlement and urbanism*, 651–6. London.

(1976). The Window of Appearance at El-Amarna, and the basic structure of the city. *J. Egypt. Archaeol.* **62**, 81–99.

(1977). The city of el-Amarna as a source for the study of urban society in ancient Egypt. *World Archaeol.* **9**, 123–39.

(1978). Imperialism and empire in New Kingdom Egypt (*c.* 1575–1087 B.C.). In P. D. A. Garnsey and C. R. Whittaker (eds.), *Imperialism in the Ancient World*, 7–57, 284–97, 368–73. Cambridge.

(1981). The character of the south suburb at Tell el-'Amarna. *Mitteilungen der Deutschen Orient-Gesellschaft zu Berlin* **113**, 81–97.

Kemp, B. J. and D. O'Connor (1974). An ancient Nile harbour. University Museum excavations at the 'Birket Habu'. *Int. J. Naut. Underwater Explor.* **3**, 101–36 and 182.

Kienitz, F. K. (1953). *Die politische Geschichte Ägyptens vom 7. bis zum 4. Jahrhundert vor der Zeitwende*. Berlin.

(1967). Die saïtische Renaissance. In E. Cassin, J. Bottero and J. Vercoutter (eds.), *Fischer Weltgeschichte, vol. IV : Die atorientalischen Reiche*, pt 3, ch. 6. Frankfort-am-Main.

Kitchen, K. A. (1965). On the chronology and history of the New Kingdom. *Chronique d'Egypte* **40–80**, 310–22.

(1968– ). *Ramesside inscriptions*, vols. I–VI. Oxford.

(1971). Punt and how to get there. *Orientalia* **40**, 184–207.

(1972). Ramesses VII and the Twentieth Dynasty. *J. Egypt. Archaeol.* **58**, 182–94.

(1973). *The Third Intermediate Period in Egypt (1100–650 B.C.)*. Warminster.

(1975–6). The great biographical stela of Setau, Viceroy of Nubia. *Orient. lovan. Periodica* **6–7**, 295–302.

(1977). Historical observations on Ramesside Nubia. In E. Endesfelder *et al.* (eds.), *Ägypten und Kusch*, 213–25. Berlin.

Krauss, R. (1976). Untersuchungen zu König Amenmesse. 1. *Stud. altägypt. Kultur* **4**, 161–99.

(1977). Untersuchungen zu König Amenmesse, 2. *Stud. altägypt. Kultur* **5**, 131–74.

Lange, K. and Hirmer, M. (1956). *Egypt: architecture, sculpture and painting*. London.

Leclant, J. (1961). *Montouemhat quatrième prophète d'Amon, prince de la ville*. Cairo.

(1972). Afrika. In H. W. Helck and E. Otto (eds.), *Lexikon der Ägyptologie*, vol. I, pt 1, 86–94. Wiesbaden.

Lefebvre, G. (1929). *Histoire des grands prêtres d'Amon de Karnak jusqu'à la XXIe Dynastie*. Paris.

Lepsius, K. R. (1844–56). *Denkmaeler aus Aegypten und Aethiopien*. 12 vols. Berlin.

Lichtheim, M. (1976). *Ancient Egyptian literature, vol. II: The New Kingdom.* California.

(1980). *Ancient Egyptian literature, vol. III: The Late Period.* California.

Lorton, D. (1973). The so-called 'vile' enemies of the King of Egypt (in the Middle Kingdom and Dynasty XVIII). *Journal of the American Research Center in Egypt* **10**, 65–70.

(1974). *The juridical terminology of international relations in Egyptian texts through Dynasty XVIII.* London and Baltimore.

Lucas, A. and J. R. Harris (1962). *Ancient Egyptian materials and industries,* 4th edn. London.

Macadam, F. L. (1955). *The Temples of Kawa,* vol. II. London.

Manetho. Translated by W. G. Waddell (1956). Loeb Classical Library, Cambridge, Mass. and London.

Martin, G. T. (1974). *The rock tombs of El-Amarna, Pt 7. The royal tomb at El-Amarna, vol. I: the objects.* London.

May, H. G. (ed.) (1965). *Oxford Bible atlas.* London, New York and Toronto.

Menu, B. (1970). *Le régime juridique des terres et du personnel attaché à la terre dans le papyrus Wilbour.* Lille.

(1971). Le régime juridique des terres en Égypte pharaonique. Moyen Empire et Nouvel Empire. *Rev. hist. Droit fr. étranger* **49**, 555–85.

Meulenaere, H. de (1967). Die dritte Zwischenzeit und das äthiopische Reich. In E. Cassin, J. Bottero and J. Vercoutter (eds.), *Fischer Weltgeschichte, vol. IV: Die altorientalischen Reiche,* 220–55. Frankfort-am-Main.

Meyer, E. (1928). Gottesstaat, Militärherrschaft und Standwesen in Ägypten. *Sitzungsberichte der preussischen Akademie der Wissenschaften zu Berlin, Phil.-hist. Kl.,* 495–532.

Naville, E. (1898). *The temple of Deir el-Bahari,* vol. III. London.

(1908). *The temple of Deir el-Bahari,* vol. VI. London.

Nelson, H. H. *et al.* (1932). *Medinet Habu, vol. II: later historical records of Ramses III. Plates.* Chicago.

Nims, C. (1966). The date of dishonoring Hatshepsut. *Z. ägypt. Sprache Altertumskunde* **93**, 97–100.

O'Connor, D. (1969). Nubian archaeological material of the First to the Second Intermediate Period. Ph.D. dissertation, University of Cambridge.

(1972a). The geography of settlement in ancient Egypt. In P. J. Ucko, R. Tringham and G. W. Dimbleby (eds.), *Man, settlement and urbanism* 681–98. London.

(1972b). A regional population in Egypt to circa 600 B.C. In B. Spooner (ed.), *Population growth: anthropological implications,* 98–100. Cambridge, Mass. and London.

(1978). Nubia before the New Kingdom. In *Africa in Antiquity, vol. I: The arts of ancient Nubia and the Sudan. The essays,* 46–61. New York.

(1982a). Cities and towns. In Museum of Fine Arts, Boston, *Egypt's golden age: the art of living in the New Kingdom 1558–1085 BC,* Boston, 17–24.

(1982b). Egypt, 1552–664 BC. In *Cambridge History of Africa,* vol. 1, 830–970. 970.

Otto, E. (1951). Die Endsituation der ägyptischen Kultur. *Die Welt als Geschichte* **11**, 203–13.

(1954). *Die biographischen Inschriften der ägyptischen Spätzeit*, vol. 2, *Probleme der Ägyptologie*, ed. H. Kees, **2**, 102–18. Leiden.

*Oxford Regional Economic Atlas* (1960). *The Middle East and North Africa.* Oxford.

Peet, T. E., C. L. Woolley *et al.* (1923). *The city of Akhenaten*, pt I. *Egypt Exploration Society, Memoir* **38**, London.

Pendlebury, J. D. S. (1951). *The city of Akhenaten*, pt III, 2 vols. *Egypt Exploration Society, Memoir* **44**. London.

Pflüger, K. (1946). The edict of king Haremhab. *J. Near East. Stud.* **5**, 260–8.

Piotrovsky, B. (1967). The early dynastic settlements of Khor-Daoud and Wadi-Allaki: the ancient route to the gold mines. *Fouilles en Nubie (1961–63), Service des Antiquités de l'Égypte.* Cairo. UNESCO, Campagne internationale pour la sauvegarde des monuments de la Nubie.

Porter, B. and R. L. Moss (1927–51). *Topographical bibliography of ancient Egyptian hieroglyphic texts, reliefs and paintings*, 7 vols., 1st ed. Oxford.

(1960–4). *Topographical bibliography of ancient Egyptian hieroglyphic texts, reliefs and paintings*, 2nd edn, vols. I and II. Oxford.

(1974). *Topographical bibliography of ancient Egyptian hieroglyphic texts, reliefs and paintings*, 2nd edn (revised and augmented by J. Malek), vol. III, pt 1. Oxford.

Posener, G. (1958a). Pour une localisation du pays Koush au Moyen Empire. *Kush* **6**, 39–65.

(1958b). [Nehasyu and Medjayu]. *Z. ägypt. Sprache Altertumskunde* **83**, 38–43.

(1960). *De la divinité du pharaon. Cahiers de la société asiatique* **15**. Paris.

(1977). L'or de Pouent. In E. Endesfelder *et al.* (eds.), *Ägypten und Kusch*, 337–42. Berlin.

Pratt, I. A. (1925). *Ancient Egypt. Sources of information in the New York Public Library.* New York.

(1942). *Ancient Egypt 1925–1941. A supplement to Ancient Egypt: sources of information in the New York Public Library.* New York.

Priese, K.-H. (1974). '*rm* und '*ʒm*, das Land Irame. Eine Beitrag zur Topographie des Sudan im Altertum. *Altorientalische Forschungen* **1**, 7–41.

Pritchard, J. B. (ed.) (1969). *Ancient Near Eastern texts relating to the Old Testament*, 3rd edn, with supplement. Princeton.

Redford, D. B. (1967). *History and chronology of the Eighteenth Dynasty of Egypt.* Toronto.

(1976). The sun-disc in Akhenaten's program: its worship and antecedents, I. *J. Am. Res. Cent. Egypt* **13**, 47–61.

Reineke, W.-F. (1977). Ein Nubien Feldzug unter Königin Hatschepsut. E. Endesfelder *et al.* (eds.), *Ägypten und Kusch*, 369–76. Berlin.

Reisner, G. A. (1920). The Viceroys of Nubia. *J. Egypt. Archaeol.* **6**, 28–55 and 73–88.

(1923). *Excavations at Kerma*, vol. IV. Cambridge, Mass.

Ricke, H., G. R. Hughes and E. F. Wente (1967). *The Beit el-Wali temple of Ramesses II.* Chicago.

Rowe, A. (1953). A contribution to the archaeology of the Western Desert: I. *Bull. John Rylands Libr. Manchester* **36**, 128–145.

(1954). A contribution to the archaeology of the Western Desert. II. *Bull. John Rylands Libr. Manchester* **36**, 484–500.

Sander-Hansen, C. E. (1940). *Das Gottesweib des Amun.* Copenhagen.

Sauneron, S. (1957). *Les prêtres de l'ancienne Égypte* Bourges.

Säve-Söderbergh, T. (1941). *Aegypten und Nubien.* Lund.

(1946). The Navy of the eighteenth Egyptian dynasty. *Uppsala Universitets Arsskrift* **6**.

(1960). The paintings in the tomb of Djehuty-hetep at Debeira. *Kush* **8**, 25–44.

(1963). The tomb of the prince of Teh-khet, Amenemhet. *Kush* **11**, 159–74.

(1969). Die Akkulturation der nubischen C-Gruppe im Neuen Reich. *Z. dt. morgenländ. Ges. (Suppl 1)* **17**, 12–20.

Schaedel, H. D. (1936). *Die Listen des grossen Papyrus Harris, ihre wirtschaftliche und politische Ausdeutung.* Glückstadt.

Schulman, A. R. (1964a). Some remarks on the military background to the Amarna period. *J. Am. Res. Cent. Egypt* **3**, 51–69.

(1964b). *Military rank, title and organisation in the Egyptian New Kingdom.* Berlin.

(1969–70). Some remarks on the alleged 'fall' of Senmut. *J. Am. Res. Cent. Egypt* **8**, 29–48.

(1976). The royal butler Ramessesemperre. *J. Am. Res. Cent. Egypt* **13**, 117–30.

Seele, K. (1959). *The Tomb of Tjanefer at Thebes.* Chicago.

Seidl, E. (1939). *Einführung in die ägyptische Rechtsgeschichte bis zum Ende des Neuen Reiches. I. Juristischer Teil.* Glückstadt, Hamburg and New York.

Sethe, K. (1909). *Die Einsetzung des Veziers unter der 18. Dynastie. Inschrift im Grabe des Rekh-mi-re' zu Schech Abd el Gurna.* Leipzig.

(1914). *Urkunden der 18. Dynasty. I.* (Translated.) Leipzig.

Sethe, K. and H. W. Helck (1906–58). *Urkunden der 18. Dynastie. Urkunden des ägyptischen Altertums,* vol. IV, pts 1–22. Leipzig and Berlin.

Shinnie, P. L. (1981). The Nilotic Sudan and Ethiopia. In *Cambridge History of Africa,* vol. I, 210–71.

Simons, J. J. (1937). *Handbook for the study of Egyptian topographical lists relating to Western Asia.* Brill.

Simpson, W. K. (1963). *Heka-Nefer.* New Haven and Philadelphia.

(ed.) (1973). *The literature of ancient Egypt an anthology of stories, instructions, and poetry,* with translations by R. O. Faulkner, E. F. Wente, Jr., and W. K. Simpson. New Haven and London.

Smith, H. S. (1969). Animal domestication and animal cult in ancient Egypt. In P. J. Ucko and G. W. Dimbleby (eds.), *The domestication and exploitation of plants and animals,* 307–14. London.

(1972). Society and settlement in ancient Egypt. In P. J. Ucko, R. Tringham and G. W. Dimbleby (eds.), *Man, settlement and urbanism,* 705–19. London.

(1976). *The fortress of Buhen: The inscriptions. Egypt Exploration Society Memoir* **48**. London.

Smith, W. S. (1965). *Interconnections in the ancient Near East:* New Haven and London.

(1981). *The art and architecture of Ancient Egypt.* Revised with additions by William Kelly Simpson. Harmondsworth.

Spalinger, A. (1974a). Esarhaddon and Egypt: an analysis of the first invasion of Egypt. *Orientalia* **43**, 295–326.

(1974b). Assurbanipal and Egypt: a source study. *J. Am. Orient. Soc.* **94**, 316–28.

(1976). Psammetichus, King of Egypt, I. *J. Am. Res. Cent. Egypt* **13**, 133–47.

Stadelmann, R. (1971). Das Grab im Tempelhof. Der Typus des Königsgrabes in der Spätzeit. *Mitt. dt. archäol. Inst. Abt. Kairo* **27**, 111–23.

(1973). Tempelpalast und Erscheinungsfenster in den Thebanische totentempeln. *Mitt. dt. archäol. Inst. Abt. Kairo* **29**, 221–42.

Steindorff, G. (1935–7). *Aniba,* 2 vols. Glückstadt.

Steindorff, G. and K. C. Seele (1957). *When Egypt ruled the East,* 2nd edn. Chicago.

Tanner, R. (1975). Bemerkungen zur Sukzession der Pharaonen in der 12., 17. und 18. Dynastie. *Z. ägypt. Sprache Altertumskunde* **102**, 50–9.

*Textes et langages de l'Égypte pharaonique,* vol. I (1973). Hommage à Jean-François Champollion. Cairo.

*Textes et langages de l'Égypte pharaonique,* vol. II (1973). Hommage à Jean-François Champollion. Cairo.

*Textes et langages de l'Égypte pharaonique,* vol. III (1974). Hommage à Jean-François Champollion. Cairo.

Théodoridès, A. (1971). The concept of law in ancient Egypt. In J. R. Harris (ed.), *The legacy of Egypt,* 2nd edn, 291–322. Oxford.

Trigger, B. (1965). *History and settlement in Lower Nubia. Yale Univ. Publs Anthrop.* **69**. New Haven.

(1976). *Nubia Under the Pharaohs.* London.

Uphill, E. (1970). The Per-Aten at Amarna. *J. Near East. Stud.* **29**, 151–66.

Vandersleyen, C. (1971). *Les Guerres d'Amosis, fondateur de la XVIII<sup>e</sup> dynastie. Monogr. Reine Elisabeth* **1**. Brussels.

van de Walle, B. (1948). *La transmission des textes littéraires égyptiens (avec une annexe de G. Posener).* Brussels.

Vandier, J. (1949). *La religion égyptienne.* 'Mana': Introduction à l'histoire des religions vol. I: Les anciennes religions orientales, pt 1, 2nd edn. Paris.

(1955). *Manuel d'archéologie égyptienne, vol. II: Les grandes époques. L'architecture religieuse et civile.* Paris.

(1958). *Manuel d'archéologie égyptienne, vol. III: Les grandes époques. La statuaire.* Paris.

(1964). *Manuel d'archéologie égyptienne, vol. IV: Bas-reliefs et peintures. Scènes de la vie quotidienne.* Paris.

Vercoutter, J. (1956). New Egyptian texts from the Sudan. *Kush* **4**, 66–82.

(1959). The gold of Kush. Two gold-washing stations at Faras East. *Kush* **7**, 120–53.

(1972). Une campagne militaire de Séti I en haute Nubie. Stele de Sai' S.579. *Revue d'égyptologie* **24**, 201–8.

(1973). La XVIII<sup>e</sup> Dynastie à Saï et en Haute Nubie. *Etudes sur l'Egypte et le Soudan anciens, Cahier de Recherches de l'Institut de Papyrologie et d'Egyptologie de Lille*, 7–38.

Wainwright, G. A. (1961). Some Sea-Peoples. *J. Egypt. Archaeol.* **47**, 71–90.

(1962). The Meshwesh. *J. Egypt. Archaeol.* **48**, 89–99.

Wenig, S. (1978). *Africa in antiquity, vol. II. The arts of ancient Nubia and the Sudan. The Catalogue.* The Brooklyn Museum.

Wente, E. F. (1966). On the suppression of the High-Priest Amenhotep. *J. Near East. Stud.* **25**, 73–87.

(1967). *Late Ramesside letters. Studies in ancient oriental civilisation* **33**. Chicago.

(1976). Tutankhamun and his world. In *Treasures of Tutankhamun*, 19–31. New York.

Wilson, J. (1951). *The burden of Egypt.* Chicago.

(1954a). Egypt. In H. Frankfort *et al.* (eds.), *Before philosphy*, 39–133. Harmondsworth.

(1954b). Authority and law in ancient Egypt. *J. Am. Orient. Soc. Suppl.* **17**: *authority and law in the ancient Near East*, 1–7.

(1955). Buto and Hierakonpolis in the geography of Egypt. *J. Near East. Stud.* **14**, 209–36.

(1969). The Hymn to the Aton. In J. B. Pritchard (ed.), *Ancient Near Eastern texts relating to the Old Testament*, 3rd edn, 370. Princeton.

(1974). Akhenaton. *New Encyclopedia Britannica, Macropaedia I*, 401–3.

Wolf, W. (1924). Amenhotep, Vizekönig von Nubien. *Zeitschrift für ägyptische Sprache und Altertumskunde* **59**, 157–8.

(1957). *Die Kunst Ägyptens: Gestalt und Geschichte.* Stuttgart.

Youssef, A. (1964). Merenptah's fourth year text at Amada. *Ann. Serv. antiquités Égypte* **58**, 272–80.

Yoyotte, J. (1952). Une épithète de Min comme explorateur des régions orientales. *Revue d'Égyptologie* **9**, 125–37.

(1956). Egypte ancienne. In *Histoire universelle, vol. I: Des origines à l'Islam, Encyclopédie de la Pléiade.* Paris.

(1961). Les principautés du Delta au temps de l'anarchie libyenne. *Mémoires publiés par les membres de l'Institut français d'archéologie orientale du Caire*, **66**, 121–81.

(1966). Das Neue Reich in Ägypten. I: Die XVIII Dynastie. In E. Cassin, J. Bottero and J. Vercoutter (eds.), *Fischer Weltgeschichte vol. III: Die altorientalischen Reiche*, pt 2, 222–60. Frankfort-am-Main.

Žaba, Z. (1950). Un nouveau fragment du sarcophage de Merymôse. *Ann. serv. antiquités Égypte* **50**, 509–14.

Zeissl, H. von (1944). *Äthiopen und Assyrer in Ägypten: Beitrage zur Geschichte der ägyptischen 'Spätzeit'. Ägyptologische Forschungen* **14**. Glückstadt and Hamburg.

Zhylarz, E. (1958). The countries of the Ethiopian empire of Kash (Kush) and Egyptian Old Ethiopia in the New Kingdom. Translated by M. Jackson. *Kush* **6**, 7–38.

Zibelius, K. (1972). *Afrikanische Orts- und Völkernamen in hieroglyphischen und hieratischen Texten.* Wiesbaden.

## 4. THE LATE PERIOD

Adams, W. Y. (1977). *Nubia, corridor to Africa*. London.

Aḥituv, S. (1978). Economic factors in the Egyptian conquest of Canaan. *Israel Exploration J.* **28**, 93–105.

Aldred, C. (1980). *Egyptian art*. London.

Allam, S. (1970). Zur Stellung der Frau im Alten Ägypten. *Das Altertum* **16**, 67–81.

(1977). Les obligations et la famille dans la société égyptienne ancienne. *Oriens Antiquus* **16**, 89–97.

(1978). Le droit égyptien ancien. État de recherches et perspectives. *Z. ägypt. Sprache Altertumskunde* **105**, 1–6.

(1981). Quelques aspects du mariage dans l'Égypte ancienne. *J. Egypt. Archaeol.* **67**, 116–35.

Amir, Mustafa el- (1948). The ΣΗΚΟΣ of Apis at Memphis. *J. Egypt. Archaeol.* **34**, 51–6.

(1964). Monogamy, polygamy, endogamy and consanguinity in ancient Egyptian marriage. *Bull. Inst. fr. archéol. orient. Cairo* **62**, 103–7.

Anthes, R. (1959). *Mit Rahineh 1955*. Philadelphia.

(1965). *Mit Rahineh 1956*. Philadelphia.

Aristotle (pseudo). *Oeconomica*. Translated by E. S. Forster in W. D. Ross (ed.), *The works of Aristotle*, vol. x, Oxford, 1972.

Arkell, A. J. (1961). *A history of the Sudan from the earliest times to 1821*, 2nd edn. London.

Atkinson, K. M. T. (1956). The legitimacy of Cambyses and Darius as kings of Egypt. *J. Amer. orient. Soc.* **76**, 167–77.

Austin, M. M. (1970). *Greece and Egypt in the Archaic Age* (*Proceedings of the Cambridge Philological Society* Suppl. 2). Cambridge.

Badawy, A. M. (1975). The approach to the Egyptian temple in the Late and Graeco-Roman periods. *Z. ägypt. Sprache Altertumskunde* **102**, 79–90.

Baedeker, K. (1914). *Egypt and the Sudan*, 7th edn. London.

Baer, K. (1973). The Libyan and Nubian kings of Egypt: notes on the chronology of Dynasties XXII to XXVI. *J. Near East. Stud.* **32**, 4–25.

Bakir, Abd el-Mohsen (1952). *Slavery in Pharaonic Egypt* (*Ann. Serv. Antiquités Égypte* Suppl. 18). Cairo.

Bakry, H. S. K. (1967). Psammētichus II and his newly-found stela at Shellâl. *Oriens Antiquus* **6**, 225–44.

(1968). A family from Saïs. *Mitt. dt. archäol. Inst. Abt. Cairo* **23**, 69–74.

(1970–1). A donation stela from Busiris during the reign of King Nekō (610–595 BC). *Studi classici e orientali* **19–20**, 325–37.

Ball, J. (1942). *Egypt in the classical geographers*. Cairo.

Barois, J. (1911). *Les irrigations en Égypte*, 2nd edn. Paris.

Barron, J. P. (1964). The sixth-century tyranny at Samos. *Classical Quarterly* n.s. **14**, 210–29.

Basch, L. (1969). Phoenician oared ships. *The Mariner's Mirror* **55**, 139–62, 227–45.

(1977). Trières grecques, phéniciennes et égyptiennes. *J. Hellenic Stud.* **97**, 1–10.

(1980). M. le Professeur Lloyd et les trières: quelques remarques. *J. Hellenic Stud.* **100**, 198–9.

Bergman, J. (1972). Zum 'Mythus vom Staat' im Alten Ägypten. In H. Biezais (ed.), *The myth of the state (Scripta instituti Donneriani Aboensis* 6), 80–102. Stockholm.

Bernand, A. (1970). *Le delta égyptien d'après les textes grecques.* I. Cairo.

Bernand, A. and O. Masson (1957). Les inscriptions grecques d'Abou-Simbel. *Rev. études grecques* **70**, 1–46.

Bernhardt, K.-H. (1977). *Der alte Libanon.* Vienna and Munich.

Bevan, E. (1968). *The house of Ptolemy,* revised edn. Chicago.

Bickerman, E. J. (1968). *Chronology of the ancient world.* London.

Bietak, M. (1975). *Tell el- Dabʻa II (Untersuchungen der Zweigstelle Kairo des österreichischen archäologischen Institutes* I). Vienna.

Bilabel, F. (1934). Polykrates von Samos und Amasis von Aegypten. *Neue Heidelberg. Jahrbücher* N.F., 129–59.

Bissing, F. W. Freiherr v. (1949). Forschungen zur Geschichte und kulturellen Bedeutung der griechischen Kolonie Naukratis in Ägypten. *Forschungen und Fortschritte* **25**, 1–2.

(1951). Naukratis. *Bull. Soc. Roy. D'Arch. d'Alexandrie* **39**, 33–82.

Blackman, A. H. (1918). Priest, Priesthood (Egyptian). In J. Hastings (ed.), *Encyclopedia of Religion and Ethics,* X, 293–302. Edinburgh and New York.

(1925). Oracles in Ancient Egypt I. *J. Egypt. Archaeol.* **11**, 249–55.

(1926). Oracles in Ancient Egypt II. *J. Egypt. Archaeol.* **12**, 176–85.

Blackman, W. S. (1927). *The Fellāhīn of Upper Egypt.* London.

Boardman, J. (1980). *The Greeks overseas,* revised edn. London.

Bohannan, P. (1969). *Social anthropology.* London.

Bonneau, D. (1964). *La crue du Nil.* Paris.

Bonnet, H. (1952). *Reallexikon der ägyptischen Religionsgeschichte.* Berlin.

(1961). Herkunft und Bedeutung der naophoren Statue. *Mitt. dt. archäol. Inst. Abt. Cairo* **17**, 91–8.

Bosse, K. (1936). *Die menschliche Figur in der Rundplastik der ägyptischen Spätzeit von der XXII. bis zur XXX. Dynastie (Ägypt. Forschungen* 1). Glückstadt, Hamburg, New York.

Bothmer, B. V. (1969). *Egyptian sculpture of the Late Period, 700 B.C.–100 A.D.* Brooklyn Museum.

Bowman, R. A. (1941). An Aramaic journal page. *Am. J. Sem. Languages* **58**, 302–13.

Braun, M. (1938). *History and romance in graeco-oriental literature.* Oxford.

Breasted, J. H. (1906–7). *Ancient records of Egypt. Historical documents from the earliest times to the Persian conquest.* 5 vols. Chicago.

Bresciani, E. (1958). La satrapia d'Egitto. *Studi classici e orientali* **7**, 153–87.

and S. Donadoni (1969). *Letteratura e poesia dell' Antico Egitto.* Turin.

Brugsch, H. K. (1879–80). *Dictionnaire géographique de l'ancienne Égypte.* Leipzig.

Brunner, H. (1956). Das Gottkönigtum der Pharaonen. *Universitas* **118**, 797–806.

(1964). *Die Geburt des Gottkönigs.* Wiesbaden.

Brunner, H. and H. Hommel (1957–8). Ein Bildnis des Amasis mit griechischer Inschrift. *Archiv für Orientforsch.* **18**, 279–87.

Burchardt, M. (1911). Datierte Denkmäler der Berliner Sammlung aus der Achämenidenzeit. *Z. ägypt. Sprache Altertumskunde* **49**, 69–80.

Butzer, K. W. (1976). *Early hydraulic civilization in Egypt. A study in cultural ecology (Prehistoric archeology and ecology series)*. Chicago and London.

*Cambridge Ancient History* (1929–53). Vol. III–VI. H. R. Hall, vol. III, (Ch. XII–XV); G. Buchanan Gray, vol. IV (Ch. I); P. N. Ure, vol. IV (Ch. IV); G. B. Gray and M. Cary, vol. IV (Ch. VII); E. M. Walker, vol. V (Ch. III); W. W. Tarn, vol. VI (Ch. I); H. R. Hall, vol. VI (Ch. VI); W. W. Tarn, vol. VI (Ch. XII).

Cameron, G. C. (1943). Darius, Egypt and the 'Lands Beyond the Sea'. *J. Near East. Stud.* **2**, 307–13.

Caminos, R. A. (1964). The Nitocris adoption stele. *J. Egypt. Archaeol.* **50**, 71–101.

Carpenter, R. (1956). A trans-Saharan caravan route in Herodotus. *Am. J. Archaeol.* **60**, 231–42.

Cavaignac, E. (1919). La milice égyptienne au VIe siècle et l'empire achéménide. *Revue égyptologique* n.s. **1**, 192–8.

Cazelles, H. (1967). Sophonie, Jérémie, et les Scythes en Palestine. *Rev. Biblique* **74**, 24–44.

Cenival, F. de (1972). *Les associations religieuses en Égypte d'après les documents démotiques (Bibliothèque d'étude* **46**). Cairo.

Černý, J. (1954). Consanguineous marriages in Pharaonic Egypt. *J. Egypt Archaeol.* **40**, 23–9.

Chamoux, F. (1953). *Cyrène sous la monarchie des Battiades*. Paris.

Champollion, J. Fr. (1868). *Lettres écrites de l'Égypte et de Nubie*. Paris.

Christophe, L. A. (1952). L'ascendance de la Divine Adoratrice. *Cahiers d'histoire égyptienne* Série IV (**3–4**), 222–33.

Cook, R. M. (1937). Amasis and the Greeks in Egypt. *J. Hellenic Stud.* **57**, 227–37.

Cooney, J. D. (1953). The portrait of an Egyptian collaborator. *Brooklyn Museum Bulletin* **15** (2), 1–16.

*Corpus inscriptionum semiticarum* (1881). I, 1. Paris.

Coulsen, W. D. E. and A. Leonard (1979). A preliminary survey of the Naukratis region in the western Nile Delta. *J. Field Archaeology* **6**, 151–68.

Couyat, J. and P. Montet (1912–13). *Les inscriptions hiéroglyphiques et hiératiques du Ouâdi Hammâmât*. Cairo.

Crawford, D. (1971). *Kerkeosiris. An Egyptian village in the Ptolemaic period*. Cambridge.

Daressy, G. (1900). Stèle de l'an III d'Amasis. *Recueil de travaux* **22**, 1–9.

Daumas, F. (1977). Le problème de la monnaie dans l'Égypte antique avant Alexandre. *Mélanges école française Rome* **89**, 425–42.

Davies, N. de Garis (1929). The town house in ancient Egypt. *Metropolitan Museum Studies* I (2), 233–55.

Davies, W. V. (1982). The origin of the Blue Crown. *J. Eg. Archaeol.* **68**, 69–76.

Davis, S. (1951). *Race-relations in Ancient Egypt*. London.

Davis, W. M. (1979). Ancient Naukratis and the Cypriotes in Egypt. *Götting. Misz.* **35**, 13–23.

(1980). The Cypriots at Naukratis. *Götting. Misz.* **41**, 7–19.

(1981). Egypt, Samos, and the archaic style in Greek sculpture. *J. Egypt. Archaeol.* **67**, 61–81.

Decker, W. (1971). Die physische Leistung Pharaos. *Untersuchungen zu Heldentum, Jagd und Leibesübungen der ägyptischen Könige.* Cologne.

(1974). La délégation des Éléens en Égypte sous la 26ᵉ dynastie (Her. II 160-Diod. I 95). *Chronique d'Égypte* **49**, 31–42.

Demisch, H. (1977). *Die Sphinx. Geschichte ihrer Darstellung von den Anfängen bis zur Gegenwart.* Stuttgart.

Derchain, P. (1962). Le rôle du roi d'Égypte dans le maintien de l'ordre cosmique. *Annales du Centre d'étude des religions* **1**, 61–73.

Diller, A. (1937). *Race mixture among the Greeks before Alexander (Illinois Studies in Language and Literature* **20** (1–2)). Urbana, Illinois.

Diodorus Siculus. *Library of History.* Translated by C. H. Oldfather *et al.*, Loeb Classical Library, Cambridge, Mass., and London.

Dothan, M. (1971). Ashdod II–III. The second and third seasons of excavation 1963, 1965. *'Atiqot* **9–10**. Jerusalem.

Dothan, M. and D. N. Freedman (1967). Ashdod I. The first season of excavations 1962. *'Atiqot* **7**, Jerusalem.

Drioton, E. and J. Vandier (1962). *L'Egypte,* 4th edn. Paris.

Dunand, M. (1975–6). Les rois de Sidon au temps des Perses. *Mélanges de l'Université Saint-Joseph (Beyrouth)* **49**, 489–99.

Dupont-Sommer, A. (1978). Les dieux et les hommes en l'île d'Éléphantine, près d'Assouan, au temps de l'empire des Perses. *Comptes Acad. Inscript. et Belles-Lettres,* 756–72.

Eddy, S. K. (1961). *The king is dead. Studies in the Near Eastern resistance to Hellenism 334–31 B.C.* Lincoln, Nebraska.

Edel, E. (1978). Amasis and Nebukadrezar II. *Götting. Misz.* **29**, 13–20.

Emery, W. B. (1965). *Egypt in Nubia.* London.

(1965–71). Preliminary reports on the excavations at North Saqqâra. *J. Egypt. Archaeol.* **51–7.**

Endesfelder, E. (1979). Zur Frage der Bewässerung im pharaonischen Ägypten. *Z. ägypt. Sprache Altertumskunde* **106**, 37–51.

Erichsen, W. (1941). Erwähnung eines Zuges nach Nubien unter Amasis in einem demotischen Text. *Klio* **34**, 56–61.

Erman, A. and U. Wilcken (1900). Die Naukratisstele. *Z. ägypt. Sprache Altertumskunde* **38**, 127–35.

Fairman, H. W. (1954). Worship and festivals in an Egyptian temple. *Bulletin of the John Rylands Library* **37** (1), 165–203.

Fakhry, A. (1942–50). *Bahria oasis.* 2 vols. Cairo.

(1944). *Siwa oasis.* Cairo.

(1973a). The search for texts in the Western Desert. In *Textes et langages de l'Égypte pharaonique, Hommages à Jean-François Champollion,* vol. II, 207–22. Cairo.

(1973b). *The oases of Egypt. Vol. I. Siwa Oasis.* Cairo.

(1974). *The oases of Egypt. Vol. II. Baḥrīyah and Farafra Oases.* Cairo.

Farag, S., G. Wahba and A. Farid (1977). Reused blocks from a temple of Amasis at Philae. A preliminary report. *Oriens Antiquus* 16, 315–24.

Farina, G. (1929). La politica religiosa di Cambise in Egitto. *Bilychnis* 33, 449–57.

Finegan, J. (1964). *Handbook of Biblical chronology.* Princeton.

Finley, M. I. (1956). *The world of Odysseus.* Harmondsworth.

Fitzmyer, J. A. (1965). The Aramaic letter of King Adon to the Egyptian Pharaoh. *Biblica* 46, 41–55.

Fleming, W. B. (1915). *History of Tyre (Columbia University Oriental Studies* 10) New York.

Frankfort, H. (1948). *Kingship and the gods.* Chicago.

(1961). *Ancient Egyptian religion.* New York.

Freedy, K. S. and D. Redford (1970). The dates in Ezekiel in relation to Biblical, Babylonian and Egyptian sources. *J. Am. orient. Soc.* 90, 462–85.

Froidefond, C. (1971). *Le mirage égyptien dans la littérature grecque d'Homère à Aristote (Publications universitaires des lettres et sciences humaines d'Aix-en-Provence).* Aix-en-Provence.

Frye, R. (1962). *The heritage of Persia.* London.

Gadd, C. J. (1923). *The fall of Nineveh.* London.

Gardiner, A. H. (1947). *Ancient Egyptian onomastica.* 3 vols. Oxford.

(1961). *Egypt of the Pharaohs.* Oxford.

Gardner, E. A. (1888). *Naukratis II.* London.

Gauthier, H. (1907–17). *Le livre des rois d'Égypte,* 5 vols. Cairo.

(1925–31). *Dictionnaire des noms géographiques contenus dans les textes hiéro-glyphiques.* 7 vols. Cairo.

(1935). *Les nomes d'Égypte depuis Hérodote jusqu'à la conquête arabe (Mémoires Inst. d'Égypte* 25). Cairo.

Ghali, I. A. (1969). *L'Égypte et les Juifs dans l'Antiquité.* Paris.

Ghirshman, R. (1965). *Iran.* Harmondsworth.

Gjerstad, E. (1934). Studies in Archaic Greek chronology. I. Naukratis. *Liverpool Annals Archaeol. Anthropol.* 21, 67–84.

Goedicke, H. (1962). Psammetik I. und die Libyer. *Mitt. dt. archäol. Inst. Abt. Kairo* 18, 26–49.

Gomaà, F. (1974). *Die libyschen Fürstentümer des Deltas vom Tod Osorkons II. bis zur Wiedervereinigung Agyptens durch Psametik I.* Wiesbaden.

Goody, J. (ed.) (1971). *Kinship (Penguin Modern Sociology Readings).* Harmondsworth.

Gostynski, T. (1975). La Libye antique et ses relations avec l'Égypte. *B. Inst. Fond. Afrique Noire* Série B, 37, 3. 473–588.

Goyon, G. (1957). *Nouvelles inscriptions rupestres du Wadi Hammamat.* Paris.

Griffith, F. Ll. (1900). *Stories of the High Priests of Memphis.* Oxford.

(1909). *Catalogue of the demotic papyri in the John Rylands Library Manchester.* 3 vols. Manchester.

Gsell, S. (1913–28). *Histoire ancienne de l'Afrique du Nord.* 8 vols. Paris.

Guilmot, M. (1962). Le Sarapieion de Memphis: étude topographique. *Chronique d'Égypte* 37, 359–81.

Gunn, B. (1927). The stela of Apries at Mîtrahîna. *Ann. Serv. Antiquités Égypte* **27**, 211–37.

(1943). Notes on the Naukratis stela. *J. Egypt. Archaeol.* **29**, 55–9.

Gyles, M. F. (1959). *Pharaonic policies and administration 663 to 323 B.C.* (*James Sprunt Studies in History and Political Science* **41**). Chapel Hill.

Habachi, L. (1943). Sais and its monuments. *Ann. Serv. Antiquités Égypte* **42**, 369–416.

(1957). *Tell Basta* (*Ann. Serv. Antiquités* Suppl. **22**). Cairo.

(1974). Psammétique II dans la région de la première cataracte. *Oriens Antiquus* **13**, 317–26.

Haight, E. H. (1955). *The life of Alexander of Macedon*. New York.

Hamilton, J. R. (1973). *Alexander the Great*. London.

Harrison, M. (1978/9). Excavations at Mendes. *Newsletter Am. Res. Cent. Egypt* **107**, 15–7.

Hartmann, F. (1923). *L'agriculture dans l'ancienne Égypte*. Paris.

Heichelheim, F. M. (1957). *An ancient economic history from the Palaeolithic Age to the migration of the Germanic, Slavic and Arabic nations*. 2 vols. Leiden.

Helck, W. (1956). *Untersuchungen zu Manetho und den ägyptischen Königslisten* (*Untersuchungen* **18**). Berlin.

(1964). Die Ägypter und die Fremden. *Saeculum* **15**, 103–14.

(1960–9). *Materialien zur Wirtschaftsgeschichte des Neuen Reiches I–VI* (*Akademie der Wissenschaften und der Literatur im Mainz. Abh. der Geistesund sozialwiss. Klasse, Jhrg. 1960–1969*). With indexes by I. Hoffmann, Wiesbaden, 1970.

(1974). *Die altägyptischen Gaue* (*Beihefte zum Tübinger Atlas des Vorderen Orients* Reihe B (5)). Wiesbaden.

(1975). *Wirtschaftsgeschichte des alten Ägypten im 3. und 2. Jahrtausend vor Chr.* Leiden.

Helck, W., E. Otto and W. Westendorf (eds.) (1975– ). *Lexikon der Ägyptologie*, I ff. Wiesbaden.

Hermann, A. (1938). *Die ägyptische Königsnovelle* (*Leipziger ägyptologische Studien* **10**). Glückstadt, Hamburg, New York.

Herodotus. Translated by A. de Selincourt, *Herodotus. The Histories*. (*The Penguin Classics*), Harmondsworth, 1972. See also Hude, C. and Lloyd, A. B.

Hill, Sir George (1940). *A history of Cyprus*, vol. 1. Cambridge.

Hinz, W. (1975). Darius und der Suezkanal. *Archaeologische Mitteilungen aus Iran* **8**, 115–21.

Hölscher, W. (1937). *Libyer und Ägypter* (*Ägypt. Forschungen* **4**). Glückstadt, Hamburg, New York.

Hoffmeier, J. K. (1981). A new insight on Pharaoh Apries from Herodotus, Diodorus and Jeremiah 46: 17. *J. Soc. Stud. Egypt. Antiquities* **11**, 165–8.

Hogarth, D. G. (1898–9). Excavations at Naucratis. *Ann. Brit. Sch. Athens* **5**, 26–97.

Hogarth, D. G., H. L. Lorimer and C. C. Edgar (1905). Naukratis, 1903. *J. Hellenic Stud.* **25**, 105–36.

Holm-Rasmussen, T. (1977). Nektanebos II and Temple M at Karnak (north). *Götting. Misz.* **26**, 37–41.

Holz, R. K. and D. Stieglitz, D. P. Hansen and E. Ochsenschlager (1980). *Mendes I*. Cairo.

Hopfner, T. (1913). *Der Tierkult der alten Ägypter (Denkschriften Wien 57 (2))*. Vienna.

Hornung, E. (1965). Die Sonnenfinsternis nach dem Tode Psammetichs I. *Z. ägypt. Sprache Altertumskunde* 92, 38–9.

(1966). *Geschichte als Fest*. Darmstadt.

Hude, C. (1927). *Herodoti Historiae (Oxford Classical Texts)*, 3rd edn. 2 vols. Oxford.

Hughes, G. R. (1952). *Saite demotic land leases (Studies in Ancient Oriental Civilization* 28). Chicago.

Jacobsohn, H. (1939). *Die dogmatische Stellung des Königs in der Theologie der alten Ägypter (Ägypt. Forschungen* 8). Glückstadt, Hamburg, New York.

Jacoby, F. (1958). *Die Fragmente der griechischen Historiker*. III. Leiden.

Janssen, J. J. (1975a). *Commodity Prices from the Ramessid period*. Leiden.

(1975b). Prolegomena to the study of Egypt's economic history during the New Kingdom. *Stud. altägypt. Kultur* 3, 127–85.

(1982). Gift-giving in Ancient Egypt as an economic feature. *J. Egypt. Archaeol.* 68, 253–8.

Jantzen, U. (1972). *Ägyptische und orientalische Bronzen aus dem Heraion von Samos (Samos* 8). Bonn.

Janvier, Y. (1978). Pour une meilleure lecture d'Hérodote: à propos de l'Égypte et du 'Périple de Néchao'. *Les Études Classiques* 46, 95–111.

Jelínková-Reymond, E. (1956). Quelques recherches sur les réformes d'Amasis. *Ann. Serv. Antiquités Égypte* 54, 251–87.

Jenkins, G. K. (1955). Greek coins recently acquired by the British Museum. *The Numismatic Chronicle* 6th series, 15, 131–56.

Johnson, J. H. (1974). The Demotic Chronicle as an historical source. *Enchoria* 4, 1–17.

Josephus. *Jewish Antiquities*. Translated by H. St. J. Thackeray *et al.*, Loeb Classical Library, Cambridge, Mass., and London.

Junge, P. J. (1944). *Dareios I. König der Perser*. Leipzig.

Kaiser, M. (1968). Herodots Begegnung mit Ägypten. In S. Morenz, *Die Begegnung Europas mit Ägypten*, 205–46. Berlin.

Kákosy, L. (1975). Les sciences à l'époque saïte et persane. *Annales Universitatis Budapestiensis, Sectio Classica*, 3, 17–22.

Kaplony, P. (1971). Bemerkungen zum ägyptischen Königtum, vor allem in der Spätzeit. *Chronique d'Égypte* 46, 250–74.

Katzenstein, H. J. (1973). *The history of Tyre*. Jerusalem.

Kees, H. (1926). Review of Fritz Heichelheim, *Die auswärtige Bevölkerung im Ptolemäerreich*. In *Göttingische Gelehrte Anzeigen* 188, 172–81.

(1933). *Ägypten (Kulturgeschichte des alten Orients)*. Munich.

(1934–6). Zur Innenpolitik der Saïtendynastie. *Nach. Ges. Wiss. Göttingen, Phil.-hist. Kl.* 1, 95–106.

(1935). Naukratis. *Paulys Real-Encyclopädie der classischen Altertumswissenschaft*, 16, 1954–66.

(1953). *Das Priestertum im ägyptischen Staat (Probleme der Ägyptologie* I). Leiden and Cologne.

(1956a). *Der Götterglaube im alten Ägypten*, 2nd edn. Berlin.

(1956b). *Totenglauben und Jenseitsvorstellungen der alten Ägypter*, 2nd edn. Berlin.

(1961). *Ancient Egypt. A cultural topography*. London.

Kemp, B. J. (1976). A note on stratigraphy at Memphis. *J. Am. Res. Cent. Egypt* **13**, 25–9.

(1977a). The early development of towns in Egypt. *Antiquity* **51**, 185–200.

(1977b). The Palace of Apries at Memphis. *Mitt. dt. archäol. Inst. Abt. Kairo* **33**, 101–8.

(1978a). Imperialism and empire in New Kingdom Egypt (*c.* 1575–1087 B.C.). In P. D. A. Garnsey and C. R. Whittaker (eds.), *Imperialism in the ancient world*, 7–57, 284–97, 368–73. Cambridge.

(1978b). A further note on the Palace of Apries at Memphis. *Götting. Misz.* **29**, 61.

Kent, R. (1953). *Old Persian*, 2nd edn. (revised). New Haven.

Kienitz, F. K. (1953). *Die politische Geschichte Ägyptens vom 7. bis zum 4. Jahrhundert vor der Zeitwende*. Berlin.

(1967). Die Saïtische Renaissance. In E. Cassin, J. Bottéro, and J. Vercoutter (eds.), *Fischer Weltgeschichte. Die altorientalischen Reiche. III. Die erste Hälfte des 1. Jahrtausends*, 256–82. Frankfurt am Main.

Kitchen, K. A. (1973). *The Third Intermediate Period in Egypt (1100–650 BC)*. Warminster.

(1977). On the princedoms of Late-Libyan Egypt. *Chronique d'Égypte* **52**, 40–8.

Klasens, A. (1945–8). Cambyses en Egypte. *Jaarber. Vooraziat-Egypt. Genoot. 'Ex Oriente Lux'* **10**, 339–49.

Kornfeld, W. (1978). Neues über die phönikischen und aramäischen Graffiti in den Tempeln von Abydos. *Anzeiger Öst. Akad. Wiss. Phil.-hist. Klasse*, **7**, 193–204.

Kraeling, E. G. (1953). *The Brooklyn Museum Aramaic papyri*, reprinted 1969. New York.

Kuhlmann, K. P. (1981). Ptolemais – queen of Nectanebo I. Notes on the inscription of an unknown princess of the XXXth dynasty. *Mitt. dt. archäol. Inst. Abt. Kairo* **37**, 267–79.

Lane, E. (1966). *The manners and customs of the modern Egyptians*, Everyman edn. London.

Leahy, A. (1977). Egyptian geography and settlement patterns. In J. Bintliff (ed.), *Mycenaean geography*, 94–7. Cambridge.

Leclant, J. and H. De Meulenaere (1957). Une statuette égyptienne à Delos. *Kêmi* **14**, 34–42.

(1961). *Montouemhat quatrième prophète d'Amon prince de la ville (Bibliothèque d'étude 35)*. Cairo.

(1968). Les relations entre l'Égypte et la Phénicie du voyage d'Ounamon à l'expédition d'Alexandre. In W. A. Ward, *The role of the Phoenicians in the interactions of Mediterranean civilizations. Papers presented to the Archaeological Symposium at the American University of Beirut, March 1967*, 9–31. Beirut.

Lefebvre, G. (1923–4). *Le tombeau de Petosiris*. 3 vols. Cairo.

Libourel, J. M. (1971). The Athenian disaster in Egypt. *Amer. J. Philology* **92**, 605–15.

Lichtheim, M. (1975). *Ancient Egyptian literature. I: The Old and Middle Kingdoms.* Berkeley and Los Angeles.

(1976). The Naucratis stele once again. In J. P. Allen and E. F. Wente (eds.), *Studies in honor of George R. Hughes,* 139–46. Chicago.

(1980). *Ancient Egyptian Literature. III: The Late Period.* Berkeley and Los Angeles.

Lindsay, J. (1976). The Babylonian kings and Edom, 605–550 B.C. *Palestine Exploration Quarterly* **108**, 23–39.

Lipinski, E. (1972). The Egypto-Babylonian war of the winter 601–600 B.C. *Annali Ist. Orient. Napoli* **32**, 235–41.

Lloyd, A. B. (1969). Perseus and Chemmis (Herodotus II 91). *J. Hellen. Stud.* **89**, 79–86.

(1972a). Triremes and the Saïte navy. *J. Egypt. Archaeol.* **58**, 268–79.

(1972b). The so-called galleys of Necho. *J. Egypt. Archaeol.* **58**, 307–8.

(1975a). *Herodotus Book II, Introduction.* Leiden.

(1975b). Were Necho's triremes Phoenician? *J. Hellenic Stud.* **95**, 45–61.

(1976). *Herodotus Book II, Commentary 1–98.* Leiden.

(1977). Necho and the Red Sea: some considerations. *J. Egypt. Archaeol.* **63**, 142–55.

(1978). Two figured ostraca from North Saqqâra. *J. Egypt. Archaeol.* **64**, 107–12.

(1980). M. Basch on triremes: some observations. *J. Hellenic Stud.* **100**, 195–8.

(1982a). Nationalist propaganda in Ptolemaic Egypt. *Historia* **31**, 33–55.

(1982b). The inscription of Udjaḥorresnet: a collaborator's testament. *J. Egypt. Archaeol.* **68**, 166–80.

Lorton, D. (1974). *The juridical terminology of international relations in Egyptian texts through Dyn. XVIII (The John Hopkins Near Eastern Studies 4).* Baltimore and London.

Lucas, A. (1962). *Ancient Egyptian materials and industries,* 4th edn. (revised by J. R. Harris). London.

Luckenbill, D. D. (1927). *Ancient records of Assyria and Babylonia.* 2 vols. Chicago.

Macfarquhar, C. F. (1966). Early Greek travellers in Egypt. *Greece and Rome* **13**, 108–16.

Magnanini, P. (1973). *Le iscrizioni fenicie dell'oriente.* Rome.

Mair, L. (1977). *An introduction to social anthropology,* 2nd edn. Oxford.

Malamat, A. (1950). The last wars of the kingdom of Judah. *J. Near East. Stud.* **9**, 218–27.

(1968). The last kings of Judah and the fall of Jerusalem. *Israel Exploration J.* **18**, 137–56.

(1973). Josiah's bid for Armageddon. The background of the Judean-Egyptian encounter in 609 B.C. *J. Ancient Near Eastern Soc. Columbia Univ.* **5**, 267–79.

(1974). Megiddo, 609 B.C.: the conflict re-examined. *Acta Antiqua* **22**, 445–9.

(1975). A twilight of Judah: in the Egyptian-Babylonian maelstrom. *Vetus Testamentum* Suppl. **28**, 123–45.

(1976). *A history of the Jewish people.* London.

Malinine, M. and J. Pirenne (1950–1). *Documents juridiques égyptiens* (Deuxieme série) (*Archives d'historie du droit oriental* **5**). 11–91.

(1953). *Choix de textes juridiques en hiératique anormal et en démotique* (*XXVᵉ– XXVIIᵉ Dynastie*). Paris.

Malinine, M., G. Posener and J. Vercoutter (1968). *Catalogue des stèles du Sérapéum de Memphis*. Paris.

(1975). Vente de tombes à l'époque saïte. *Rev. Égypt.* **27**, 164–74.

Mallet, D. (1888). *Le culte de Neit à Saïs*. Paris.

(1893). *Les premiers établissements des grecs en Égypte*. Paris.

(1922). *Les rapports des grecs avec l'Égypte*. Cairo.

Manetho. Translated by W. G. Waddell. (1940). Loeb Classical Library, Cambridge, Mass., and London. (See also Jacoby, F.)

Masson, O. (1969). Les Cariens en Égypte. *Bull. Soc. français Égyptol.* **56**, 25–36.

(1971). Les Chypriotes en Égypte. *Bull. Soc. français Égyptol.* **60**, 28–46.

Masson, O. and J. Yoyotte (1956). *Objets pharaoniques à inscription carienne* (*Bibliothèque d'etude* **15**). Cairo.

Matthiae Scandone, G. (1967). Il tempio di Neith in Sais e gli dei ΣΥΝΝΑΟΙ in epoca tarda. *Oriens Antiquus* **6**, 145–68.

Mauny, R. (1976). Le périple de l'Afrique par les Phéniciens de Nechao vers 600 av. J.-C. *Archeologia* **96**, 44–5.

Mauss, M. (1954). *The gift: forms and functions of exchange in archaic societies*. London.

Mazzarino. S. (1947). *Fra oriente ed occidente, ricerche di storia greca archaica*. Florence.

Meiggs, R. (1963). The crisis of Athenian imperialism. *Harvard Stud. Class. Phil.* **67**, 1–36.

(1972). *The Athenian empire*. Oxford.

Menu, B. (1977). Les rapports de dépendance en Égypte à l'époque saïte et perse. *Rev. hist. Droit fr. étranger* **55**, 391–401.

Meulenaere, H. De (1951). *Herodotos over de 26ste Dynastie* (*Bibliothèque du Muséon* **27**). Louvain.

(1964). De vestiging van de Saïtische dynastie. *Orientalia Gandensia* **I**, 95–103.

(1967). Die Dritte Zwischenzeit und das äthiopische Reich. In E. Cassin, J. Bottéro, and J. Vercoutter (eds.), *Fischer Weltgeschichte. Die altorientalischen Reiche. III. Die erste Hälfte des I. Jahrtausends*, 220–55. Frankfurt am Main.

(1968). Le famille du roi Amasis. *J. Egypt. Archaeol.* **54**, 183–7.

(1975–6). Le clergé abydénien d'Osiris à la Basse Époque. *Orientalia Lovaniensia Periodica* **6–7** (*Miscellanea Vergote*), 133–51.

Meulenaere, H. De and P. Mackay (1976). *Mendes II*. Warminster.

Meyer, E. (1915). Ägyptische Dokumente aus der Perserzeit. *Sitz. preuss. Ak. Wiss. Phil.-hist. Klasse* **16**, 287–311.

(1928). Gottesstaat, Militärherrschaft und Ständewesen in Ägypten. *Sitz. preuss. Ak. Wiss. Phil.-hist. Klasse* **28**, 495–532.

Millard, A. R. (1979). The Scythian problem. In J. Ruffle *et al.* (eds.), *Orbis Aegyptiorum Speculum. Glimpses of Ancient Egypt*, 119–22. Warminster.

Mitchell, B. (1975). Herodotus and Samos. *J. Hellen. Stud.* **95**, 75–91.

Montet, P. (1957–61). *Géographie de l'Égypte ancienne.* 2 vols. Paris.

Morenz, S. (1960). *Ägyptische Religion.* Stuttgart.

Moret, A. (1902a). *Du caractère religieux de la royauté pharaonique* (*Annales du Musée Guimet. Bibliothèque d'études* 15). Paris.

(1902b). *Le rituel du culte divin journalier en Égypte.* Paris.

Müller, C. (1975). VIII. Drei Stelenfragmente. In W. Kaiser *et al.*, Stadt und Tempel von Elephantine. Fünfter Grabungsbericht. *Mitt. dt. archäol. Inst. Abt. Kairo* 31, 80–4.

Müller, H. (1938). *Die formale Entwicklung der Titulatur der ägyptischen Könige* (*Ägypt. Forschungen* 7). Glückstadt, Hamburg, New York.

Müller, W. (no date). *Die Umsegelung Afrikas durch phönizische Schiffer ums Jahr 600 v. Christ. Geb.* Rathenow.

Murnane, W. J. (1977). *Ancient Egyptian coregencies* (*Studies in Ancient Oriental Civilization* 40). Chicago.

Muszynski, M. (1976). Les papyrus démotiques de Ricci. *Enchoria* 6, 19–27.

(1977). Les 'associations religieuses' en Égypte d'après les sources hiéroglyphiques, démotiques et grecques. *Orientalia Lovaniensia Periodica* 8, 145–74.

Naville, E. (1891). *Bubastis.* London.

(1892). *The festival hall of Osorkon II in the great temple of Bubastis.* London.

(1903). *The store-city of Pithom,* 4th edn. London.

Oldfather *et al. Diodorus Siculus.* Leob Classical Library, Cambridge, Mass. and London.

Olmstead, A. T. (1959). *History of the Persian empire.* Chicago and London.

Oren, E. (1977). Report on excavations at 'Migdol' (in Hebrew). *Qadmoniot* 10, 71–6.

(1979). Stratopeda – Biblical Migdol? A new fortress of the archaic period in the eastern Nile Delta. *Greece and Italy in the Classical World* (*Acta of the XI International Congress of Classical Archaeology, London, 3–9 September 1978*), 199. London.

Otto, E. (1954). *Die biographischen Inschriften der ägyptischen Spätzeit* (*Probleme der Ägyptologie* 2). Leiden.

Otto, W. (1905–8). *Priester und Tempel im hellenistischen Ägypten.* 2 vols. Leipzig and Berlin.

Parke, H. W. (1933). *Greek mercenary soldiers.* Oxford.

Parker, R. A. (1957). The length of the reign of Amasis and the beginning of the Twenty-sixth Dynasty. *Mitt. dt. archäol. Inst. Abt. Kairo* 15, 208–14.

(1962). *A Saite oracle papyrus from Thebes.* Providence.

Parker, R. A. and W. H. Dubberstein (1956). *Babylonian chronology 626 B.C.–A.D. 75* (*Brown University Studies* 19). Providence.

Parlebas, J. (1977). Les égyptiens et la ville d'après les sources littéraires et archéologiques. *Ktèma* 2, 49–57.

Pernigotti, S. (1974). Ricerche su personaggi egiziani di epoca etiopica e saitica. *Aegyptus* 54, 141–56.

(1978). A proposito di Sais e delle sue divinità. *Studi classici e orientali* 28, 223–35.

Pestman, P. (1961). *Marriage and matrimonial property in Ancient Egypt.* Leiden.

Petrie, W. M. F. (1886). *Naukratis I (1884–5)*. London.
(1888). *Tanis II. Nebesheh (Am) and Defenneh (Tahpanhes)*. London.
(1905). *A history of Egypt, vol. III. From the XIXth to the XXXth Dynasties.* London.
Petrie, W. M. F. and J. H. Walker (1909a). *Memphis I*. London.
(1909b). *The palace of Apries (Memphis II)*. London.
Petrie, W. M. F., E. Mackay and G. Wainwright (1910). *Meydum and Memphis III*. London.
Petrie, W. M. F., G. A. Wainwright and A. H. Gardiner (1913). *Tarkhan I and Memphis V*. London.
Picard, Ch. (1957). La thoraké d'Amasis. In *Hommages à Waldemar Deonna. Collection Latomus* **28**, 363–70.
Pirenne, J. (1963). *Histoire de la civilisation de l'Égypte ancienne*, vol. III. Paris.
Pirenne, J. and A. Théodoridès (1966). Droit égyptien. (*Introduction bibliographique à l'histoire du droit et à l'ethnologie juridique*). Brussels.
Poidebard, A. (1939). *Un grand port disparu. Tyr*. Paris.
Porten, B. (1968). *Archives from Elephantine*. Berkeley and Los Angeles.
Porten B. and J. C. Greenfield (1974). *Jews of Elephantine and Arameans of Syene (5th century BC)*. Jerusalem.
Porter, B. and R. L. B. Moss (1927–51). *Topographical bibliography of ancient Egyptian hieroglyphic texts, reliefs and paintings*, 7 vols. Oxford.
(1960–4). *Topographical bibliography of ancient Egyptian hieroglyphic texts, reliefs and paintings*, 2nd edn., vols. I and II. Oxford.
(1974). *Topographical bibliography of ancient Egyptian hieroglyphic texts, reliefs and paintings*, 2nd edn. (revised and augmented by J. Málek), vol. III, pt. 1. Oxford.
Posener, G. (1934). Notes sur la stèle de Naucratis. *Ann. Serv. Antiquités Égypte* **34**, 141–8.
(1936). *La première domination perse en Égypte (Bibliothèque d'etude* **11**). Cairo.
(1938). Le canal du Nil à la Mer Rouge avant les Ptolemées. *Chronique d'Égypte* **13**, 259–73.
(1947). Les douanes de la Méditerranée dans l'Égypte saïte. *Revue de Philologie* **21**, 117–31.
(1956). *Littérature et politique dans l'Égypte de la XXIIᵉ dynastie*. Paris.
(1957). Le conte de Néferkarê et du general Siséné (recherches littéraires VI). *Rev. Égypt*, **11**, 119–37.
(1960). *De la divinité du pharaon*. Paris.
Prinz, H. (1908). *Funde aus Naukratis (Klio Beiheft* **7**).
Pritchard, J. B. (ed.) (1969). *Ancient Near Eastern texts relating to the Old Testament*, 3rd edn. Princeton.
Ranke, H. (1943). Eine spätsaïtische Statue in Philadelphia. *Mitt. dt. archäol. Inst. Abt. Kairo* **12**, 107–38.
Ray, J. D. (1972). The house of Osorapis. In P. Ucko, R. Tringham, and G. W. Dimbleby (eds.), *Man, settlement and urbanism*, 699–704. London.
(1976). *The archive of Hor*. London.
(1981). Ancient Egypt. In M. Loewe and C. Blacker (eds.), *Divination and Oracles*, 174–90. London.

(1982). The Carian inscriptions from Egypt. *J. Egypt Archaeol.* **68**, 181–98.

Redford, D. B. (1977a). The oases in Egyptian history to classical times. Part IV. *c.* 1000 B.C.–*c.* 630 B.C. *Newsl. Soc. Stud. Egypt. Antiquities* 7(4), 7–10.

(1977b). Some observations on Egyptian chronology of the eighth and seventh centuries B.C. *Am. J. Archaeol.* **81**, 82–3.

Ritner, R. K. (1980). Khababash and the Satrap Stela – a grammatical rejoinder. *Z. ägypt. Sprache Altertumskunde* **107**, 135–7.

Roeder, G. (1927). *Altägyptische Erzählungen und Märchen.* Jena.

(1960). *Kulte, Orakel und Naturverehrung im alten Ägypten.* Zürich and Stuttgart.

Röllig, W. (1974). Politische Heiraten im Alten Orient. *Saeculum* **25**, 11–23.

Rostovtzeff, M. (1953). *The social and economic history of the Hellenistic world.* 3 vols. Oxford.

Russmann, E. R. (1974). *The representation of the king in the XXVth dynasty (Monographies Reine Élisabeth).* Brussels and Brooklyn.

Ruszczyc, B. (1976). Le temple d'Amasis à Tell-Atrib. *Études et Travaux* **9**, 117–27.

Säve-Söderbergh, T. (1941). *Ägypten und Nubien: ein Beitrag zur Geschichte altägyptischer Aussenpolitik.* Lund.

Saffirio, L. (1972). L'alimentazione umana nell-antico Egitto. *Aegyptus* **52**, 19–66.

Salmon, P. (1965). *La politique égyptienne d'Athènes (VIe et Ve siècles avant J.-C.).* Brussels.

Sauneron, S. and J. Yoyotte. (1952a). La campagne nubienne de Psammétique II et sa signification historique. *Bull. Inst. fr. archéol. orient. Caire* **50**, 157–207.

(1952b). Sur la politique palestinienne des rois saïtes. *Vetus Testamentum* **2**, 131–6.

(1957). *Les prêtres de l'ancienne Égypte.* Bourges.

(1959). L'avis des égyptiens sur la cuisine soudanaise. *Kush* **7**, 63–70.

(1964). Villes et légendes d'Égypte. VI. A propos du 'toponyme' Achérou (*išrw*). *Bull. Inst. fr. archéol. orient. Caire* **62**, 50–7.

Sayed, R. el- (1974). Quelques éclaircissements sur l'histoire de la XXVIe dynastie, d'après la statue du Caire CG. 658. *Bull. Inst. fr. archéol. orient. Caire* **74**, 29–44.

(1975). *Documents relatifs à Saïs et ses divinités (Bibliothèque d'étude 69).* Cairo.

(1976). Deux aspects nouveaux du culte à Saïs – un prophète du nain de Neïth – des châteaux d'Ageb. *Bull. Inst. fr. archéol. orient. Caire* **76**, 91–100.

(1977). Au sujet de la statue Caire CG. 662. *Bull. Inst. fr. archéol. orient. Caire* **77**, 101–111.

(1978). A propos de l'activité d'un fonctionnaire du temps de Psammétique I à Karnak d'après la stèle du Caire 2747. *Bull. Inst. fr. archéol. orient. Caire* **78**, 459–76.

Schäfer, H. (1897). Noch einmal die Inschrift von Neapel. In *Aegyptiaca. Festschrift für Georg Ebers*, 92–8. Leipzig.

(1899). Bruchstück eines koptischen Romans über die Eroberung Aegyptens durch Kambyses. *Sitz. preuss. Ak. Wiss. Phil.-hist. Klasse* **38**, 727–44.

(1904). Die Auswanderung der Krieger unter Psammetich I. und der Söldneraufstand in Elephantine unter Apries. *Klio* 4, 152–63.

Schaefer, H. (1952). Die verwassungsgeschichtliche Entwicklung Kyrenes im ersten Jahrhundert nach seiner Begründung. *Rheinisches Museum* 95, 135–70.

Schenkel, W. (1965). *Memphis, Herakleopolis, Theben (Ägyptologische Abhandlungen* 12). Wiesbaden.

Schiwek, H. (1962). Der persische Golf als Schiffahrts- und Seehandelsroute in Achämenidischer Zeit und in der Zeit Alexanders des Großen. *Bonner Jahrbücher* 162, 4–97.

Schlott, A. (1969). *Die Ausmaße Ägyptens nach altägyptischen Texten.* Diss. Tübingen.

Schnibel, M. (1925). *Die Landwirtschaft im hellenistischen Ägypten.* Munich.

Schott, S. (1967). R$\check{s}$-N.t und M$\underline{h}$-N.t als Häuser der Neith. *Rev. Égypt.* 19, 99–110.

Schwab-Schlott, A. (1972). Altägyptische Texte über die Ausmaße Ägyptens. *Mitt. dt. archäol. Inst. Abt. Kairo* 28, 109–13.

Schwartz, J. (1949). Les conquérants perses et la littérature égyptienne. *Bull. Inst. fr. archéol. orient. Caire* 48, 65–80.

Schweitzer, U. (1948). *Löwe und Sphinx im alten Ägypten (Ägypt. Forschungen* 15). Glückstadt and Hamburg.

Seidl, E. (1966). Die Unterhaltspflicht der Töchter und die Kaufehe in den Papyrusurkunden. *Atti dell' 11$^{mo}$ congresso internazionale dei Pairologia, Milano, 2–8 sett. 1965,* 1949–55. Milan.

(1968). *Ägyptische Rechtsgeschichte der Saiten- und Perserzeit (Ägypt. Forschungen* 20), 2nd edn. Glückstadt.

Senac, R. (1967). Le périple africain par la flotte de Néchao. *La Revue Maritime* 241, 281–93.

Seton-Williams, M. V. (1965–7, 1969). Preliminary reports on the excavations at Tell el-Farâ$^{c}$in (Buto). *J. Egypt. Archaeol.* 51–3, 55.

Simpson, W. K. (ed.) (1973). *The literature of Ancient Egypt.* New Haven and London.

(1982). Egyptian sculpture and two-dimensional representation as propaganda. *J. Egypt. Archaeol.* 68, 266–71.

Smith, E. Marion (1926). Naukratis, a chapter in the history of the Hellenization of Egypt. *J. Soc. Orient. Research* 10, 119–206.

Smith, H. S. (1974a). La mère d'Apis. Fouilles récentes de l'Egypt Exploration Society à Saqqara-nord. *Bull. Soc. français Égyptol.* 70–1, 11–27.

(1974b). *A visit to Ancient Egypt. Life at Memphis & Saqqara (c. 500–30 BC).* Warminster.

(1976). Aspects of the study of the Egyptian city. In D. Wildung, (ed.), *First International Congress of Egyptology. Cairo, October 2–10, 1976, Abstracts of Papers,* 112–4. Munich.

Spalinger, A. (1974). Assurbanipal and Egypt: a source study. *J. Am. Orient. Soc.* 94, 316–28.

(1976a). Foreign policy of the Saites – Egypt and Babylon. In D. Wildung (ed.), *First International Congress of Egyptology. Cairo, October 2–10, 1976. Abstracts of Papers,* 117. Munich.

(1976b). Psammetichus, king of Egypt: I. *J. Am. Res. Cent. Egypt* **13**, 133–47.

(1977a). The concept of kingship in Dynasty XXVI. *Newsletter Am. Res. Cent. Egypt* **99/100**, 9.

(1977b). Egypt and Babylonia: a survey (*c.* 620 B.C. – 550 B.C.). *Stud. altägypt. Kultur* **5**, 221–44.

(1978a). The concept of the monarchy during the Saite epoch – an essay of synthesis. *Orientalia* **47**, 12–36.

(1978b). The date of the death of Gyges and its historical implications. *J. Am. Orient. Soc.* **98**, 400–9.

(1978c). The foreign policy of Egypt preceding the Assyrian conquest. *Chronique d'Égypte* **53**, 22–47.

(1978d). The reign of King Chabbash: an interpretation. *Z. ägypt. Sprache Altertumskunde* **105**, 142–54.

(1980). Addenda to 'The Reign of King Chabbash: an Interpretation' (ZÄS 105, 1978, pp. 142–154). *Z. ägypt. Sprache Altertumskunde* **107**, 87.

Spencer, A. J. (1979). The brick foundations of Late-Period peripteral temples and their mythological origins. In J. Ruffle *et al.* (eds.), *Orbis Aegyptiorum Speculum. Glimpses of Ancient Egypt*, 132–7. Warminster.

Spiegelberg, W. (1907). *Der Papyrus Libbey (Schriften der Wissenschaftlichen Gesellschaft in Straßburg)*. Strasbourg.

(1910). *Der Sagenkreis des Königs Petubastis (Demotische Studien 3)* Leipzig.

(1914). *Die sogenannte Demotische Chronik des Pap. 215 der Bibliothèque National zu Paris (Demotische Studien 7)*. Leipzig.

Stadelmann, R. (1971). Das Grab im Tempelhof. Der Typus des Königsgrabes in der Spätzeit. *Mitt. dt. archäol. Inst. Abt. Kairo* **27**, 111–23.

Strabo. Translated by H. L. Jones. Loeb Classical Library, Cambridge, Mass., and London.

Struve, W. (1932). Die Hermotybier. In *Studies presented to F. Ll. Griffith*, 369–72. London.

Tanner, R. (1967). Untersuchungen zur ehe- und erbrechtlichen Stellung der Frau im pharaonischen Ägypten. *Klio* **49**, 5–37.

Théodoridès, A. (1975). Les relations de l'Égypte pharaonique avec ses voisins. *Rev. Int. Droits Antiquité* **22**, 87–140.

(1976). Le droit matrimonial dans l'Égypte pharaonique. *Rev. Int. Droits Antiquité* **23**, 15–55.

Traunecker, C. (1979). Essai sur l'histoire de la XXIX<sup>e</sup> dynastie. *Bull. Inst. fr. archéol. orient. Caire.* **79**, 395–436.

Traunecker, C., F. Le Saout, and O. Masson (1981). *La chapelle d'Achôris à Karnak*, II (Recherche sur les grandes civilisations, Synthèse no. 5). Paris.

Tresson, P. (1930). La stèle de Naples. *Bull. Inst. fr. archéol. Caire* **30**, 369–91.

(1931). Sur deux monuments égyptiens inédits de l'époque d'Amasis et de Nectanébo I<sup>er</sup>. *Kêmi* **4**, 126–50.

Trigger, B. (1976). *Nubia under the Pharaohs*. London.

Ucko, P. J., R. Tringham and G. W. Dimbleby (eds.) (1972). *Man, settlement and urbanism*. London.

Vandier, J. (1949). *La religion égyptienne*, 2nd edn. Paris.

(1963). Une tête royale de l'époque saïte. *Z. ägypt. Sprache Altertumskunde* **90**, 115–18.

Vittmann, G. (1974). Zwei Königinnen der Spätzeit namens Chedebnitjerbōne. *Chronique d'Égypte* **49**, 43-51.

(1975). Die Familie der saitschen Könige. *Orientalia* **44**, 375-87.

(1977). Neues zu Pabasa, Obermajordomus der Nitokris. *Stud. altägypt. Kultur* **5**, 245-64.

(1978). *Priester und Beamte im Theben der Spätzeit*. Vienna.

Wainwright, G. A. (1952). The date of the rise of Meroë. *J. Egypt. Archaeol.* **38**, 75-7.

Walcot, P. (1970). *Greek peasants, ancient and modern. A comparison of social and moral values*. Manchester.

Wałek-Czernecki, T. (1941). La population de l'Égypte à l'époque saïte. *Bull. Inst. Ég.* **23**, 37-62.

Wâsif, F. M. (1974). Soundings on the borders of ancient Sais. *Oriens Antiquus* **13**, 327-8.

Wessetzky, W. (1942). Zur Deutung des 'Orakels' in der sogenannten Demotischen Chronik. *Wien. Z. Kunde Morgenlandes* **49**, 161-71.

(1963). Die Familiengeschichte des Peteêse als historische Quelle für die Innenpolitik Psametiks I. *Z. äg. Sprache Altertumskunde* **88**, 69-73.

(1977). An der Grenze von Literatur und Geschichte. In J. Assmann *et al.* (eds.), *Fragen an die altägyptische Literatur*, 499-502. Wiesbaden.

Wiedemann, A. (1880). *Geschichte Ägyptens von Psammetich I. bis auf Alexander den' Grossen*. Leipzig.

(1886). Les castes en Égypte. *Le Muséon* **5**, 79-102.

(1912). *Der Tierkult der alten Ägypter (Der alte Orient* **14**(1)). Leipzig.

Wilkinson, Sir John Gardner (1842). A tour to Bubastis, Sebennytus and Menzaleh. *Miscellanea Aegyptiaca*. Alexandria.

Willcocks, W. and J. I. Craig (1913). *Egyptian irrigation*, 3rd edn. London.

Winnicki, J. K. (1977). Die Kalasirier der spätdynastischen und der ptolemäischen Zeit. *Historia* **26**, 257-68.

Winter, E. (1978). *Der Apiskult im Alten Ägypten*. Mainz.

Wiseman, D. J. (1961). *Chronicles of Caldaean kings (626-556 BC) in the British Museum*. London.

Woolley, C. L. *et al.* (1914-52). *Carchemish*. 3 vols. London.

Yoyotte, J. (1951a). Le martelage des noms royaux éthiopiens par Psammétique II. *Rev. Égypt.* **8**, 215-39.

(1951b). Sur le voyage asiatique de Psammétique II. *Vetus Testamentum* **1**, 140-4.

Zauzich, K. (1972). *Einige Karische Inschriften aus Ägypten und ihre Deutung nach der Entzifferung der Karischen Schrift*. Wiesbaden.

Zeissl, H. von (1944). *Äthioper und Assyrer in Ägypten (Ägypt. Forschungen* **14**). Glückstadt and Hamburg.

# INDEX

Lightning Source UK Ltd.
Milton Keynes UK
UKOW06f1338170615

253655UK00009B/380/P